CLYMER®

YAMAHA

BANSHEE • 1987-2004

The world's finest publisher of mechanical how-to manuals

PRIMEDIA
Information Data Products
P.O. Box 12901, Overland Park, Kansas 66282-2901

FIRST EDITION
First Printing July, 1995
Second Printing November, 1997
Third Printing November, 1998

SECOND EDITION
First Printing July, 1999
Second Printing June, 2000
Third Printing January, 2001
Fourth Printing August, 2001

THIRD EDITION
First Printing May, 2002

FOURTH EDITION
First Printing June, 2003

FIFTH EDITION
First Printing October, 2004

Printed in U.S.A.

ISBN: 0-89287-917-3

Library of Congress: 2004113152

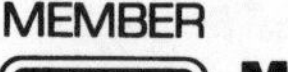

TECHNICAL PHOTOGRAPHY: Ron Wright. Yamaha Banshee courtesy of Anthony Pacini. Additional photographic and research assistance courtesy of Clawson Motorsports, Fresno, California.

TECHNICAL ILLUSTRATIONS: Steve Amos

WIRING DIAGRAMS: Robert Caldwell.

PRODUCTION: Dylan Goodwin.

TOOLS AND EQUIPMENT: K & L Supply Co. at www.klsupply.com.

COVER: Banshees (2003 model front cover/1994 model back cover) photographed by Mark Clifford Photography at www.markclifford.com

PRIMEDIA
Business Magazines & Media
P.O. Box 12901, Overland Park, KS 66282-2901 • 800-262-1954 • 913-967-1719

The following books and guides are published by PRIMEDIA Business Directories & Books.

More information available at *primediabooks.com*

CONTENTS

QUICK REFERENCE DATA

ATV INFORMATION

MODEL:______________________________ YEAR:__________

VIN NUMBER:______________________________

ENGINE SERIAL NUMBER:______________________________

CARBURETOR SERIAL NUMBER OR I.D. MARK:______________________________

TIRE INFLATION PRESSURE

	Standard psi (kPa)	Minimum psi (kPa)
Front		
1987-1990	4.3 (30)	3.8 (27)
1991-on	4.3 (30)	3.8 (27)
Rear		
1987-1990	3.6 (25)	3.1 (22)
1991-on	4.3 (30)	3.1 (22)

RECOMMENDED LUBRICANTS AND FUEL

Engine oil	Yamalube "R", Castrol R30 or equivalent 2-stroke oil
Transmission	SAE 10W30 motor oil
Air filter	Foam air filter oil
Drive chain*	Non-tacky O-ring chain lubricant or SAE 30-50 weight engine motor oil
Brake fluid	DOT 4
Steering and suspension lubricant	Lithium base grease
Fuel	Regular gasoline with octane rating of at least 90
Control cables	Cable lube**

*Use kerosene to clean drive chain.

**Do not use drive chain lubricant to lubricate control cables.

FUEL/OIL PREMIX RATIO

Oil type	Premix Ratio	
Castol R30	20:1	
Yamalube "R" or equivalent	24:1	
Ratio 20:1 Gasoline (gal.)	**Oil oz.**	**Oil ml**
1	6.4	190
2	12.8	380
3	19.2	570
4	25.6	760
5	32	945

(continued)

FUEL/OIL PREMIX RATIO (continued)

Ratio 24:1 Gasoline (gal.)	Oil oz.	Oil ml
1	5.3	157
2	10.7	316
3	16.0	473
4	21.3	630
5	26.7	790

FUEL TANK CAPACITY

	U.S. gal	Liters	Imp. gal.
Total	3.17	12	2.64
Reserve	0.66	2.5	0.55

COOLANT CAPACITY*

	Liters	U.S. qt.	Imp. qt.
Total amount	2.5	2.64	2.20
Reservoir tank	0.28	0.30	0.25

*Mixing ratio is 50% coolant to 50% water.

SPARK PLUGS AND GAP

Plug range	Type and heat range
Hotter	NGK BR7ES
Standard	NGK BR8ES
Colder	NGK BR9ES
Spark plug gap	0.7-0.8 mm (0.028-0.032 in.)

TUNE-UP SPECIFICATIONS

Ignition timing	17 BTDC @ 1,200 rpm*
Carburetor adjustment	
Pilot air screw	2.0 turns out
Engine Idle speed	1,450-1,550 rpm

*See text for inspection procedure.

GENERAL DIMENSIONS

	mm	in.
Overall length	1,855	73
Overall width	1,100	43.3
Overall height	1,080	42.5
Seat height		
1987-1989	780	30.7
1990-on	800	31.4
Wheel base	1,280	50.4
Minimum ground clearance	135	5.31
Minimum turning radius	3,600	142

WEIGHT SPECIFICATIONS*

	kg	lbs.
1987-1989	182	401
1990	185	408
1991-on	186	410

*With oil and fuel tank full.

CLYMER®

YAMAHA

BANSHEE • 1987-2004

INTRODUCTION

While most manufacturers have abandoned the two-stroke ATV, Yamaha refuses to stop producing the industry's only twin-cylinder, two-stroke powered machine. The one-off Banshee, an appropriate name if you've ever heard the engine's howl at full throttle, continues to thrill those that seek a mount with a little more spirit than the typical four-stroke powered ATV. With a powerband that features an almost non-existent lower end, thankfully the clutch has proven durable, and 'whoa Nellie' top end, the Banshee is definitely not for the faint hearted. For those looking for a docile trail machine, look elsewhere, because this machine has a pedigree of desert rally and hill climbing victories.

The 347 cc water-cooled engine's power is mated to a six-speed transmission sans reverse. Performance suspension features 9.1 inches of travel up front and 8.7 inches in the rear. Hydraulic disc brakes (two upfront–one in the rear) help control the demon's torque. And if the out of the box performance is insufficient, the Banshee is supported by a wealth of aftermarket specialists who provide pipes, cylinders, carb kits, etc. to take the machine into another stratosphere.

With a long production run and steady sales it is little wonder, despite the Banshee's critics, that Yamaha has continued to produce this unique and exciting machine.

CHAPTER ONE

GENERAL INFORMATION

This detailed, comprehensive manual covers the 1987-2003 Yamaha YFZ350 Banshee.

Troubleshooting, tune-up, maintenance and repair are not difficult, if you know what tools and equipment to use and what to do. Step-by-step instructions guide you through jobs ranging from simple maintenance to complete engine and suspension overhaul.

This manual can be used by anyone from a first time do-it-yourselfer to a professional mechanic. Detailed drawings and clear photographs give you all the information you need to do the work right.

Some of the procedures in this manual require the use of special tools. The resourceful mechanic can, in many cases, think of acceptable substitutes for special tools—there is always another way. This can be as simple as using a few pieces of threaded rod, washers and nuts to remove or install a bearing or as complex as fabricating a tool from scrap material. However, using a substitute for a special tool is not recommended as it can be dangerous and may damage the part. If you find that a tool can be designed and safely made, but will require some type of machine work, you may want to search out a local community college or high school that has a machine shop curriculum. Shop teachers sometimes welcome outside work that can be used as practical shop applications for advanced students.

Table 1 lists model coverage with engine serial numbers.

Table 2 lists general vehicle dimensions.

Table 3 lists weight specifications.

Table 4 lists decimal and metric equivalents.

Table 5 lists conversion tables.

Table 6 lists general torque specifications.

Table 7 lists technical abbreviations.

Table 8 lists metric tap drill sizes.

Table 9 lists windchill factors.

Tables 1-9 are at the end of the chapter.

MANUAL ORGANIZATION

This chapter provides general information and discusses equipment and tools useful both for preventive maintenance and troubleshooting.

Chapter Two provides methods and suggestions for quick and accurate diagnosis and repair of problems. Troubleshooting procedures discuss typical symptoms and logical methods to pinpoint the trouble.

Chapter Three explains all periodic lubrication and routine maintenance necessary to keep your

Yamaha operating well. Chapter Three also includes recommended tune-up procedures, eliminating the need to consult constantly other chapters on the various assemblies.

Subsequent chapters describe specific systems such as the engine top end, engine bottom end, clutch, transmission, fuel, exhaust, electrical, suspension, drive train, steering and brakes. Each chapter provides disassembly, repair, and assembly procedures in simple step-by-step form. If a repair is impractical for a home mechanic, it is so indicated. It is usually faster and less expensive to take such repairs to a Yamaha dealer or competent repair shop. Specifications concerning a particular system are included at the end of the appropriate chapter.

NOTES, CAUTIONS AND WARNINGS

The terms NOTE, CAUTION and WARNING have specific meanings in this manual. A NOTE provides additional information to make a step or procedure easier or clearer. Disregarding a NOTE could cause inconvenience, but would not cause damage or personal injury.

A CAUTION emphasizes areas where equipment damage could occur. Disregarding a CAUTION could cause permanent mechanical damage; however, personal injury is unlikely.

A WARNING emphasizes areas where personal injury or even death could result from negligence. Mechanical damage may also occur. WARNINGS *are to be taken seriously*. In some cases, serious injury and death has resulted from disregarding similar warnings.

SAFETY FIRST

Professional mechanics can work for years and never sustain a serious injury. If you observe a few rules of common sense and safety, you can enjoy many safe hours servicing your own machine. If you ignore these rules you can hurt yourself or damage the equipment.

1. *Never* use gasoline as a cleaning solvent.

2. *Never* smoke or use a torch in the vicinity of flammable liquids, such as cleaning solvent, in open containers.

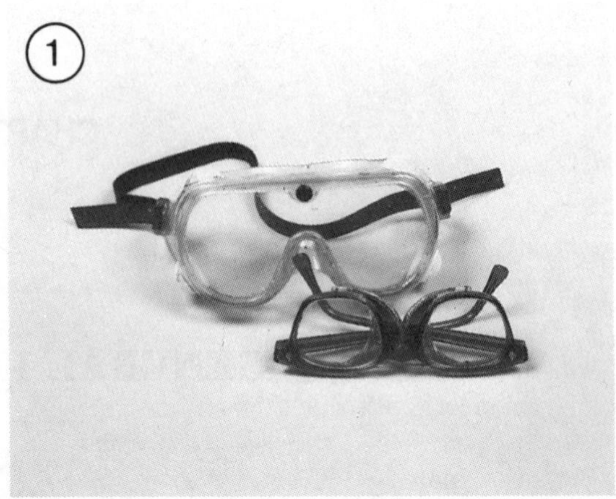

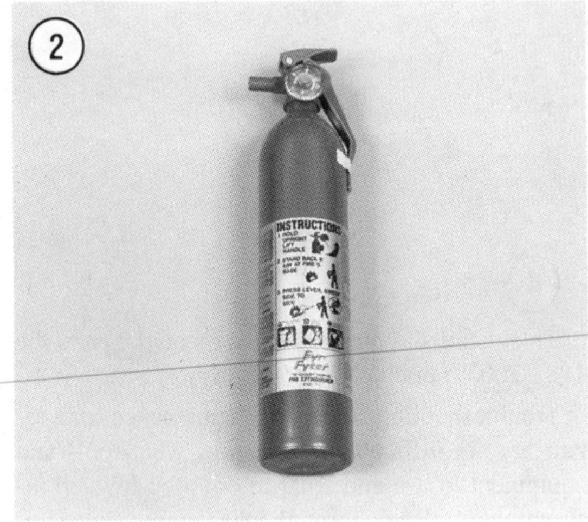

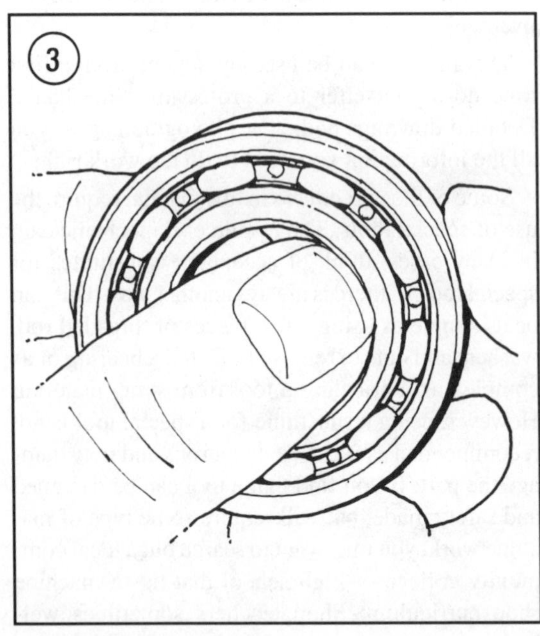

3. If welding or brazing is required on the machine, remove the fuel tank and rear shock to a safe distance, at least 50 ft. (15 m) away.

4. Use the proper sized wrenches to avoid damage to fasteners and injury to yourself.

5. When loosening a tight or stuck nut, be guided by what would happen if the wrench should slip. Be careful; protect yourself accordingly.

6. When replacing a fastener, make sure to use one with the same measurements and strength as the old one. Incorrect or mismatched fasteners can result in damage to the vehicle and possible personal injury. Beware of fastener kits that are filled with cheap and poorly made nuts, bolts, washers and cotter pins. Refer to *Fasteners* in this chapter for additional information.

7. Keep all hand and power tools in good condition. Wipe greasy and oily tools after using them. They are difficult to hold and can cause injury. Replace or repair worn or damaged tools.

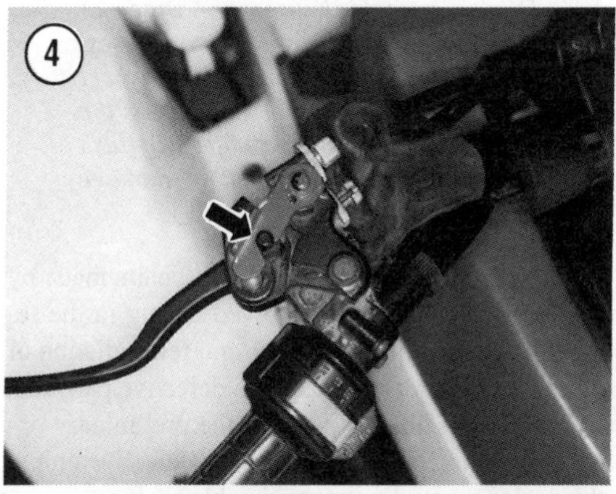

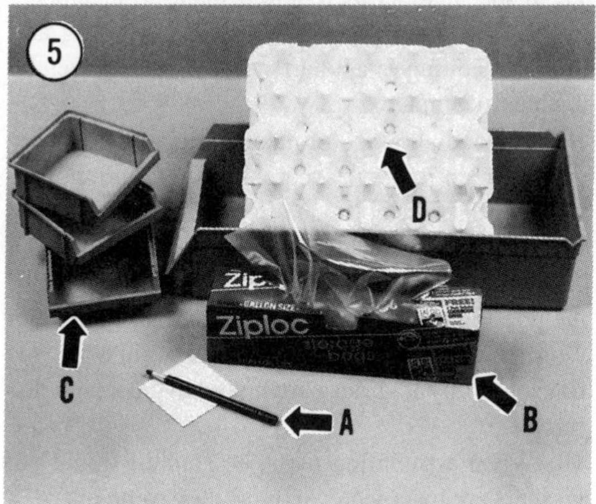

8. Keep your work area clean and uncluttered.

9. Wear safety goggles (**Figure 1**) during all operations involving drilling, grinding, the use of a cold chisel or *anytime* you feel unsure about the safety of your eyes. Safety goggles should also be worn anytime solvent and compressed air is used to clean parts.

10. Keep an approved fire extinguisher (**Figure 2**) nearby. Be sure it is rated for gasoline (Class B) and electrical (Class C) fires.

11. When drying bearings or other rotating parts with compressed air, never allow the air jet to rotate the bearing or part. The air jet is capable of rotating them at speeds far in excess of those for which they were designed. The bearing or rotating part is very likely to disintegrate and cause serious injury and damage. To prevent bearing damage when using compressed air, hold the inner bearing race by hand (**Figure 3**).

SERVICE HINTS

Most of the service procedures covered are straightforward and can be performed by anyone reasonably handy with tools. It is suggested, however, that you consider your own capabilities carefully before attempting any operation involving major disassembly of the engine assembly.

Take your time and do the job right. Do not forget that a newly rebuilt engine must be broken-in the same way as a new one. Refer to *Engine Break-in* in Chapter Five.

1. "Front," as used in this manual, refers to the front of the vehicle; the front of any component is the end closest to the front of the vehicle. The "left-" and "right-hand" sides refer to the position of the parts as viewed by a rider sitting on the seat facing forward. For example, the throttle control is on the right-hand side. These rules are simple, but confusion can cause a major inconvenience during service.

2. Whenever servicing the engine or clutch, or when removing a suspension component, the vehicle should be secured in a safe manner and the parking brake (**Figure 4**) applied.

3. Tag all similar internal parts for location and mark all mating parts for position (A, **Figure 5**). Record number and thickness of any shims as they are removed. Small parts such as bolts can be iden-

tified by placing them in plastic sandwich bags (B, **Figure 5**). Seal and label them with masking tape.

4. Place parts from a specific area of the engine (e.g. cylinder head, cylinder, clutch, shift mechanism, etc.) into plastic boxes (C, **Figure 5**) to keep them separated.

5. When disassembling transmission shaft assemblies, use an egg flat (the type that restaurants get their eggs in) (D, **Figure 5**) and set the parts from the shaft in one of the depressions in the same order in which they were removed.

6. Wiring should be tagged with masking tape and marked as each wire is removed. Again, do not rely on memory alone.

7. Finished surfaces should be protected from physical damage or corrosion. Keep gasoline and brake fluid off painted surfaces.

8. Use penetrating oil on frozen or tight bolts, then strike the bolt head a few times with a hammer and punch (use a screwdriver on screws). Avoid the use of heat where possible, as it can warp, melt or affect the temper of parts. Heat also ruins finishes, especially paint and plastics.

9. No parts removed or installed (other than bushings and bearings) in the procedures given in this manual should require unusual force during disassembly or assembly. If a part is difficult to remove or install, find out why before proceeding.

10. Cover all openings after removing parts or components to prevent dirt, small tools, etc. from falling in.

11. Read each procedure *completely* while looking at the actual parts before starting a job. Make sure you *thoroughly* understand what is to be done and then carefully follow the procedure, step by step.

12. Recommendations are occasionally made to refer service or maintenance to a Yamaha dealer or a specialist in a particular field. In these cases, the work will be done more quickly and economically than if you performed the job yourself.

13. In procedural steps, the term "replace" means to discard a defective part and replace it with a new or exchange unit. "Overhaul" means to remove, disassemble, inspect, measure, repair or replace defective parts, reassemble and install major systems or parts.

14. Some operations require the use of a hydraulic press. It is wiser to have these operations performed by a shop equipped for such work, rather than to try to do the job yourself with makeshift equipment that may damage your machine.

15. Repairs go much faster and easier if your machine is clean before you begin work. There are many special cleaners on the market, like Bel-Ray Degreaser, for washing the engine and related parts. Follow the manufacturer's directions on the container for the best results. Clean all oily or greasy parts with cleaning solvent as you remove them. See *Washing the Vehicle* in this chapter.

CAUTION

Do not spray the vehicle with a degreaser or similar chemical while the O-ring drive chain is installed; otherwise, these chemicals can cause the O-rings in the chain to swell, permanently damaging the chain.

WARNING

Gasoline is highly flammable. Do not use gasoline to clean parts as an explosion and fire may occur.

CAUTION

Don't direct high pressure water at steering bearings, carburetor hoses, suspension linkage components, wheel bearings, electrical components or the O-ring drive chain. The water will flush grease out of the bearings or damage the seals.

16. Much of the labor charges for repairs made by dealers are for the time involved during in the removal, disassembly, assembly, and reinstallation of other parts in order to reach the defective part. It is frequently possible to perform the preliminary operations yourself and then take the defective unit to the dealer for repair at considerable savings.

17. If special tools are required, make arrangements to get them before you start. It is frustrating and time-consuming to get partly into a job and then be unable to complete it.

18. Make diagrams (or take a Polaroid picture) wherever similar-appearing parts are found. For instance, crankcase bolts are often not the same length. You may think you can remember where everything came from—but mistakes are costly. There is also the possibility that you may be sidetracked and not return to work for days or even weeks—in which the time carefully laid out parts may have become disturbed.

19. When assembling parts, be sure all shims and washers are installed exactly as they came out.

20. Whenever a rotating part butts against a stationary part, look for a shim or washer. Use new gaskets if there is any doubt about the condition of the old ones. A thin coat of oil on nonpressure type gaskets may help them seal more effectively.

21. High spots may be sanded off a piston with sandpaper, but fine emery cloth and oil will do a much more professional job.

22. Carbon can be removed from the cylinder head, the piston crowns and the exhaust ports with a suitable wire wheel. Do *not* scratch machined surfaces. Wipe off the surface with a clean cloth when finished.

23. Heavy grease can be used to hold small parts in place if they tend to fall out during assembly. However, keep grease and oil away from electrical and brake components.

WASHING THE VEHICLE

Since the Banshee is an off-road vehicle, and if you are using it often and maintaining it properly, you will spend a lot of time cleaning it. After riding it in extremely dirty areas, wash it down thoroughly. Doing this will make maintenance and service procedures quick and easy. More important, proper cleaning will prevent dirt from falling into critical areas undetected. Failing to clean the vehicle or cleaning it incorrectly will add to your maintenance costs and shop time because dirty parts wear out prematurely. It's unthinkable that your vehicle could break because of improper cleaning, but it can happen.

When cleaning your Yamaha, you will need a few tools, shop rags, scrub brush, bucket, liquid cleaner and access to water. Many riders use a coin-operated car wash. Coin-operated car washes are convenient and quick, but with improper use, the high water pressures can do more damage than good to your vehicle.

NOTE

Simple Green is a safe biodegradable, nontoxic and nonflammable liquid cleaner. It works well for washing your vehicle and removing grease and oil from engine and suspension parts. Simple Green can be purchased through some supermarkets, hardware, garden and discount supply houses. Follow the directions on the container for recommended dilution ratios.

When cleaning your vehicle, and especially when using a spray type degreaser, remember that what goes on the vehicle will rinse off and drip onto your driveway or into your yard. If you can, use a degreaser at a coin-operated car wash. If you are cleaning your vehicle at home, place thick cardboard or newspapers underneath the vehicle to catch the oil and grease deposits that are rinsed off.

1. Place the vehicle on level ground and set the parking brake.
2. Check the following before washing the vehicle:
   a. Make sure the gas filler cap is screwed on tightly.
   b. Make sure the engine oil cap is on tight.
   c. Plug the silencer openings with pipe plugs or rags.
   d. Remove the seat and cover the air box with plastic.
   e. If you are going to use some type of chemical degreaser to clean your Yamaha, first remove the O-ring drive chain.
3. Wash the vehicle from top to bottom with soapy water. Use the scrub brush to get excess dirt out of the wheel rims and engine crannies. Concentrate on the upper controls, engine, side panels and gas tank during this wash cycle. Don't forget to wash dirt and mud from underneath the fenders, suspension and engine crankcase.
4. Next, concentrate on the frame tube members, outer airbox areas, suspension linkage, rear shock and swing arm.
5. Direct the hose underneath the engine and swing arm. Wash this area thoroughly.
6. Finally, rinse using cold water without soap and spray the entire vehicle again. Use as much time and care when rinsing the vehicle as when washing it. Built up soap deposits will quickly corrode electrical connections and remove the natural oils from tires, causing premature cracks and wear. Make sure you thoroughly rinse the vehicle off.
7. Tip the vehicle from side to side to allow any water that has collected on horizontal surfaces to drain off.
8. Remove the seat and remove the plastic cover from around the air box.
9. Remove the pipe plugs or rags from the silencer openings.

10. If you are washing the vehicle at home, start the engine. Idle the engine to burn off any internal moisture.

11. Before taking the vehicle into the garage, wipe it dry with a soft cloth or chamois. Inspect the machine as you dry it for further signs of dirt and grime. Make a quick visual inspection of the frame and other painted pieces. Spray any worn-down spots with WD-40 or Bel-Ray 6-in-1 to prevent rust from building on the bare metal. When the vehicle is back at your work area you can repaint the bare areas with touch-up paint after cleaning off the WD-40. A quick shot from a touch-up paint can each time you work on the vehicle will keep it looking sharp and stop rust from building and weakening parts.

TORQUE SPECIFICATIONS

The materials used in the manufacture of your Yamaha can be subjected to uneven torque stresses if the fasteners used to hold the sub-assemblies are not installed and torqued correctly. Improper bolt tightening can cause cylinder head warpage, crankcase leaks, premature bearing and seal failure and suspension failure from loose or missing fasteners. An accurate torque wrench (described in this chapter) should be used together with the torque specifications listed at the end of most chapters.

Torque specifications throughout this manual are given in Newton-meters (N•m) and foot-pounds (ft.-lb.).

Existing torque wrenches calibrated in meter kilograms can be used by performing a simple conversion. All you have to do is move the decimal point one place to the right; for example, 3.5 mkg = 35 N•m. This conversion is accurate enough for mechanical work even though the exact mathematical conversion is 3.5 mkg = 34.3 N•m.

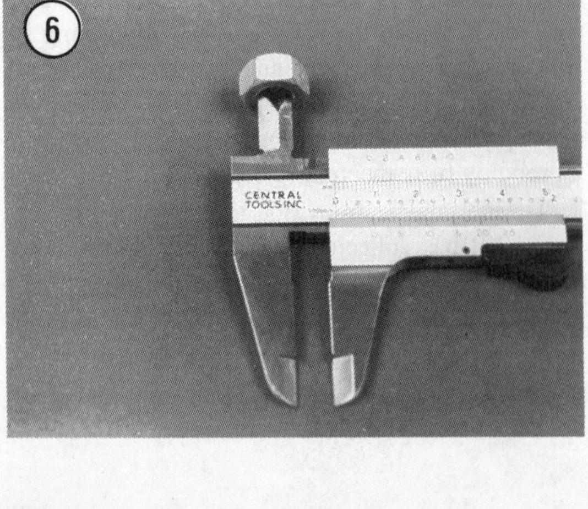

Refer to **Table 6** for standard torque specifications for various size screws, bolts and nuts that may not be listed in the respective chapters. To use the table, first determine the size of the bolt or nut. Use a vernier caliper and measure the inside dimension of the threads of the nut (**Figure 6**) and across the threads for a bolt (**Figure 7**).

FASTENERS

The materials and designs of the various fasteners used on your Yamaha are not arrived at by chance or accident. Fastener design determines the type of tool required to work the fastener. Fastener material is carefully selected to decrease the possibility of physical failure.

Nuts, bolts and screws are manufactured in a wide range of thread patterns. To join a nut and bolt, the diameter of the bolt and the diameter of the hole in

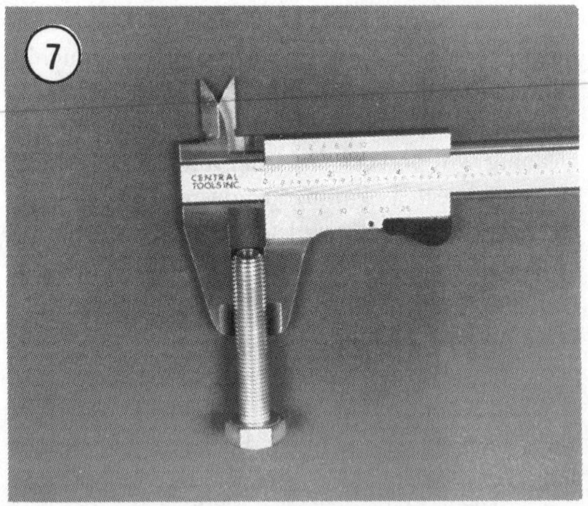

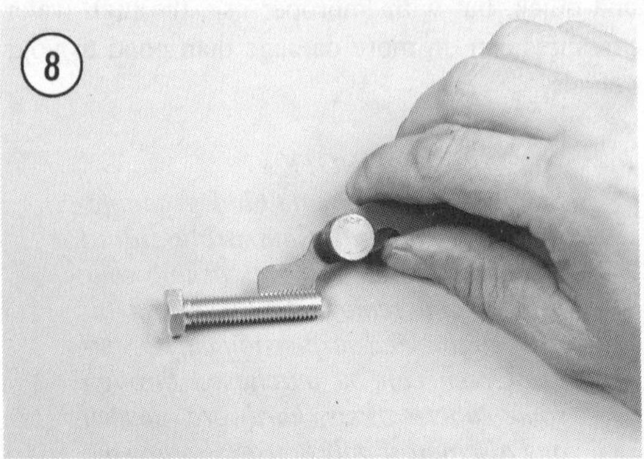

the nut must be the same. It is just as important that the threads on both be properly matched.

The best way to tell if the threads on 2 fasteners are matched is to turn the nut on the bolt (or the bolt into the threaded hole in a piece of equipment) with fingers only. Be sure both pieces are clean. If much force is required, check the thread condition on each fastener. If the thread condition is good but the fasteners jam, the threads are not compatible. A thread pitch gauge (**Figure 8**) can also be used to determine pitch. Yamaha ATV's and motorcycles are manufactured with ISO (International Organization for Standardization) metric fasteners. The threads are cut differently than that of American fasteners (**Figure 9**).

Most threads are cut so that the fastener must be turned clockwise to tighten it. These are called right-hand threads. Some fasteners have left-hand threads; they must be turned counterclockwise to be tightened. Left-hand threads are used in locations where normal rotation of the equipment would tend to loosen a right-hand threaded fastener.

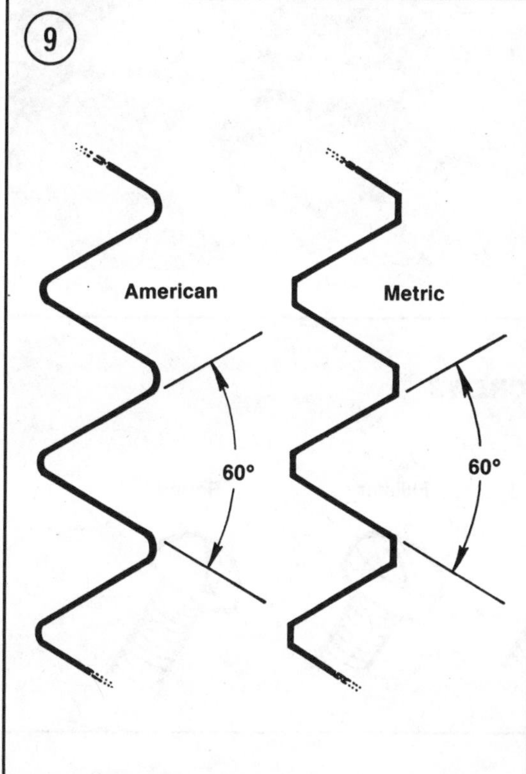

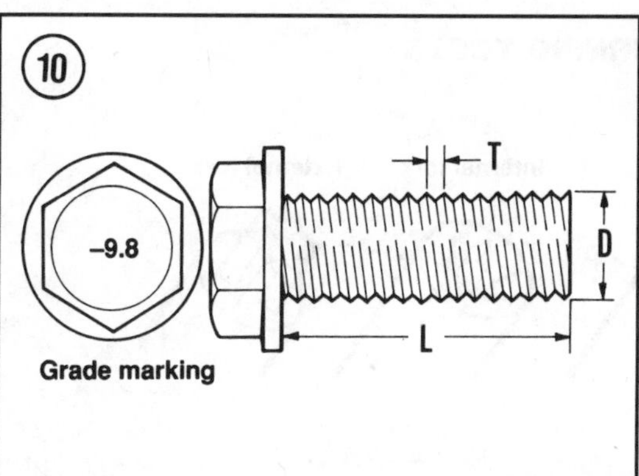

ISO Metric Screw Threads (Bolts, Nuts and Screws)

ISO (International Organization for Standardization) metric threads come in 3 standard thread sizes: coarse, fine and constant pitch. The ISO coarse pitch is used for most all common fastener applications. The fine pitch thread is used on certain precision tools and instruments. The constant pitch thread is used mainly on machine parts and not for fasteners. The constant pitch thread, however, is used on all metric thread spark plugs.

Metric screws and bolts are classified by length (L, **Figure 10**), nominal diameter (D) and distance between thread crests (T). A typical bolt might be identified by the numbers 8-1.25 × 130, which would indicate that the bolt has a nominal diameter of 8 mm, the distance between thread crests is 1.25 mm and bolt length is 130 mm.

The strength of metric screws and bolts is indicated by numbers located on the top of the screw or bolt as shown in **Figure 10**. The higher the number the stronger the screw or bolt. Unnumbered screws or bolts are the weakest.

CAUTION

Do not install fasteners with a lower strength grade classification than installed originally by the manufacturer. Doing so may cause engine or equipment failure and possible injury.

The measurement across 2 flats on the head of the bolt indicates the proper wrench size to be used. **Figure 7** shows how to determine bolt diameter.

When purchasing a bolt from a dealer or parts store, it is important to know how to specify bolt length. The correct way to measure bolt length is by measuring the length starting from underneath the bolt head to the end of the bolt (**Figure 11**). Always measure bolt length in this manner to avoid purchasing bolts that are too long.

Machine Screws

There are many different types of machine screws. **Figure 12** shows a number of screw heads requiring different types of turning tools. Heads are also designed to protrude above the metal (round) or to be slightly recessed in the metal (flat). See **Figure 13**.

Nuts

Nuts are manufactured in a variety of types and sizes. Most are hexagonal (6-sided) and fit on bolts, screws and studs with the same diameter and pitch.

Figure 14 shows several types of nuts. The common nut is generally used with a lockwasher. Self-locking nuts have a nylon insert which prevents the nut from loosening; no lockwasher is required. Wing nuts are designed for fast removal by hand. Wing nuts are used for convenience in non-critical locations.

To indicate the size of a metric nut, manufacturers specify the diameter of the opening and the thread

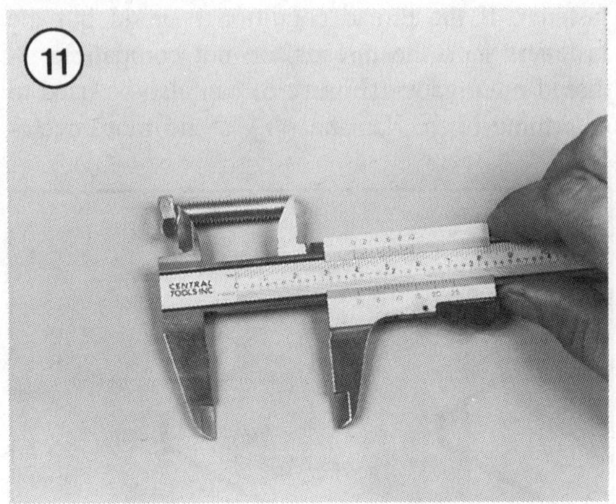

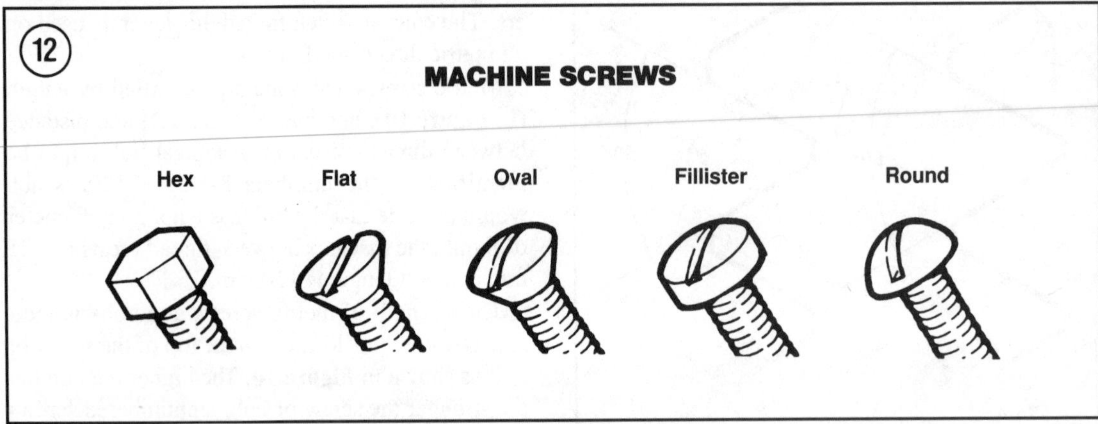

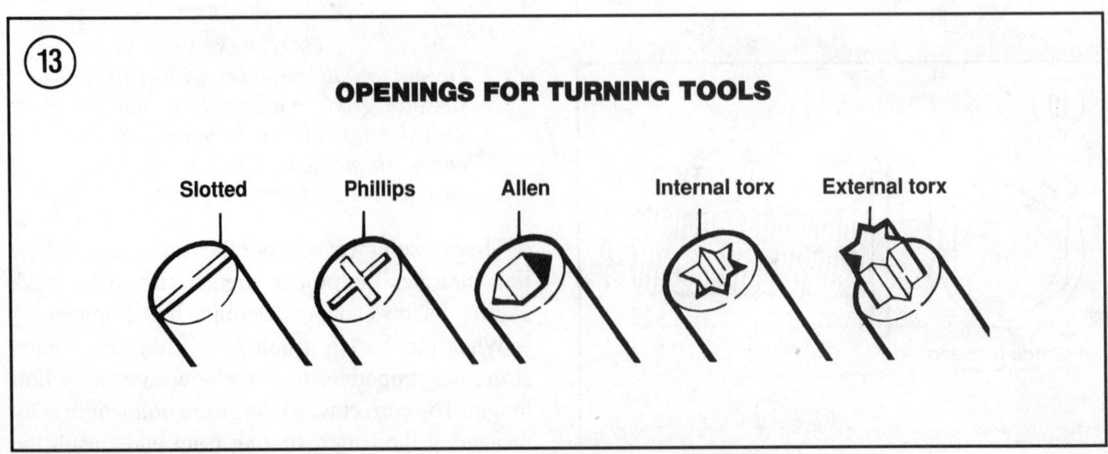

pitch. This is similar to bolt specifications, but without the length dimension. The measurement across 2 flats on the nut indicates the proper wrench size to be used (**Figure 15**).

Self-Locking Fasteners

Several types of bolts, screws and nuts incorporate a system that develops an interference between the bolt, screw, nut or tapped hole threads. Interference is achieved in various ways: by distorting threads, coating threads with dry adhesive or nylon, distorting the top of an all-metal nut, using a nylon insert in the center or at the top of a nut, etc.

Self-locking fasteners offer greater holding strength and better vibration resistance. Some self-locking fasteners can be reused if in good condition. Others, like the nylon insert nut, form an initial locking condition when the nut is first installed; the nylon forms closely to the bolt thread pattern, thus reducing any tendency for the nut to loosen. When the nut is removed, the locking efficiency is greatly reduced. For greatest safety, self-locking fasteners should be discarded and new ones installed whenever components are removed or disassembled.

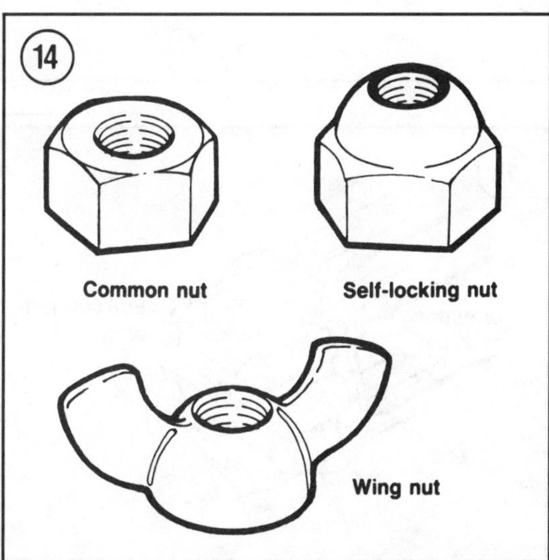

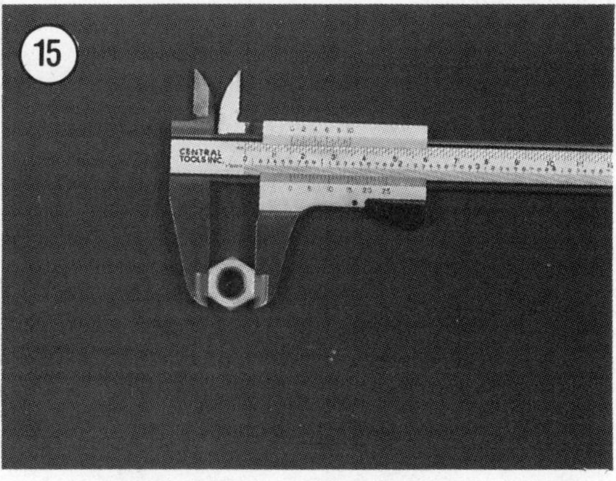

Washers

There are 2 basic types of washers: flat washers and lockwashers. Flat washers are simple discs with a hole to fit a screw or bolt. Lockwashers are designed to prevent a fastener from working loose due to vibration, expansion and contraction. **Figure 16** shows several types of lockwashers. Washers are also used in the following functions:

a. As spacers.

b. To prevent galling or damage of the equipment by the fastener.

c. To help distribute fastener load during torquing.

d. As seals.

Note that flat washers are often used between a lockwasher and a fastener to provide a smooth bearing surface. This allows the fastener to be turned easily with a tool.

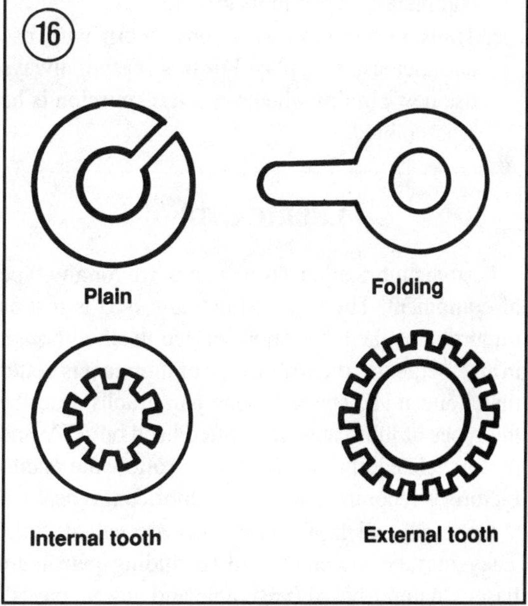

Cotter Pins

Cotter pins (**Figure 17**) are used to secure special kinds of fasteners. The threaded stud must have a hole in it; the nut or nut lock piece has castellations around which the cotter pin ends wrap. Cotter pins should *not* be reused after removal.

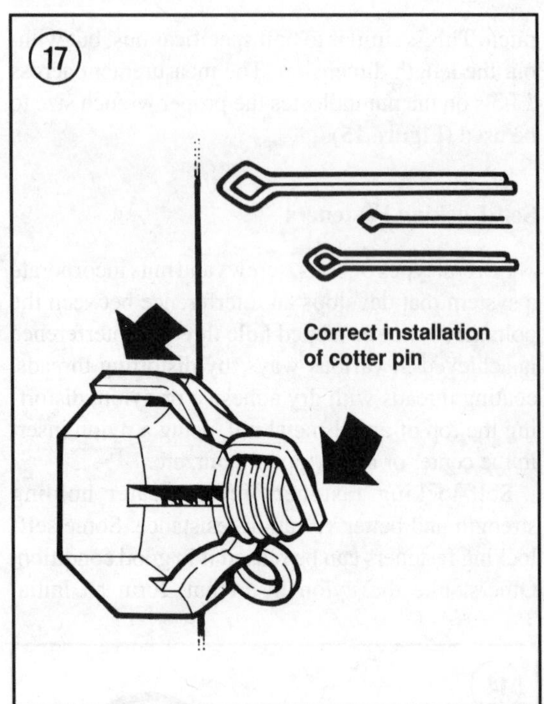

Circlips

Circlips can be internal or external design. They are used to retain items on shafts (external type) or within tubes (internal type). In some applications, circlips of varying thicknesses are used to control the end play of parts assemblies. These are often called selective circlips. Circlips should be replaced during installation, as removal weakens and deforms them.

Two basic styles of circlips are available: machined and stamped circlips. Machined circlips (**Figure 18**) can be installed in either direction (shaft or housing) because both faces are machined, thus creating two sharp edges. Stamped circlips (**Figure 19**) are manufactured with one sharp edge and one rounded edge. When installing stamped circlips in a thrust situation (transmission shafts, fork tubes, etc.), the sharp edge must face away from the part producing the thrust. When installing circlips, observe the following:

a. Compress or expand circlips only enough to install them.
b. After the circlip is installed, make sure it is completely seated in its groove.
c. Transmission circlips become worn with use and increase side play. For this reason, always use new circlips whenever a transmission is be reassembled.

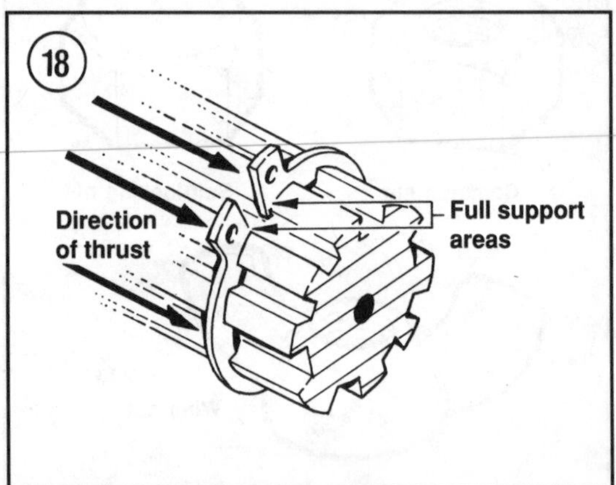

LUBRICANTS

Periodic lubrication assures long life for any type of equipment. The *type* of lubricant used is just as important as the lubrication service itself, although in an emergency, the wrong type of lubricant is better than none at all. The following paragraphs describe the types of lubricants most often used on ATV and motorcycle equipment. Be sure to follow the manufacturer's recommendations for lubricant types.

Generally, all liquid lubricants are called "oil." They may be mineral-based (including petroleum bases), natural-based (vegetable and animal bases),

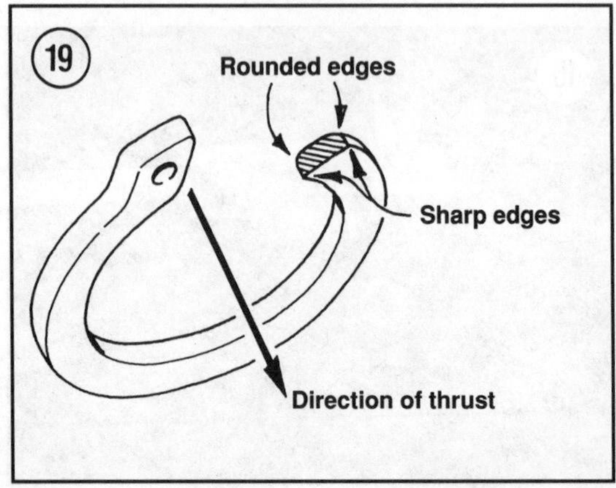

synthetic-based or emulsions (mixtures). "Grease" is an oil to which a thickening base has been added so that the end product is semi-solid. Grease is often classified by the type of thickener added; lithium soap is commonly used.

2-cycle Engine Oil

Lubrication for a two-stroke engine is provided by oil mixed with the incoming air/fuel mixture. Some of the oil mist settles out in the crankcase, lubricating the crankshaft and the connecting rod lower end. The rest of the oil enters the combustion chamber to lubricate the piston rings and cylinder walls. This oil is burned during the combustion process.

Engine oil must have several special qualities to work well in a 2-stroke engine. It must mix easily and stay in suspension in gasoline. When burned, it can't leave behind excessive deposits. It must be appropriate for the high temperatures associated with with 2-stroke engines.

In addition to oil grade, manufacturers specify the ratio of gasoline to oil required during break-in and normal engine operation. Using too little oil will cause excessive engine wear and overheating and result in seizure. Too much oil will cause excessive carbon build-up in the combustion chamber and exhaust port.

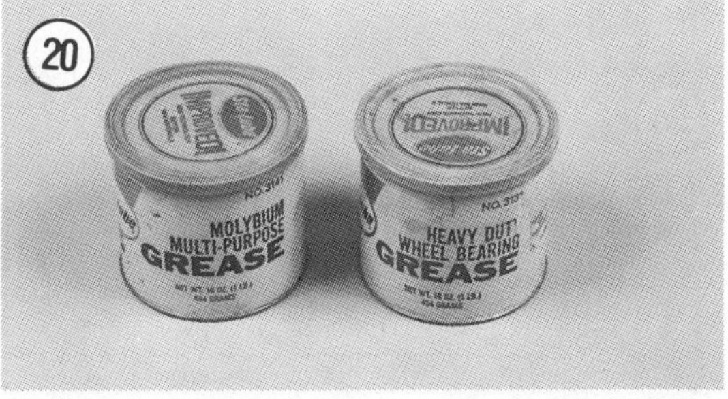

4-cycle Oil

Four-cycle oil used in your Yamaha lubricates the transmission and clutch components. Gears tend to shear the polymers in the oil which control viscosity. For this reason, you should always use an oil designed specifically for motorcycle and ATV use. Motorcycle and ATV gear oil contain additional amounts of EP (extra pressure) additives to prevent oil shear. The SAE and API oil ratings do not address this unique need.

NOTE

The oil viscosity numbers on motorcycle and ATV designated gear oil differ from regular SAE numbers. Refer to the application numbers on the back of the oil can (specified for motorcycle and ATV use) when cross-referencing oil viscosity.

Grease

Greases are graded by the National Lubricating Grease Institute (NLGI). Greases are graded by number according to the consistency of the grease; these range from No. 000 to No. 6, with No. 6 being the most solid. A typical multipurpose grease is NLGI No. 2. For specific applications, equipment manufacturers may require grease with an additive such as molybdenum disulfide (MOS2) (**Figure 20**).

THREADLOCK

A threadlock should be used to help secure many of the fasteners used on your Yamaha. A threadlock will lock fasteners against vibration loosening and seal against leaks. Loctite 242 (blue) and 271 (red) are recommended for many threadlock requirements described in this manual (**Figure 21**). There are other quality threadlock brands on the market.

EXPENDABLE SUPPLIES

Certain expendable supplies are required during maintenance and repair work. These include grease, oil, gasket cement, wiping rags and cleaning solvent. Ask your dealer for the special locking compounds, silicone lubricants and other products which make vehicle maintenance simpler and easier. Cleaning solvent or kerosene is available at some service stations, paint or hardware stores.

WARNING
Solvent soaked rags stored in an open container or piled on the floor can ignite from spontaneous combustion. Store rags and similar materials in a covered metal container until they can be washed or discarded; otherwise, a fire may occur, causing loss of the workshop or building and severe personal injury.

NOTE
To avoid absorbing solvent and other chemicals into your skin while cleaning parts, wear a pair of petroleum-resistant rubber gloves. These can be purchased through industrial supply houses or well-equipped hardware stores.

PARTS REPLACEMENT

Yamaha makes frequent changes during a model year, some minor, some relatively major. When you order parts from the dealer or other parts distributor, always order by frame and engine numbers. The frame serial number is stamped on the left-hand lower frame member (**Figure 22**). The engine number is stamped on a raised pad on the left-hand side of the upper crankcase (**Figure 23**). The first 3 digits are for model identification. The remaining digits are production numbers.

Write the numbers down and carry them with you. Compare new parts to old before purchasing them. If they are not alike, have the parts manager explain the difference to you. **Table 1** lists engine serial numbers for the models covered in this manual.

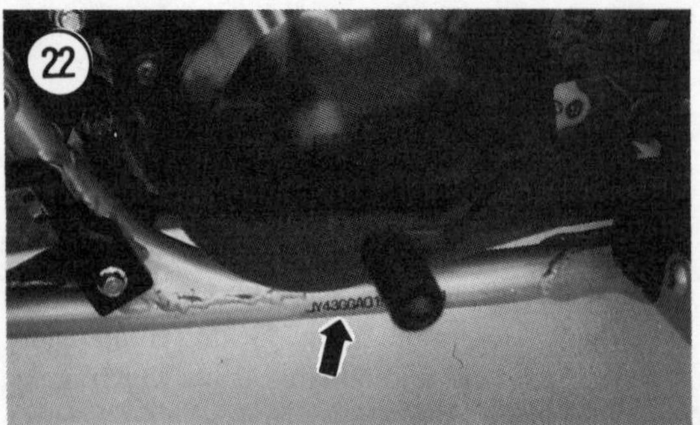
22

BASIC HAND TOOLS

Many of the procedures in this manual can be carried out with simple hand tools and test equipment familiar to the average home mechanic. Keep your tools clean and in a tool box. Keep them organized with the sockets and related drives together, the open-end combination wrenches together, etc. After using a tool, wipe off dirt and grease with a clean cloth and return the tool to its correct place.

Top-quality tools are essential; they are also more economical in the long run. If you are now starting to build your tool collection, stay away from the "advertised specials" featured at some parts houses, discount stores and chain drug stores. These are usually a poor grade tool that can be sold cheaply and that is exactly what they are—*cheap*. They are usually made of inferior material, and are thick,

23

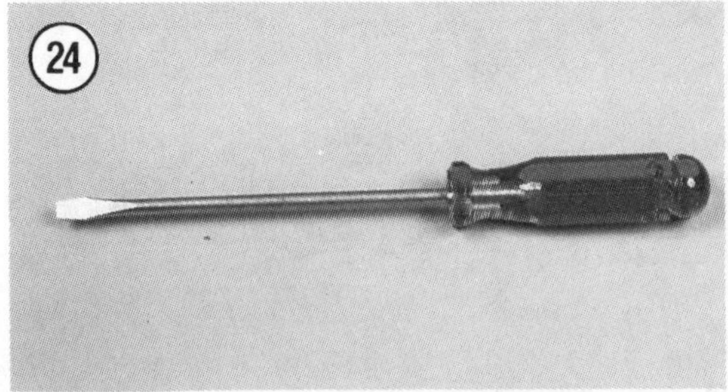
24

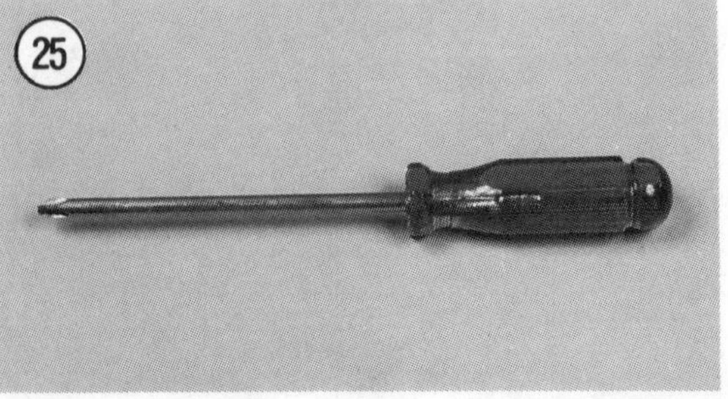
25

heavy and clumsy. Their rough finish makes them difficult to clean and they usually don't last very long. If it is ever your misfortune to use such tools, you will probably find out that the wrenches do not fit the heads of bolts and nuts correctly and damage the fastener.

Quality tools are made of alloy steel and are heat treated for greater strength. They are lighter and better balanced than cheap ones. Their surface is smooth, making them a pleasure to work with and easy to clean. The initial cost of good quality tools may be more but they are cheaper in the long run. Don't try to buy everything in all sizes in the beginning; do it a little at a time until you have the necessary tools.

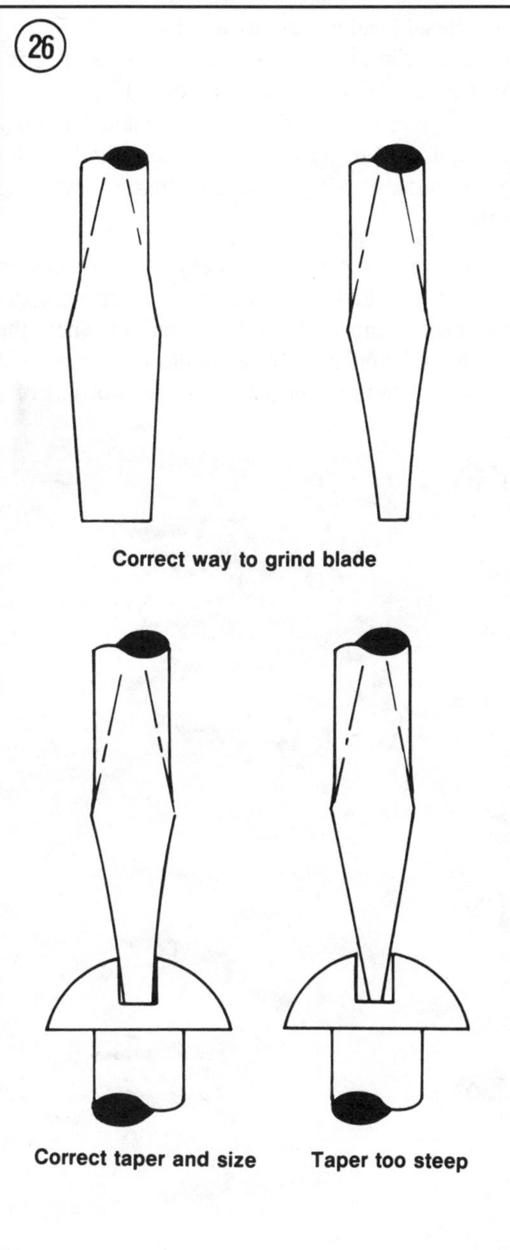

Screwdrivers

The screwdriver is a very basic tool, but if used improperly it will do more damage than good. The slot on a screw has a definite dimension and shape. A screwdriver must be selected to conform with that shape. Use a small screwdriver for small screws and a large one for large screws or the screw head will be damaged.

Two basic types of screwdriver are required: common (flat-blade) screwdrivers (**Figure 24**) and Phillips screwdrivers (**Figure 25**).

Screwdrivers are available in sets which often include an assortment of common and Phillips blades. If you buy them individually, buy at least the following:

a. Common screwdriver—5/16 × 6 in. blade.
b. Common screwdriver—3/8 × 12 in. blade.
c. Phillips screwdriver—size 2 tip, 6 in. blade.
d. Phillips screwdriver—size 3 tip, 6 and 10 in. blade.

Use screwdrivers only for driving screws. Never use a screwdriver for prying or chiseling metal. Do not try to remove a Phillips or Allen head screw with a common screwdriver (unless the screw has a combination head that will accept either type); you can damage the head so that the proper tool will be unable to remove it.

Keep screwdrivers in the proper condition and they will last longer and perform better. Always keep the tip of a common screwdriver in good condition. **Figure 26** shows how to grind the tip to the proper shape if it becomes damaged. Note the symmetrical sides of the tip.

Pliers

Pliers come in a wide range of types and sizes. Pliers are useful for cutting, bending and crimping. They should never be used to cut hardened objects or to turn bolts or nuts. **Figure 27** shows several pliers useful in ATV and motorcycle repair.

Each type of pliers has a specialized function. Slip-joint pliers are general purpose pliers and are used mainly for holding things and for bending.

Needlenose pliers are used to hold or bend small objects. Channel lock pliers can be adjusted to hold various sizes of objects; the jaws remain parallel to grip around objects such as pipe or tubing. There are many more types of pliers. The ones described here are most suitable for vehicle repairs.

Vise-grip Pliers

Vise-grip pliers (**Figure 28**) are used to hold objects very tightly like a vise. However, avoid using them unless absolutely necessary since their sharp jaws will permanently scar any objects which are held. Vise-grip pliers are available in many types for more specific tasks.

Circlip Pliers

Circlip pliers (**Figure 29**) are special in that they are only used to remove circlips from shafts or within engine or suspension housings. When purchasing circlip pliers, there are two kinds to distinguish from. External pliers (spreading) are used to remove circlips that fit on the outside of a shaft. Internal pliers (squeezing) are used to remove circlips which fit inside a gear or housing.

WARNING
Circlips can slip and "fly off" when removing and installing them. To prevent eye injury, wear safety glasses.

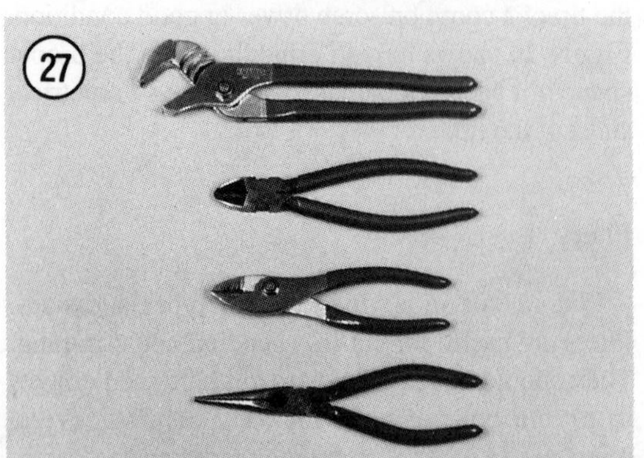
27

Box-end, Open-end and Combination Wrenches

Box-end, open-end and combination wrenches are available in sets or separately in a variety of sizes. On open and box end wrenches, the number stamped near the end refers to the distance between 2 parallel flats on the hex head bolt or nut. On combination wrenches, the number is stamped near the center.

Box-end wrenches require clear overhead access to the fastener but can work well in situations where the fastener head is close to another part. They grip on all six edges of a fastener for a very secure grip. They are available in either 6-point or 12-point. The 6-point gives superior holding power and durability but requires a greater swinging radius. The 12-point works better in situations with limited swinging radius.

Open-end wrenches are speedy and work best in areas with limited overhead access. Their wide flat jaws make them unstable for situations where the bolt or nut is sunken in a well or close to the edge of a casting. These wrenches grip only two flats of a

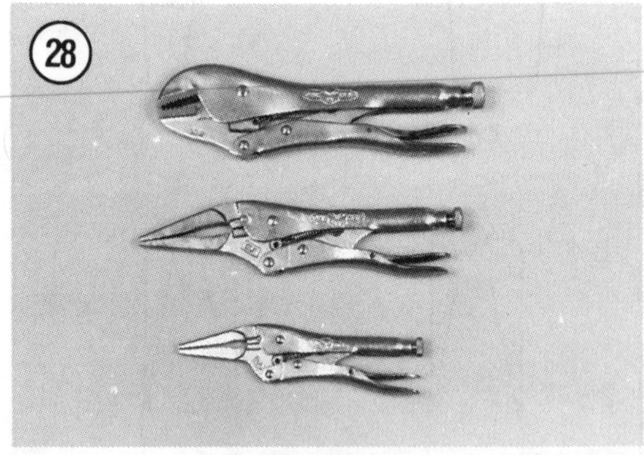
28

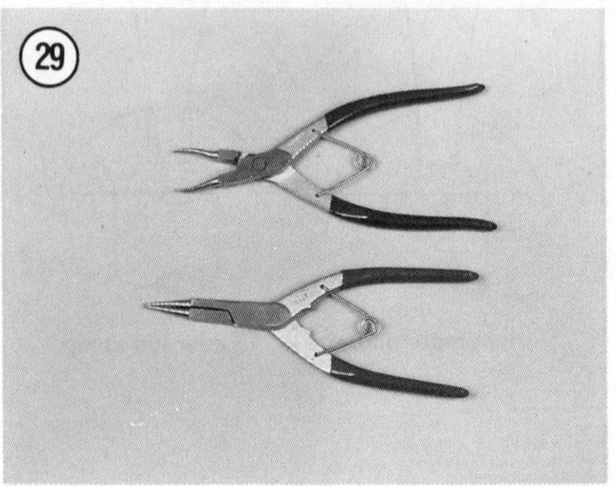
29

fastener so if either the fastener head or the wrench jaws are worn, the wrench may slip off.

Combination wrenches (**Figure 30**) have open-end on one side and box-end on the other with both ends being the same size. These wrenches are favored by professionals because of their versatility.

Adjustable (Crescent) Wrenches

An adjustable wrench (sometimes called crescent wrench) can be adjusted to fit nearly any nut or bolt head which has clear access around its entire perimeter. Adjustable wrenches (**Figure 31**) are best used as a backup wrench to keep a large nut or bolt from turning while the other end is being loosened or tightened with a proper wrench.

Adjustable wrenches have only two gripping surfaces which make them more subject to slipping off the fastener and damaging the part and possibly injuring your hand. The fact that one jaw is adjustable only aggravates this shortcoming.

These wrenches are directional; the solid jaw must be the one transmitting the force. If you use the adjustable jaw to transmit the force, it will loosen and possibly slip off.

Adjustable wrenches come in all sizes but something in the 6 to 8 in. range is recommended as an all-purpose wrench.

Socket Wrenches

This type is undoubtedly the fastest, safest and most convenient to use. Sockets which attach to a ratchet handle (**Figure 32**) are available with 6-point or 12-point openings and 1/4, 3/8, 1/2 and 3/4 in. drives. The drive size indicates the size of the square hole which mates with the ratchet handle (**Figure 33**).

Allen Wrenches

Allen wrenches are available in sets or separately in a variety of sizes. These sets come in SAE and metric size, so be sure to buy a metric set. Allen bolts are sometimes called socket bolts. Sometimes the bolts are difficult to reach, and it is suggested that a variety of Allen wrenches be purchased (e.g. socket

30

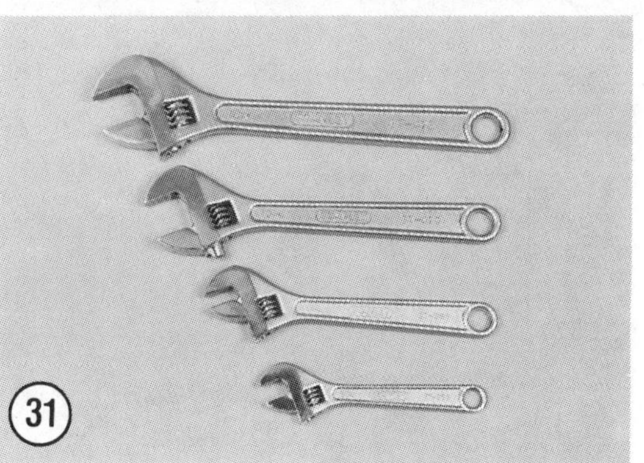

31

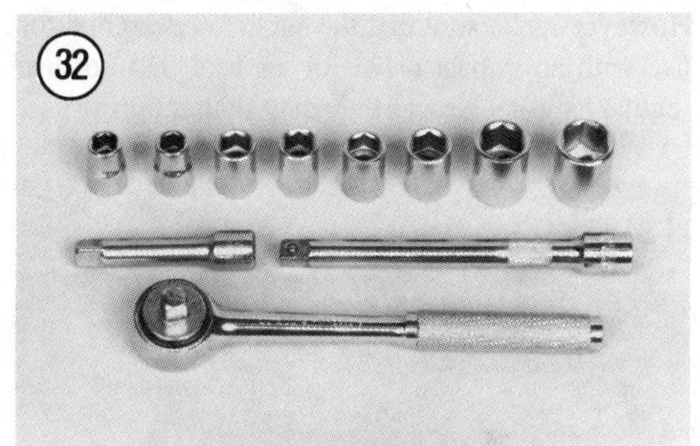

32

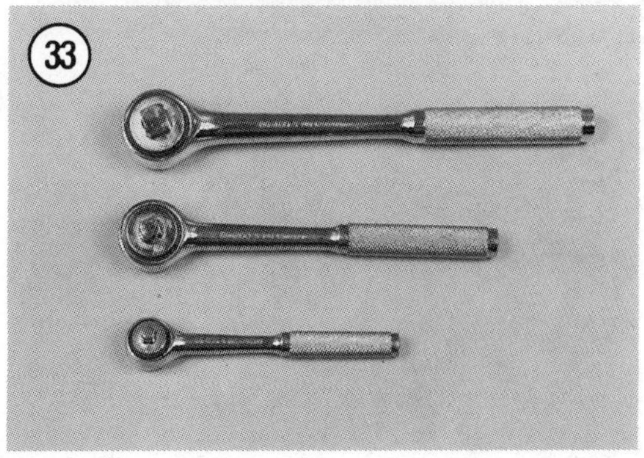

33

driven, T-handle and extension type) as shown in **Figure 34**.

Torque Wrench

A torque wrench is used with a socket to measure how tightly a nut or bolt is installed. They come in a wide price range and with either 1/4, 3/8 or 1/2 in. square drive (**Figure 35**). The drive size indicates the size of the square drive which mates with the socket.

Impact Driver

This tool might have been designed with the ATV and motorcycle rider in mind. This tool makes removal of fasteners easy and eliminates damage to bolts and screw slots. Impact drivers and interchangeable bits (**Figure 36**) are available at most large hardware, motorcycle or auto parts stores. Don't purchase a cheap one as they do not work as well and require more force (the "use a larger hammer" syndrome) than a moderately priced one. Sockets can also be used with a hand impact driver. However, make sure that the socket is designed for use with an impact driver or air tool. Do not use regular hand sockets, as they may shatter during use.

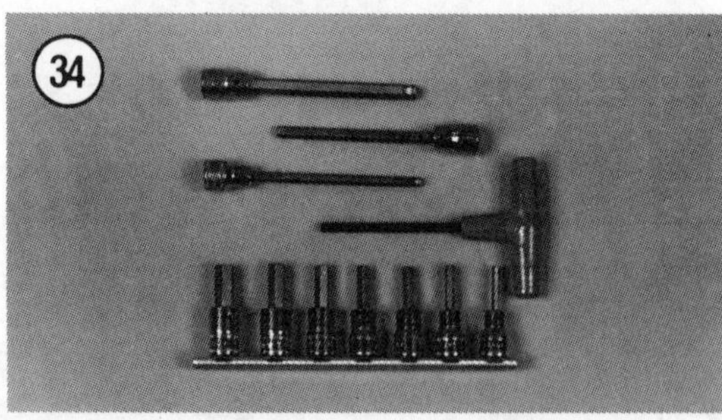
34

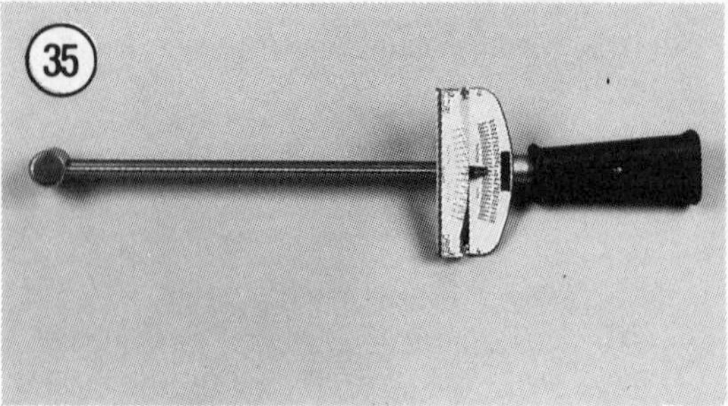
35

Hammers

The correct hammer (**Figure 37**) is necessary for repairs. Use only a hammer with a face (or head) of rubber or plastic or the soft-faced type that is filled with buckshot. These are sometimes necessary in engine teardowns. *Never* use a metal-faced hammer on engine or suspension parts, as severe damage will result in most cases. You can always produce the same amount of force with a soft-faced hammer. A

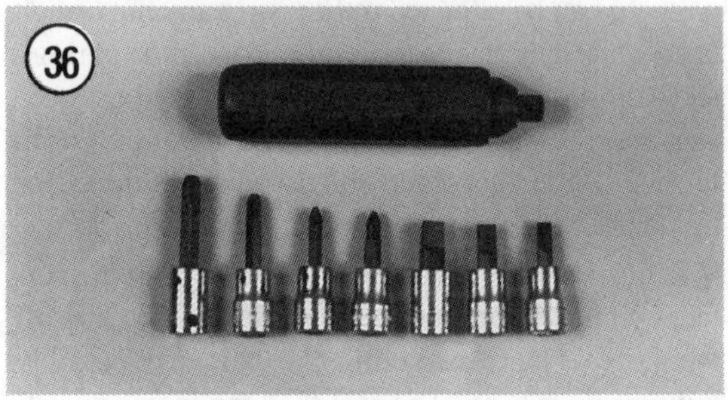
36

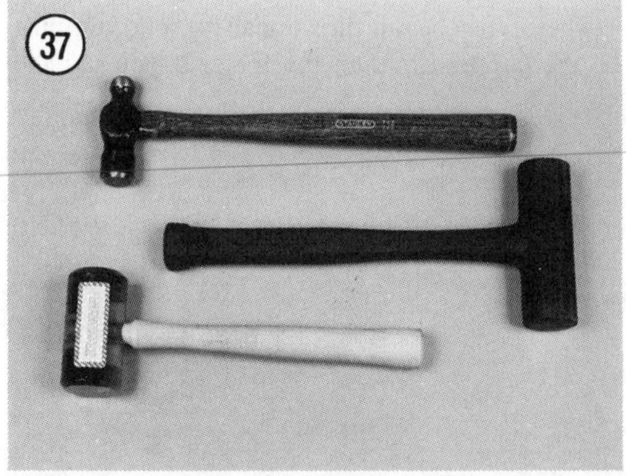
37

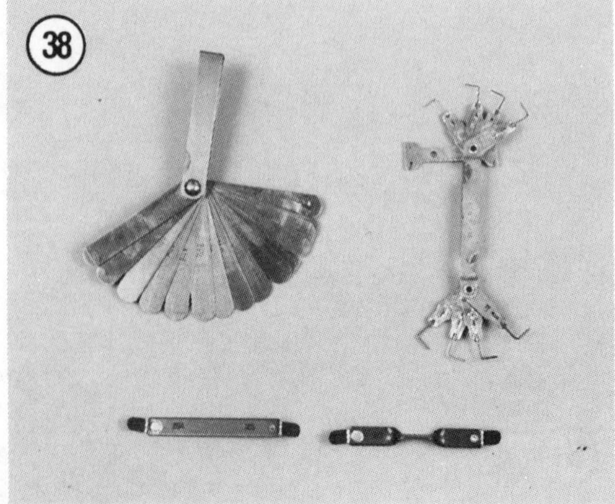
38

metal-faced hammer, however, is required when using a hand impact driver.

PRECISION MEASURING TOOLS

Measurement is an important part of engine and suspension service. When performing many of the service procedures in this manual, you will be required to make a number of measurements. These include basic checks such as valve clearance, engine compression and spark plug gap. As you get deeper into engine disassembly and service, measurements will be required to determine the size and condition of the piston and cylinder bore, valve and guide wear, camshaft wear, crankshaft runout and so on. When making these measurements, the degree of accuracy will dictate which tool is required. Precision measuring tools are expensive. If this is your first experience at engine or suspension service, it may be more worthwhile to have the checks made at a Yamaha dealer or machine shop. However, as your skills and enthusiasm increase for doing your own service work, you may want to begin purchasing some of these specialized tools. The following is a description of the measuring tools required during engine and suspension overhaul.

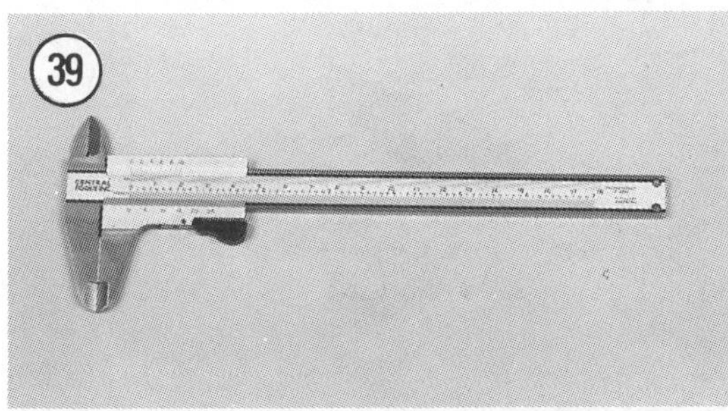
39

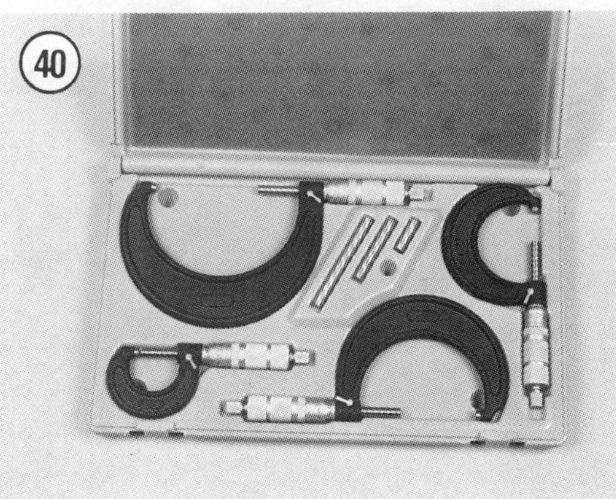
40

Feeler Gauge

Feeler gauges come in assorted sets and types (**Figure 38**). The feeler gauge is made of either a piece of a flat or round hardened steel of a specified thickness. Wire gauges are used to measure spark plug gap. Flat gauges are used for all other measurements.

Vernier Caliper

This tool (**Figure 39**) is invaluable when reading inside, outside and depth measurements with close precision. It can be used to measure clutch spring length and the thickness of clutch plates, shims and thrust washers.

Outside Micrometers

One of the most reliable tools used for precision measurement is the outside micrometer (**Figure 40**). Outside micrometers are required to measure valve shim thickness, piston diameter and valve stem diameter. Outside micrometers are also used with other tools to measure the cylinder bore and the valve guide inside diameters. Micrometers can be purchased individually or as a set.

Dial Indicator

Dial indicators (**Figure 41**) are precision tools used to check dimension variations on machined parts such as transmission shafts and axles and to check crankshaft and axle shaft end play. Dial indicators are available with various dial types for different measuring requirements.

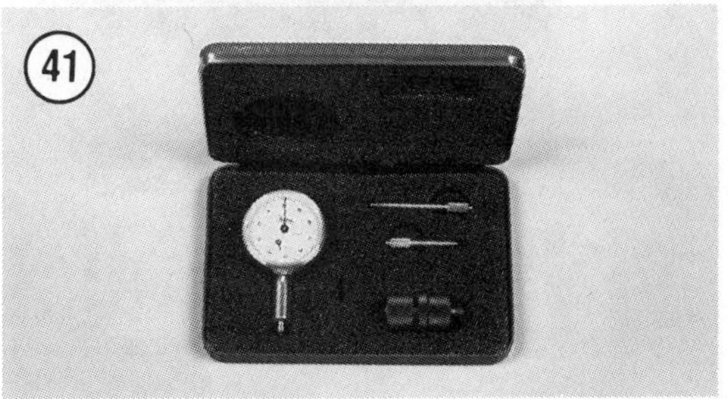
41

Cylinder Bore Gauge

The cylinder bore gauge is a very specialized precision tool. The gauge set shown in **Figure 42** is comprised of a dial indicator, handle and a number of length adapters to adapt the gauge to different bore sizes. The bore gauge can be used to make cylinder bore measurements such as bore size, taper and out-of-round. Depending on the bore gauge, it can sometimes be used to measure brake caliper and master cylinder bore sizes. An outside micrometer must be used together with the bore gauge to determine bore dimensions.

Small Hole Gauges

A set of small hole gauges allow you to measure a hole, groove or slot ranging in size up to 13 mm (0.500 in.). A small hole gauge is required to measure valve guide, brake caliper and brake master cylinder bore diameters. An outside micrometer must be used together with the small hole gauge to determine bore dimensions.

Compression Gauge

An engine with low compression cannot be properly tuned and will not develop full power. A compression gauge (**Figure 43**) measures engine compression. The one shown has a flexible stem with an extension that can allow you to hold it while kicking the engine over. Open the throttle all the way when checking engine compression. See Chapter Three.

42

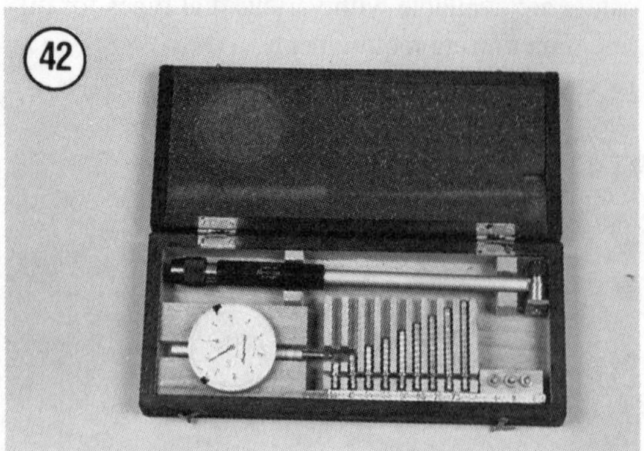

Strobe Timing Light

This instrument is useful for checking ignition timing. By flashing a light at the precise instant the spark plug fires, the position of the timing mark can be seen. The flashing light makes a moving mark appear to stand still opposite a stationary mark.

Suitable lights range from inexpensive neon bulb types to powerful xenon strobe lights (**Figure 44**). A light with an inductive pickup is recommended to

43

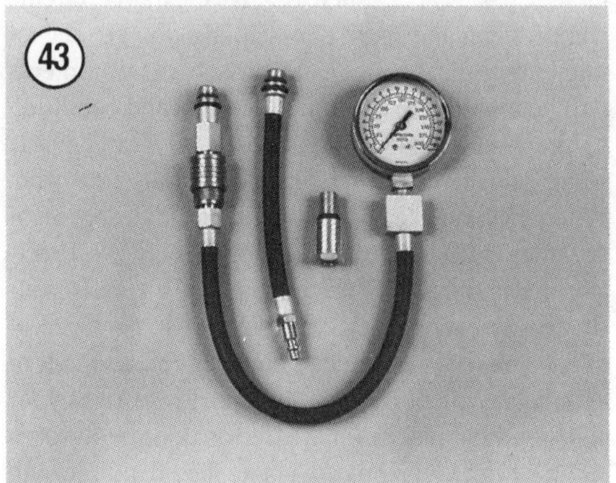

44

45

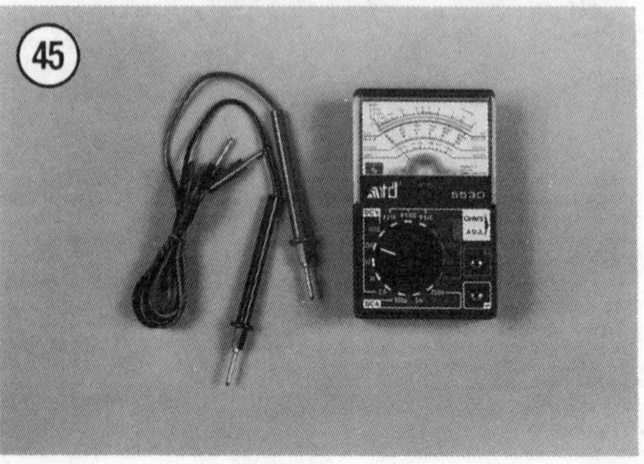

eliminate any possible damage to ignition wiring. Use according to manufacturer's instructions.

Multimeter or VOM

This instrument (**Figure 45**) is invaluable for electrical system troubleshooting. See *Component Testing* in Chapter Nine for its use.

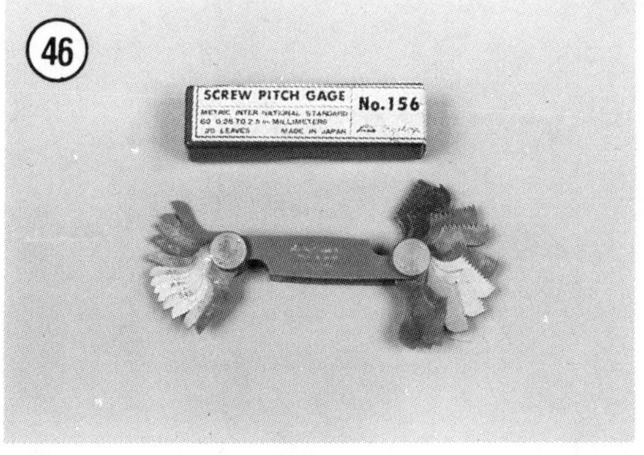

46

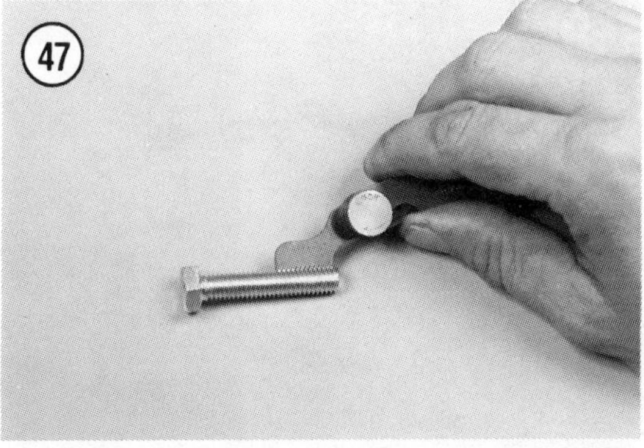

47

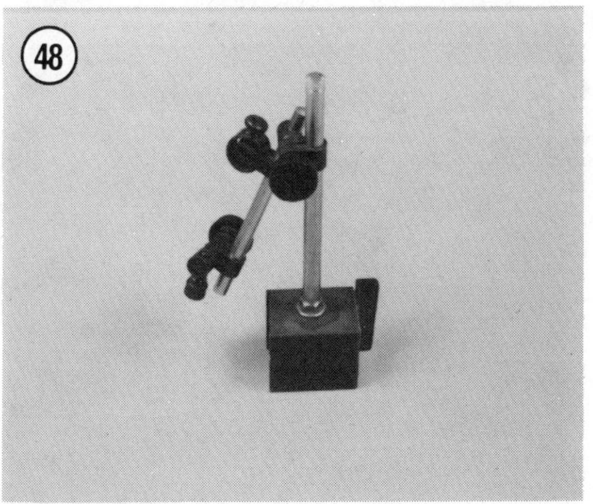

48

Screw Pitch Gauge

A screw pitch gauge (**Figure 46**) determines the thread pitch of bolts, screws, studs, etc. The gauge is made up of a number of thin plates. Each plate has a thread shape cut on one edge to match one thread pitch. When using a screw pitch gauge to determine a thread pitch size, try to fit different blade sizes onto the bolt thread until both threads match (**Figure 47**).

Magnetic Stand

A magnetic stand (**Figure 48**) is used to hold a dial indicator securely when checking the runout of a round object or when checking the end play of a shaft.

V-Blocks

V-blocks (**Figure 49**) are precision ground blocks used to hold a round object when checking its runout or condition. In ATV and motorcycle repair, V-blocks can be used when checking the runout of such items as the rear axle and crankshaft.

SPECIAL TOOLS

A few special tools may be required for major service. These are described in the appropriate chapters and are available either from a Yamaha dealer or other manufacturers as indicated.

This section describes special tools unique to this type of vehicle's service and repair.

49

The Grabbit

The Grabbit (**Figure 50**) is a special tool used to hold the clutch boss when removing the clutch nut and to secure the drive sprocket when removing the sprocket nut.

Flywheel Puller

A flywheel puller (**Figure 51**) is required to remove the flywheel. Flywheel removal is necessary for stator plate service. In addition, when disassembling the engine, the flywheel must be removed before the crankcases can be split. There is no satisfactory substitute for this tool. Because the flywheel is a tapered fit on the crankshaft, makeshift removal often results in crankshaft and flywheel damage. Don't think about removing the flywheel without this tool. This tool can be ordered through Yamaha dealers (part No. YM-01189).

Rear Axle Nut Wrench

The 50 mm rear axle nuts require a rear axle nut wrench (**Figure 52**) for their removal and installation. This tool can be ordered through Yamaha dealers (part No. YM-37132).

MECHANIC'S TIPS

Removing Frozen Nuts and Screws

When a fastener rusts and cannot be removed, several methods may be used to loosen it. First, apply penetrating oil such as Liquid Wrench or WD-40 (available at hardware or auto supply stores). Apply it liberally and let it penetrate for 10-15 minutes. Rap the fastener several times with a small hammer; do not hit it hard enough to cause damage. Reapply the penetrating oil if necessary.

For frozen screws, apply penetrating oil as described, then insert a screwdriver in the slot and rap the top of the screwdriver with a hammer. This loosens the rust so the screw can be removed in the normal way. If the screw head is too chewed up to use this method, grip the head with vise-grip pliers and twist the screw out.

Avoid applying heat unless specifically instructed, as it may melt, warp or remove the temper from parts.

Removing Broken Screws or Bolts

When the head breaks off a screw or bolt, several methods are available for removing the remaining portion.

If a large portion of the remainder projects out, try gripping it with vise-grip pliers. If the projecting

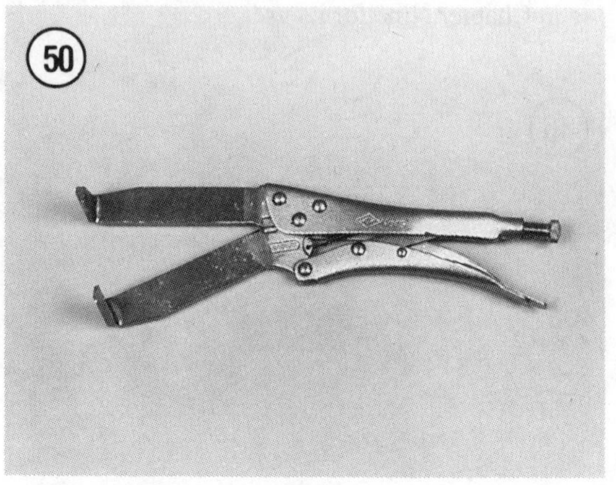

50

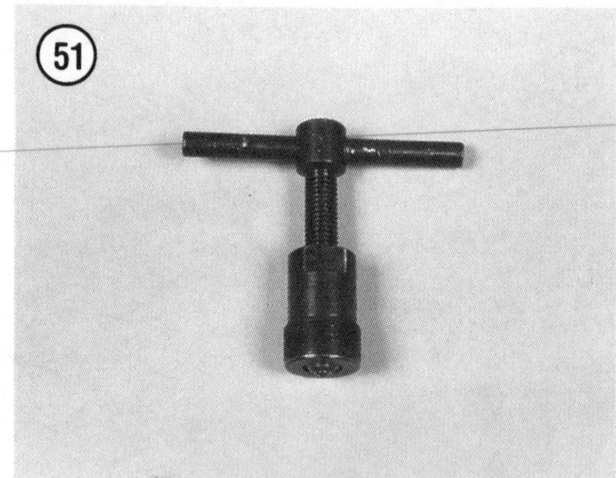

51

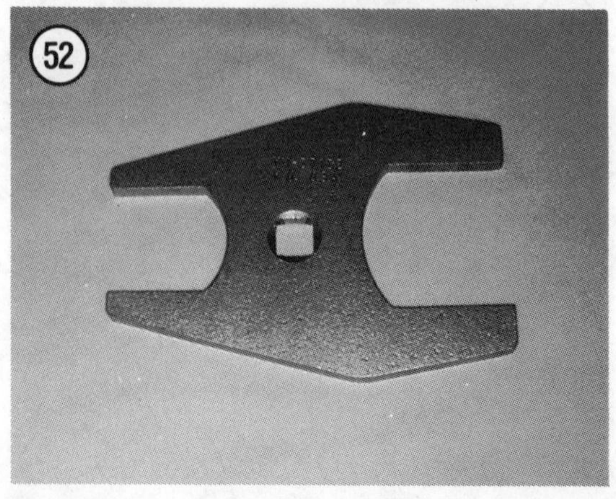

52

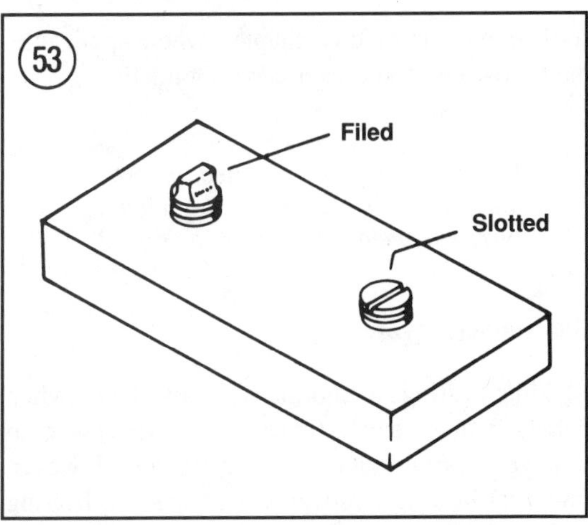

portion is too small, file it to fit a wrench or cut a slot in it to fit a screwdriver. See **Figure 53**.

If the head breaks off flush, use a screw extractor. To do this, centerpunch the exact center of the remaining portion of the screw or bolt. Drill a small hole in the screw and tap the extractor into the hole. Back the screw out with a wrench on the extractor. See **Figure 54**.

Remedying Stripped Threads

Occasionally, threads are stripped through carelessness or impact damage. Often the threads can be

54

REMOVING BROKEN SCREWS AND BOLTS

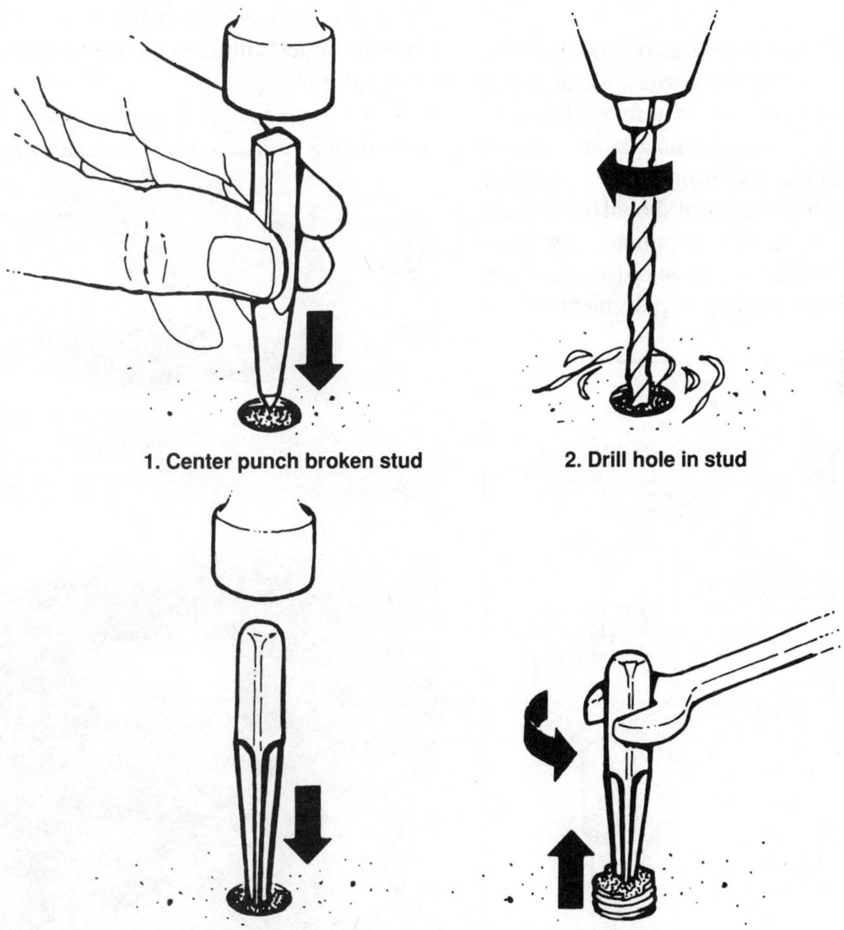

1. Center punch broken stud

2. Drill hole in stud

3. Tap in screw extractor

4. Remove broken stud

cleaned up by running a tap (for internal threads on nuts) or die (for external threads on bolts) through the threads. See **Figure 55**. To clean or repair spark plug threads, a spark plug tap can be used (**Figure 56**).

NOTE
*Tap and dies can be purchased individually or in a set as shown in **Figure 57**.*

If an internal thread is damaged, it may be necessary to install a thread insert; see **Figure 58**, typical. Follow the manufacturer's instructions when installing their insert.

If it is necessary to drill and tap a hole, refer to **Table 8** for metric tap drill sizes.

BALL BEARING REPLACEMENT

Ball bearings (**Figure 59**) are used throughout the engine and chassis to reduce power loss, heat and noise resulting from friction. Because ball bearings are precision made parts, they must be maintained by proper lubrication and maintenance. When a bearing is found to be damaged, it should be replaced immediately. However, when installing a new bearing, care should be taken to prevent damage to the new bearing. While bearing replacement is described in the individual chapters where applicable, the following should be used as a guideline.

NOTE
Unless otherwise specified in procedure, install bearings with the manufacturer's name and size code facing out.

Bearing Removal

While bearings are normally removed only when damaged, there may be times when it is necessary to remove a bearing that is in good condition. However, improper bearing removal will damage the bearing and maybe the shaft or case half. Note the following when removing bearings.

1. When using a puller to remove a bearing on a shaft, care must be taken so that shaft damage does not occur. Always place a piece of metal between the end of the shaft and the puller screw. In addition, place the puller arms next to the inner bearing race. See **Figure 60**.
2. When using a hammer to remove a bearing on a shaft, do not strike the hammer directly against the

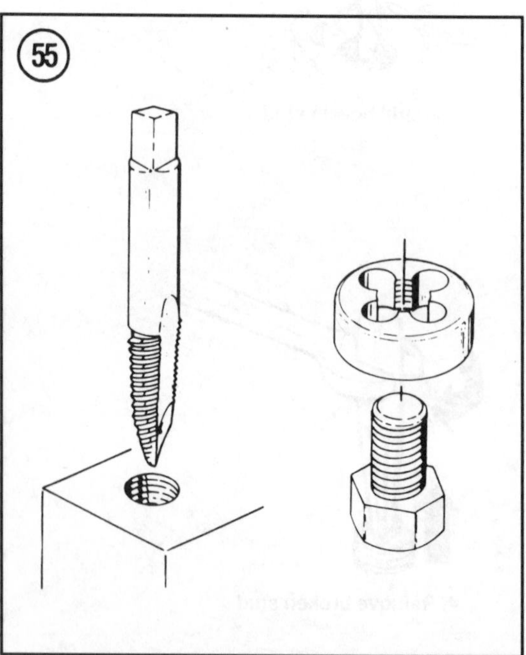

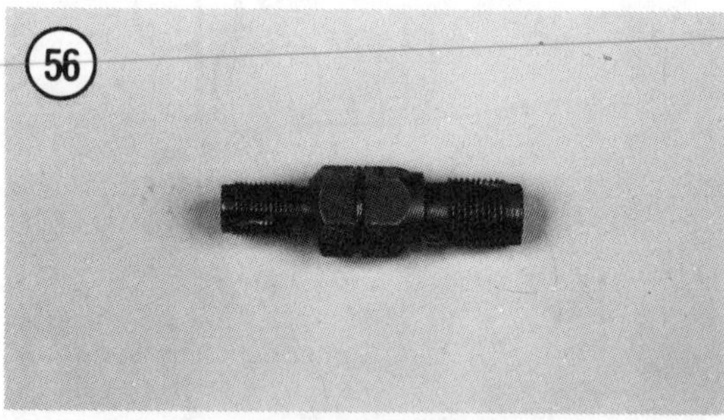

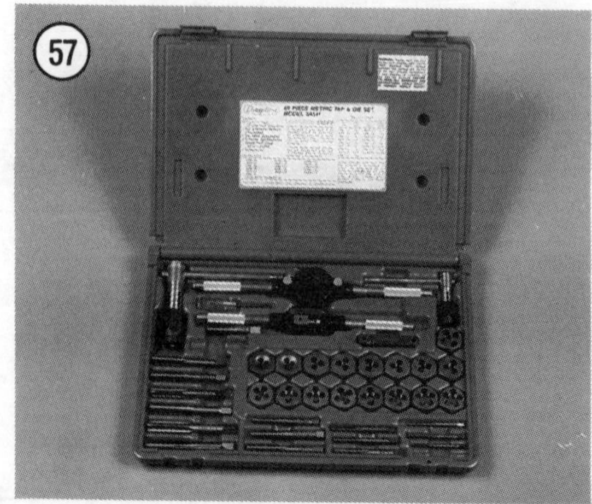

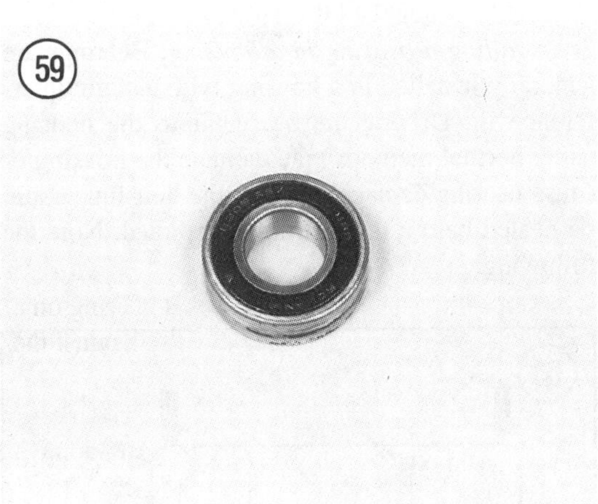

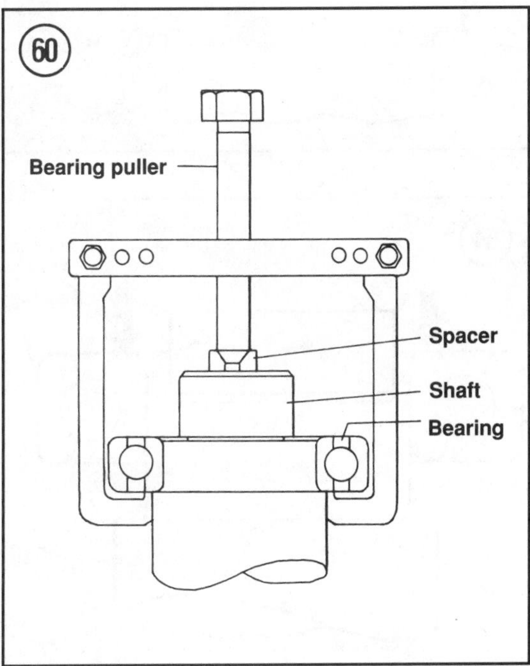

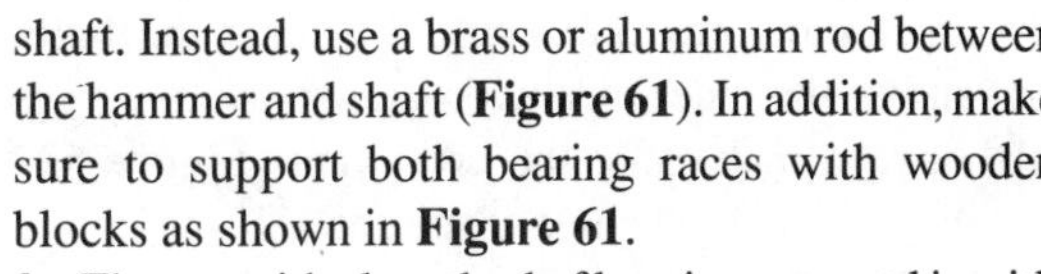

shaft. Instead, use a brass or aluminum rod between the hammer and shaft (**Figure 61**). In addition, make sure to support both bearing races with wooden blocks as shown in **Figure 61**.

3. The most ideal method of bearing removal is with a hydraulic press. However, certain procedures must be followed or damage may occur to the bearing, shaft or bearing housing. Note the following when using a press:

   a. Always support the inner and outer bearing races with a suitable size wooden or aluminum spacer (**Figure 62**). If you only support the

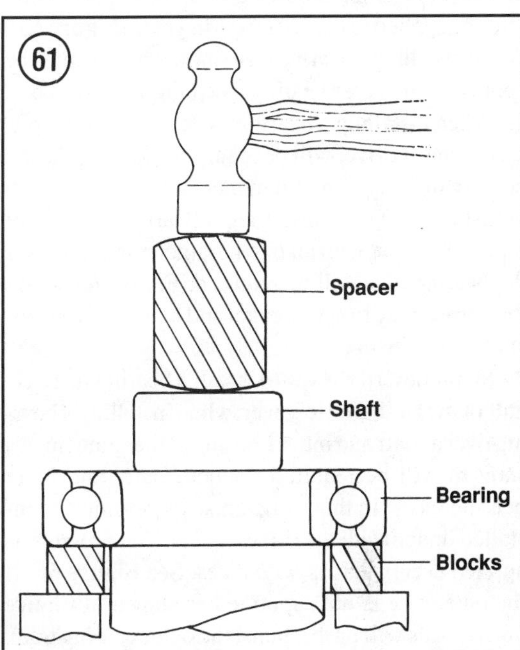

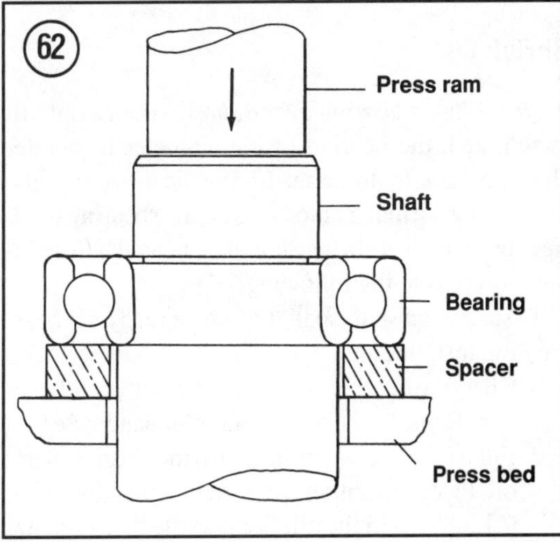

outer race, pressure applied against the balls and/or the inner race will damage them.

b. Always make sure the press ram (**Figure 62**) aligns with the center of the shaft. If the ram is not centered, it may damage the bearing and/or shaft.
c. The moment the shaft is free of the bearing, it will drop to the floor. Secure or hold the shaft to prevent it from falling.

Bearing Installation

1. When installing a bearing in a housing, pressure must be applied to the *outer* bearing race (**Figure 63**). When installing a bearing on a shaft, pressure must be applied to the *inner* bearing race (**Figure 64**).
2. When installing a bearing as described in Step 1, some type of driver will be required. Never strike the bearing directly with a hammer or the bearing will be damaged. When installing a bearing, a piece of pipe or a socket with an outer diameter that matches the bearing race will be required. **Figure 65** shows the correct way to use a socket and hammer when installing a bearing.
3. Step 1 describes how to install a bearing in a case half or over a shaft. However, when installing a bearing over a shaft and into a housing at the same time, a snug fit will be required for both outer and inner bearing races. In this situation, a spacer must be installed underneath the driver tool so that pressure is applied evenly across *both* races. See **Figure 66**. If the outer race is not supported as shown in **Figure 66**, the balls will push against the outer bearing track and damage it.

Shrink Fit

1. *Installing a bearing over a shaft*: When a tight fit is required, the bearing inside diameter is smaller than the shaft. In this case, driving the bearing on the shaft using normal methods may cause bearing damage. Instead, the bearing should be heated before installation. Note the following:
   a. Secure the shaft so that it can be ready for bearing installation.
   b. Clean the bearing surface on the shaft of all residue. Remove burrs with a file or sandpaper.
   c. Fill a suitable pot or beaker with clean mineral oil. Place a thermometer (rated higher than 120° C [248° F]) in the oil. Support the thermometer so that it does not rest on the bottom or side of the pot.
   d. Remove the bearing from its wrapper and secure it with a piece of heavy wire bent to hold it in the pot. Hang the bearing in the pot so that it does not touch the bottom or sides of the pot.
   e. Turn the heat on and monitor the thermometer. When the oil temperature rises to approximately 120° C (248° F), remove the bearing from the pot and quickly install it. If necessary, place a socket on the inner bearing race and tap the bearing into place. As the bearing chills, it will tighten on the shaft so you must work quickly when installing it. Make sure the bearing is installed all the way.
2. *Installing a bearing in a housing*: Bearings are generally installed in a housing with a slight interference fit. Driving the bearing into the housing using normal methods may damage the housing or cause bearing damage. Instead, the housing should be heated before the bearing is installed. Note the following:

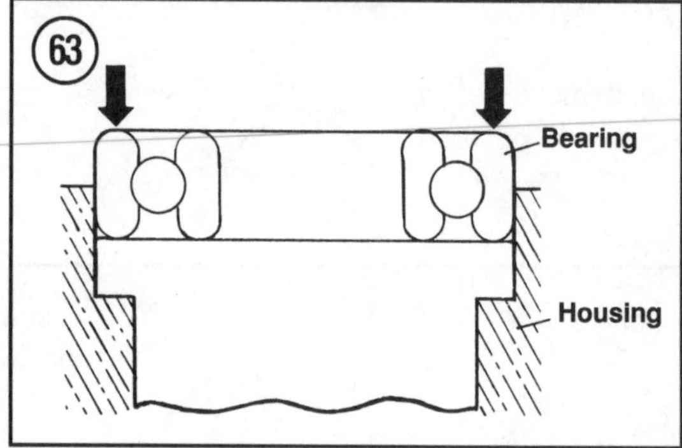

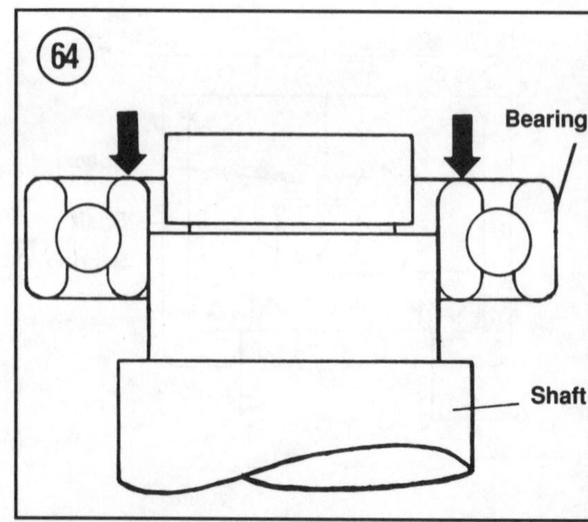

CAUTION
Before heating the cases to remove the bearings, wash the cases thoroughly with detergent and water. Rinse and rewash the cases as required to remove all traces of oil and other chemical deposits.

a. The housing must be heated to a temperature of about 212° F (100° C) in an oven or on a hot plate. An easy way to check to see that it is at the proper temperature is to drop tiny drops of water on the case; if they sizzle and evaporate immediately, the temperature is correct. Heat only one housing at a time.

CAUTION
Do not heat the housing with a torch (propane or acetylene)—never bring a flame into contact with the bearing or housing. The direct heat will destroy the case hardening of the bearing and will likely warp the housing.

b. Remove the housing from the oven or hot plate. Hold the housing with a kitchen pot holder, heavy gloves, or heavy shop cloths—*it is hot.*

NOTE
Remove and install bearings with a bearing driver, socket or piece of pipe of the correct diameter.

c. Hold the housing with the bearing side down and tap the bearing out. Repeat for all bearings in the housing.

d. Prior to heating the bearing housing, place the new bearing in a freezer, if possible. Chilling a bearing will slightly reduce its outside diameter while the heated bearing housing assembly is slightly larger due to heat expansion. This will make bearing installation much easier.

NOTE
Unless otherwise specified in procedure, install bearings with the manufacturer's name and size code facing out.

e. While the housing is still hot, install the new bearing(s) into the housing. Install the bearings by hand, if possible. If necessary, lightly tap the bearing(s) into the housing with a socket placed on the outer bearing race. *Do not* install new bearings by driving on the inner bearing race. Install the bearing(s) until it seats completely.

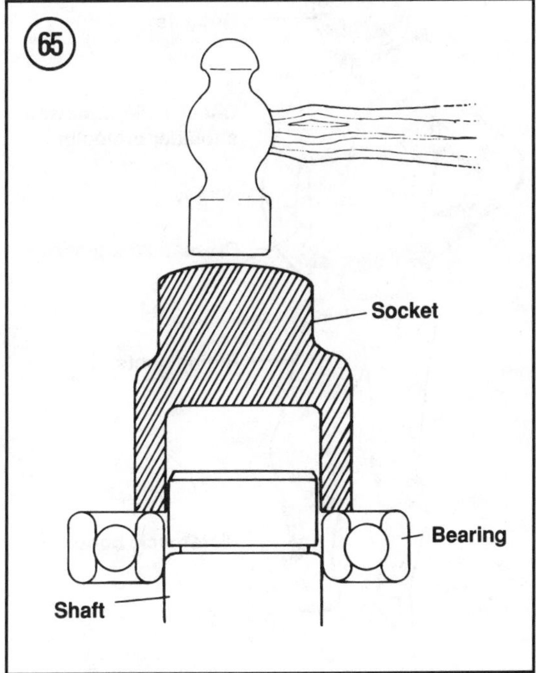

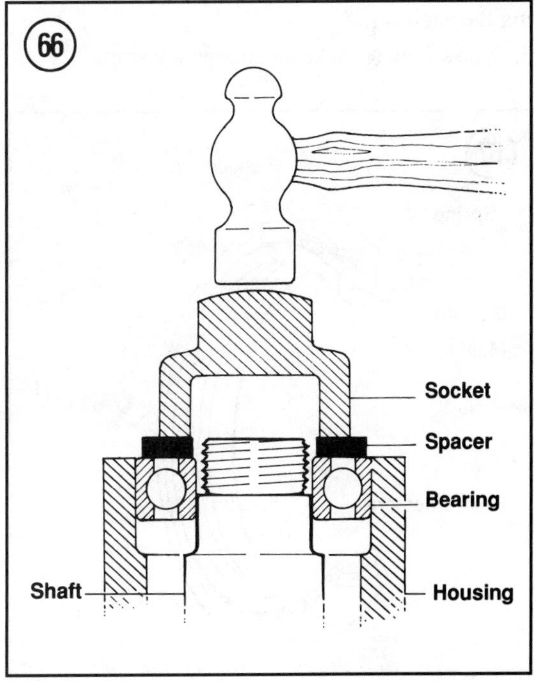

OIL SEALS

Oil seals (**Figure 67**) are used to contain oil, water, grease or combustion gasses in a housing or shaft. Improper removal of a seal can damage the housing or shaft. Improper installation of the seal can damage the seal. Note the following:

a. Prying is generally the easiest and most effective method of removing a seal from a housing. However, always place a rag underneath the pry tool to prevent damage to the housing.
b. Waterproof grease should be packed in the seal lips before the seal is installed.
c. Oil seals should always be installed so that the manufacturer's numbers or marks face out.
d. Oil seals should be installed with the driver placed on the outside of the seal as shown in **Figure 68**. Make sure the seal is driven squarely into the housing. Never install a seal by hitting against the top of the seal with a hammer.

RIDING SAFETY

General Tips

1. Read your owner's manual and know your machine.
2. Check the throttle and brake controls before starting the engine.
3. Know how to make an emergency stop.
4. Never add fuel while anyone is smoking in the area or when the engine is running.
5. Never wear loose scarves, belts or boot laces that could catch on moving parts.
6. Always wear eye and head protection and protective clothing to protect your *entire* body (**Figure 69**). Today's riding apparel is very stylish and you will be ready for action as well as being well protected.

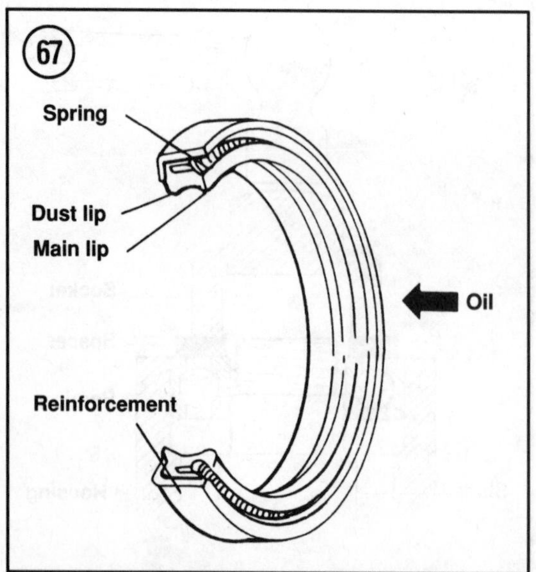

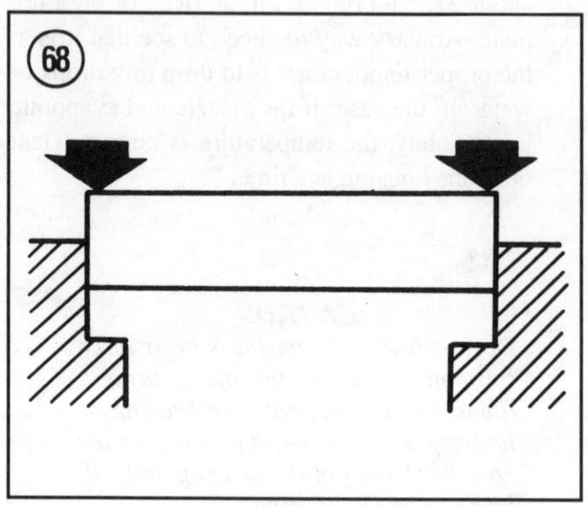

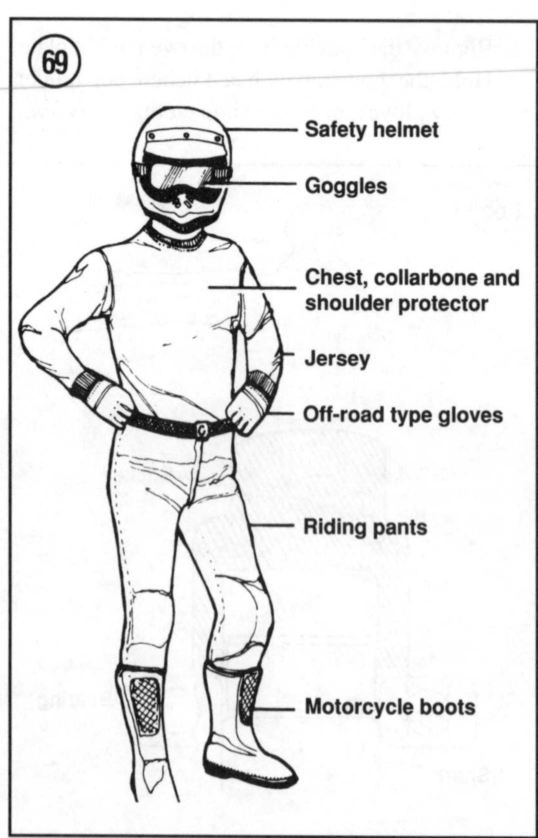

7. Riding in the winter months requires a good set of clothes to keep your body dry and warm, otherwise your entire trip may be miserable. If you dress properly, moisture will evaporate from your body. If you become too hot and if your clothes trap the moisture, you will become cold. **Figure 70** shows some recommended inner and outer layers of cold weather clothing. Even mild temperatures can be very uncomfortable and dangerous when combined with a strong wind or traveling at high speed. See **Table 9** for wind chill factors. Always dress according to what the wind chill factor is, not the ambient temperature.

8. Never allow anyone to operate the vehicle without proper instruction. This is for their bodily protection and to keep your machine from damage or destruction.

9. Use the "buddy system" for long trips, just in case you have a problem or run out of gas.

10. Never attempt to repair your machine with the engine running except when necessary for certain tune-up procedures.

11. Check all of the machine components and hardware frequently, especially the wheels and the steering.

Operating Tips

1. Never operate the machine in crowded areas or steer toward persons.
2. Avoid dangerous terrain.
3. Cross highways (where permitted) at a 90° angle after looking in both directions. Post traffic guards if crossing in groups.
4. Do not ride the vehicle on or near railroad tracks. Engine and exhaust noise can drown out the sound of an approaching train.
5. Keep the headlight and taillight free of dirt and never ride at night without the headlight and taillight ON.
6. Do not ride your Yamaha without the seat and fenders in place.
7. Always steer with both hands.
8. Be aware of the terrain and avoid operating the Yamaha at excessive speed.
9. Do not panic if the throttle sticks. Turn the engine stop switch (**Figure 71**) to the OFF position.
10. Do not speed through wooded areas. Hidden obstructions, hanging tree limbs, unseen ditches and even wild animals and hikers can cause injury and damage to you and your Yamaha.
11. Do not tailgate. Rear end collisions can cause injury and machine damage.

12. Do not mix alcoholic beverages or drugs with riding—ride straight.
13. Keep both feet on the foot pegs. Do not permit your feet to hang out to stabilize the machine when making turns or in near spill situations; broken limbs could result.
14. Check your fuel supply regularly. Do not travel farther than your fuel supply will permit you to return.
15. Check to make sure that the parking brake is *completely released* while riding. If left on, the rear brake pads will be damaged.

Table 1 STARTING ENGINE AND FRAME SERIAL NUMBERS

Year and model number	Engine/frame serial No. starting number
1987 YFZ350T	2GU-000101-030100
1988 YFZ350U	2GU-030101-on
1989 YFZ350W	3GG-000101-on
1990 YFZ350A	3GG-010101-024100
1990 YFZ350A	3GG-024101-025100
1991 YFZ350B	3GG-025101-on
1992 YFZ350D	3GG-036101-on
1993 YFZ350E	3GG-049101-on
1994 YFZ350F	3GG-059101-on
1995 YFZ350G	3GG-069101-on
1996 YFZ350H	3GG-079101-on
1997 YFZ350J	3GG-089101-on
1998 YFZ350K	3GG-130101-on
1999 YFZ350L	3GG-150917-on
2000 YFZ350M	NA
2001 YFZ350N	NA
2002 YFZ350P	NA
2003 NA	NA
2004 NA	NA

Table 2 GENERAL DIMENSIONS

	mm	in.
Overall length	1,855	73
Overall width	1,100	43.3
Overall height	1,080	42.5
Seat height		
1987-1989	780	30.7
1990-on	800	31.4
Wheelbase	1,280	50.4
Minimum ground clearance	135	5.31
Minimum turning radius	3,600	142

Table 3 WEIGHT SPECIFICATIONS*

	kg	lbs.
1987-1989	182	401
1990	185	408
1991-on	186	410

* With oil and fuel tank full.

Table 4 DECIMAL AND METRIC EQUIVALENTS

Fractions	Decimal in.	Metric mm	Fractions	Decimal in.	Metric mm
1/64	0.015625	0.39688	33/64	0.515625	13.09687
1/32	0.03125	0.79375	17/32	0.53125	13.49375
3/64	0.046875	1.19062	35/64	0.546875	13.89062
1/16	0.0625	1.58750	9/16	0.5625	14.28750
5/64	0.078125	1.98437	37/64	0.578125	14.68437
3/32	0.09375	2.38125	19/32	0.59375	15.08125
7/64	0.109375	2.77812	39/64	0.609375	15.47812
1/8	0.125	3.1750	5/8	0.625	15.87500
9/64	0.140625	3.57187	41/64	0.640625	16.27187
5/32	0.15625	3.96875	21/32	0.65625	16.66875
11/64	0.171875	4.36562	43/64	0.671875	17.06562
3/16	0.1875	4.76250	11/16	0.6875	17.46250
13/64	0.203125	5.15937	45/64	0.703125	17.85937
7/32	0.21875	5.55625	23/32	0.71875	18.25625
15/64	0.234375	5.95312	47/64	0.734375	18.65312
1/4	0.250	6.35000	3/4	0.750	19.05000
17/64	0.265625	6.74687	49/64	0.765625	19.44687
9/32	0.28125	7.14375	25/32	0.78125	19.84375
19/64	0.296875	7.54062	51/64	0.796875	20.24062
5/16	0.3125	7.93750	13/16	0.8125	20.63750
21/64	0.328125	8.33437	53/64	0.828125	21.03437
11/32	0.34375	8.73125	27/32	0.84375	21.43125
23/64	0.359375	9.12812	55/64	0.859375	22.82812
3/8	0.375	9.52500	7/8	0.875	22.22500
25/64	0.390625	9.92187	57/64	0.890625	22.62187
13/32	0.40625	10.31875	29/32	0.90625	23.01875
27/64	0.421875	10.71562	59/64	0.921875	23.41562
7/16	0.4375	11.11250	15/16	0.9375	23.81250
29/64	0.453125	11.50937	61/64	0.953125	24.20937
15/32	0.46875	11.90625	31/32	0.96875	24.60625
31/64	0.484375	12.30312	63/64	0.984375	25.00312
1/2	0.500	12.70000	1	1.00	25.40000

Table 5 CONVERSION TABLES

Multiply	By	To get equivalent of
Length		
Inches	25.4	Millimeter
Inches	2.54	Centimeter
Miles	1.609	Kilometer
Feet	0.3048	Meter
Millimeter	0.03937	Inches
Centimeter	0.3937	Inches
Kilometer	0.6214	Mile
Meter	0.0006214	Mile
Fluid volume		
U.S. quarts	0.9463	Liters
U.S. gallons	3.785	Liters
U.S. ounces	29.573529	Milliliters
Imperial gallons	4.54609	Liters
Imperial quarts	1.1365	Liters
Liters	0.2641721	U.S. gallons
Liters	1.0566882	U.S. quarts
Liters	33.814023	U.S. ounces
Liters	0.22	Imperial gallons
Liters	0.8799	Imperial quarts
Milliliters	0.033814	U.S. ounces
Milliliters	1.0	Cubic centimeters
Milliliters	0.001	Liters
Torque		
Foot-pounds	1.3556	Newton-meters
Foot-pounds	0.138255	Meters-kilograms
Inch-pounds	0.1130	Newton-meters
Newton-meters	0.7375622	Foot-pounds
Newton-meters	8.8507	Inch-pounds
Meters-kilograms	7.2330139	Foot-pounds
Volume		
Cubic inches	16.387064	Cubic centimeters
Cubic centimeters	0.0610237	Cubic inches
Temperature		
Fahrenheit	(F – 32) × 0.556	Centigrade
Centigrade	(C × 1.8) + 32	Fahrenheit
Weight		
Ounces	28.3495	Grams
Pounds	0.4535924	Kilograms
Grams	0.035274	Ounces
Kilograms	2.2046224	Pounds
Pressure		
Pounds per square inch	0.070307	Kilograms per square centimeter
Kilograms per square centimeter	14.223343	Pounds per square inch
Speed		
Miles per hour	1.609344	Kilometers per hour
Kilometers per hour	0.6213712	Miles per hour

Table 6 GENERAL TORQUE SPECIFICATIONS

Thread diameter	N•m	ft.-lb.
5 mm	3.4-4.9	30-43 in.-lb.
6 mm	5.9-7.8	52-69 in.-lb.
8 mm	14-19	10.0-13.5

(continued)

Table 6 GENERAL TORQUE SPECIFICATIONS (continued)

Thread diameter	N•m	ft.-lb.
10 mm	25-39	19-25
12mm	44-61	33-45
14 mm	73-98	54-72
16 mm	115-155	83-115
18 mm	165-225	125-165
20 mm	225-325	165-240

Table 7 TECHNICAL ABBREVIATIONS

ABDC	After bottom dead center
ATDC	After top dead center
BBDC	Before bottom dead center
BDC	Bottom dead center
BTDC	Before top dead center
C	Celsius (Centigrade)
cc	Cubic centimeters
CDI	Capacitor disharge ignition
cu. in.	Cubic inches
F	Fahrenheit
ft.-lb.	Foot-pounds
gal.	Gallons
hp	Horsepower
in.	Inches
kg	Kilogram
kg/cm^2	Kilograms per square centimeter
kgm	Kilogram meters
km	Kilometer
l	Liter
m	Meter
mm	Millimeter
N•m	Newton-meters
oz.	Ounce
psi	Pounds per square inch
pts.	Pints
qt.	Quarts
rpm	Revolutions per minute

Table 8 METRIC TAP DRILL SIZES

Metric tap (mm)	Drill size	Decimal equivalent	Nearest fraction
3 × 0.50	No. 39	0.0995	3/32
3 × 0.60	3/32	0.0937	3/32
4 × 0.70	No. 30	0.1285	1/8
4 × 0.75	1/8	0.125	1/8
5 × 0.80	No. 19	0.166	11/64
5 × 0.90	No. 20	0.161	5/32
6 × 1.00	No. 9	0.196	13/64
7 × 1.00	16/64	0.234	15/64
8 × 1.00	J	0.277	9/32
8 × 1.25	17/64	0.265	17/64
9 × 1.00	5/16	0.3125	5/16
9 × 1.25	5/16	0.3125	5/16

(continued)

Table 8 METRIC TAP DRILL SIZES (continued)

Metric tap (mm)	Drill size	Decimal equivalent	Nearest fraction
10 × 1.25	11/32	0.3437	11/32
10 × 1.50	R	0.339	11/32
11 × 1.50	3/8	0.375	3/8
12 × 1.50	13/32	0.406	13/32
12 × 1.75	13/32	0.406	13/32

Table 9 WINDCHILL FACTORS

Estimated wind speed in mph	Actual thermometer reading (°F)											
	50	40	30	20	10	0	−10	−20	−30	−40	−50	−60
	Equivalent temperature (°F)											
Calm	50	40	30	20	10	0	−10	−20	−30	−40	−50	−60
5	48	37	27	16	6	−5	−15	−26	−36	−47	−57	−68
10	40	28	16	4	−9	−21	−33	−46	−58	−70	−83	−95
15	36	22	9	−5	−18	−36	−45	−58	−72	−85	−99	−112
20	32	18	4	−10	−25	−39	−53	−67	−82	−96	−110	−124
25	30	16	0	−15	−29	−44	−59	−74	−88	−104	−118	−133
30	28	13	−2	−18	−33	−48	−63	−79	−94	−109	−125	−140
35	27	11	−4	−20	−35	−49	−67	−82	−98	−113	−129	−145
40	26	10	−6	−21	−37	−53	−69	−85	−100	−116	−132	−148
*	Little danger (for properly clothed person)				Increasing danger			Great danger				
					• Danger from freezing of exposed flesh •							

*Wind speeds greater than 40 mph have little additional effect.

CHAPTER TWO

TROUBLESHOOTING

Diagnosing mechanical problems is relatively simple if you use orderly procedures and keep a few basic principles in mind. The first step in any troubleshooting procedure is to define the symptoms as closely as possible and then localize the problem. Subsequent steps involve testing and analyzing those areas which could cause the symptoms. A haphazard approach may eventually solve the problem, but it can be very costly in terms of wasted time and unnecessary parts replacement.

Proper lubrication, maintenance and periodic tune-ups as described in Chapter Three will reduce the necessity for troubleshooting. Even with the best of care, however, all vehicles are prone to problems which will require troubleshooting.

Never assume anything. Do not overlook the obvious. If the engine won't start, is the engine stop switch shorted out? Is the engine flooded with fuel from using the choke too much?

If the engine suddenly quits, what sound did it make? Consider this and check the easiest, most accessible problem first. If the engine sounded like it ran out of fuel, check to see if there is fuel in the tank. If there is fuel in the tank, is it reaching the carburetors? If not, the fuel tank vent hose may be plugged, preventing fuel from flowing from the fuel tank to the carburetors. If only one cylinder is firing, refer your checks to the other cylinder—spark plug, fuel flow to that cylinder's carburetor, ignition system wiring, etc.

If nothing obvious turns up in a quick check, look a little further. Learning to recognize and describe symptoms will make repairs easier for you or a mechanic at the shop. Describe problems accurately and fully.

Gather as many symptoms as possible to aid in diagnosis. Note whether the engine lost power gradually or all at once, what color smoke came from the exhaust and so on. Remember that the more complicated a machine is, the easier it is to troubleshoot because symptoms point to specific problems.

After the symptoms are defined, areas which could cause problems are tested and analyzed.

Guessing at the cause of a problem may provide the solution, but it can easily lead to frustration, wasted time and a series of expensive, unnecessary parts replacements.

You do not need fancy equipment or complicated test gear to determine whether repairs can be attempted at home. A few simple checks could save a large repair bill and lost time while the bike sits in a dealer's service department. On the other hand, be realistic and do not attempt repairs beyond your abilities. Service departments tend to charge heavily for putting together a disassembled engine that may have been abused. Some won't even take on such a job—so use common sense and don't get in over your head.

OPERATING REQUIREMENTS

An engine needs 3 basics to run properly: correct fuel/air mixture, compression and a spark at the right time (**Figure 1**). If one basic requirement is missing, the engine will not run.

NOTE
The operational sequence of a two-stroke engine is illustrated in Chapter Four.

If the vehicle has been sitting for any length of time and refuses to start, check and clean the spark plugs. If the plugs are not fouled, look to the fuel delivery system. This includes the fuel tank, fuel shutoff valve, in-line fuel filters (if used) and fuel lines. If the vehicle sat for a while with fuel in the carburetors, fuel deposits may have gummed up carburetor jets and air passages. Gasoline tends to lose its potency after standing for long periods, and as it evaporates, the mixture becomes richer. Condensation may cause the gasoline to be contaminated with water. Drain the old fuel and try starting with a fresh tankful.

TROUBLESHOOTING INSTRUMENTS

Chapter One lists the instruments needed and instruction on their use.

STARTING THE ENGINE

When your engine refuses to start, frustration can cause you to forget basic starting principles and procedures. The following outline will guide you through basic starting procedures. In all cases, make sure that there is an adequate supply of properly mixed fuel in the tank.

Starting a Cold Engine

WARNING
Prior to starting the engine in freezing weather, check that the throttle cables and carburetor throttle valves (slides)

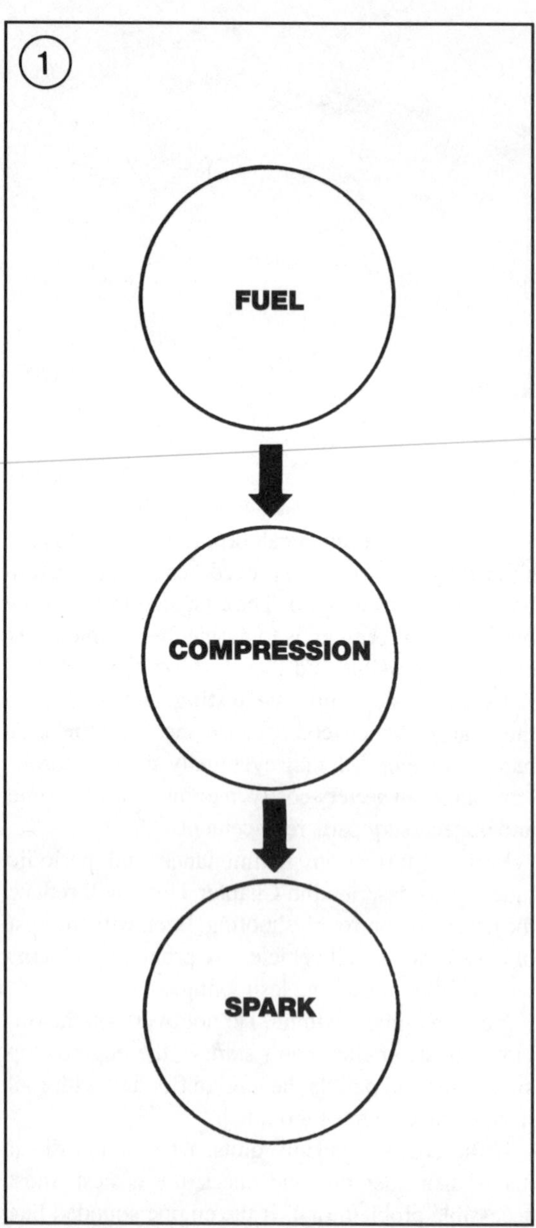

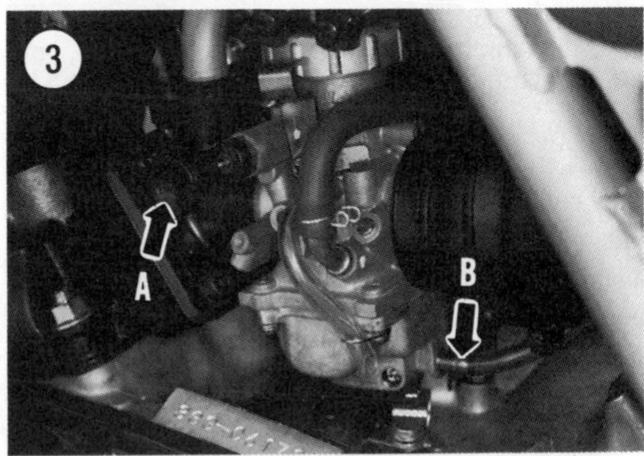

move freely. Do not start or ride the vehicle if the throttle cables appear sluggish or tight as a stuck cable can cause you to lose control.

1. Shift the transmission into NEUTRAL.

2. Rock the vehicle back and forth. This will help to mix the fuel in the tank.

3. Turn the fuel valve to the ON position (**Figure 2**).

4. Pull the choke knob (A, **Figure 3**) out to the detent position that matches the ambient temperature range shown in **Figure 4**.

5. With the throttle completely *closed*, kick the engine over.

6. When the engine starts, set the choke to its 2nd detent position (if it is not already there) and work the throttle slightly to keep it running.

7. Idle the engine for approximately a minute or until the throttle responds cleanly and the choke can be closed. In severely cold weather, the engine should be sufficiently warmed to prevent cold seizure.

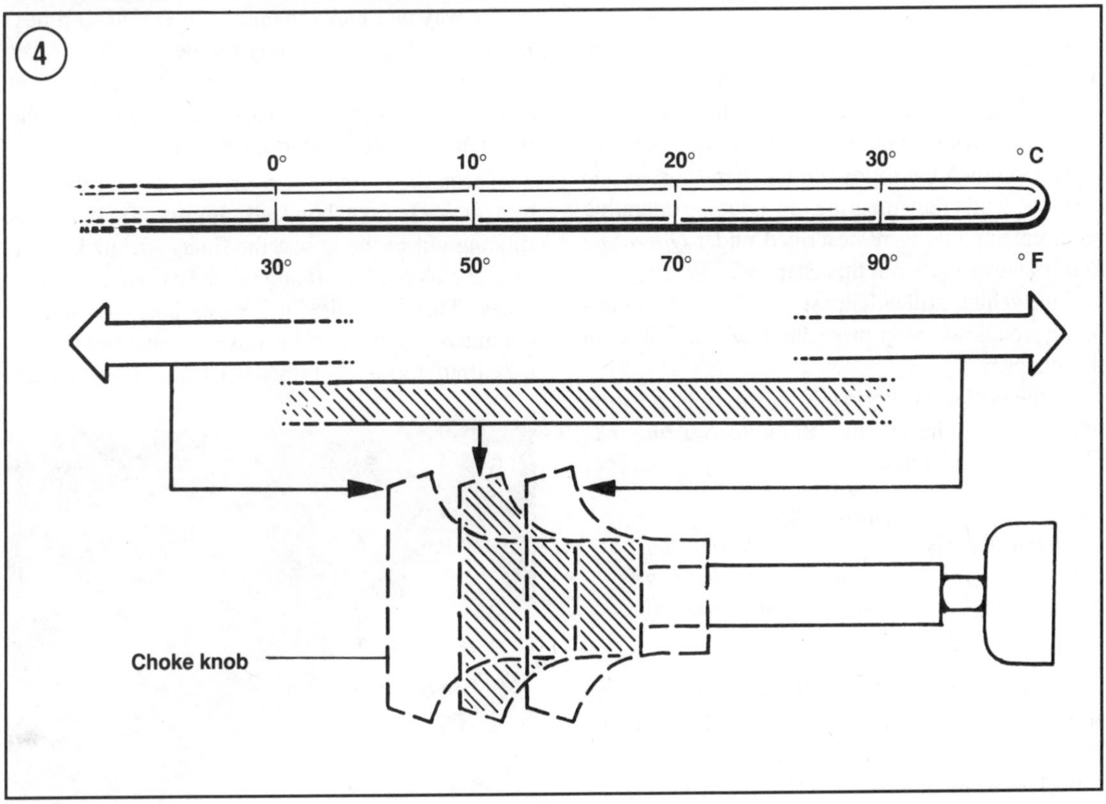

4

0° 10° 20° 30° °C

30° 50° 70° 90° °F

Choke knob

Starting a Warm or Hot Engine

1. Shift the transmission into NEUTRAL.
2. Turn the fuel valve on (**Figure 2**).
3. Make sure the choke is closed. The choke knob (A, **Figure 3**) should be pushed all the way in. See **Figure 4**.
4. Open the throttle slightly and kick the engine over.

Starting a Flooded Engine

If the engine will not start and there is a strong gasoline smell, the engine may be flooded. If so, open the throttle all the way and kick the engine over until it starts. Do *not* pull out the choke knob.

NOTE
*If the engine refuses to start, check the carburetor overflow hoses attached to the fitting at the bottom of each float bowl (B, **Figure 3**). If fuel is running out of the hoses, the floats are stuck open, allowing the carburetors to overfill.*

STARTING DIFFICULTIES

When the engine turns over but is difficult to start, won't start at all, or runs on one cylinder only, it doesn't help to wear out your leg on the kick starter. Check for obvious problems before getting out your tools. Go down the following list step-by-step. Do each one while remembering the 3 engine operating requirements that were described under *Operating Requirements* earlier in this chapter.

If the vehicle still will not start, refer to the appropriate troubleshooting procedures which follow in this chapter.

1. Is the choke (A, **Figure 3**) in the right position when starting the engine? Refer to *Starting The Engine* in this chapter.

WARNING
Gasoline is highly flammable. Do not use an open flame to check its level in the tank as an explosion and fire will occur.

2. Is there fuel in the tank? Remove the filler cap and rock the vehicle. Listen for fuel sloshing around. Is the fuel/oil mixture correct? Has the vehicle been sitting long enough for the fuel mixture to deteriorate? If in doubt, drain the fuel and fill with a fresh, correctly mixed fuel/oil mixture. Check that the fuel tank vent tube (**Figure 5**) is not clogged. Remove the tube from the filler cap, wipe off one end and blow through it.

NOTE
Mix the fuel in the correct ratio as listed in Chapter Three. Too little oil will cause premature wear and engine damage. Too much oil will cause excessive smoking, spark plug fouling or engine damage.

3. If the tank has fuel and the mixture is fresh, pull off the fuel line at both carburetors and insert it into a clear, glass container. Turn the fuel valve on (**Figure 2**) and see if fuel flows freely. If fuel does not flow out and there is a fuel filter installed in the fuel line, remove the filter and turn the fuel valve to ON again. If fuel flows, the filter is clogged and should be replaced. If no fuel comes out, the fuel valve may be shut off, blocked by foreign matter, or the fuel cap vent may be plugged.
4. If you suspect that the cylinder is flooded, or there is a strong smell of gasoline, open the throttle all the way and kick the engine over several times. If the cylinders are severely flooded (fouled or wet spark plug), remove both plugs and dry the base and electrode thoroughly with a soft cloth. Reinstall the plugs and attempt to start the engine.
5. Check the carburetor overflow hose on the bottom of each float bowl (B, **Figure 3**). If fuel is running out of the hoses, the floats are stuck open. Turn the fuel valve off and tap the carburetors a few times. Then turn the fuel valve back on. If fuel continues to run out of the hose, remove and service the carburetors as described in Chapter Eight. Check

the carburetor vent hoses to make sure they are clear. Check the end of the hoses for contamination.

NOTE
Now that you have determined that fuel is reaching the carburetors, the fuel system could still be the problem. The jets (pilot and main) could be clogged or the air filter could be severely restricted. However, before removing the carburetors, continue with Step 6 to make sure that the engine has an adequate spark.

6. Are both spark plug caps (**Figure 6**) on tight? Push each plug cap on its spark plug and slightly rotate it to clean the electrical connection between the plug and the connector. Also check that the high-tension lead ends at the coil and plug cap are pushed in all the way.

NOTE
If the engine will still not start, perform Step 7.

7. Perform a spark test as described under *Engine Fails to Start (Spark Test)* in this chapter. If there is a strong spark, perform Step 8. If there is no spark or if the spark is very weak, test the ignition system as described under *Ignition System Troubleshooting* in this chapter.

6

7

NOTE
The ignition system is equipped with a throttle override system (T.O.R.S.). If the T.O.R.S. system is inoperative, the spark plugs will not fire. If there is no spark, check the T.O.R.S. system as described under ***Ignition System Troubleshooting*** *in this chapter.*

NOTE
If the fuel and ignition systems are working properly, the mechanical system should be checked next. Unless the engine seized or experienced some other type of problem, mechanical problems generally occur over a period of time. Isolate the mechanical system to one of these areas: top end, bottom end, clutch or transmission. The top and bottom end (as they relate to engine compression) will be covered in Step 8. Clutch and transmission problems are covered in this chapter.

8. Check cylinder compression as follows:
   a. Turn the fuel valve off.
   b. Make sure the ignition switch is turned off.
   c. Remove and ground both spark plugs against the cylinder head; see **Figure 7**.
   d. Put your finger tightly over one of the spark plug holes.
   e. Operate the kickstarter. As the piston comes up on the compression stroke, rising pressure in the cylinder should force your finger off of the spark plug hole. This indicates that the cylinder probably has sufficient cylinder compression to start the engine. Repeat for the opposite cylinder.

NOTE
Engine compression can be checked more accurately with a compression gauge as described under ***Tune-up*** *in Chapter Three.*

NOTE
If the cylinder compression is sufficient, the engine may be suffering from a loss of crankcase pressure. During two-

stroke operation, the air/fuel mixture is compressed twice, first in the crankcase and then in the combustion chamber. Crankcase pressure forces the air/fuel mixture to flow from the crankcase chamber through the transfer ports and into the combustion chamber. Before continuing, perform the ***Two-Stroke Crankcase Pressure Test*** *described in this chapter.*

ENGINE STARTING TROUBLES

An engine that refuses to start or is difficult to start is very frustrating. More often than not, the problem is very minor and can be found with a simple and logical troubleshooting approach.

The following items show a beginning point from which to isolate engine starting problems.

Engine Fails to Start (Spark Test)

Perform the following spark test to determine if the ignition system is operating properly.

1. Disconnect the plug cap (**Figure 6**) from each spark plug.
2. Clean all dirt and debris away from each spark plug.

CAUTION
Dirt that falls into the cylinder will cause rapid piston, piston ring and cylinder wear.

3. Loosen and remove both spark plugs (**Figure 6**).
4. Insert the spark plug into its cap and touch the spark plug base against the cylinder head to ground it (**Figure 7**). Position both spark plugs so that you can see the electrodes.

WARNING
Turning the engine over with the spark plugs removed will allow fuel to be ejected through the spark plug holes. When making a spark plug test, do not place the spark plugs next to the open spark plug holes because the air/fuel mixture in the cylinders may ignite and cause a fire or explosion to occur.

5. Turn the ignition switch to ON and the engine stop switch to RUN.

WARNING
Do not hold a spark plug, wire or connector—a serious electrical shock may result.

6. Turn the engine over with the kickstarter. A fat blue spark should be evident across both spark plug electrodes.
7. If the spark is good, check for one or more of the following possible malfunctions:
   a. Obstructed fuel line or fuel filter.
   b. Low compression or engine damage.
   c. Flooded engine.

8A. If there is no spark at both spark plugs, check for one or more of the following:
   a. A faulty throttle override system (T.O.R.S.) will prevent the engine from starting. Refer to *Ignition System Troubleshooting* in this chapter.
   b. Fouled or wet spark plugs.
   c. Loose or damaged high tension wiring connections (at coil and plug cap).
   d. Faulty ignition coil or faulty ignition coil ground wire connection.
   e. Faulty CDI unit.
   f. Sheared flywheel key.
   g. Loose flywheel nut.
   h. Loose or dirty electrical connections.

8B. If there is no spark at one spark plug only, check for one or more of the following:
   a. Fouled or wet spark plug.
   b. Loose or damaged high tension wiring connection (at coil and plug cap).

NOTE
If the engine backfires when attempting to start it, the ignition timing is probably incorrect. Incorrect ignition timing can be caused by a loose flywheel (rotor), loose stator plate mounting screws or a faulty ignition component. If you find that the stator plate and flywheel are tight, check ignition timing as described in Chapter Three.

Engine is Difficult to Start

If the vehicle has spark, compression and fuel, but it is difficult to start, check for one or more of the following possible malfunctions:

1. Incorrect air/fuel mixture:
   a. Clogged air filter element.
   b. Incorrect carburetor adjustment.

c. Clogged pilot jets.
d. Clogged air passage.
2. Engine flooded:
a. Incorrect starting procedures.
b. Incorrect fuel level (too high).
c. Worn fuel valve and seat assembly.
d. Fuel valve stuck open.
e. Damaged float.
3. No fuel flow:
a. Clogged fuel line.
b. Clogged fuel filter (if used).
c. Clogged fuel valve.
d. Clogged or restricted fuel valve.
e. Clogged fuel tank cap vent hose.
f. Fuel valve turned off.
4. Weak spark:
a. Fouled or wet spark plugs.
b. Loose or damaged spark plug cap connection.
c. Loose or damaged high tension wiring connections (at coil and plug cap).
d. Faulty ignition coil.
e. Faulty CDI.
f. Faulty pickup coil.
g. Sheared flywheel key.
h. Loose flywheel nut.
i. Loose electrical connections.
j. Dirty electrical connections.
5. Low engine compression:
a. Loose spark plug or missing spark plug gasket.
b. Stuck piston rings.
c. Excessive piston ring wear.
d. Excessively worn piston and/or cylinder.
e. Loose cylinder head fasteners.
f. Cylinder head incorrectly installed and/or torqued down.
g. Warped cylinder head.
h. Blown head gasket.
i. Blown base gasket.
j. Loose cylinder nuts.
6. Excessively worn or broken reed valve(s).

Engine Will Not Turn Over

If the engine will not turn over because of a mechanical problem, check for one or more of the following possible malfunctions.

a. Defective kickstarter and/or gear.
b. Broken kickstarter return spring.
c. Damaged kickstarter ratchet gear.
d. Seized or damaged idler gear.
e. Seized piston(s).
f. Broken piston skirt—chunks of piston are wedged between the crankshaft and crankcase.
g. Seized crankshaft bearings.
h. Seized connecting rod small end bearing.
i. Seized connecting rod big end bearing.
j. Broken connecting rod.
k. Seized primary drive gear/clutch assembly.

ENGINE PERFORMANCE

In the following check list, it is assumed that the engine runs, but is not operating at peak performance. This will serve as a starting point from which to isolate a performance malfunction.

Engine Will Not Idle or the Throttle Appears Stuck Open

a. Damaged throttle cable.
b. Contaminated or damaged throttle lever.
c. Incorrect throttle cable routing or adjustment.

Engine Will Not Idle

a. Incorrect carburetor adjustment.
b. Clogged pilot jets.
c. Obstructed fuel line or fuel shutoff valve.
d. Fouled or improperly gapped spark plugs.
e. Leaking head gasket.

Poor Low Speed Performance

Check for one or more of the following possible malfunctions:

1. Incorrect air/fuel mixture:
a. Clogged air filter element.
b. Incorrect carburetor adjustment.
c. Clogged pilot jets.
d. Clogged carburetor air passages.
e. Loose or cracked air filter duct hose.
f. Loose carburetor hose clamps.
g. Clogged fuel tank cap vent hose.
h. Carburetor choke stuck open.
i. Incorrect fuel level (too high or too low).
2. Weak spark:
a. Fouled or wet spark plugs.
b. Incorrect spark plug heat range.
c. Loose or damaged spark plug cap connections.

d. Loose or damaged high tension wiring connections (at coil and plug cap).
e. Faulty ignition coil.
f. Faulty CDI unit.
g. Faulty pickup coil.
h. Loose electrical connections.
i. Dirty electrical connections.

3. Low engine compression:
a. Loose spark plug or missing spark plug gasket.
b. Stuck piston ring(s).
c. Excessive piston ring wear.
d. Excessively worn piston and/or cylinder.
e. Loose cylinder head fasteners.
f. Cylinder head incorrectly installed and/or torqued down.
g. Warped cylinder head.
h. Blown head gasket.
i. Blown base gasket.
j. Loose cylinder nuts.
k. Severely damaged reed valve assembly.

4. Excessively worn or broken reed valve(s).

5. Brake drag. Refer to *Brakes* in this chapter for additional information.

Poor High Speed Performance

Check for one or more of the following possible malfunctions:

1. Incorrect air/fuel mixture:
a. Clogged air filter element.
b. Clogged carburetor air vent tubes.
c. Incorrect jet needle clip position.
d. Incorrect main jets.
e. Clogged main jets.
f. Worn jet needle and/or needle jet.
g. Clogged air jet or air passage.
h. Loose or cracked air filter duct hose.
i. Loose carburetor hose clamps.
j. Clogged fuel tank cap vent hose.
k. Worn fuel valve and seat.
l. Incorrect fuel level (too high or too low).
m. Clogged fuel line.
n. Clogged fuel filter.
o. Clogged fuel valve.
p. The fuel mixture is contaminated with water.

2. If the engine rpm drops off or cuts out abruptly:
a. Clogged air filter element.
b. Damaged exhaust system.
c. Clogged exhaust system.
d. Clutch slippage.
e. Clogged main jets.
f. Incorrect fuel level (too high or too low).
g. Choke valve partially stuck.
h. Throttle valve does not open all the way.
i. Brake drag.
j. Engine overheating.
k. The fuel mixture is contaminated with water.
l. Defective parking brake switch (1997-on models).

NOTE

With the parking brake applied the CDI limits engine speed to 2300 rpm by causing a misfire condition.

3. Low engine compression:
a. Loose spark plug or missing spark plug gasket.
b. Stuck piston ring.
c. Excessive piston ring wear.
d. Excessively worn piston and/or cylinder.
e. Loose cylinder head fasteners.
f. Cylinder head incorrectly installed and/or torqued down.
g. Warped cylinder head.
h. Blown head gasket.
i. Blown base gasket.
j. Loose cylinder nuts.
k. Broken reed valve(s).

Engine Overheating

Check for one or more of the following possible malfunctions:

1. Low coolant level. Visually check the system for leaks.

2. Coolant deterioration:
a. Engine coolant contains additives to prevent cooling system corrosion. Replace the coolant at the intervals specified in Chapter Three.
b. Contaminated coolant has a unique smell. If the coolant gives off an abnormal smell, exhaust gas may be leaking into the engine water jacket. See Chapter Three.

CAUTION

A blown or defective cylinder head gasket or warped cylinder head will allow exhaust gas to leak into the engine water jacket. Acids, formed by the mixing of coolant water and gas, corrode the cylinder head and cylinder mating surfaces. During acceleration, leaking exhaust gases force coolant away from the damaged gasket area, causing the effected area to overheat. When the engine speed is reduced, coolant that was diverted during acceleration, returns to the overheated area. This abrupt temperature change can warp the cylinder head and cylinder mating surfaces. Extra pressure in the radiator will also cause the pressure valve in the radiator cap to open and release coolant.

3. Faulty cooling system:
   a. Faulty radiator cap.
   b. Defective water pump.
   c. Clogged radiator and engine coolant passages.
   d. Collapsed coolant hoses.
4. Other causes of engine overheating that have nothing to do with the cooling system are:
   a. Excessive carbon buildup in the combustion chambers.
   b. Incorrect air/fuel mixture.
   c. Clutch slippage.
   d. Brake drag.
   e. Transmission oil level too high.

Black Exhaust and Engine Runs Roughly

a. Clogged air filter element.
b. Carburetor adjustment incorrect—mixture too rich.
c. Carburetor floats damaged or incorrectly adjusted.
d. Choke not operating correctly.
e. Water or other contaminants in fuel.
f. Excessive piston-to-cylinder clearance.

Engine Loses Power

a. Carburetor incorrectly adjusted.
b. Engine overheating.
c. Ignition timing incorrect due to improper timing or defective ignition component(s).
d. Incorrectly gapped spark plugs.
e. Obstructed silencers.
f. Brake drag.

Engine Lacks Acceleration

a. Incorrect carburetor adjustment.
b. Clogged fuel line.
c. Ignition timing incorrect due to improper timing or faulty ignition component(s).
d. Brake drag.

ENGINE

Engine problems are generally symptoms of something wrong in another system, such as ignition, fuel or starting.

Preignition

Preignition is the premature burning of fuel and is caused by hot spots in the combustion chamber. The fuel actually ignites before it is supposed to. Glowing deposits in the combustion chamber, inadequate cooling or an overheated spark plug can all cause preignition. This is first noticed in the form of a power loss but will eventually result in extended damage to the internal parts of the engine because of higher combustion chamber temperatures.

Detonation

Commonly called "spark knock" or "fuel knock," detonation is the violent explosion of fuel in the combustion chamber prior to the proper time of combustion. Severe damage can result. Use of low octane gasoline is a common cause of detonation.

Even when high octane gasoline is used, detonation can still occur if the engine is improperly timed. Other causes are over-advanced ignition timing, lean fuel mixture at or near full throttle, inadequate engine cooling, or the excessive accumulation of deposits on the pistons and combustion chambers.

Power Loss

Several factors can cause a lack of power and speed. Look for a clogged air filter or fouled or damaged spark plug(s). A piston or cylinder that is galling, incorrect piston clearance or worn or stuck piston rings may be responsible. Look for loose bolts, defective gaskets or leaking machined mating surfaces on the cylinder head, cylinder blocks and crankcase. Also check the crankshaft seals; refer to *Two-Stroke Crankcase Pressure Test* in this chapter.

If the engine seems to operate correctly but you are experiencing performance related problems, check the front and rear brakes for dragging or damage.

Piston Seizure

This is caused by incorrect bore clearance, piston rings with an improper end gap, compression leak, incorrect engine oil, spark plug of the wrong heat range, incorrect ignition timing or the use of an incorrect air/fuel mixture. Overheating from any cause may result in piston seizure.

Piston Slap

Piston slap is an audible slapping or rattling noise resulting from excessive piston-to-cylinder clearance. When allowed to continue, piston slap will eventually cause the piston skirt to shatter. In some cases, a shattered piston will cause some form of secondary engine damage.

This type of damage can be prevented by measuring the cylinder bores and piston diameters at specified intervals, and by close visual inspection of all top end components, checking each part for scuff marks, scoring, cracks and other signs of abnormal wear. Replace parts that exceed wear limits or show damage.

ENGINE NOISES

1. *Knocking or pinging during acceleration*— Caused by using a lower octane fuel than recommended. May also be caused by poor fuel available at some "discount" gasoline stations. Pinging can also be caused by spark plugs of the wrong heat range or incorrect carburetor jetting. Refer to *Correct Spark Plug Heat Range* in Chapter Three. Check also for excessive carbon buildup in the combustion chambers or incorrect ignition timing.
2. *Slapping or rattling noises at low speed or during acceleration*— May be caused by piston slap, i.e., excessive piston-cylinder wall clearance. Check also for a bent connecting rod or worn piston pin and/or piston pin holes in the piston.
3. *Knocking or rapping while decelerating*— Usually caused by excessive rod bearing clearance.
4. *Persistent knocking and vibration or other noise*— Usually caused by worn main bearings. If the main bearings are okay, consider the following:
   a. Loose engine mounts.
   b. Cracked frame.
   c. Leaking cylinder head gasket.
   d. Exhaust pipe leakage at cylinder head.
   e. Stuck piston ring.
   f. Broken piston ring.
   g. Partial engine seizure.
   h. Excessive small end connecting rod bearing clearance.
   i. Excessive big end connecting rod bearing clearance.
   j. Excessive crankshaft runout.
   k. Worn or damaged primary drive gear.
5. *Rapid on-off squeal*— Compression leak around cylinder head gasket or spark plug.

FUEL SYSTEM

Many riders automatically assume that the carburetors are at fault when the engine does not run properly. While fuel system problems are not uncommon, carburetor adjustment is seldom the answer. In many cases, adjusting the carburetors only compounds the problem by making the engine run worse.

Fuel system troubleshooting should start at the fuel tank and work through the system, reserving the carburetors as the final point. Most fuel system problems result from plugged fuel filters or fuel valve, sour fuel or dirty carburetors. Fuel system troubleshooting is covered thoroughly under *Starting Difficulties, Engine Starting Troubles* and *Engine Performance* in this chapter.

Carburetor chokes can also present problems. A choke stuck open will show up as a hard starting problem; one that sticks closed will result in a flooding condition. Check the choke operation; push and pull the choke knob in the carburetor (A, **Figure 3**). The choke should move between its OFF and ON positions without binding or sticking in one position. If necessary, remove the choke (Chapter Eight) and inspect it for severe wear or damage.

IGNITION SYSTEM

All models are equipped with a capacitor discharge ignition (CDI) system (**Figure 8**). This solid state system uses no contact breaker point or other moving parts. Because of the solid state design, problems with the capacitor discharge system are relatively few. However, when problems arise they stem from one of the following:

a. Weak spark.
b. No spark.

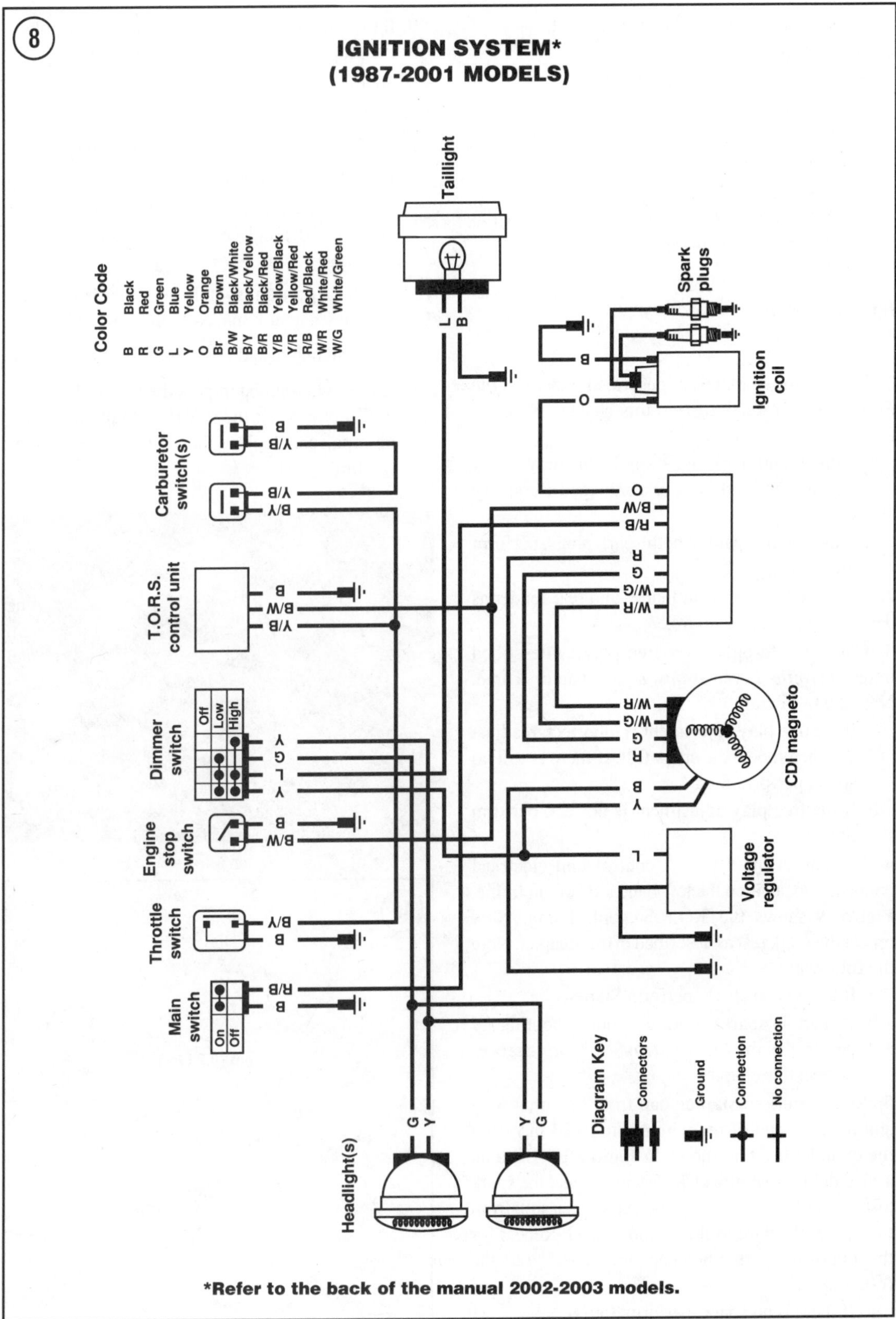
8
IGNITION SYSTEM*
(1987-2001 MODELS)
Color Code
B Black
R Red
G Green
L Blue
Y Yellow
O Orange
Br Brown
B/W Black/White
B/Y Black/Yellow
B/R Black/Red
Y/B Yellow/Black
Y/R Yellow/Red
R/B Red/Black
W/R White/Red
W/G White/Green
Taillight
Spark plugs
Ignition coil
Carburetor switch(s)
T.O.R.S. control unit
Dimmer switch
Off
Low
High
Engine stop switch
Throttle switch
Main switch
On
Off
CDI magneto
Voltage regulator
Headlight(s)
Diagram Key
Connectors
Ground
Connection
No connection
*Refer to the back of the manual 2002-2003 models.

It is possible to check CDI systems that:

a. Do not spark.
b. Have broken or damaged wires.
c. Have a weak spark.

It is difficult to check CDI systems that malfunction due to:

a. Vibration problems.
b. Components that malfunction only when the engine is hot or under a load.

Ignition System Troubleshooting

1. Perform the spark test as described under *Engine Fails to Start (Spark Test)* in this chapter. Note the following:
   a. If there is no spark at one spark plug only, check for a fouled spark plug or a damaged secondary wire.
   b. If there is no spark at both spark plugs, perform Step 2.
2. Remove the seat, front fender and rear fender as described in Chapter Fourteen.
3. Check the throttle lever free play as described under *Throttle Lever Adjustment* Chapter Three. Note the following:
   a. If the free play adjustment is incorrect, readjust and then repeat the spark test. If there is still no spark, perform Step 4.
   b. If the free play adjustment is correct, perform Step 4.
4. Disconnect the T.O.R.S. control unit electrical connector located on the left-hand side of the frame. **Figure 9** shows the T.O.R.S. control unit. Now repeat the spark test as described in this chapter. Note the following:
   a. If there is no spark, perform Step 5.
   b. If there is spark, continue troubleshooting by performing the *T.O.R.S. Troubleshooting* procedure in this chapter.
5. Remove the spark plug cap from one plug wire and hold the end of the wire 6 mm (0.24 in.) from the cylinder head as shown in **Figure 10**. Have an assistant kick over the kickstarter to repeat the spark test. A fat blue spark should be evident passing from the end of the wire to the cylinder head. Repeat for the opposite spark plug cap and wire. Note the following:
   a. If there is no spark, perform Step 6.
   b. If there is a spark, the plug cap is faulty. Replace the plug cap and repeat the spark test.
6. Test the engine stop switch as described under *Switches* in Chapter Nine. Note the following:
   a. If the switch tested good, perform Step 7.
   b. If the switch failed to pass the test as described in Chapter Nine, the switch is faulty and must be replaced. Replace the switch and retest the ignition system.
7. Test the ignition switch as described under *Switches* in Chapter Nine. Note the following:
   a. If the switch tested good, perform Step 8.
   b. If the switch failed to pass the test as described in Chapter Nine, the switch is faulty and must be replaced. Replace the switch and retest the ignition system.

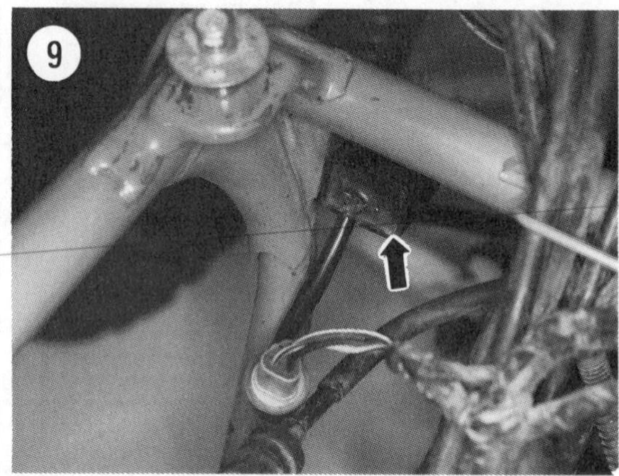

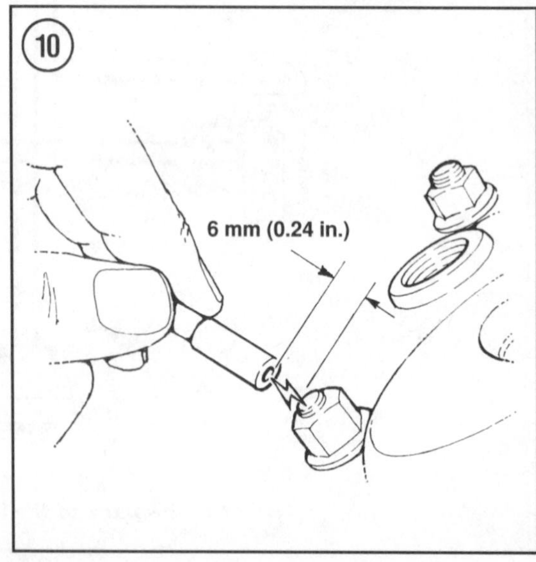

8. Test the ignition coil secondary and primary resistance as described under *Ignition Coil Testing* in Chapter Nine. Note the following:
   a. If the ignition coil tested good, perform Step 9.
   b. If the ignition coil failed to pass the tests described in Chapter Nine, the ignition coil is faulty and must be replaced. Replace the ignition coil and retest the ignition system.
9. Test the source and pickup coils as described under *Stator Coil Testing* in Chapter Nine. Note the following:
   a. If both coils tested good, perform Step 10.
   b. If one or both coils tested incorrectly, the stator coil is faulty and must be replaced. Replace the stator coil assembly and retest the ignition system.
10. If you have not been able to locate the damaged component, check the ignition system wiring harness and connectors. Check for damaged wires or loose, dirty or damaged connectors. If the wiring and connectors are okay, the CDI unit is faulty and must be replaced.
11. Install all parts previously removed.

11

THROTTLE OVERRIDE SYSTEM (T.O.R.S.)

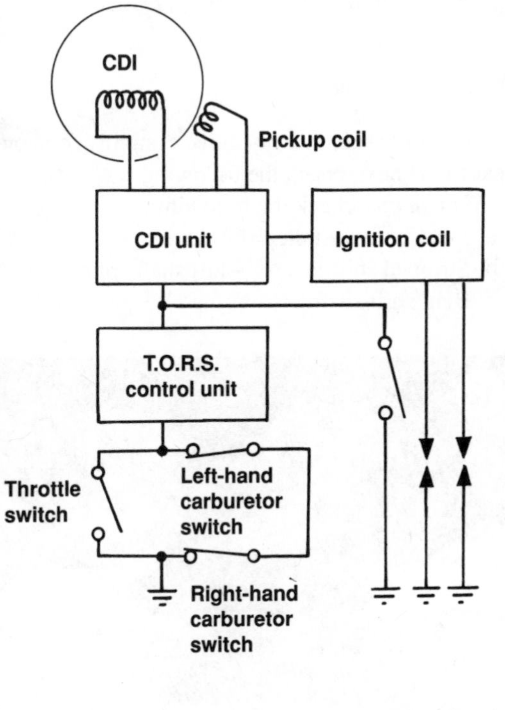

Throttle Override System (T.O.R.S.) Troubleshooting

The throttle override circuit of the ignition system consists of the T.O.R.S. control unit, throttle lever switch and the left- and right-hand carburetor switches (**Figure 11**). A faulty throttle override system will prevent the ignition system from operating.

Prior to troubleshooting the T.O.R.S. system, perform the *Ignition System Troubleshooting* procedure in this chapter to determine if the T.O.R.S. system is inoperative. If so, perform the following procedures to isolate the damaged component(s).

1. Test the throttle lever switch as described under *Switches* in Chapter Nine. Note the following:
   a. If the throttle lever switch tested good, perform Step 2.
   b. If the throttle lever switch failed to pass the tests described in Chapter Nine, the throttle lever switch is faulty and must be replaced. Replace the throttle lever and retest the ignition system.
2. Test the left- and right-hand carburetor switches as described under *Switches* in Chapter Nine. Note the following:
   a. If both switches tested good, perform Step 3.
   b. If one or both switches tested incorrectly, replace the T.O.R.S. housing (Chapter Eight) and retest the ignition system.
3. If you have not been able to locate the damaged component, check the T.O.R.S. system wiring harness and connectors. Check for damaged wires or loose, dirty or damaged connectors. If the wiring and connectors are okay, the T.O.R.S. control unit (**Figure 9**) is faulty and must be replaced.

ENGINE OVERHEATING

Engine overheating is a serious problem in that it can quickly cause engine seizure and damage. The following section groups 6 main systems with probable causes that can lead to engine overheating.

1. *Ignition system*—check the following:
   a. Incorrect spark plug gap.
   b. Incorrect spark plug heat range; see Chapter Three.
   c. Faulty CDI unit/incorrect ignition timing.

2. *Engine compression system*—check the following:
   a. Cylinder head gasket leakage.
   b. Heavy carbon build-up in combustion chamber.
3. *Engine cooling system*—check the following:
   a. Restricted coolant passage to radiator (**Figure 12**).
   b. Low coolant level.
   c. Damaged water pump (impeller, oil seal and bearing). See **Figure 13**.
   d. Faulty radiator cap.
   e. Contaminated coolant passages (cooling system and engine).
   f. Leaking water pump oil seal.
   g. Damaged cylinder head gasket.
   h. Warped cylinder head.
   i. Leaking or damaged radiator and/or coolant hoses.
4. *Engine lubrication system*—check the following:
   a. Incorrect fuel/oil mixture ratio.
   b. Wrong type of engine oil.
5. *Fuel system*—check the following:
   a. Clogged air filter element.
   b. Incorrect float level.
   c. Incorrect carburetor adjustment or jetting.
6. *Brake and rear axle*—check for:
   a. Brake drag.
   b. Damaged or partially seized rear axle bearings.

CLUTCH

The 2 basic clutch troubles are:

a. Clutch slipping.
b. Clutch dragging.

All clutch troubles, except adjustments, require partial engine disassembly to identify and cure the problem. Refer to Chapter Six for procedures.

Clutch Slipping

1. *Clutch wear or damage*—check the following:
   a. Weak or damaged clutch springs.
   b. Worn friction plates.
   c. Warped steel plates.
   d. Loose clutch springs.
   e. Incorrectly assembled clutch.
   f. Incorrect clutch adjustment.
2. *Clutch/transmission*—check for the following:
   a. Low oil level.
   b. Oil additives.
   c. Low viscosity oil.

Clutch Dragging

1. *Clutch wear or damage*—check the following:
   a. Warped steel plates.
   b. Swollen friction plates.
   c. Warped pressure plate.
   d. Incorrect clutch spring tension.
   e. Incorrectly assembled clutch.
   f. Loose clutch nut.
   g. Burnt primary driven gear bushing.
   h. Damaged clutch boss.
   i. Incorrect clutch adjustment.
2. *Clutch/transmission oil*—check for the following:
   a. Oil level too high.
   b. High viscosity oil.

TRANSMISSION

The basic transmission troubles are:

a. Difficult shifting.
b. Gears pop out of mesh.

Transmission symptoms are sometimes hard to distinguish from clutch symptoms. Be sure that the clutch is not causing the trouble before working on the transmission.

Difficult Shifting

If the shift shaft does not move smoothly from one gear to the next, check the following.

1. *Shift shaft*—check the following:
   a. Incorrectly installed shift lever.
   b. Stripped shift lever-to-shift shaft splines.
   c. Bent shift shaft.

d. Damaged shift shaft return spring.
e. Damaged shift shaft where it engages the shift drum.

2. *Stopper lever*—check the following:
   a. Seized or damaged stopper lever roller.
   b. Broken stopper lever spring.
   c. Loose stopper lever mounting bolt.
3. *Shift drum and shift forks*—check the following:
   a. Bent shift fork(s).
   b. Damaged shift fork guide pin(s).
   c. Seized shift fork (on shaft).
   d. Broken shift fork or shift fork shaft.
   e. Severely worn or damaged shift drum groove(s).
   f. Damaged shift drum bearing.

Gears Pop Out Of Mesh

If the transmission shifts into gear but then slips or pops out, check the following:

1. *Shift shaft*—check the following:
   a. Incorrect shift lever position/adjustment.
   b. Stopper lever fails to move or set properly.
2. *Shift drum*—check the following:
   a. Incorrect thrust play.
   b. Severely worn or damaged shift drum groove(s).
3. *Shift forks*—check the following:
   a. Bent shift fork(s).
4. *Transmission*—check the following:
   a. Worn or damaged gear dogs.
   b. Excessive gear thrust play.
   c. Worn or damaged shaft circlips or thrust washers.

13

DRIVE TRAIN NOISE

This section deals with noises that are restricted to the drive train assembly—drive chain, clutch and transmission. While some drive train noises have little meaning, abnormal noises are a good indicator of a developing problem. The problem is recognizing the difference between a normal and abnormal noise. One thing that is in your favor, however, is that by maintaining and riding your Yamaha, you become accustomed to the normal noises that occur during engine starting and when riding. A new noise, no matter how minor, should be investigated.

1. *Drive chain noise*— Normal drive chain noise can be considered a low-pitched, continuous whining sound. The noise will vary, depending on the speed of the vehicle and the terrain you are riding on, as well as proper lubrication, wear (both chain and sprockets) and alignment. When checking abnormal drive chain noise, consider the following:
   a. *Inadequate lubrication*—a dry chain will give off a loud whining sound. Clean and lubricate the drive chain at regular intervals; see Chapter Three and Chapter Eleven.
   b. *Incorrect chain adjustment*—check and adjust the drive chain as described in Chapter Three.
   c. *Worn chain*—chain wear should be checked at regular intervals, and replaced when it's overall length exceeds the wear limit specified in Chapter Three.
   d. *Worn or damaged sprockets*—Worn or damaged sprockets will accelerate chain wear. Inspect the sprockets carefully as described in Chapter Three.
   e. *Worn, damaged or missing drive chain rollers*—Chain rollers are in constant contact with the chain. They should be checked often for loose, damaged or missing parts. A missing chain roller will increase chain slack and may cause rapid wear against the frame or swing arm.
   f. *Worn swing arm/chain protector*—A damaged or worn through protector will allow the chain to act much like a chain saw and grind away at the swing arm or frame. Chain wear will also increase rapidly. A new, regular clicking or grinding noise may point to a worn through protector. Inspect the protector(s) regularly. Replace worn protectors before the chain wears through and causes expensive swing arm damage.

2. *Clutch noise*— Any noise that develops in the clutch should be investigated. First, drain the clutch/transmission oil, checking for bits of metal or clutch plate material. If the oil looks and smells okay, remove the clutch cover and clutch (Chapter Six) and check for the following:

a. Worn or damaged clutch housing gear teeth.
b. Excessive clutch housing axial play.
c. Excessive clutch housing-to-friction plate clearance.
d. Excessive clutch housing gear-to-primary drive gear backlash.

3. *Transmission noise*— The transmission will exhibit more normal noises than the clutch, but like the clutch, a new noise in the transmission should be investigated. Drain the clutch/transmission oil into a clean container. Wipe a small amount of oil on a finger and rub the finger and thumb together. Check for the presence of metallic particles. Inspect the drain container for signs of water separation from the oil. Some transmission associated noises are caused by:

a. Insufficient transmission oil level.
b. Contaminated transmission oil.
c. Transmission oil viscosity too thin. A too thin "oil viscosity" will raise the transmission operating temperature.
d. Worn transmission gear(s).
e. Chipped or broken transmission gear(s).
f. Excessive gear side play.
g. Worn or damaged crankshaft-to-transmission bearing(s).

4. If metallic particles are found in Step 2 or Step 3, remove the clutch cover and inspect the clutch, kickstarter, idler gear and primary drive gear assemblies for damage. Remove the clutch cover as described in Chapter Six.

NOTE

If you cannot find any damage with the assemblies described in Step 4, it may be necessary to disassemble the engine and inspect the transmission and internal shifting mechanism for damage.

TWO-STROKE CRANKCASE PRESSURE TEST

Many owners of 2-stroke vehicles are plagued by hard starting and generally poor engine operation, for which there seems to be no cause. Carburetion and ignition systems may be good, and compression tests may show that all is well in the engine's upper end.

What a compression test does not show is lack of primary compression. The crankcase in a 2-stroke engine must be alternately under pressure and vac-

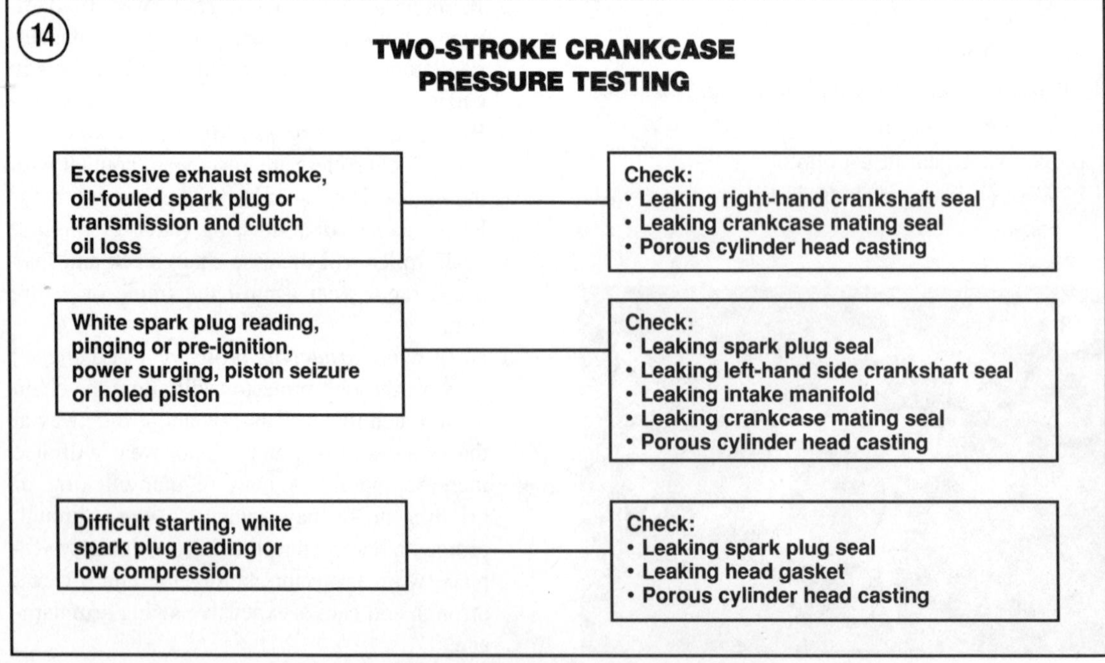

uum. After the piston closes the intake port, further downward movement of the piston causes the entrapped mixture to be pressurized so that it can rush quickly into the cylinder when the scavenging ports are opened. Upward piston movement creates a slight vacuum in the crankcase, enabling the air/fuel mixture to be drawn in from the carburetor.

NOTE

The operational sequence of a two-stroke engine is illustrated in Chapter Four.

If crankcase seals or cylinder gaskets leak, the crankcase cannot hold pressure or vacuum, and proper engine operation becomes impossible. Any other source of leakage such as a defective cylinder base gasket or porous or cracked crankcase castings will result in the same conditions. See **Figure 14**.

It is possible, however, to test for and isolate engine pressure leaks. The test is simple but requires special equipment. A typical 2-stroke pressure test kit is shown in **Figure 15**. The test kit is used to seal off all natural engine openings, then air pressure is applied. If the engine does not hold air, a leak or leaks is indicated. Then it is only necessary to locate and repair all leaks.

NOTE

Because of the labyrinth seal installed on the crankshaft, the cylinders cannot be checked individually. When you pump up one cylinder you will also be pumping up the opposite cylinder. Block off both cylinders before applying pressure during testing.

The following procedure describes a typical pressure test.

1. Remove the exhaust pipes as described in Chapter Eight.
2. Remove both carburetors as described in Chapter Eight.

NOTE

*Do **not** remove the intake manifolds from the cylinder blocks. The manifolds should remain on the engine during this test as they are a common source of air leaks.*

3. Remove the flywheel and stator plate (Chapter Nine) to access the left-hand oil seal (**Figure 16**).

NOTE

Step 4 and Step 5 describe how to block off of the engine openings (intake, exhaust and spark plug). The tester assembly shown in this procedure blocks off the intake manifold completely, while the tester gauge is installed in one of the spark plug holes.

4. Take a rubber plug and push it tightly into the intake manifold (**Figure 17**). Then tighten the car-

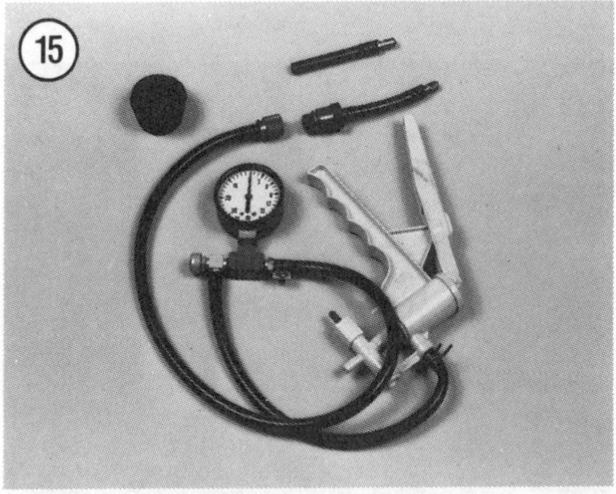
15

16

17

buretor clamp screw securely. Repeat for the opposite intake manifold.

NOTE
***Figure 18** shows the exhaust ports blocked off with expandable rubber plugs. These plugs come in a number of different sizes, so purchase one that is slightly smaller than the exhaust ports inside diameter. In order for an expandable plug to make a tight seal, the exhaust port must be clean.*

5. Block off the exhaust ports, using suitable adapters and fittings. When using expandable plugs (**Figure 18**), insert the expandable portion of the plug into the exhaust port. The outer washer on the plug should not contact the port opening. Then tighten the wingnut securely, watching how the plug seals around the port opening. You may have to loosen the wingnut and reposition the plug a few times to get it to seal properly.
6. Remove one of the spark plugs and install the pressure gauge adaptor into the spark plug hole (**Figure 19**). Connect the pressurizing lever and gauge to the pressure fitting, then squeeze the lever until the gauge indicates approximately 41.3-48.3 kPa (6-7 psi).

CAUTION
Do not apply more than 48.3 kPa (7 psi); otherwise, damage to the crankshaft oil seals may occur.

7. Read the pressure gauge (**Figure 20**). If the engine is in good condition, pressure should not drop more than 6.9 kPa (1 psi) in several minutes. A good rule of thumb is that an engine should hold six pounds of air for six minutes. Any immediate pressure loss or a pressure loss of 6.9 kPa (1 psi) in 1 minute indicates serious sealing problems.

Before condemning the engine, first be sure that there are no leaks in the test equipment or sealing plugs. Check the equipment sealing points with a small brush and soap suds solution. When all of the test equipment is air tight, go over the entire engine carefully. You may be able to hear large leaks, but generally, leaks are found by applying the soap suds solution to all sealing areas on the engine. Possible leakage points are listed in **Figure 14**. Note the following:

a. Left-hand crankshaft seal (**Figure 16**).
b. Right-hand crankshaft seal (**Figure 21**). To check this seal with the clutch cover installed on the engine, apply the soap suds solution to the open end of the transmission breather tube. (**Figure 22** shows the breather tube nozzle with the tube removed.) If the tube blows bubbles, the right-hand crankshaft seal is leaking. A damaged seal will allow oil to be drawn into the crankcase, causing excessive smoking and spark plug fouling. Before tearing the engine down, confirm the seal's condition by removing the clutch (do not remove the primary drive gear assembly) as described in Chapter Six and pressure checking the engine again with the seal exposed.

NOTE
*The primary drive gear (**Figure 21**) must be installed on the crankshaft when pressure testing the engine.*

8. When a leak is detected, it must be repaired or the damaged part replaced. Then, perform this test again. There may still be a leak at some other point on the engine.

18

19

HANDLING

Poor handling will reduce overall performance and may cause you to crash. If you are experiencing poor handling, check the following items:

1. *Handlebars*—check the following:
   a. Loose or damaged handlebar clamps.
   b. Incorrect handlebar clamp installation.
   c. Bent or cracked handlebar.
2. *Tires*—check the following:
   a. Incorrect tire pressure.
   b. Uneven tire pressure (both sides).
   c. Worn or damaged tires.
3. *Wheels*—check the following:
   a. Loose or damaged hub bearings.
   b. Loose or bent wheel axle.
   c. Damaged wheel.
   d. Loose wheel nuts.
   e. Excessive wheel runout.
4. *Steering*—check the following:
   a. Incorrect toe-in adjustment.
   b. Damaged steering shaft.
   c. Damaged steering shaft bearing or bearing blocks.
   d. Incorrectly installed steering shaft.
   e. Bent tie rods.
   f. Damaged steering knuckles.
   g. Bent upper and/or lower arm(s).
5. *Swing arm*—check the following:
   a. Damaged swing arm.
   b. Severely worn or damaged swing arm bearings.
   c. Improperly tightened swing arm pivot shaft.
   d. Damaged axle bearing housing.
   e. Damaged relay arm and/or connecting rod.
   f. Severely worn or damaged relay arm and/or connecting rod.
6. *Rear axle*—check the following:
   a. Loose rear axle mounting bolts.
   b. Seized or otherwise damaged rear axle bearings.
   c. Bent rear axle.
   d. Loose or damaged rear axle bearing housing.
7. *Shock absorber(s)*—check the following:
   a. Damaged damper rod.
   b. Leaking damper housing.
   c. Sagged shock spring(s).
   d. Incorrect shock adjustment.
   e. Loose or damaged shock mount bolts.
8. *Frame*—check the following:
   a. Damaged frame.
   b. Cracked or broken engine mount brackets.

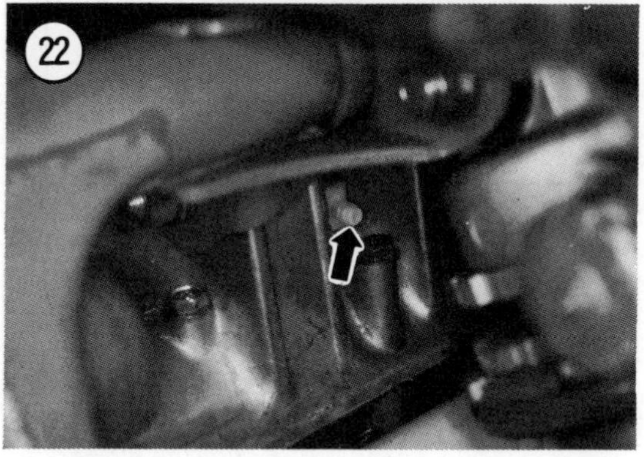

FRAME NOISE

Noises that can be traced to the frame or suspension are usually caused by loose, worn or damaged parts. Various noises that are related to the frame are listed below:

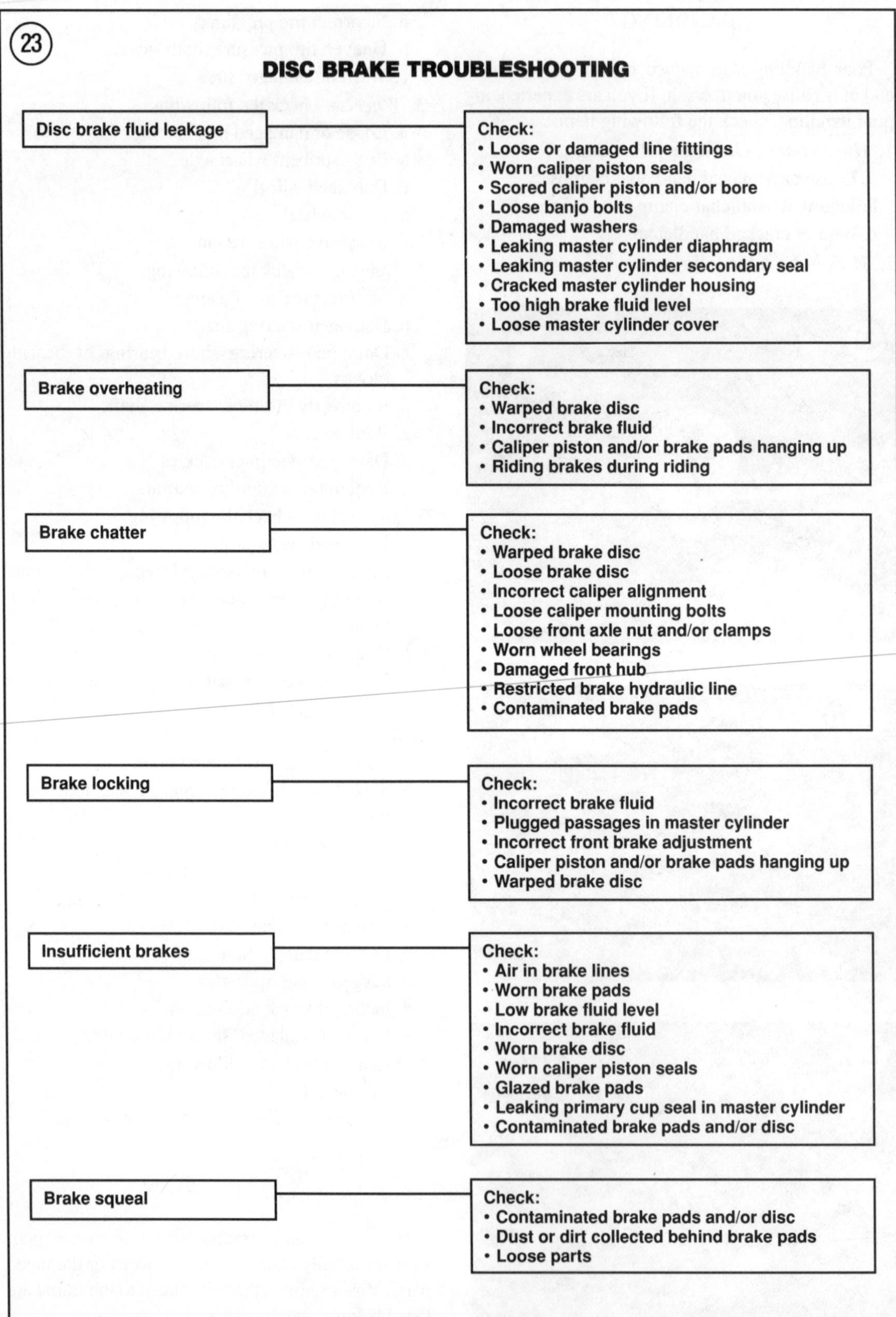
23
DISC BRAKE TROUBLESHOOTING
Disc brake fluid leakage
Check:
• Loose or damaged line fittings
• Worn caliper piston seals
• Scored caliper piston and/or bore
• Loose banjo bolts
• Damaged washers
• Leaking master cylinder diaphragm
• Leaking master cylinder secondary seal
• Cracked master cylinder housing
• Too high brake fluid level
• Loose master cylinder cover
Brake overheating
Check:
• Warped brake disc
• Incorrect brake fluid
• Caliper piston and/or brake pads hanging up
• Riding brakes during riding
Brake chatter
Check:
• Warped brake disc
• Loose brake disc
• Incorrect caliper alignment
• Loose caliper mounting bolts
• Loose front axle nut and/or clamps
• Worn wheel bearings
• Damaged front hub
• Restricted brake hydraulic line
• Contaminated brake pads
Brake locking
Check:
• Incorrect brake fluid
• Plugged passages in master cylinder
• Incorrect front brake adjustment
• Caliper piston and/or brake pads hanging up
• Warped brake disc
Insufficient brakes
Check:
• Air in brake lines
• Worn brake pads
• Low brake fluid level
• Incorrect brake fluid
• Worn brake disc
• Worn caliper piston seals
• Glazed brake pads
• Leaking primary cup seal in master cylinder
• Contaminated brake pads and/or disc
Brake squeal
Check:
• Contaminated brake pads and/or disc
• Dust or dirt collected behind brake pads
• Loose parts

1. *Disc brake noise*— A screeching sound during braking is the most common disc brake noise. Some other disc brake associated noises can be caused by:
   a. Glazed brake pad surface.
   b. Severely worn brake pads.
   c. Warped brake disc.
   d. Loose brake disc mounting bolts.
   e. Loose or missing brake caliper mounting bolts.
   f. Damaged brake caliper.
2. *Rear shock absorber noise*— Check for the following:
   a. Loose shock absorber mounting bolts.
   b. Cracked or broken shock spring.
   c. Damaged shock absorber.
3. Some other frame associated noises are caused by:
   a. Broken frame.
   b. Broken swing arm.
   c. Loose engine mounting bolts.
   d. Damaged steering bearing.
   e. Loose mounting bracket(s).

BRAKES

The front and rear disc brake units are critical to riding performance and safety. The brakes should be inspected frequently and any problems located and repaired immediately. When replacing or refilling the brake fluid, use only DOT 4 brake fluid from a closed and sealed container. See Chapter Thirteen for additional information on brake fluid and disc brake service. The troubleshooting procedures in **Figure 23** will help you isolate the majority of disc brake troubles.

When checking brake pad wear, check that the brake pads in each caliper contact the disc squarely. If one of the brake pads is wearing unevenly, suspect a warped or bent brake disc or damaged caliper.

CHAPTER THREE

LUBRICATION, MAINTENANCE AND TUNE-UP

The performance and service life of your Yamaha Banshee depends on regular maintenance. This chapter covers all of the regular maintenance required to keep your Yamaha in top shape. Regular maintenance is something you can't afford to ignore. Neglecting regular maintenance will reduce the engine life and performance of your Yamaha.

This chapter explains lubrication, maintenance and tune-up procedures required for the Yamaha YFZ350 models described in this manual. **Table 1** is a suggested maintenance schedule. **Tables 1-11** are at the end of the chapter.

NOTE

Due to the number of models and years covered in this book, be sure to follow the correct procedure and specifications for your specific model and year. Also use the correct quantity and type of fluid as indicated in the tables.

PRE-RIDE CHECKLIST

The following checks should be performed prior to the first ride of the day.

1. Inspect all fuel lines and fittings for wetness.
2. Make sure the fuel tank is full and has the correct fuel/oil mixture. Refer to *Engine Lubrication* in this chapter.
3. Make sure the clutch/transmission oil level is correct; add oil if necessary.
4. Make sure the air filter is clean.
5. Check the operation of the clutch and adjust if necessary.
6. Check the throttle and the brake levers. Make sure they operate properly with no binding.
7. Check the brake fluid level in the front and rear master cylinder reservoirs; add DOT 4 brake fluid if necessary.
8. Inspect the front and rear suspension; make sure it has a good solid feel with no looseness.
9. Check chain adjustment and adjust if necessary.
10. Check tire pressure. Refer to **Table 2**.
11. Check the exhaust system for leaks or damage.
12. Check the tightness of all fasteners, especially engine and suspension mounting hardware.
13. Make sure the headlights and taillight work.
14. Check the coolant level with the engine cold. Check the cooling system for leaks.

SERVICE INTERVALS

The services and intervals shown in **Table 1** are recommended by the factory. Strict adherence to these recommendations will insure long service from your Yamaha. However, if the vehicle is run in an area of high humidity, the lubrication and service must be done more frequently to prevent possible rust damage. This is especially true if you have run the Yamaha through water (especially saltwater) and sand.

For convenience when maintaining your vehicle, most of the services shown in **Table 1** are described in this chapter. However, some procedures which require more than minor disassembly or adjustment are covered elsewhere in the appropriate chapter.

TIRES AND WHEELS

Tire Pressure

Tire pressure should be checked and adjusted to maintain the smoothness of the tire, good traction and handling and to get the maximum life out of the tire. A simple, accurate gauge (**Figure 1**) can be purchased for a few dollars and should be carried in your tool box. The appropriate tire pressures are listed in **Table 2**.

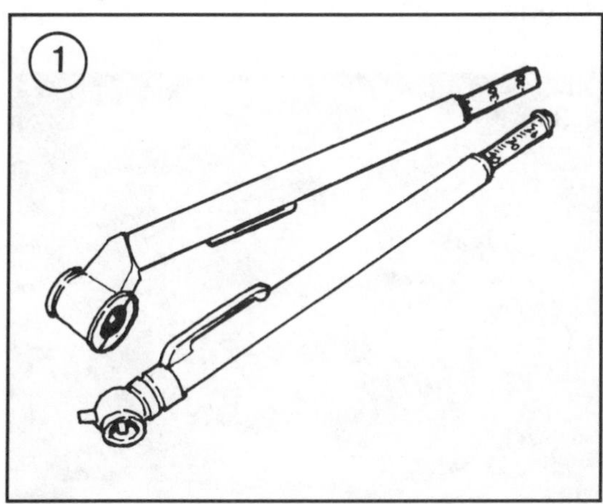

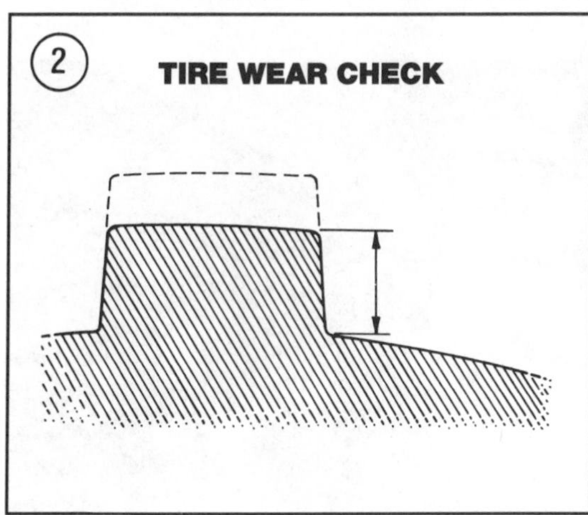

NOTE

*The tire pressure specifications listed in **Table 2** are for the stock tires that originally come equipped on your Yamaha. If you have installed different tires, follow the tire pressure recommendations specified by the tire manufacturer.*

WARNING

Inflate both rear tires to the same pressure. Operating the vehicle with unequal air pressure will cause it to run toward one side. This will cause poor handling.

CAUTION

*Do not over inflate the stock tires as they will be permanently distorted and damaged. If overinflated, they will bulge out similar to inflating an inner tube that is not within the constraints of a tire. If this happens, the tire **will not** return to its original contour.*

Tire Inspection

The tires take a lot of punishment due to the variety of terrain in which they are subjected. Inspect them periodically for excessive wear, cuts, abrasions, etc. If you find a nail or other object in the tire, mark its location with a light crayon prior to removing it. This will help locate the hole for repair. Refer to Chapter Eleven for tire changing and repair information.

Measure tire wear with a ruler as shown in **Figure 2**. To obtain an accurate measurement of tire wear, measure a number of different knobs around the tire. The maximum tire wear limit for stock front and rear tires is 3.0 mm (0.12 in.). If your measurements determine that a tire is worn out, replace it as described in Chapter Eleven.

WARNING

Do not operate your vehicle with worn out tires. Worn out tires can cause you to loose control. Replace worn out tires immediately.

Rim Inspection

Frequently inspect the condition of the wheel rims, especially the outer side (**Figure 3**). If the wheel has hit a tree or large rock, rim damage may be sufficient to cause an air leak or knock it out of alignment. Improper wheel alignment can cause severe vibration and result in an unsafe riding condition.

Make sure the 4 lug nuts (**Figure 3**) are securely in place on all wheels. If they are loose or lost—it's good-bye wheel. Tighten lug nuts to the torque specification listed in **Table 3**.

LUBRICANTS

Transmission Oil

Oil is graded according to its viscosity, which is an indication of how thick it is. The Society of Automotive Engineers (SAE) system distinguishes oil viscosity by numbers,called "weights." Thick (heavy) oils have higher viscosity numbers than thin (light) oils. For example, a 5 weight (SAE 5) oil is a light oil while a 90 weight (SAE 90) oil isrelatively heavy. The viscosity of the oil has nothing to do with its lubricating properties.

Grease

A good-quality grease—preferably waterproof—should be used for many of the parts which require grease. Water does not wash grease off parts as easily as it washes off oil. In addition, grease maintains its lubricating qualities better than oil on long and strenuous events.

CLEANING SOLVENT

A number of solvents can be used to remove old dirt, grease and oil. See your dealer or an auto parts store.

WARNING

***Never use gasoline** as a cleaning solvent. Gasoline is extremely volatile and contains tremendously destructive potential energy. The slightest spark from metal parts accidentally hitting, or a tool slipping, could cause a fatal explosion.*

ENGINE LUBRICATION

WARNING

Serious fire hazards always exist around gasoline. Do not allow smoking in areas where fuel is being mixed or while refueling your machine. Always have a fire extinguisher, rated for gasoline and electrical fires, within reach just to play it safe.

The engines in all models are lubricated by oil mixed with gasoline. Refer to **Table 4** for recommended oil and fuel types. Mix the oil and gasoline thoroughly in a separate clean, sealable container larger than the quantity being mixed to allow room for agitation. Always measure the quantities exactly. **Table 5** lists fuel/oil mixture ratios for all models. Fuel capacity for the various models is given in **Table 6**. Use a good grade of premium fuel rated at 90+ octane.

3

4

CAUTION
Do not mix castor bean oils with petroleum lubricants. A gum will form and may cause serious engine damage.

WARNING
Do not reuse the baby bottle for drinking purposes.

Use a *discarded* baby bottle with graduations in both milliliters (ml) and fluid ounces (oz.) on the side. Pour the required amount of oil into the mixing container and add approximately 1/2 the required amount of gasoline. Agitate the mixture thoroughly, then add the remaining fuel and agitate again until all is mixed well.

To avoid any contaminants entering into the fuel system, use a funnel with a filter when pouring the fuel into the fuel tank.

PERIODIC LUBRICATION

Clutch/Transmission Oil Checking and Changing

The oil poured into the clutch cover lubricates both the clutch and transmission. Proper operation and long service for the clutch and transmission require clean oil. Oil should be changed at the intervals indicated in **Table 1**. Check the oil level frequently and add as necessary to maintain the correct level. Refer to **Table 7** for oil capacities.

Try to use the same brand of oil. Do not mix 2 brand types at the same time as they all vary slightly in their composition. Use of oil additives is not recommended as it may cause clutch slippage.

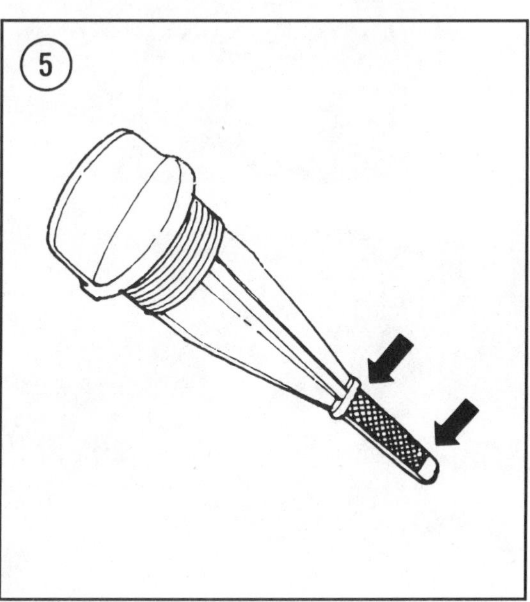

Checking

1. Park the vehicle on a level surface and set the parking brake.
2. Start the engine and let it warm up approximately 2-3 minutes. Shut it off. Wait a few minutes to allow the oil to drain down into the engine.
3. Unscrew the dipstick (**Figure 4**) and remove it from the clutch cover.
4. Wipe the dipstick clean and reinsert the dipstick into the threads in the hole; do *not* screw it in.
5. Remove the dipstick and check the oil level. The level should be between the 2 lines (**Figure 5**) and not above the upper one. If the level is below the lower line, add the recommended type engine oil (**Table 4**) to correct the level. Do not overfill.

CAUTION
If the oil level is too high, remove the oil fill cap and siphon out the excess oil.

Changing

To drain the oil, you need the following:

a. Drain pan.
b. Funnel.
c. Can opener or pour spout.
d. Oil; see **Table 4** and **Table 7**.
e. Hand tools.

There are a number of ways to discard the old oil safely.

The easiest way is to pour it from the drain pan into a half-gallon plastic bleach or milk bottle. Tighten the cap and take the oil to a service station or oil retailer for recycling. *Do not* discard the oil in your household trash or pour it onto the ground.

1. Park the vehicle on a level surface and set the parking brake.
2. Start the engine and let it reach operating temperature.
3. Shut the engine off and put a 2 quart or larger drain pan under the engine.

4. Wipe all dirt and debris from around the drain plug. Then remove the drain plug (**Figure 6**) and sealing washer. If the washer is not on the drain plug, it may have dropped into the oil pan or it may be stuck to the crankcase. Remove the oil fill cap to help speed up the flow of oil.
5. Replace the sealing washer if crushed or damaged.
6. Replace the drain plug if the hex portion on the plug is starting to round off.
7. Install the drain plug and washer and tighten to the torque specification in **Table 3**.
8. Fill the transmission with the correct weight and quantity oil (**Table 4** and **Table 7**).
9. Screw in the oil fill cap and start the engine. Let it idle for 2-3 minutes. Check for leaks.
10. Turn the engine off and check the oil level as described in this chapter. Adjust the level if necessary.

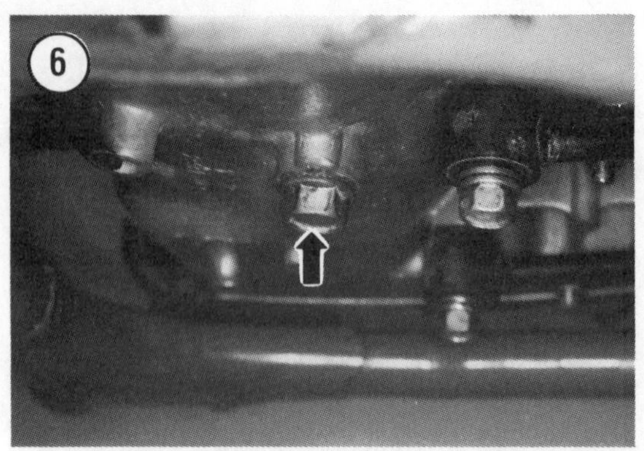
6

7

Control Cable Lubrication

The clutch, throttle and parking brake cables should be cleaned and lubricated at the intervals indicated in **Table 1**. In addition, the cables should be checked for kinks and signs of wear and damage or fraying that could cause the cables to fail or stick. Cables are expendable items and won't last forever under the best of conditions.

The most positive method of control cable lubrication involves the use of a cable lubricator like the one shown in **Figure 7**. A can of cable lube or a general lubricant is also required.

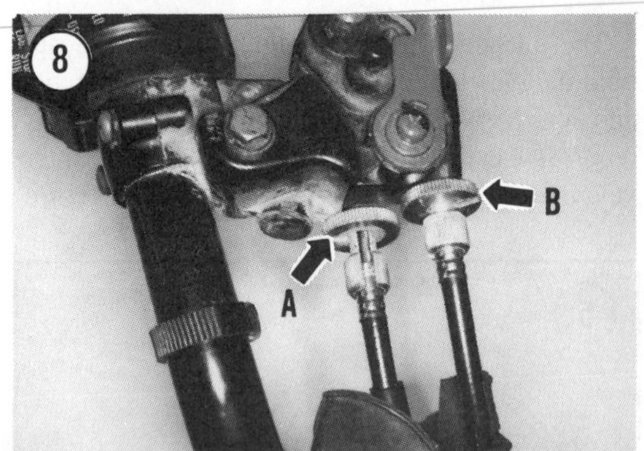

8

WARNING

Do not use chain lube as a cable lubricant. Chain lube may cause the cables to stick and bind in their housings. Stuck throttle cables may cause you to loose control and crash.

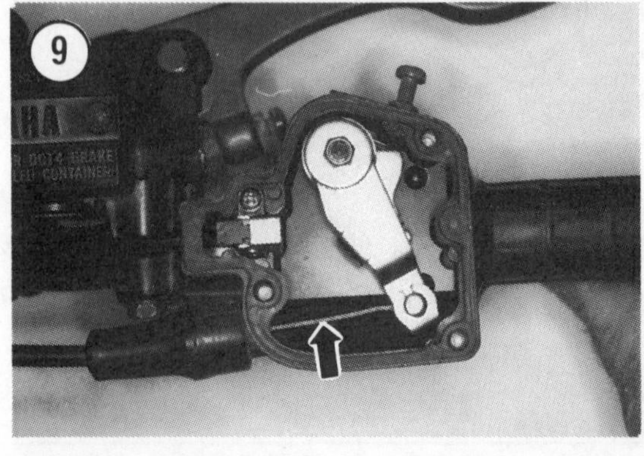
9

1. Loosen the clutch cable adjuster at the handlebar and disconnect the clutch cable (A, **Figure 8**).
2. Disconnect the parking brake cable (B, **Figure 8**) at the handlebar.
3. To disconnect the throttle cables:
   a. Disconnect the upper throttle cable from the throttle lever assembly (**Figure 9**).
   b. Disconnect the lower throttle cables (A, **Figure 10**) from the T.O.R.S. housings (B, **Figure 10**)

as described under *Throttle Valve/T.O.R.S. Housing Removal* in Chapter Eight.

c. Separate the 2 lower throttle cables from the cable junction housing.

4. Attach a cable lubricator to the end of the cable following the manufacturer's instructions (**Figure 11**).

5. Insert the nozzle of the lubricant can into the lubricator, press the button on the can and hold down until the lubricant begins to flow out of the other end of the cable.

NOTE
Place a shop cloth at the end of the cable to catch the lubricant as it runs out.

6. Disconnect the lubricator.

7. Apply a light coat of grease to the cable ends before reconnecting them.

8. Reconnect the cables and adjust the cables as described in this chapter. Attach the throttle cables and install the T.O.R.S. housing as described under *Throttle Valve/T.O.R.S. Housing Reassembly* in Chapter Eight.

9. Operate the throttle, checking that it opens and closes both throttle valves smoothly with no binding.

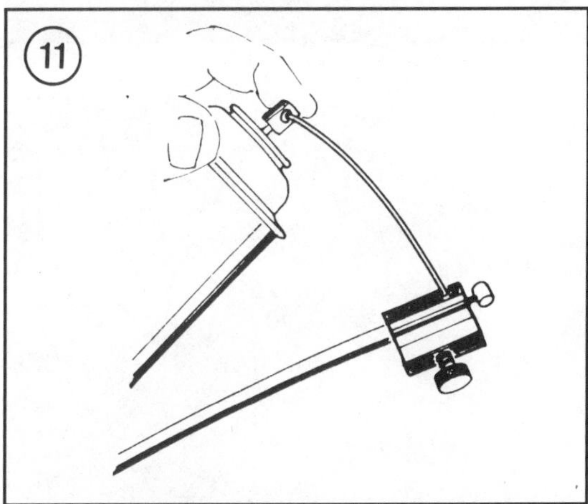

Clutch and Brake Lever Pivot Bolt Lubrication

Periodically, remove the clutch and brake lever pivot bolts and lubricate the bolts with 10W-30 motor oil.

Drive Chain Lubrication

All models are equipped with an O-ring drive chain (**Figure 12**). A properly maintained chain will provide maximum service life and reliability.

1. Support the vehicle with both rear wheels off the ground.

2. Shift the transmission into NEUTRAL.

3. Externally lubricate the chain with an SAE 30-50 weight motor oil or a good grade of chain lubricant (non-tacky) specifically formulated for O-ring chains, following the manufacturer's instructions.

CAUTION
Do not use a tacky chain lubricant on O-ring chains. Dirt and other abrasive materials that stick to the lubricant will grind against the O-rings and damage them. An O-ring chain is pre-lubricated during its assembly at the factory. External oiling is only required to prevent chain rust and to keep the O-rings pliable.

4. Wipe off all excess oil from the rear bearing housing and axle.
5. Check that the master link is properly installed and secured.

Front and Rear Suspension Lubrication (Grease Fitting)

The following components should be lubricated with a grease gun equipped with lithium base grease:

NOTE
Prior to and then after lubricating the following components, wipe off the grease fittings with a clean rag.

a. Upper arm pivot bolt (**Figure 13**).
b. Lower arm pivot bolts (**Figure 14**).
c. Both connecting rod pivot bolts (**Figure 15**).
d. Relay arm pivot bolt (**Figure 16**).

Upper Steering Bearing Block and Dust Seals

While not a part of the periodic maintenance schedule, the upper steering bearing block and oil seals (**Figure 17**) should be removed, cleaned and lubricated during the riding season. Refer to Chapter Eleven for service procedures.

Lower Steering Bearing

A double-sealed lower steering bearing (**Figure 18**) is used on all models. The bearing boss on the frame is not equipped with a grease fitting. Periodic lubrication is not required. When inspecting the steering shaft for excessive play, inspect the upper and lower bearing oil seals (**Figure 19**) for damage. Replace damaged oil seals as described in Chapter Eleven.

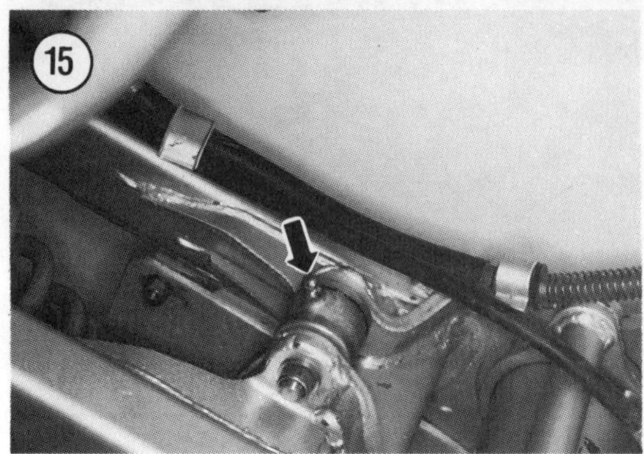

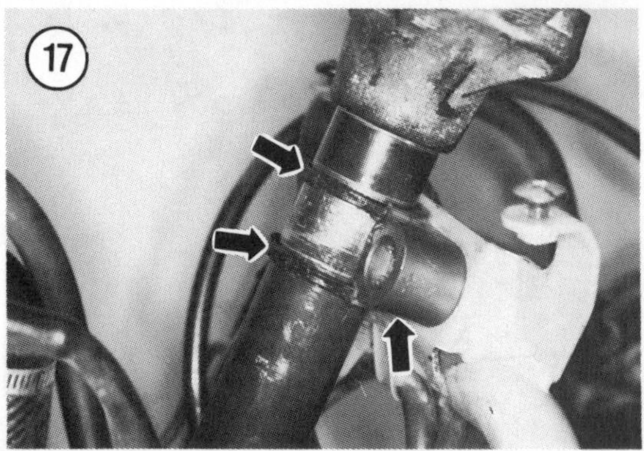

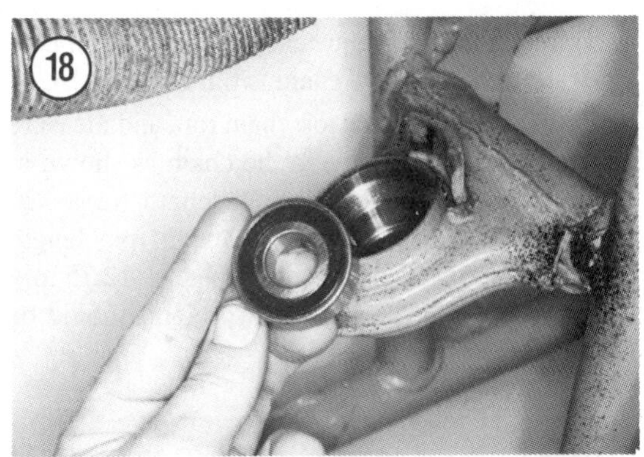

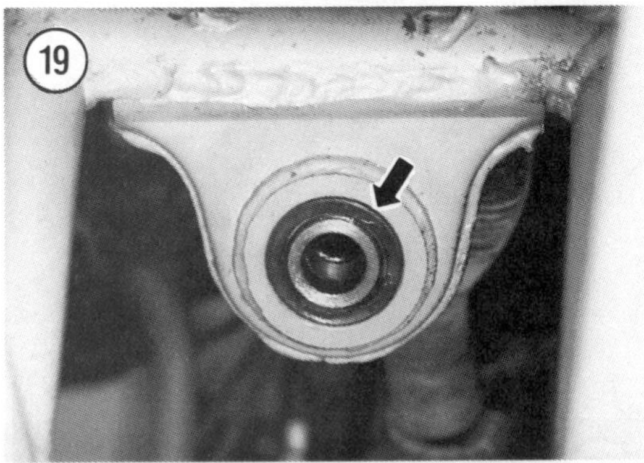

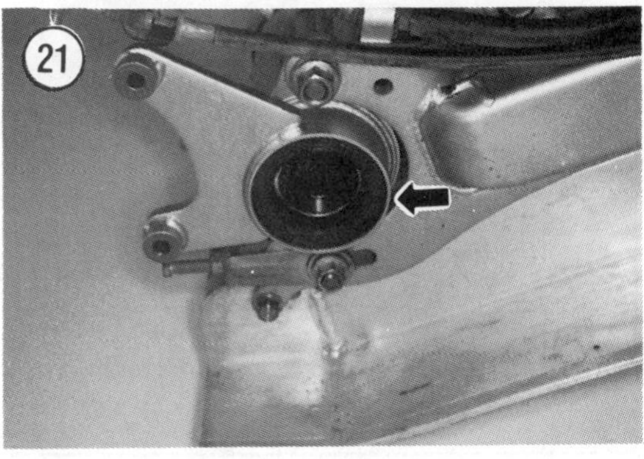

Front Hub Wheel Bearings

The front hub wheel bearings (**Figure 20**) should be lubricated with a lithium base grease. New oil seals should be installed after lubricating the bearings. Refer to Chapter Eleven for service.

Rear Axle Bearings and Oil Seals

Double sealed rear axle bearings are installed in the axle housing. Periodic lubrication of the bearings is not required. Periodically, inspect the outer oil seals (**Figure 21**). Severely worn or damaged oil seals should be replaced immediately; leaking oil seals (**Figure 22**) allow dirt, water and sand to enter the axle housing, damaging the bearing and causing rust and corrosion to build on the axle and center hub spacer. If dirt has entered the axle housing, the housing should be removed and disassembled; refer to Chapter Twelve.

Whenever the rear axle has been removed, pack the oil seal lips with grease before reinstalling the axle.

Swing Arm Bearing Assembly Lubrication

The swing arm bearing assembly (**Figure 23**, typical) should be lubricated at the intervals speci-

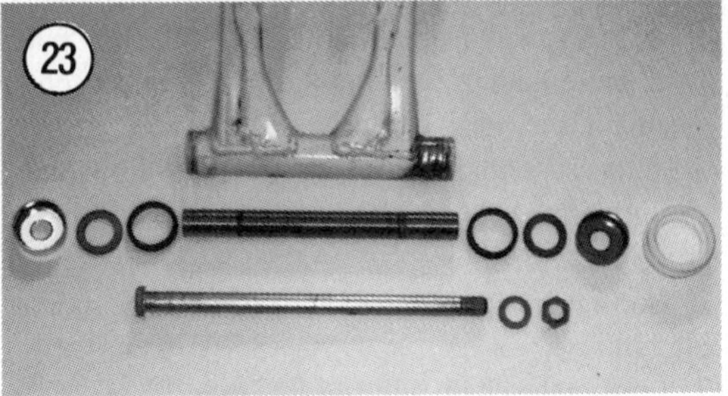

fied in **Table 1**. The swing arm must be removed and partially disassembled to lubricate the bearings—do not remove the needle bearings (**Figure 24**) for periodic lubrication. Refer to Chapter Twelve for service procedures.

Rear Shock Absorber Bearing and Pivot Bolt Lubrication

The shock absorber bearings and pivot bolts should be lubricated at the intervals indicated in **Table 1**. The shock absorber must be removed to lubricate these parts. Do not remove the bearings for periodic lubrication. Refer to Chapter Twelve.

Rear Brake Pedal Pivot Shaft Lubrication

Remove the rear brake pedal and lubricate the pivot shaft (**Figure 25**) with waterproof grease. Reverse to install. Inspect the pedal return spring for weakness or damage.

PERIODIC MAINTENANCE

Periodic maintenance intervals are listed in **Table 1**.

Drive Chain Cleaning

Refer to *Drive Chain* in Chapter Twelve.

Drive Chain/Sprockets Wear Inspection

The drive chain should be checked frequently and replaced when excessively worn or damaged.

A quick check will give you an indication of when to measure chain wear. At the rear sprocket, pull one of the links away from the sprocket. If the link pulls away more than 1/2 the height of a sprocket tooth, the chain is excessively worn (**Figure 26**).

To measure chain wear, perform the following:

1. Support the vehicle with both rear wheels off the ground.
2. Loosen the upper and lower axle housing mounting bolts.
3. Loosen the chain adjuster locknuts.
4. Tighten the chain adjusters to move the rear axle rearward until the drive chain is tight (no slack).
5. Lay a scale along the top chain run, and measure the length of any 21 pins in the chain as shown in **Figure 27**. The nominal 21-pin length for a 520 chain is 318 mm (12.5 in.). If the 21-pin length measurement meets or exceeds 327 mm (12.75 in.), the drive chain is excessively worn and should be replaced.

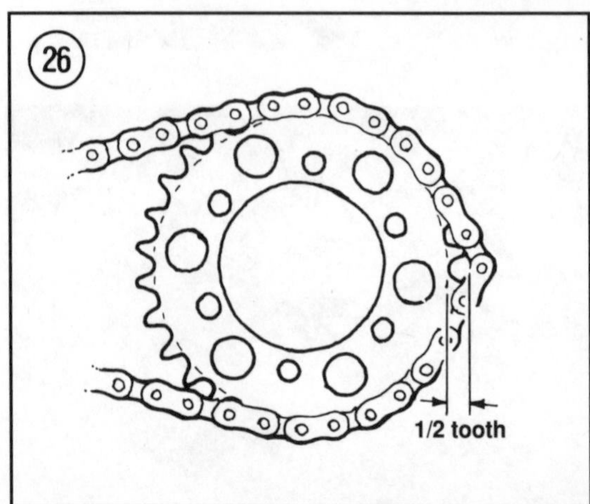

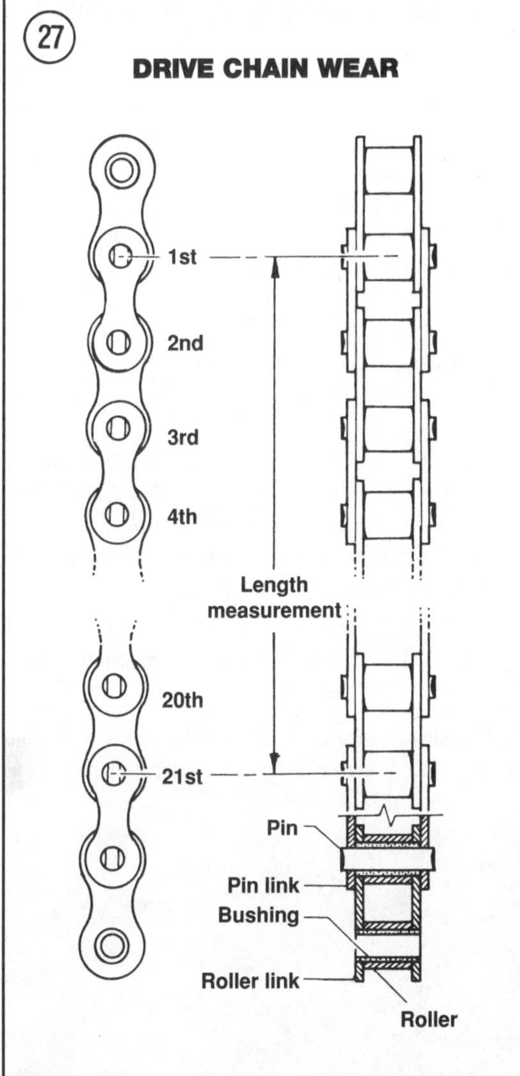

6. Check the inner plate chain faces. They should be lightly polished on both sides. If they show considerable uneven wear on one side, the sprockets are not aligned. Severe wear requires chain and sprocket replacement.

7. If the drive chain is worn, inspect the drive and driven sprockets for the following defects:

   a. Undercutting or sharp teeth.

   b. Broken teeth.

8. If wear is evident, replace the chain and sprockets as a set, or you'll soon wear out a new drive chain.

9. Adjust the drive chain as described in this chapter.

3

Drive Chain Adjustment

The drive chain must have adequate play so that the chain is not strung tight when the swing arm is horizontal. On the other hand, too much play may cause the chain to jump off the sprockets with potentially disastrous results.

When riding in mud and sand, the dirt buildup will make the chain tighter. Recheck chain play and readjust as required.

The drive chain should be checked and adjusted prior to each ride. Drive chain free play is listed in **Table 8**.

1. Support the vehicle with both rear wheels off the ground.

2. Spin the rear axle and check the chain tightness at several spots in the middle of the upper chain run (**Figure 28**). Because the chain wears unevenly, you will find that the chain's tightness will vary along its

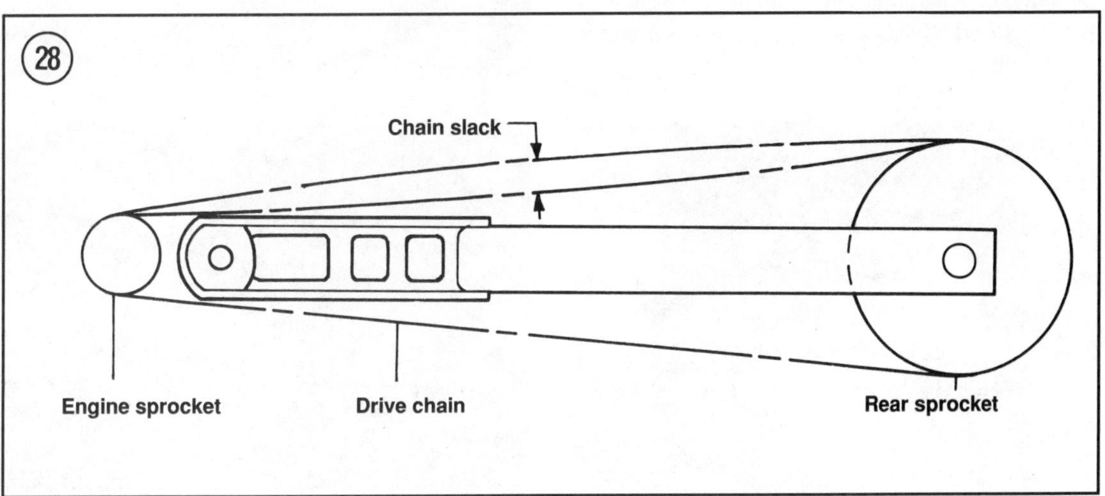

length. Check and adjust the chain at its *tightest* point.

3. Compare the drive chain free play with the specification listed in **Table 8**. If necessary, adjust the drive chain as follows.

CAUTION
When adjusting the drive chain, rear axle alignment must be maintained. A misaligned rear axle can cause poor handling and pulling to one side or the other, as well as increased chain and sprocket wear. All models have wheel alignment marks on the axle housing and chain adjusters.

4. Loosen the upper and lower axle housing bolts or the bolts and nuts. See **Figure 29**, typical.

NOTE
The axle housing on 1987-1988 models uses 4 mounting bolts. The axle housing on 1989-on models uses 2 long bolts and nuts.

5. Loosen the chain adjuster locknuts and turn the adjuster bolts so that the same mark on each adjuster aligns with the axle housing marks. See **Figure 30**. Recheck chain free play.

6. When chain free play is correct, check wheel alignment by sighting along the chain from the rear sprocket. It should leave the sprocket in a straight line. If it is cocked to one side or the other, adjust wheel alignment by turning one adjuster or the other. Recheck chain play.

7. Tighten the upper and lower axle housing bolts (and nuts) to the torque specification in **Table 3**.

8. Check and adjust the rear brake as described in this chapter.

Drive Chain Guard, Rollers and Chain Slider Replacement

Inspect the chain guide, rollers (**Figure 31**) and swing arm chain slider to make sure that none are missing or severely damaged. Running the vehicle with damaged parts can cause frame and swing arm damage. To replace the chain slider, remove the swing arm as described in Chapter Twelve.

Front Brake Lever Adjustment (1987-2001 Models)

Brake pad wear in the caliper is automatically adjusted as the pistons move forward in the calipers. Reduced clearance can cause brake drag and premature brake pad wear. Free play is the distance the lever travels from the at-rest position to the applied position.

On 2002 models, there should be no play. If play is evident, bleed the brake.

1. Measure the front brake lever free play at the *end* of the brake lever (**Figure 32**). Correct free play is

4-8 mm (5/32-51/64 in.). If free play is incorrect, perform Step 2.

2. Loosen the locknut (A, **Figure 33**) and turn the adjuster bolt (B, **Figure 33**) in or out to set free play within prescribed range listed in Step 1. Tighten locknut and remeasure free play.

Rear Brake Pedal Height Adjustment

Brake pedal height is the only adjustment provided on the rear brake system. The brake pedal height adjustment maintains the proper amount of brake pedal free play. Free play is the distance the pedal travels from the at-rest position to the applied position when the pedal is lightly depressed.

1. Park the vehicle on level ground.
2. Measure the distance from the top of the footpeg to the top of the brake pedal (**Figure 34**). This measurement is brake pedal height. The correct brake pedal height measurement is 10 mm (0.4 in.). If adjustment is necessary, perform Step 3.
3. Loosen the master cylinder locknut (A, **Figure 35**) and turn the adjusting bolt (B, **Figure 35**) in or out to achieve the correct brake pedal height position. Tighten the locknut and recheck the height adjustment.

WARNING

After tightening the locknut in Step 3, check the position of the adjuster bolt through the hole in the clevis (C, ***Figure 35****). The end of the adjuster bolt must be visible within the hole as shown in* ***Figure 36****. If not, rear brake failure may occur if the bolt backs out of the clevis. This could cause you to lose control.*

4. Support the vehicle with both rear wheels off the ground.
5. Rotate the rear axle and check for brake drag. Also operate the pedal several times to make sure it returns to the at-rest position immediately after release.
6. Lower the rear wheels back onto the ground.

Brake Fluid Level Check

The brake fluid level in each reservoir should always be kept at its maximum level. See **Figure 37**

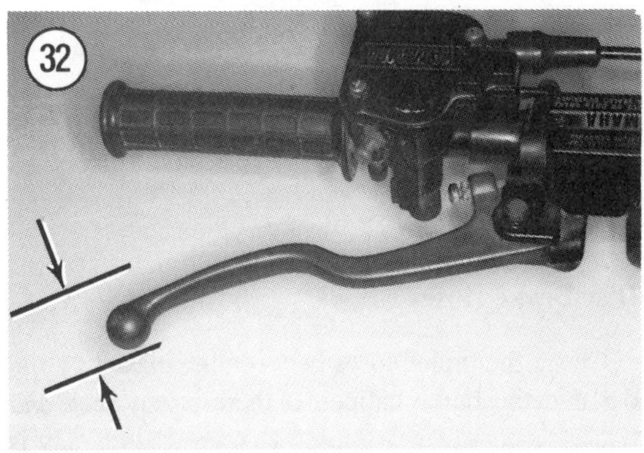

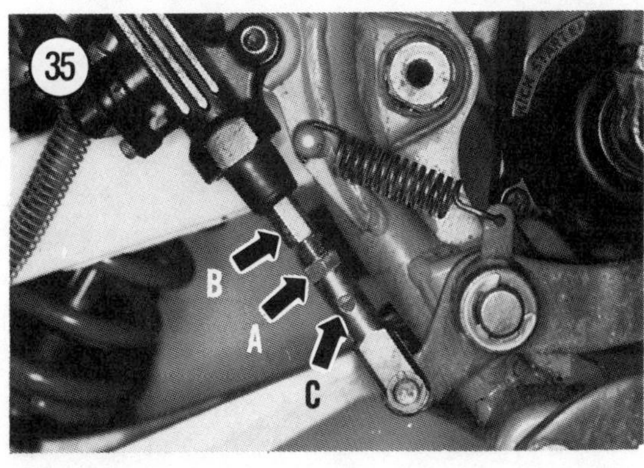

(front) and **Figure 38** (rear). If the brake fluid drops below half-full, correct by adding fresh DOT 4 brake fluid.

WARNING
If the brake fluid level lowers rapidly, check the brake hose and fittings.

1. Park the vehicle on level ground and set the parking brake.
2. Clean any dirt from the cover prior to removing the cover.
3A. *Front*: Perform the following:
   a. Turn the handlebar so that the master cylinder reservoir is level.
   b. Remove the 2 top cover screws and remove the cover (**Figure 37**) and diaphragm.
3B. *Rear*: Perform the following:
   a. Remove the reservoir cover, if equipped.
   b. Unscrew the cover (**Figure 38**) and remove it and the diaphragm.

WARNING
Use brake fluid clearly marked DOT 4 and specified for disc brakes. Others may vaporize and cause brake failure. Do not intermix different brands or types of brake fluid as they may not be compatible. Do not intermix a silicone based (DOT 5) brake fluid as it can cause brake component damage leading to brake system failure.

CAUTION
Be careful when handling brake fluid. Do not spill it on painted or plastic surfaces as it will destroy the surface. Wash the area immediately with soap and water and thoroughly rinse it off.

4. Add fresh DOT 4 brake fluid from a sealed container.
5. Reinstall the diaphragm and top cover. On front master cylinders, install the screws and tighten securely.

Disc Brake Hoses

Check the brake hoses between the master cylinder and the brake caliper. If there is any leakage,

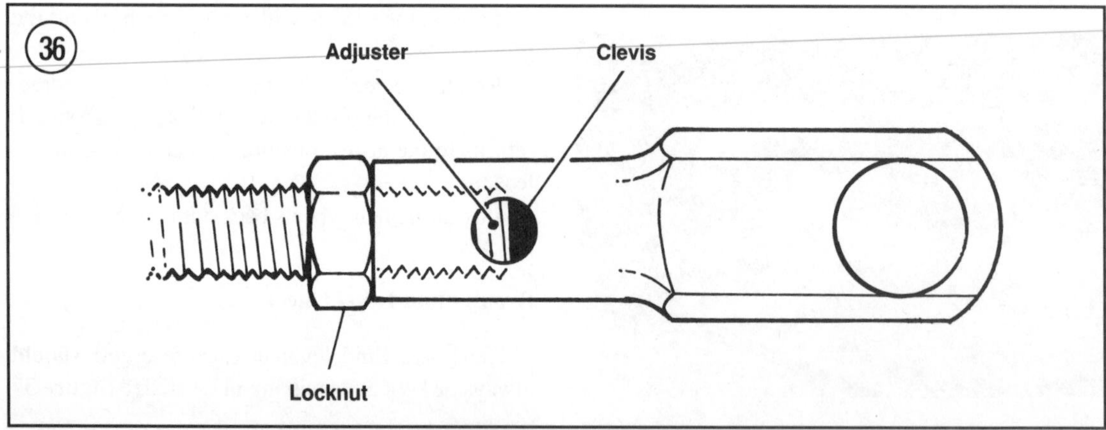

tighten the bolt or hose and then bleed the brake as described in Chapter Thirteen. If this does not stop the leak or if a brake line is obviously damaged, cracked or chafed, replace the brake hose and bleed the system (Chapter Thirteen).

Replace the brake hoses at the intervals specified in **Table 1**.

Disc Brake Pad Wear

Replace the brake pads when the lining thickness is worn to the wear limit specified in Chapter Thirteen, when the pads show uneven wear and scoring or if there is grease or oil on the friction surface; see **Figure 39** (front) and **Figure 40** (rear). Check the disc for scoring and warpage. Refer to Chapter Thirteen.

Disc Brake Fluid Change

Every time the reservoir cap is removed, a small amount of dirt and moisture enters the brake fluid. The same thing happens if a leak occurs or any part of the hydraulic system is loosened or disconnected.

Dirt can clog the system and cause unnecessary wear. Water in the brake fluid vaporizes at high temperature, impairing the hydraulic action and reducing the brake's stopping ability.

To maintain peak performance, change the brake fluid every year or when rebuilding a caliper or master cylinder. To change brake fluid, follow the brake bleeding procedure in Chapter Thirteen.

WARNING

Use brake fluid clearly marked DOT 4 only. Others may vaporize and cause brake failure. Dispose of any used fluid according to local EPA regulations—never reuse brake fluid. Contaminated brake fluid can cause brake failure.

Brake Master Cylinder (Front and Rear)

The master cylinder piston assembly should be replaced whenever the master cylinder is leaking or disassembled. Refer to Chapter Thirteen for service procedure.

Brake Caliper (Front and Rear)

The brake caliper piston seals (dust and piston) should be replaced whenever the caliper is leaking or disassembled. Refer to Chapter Thirteen for service procedures.

Parking Brake Check and Adjustment

The parking brake lever (A, **Figure 41**) is an integral part of the right-hand clutch lever assembly.

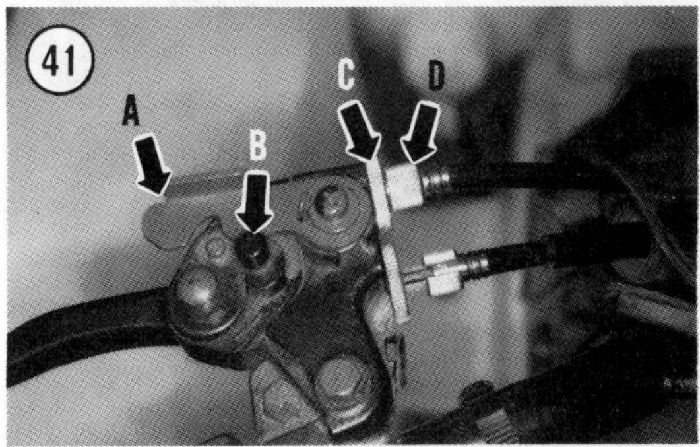

The cable operated parking brake locks the rear wheels only.

1. To set and check the parking brake:
   a. Depress the parking brake button (B, **Figure 41**) and pull in the clutch lever.
   b. While pulling the clutch lever in, move the parking brake lever over so that the notch in the lever contacts the locking pin mounted on the clutch lever assembly. Then release the clutch lever, making sure that the parking brake lever engages the pin as shown in **Figure 42**. The parking brake is now set.
   c. With the parking brake set and with the transmission in NEUTRAL, you should not be able to roll the vehicle forward or backward. If the parking brake does not hold, adjust it, starting with Step 2.
2. Release the parking brake.
3. Loosen the parking brake adjuster locknut (C, **Figure 41**) and turn the adjuster (D) in to provide as much cable slack as possible.
4. Loosen the parking brake cable adjuster locknut on the rear brake caliper (A, **Figure 43**) and back the adjuster bolt (B, **Figure 43**) out.
5. Slowly screw the adjuster bolt (B, **Figure 43**) into the caliper until it feels tight, then back it out 1/4 turn. Hold the adjuster bolt and tighten the locknut (A, **Figure 43**) securely.
6. Adjust the parking brake cable length as follows:

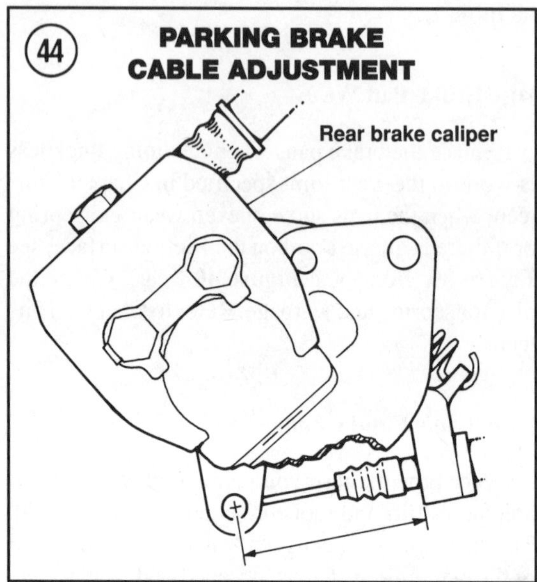

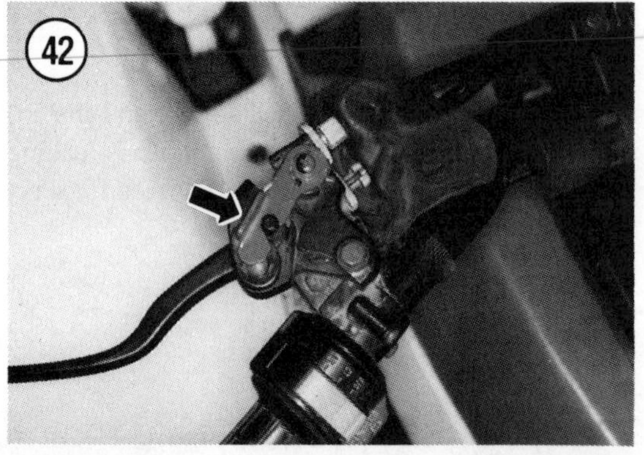

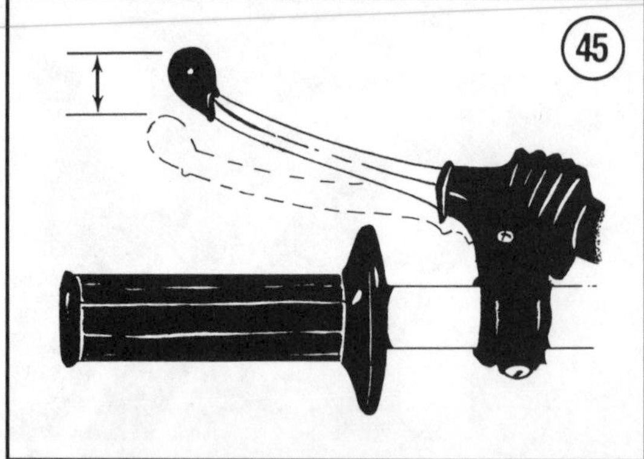

a. At the handlebar, turn the parking brake cable adjuster out (D, **Figure 41**) to obtain a parking brake cable length (at the rear caliper) of 46-50 mm (1.81-1.97 in.) as shown in **Figure 44**.
b. Tighten the adjuster locknut (C, **Figure 41**).

7. Support the vehicle with both rear wheels off the ground.
8. With the parking brake off, make sure the rear axle rotates freely. There should be no brake drag.

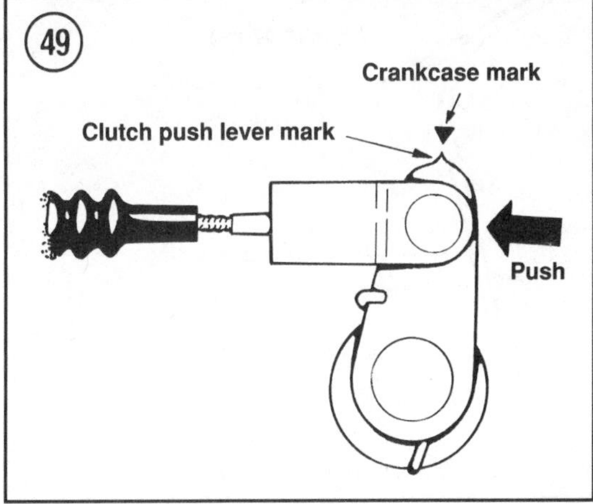

Then set the parking brake and check that the rear axle is locked.

9. If there is brake drag or if the rear axle is not locked, readjust the parking brake.
10. Lower the vehicle so that both rear wheels are on the ground.

3

Clutch Adjustment

Clutch adjustment takes up slack caused by cable stretch and clutch plate wear. Insufficient free play will cause clutch slippage and rapid clutch plate wear.

Clutch free play adjustment

1. Measure the clutch lever free play at the *end* of the clutch lever; see **Figure 45**. Correct free play is 10-15 mm (0.4-0.6 in.). If free play is incorrect, perform Step 2.
2. At the clutch lever loosen the locknut (A, **Figure 46**) and turn the adjuster (B) in or out to obtain the correct amount of free play. Tighten the locknut.
3. If the proper amount of free play cannot be achieved at the clutch lever adjuster, perform the *Clutch Mechanism Adjustment*.

Clutch mechanism adjustment

If you cannot obtain the correct clutch adjustment with the cable adjuster, adjust the clutch mechanism as follows.

1. Park the vehicle on a level surface and set the parking brake.
2. Remove the clutch cover as described in Chapter Six.
3. At the clutch lever, loosen the locknut (A, **Figure 46**) and turn the adjuster (B) in all the way to obtain as much cable slack as possible.
4. At the clutch pressure plate, hold the clutch mechanism adjuster with a screwdriver and loosen the locknut (**Figure 47**).
5. Move the clutch push lever (A, **Figure 48**) toward the front of the engine until it stops and hold in this position.
6. Turn the adjuster (**Figure 47**) to align the mark on the end of the clutch push lever with the cast mark on the crankcase (B, **Figure 48**). See **Figure 49**.

Hold the adjuster in this position and tighten the locknut (**Figure 47**).

7. Perform the *Clutch Free Play Adjustment* to complete clutch adjustment.

8. If the proper amount of free play cannot be achieved by using this adjustment procedure, either the clutch cable has stretched to the point that it needs to be replaced or the friction discs are worn and need replaced. Refer to Chapter Six for cable and clutch plate replacement.

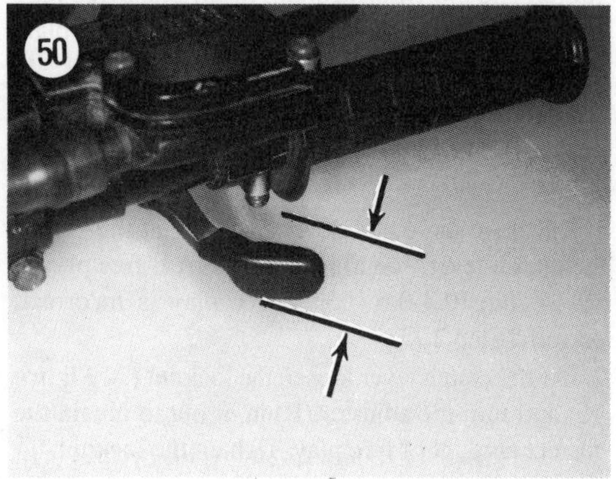

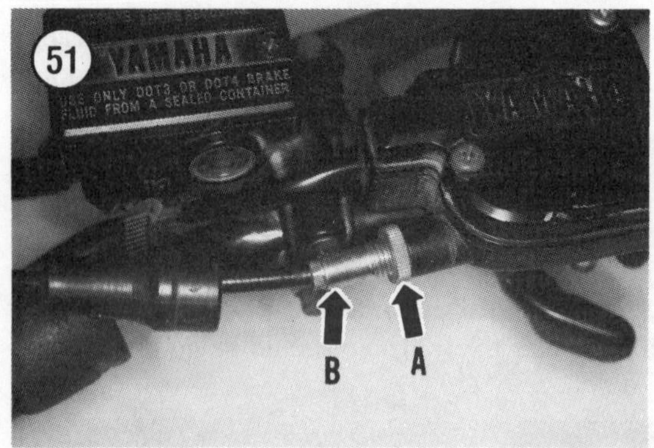

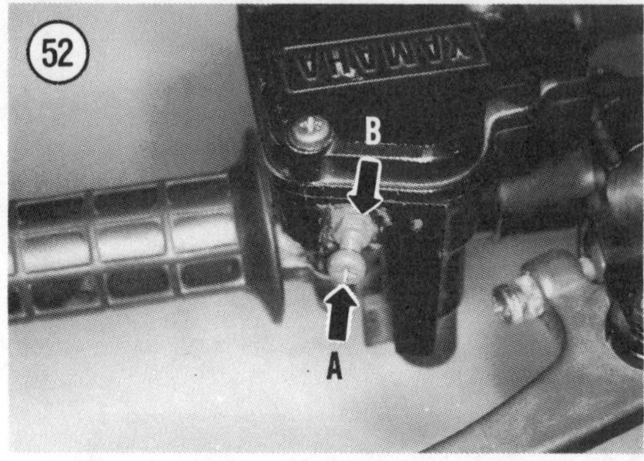

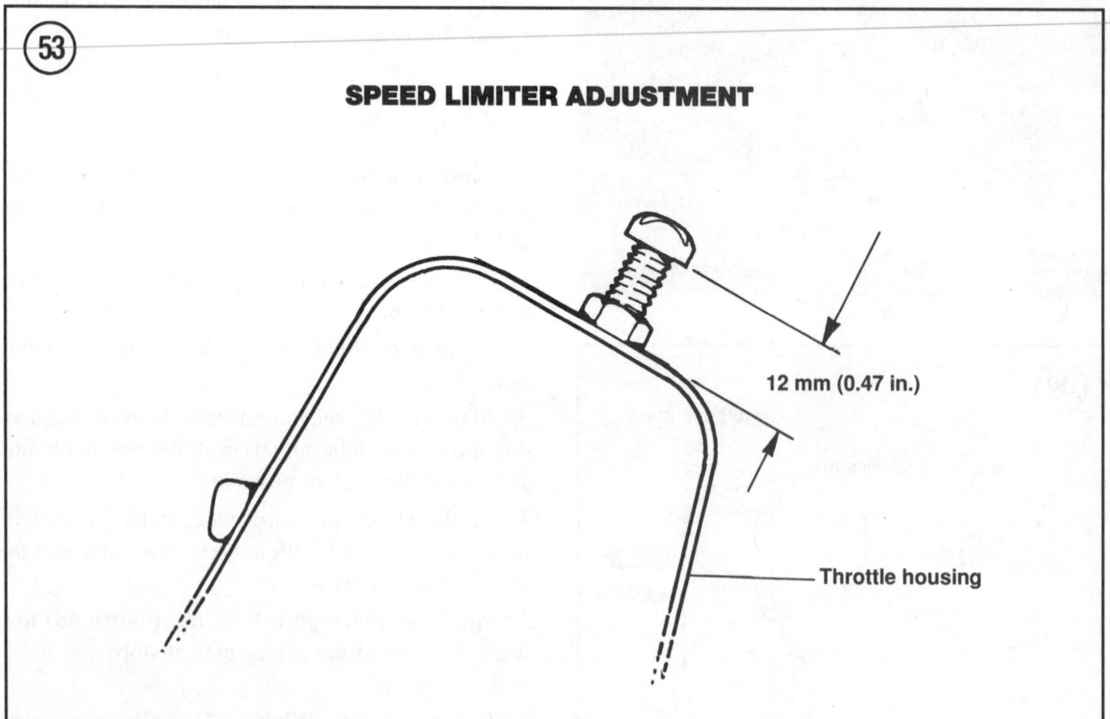

53

SPEED LIMITER ADJUSTMENT

12 mm (0.47 in.)

Throttle housing

Throttle Lever Adjustment

The throttle cable free play should be checked at the interval indicated in **Table 1** or whenever it seems excessively tight or loose. In time, the throttle cable free play will become excessive from cable stretch. This will delay throttle response and affect low speed operation. On the other hand, if there is no throttle cable free play, an excessively high idle can result.

1. Check carburetor synchronization as described under *Carburetor Synchronization* in this chapter. Adjust if necessary.

2. Measure throttle lever free play. Yamaha specifies a throttle free play of 4-6 mm (0.16-0.24 in.) measured at the tip of the throttle lever (**Figure 50**). If incorrect, continue with Step 3.

3. Slide the rubber cover away from the cable adjuster.

4. Loosen the locknut (A, **Figure 51**) and turn the adjuster (B, **Figure 51**) until the correct amount of free play is achieved.

5. Tighten the locknut (A, **Figure 51**) and slide back the rubber boot.

6. If the throttle cable cannot be adjusted properly, the upper throttle cable assembly has stretched excessively and must be replaced.

7. Make sure the throttle lever rotates freely from a fully closed to fully open position.

8. Start the engine and allow it to idle in NEUTRAL. Turn the handlebar from side-to-side. If the idle increases, the throttle cable is routed incorrectly or there is not enough cable free play.

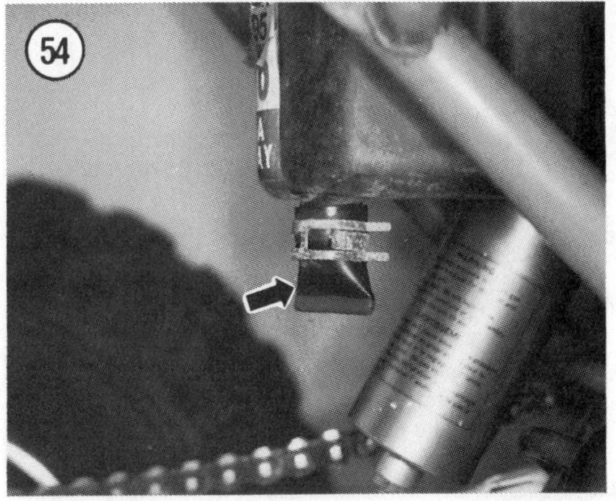

WARNING
A sticking throttle cable(s) can cause you to lose control. Do not ride the vehicle until the throttle lever and cables operate correctly.

Speed Limiter Adjustment

The throttle housing is equipped with a speed limiter (A, **Figure 52**) that can be set to prevent the rider from opening the throttle all the way. The speed limiter can be set for beginning riders or to control engine rpm when breaking in a new engine.

The speed limiter adjustment is set by varying the length of the speed limiter screw, measured from the throttle housing to the bottom of the screw head; see **Figure 53**. The standard speed limiter setting is 12 mm (0.47 in.)

1. Check throttle cable free play as described in this chapter. If necessary, adjust throttle cable free play, then continue with Step 2.

2. Loosen the locknut (B, **Figure 52**).

3. Turn the speed limiter screw (A, **Figure 52**) in or out as required. Do not exceed the 12 mm (0.47 in.) adjustment limit. Tighten the locknut (B, **Figure 52**).

WARNING
Do not operate the vehicle with the speed limiter screw removed from the housing. Do not exceed the 12 mm (0.47 in.) adjustment limit. If you are adjusting the speed limiter for a new rider, start and ride the vehicle yourself, making sure it is positioned where you want it.

Air Filter Housing Check Hose

A check hose is mounted in the bottom of the air box (**Figure 54**). When the check hose becomes contaminated with dirt and water, check the air box and air filter for contamination.

Air Filter

A clogged air filter will decrease the efficiency and life of the engine. Never run the ATV without an air filter properly installed. Even minute particles of

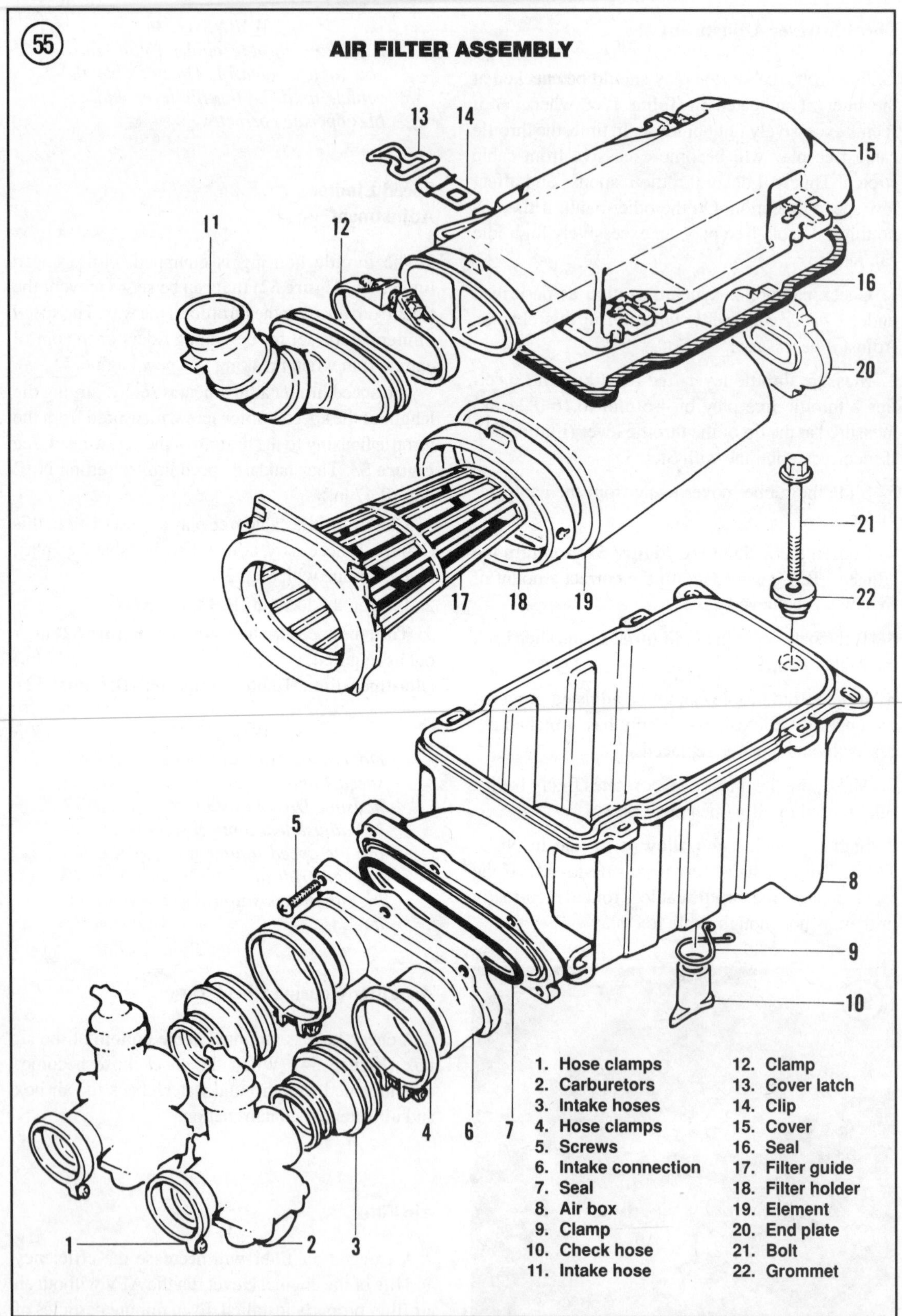
55
AIR FILTER ASSEMBLY
1
2
3
4
5
6
7
8
9
10
11
12
13
14
15
16
17
18
19
20
21
22
1. Hose clamps
2. Carburetors
3. Intake hoses
4. Hose clamps
5. Screws
6. Intake connection
7. Seal
8. Air box
9. Clamp
10. Check hose
11. Intake hose
12. Clamp
13. Cover latch
14. Clip
15. Cover
16. Seal
17. Filter guide
18. Filter holder
19. Element
20. End plate
21. Bolt
22. Grommet

dust can cause severe internal engine wear and clogging of carburetor passages.

Figure 55 is an exploded view of the air filter assembly.

1. Remove the seat as described in Chapter Fourteen.
2. Disconnect the air filter cover latches and remove the cover (**Figure 56**).
3. Remove the air filter assembly (**Figure 57**).
4. Remove the end plate (**Figure 58**) and slide off the filter holder (A, **Figure 59**).

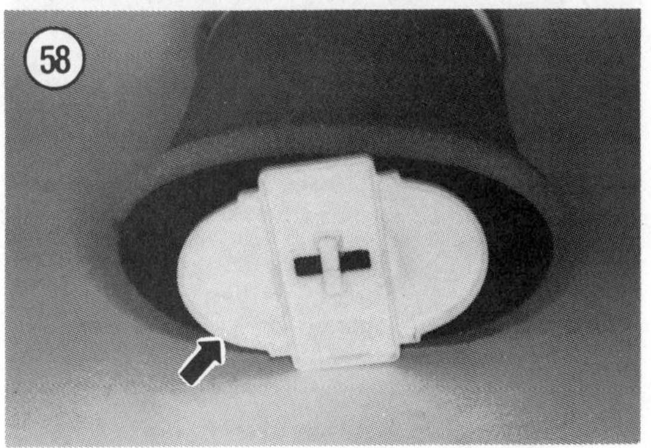

5. Slide the air filter element off of the filter guide (**Figure 60**).
6. Use a flashlight and check the air box-to-carburetor boot inside diameter for dirt or other abrasive materials that may have passed through the air filter.
7. Wipe the inside of the air box with a clean rag. If you cannot clean the air box with it mounted on the frame, remove the air box and clean thoroughly with solvent. Then clean with hot soapy water and rinse with water from a garden hose. Remove and install the air box as described in Chapter Eight.
8. Inspect all fittings and connections from the air box to each carburetor. Check each hose clamp for tightness.

WARNING
Gasoline is highly flammable. Do not clean the air filter element with gasoline as an explosion and fire may occur.

9. Clean the filter element with a filter solvent to remove oil and dirt, then allow to dry. If you are using an accessory air filter, the manufacturer may sell or recommend an air filter cleaning solvent.

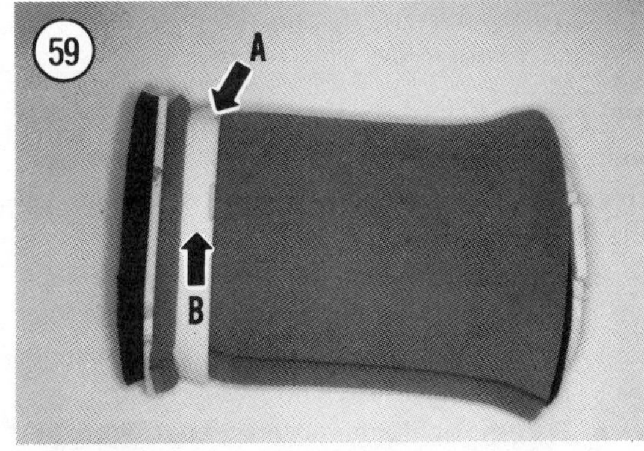

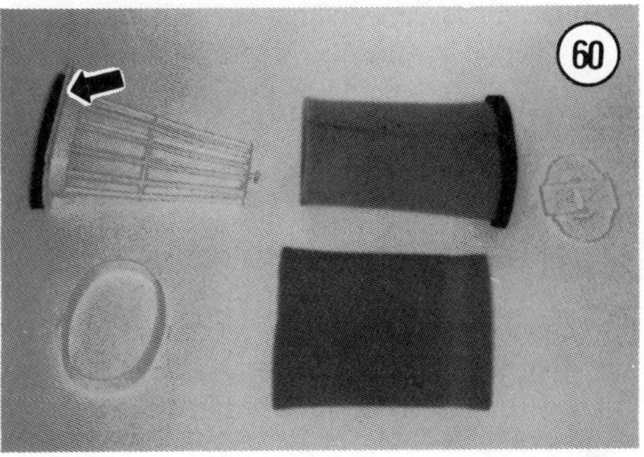

3

10. Fill a clean pan with liquid cleaner and warm water.

CAUTION
Do not wring or twist the air filter when cleaning it. This harsh action could damage a filter pore or tear the filter loose at a seam. This would allow unfiltered air to enter the engine and cause severe and rapid wear.

11. Submerge the filter into the cleaning solution and gently work the cleaner into the filter pores. Gently soak and squeeze the filter to clean it.
12. Rinse the filter under warm water while soaking and gently squeezing it.
13. Repeat Steps 11 and 12 two or three times or until there are no signs of dirt being rinsed from the filter.
14. After cleaning the element, inspect it carefully. If it is torn or broken in any area it should be replaced. Do not run with a damaged element as it may allow dirt to enter the engine and cause severe engine wear.
15. Set the filter aside and allow it to dry thoroughly.
16. Clean the end plate, filter guide and filter holder in solvent and dry thoroughly.

CAUTION
A damp filter will not trap fine dust. The filter must be dry when oiling it.

17. Properly oiling an air filter element is a messy job. You may want to wear a pair of disposable rubber gloves when performing this procedure. Oil the filter as follows:
  a. Purchase a box of gallon size storage bags. The bags can be used when cleaning the filter as well as for storing engine and carburetor parts during disassembly.
  b. Place the air filter into a storage bag (**Figure 61**).
  c. Pour foam air filter oil onto the filter to soak it.
  d. Gently squeeze and release the filter to soak filter oil into the filter's pores. Repeat until all of the filter's pores are discolored with the oil.
  e. Remove the filter from the bag and check the pores for uneven oiling. This is indicated by light or dark areas on the filter. If necessary, soak the filter and squeeze it again.
  f. When the oil is evenly distributed, squeeze the filter a final time.

18. Apply some wheel bearing grease to the filter guide where it seats against the filter; see arrow in **Figure 60**.
19. Remove the filter from the bag and slide it onto the filter guide. Position the end of the filter so that the hook on the end of the filter guide is pushed through the slot in the end of the filter.
20. Slide the filter holder (A, **Figure 59**) over the air filter so that the arrow mark on the filter holder faces forward; see B, **Figure 59**.
21. Align the slot in the end plate with the hook on the filter guide and install the end plate onto the filter. Then turn the end plate 90 to lock it (**Figure 58**).
22. Apply an even coat of wheel bearing grease onto the filter's sealing surface.
23. Install the air filter into the air box. The 2 arrows on the filter guide must be facing up (**Figure 62**) when installing the air filter. See **Figure 57**.

CAUTION
The filter assembly must seat in the groove in the air box so the cover can lock it in place. Improper installation will result in leakage around the filter.

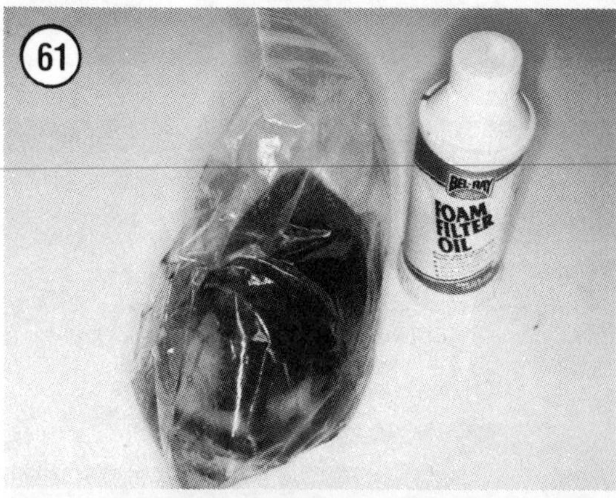

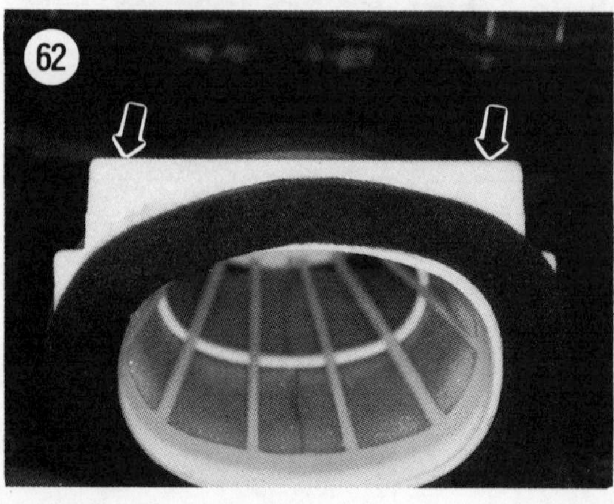

24. Install the air filter cover (**Figure 56**), locking the air filter assembly in place. Lock the cover latches.
25. Install and secure the seat.

Fuel Line Inspection

Inspect the fuel line from the fuel tank to the carburetor and then the interconnecting hose to both carburetors. Replace the fuel line if it is cracked or starting to deteriorate. Make sure the small hose clamps are in place and holding securely. Check that the overflow and vent tubes are in place.

WARNING
Gasoline is highly flammable. A damaged or deteriorated fuel line presents a very dangerous fire hazard to both the rider and the machine.

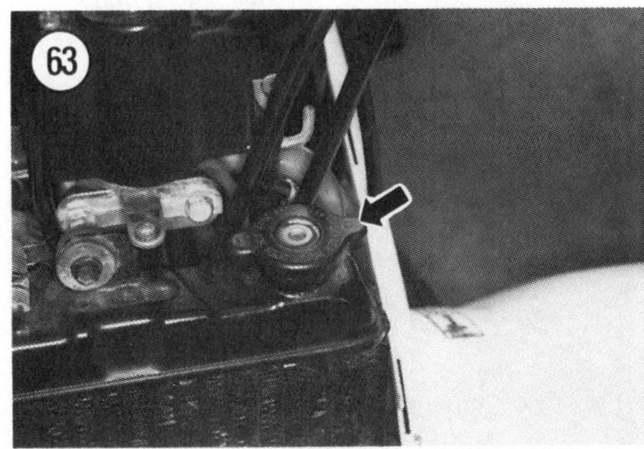
63

64

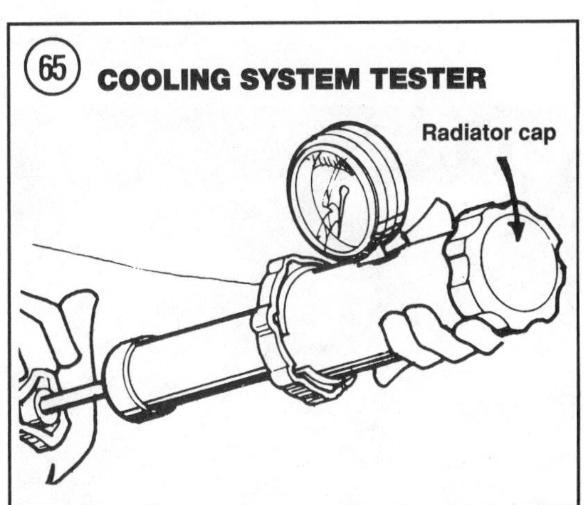

65 COOLING SYSTEM TESTER

Cooling System Inspection

Once a year, or whenever troubleshooting the cooling system, the following items should be checked. If you do not have the test equipment, the tests can be done by a Yamaha dealer, radiator shop or service station.

WARNING
Do not remove the radiator cap, coolant drain bolts or disconnect any hose while the engine and radiator are hot. Scalding fluid and steam may be blown out under pressure and cause serious injury.

1. Remove the front panel as described in Chapter Fourteen.
2. With the engine cold, remove the radiator cap (**Figure 63**).
3. Check the rubber washers on the radiator cap (**Figure 64**). Replace the cap if the washers show signs of deterioration, cracking or other damage. If the radiator cap is okay, perform Step 4.
4. Have the radiator cap pressure tested (**Figure 65**). The specified radiator cap relief pressure is 93-123 kPa (13.5-17.8 psi). The cap must be able to sustain this pressure for 1 minute. Replace the radiator cap if it does not hold pressure.

CAUTION
Do not exceed the maximum cooling system pressure listed in Step 5; otherwise, damage to the cooling system may occur.

5. Leave the radiator cap off and have the entire cooling system pressure tested. The specified cooling system test pressure is 98.1 kPa (14 psi). The system must be able to hold this pressure for 1 minute. If the system does not hold pressure, replace or repair any damaged components.

6. Check all cooling system hoses for damage or deterioration. Replace any hose that is questionable. Make sure all hose clamps are tight.
7. Carefully clean any dirt, mud, bugs, etc. from the radiator core. Use a whisk broom, compressed air or low-pressure water from a garden hose. Straighten bent radiator fins with a screwdriver.
8. Check the radiator for clogged or damaged fins. If more than 20% of the radiator fin area is damaged, repair or replace the radiator.
9. Reinstall the radiator cap and front panel.

Coolant Check

The coolant reserve tank is mounted underneath the seat and behind the air box (**Figure 66**).

1. With the engine cold, visually check the coolant level in the coolant reserve tank (**Figure 66**). The level should be between the "FULL" and "LOW" marks.
2. To add coolant:
   a. Remove the seat as described in Chapter Fourteen.

NOTE
If the reserve tank is empty, there may be a leak in the cooling system. Remove the radiator cap (with engine cold) and check the coolant level in the radiator.

   b. Remove the coolant reserve tank cap (**Figure 67**) and add a 50:50 mixture of distilled water and antifreeze into the reserve tank (not the radiator) to bring the level to the "FULL" mark.
   c. Reinstall the reserve tank cap and seat.

WARNING
Do not remove the radiator cap when the engine is hot. The coolant is under pressure and scalding and severe burns could result.

Coolant

Only a high-quality ethylene glycol-based antifreeze compounded for aluminum block engines should be used. Do not use an alcohol-based antifreeze. The antifreeze should be mixed with water in a 50:50 ratio. Coolant capacity is listed in **Table 9**. When mixing antifreeze with water, make sure to use only soft or distilled water. Never use tap or saltwater as this will damage engine parts. Distilled water can be purchased at supermarkets in gallon containers.

Coolant Change

The cooling system should be completely drained and refilled at the intervals indicated in **Table 1**.

WARNING
Antifreeze has been classified as an environmental toxic waste by the EPA and cannot be legally disposed of by flush-

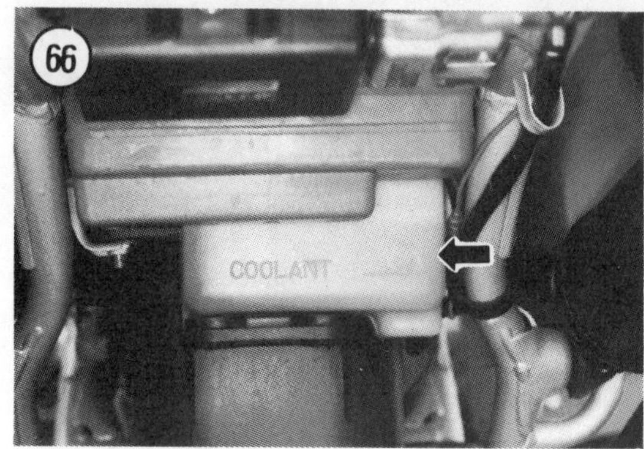

ing down a drain or pouring it onto the ground. Place antifreeze in a suitable container and dispose of it according to local EPA regulations. Do not store coolant where it is accessible to children or animals.

The following procedure must be performed when the engine is *cold*.

CAUTION

Coolant can damage painted surfaces. Wash immediately with soapy water and rinse thoroughly with clean water.

1. Remove the front panel as described in Chapter Fourteen.
2. With the engine cold, remove the radiator cap (**Figure 63**).

NOTE

Drain engine coolant into a clean container.

3. Remove the left-hand cylinder block coolant drain bolt (**Figure 68**) and washer and allow the coolant in the cylinder to drain out. Catch the coolant with a clean drain pan.
4. Repeat Step 3 for the right-hand cylinder block coolant drain bolt.
5. Remove the hose clamp and inlet hose (**Figure 69**) from the water pump hose nozzle and allow the coolant in the radiator to drain out. Catch the coolant with a clean drain pan.
6. Remove the drain pan with coolant and set it aside. Place another pan underneath the inlet hose opening.
7. Flush the cooling system with clean tap water directed through the radiator filler neck. Allow this water to drain completely.
8. Reinstall the cylinder block coolant drain bolts and washers (**Figure 68**). Tighten both coolant drain bolts to the torque specification in **Table 3**.
9. Reconnect the inlet hose to the water pump hose nozzle. Secure the hose with the hose clamp. See **Figure 69**.
10. Remove the coolant reserve tank (**Figure 70**) and pour out the old coolant. Reinstall the tank.
11. Refill the radiator. Add coolant slowly through the radiator filler neck. Use a 50:50 mixture of antifreeze and distilled water. Radiator capacity is listed in **Table 9**. Fill to the radiator filler neck—just below the reserve tank tube opening (**Figure 71**). Do not install the radiator cap at this time.
12. If empty, fill the coolant reserve tank (**Figure 66**) to the "FULL" mark.

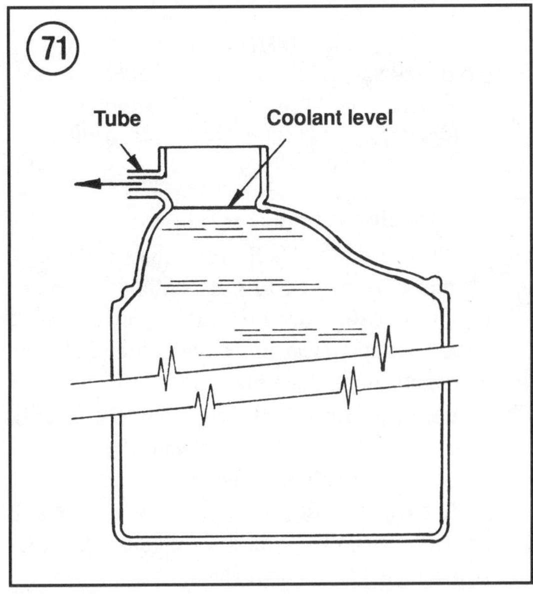

3

13. Start the engine and let it run at idle speed until the engine reaches normal operating temperature. Make sure there are no air bubbles in the coolant and that the coolant level stabilizes at the correct level (**Figure 71**). Add coolant as necessary.
14. Install the radiator cap.
15. Add coolant to the coolant reserve tank (**Figure 66**), as necessary.
16. After the engine has cooled, readjust the coolant level in the reserve tank as required.

Steering System and Front Suspension Inspection

The steering system and front suspension should be checked at the interval indicated in **Table 1**.

1. Park the vehicle on level ground and set the parking brake.
2. Visually inspect all components of the steering system. Pay close attention to the tie rods and steering shaft, especially after a hard spill or collision. If damage is apparent, the steering components must be repaired. Refer to service procedures described in Chapter Eleven.
3. Check the tightness of the handlebar holder bolts.
4. Make sure the front wheel lug nuts and axle nuts are tight and that the cotter pins are in place.
5. Check that the cotter pins are in place on all steering components. If any cotter pin is missing, check the nut(s) for looseness. Torque the nut(s) and install new cotter pins.

CAUTION
If any of the previously mentioned bolts and nuts are loose, refer to Chapter Eleven for correct procedures and torque specifications.

6. Check steering shaft play as follows:
   a. To check steering shaft radial play, move the handlebar from side-to-side (without attempting to move the wheels). If radial play is excessive, the upper steering bearings are probably worn and should be replaced.
   b. To check steering shaft thrust play, lift up and then push down on the handlebar. If excessive thrust play is noted, check the lower steering shaft nut for looseness. If the nut is torqued properly, then the lower steering shaft bearing is worn and should be replaced.
   c. Replace worn or damaged steering shaft parts as described in Chapter Eleven.
7. Check steering knuckle and tie rod ball joints as follows:
   a. Turn the handlebar quickly from side-to-side. If there is appreciable looseness between the handlebar and tires, check the ball joints for severe wear or damage.
   b. Replace worn or damaged steering knuckle and tie rod components as described in Chapter Eleven.

CAUTION
Do not reuse cotter pins. Where removed, new cotter pins must be installed.

Toe-in Adjustment

Toe-in is a condition where the front of the tires are closer together than the back; see **Figure 72**. The front wheel toe-in alignment should be checked after servicing the front steering assembly and periodically through the riding season.

1. Toe-in is adjusted by changing the length of the tie rods.
2. Inflate all 4 tires to the recommended tire pressure specified in **Table 2**.
3. Park the vehicle on level ground and set the parking brake. The raise and support the front end so that both front tires just clear the ground.
4. Turn the handlebar so that the wheels are at the straight-ahead position.

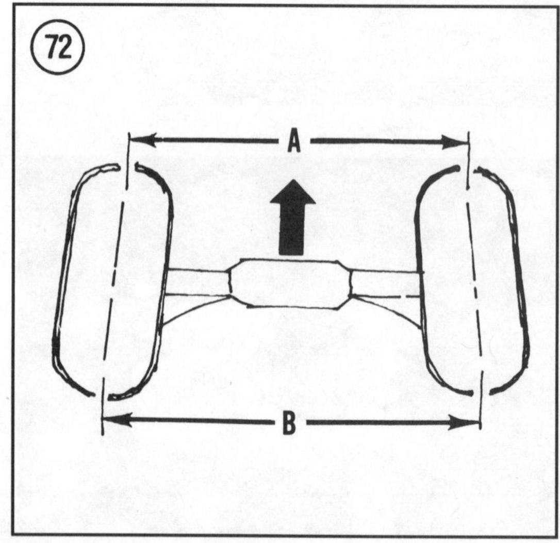

5. Using a ruler, carefully measure the distance between the center of both front tires as shown in A, **Figure 72**. Mark the tires with a piece of chalk at these points. Write down the measurement.

6. Turn each tire exactly 180° and measure the distance between the center of both front tires at B, **Figure 72**. Write down the measurement.

7. Subtract the measurement in Step 5 from Step 6 as shown in **Figure 72**. Toe-in is correct if the difference is 0-10 mm (0-0.39 in.). If the toe-in is incorrect, proceed to Step 8.

8. Loosen the locknuts securing each tie rod. See **Figure 73** and **Figure 74**.

NOTE
Turn both tie rods the same number of turns. This ensures that the tie rod length for both sides will remain the same.

9. Use a wrench on the flat portion of the tie rods and slowly turn both tie rods the *same* amount until the toe-in measurement is correct.

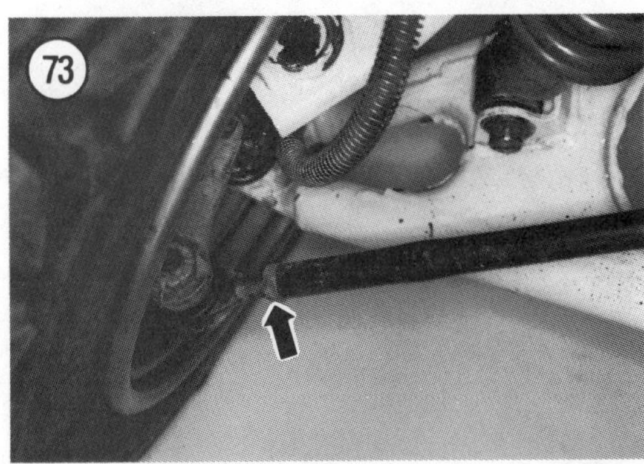

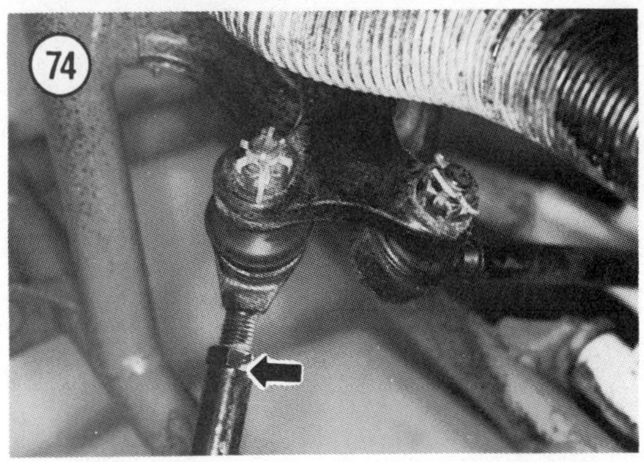

WARNING
If the tie rod lengths are different, the vehicle will tend to drift to the left or right, even though the handlebar is pointed straight-ahead. This may cause you to loose control and crash. If you cannot adjust the toe-in properly, have a dealer inspect the front end and then adjust the toe-in for you.

10. When the toe-in adjustment is correct, hold each tie rod in place and tighten the locknuts to the torque specification in **Table 3**.

Front Hub Bearings

The front hub bearings should be inspected for excessive wear or damage at the intervals specified in **Table 1**. Refer to *Front Hub Wheel Bearings* under *Periodic Lubrication* in this chapter for bearing and oil seal lubrication.

1. Park the vehicle on a level surface and set the parking brake. Support the vehicle with both front wheels off the ground.
2. Turn both front wheels by hand. The wheels should turn smoothly with no roughness, excessive noise, excessive play or other abnormal conditions.
3. If necessary, service the front hub bearings as described in Chapter Eleven.

Rear Axle Housing Bearings

The rear axle housing bearings should be inspected for excessive wear or damage at the intervals specified in **Table 1**. Refer to *Rear Axle Bearings and Oil Seals* under *Periodic Lubrication* in this chapter for bearing and oil seal lubrication.

1. Park the vehicle on a level surface and block the front wheels so that the vehicle cannot roll in either direction. Support the vehicle with both rear wheels off the ground.
2. Turn the rear axle by hand. The axle should turn smoothly with no roughness, excessive noise, excessive play or other abnormal conditions.
3. If necessary, service the axle housing bearings as described in Chapter Twelve.

Lighting Equipment

At the intervals listed in **Table 1**, check the front and rear lights for proper operation.

Carburetor Cleaning

At the specified intervals, remove, disassemble and clean the carburetors as described in Chapter Eight.

Nuts, Bolts, and Other Fasteners

Constant vibration can loosen many of the fasteners on the Banshee. Check the tightness of all fasteners, especially those on:

a. Engine mounting hardware.
b. Engine crankcase covers.
c. Handlebar.
d. Gearshift lever.
e. Brake pedal and lever.
f. Exhaust system.

NON-SCHEDULED MAINTENANCE

Fuel Valve Cleaning

Periodically, remove and clean the fuel valve (**Figure 75**) as described in Chapter Eight.

Sprocket Bolt Tightness

Check the driven sprocket bolts and nuts for looseness. Tighten the nuts to the torque specification listed in **Table 12**.

Exhaust System

Refer to Chapter Eight for service and repair procedures.

1. Inspect the exhaust pipe for cracks or dents which could alter performance.
2. Check all of the exhaust pipe fasteners and mounting points for loose or damaged parts.

Handlebar

Inspect the handlebar weekly for any sign of damage. A bent or damaged handlebar should be replaced. The knurled section of the bar should be very rough. Keep the clamps clean with a wire brush. Any time that the bars slip in the clamps they should be removed and wire brushed clean to prevent small balls of aluminum from gathering in the clamps and reducing gripping abilities.

NOTE
When installing aluminum handlebars, follow the manufacturer's directions.

Handlebar Grips

Inspect the handlebar grips (**Figure 76**) for tearing, looseness or severe wear. Install new grips when required, safety wiring the grips to prevent them from slipping. Follow manufacturer's instructions when installing grips.

Frame Inspection

Routinely inspect the frame for cracks or other damage.

ENGINE TUNE-UP

The number of definitions of the term "tune-up" is probably equal to the number of people defining

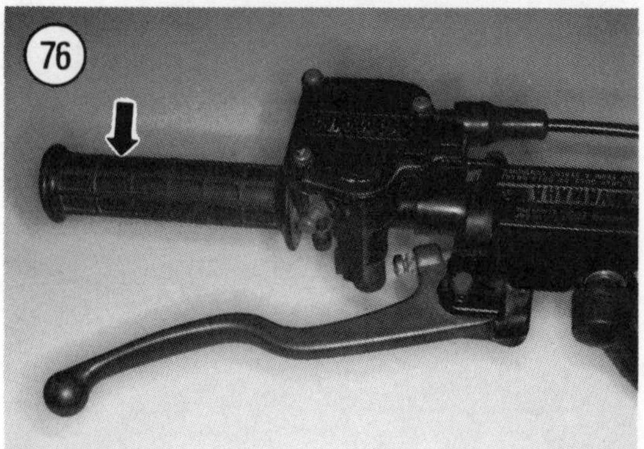

it. For the purposes of this book, a tune-up is general adjustment and maintenance to insure peak engine performance.

The following paragraphs discuss each facet of a proper tune-up which should be performed in the order given. Unless otherwise specified, the engine should be thoroughly cool before starting any tune-up procedure.

Have the new parts on hand before you begin.

To perform a tune-up on your Yamaha, you will need the following tools and equipment:

a. 14 mm spark plug wrench.
b. Socket wrench and assorted sockets.
c. Phillips head screwdriver.
d. Spark plug gap gauge and gapper tool.
e. Timing light.

Cylinder Compression

A cylinder cranking compression check is one of the quickest ways to check the internal condition of the engine: rings, head gasket, etc. It's a good idea to check compression at each tune-up, write it down, and compare it with the reading you get at the next tune-up. This will help you spot any developing problems.

1. Warm the engine to normal operating temperature. Then turn the engine off.
2. Remove both spark plugs.
3. Thread or insert the tip of a compression gauge into the cylinder head spark plug hole (**Figure 77**). Make sure the gauge is seated properly.

NOTE
The engine stop switch must be in the OFF position when performing Step 4.

4. Hold the throttle wide open and turn the engine over with the kickstarter for several revolutions until the gauge needle levels off at its highest reading. Record the highest reading on the gauge.
5. Repeat for the opposite cylinder.
6. Interpret results as follows:
   a. Yamaha does not list engine compression specifications. However, checking compression allows you to compare the left- and right-hand cylinder readings.
   b. Compare the compression readings for both cylinders. The readings must be within 10% of each other.
   c. If the compression readings vary by more than 10%, the cylinder with the lower reading may be suffering from piston ring, piston or cylinder wear.
   d. If both compression readings are significantly low, the engine may be suffering from a blown head gasket, light seizure or top end wear (pistons, rings and cylinders).
7. If the readings are low, perform the *Two-Stroke Crankcase Pressure Test* in Chapter Two. This test will show you if there is a loss of compression at some other engine point.

Correct Spark Plug Heat Range

Spark plugs are available in various heat ranges—hotter or colder than the plugs originally installed at the factory.

Select plugs of the heat range designed for the loads and conditions under which your Yamaha will operating under. Use of incorrect heat ranges can cause the plug to foul, overheating and piston damage.

In general, use a hot plug for low speeds and low temperatures. Use a cold plug for high speeds, high engine loads and high temperatures. The plug should operate hot enough to burn off unwanted deposits, but not so hot that they burn themselves or cause preignition. A spark plug of the correct heat range will show a light tan color on the portion of the insulator within the cylinder after the plug has been in service.

The reach (length) of a plug is also important. A too short plug will cause excessive carbon build-up, hard starting and plug fouling. A too long plug will cause overheating or may contact the top of the piston. Both conditions will cause engine damage. See **Figure 78**.

The standard heat range spark plug for the various models is listed in **Table 10**.

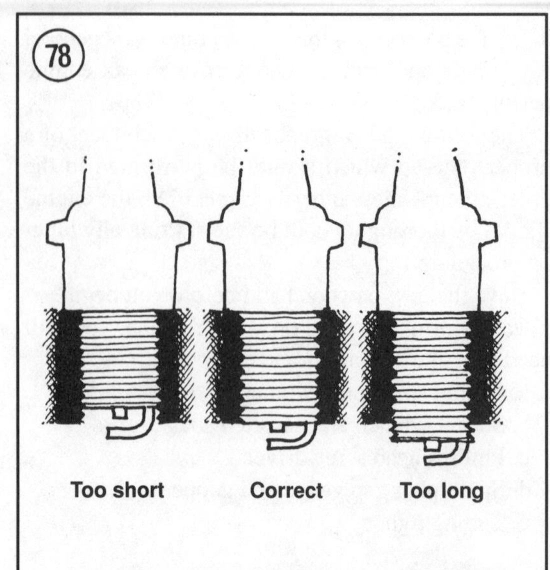

Spark Plug Removal

CAUTION

Whenever the spark plug is removed, dirt around it can fall into the plug hole. This can cause expensive engine damage.

1. Grasp the spark plug lead (**Figure 79**) as near the plug as possible and pull it off the plug. If it is stuck to the plug, twist it slightly to break it loose.
2. Blow away any dirt that has collected around the spark plug.
3. Remove the spark plug with a spark plug socket.

NOTE

If the plug is difficult to remove, apply penetrating oil, like WD-40 or Liquid Wrench, around the base of the plug and let it soak in about 10-20 minutes.

4. Inspect the plug carefully. Look for a broken center porcelain, excessively eroded electrodes, and excessive carbon or oil fouling. See *Reading Spark Plugs* in this chapter.

Gapping and Installing the Plug

A new spark plug should be carefully gapped to ensure a reliable, consistent spark. You must use a special spark plug gap gauge and gapper tool.

1. Remove the new spark plug from the box. If necessary, screw the small adapter onto the end of the plug (**Figure 80**).
2. Insert a wire gap gauge between the center and side electrode (**Figure 81**). The correct gap is listed in **Tables 10**. If the gap is correct, you will feel a slight drag as you pull the wire through. If there is no drag, or the gauge won't pass through, bend the side electrode with a gapper tool (**Figure 82**) to set the proper gap.
3. Apply anti-seize to the plug threads before installing the spark plug.

NOTE

Anti-seize can be purchased at most automotive parts stores.

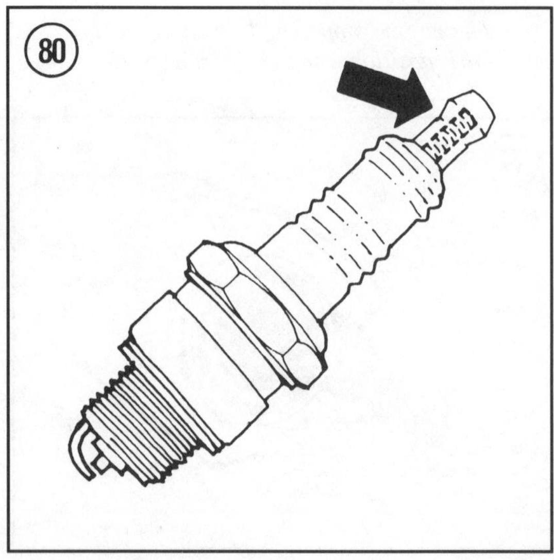

4. Screw the spark plug in by hand until it seats. Very little effort should be required. If force is necessary, you have the plug cross-threaded. Unscrew it and try again.

CAUTION
Do not overtighten the spark plugs. This will crush the gaskets and destroy their sealing ability.

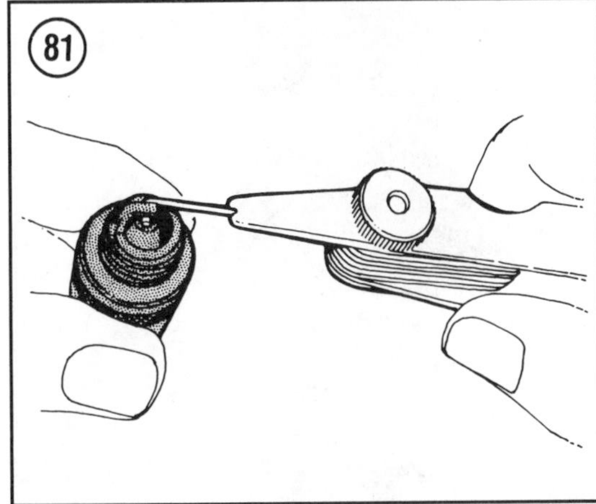

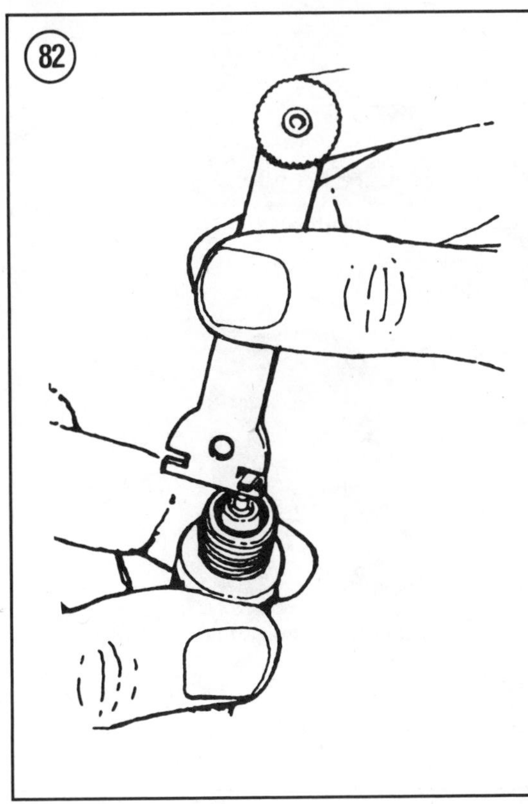

5. Use a spark plug wrench and tighten the spark plug to the torque specification in **Table 3**. If you do not have a torque wrench, tighten the plug an additional 1/4 to 1/2 turn after the gasket has made contact with the head. If you are installing an old, regapped plug and reusing the old gasket, only tighten an additional 1/4 turn.
6. Install the spark plug caps. Make sure each cap fits tightly on its spark plug.

CAUTION
Make sure both spark plug wires are pulled away from the exhaust pipe.

Reading Spark Plugs

Much information about engine and spark plug performance can be determined by careful examination of the spark plug. This information is more valid after performing the following steps.
1. Ride the vehicle a short distance at full throttle.
2. Push the engine stop switch to OFF before closing the throttle and simultaneously pull in the clutch or shift to neutral; coast and brake to a stop.
3. Remove the spark plugs and examine them. Compare the spark plugs to the plugs shown in **Figure 83** and note the following:

Normal condition

If the plug has a light tan- or gray-colored deposit and no abnormal gap wear or erosion, good engine, carburetor adjustment and ignition condition are indicated. The plug in use is of the proper heat range and may be serviced and returned to use.

Carbon fouled

Soft, dry, sooty deposits covering the entire firing end of the plug are evidence of incomplete combustion. Even though the firing end of the plug is dry, the plug's insulation decreases. An electrical path is formed that lowers the voltage from the ignition system. Engine misfiring is a sign of carbon fouling. Carbon fouling can be caused by one or more of the following:

a. Too-rich fuel mixture.
b. Spark plug heat range too cold.
c. Clogged air filter.
d. Over-retarded ignition timing.

83

SPARK PLUG CONDITIONS

Normal

Gap Bridged

Carbon Fouled

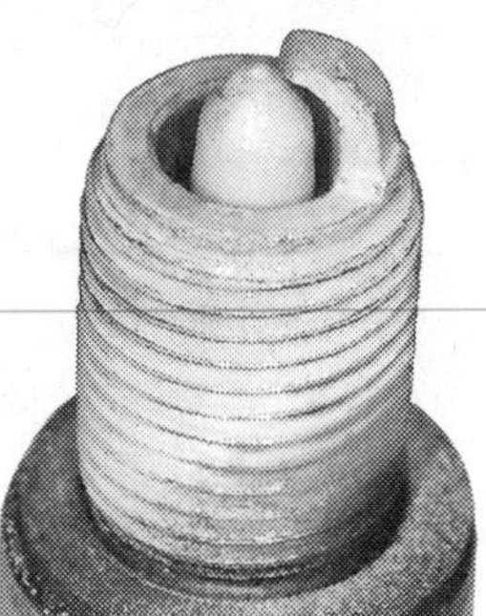
Overheated

Oil Fouled

Sustained Preignition

e. Ignition component failure.
f. Low engine compression.
g. Prolonged idling.

Oil fouled

The tip of an oil fouled plug has a black insulator tip, a damp oily film over the firing end and a carbon layer over the entire nose. The electrodes will not be worn. Common causes for this condition are:

a. Rich air/fuel mixture.
b. Low idle speed or prolonged idling.
c. Ignition component failure.
d. Spark plug heat range too cold.
e. Engine still being broken in.

Oil fouled spark plugs may be cleaned in an emergency, but is better to replace them. It is important to correct the cause of fouling before the engine is returned to service.

Gap bridging

Plugs with this condition exhibit gaps shorted out by combustion deposits between the electrodes. If this condition is encountered, check for an improper oil type or excessive carbon in the combustion chamber. Be sure to locate and correct the cause of this condition.

Overheating

Badly worn electrodes and premature gap wear are signs of overheating, along with a gray or white "blistered" porcelain insulator surface. The most common cause for this condition is using a spark plug of the wrong heat range (too hot). If you have not changed to a hotter spark plug and the plug is overheated, consider the following causes:

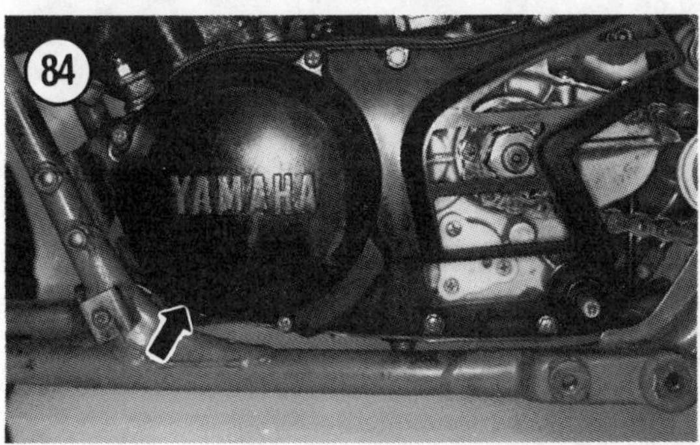

a. Lean air/fuel mixture.
b. Ignition timing too advanced.
c. Engine lubrication system malfunction.
d. Engine air leak.
e. Improper spark plug installation (too tight).
f. No spark plug gasket.
g. Cooling system malfunction.

Worn out

Corrosive gases formed by combustion and high voltage sparks have eroded the electrodes. Spark plugs in this condition require more voltage to fire under hard acceleration. Replace with new spark plugs.

Preignition

If the electrodes are melted, preignition is almost certainly the cause. Check for carburetor mounting or intake manifold leaks and over-advanced ignition timing. It is also possible that the wrong heat range plugs (too hot) are being used. Find the cause of the preignition before returning the engine into service.

Ignition Timing

All models are equipped with a nonadjustable capacitor discharge ignition system (CDI). While the ignition timing is not adjustable, it should be checked periodically to make sure all components of the ignition system are functioning properly. Ignition system components that malfunction can cause incorrect ignition timing. This can cause a drastic loss of engine performance and efficiency. It may also cause overheating. The ignition should also be checked when the engine is difficult to start if it is operating with reduced engine performance.

Before starting on this procedure, check all electrical connections related to the ignition system. Make sure all connections are tight and free from corrosion and that all ground connections are clean and tight.

1. Start the engine and let it warm up approximately 2-3 minutes.
2. Park the vehicle on level ground and apply the parking brake, shut off the engine.
3. Remove the left-hand footpeg and shift lever.
4. Remove the left-hand crankcase cover (**Figure 84**) and gasket.

5. Connect a portable tachometer following its manufacturer's instructions.

6. Connect a timing light following its manufacturer's instructions.

7. Restart the engine and let it run at the idle speed indicated in **Table 11**. If necessary, adjust the idle speed as described in this chapter.

8. Aim the timing light (**Figure 85**) at the fixed index mark mounted on the stator plate (**Figure 86**) and pull the trigger. The timing is correct if the firing range marked on the flywheel is aligned with the fixed index mark on the stator plate; see **Figure 87**.

9. Turn the engine off.

10. If timing is incorrect, note the following:

   a. Check for a loose or damaged flywheel or sheared flywheel key. Then check for a loose or damaged pickup coil (**Figure 88**). If these parts are okay, remove the flywheel (Chapter Nine) and check the stator plate for loose mounting screws.

   b. If all of the electrical components are tight, test the ignition system electrical components as described in Chapter Nine.

11. Disconnect the timing light and portable tachometer.

12. Install the gasket and the left-hand crankcase cover.

13. Install the shift lever and the left-hand footpeg. Tighten the footpeg mounting bolts to the torque specification in **Table 3**.

Carburetor Synchronization (And Lower Throttle Cable Adjustment)

For optimum engine performance, the throttle valve opening on each carburetor must be the same. To do this, the carburetors are adjusted so that the throttle valves (**Figure 89**) open at the same precise moment. This synchronizes the carburetors so that the same air/fuel mixture ratio is delivered to each cylinder. If the throttle valve on one carburetor opens earlier, that cylinder will be forced to work harder.

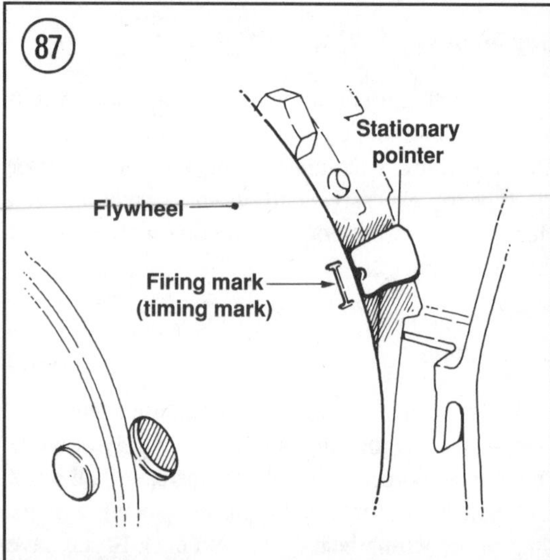

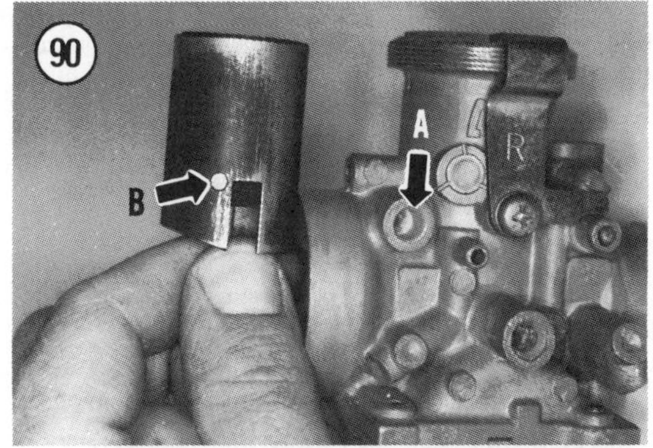

This will cause spark plug fouling, overheating and rough engine operation.

On the stock YFZ350 carburetors, carburetor synchronization is checked by using the inspection window (A, **Figure 90**) installed in each carburetor housing and the index mark (B, **Figure 90**) machined in each throttle valve.

Due to throttle cable stretch and linkage wear, carburetor synchronization should be checked at each tune-up or when troubleshooting a rough running engine.

1. Park the vehicle on a level surface and set the parking brake.
2. Remove the fuel tank as described in Chapter Eight.
3. Operate the throttle lever (**Figure 91**) a few times.
4. Push the throttle lever (**Figure 91**) until the right-hand throttle valve index mark (B, **Figure 90**) is centered in the right-hand carburetor inspection window; see **Figure 92**. Hold the throttle lever in this position and check the left-hand throttle valve index mark in the left-hand carburetor window. If the left- and right-hand index marks are in the same position, the carburetors are synchronized. If not, perform Step 5.
5. To synchronize the carburetors:
   a. Slide the rubber boots (A, **Figure 93**) off of the left- and right-hand carburetor adjusters.

NOTE

*Make all adjustments with the left-hand carburetor adjuster (B, **Figure 93**). Do not adjust the right-hand carburetor adjuster (C, **Figure 93**).*

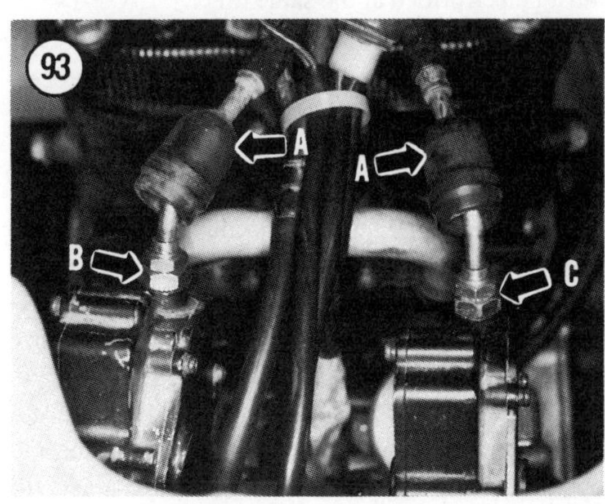

b. Loosen the left-hand carburetor adjuster locknut (A, **Figure 94**).
c. Push the throttle lever until the right-hand throttle valve index mark is centered in the right-hand carburetor inspection window; see **Figure 92**.
d. Turn the adjuster (B, **Figure 94**) in or out to center the left-hand throttle valve index mark.
e. Tighten the locknut (A, **Figure 94**) and recheck carburetor synchronization.
f. Slide the rubber boots over the carburetor adjusters.

6. Install the fuel tank as described in Chapter Eight.
7. Perform the *Idle Speed Adjustment* procedure in this chapter to set idle speed.
8. Perform the *Throttle Lever Adjustment* procedure in this chapter to adjust throttle lever free play.
9. Start the engine and allow to idle. Open and close the throttle a couple of times; check for variation in idle speed.

WARNING

With the engine idling, move the handlebar from side-to-side. If idle speed increases during this movement, the throttle cable assembly may be damaged or incorrectly routed through the frame. Correct this problem immediately. Do not ride the vehicle in this unsafe condition.

Idle Speed Adjustment

This procedure sets the engine idle speed and adjusts the pilot air screws. While the idle speed and pilot air screw setting are separate adjustments, they must be performed at the same time.

1. Make sure the air filter is clean.
2. Perform the *Carburetor Synchronization* procedure in this chapter.
3. Remove the seat as described in Chapter Fourteen.
4. Connect a tachometer to the engine following its manufacturer's instructions.
5. Turn each pilot air screw in (clockwise) until they lightly seat. Then turn each pilot air screw out (counterclockwise) the number of turns listed under *Pilot Air Screw* in **Table 11**. See **Figure 95**.
6. Start the engine and allow to warm to normal operating temperature.

NOTE

*The idle speed screws (**Figure 96**) were preset at the factory. When adjusting idle speed, turn the left- and right-hand idle speed screws the same number of turns.*

7. Adjust the idle speed by turning the left- and right-hand idle speed screws (**Figure 96**) in or out until the idle speed listed in **Table 11** is obtained.
8. Turn the engine off and disconnect the tachometer.
9. Install and secure the seat.
10. Perform the *Throttle Lever Adjustment* procedure in this chapter to adjust throttle lever free play.

STORAGE

Several months of inactivity can cause serious problems and a general deterioration of the vehicle's condition. This is especially true in areas of weather extremes. During the winter months it is advisable to prepare your Banshee for lay-up.

Selecting a Storage Area

Most riders store their ATV's in their home garages. If you do not have a home garage, facilities suitable for long-term storage are readily available for rent or lease in most areas. In selecting a building, consider the following points.

1. The storage area must be dry, free from dampness and excessive humidity. Heating is not necessary, but the building should be well insulated to minimize extreme temperature variations.
2. Buildings with large window areas should be avoided, or such windows should be masked (also a good security measure) if direct sunlight can fall on the vehicle.

Preparing Vehicle for Storage

Careful preparation will minimize deterioration and make it easier to restore the vehicle to service later. Use the following procedure.

1. Wash the vehicle completely. Make certain to remove all dirt in all the hard to reach parts. Completely dry all parts of the vehicle to remove all moisture.
2. Run the engine for about 20-30 minutes to warm up the oil in the clutch and transmission. Drain the oil, regardless of the time since the last oil change. Refill with the normal quantity and type of oil.
3. Drain all gasoline from the fuel tank, interconnecting hose, and the carburetor.
4. Clean and lubricate the drive chain and control cables; refer to specific procedures in this chapter and in Chapter Eleven.

5. Remove the spark plugs and add about one teaspoon of engine oil into each cylinder. Reinstall the spark plugs and turn the engine over to distribute the oil to the cylinder walls and pistons.
6. Tape or tie a plastic bag over the end of each silencer to prevent the entry of moisture.
7. Check the tire pressure, inflate to the correct pressure and move the vehicle to the storage area. Place it securely on a stand with all 4 wheels off the ground.
8. Cover the vehicle with a tarp, blanket or heavy plastic. Place this cover over the vehicle mainly as a dust cover—do not wrap it tightly, especially any plastic material, as it may trap moisture causing condensation. Leave room for air to circulate around the vehicle.

Inspection During Storage

Try to inspect the vehicle weekly while in storage. Any deterioration should be corrected as soon as possible. For example, if corrosion is observed, cover the corroded area with a light coat of grease or silicone spray.

Kick the engine over a couple of times. Don't start it.

Restoring Vehicle to Service

A vehicle that has been properly prepared and stored in a suitable area requires only light maintenance to restore to service. It is advisable, however, to perform a spring tune-up.

1. Before removing the vehicle from the storage area, reinflate the tires to the correct pressures. Air loss during storage may have nearly flattened the tires.
2. When the vehicle is brought to the work area, refill the fuel tank with a fresh fuel/oil mixture as described in this chapter.
3. Start the engine.
4. Perform the standard tune-up as described earlier in this chapter.
5. Check the operation of the engine stop switch. Oxidation of the switch contacts during storage may make it inoperative.
6. Clean and test ride the vehicle.

Table 1 MAINTENANCE AND LUBRICATION SCHEDULE

Initial 1st month or after engine or suspension break-in	Change clutch/transmission oil Inspect and clean spark plug; regap if necessary Inspect cooling system Clean and re-oil air filter Remove and clean carburetors Reinstall carburetor and adjust Check condition of throttle, clutch and parking brake cables; replace damaged cable(s) if necessary Lubricate throttle, clutch and parking brake cables Check throttle operation; adjust if necessary Check front and rear brake operation; adjust if necessary Check front and rear brake fluid level; refill as necessary Check clutch operation and adjustment; adjust if necessary Lubricate drive chain Check drive chain alignment and free play; adjust if necessary Lubricate steering shaft bearings Check steering shaft play; adjust if necessary Check front suspension components for looseness or damage Lubricate front suspension components Check rear suspension components for looseness or damage Lubricate rear suspension components Inspect tire condition and wear; replace if necessary Check tire air pressure; adjust if necessary Check wheel runout Inspect front wheel bearings; lubricate or replace as required Inspect rear axle housing bearings; replace as required Check and tighten all fasteners Check lighting equipment
Every 30 days of operation	Check fuel hoses for cracks or damage; replace if necessary Inspect and clean spark plug; regap if necessary Inspect cooling system Clean and re-oil air filter Remove and clean carburetors Reinstall carburetor and adjust Check condition of throttle, clutch and parking brake cables; replace damaged cable(s) if necessary Lubricate throttle, clutch and parking brake cables Check throttle operation; adjust if necessary Check front and rear brake operation; adjust if necessary Check front and rear brake fluid level; refill as necessary Check clutch operation and adjustment; adjust if necessary Inspect drive chain guards and rollers for severe wear or damage; replace if necessary Lubricate drive chain Check drive chain alignment and free play; adjust if necessary Lubricate steering shaft bearings

(continued)

Table 1 MAINTENANCE AND LUBRICATION SCHEDULE (continued)

Every 30 days of operation (continued)	Check steering shaft play; adjust if necessary Check front suspension components for looseness or damage Lubricate front suspension components Check rear suspension components for looseness or damage Lubricate rear suspension components Inspect tire condition and wear; replace if necessary Check tire air pressure; adjust if necessary Check wheel runout Inspect front wheel bearings; replace as required Inspect rear axle housing bearings; lubricate or replace as required Check and tighten all fasteners Clean frame and inspect for bent or damaged components Check lighting equipment
Once a year	Change clutch/transmission oil Lubricate steering shaft bearings Change coolant
Every 4 years	Replace brake hoses, or when found to be cracked or damaged

* Consider this maintenance schedule as a guide to general maintenance and lubrication intervals. Harder than normal use (racing) and exposure to mud, water, sand, high humidity, etc. will dictate more frequent attention to most maintenance items.

Table 2 TIRE INFLATION PRESSURE

	Standard psi (kPa)	**Minimum psi (kPa)**
Front		
1987-1990	4.3 (30)	3.8 (27)
1991-on	4.3 (30)	3.8 (27)
Rear		
1987-1990	3.6 (25)	3.1 (22)
1991-on	4.3 (30)	3.1 (22)

Table 3 MAINTENANCE TORQUE SPECIFICATIONS

	N•m	**ft.-lb.**
Oil drain plug	20	14
Coolant drain bolts	14	10
Left-hand crankcase cover	7	5.1
Spark plug	20	14
Cylinder head	28	20
Parking brake locknut	16	11
Rear axle housing		
Upper bolts	120	85
Lower bolts	60	43
Chain adjuster locknuts	16	11
Wheel lug nuts	45	32
Tie-rod locknuts	30	22
Footpeg mounting bolts	55	40

Table 4 RECOMMENDED LUBRICANTS AND FUEL

Engine oil	Yamalube "R", Castrol R30 or equivalent 2-stroke oil
Transmission	SAE 10W30 motor oil
Air filter	Foam air filter oil
Drive chain*	Non-tacky O-ring chain lubricant or SAE 30-50 weight engine motor oil
Brake fluid	DOT 4
Steering and suspension lubricant	Lithium base grease
Fuel	Regular gasoline with octane rating of at least 90
Control cables	Cable lube**

* Use kerosene to clean drive chain.
** Do not use drive chain lubricant to lubricate control cables.

Table 5 FUEL/OIL PREMIX RATIO

Oil type	Premix ratio	
Castrol R30	20:1	
Yamalube "R" or equivalent	24:1	
Ratio 20:1 Gasoline (gal.)	**Oil oz.**	**Oil ml**
1	6.4	190
2	12.8	380
3	19.2	570
4	25.6	760
5	32	945
Ratio 24:1 Gasoline (gal.)	**Oil oz.**	**Oil ml**
1	5.3	157
2	10.7	316
3	16.0	473
4	21.3	630
5	26.7	790

Table 6 FUEL TANK CAPACITY

	U.S. gal	Liters	Imp gal.
Total	3.17	12	2.64
Reserve	0.66	2.5	0.55

Table 7 CLUTCH/TRANSMISSION OIL CAPACITY

	Liters	U.S. qt.	Imp. qt.
Oil change	1.5	1.6	1.3
Total amount (engine rebuild)	1.7	1.8	1.5

Table 8 DRIVE CHAIN FREE PLAY MEASUREMENT

	mm	in.
Free play	15	0.6

Table 9 COOLANT CAPACITY*

	Liters	U.S. qt.	Imp. qt.
Total amount	2.5	2.64	2.20
Reservoir tank	0.28	0.30	0.25

* Mixing ratio is 50% coolant to 50% water.

Table 10 SPARK PLUGS AND GAP

Plug range	Type and heat range
Hotter	NGK BR7ES
Standard	NGK BR8ES
Colder	NGK BR9ES
Spark plug gap	0.7-0.8 mm (0.028-0.032 in.)

Table 11 TUNE-UP SPECIFICATIONS

Ignition timing	17 BTDC @ 1,200 rpm*
Carburetor adjustment	
Pilot air screw	2.0 turns out
Engine idle speed	1,450-1,550 rpm

* See text for inspection procedure.

CHAPTER FOUR

ENGINE TOP END

This chapter covers information to service the cylinder head, cylinder blocks, pistons, piston rings and reed valve assemblies. Engine lower end service (crankshaft, transmission removal and installation, shift drum and shift forks) is covered in Chapter Five. Clutch, primary drive and kickstarter service is covered in Chapter Six. Transmission disassembly is covered in Chapter Seven.

Prior to removing and disassembling the engine top end, clean the entire engine. It is easier to work on a clean engine and you will do a better job.

Make certain that you have all the necessary tools available and purchase replacement parts prior to disassembly. Also make sure you have a clean place to work.

It is a good idea to identify and mark parts as they are removed so that errors will be avoided during assembly and installation. Clean all parts thoroughly upon removal, then place them in trays or boxes with their associated mounting hardware. Do not rely on memory alone as it may be days or weeks before you complete the job. In the text there is frequent mention of the left-hand and right-hand side of the engine. This refers to the engine as it sits in the frame, not as it sits on your workbench.

Engine specifications are listed in **Tables 1-4** at the end of the chapter.

ENGINE PRINCIPLES

Figure 1 explains how a typical 2-stroke engine works. This is helpful when troubleshooting or repairing the engine.

ENGINE LUBRICATION

Engine lubrication is provided by the fuel/oil mixture used to power the engine. Refer to Chapter Three for oil and ratio recommendations.

CLEANLINESS

Repairs go much faster and easier if your engine is clean before you begin work. This is especially important when servicing the engine. If the top end is being serviced while the engine is installed in the frame, note that dirt trapped underneath the fuel tank or upper frame tube can fall into cylinders or crankcase openings; remove the fuel tank and wrap the frame with a large, clean towel. There are special cleaners for washing the engine and related parts. Just spray or brush on the cleaning solution, let it stand, then rinse it away with a garden hose; see Chapter One.

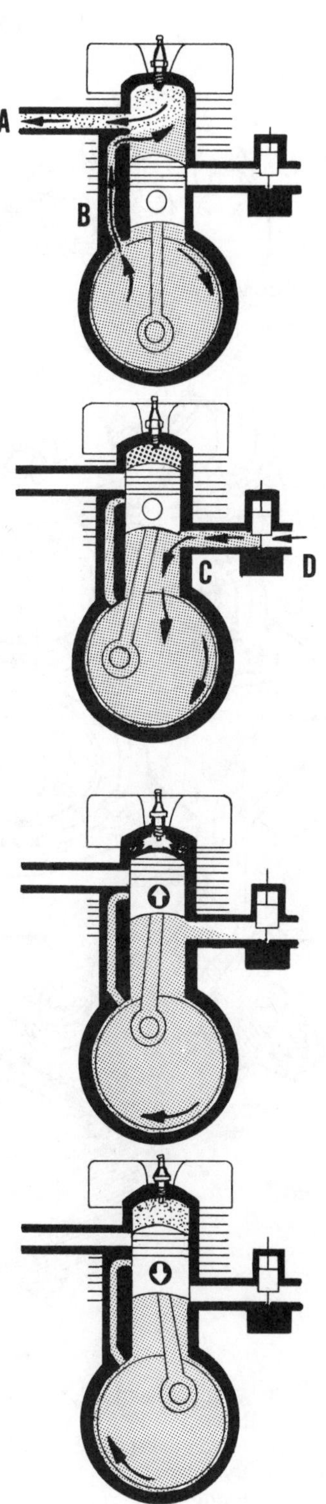

2-STROKE OPERATING PRINCIPLES

The crankshaft in this discussion is rotating in a clockwise direction.

As the piston travels downward, it uncovers the exhaust port (A) allowing the exhaust gases, which are under pressure, to leave the cylinder. A fresh fuel/air charge, which has been compressed slightly, travels from the crankcase into the cylinder through the transfer port (B). Since this charge enters under pressure, it also helps to push out the exhaust gases.

While the crankshaft continues to rotate, the piston moves upward, covering the transfer port (B) and exhaust port (A). The piston is now compressing the new fuel/air mixture and creating a low pressure area in the crankcase at the same time. As the piston continues to travel, it uncovers the intake port (C). A fresh fuel/air charge, from the carburetor (D) is drawn into the crankcase through the intake port, because of the low pressure within it.

Now, as the piston almost reaches the top of its travel, the spark plug fires, thus igniting the compressed fuel/air mixture. The piston continues to top dead (TDC) and is pushed downward by the expanding gases.

As the piston travels down, the exhaust gases leave the cylinder and the complete cycle starts all over again.

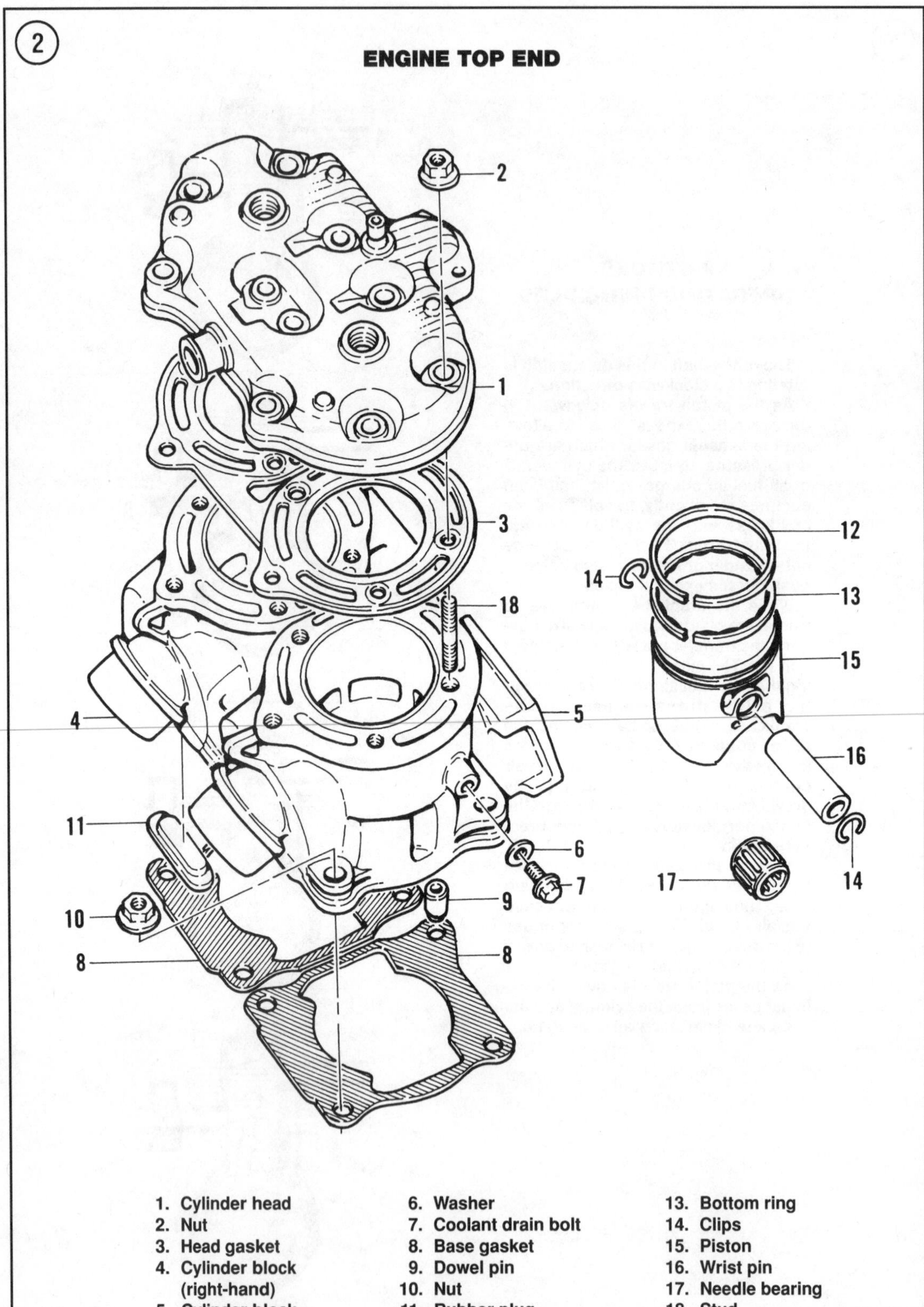

1. Cylinder head
2. Nut
3. Head gasket
4. Cylinder block (right-hand)
5. Cylinder block (left-hand)
6. Washer
7. Coolant drain bolt
8. Base gasket
9. Dowel pin
10. Nut
11. Rubber plug
12. Top ring
13. Bottom ring
14. Clips
15. Piston
16. Wrist pin
17. Needle bearing
18. Stud

CYLINDER HEAD

A single cylinder head is bolted to the top of the cylinder blocks. A single gasket separates the cylinder head and cylinders. See **Figure 2**.

If the engine is being disassembled for inspection purposes, first check engine compression as described under *Cylinder Compression* in Chapter Three. Then check for engine primary compression leaks as described under *Two-Stroke Crankcase Pressure Test* in Chapter Two. Record the results of each test.

Removal

CAUTION
To prevent warpage and damage to any component, remove the cylinder head only when the engine is cold.

1. Remove the seat as described in Chapter Fourteen.
2. Remove the fuel tank as described in Chapter Eight.

3

4

3. Remove the exhaust system as described in Chapter Eight.
4. Drain the cooling system as described under *Coolant Change* in Chapter Three.
5. Disconnect the spark plug caps at each spark plug.

CAUTION
Do not pry the coolant hoses off in the following steps. If you can't remove a hose, cut the hose so that you don't damage the cylinder head hose pipe(s).

6. Disconnect the outlet coolant hose (**Figure 3**) at the front of the cylinder head.
7. Disconnect the bypass hose (A, **Figure 4**) at the rear of the cylinder head.
8. Remove the 2 Allen bolts securing the inlet hose nozzle to the bottom of the cylinder head (B, **Figure 4**).
9. Remove the spark plugs.

NOTE
The cylinder head torque sequence numbers (1-10) are embossed into the cylinder head, next to their respective cylinder stud.

10. Loosen the cylinder head nuts, starting with No. 10 and working toward No. 1 (**Figure 5**). Loosen each nut 1/2 turn at a time until they are all loose, then remove them from the cylinder studs.

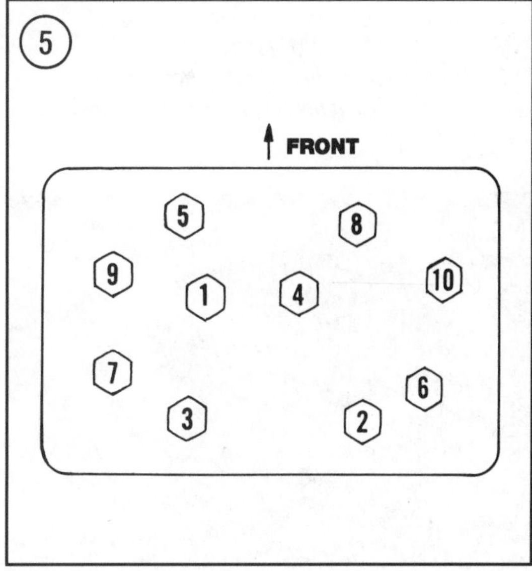

5

4

11. Lift the cylinder head (**Figure 6**) off the cylinder blocks. If the head is stuck, lightly tap it with a plastic-tipped hammer. Do not pry the head off. Place the cylinder head on a suitable surface so that the gasket surface is not damaged.

NOTE
Do not pry the head if it is stuck. Sometimes it is possible to loosen the head with engine compression. Rotate the engine with the kickstarter (with both spark plugs installed). As the pistons reach top dead center (TDC) on their compression stroke, the head may pop loose.

12. Visually check the head and gasket for signs of coolant leakage.
13. Remove the cylinder head gasket (A, **Figure 7**) and discard it.
14. Cover the cylinder openings with clean shop rags.
15. Remove all gasket residue from the hose joint gasket surface (**Figure 8**).
16. Remove all gasket residue from the cylinder block gasket surfaces.
17. Inspect the cylinder head as described in this chapter.

Inspection

1. Soak the cylinder head in solvent to soften the gasket residue and carbon deposits.

CAUTION
Do not clean the cylinder head gasket surface with a power-driven wire brush or scraper.

6

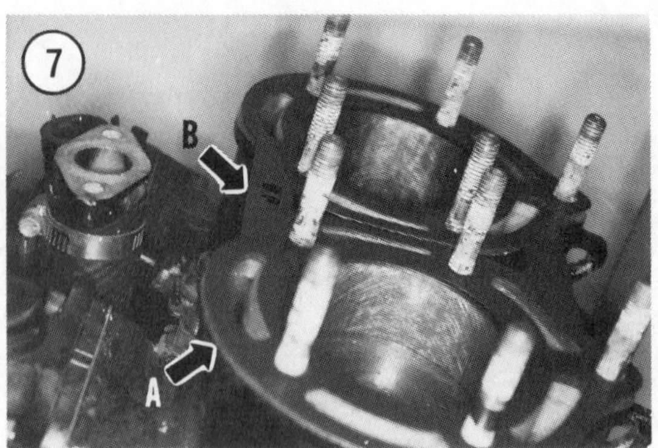

7

8

9

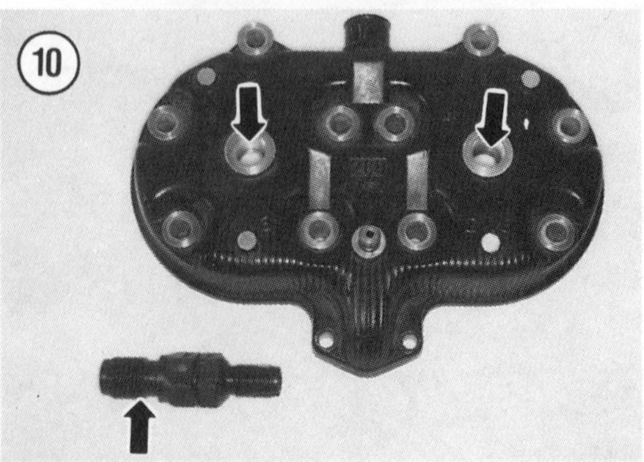
10

2. Remove gasket residue with a suitable scraper.
3. Remove carbon deposits from the cylinder head combustion chambers (**Figure 9**) with a suitable scraper or wire brush.
4. Using a 14 × 1.25 mm tap, clean the spark plug threads in the cylinder head (**Figure 10**). Lubricate the tap with kerosene or an aluminum tapping fluid.
5. Check the hose nozzle (**Figure 11**) on the cylinder head for cracks, looseness or other damage. This nozzle is an integral part of the cylinder head and is not available as a replacement item.

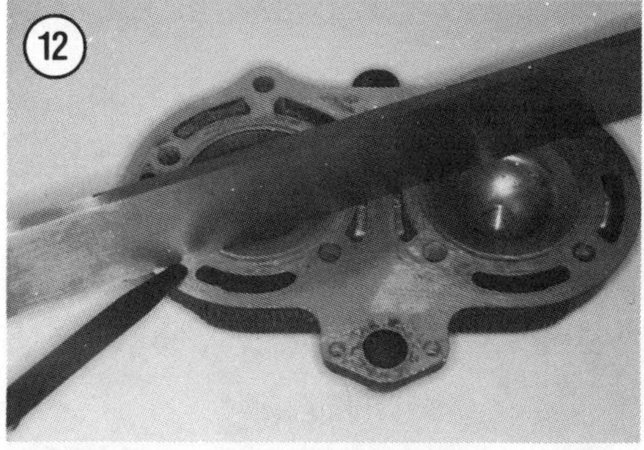

6. Reclean the cylinder head in solvent. Then blow dry with compressed air.
7. Place a straightedge lengthwise across the cylinder head sealing surface (**Figure 12**) and measure warpage with a feeler gauge. If you can insert a 0.03 mm (0.012 in.) feeler gauge between the straightedge and sealing surface at any point, resurface the cylinder head as described in Step 8.
8. To lightly resurface the cylinder head:
   a. Tape a piece of 400-600 grit wet emery sandpaper onto a piece of thick plate glass or surface plate (**Figure 13**).

NOTE

Wet the sandpaper with a soap and water solution when resurfacing the cylinder head in the following steps.

   b. Slowly resurface the head by moving it in figure-eight patterns on the sandpaper. See **Figure 14**.
   c. Rotate the head several times to avoid removing too much material from one side. Check progress often with the straightedge and feeler gauge.
   d. If the cylinder head warpage still exceeds the service limit, it will be necessary to have the head resurfaced by a machine shop. Note that removing excessive amounts of material from the cylinder head mating surface will change the compression ratio. Consult with the machinist on how much material was removed.
9. Replace any cylinder head nuts that are stripped, damaged or show other defects. Replace fasteners as a set.

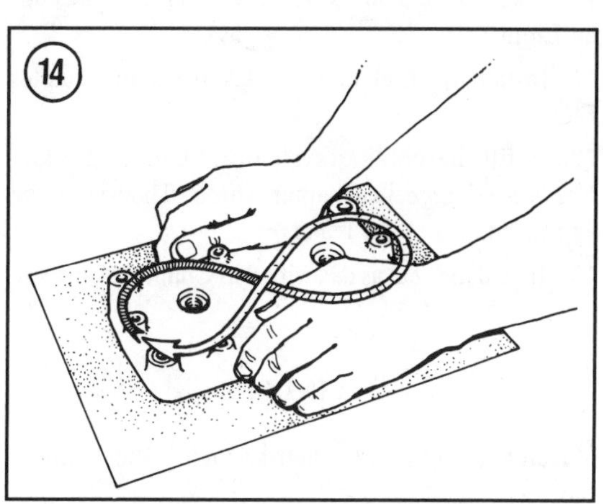

4

10. Clean the flange surface of the cylinder head nuts on the same surface plate arrangement described in Step 8. Then clean the nuts in solvent and dry with compressed air.

Installation

1. Remove all gasket residue from the cylinder head and cylinder mating surfaces.
2. Install a new head gasket over the cylinder head studs, making sure the gasket fits correctly. Install the gasket with its "UP" mark facing up as shown in B, **Figure 7**.
3. Install the cylinder head (**Figure 6**) onto the cylinder blocks.
4. Install the cylinder head nuts. Tighten finger-tight.
5. Referring to **Figure 5**, tighten the cylinder head nuts in numerical order. Tighten the nuts in 2-3 stages to the torque specification listed in **Table 4**.
6. Install the spark plugs and tighten to the torque specification in **Table 4**. Reconnect the spark plug caps.
7. Install a new gasket onto the inlet hose nozzle and secure the nozzle to the cylinder head with the 2 Allen bolts (**Figure 15**). Tighten the inlet hose nozzle Allen bolts to the torque specification in **Table 4**.
8. Install the bypass hose (A, **Figure 4**) onto the cylinder head nozzle. Secure the hose with the hose clamp.
9. Install the outlet hose onto the front cylinder head hose nozzle (**Figure 3**). Secure the hose with the hose clamp.
10. Install the exhaust system as described in Chapter Eight.
11. Install the fuel tank as described in Chapter Eight.
12. Refill the cooling system as described under *Coolant Change* in Chapter Three. Then start the engine and check for leaks.
13. Install the seat as described in Chapter Fourteen.

CYLINDERS

Refer to **Figure 2** when servicing the cylinder blocks.

Removal

1. Remove the carburetors as described in Chapter Eight.
2. Remove the pipe (**Figure 16**) from the intake manifolds.
3. Remove the cylinder head as described in this chapter.
4. Loosen the cylinder base nuts (**Figure 17**) in a crisscross pattern. Remove the nuts.
5. Loosen the cylinder by tapping around the perimeter with a rubber or plastic mallet.

15

16

17

6. Rotate the engine so the piston is at the bottom of its stroke. Pull the cylinder straight up and off the crankcase studs and piston, making sure to hold the piston when released from the cylinder so that the rod doesn't fall against the engine case.

CAUTION
When removing the second cylinder in Step 7, do not twist the cylinder so far that the piston rings could snap into the intake port. This would cause the cylinder to bind and may damage the piston rings and piston. If this should happen, remove the reed valve assembly and push the rings back into position.

7. Repeat for the opposite cylinder.
8. Remove the cylinder base gaskets and discard them.
9. Locate and remove the cylinder dowel pins, if necessary.
10. If necessary, remove the pistons and piston rings as described in this chapter.

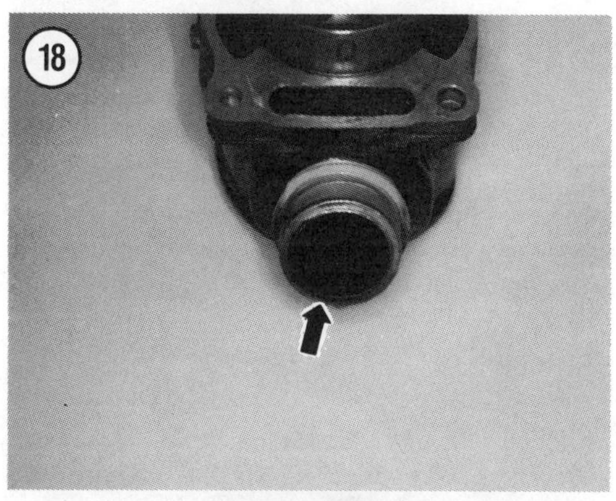
18

11. Place a clean shop cloth into the crankcase openings to prevent the entry of foreign material.
12. If necessary, remove and inspect the reed valve assemblies as described in this chapter.

Inspection

1. Remove all gasket residue from the top and bottom gasket surfaces with a gasket scraper.
2. Remove all carbon residue from the exhaust port (**Figure 18**).
3. Flush the cylinder coolant passages to remove all sludge and other residue.
4. Check the cylinder mating surface with a feeler gauge and straightedge. Check for low spots around the mating surface. Yamaha does not list a cylinder warp limit.

4

Cylinder Block Coolant Rubber Plug Replacement

A rubber plug (A, **Figure 19**) is installed in the bottom of each cylinder block (on the exhaust side) to block off the cylinder's coolant passage.

1. Check the rubber plug (A, **Figure 19**) in the bottom of the cylinder block for coolant leakage. If the plug is leaking, coolant will show up on the base gasket; see B, **Figure 19**. If the rubber plug is damaged, loose or leaking, replace it as follows.
2. Thread a sheet metal screw into the rubber plug. Then grasp the screw with a pair of pliers and pull the plug out of the cylinder block (**Figure 20**). Do not pry the plug out with a screwdriver or similar tool.

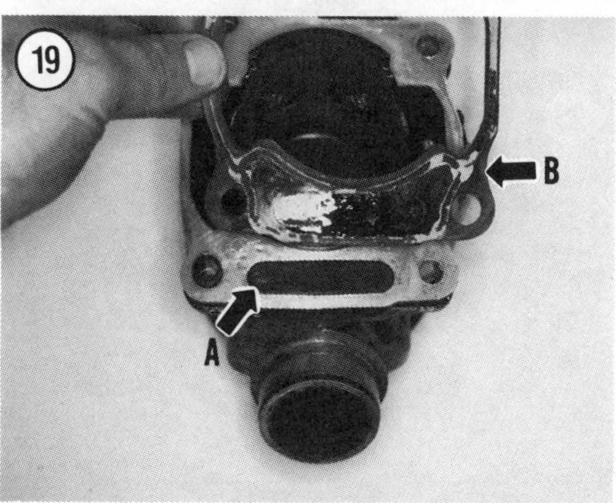

19

20

3. Clean the water port opening (**Figure 21**) in the cylinder block. Remove all coolant residue and rust.

4. Apply a light coat of Gasgacinch sealer to the new plug's sealing surface (**Figure 22**), following the manufacturer's instructions.

5. Install the rubber plug into the cylinder port opening (**Figure 23**). The plug must be flush with or slightly below the cylinder block base gasket surface. See **Figure 24**. Allow the sealer to set up before installing the cylinder block; refer to the sealer manufacturer's instructions for drying time.

Cylinder Bore Measurement

Accurate cylinder measurement requires a bore gauge and micrometer. If you don't have the right tools, have your dealer or a machine shop take the measurements.

1. Wash the cylinder block in solvent and dry with compressed air. The cylinder bore must be cleaned before attempting any measurement as incorrect readings may be obtained.

2. Check the cylinder wall for deep scratches, uneven wear, seizure or other damage; if evident, the cylinder should be rebored.

3. Measure the cylinder bore with a bore gauge (**Figure 25**) or an inside micrometer at the 3 points shown in **Figure 26**. Measure in line with the piston pin and at 90° to the pin. If the taper or out-of-round is greater than the specifications listed in **Table 2**, the cylinder must be rebored to the next oversize and

21

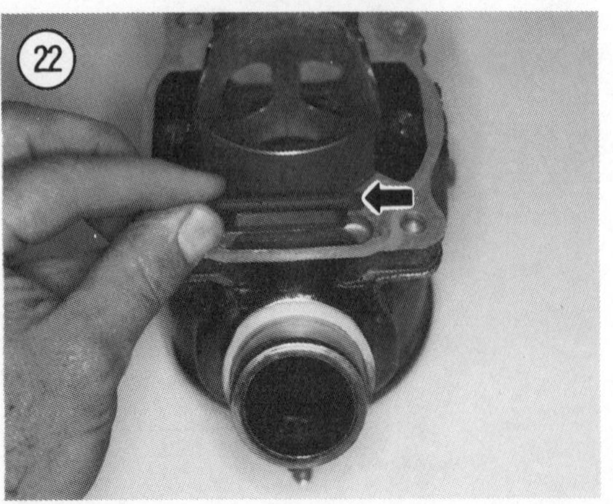
22

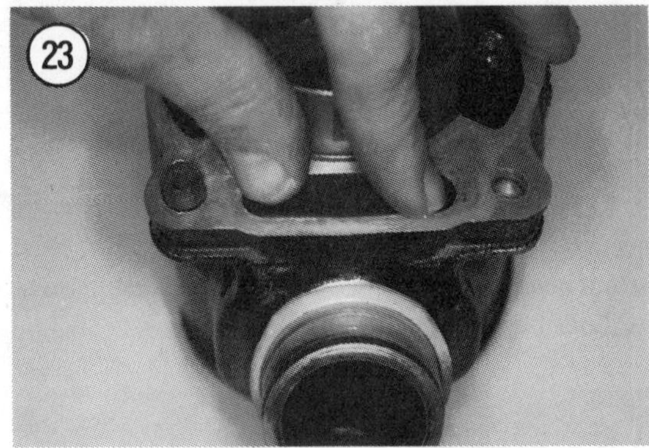
23

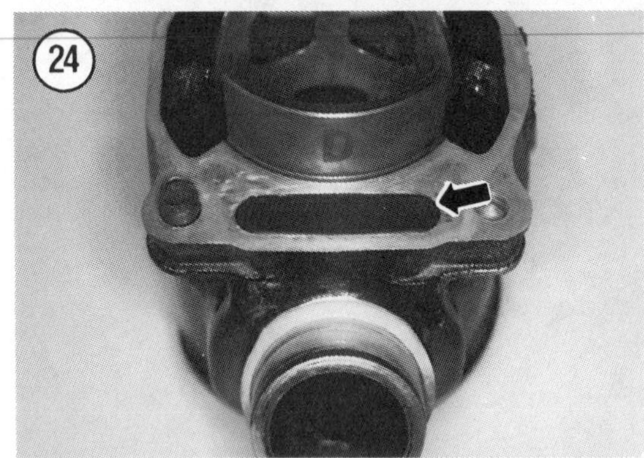
24

25

new piston and rings installed. When determining bore diameter, use the largest bore diameter measurement obtained.

NOTE
*New pistons should be obtained before boring the cylinders. Each cylinder must be bored to match one piston only (**Figure 27**). Piston-to-cylinder clearance is specified in **Table 2**.*

4. Clean the cylinder bore as described under *Cylinder Bore Cleaning* in this chapter.
5. Repeat for the other cylinder.
6. When installing a cylinder that has been honed or bored, give the vehicle the same break-in procedure you would use on a new machine.

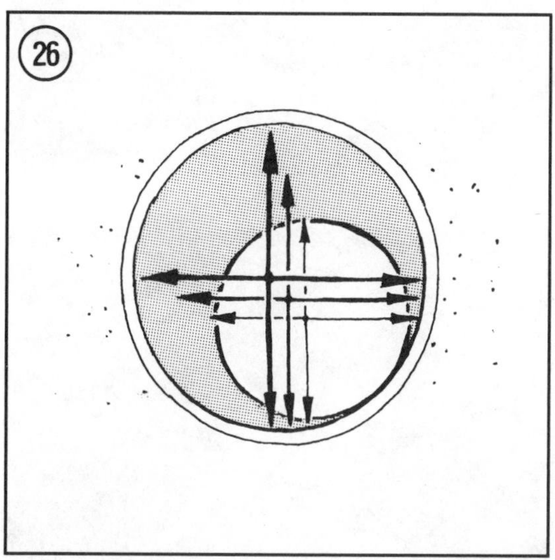

Cylinder Studs

Check the cylinder studs (**Figure 28**) for thread damage or looseness. If thread damage is minor, chase the threads with the correct size metric die. If the studs are damaged or loose, remove them with a stud remover. Coat the bottom half of a new stud with Loctite 271 (red). Follow Loctite's directions on cure time before installing the cylinder head and cylinder head nuts.

Cylinder Bore Cleaning

After the cylinder block has been serviced, wash the cylinder wall in a hot soap-and-water solution. This is the only way to clean the cylinder wall of the fine grit material left from the bore or honing job. After washing the cylinder wall, run a clean white cloth through the cylinder; the cloth should show no traces of grit or other abrasive materials. If the cloth shows traces of abrasive material, rewash the cylinder wall until the cloth comes out clean. Dry the cylinder with compressed air and lubricate the cylinder wall with clean engine oil to prevent the cylinder wall from rusting.

Installation

1. Check that the top surface of the crankcase and both cylinder surfaces are clean prior to installation.
2. Clean the cylinder bore as described under *Cylinder Bore Cleaning* in this chapter.
3. Install the reed valve assemblies, if removed, as described in this chapter.
4. Install the dowel pins, if removed.
5. Install the base gaskets as follows:

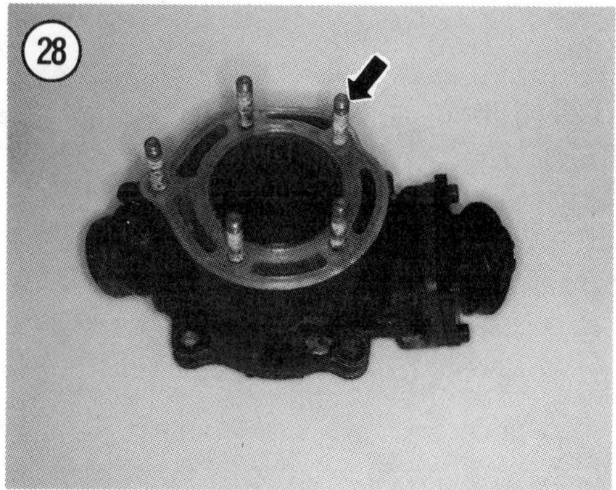

a. Factory base gaskets have a sealer applied to one side (**Figure 29**).
b. Align the base gasket with the crankcase studs and install it (**Figure 30**). Repeat for the opposite base gasket.

6. Check that the piston pin clips (**Figure 31**) are seated in the piston grooves completely.
7. Position the piston rings so that their end gaps are centered around the locating pins in the piston ring grooves as shown in **Figure 32**.
8. Lightly oil the piston rings, piston and cylinder bore with engine oil.
9. Install a piston holding fixture under the piston. Then rotate the crankshaft until the piston skirt seats against the fixture. See **Figure 33**.

NOTE
A piston holding fixture can be made out of wood as shown in ***Figure 34****.*

10. Start the cylinder down over the piston *with the exhaust port facing forward.* See **Figure 35**.

CAUTION
*Make sure to insert the cylinder over the inner rear cylinder stud (longer stud) when installing the cylinder (****Figure 36****). If you are only looking at the shorter studs, you can miss the longer rear stud and slide the cylinder down on the piston too far. You can then twist the cylinder and break a ring as it pops into the intake port.*

NOTE
*When installing the cylinder in Step 11, make frequent checks to ensure that the piston ring end gaps are centered around the piston locating pins (****Figure 32****).*

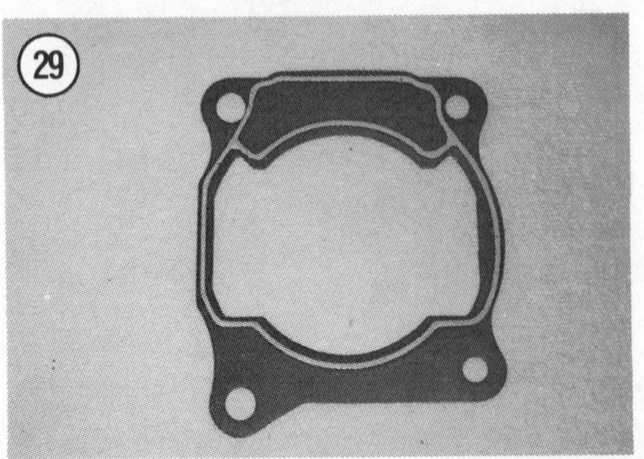
29

30

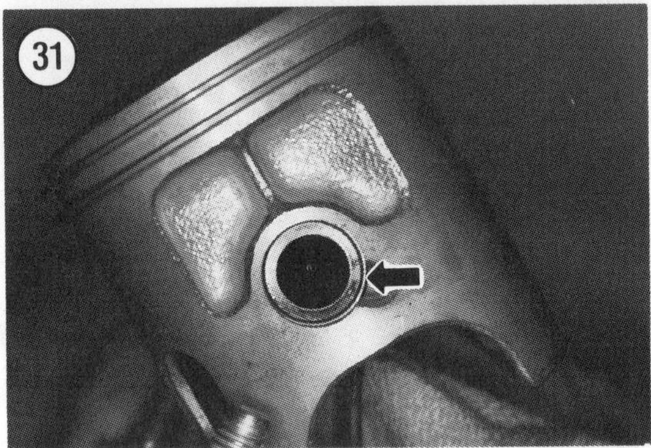
31

32

33

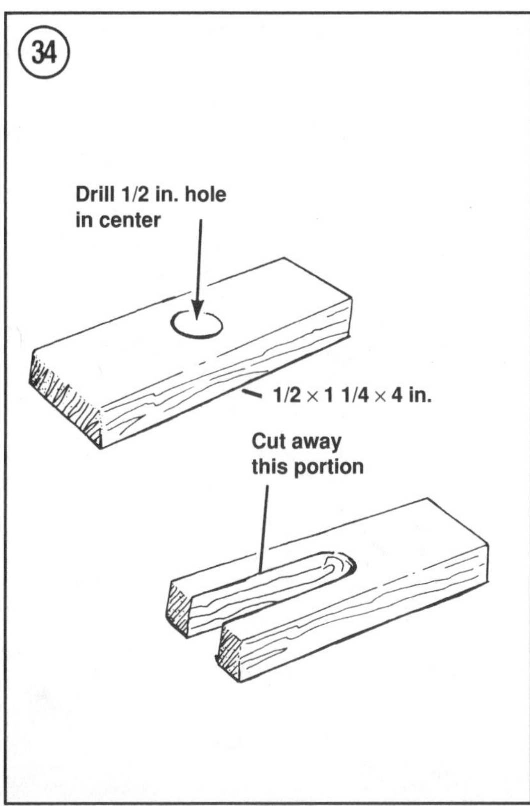

11. Compress each ring, first the top and then the bottom, with your fingers, as the cylinder starts to slide over it.

12. Slide the cylinder down until it bottoms on the piston holding fixture.

13. Remove the piston holding fixture and slide the cylinder into place on the crankcase (**Figure 37**).

14. Hold the cylinder in place with one hand and operate the kickstarter lever with your other hand. If the piston catches or stops in the cylinder, the piston rings were not lined up properly. The piston should move up and down the cylinder bore smoothly.

NOTE
If the rings were not lined up, remove the cylinder and check for damage.

15. Install the cylinder base nuts (**Figure 17**) and tighten them finger-tight.

16. Repeat to install the opposite cylinder.

17. Temporarily install the cylinder head (**Figure 38**), checking that the cylinder head slides over the cylinder studs smoothly and with no binding. Then tighten each of the cylinder base nuts (**Figure 17**) snug with a wrench. Remove the cylinder head.

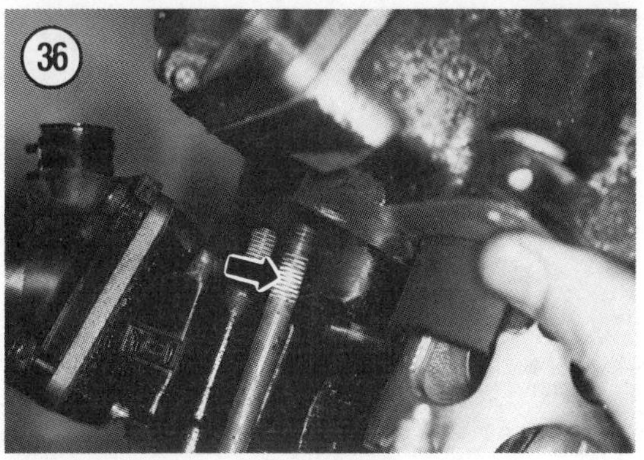

18. Tighten the cylinder base nuts in a crisscross pattern (**Figure 39**) to the torque specification in **Table 4**.
19. Install the cylinder head as described in this chapter.
20. Insert the pipe (**Figure 16**) into the intake manifolds.
21. Install the carburetors as described in Chapter Eight.
22. Follow the *Break-in Procedure* in this chapter if new parts were installed (pistons, rings, cylinder, etc.).

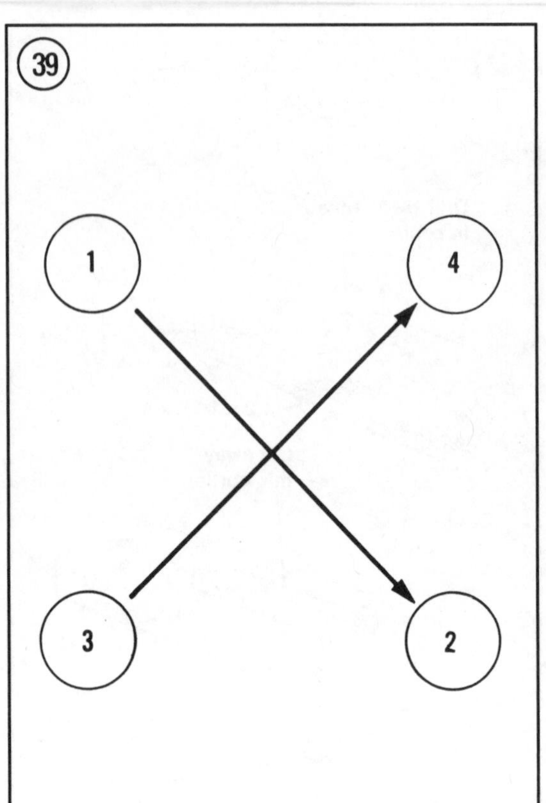

PISTONS, WRIST PINS AND PISTON RINGS

The pistons are made of an aluminum alloy. The wrist pins are a precision fit and held in place by a clip at each end. A caged needle bearing is used on the small end of each connecting rod. See **Figure 40**.

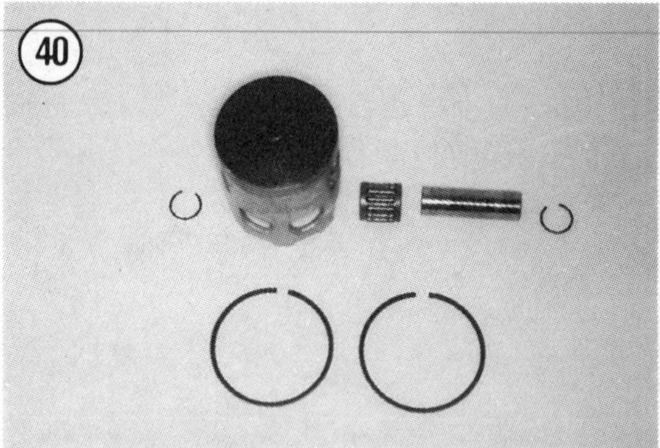

Piston and Piston Ring Removal

1. Remove the cylinder head and cylinder blocks as described in this chapter.
2. Wrap a clean shop cloth under the piston so that the clips cannot fall into the crankcase.

WARNING
Safety glasses should be worn when performing Step 3.

3. Using needlenose pliers, remove the clips from each side of the wrist pin bore (**Figure 41**). Hold your thumb over one edge of the clip when removing it to prevent it from springing out.
4. Use a proper size wooden dowel or socket extension and push out the wrist pin (A, **Figure 42**).

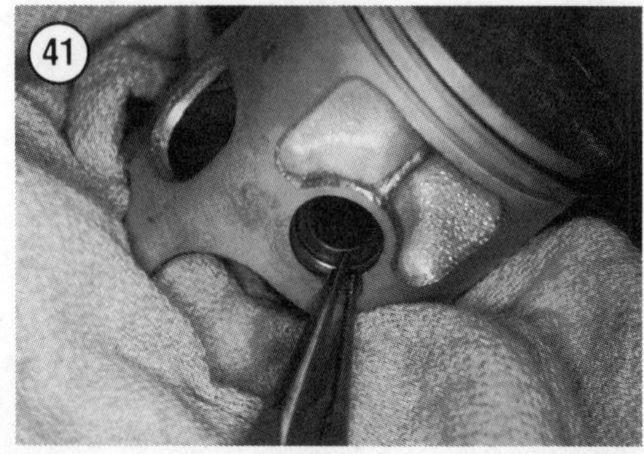

CAUTION
If the engine ran hot or seized, the wrist pin may be difficult to remove. However, do not drive the wrist pin out of the piston. This will damage the piston, needle bearing and connecting rod. If the wrist pin will not push out by hand, remove it as described in Step 5.

5. If the wrist pin is tight, fabricate the tool shown in **Figure 43**. Assemble the tool onto the piston and pull the wrist pin out of the piston. Make sure to

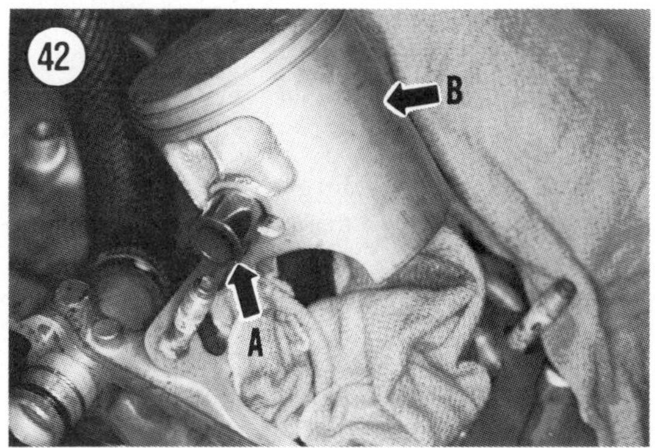

42

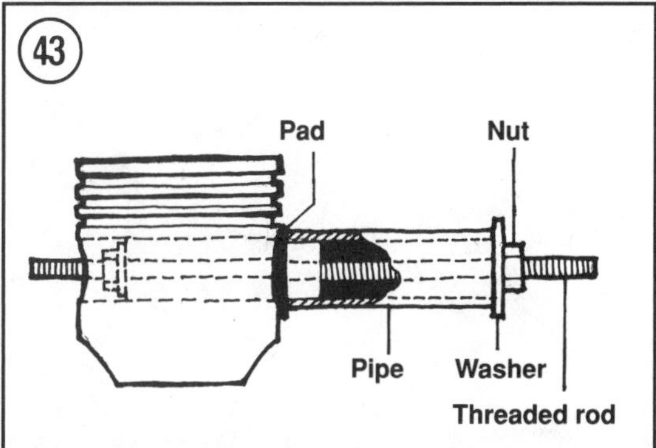

43

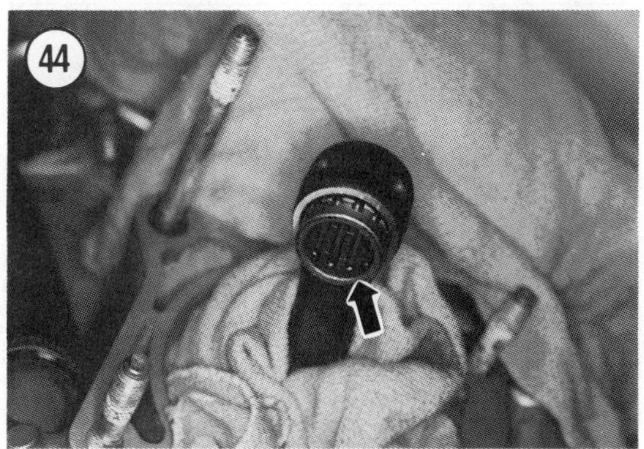

44

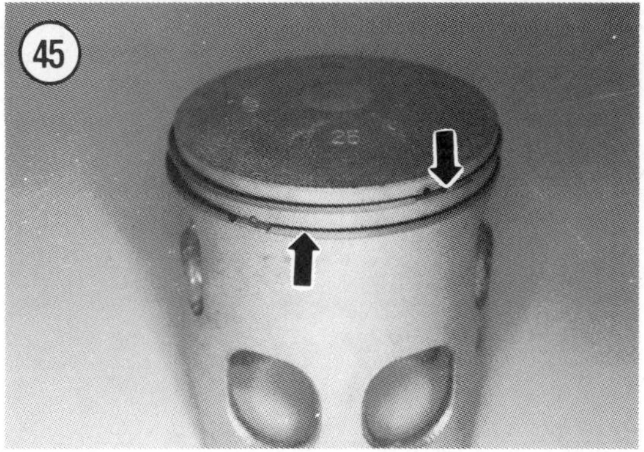

45

install a pad between the piston and piece of pipe to avoid scoring the side of the piston.

NOTE
If you intend to reuse the pistons, identify the pistons with an "L" (left-hand) or "R" (right-hand) so that you can install them in their original position.

6. Lift the piston (B, **Figure 42**) off the connecting rod.

7. Remove the needle bearing from the connecting rod (**Figure 44**).

8. Repeat for the opposite piston.

9. If the piston is going to be left off for some time, place a piece of foam insulation tube, or shop cloth, over the end of the rod to protect it.

10. Before removing the piston rings, check the piston rings for sticking in the piston ring lands. The piston rings should have free movement. If not, excessive carbon may have caused the rings to stick. This reduces engine compression and can cause piston and cylinder bore damage.

NOTE
*If you intend to reuse the piston rings (**Figure 45**), identify and store the rings in a container so that they can be reinstalled in their original ring groove.*

11. Remove the top ring by spreading the ends with your thumbs just enough to slide it up over the piston (**Figure 46**). Repeat for the bottom ring.

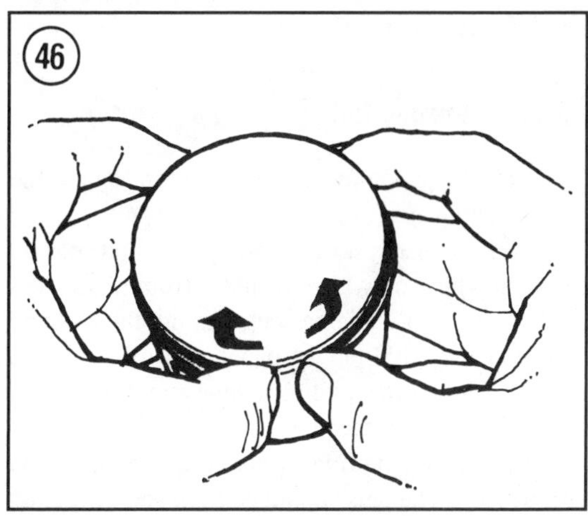

46

4

Wrist Pin and Needle Bearing Inspection

1. Clean the needle bearing (A, **Figure 47**) in solvent and dry thoroughly. Use a magnifying glass and inspect the bearing cage for cracks at the corners of the needle slots and inspect the needles themselves for cracking. If any cracks are found, the bearing must be replaced.
2. Check the wrist pin (B, **Figure 47**) for wear, scoring or chrome flaking. Also check the wrist pin for cracks along its outer surface and both ends. Replace the wrist pin if necessary.
3. Oil the needle bearing and pin and install them in the connecting rod. Slowly rotate the pin and check for radial and axial play (**Figure 48**). If any play exists, the pin and bearing should be replaced, providing the rod bore is in good condition; refer to *Connecting Rod Inspection*. If the condition of the rod bore is in question, the old pin and bearing can be checked with a new connecting rod.

CAUTION
If there are signs of piston seizure or overheating, replace the wrist pin and bearing. These parts have been weakened from excessive heat and may fail later.

Connecting Rod Inspection

1. Wipe the wrist pin bore in the connecting rod with a clean rag and check it for galling, scratches, or any other signs of wear or damage. If any of these conditions exist, replace the connecting rod as described in Chapter Five.
2. Measure connecting rod bearing play and small end free play as described in Chapter Five.

Piston and Piston Ring Inspection

1. Check the piston for cracks at the top edge of the transfer cutaways (**Figure 49**).
2. Check the piston skirt (**Figure 50**) for galling and abrasion which may have resulted from piston seizure. If light galling is present, smooth the affected area with No. 400 emery paper and oil or a fine oilstone. However, if galling is severe or if the piston is deeply scored, replace it.
3. Check the piston ring locating pins in the piston (**Figure 51**). The pins should be tight and the piston should show no signs of cracking around the pin. If any one locating pin is loose, replace the piston. A loose pin will fall out and cause severe engine damage.
4. Check the wrist pin clip grooves in the piston for cracks or other damage that could allow a wrist pin clip to fall out. This would cause severe engine damage. Replace the piston if either groove shows signs of wear or damage.
5. Observe the condition of the piston crown (**Figure 52**). Normal carbon buildup can be removed

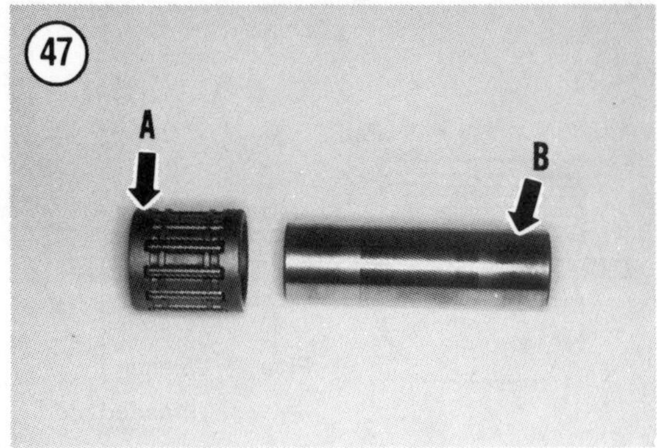

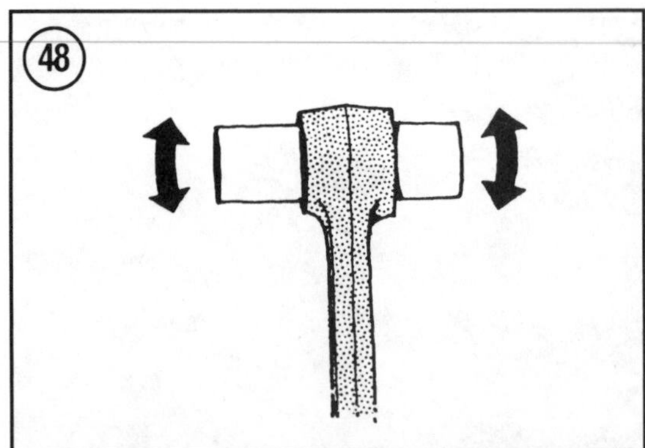

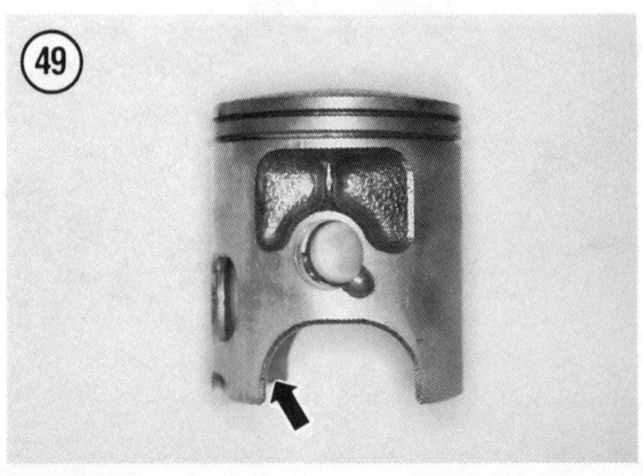

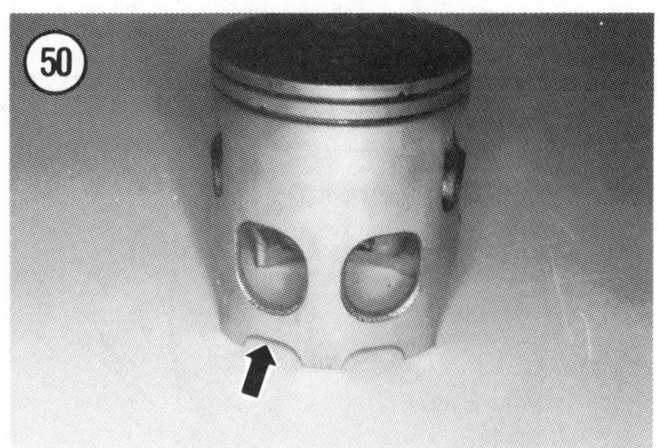

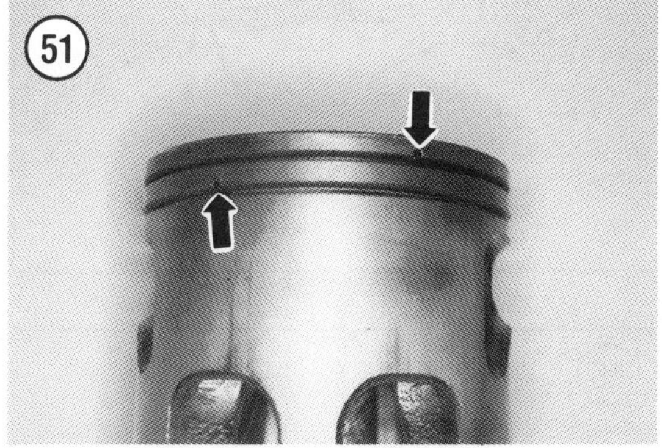

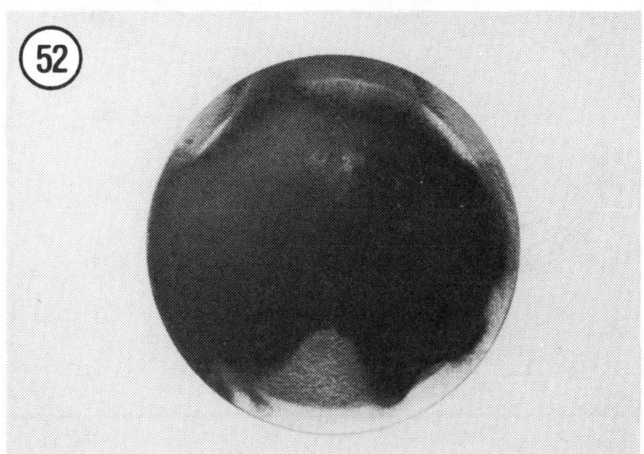

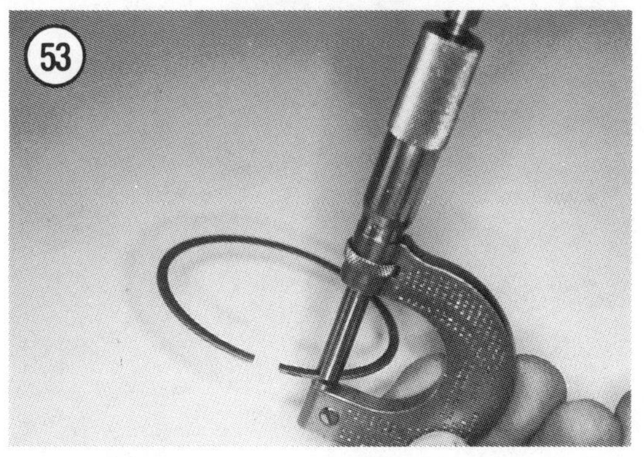

with a wire wheel mounted on a drill press. If the piston shows signs of overheating, pitting or other abnormal conditions, the engine may be experiencing preignition or detonation; both conditions are discussed in Chapter Two.

NOTE
Maintaining proper piston ring end gap helps to ensure peak engine performance. Excessive ring end gap reduces engine performance and can cause overheating. Insufficient ring end gap will cause the ring ends to butt together and cause the ring to break. This would cause severe engine damage.

NOTE
*The upper and lower piston rings are different. To identify the rings, measure their thickness with a caliper or micrometer (**Figure 53**) and compare to the piston ring sectional dimensions listed in **Table 3**.*

NOTE
*For the piston ring end gap measurement to be accurate in Step 6, the cylinder bore inside diameter must be within standard service specifications. Measure the cylinder bore as described under **Cylinder Bore Measurement** in this chapter.*

6. Measure piston ring end gap. Place a ring into the bottom of the cylinder and push it in to a point where cylinder wear is minimal. Measure the gap with a flat feeler gauge (**Figure 54**) and compare to the service limit in **Table 2**. Replace worn out rings.

NOTE
When installing new rings, measure their end gap in the same manner as for old ones.

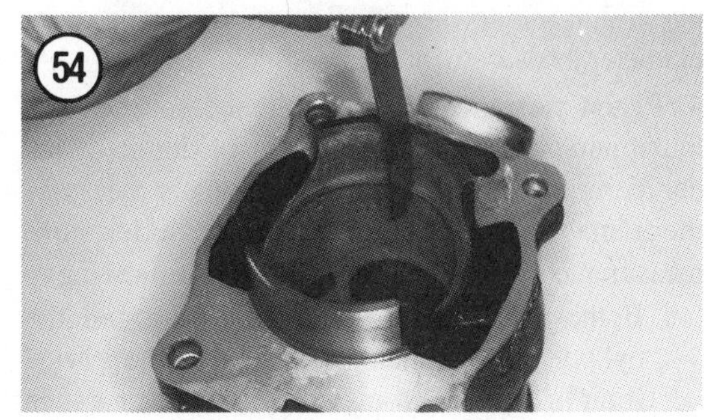

7. Carefully remove all carbon buildup from the ring grooves with a broken ring (**Figure 55**). Inspect the grooves (**Figure 51**) carefully for burrs, nicks, or broken and cracked lands. Recondition or replace the piston if necessary.

8. Install the piston rings onto the piston as described in this chapter. Then measure the side clearance of each ring in its groove with a flat feeler gauge (**Figure 56**) and compare to the service limit in **Table 2**. If the clearance is greater than specified, the rings must be replaced, and if the clearance is still excessive with the new rings, the piston must also be replaced.

9. If the piston appears okay, measure the piston outside diameter as described under *Piston/Cylinder Clearance* in this chapter.

10. If new piston rings are required, the engine should be broken in as if it were new. Refer to *Engine Break-In* in Chapter Five.

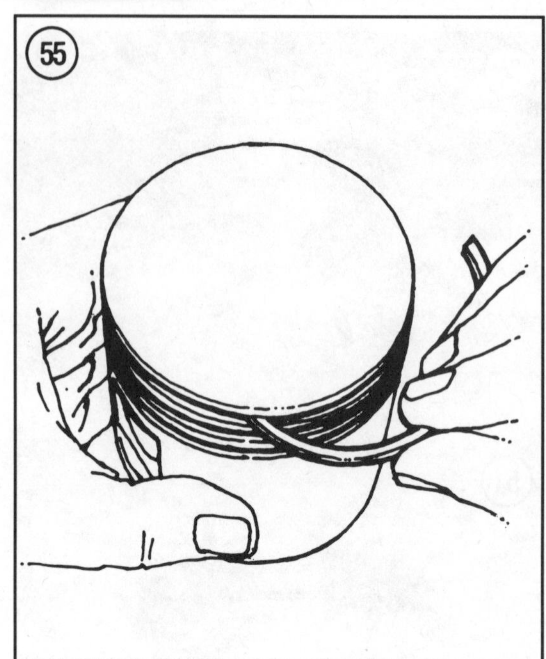

Piston/Cylinder Clearance

A micrometer and bore gauge or inside micrometer (**Figure 57**) are required to measure accurately piston-to-cylinder clearance. If these tools are not available, have the measurements performed by a dealer or machine shop.

1. Wash the piston and cylinder bore in solvent and then dry with compressed air. The cylinder bore and piston skirt must be cleaned thoroughly before attempting any measurement to prevent incorrect readings.

2. Measure the piston diameter at a 90° angle to the piston pin at a point 10 mm (0.39 in.) above the bottom edge of the piston skirt. See **Figure 58**. Record the measurement.

3. Measure the cylinder bore with a bore gauge (**Figure 59**) or an inside micrometer at the 3 points shown in **Figure 60**. Measure in line with the piston pin and at 90° to the pin. Record the largest bore diameter measurement obtained.

4. Piston clearance is the difference between the maximum piston diameter and the maximum cylinder diameter. Subtract the piston diameter measurement made in Step 2 from the cylinder bore measurement made in Step 3. Note the following:

   a. If the piston clearance is excessive and the cylinder bore diameter is not worn to the service limit in **Table 2**, you can correct the clearance

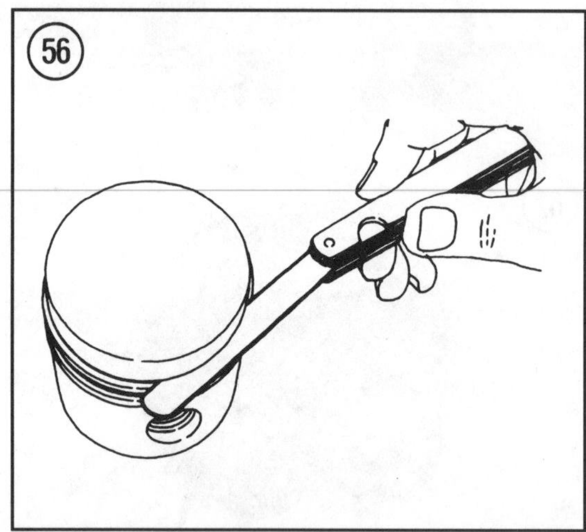

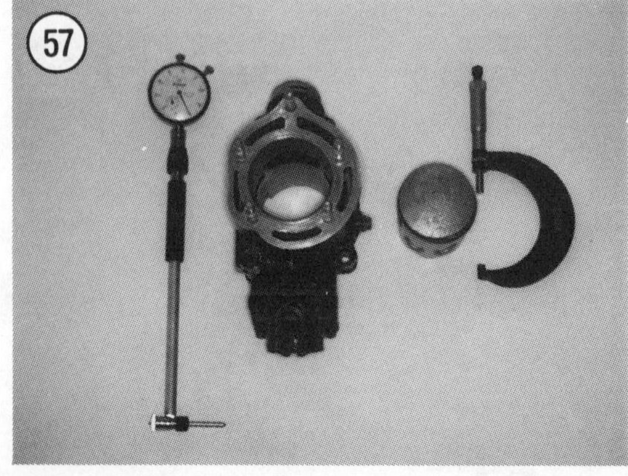

by installing a new piston of the same original diameter.

b. If the clearance is excessive because of a worn cylinder, the cylinder should be bored to match a piston of the next oversize.

5. When installing a new cylinder (or liner), piston and rings, give the vehicle the same break-in procedure you would use on a new machine. Refer to *Engine Break-In* in Chapter Five.

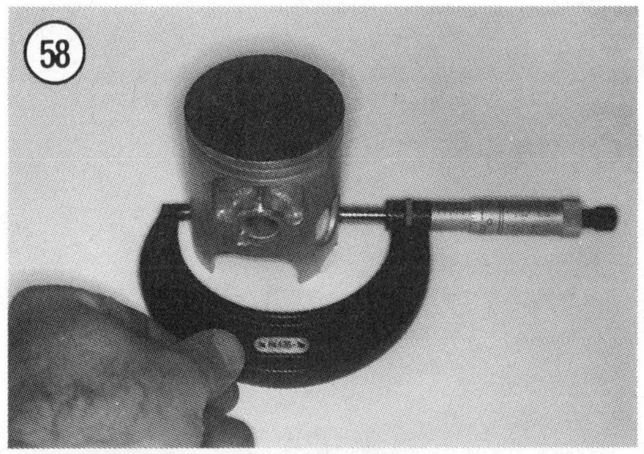

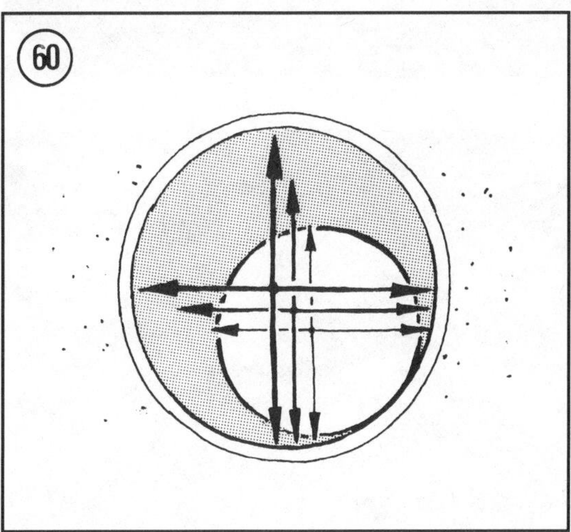

Piston Ring Installation

1. Prior to installing the piston rings, wash the piston and rings in hot soapy water. Then rinse with cold water and dry with compressed air.
2. Identify the piston rings as follows:
   a. If you are installing used rings, install them by referring to your identification marks made during removal.
   b. If you are installing new rings, note that the upper and lower rings are different. To identify the rings, measure their thickness with a caliper or micrometer (**Figure 53**) and compare to the piston ring sectional dimensions listed in **Table 3**.
3. Install the piston rings, first the bottom one, then the top, by carefully spreading the ends of the ring with your thumbs and slipping the ring over the top of the piston (**Figure 61**). Make sure that the marks on the piston rings are toward the top of the piston.

Piston Installation

1. Install the piston rings as described in the previous section.

WARNING
Safety glasses should be worn when performing Step 2.

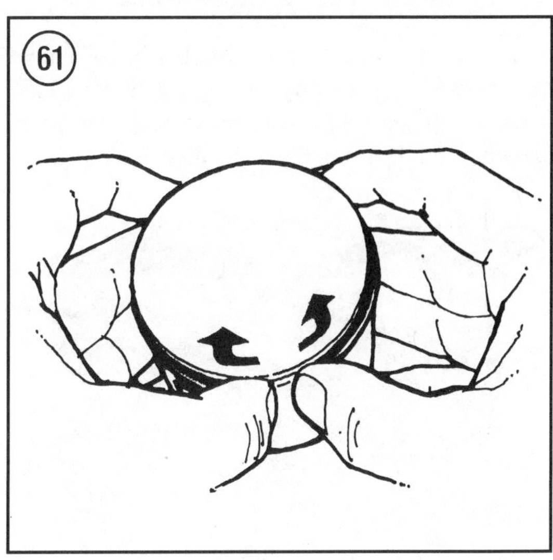

4

2. Install a new wrist pin circlip into the *inner* wrist pin circlip groove (**Figure 62**) in each piston. Make sure each circlip seats in its groove completely
3. Apply assembly oil to the needle bearing and install it in the connecting rod (**Figure 63**).
4. Oil the wrist pin and slide it into the piston until the end of it extends slightly beyond the inside of the boss as shown in **Figure 64**.
5. Place the piston over the connecting rod with the arrow on the piston crown (**Figure 65**) pointing *forward*. Line up the wrist pin with the bearing and push the pin (**Figure 66**) into the piston until it is even with the wrist pin clip grooves.
6. Wrap a clean shop cloth under the piston so that the clips cannot fall into the crankcase.

WARNING
Safety glasses should be worn when performing Step 7.

7. Install a *new* wrist pin circlip (**Figure 67**) into the outer wrist pin circlip groove. Make sure the circlip seats in its groove completely. Note that the inner piston circlips were installed during Step 2.
8. Repeat Steps 3-7 for the opposite piston.
9. Make sure the end gaps of the piston rings are aligned with the locating pins in the ring grooves (**Figure 68**).
10. Install the cylinder blocks as described in this chapter.
11. Follow the *Break-in Procedure* in Chapter Five if new pistons or rings were installed.

REED VALVE ASSEMBLY

A reed valve assembly is installed in the intake tract between each carburetor and cylinder block (**Figure 69**). Particular care must be taken when handling and repairing the reed valve assembly.

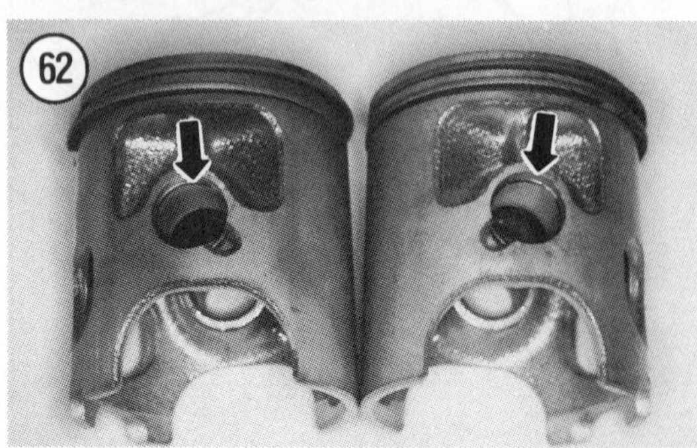
62

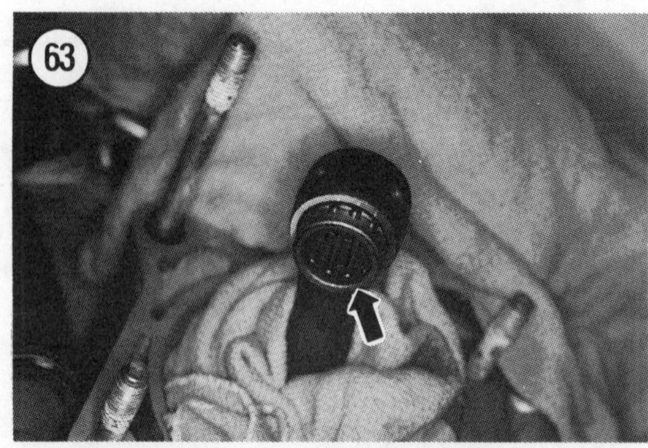
63

64

65

66

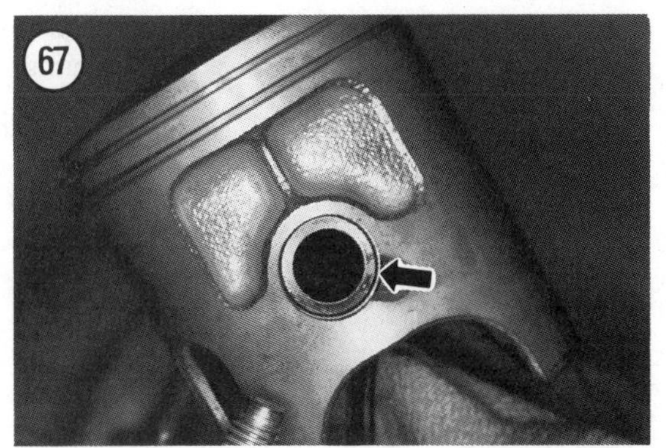

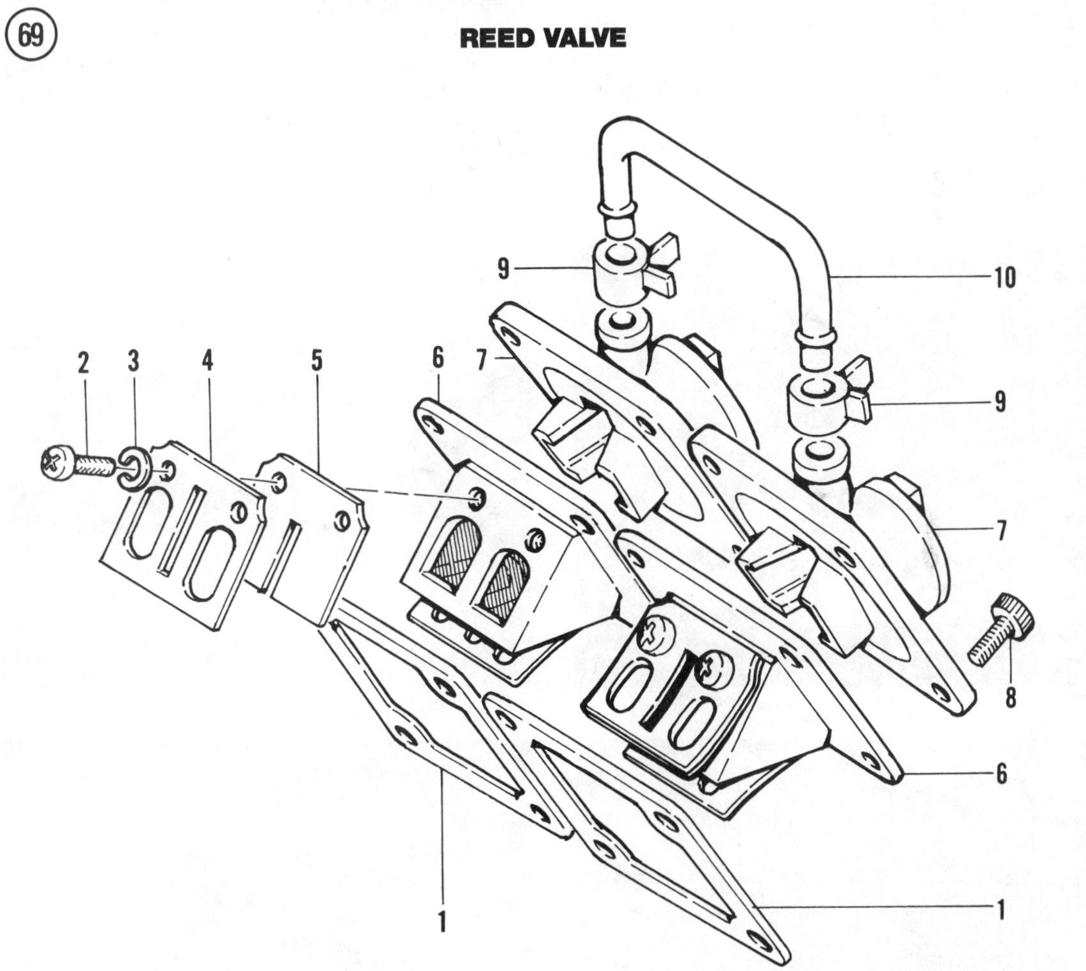

1. Gasket
2. Screw
3. Lockwasher
4. Reed stop
5. Reed valve
6. Reed block
7. Intake manifold
8. Bolt
9. Clamp
10. Pipe

NOTE
If the engine is equipped with an aftermarket reed valve, refer to its manufacturer's instructions on removal, installation and inspection procedures.

Removal

The reed valve can be serviced with the cylinder removed or installed on the engine.

1. If the reed valve (A, **Figure 70**) is going to be removed with the cylinder installed on the engine, note the following:
   a. Clean the area around the reed valve and cylinder.
   b. Remove the carburetor (B, **Figure 70**) as described in Chapter Eight.
   c. Remove the pipe (C, **Figure 70**) from the intake manifolds.
2. Note the position of any hose clamps or guides mounted on the reed valve for reference during reassembly.
3. Remove the bolts securing the intake manifold (**Figure 71**) to the cylinder block and remove the reed valve assembly. See **Figure 72**.
4. Discard the reed cage gasket. If a sealer was used, carefully remove all residue from all mating surfaces.
5. Clean and inspect the reed valve assembly as described in this chapter.

Inspection and Replacement

1. Clean the reed valve assembly in solvent and dry thoroughly.
2. Carefully examine the reed valve assembly (**Figure 73**) for visible signs of wear, breakage, cracks, distortion or other damage.

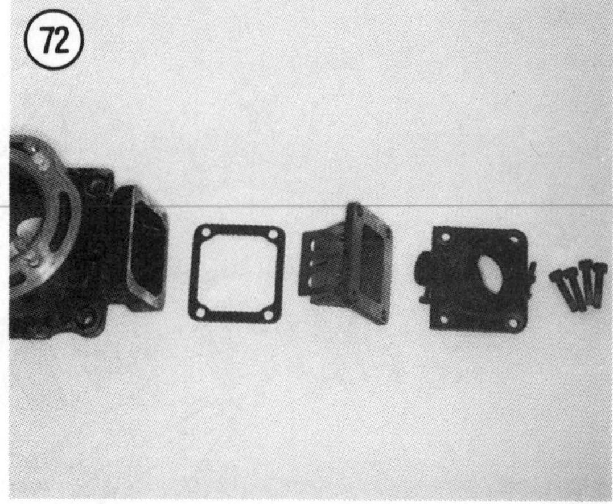

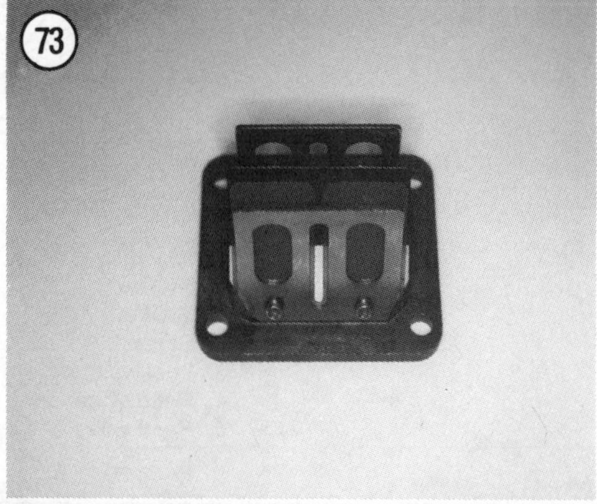

3. Use a flat feeler gauge and measure the clearance between the reed valve and the reed block (**Figure 74**). If the clearance exceeds the service limit dimension in **Table 2**, the reed valves must be replaced.

4. Measure the reed stop height as shown in **Figure 75**. If the height distance is not within the specification listed in **Table 2**, replace the reed stop.

5. Remove the screws securing the reed stop to the reed block. Be careful that the screwdriver does not slip off and damage the reed valves.

6. Carefully examine the reed valves, reed stop, and gasket. Check for signs of cracks, metal fatigue, distortion, or foreign matter damage. Pay particular attention to the rubber gasket seal. The reed stop and reed plates are available as replacement parts, but if the rubber gasket seal is damaged, replace the reed block assembly.

7. Check the threaded holes in the reed cage.

8. Reassemble the unit. Align the cut corner in the reed valve with the cut corner on the reed stop (**Figure 76**). Apply Loctite 242 (blue) to the screw threads prior to installation and tighten securely.

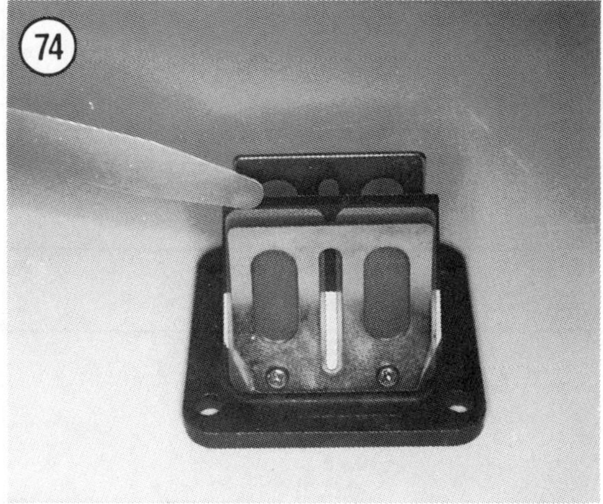

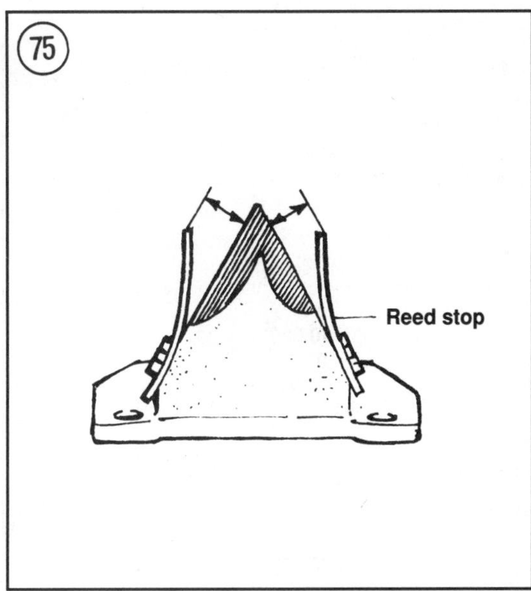

Installation

1. Install a new gasket (A, **Figure 77**) onto the reed block and insert the reed block (B, **Figure 77**) into the cylinder.

2. Install the intake manifold onto the cylinder so that the pipe openings face toward the top as shown in **Figure 71**.

3. Install the intake manifold mounting bolts and tighten evenly in a crisscross pattern to the torque specification in **Table 4**.

4. Repeat to install the opposite intake manifold assembly.

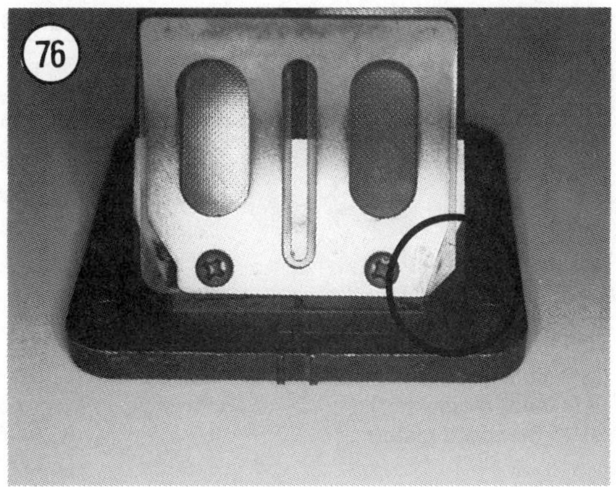

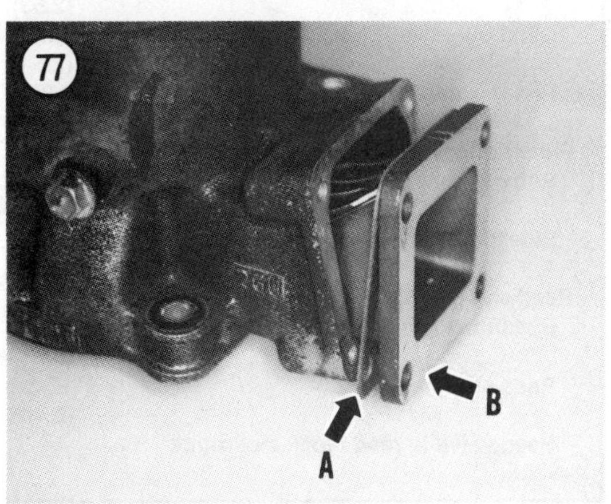

4

5. If the cylinder blocks are installed on the engine, perform the following:
   a. Install the pipe (C, **Figure 70**) into the intake manifolds. Secure the pipe with its hose clamps.

NOTE
*Prior to installing the carburetors, perform the **Two-Stroke Crankcase Pressure Test** procedure in Chapter Two to make sure the intake manifolds are not leaking. If the manifolds are leaking, remove them and apply a sealer to the gaskets.*

   b. Install carburetors (B, **Figure 70**) as described in Chapter Eight.

Table 1 GENERAL ENGINE SPECIFICATIONS

Engine type	Liquid cooled, 2-stroke twin
Induction system	Reed valve
Displacement	347 cc
Bore × stroke	64 × 54 mm (2.520 × 2.126 in.)
Compression ratio	6.5:1
Starting system	Kick starter
Engine lubrication	Premix
Air filter type	Wet type element

Table 2 ENGINE SERVICE SPECIFICATIONS

	New mm (in.)	Service limit mm (in.)
Cylinder head warp limit	—	0.03 (0.0012)
Cylinder		
Bore size	64.00-64.02 (2.520-2.521)	64.1 (2.524)
Taper limit	—	0.05 (0.002)
Out of round limit	—	0.01 (0.0004)
Piston		
Outer diameter		
Standard piston	63.94-64.00 (2.517-2.521)	—
1st oversize	64.25 (2.53)	—
2nd oversize	64.50 (2.54)	—
Piston clearance	0.060-0.065 (0.0024-0.0026)	—
Piston rings		
End gap	0.30-0.45 (0.012-0.018)	0.5 (0.020)
Side clearance	0.02-0.06 (0.0008-0.0024)	0.12 (0.0047)
Reed valve		
Reed thickness	0.37-0.47 (0.0146-0.0185)	—
Reed stop height	10.3-10.7 (0.406-0.421)	—
Reed valve to reed block clearance	—	0.5 (0.02)

Table 3 PISTON RING SECTIONAL DIMENSIONS

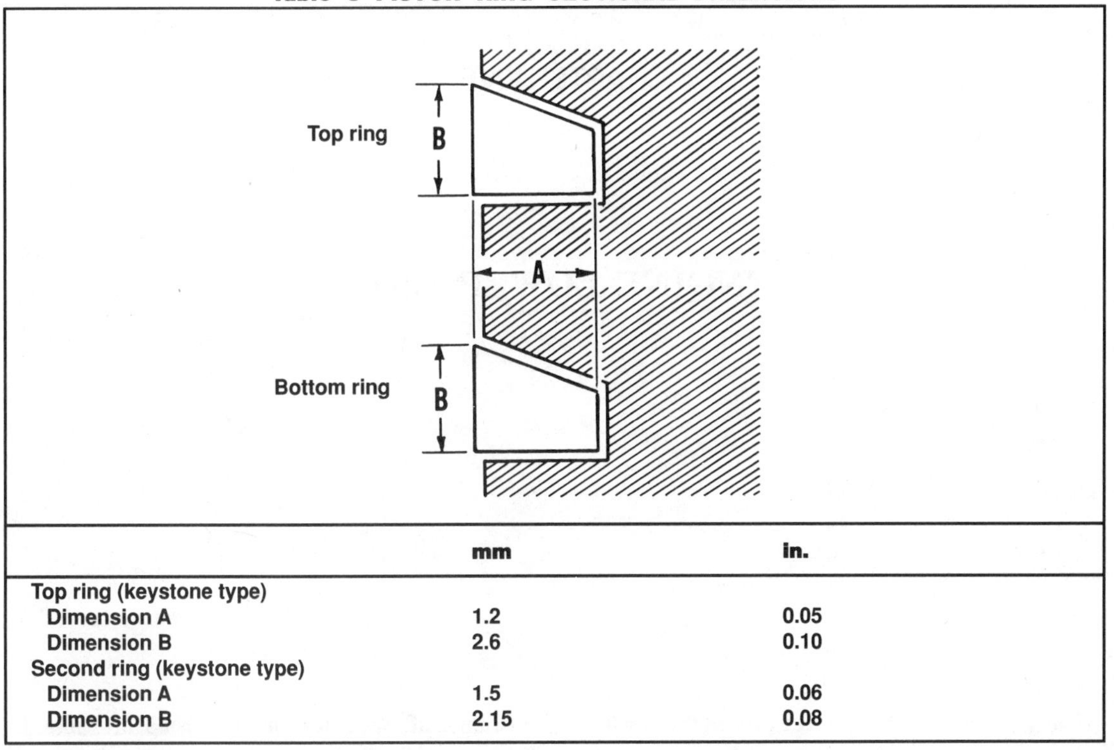

	mm	in.
Top ring (keystone type)		
Dimension A	1.2	0.05
Dimension B	2.6	0.10
Second ring (keystone type)		
Dimension A	1.5	0.06
Dimension B	2.15	0.08

Table 4 ENGINE TIGHTENING TORQUE

	N•m	ft.-lb.
Cylinder head nuts	28	20
Cylinder base nuts	28	20
Intake manifold mounting bolts	10	7.4
Spark plug	20	14
Inlet hose nozzle Allen bolts	12	8

CHAPTER FIVE

ENGINE LOWER END

This chapter describes service procedures for the following lower end components:

a. Crankcases.
b. Crankshaft.
c. Connecting rods.
d. Transmission (removal and installation).
e. Internal shift mechanism (removal and installation).

Before removing and disassembling the crankcase, clean the engine and frame with a good grade commercial degreaser, like Gunk or Bel-Ray engine degreaser or equivalent. It is easier to work on a clean engine and you will do a better job.

Make certain that you have all the necessary tools available, especially any special tool(s), and purchase replacement parts prior to disassembly. Also make sure you have a clean place to work.

It is a good idea to identify and mark parts as they are removed so that errors will be avoided during assembly and installation. Clean all parts thoroughly upon removal, then place them in trays or boxes with their associated mounting hardware. Do not rely on memory alone as it may be days or weeks before you complete the job. In the text there is frequent mention of the left-hand and right-hand side of the engine. This refers to the engine as it sits in the vehicle's frame, not as it sits on your workbench.

Crankshaft specifications are listed in **Table 1**. **Table 1** and **Table 2** are at the end of the chapter.

SERVICING ENGINE IN FRAME

Some of the components can be serviced while the engine is mounted in the frame (the frame is a great holding fixture—especially for breaking loose stubborn bolts and nuts):

a. Cylinder head.
b. Cylinder blocks.
c. Pistons.
d. Carburetors.
e. Reed valves.

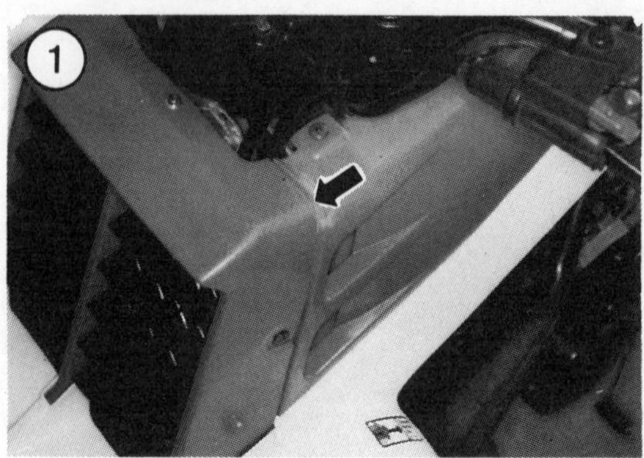

f. Flywheel and stator plate.
g. Water pump.
h. Clutch.
i. External shift mechanism.
j. Primary drive gear.
k. Kickstarter and idler gear.

ENGINE

Removal

If the engine is to be removed for non-engine related service, engine disassembly is not required. Instead, remove the engine as a unit. If service requires crankcase disassembly, use the frame as a holding tool and remove all of the engine sub-assemblies while the engine is mounted in the frame. After the sub-assemblies are removed, the crankcase can be removed as a unit and then serviced as required.

1. Park the vehicle on a level surface and set the parking brake.
2. If the engine is going to be disassembled, drain the clutch/transmission oil as described in Chapter Three.

3. Remove the seat as described in Chapter Fourteen.
4. Remove the radiator cover (**Figure 1**).
5. Remove the fuel tank as described in Chapter Eight.
6. Remove the front and rear fenders as described in Chapter Fourteen.
7. Remove the exhaust system as described in Chapter Eight.
8. Remove the carburetors as described in Chapter Eight.
9. Disconnect the spark plugs caps at each spark plug.
10. Drain the cooling system as described in Chapter Three.

CAUTION
Do not pry the coolant hoses off in the following steps. If you cannot remove a hose, cut the hose so that you don't damage the cylinder head hose pipe(s).

11. Loosen the hose clamp on the outlet hose at the front of the cylinder head (**Figure 2**). Then twist the hose and disconnect it from the cylinder head.
12. Open the bypass hose clamp (A, **Figure 3**) with a pair of pliers and slide it up the hose. Then twist the hose and remove it from the cylinder head.
13. Remove the 2 Allen bolts securing the inlet hose nozzle to the bottom of the cylinder head (B, **Figure 3**).
14. Loosen the clutch cable at the handlebar. Then remove the clutch cable mounting bracket bolt at the engine and disconnect the clutch cable at the release lever (**Figure 4**). Move the cable away from the engine.
15. Remove the shift lever pinch bolt and remove the shift lever.

16. Remove the drive sprocket as described in this chapter.
17. If you are going to disassemble the crankcases, remove the following engine sub-assemblies:
  a. Cylinder head (Chapter Four).
  b. Cylinder blocks (Chapter Four).
  c. Pistons (Chapter Four).
  d. Flywheel (Chapter Nine).
  e. Stator coils (Chapter Nine).
  f. Water pump (Chapter Ten).
  g. Clutch (Chapter Six).
  h. Kickstarter and idler gear (Chapter Six).
  i. Primary drive gear (Chapter Six).
  j. External shift mechanism (Chapter Six).
18. Disconnect the stator plate electrical leads (**Figure 5**).
19. Disconnect the rear master cylinder push rod from the rear brake pedal.
20. Disconnect the breather hose from the crankcase.
21. Remove the bolts and washers (A, **Figure 6**) securing the tension rods to the engine. Then loosen the front tension rod bolt (B, **Figure 6**) and pivot the tension rod away from the engine. Repeat for the opposite tension rod.
22. Prior to removing an assembled engine, perform the following:
  a. Remove the front tension rod mounting bracket bolts (**Figure 7**) and remove both tension rods.
  b. Place a hydraulic jack, with a piece of wood to protect the crankcase, under the engine.
23. Remove the front engine mounting nut and bolt (**Figure 8**).
24. Remove the 2 front engine mounting brackets (**Figure 9**).

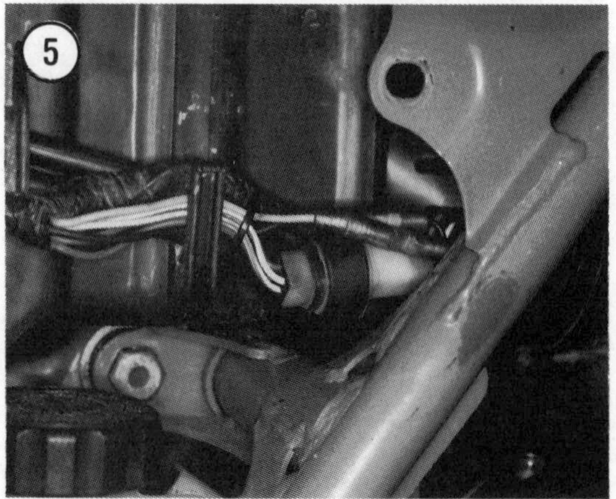

25. Remove the rear engine mounting nut and bolt (**Figure 10**).
26. Remove the engine from the right-hand side.

Cleaning and Inspection

1. Clean all of the engine mount bolts, nuts and mounting brackets in solvent and dry thoroughly.
2. Replace worn, bent or damaged fasteners.

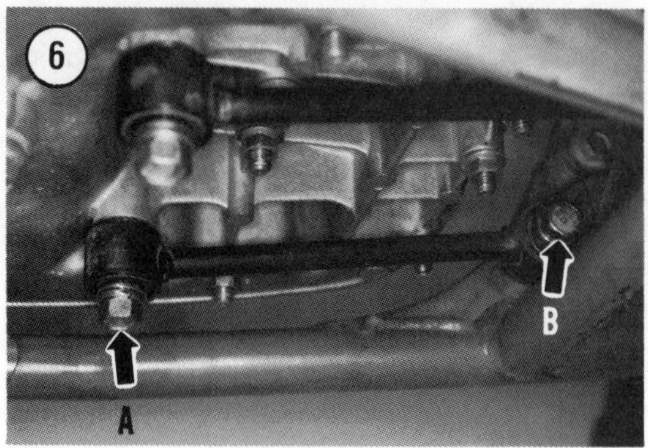

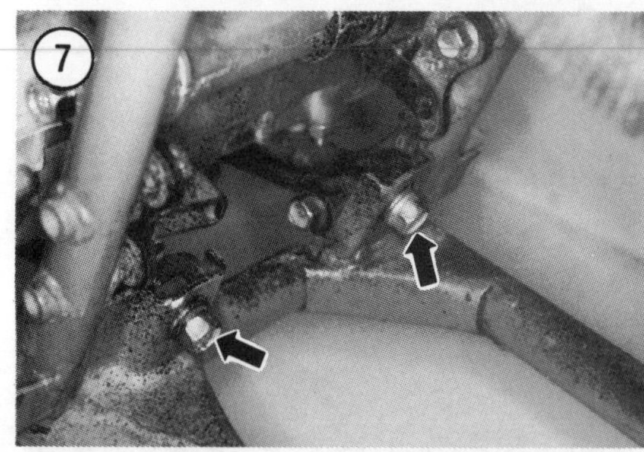

3. Clean the drive sprocket, lockwasher and nut in solvent and dry thoroughly. Inspect the sprocket for wear as described in Chapter Twelve.
4. Check the coolant hoses for cracks, leakage or other damage. Replace if necessary.
5. Check the wire harness routing in the frame. Check the harness cover and wires for chafing or other damage.
6. Clean all of the disconnected electrical connectors with contact cleaner.
7. Check all of the frame engine mount brackets for cracks or other damage.
8. Clean the air filter as described in Chapter Three.
9. Inspect the tension rods (**Figure 11**). If a tension rod is bent, cracked or if its rubber bushings have deteriorated, replace the tension rod(s).

Engine Installation

1. Apply a thin coat of grease to all engine mount bolts before installing them.

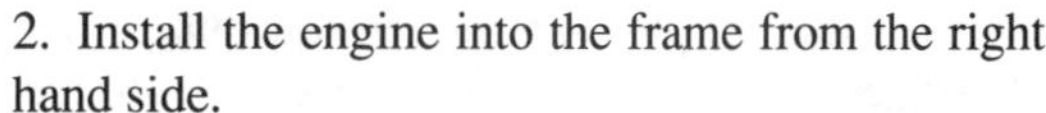

2. Install the engine into the frame from the right-hand side.
3. Install the rear engine mounting bolt (**Figure 10**) from the right-hand side. Install the nut finger-tight.
4. Install 2 front engine mounting brackets (**Figure 9**). Tighten the bolts finger-tight.
5. Install the front engine mounting bolt (**Figure 8**) from the right-hand side. Install the nut finger-tight.
6. Tighten the rear engine mounting bolt (**Figure 10**) to the torque specification in **Table 2**.
7. Tighten the front engine mounting bolts (**Figure 8**) to the torque specification in **Table 2**.
8. Tighten the engine mounting bracket (**Figure 9**) bolts to the torque specification in **Table 2**.
9. Install and tighten tension rods as follows:
   a. If the tension rods were removed, install them so that the rear end (engine side) is angled toward the engine as shown in **Figure 12**. Then tighten the tension rod mounting bracket bolts (**Figure 7**) finger-tight.
   b. Install a lockwasher and flat washer onto the tension rod mounting bolt (A, **Figure 13**) and

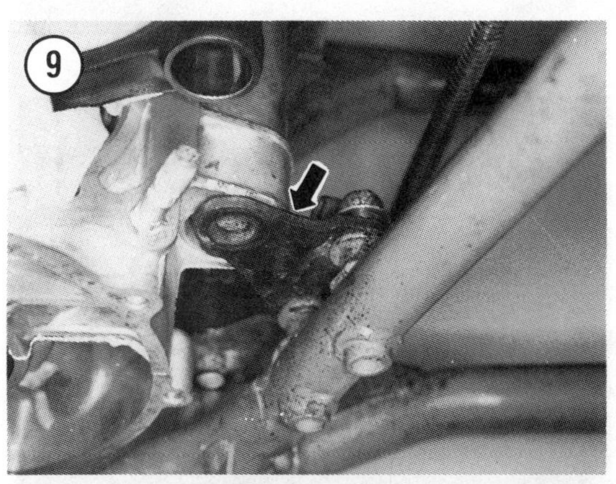

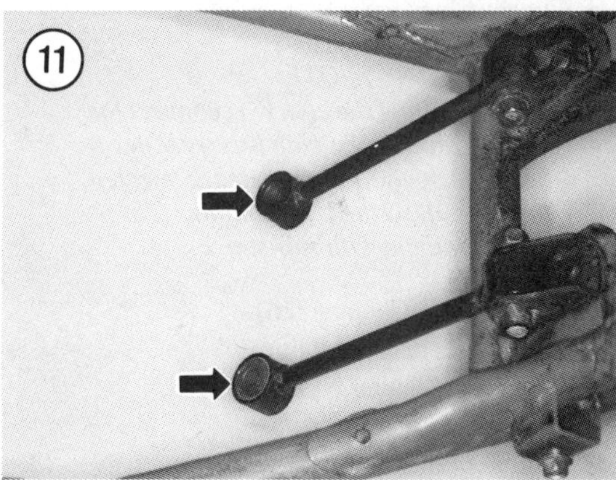

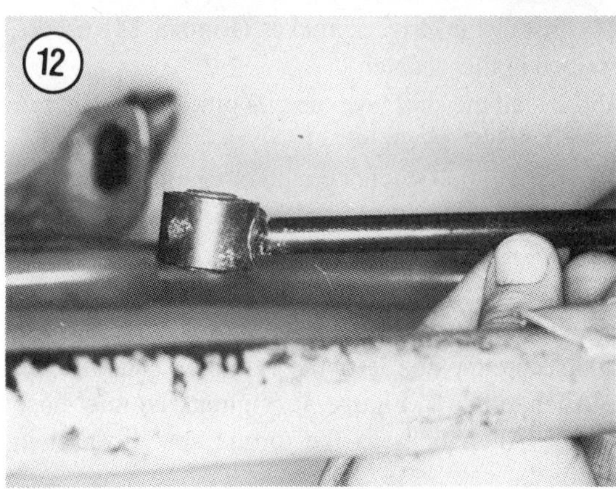

insert the bolt through the tension rod. Install the second flat washer (B, **Figure 13**) onto the bolt as shown.

c. Hand-thread the rear tension rod mounting bolt (**Figure 6**) into the engine and tighten to the torque specification in **Table 2**.
d. Tighten the front tension rod mounting bolt (**Figure 6**) to the torque specification in **Table 2**.
e. Tighten the tension rod mounting bracket bolts (**Figure 7**) to the torque specification in **Table 2**.

10. Reconnect the breather hose at the crankcase.
11. Reconnect the rear master cylinder at the rear brake pedal using a new cotter pin. Bend the cotter pin arms over to lock it in place.
12. Apply Dielectric grease to the stator plate electrical leads and reconnect them (**Figure 5**).
13. If the engine was partially disassembled, install the following engine sub-assemblies:

a. External shift mechanism (Chapter Six).
b. Primary drive gear (Chapter Six).
c. Kickstarter and idler gear (Chapter Six).
d. Clutch (Chapter Six).

NOTE
After installing the clutch, reconnect the clutch cable at the clutch release lever and adjust the clutch release mechanism as described in Chapter Three. Then continue with sub-step e.

e. Water pump (Chapter Ten).
f. Stator coils (Chapter Nine).
g. Flywheel (Chapter Nine).
h. Pistons (Chapter Four).
i. Cylinder blocks (Chapter Four).
j. Cylinder head (Chapter Four).

14. Install the drive sprocket (**Figure 14**) as described in this chapter.
15. Install the shift lever and its pinch bolt. Tighten the pinch bolt securely.
16. If the clutch was not previously removed, reconnect the clutch cable at the engine release lever (**Figure 4**). Then adjust the clutch as described in Chapter Three.
17. Install a new gasket onto the inlet hose nozzle and secure the nozzle to the cylinder head with the 2 Allen bolts (B, **Figure 3**). Tighten the inlet hose nozzle Allen bolts to the torque specification in **Table 2**.
18. Install the bypass hose (A, **Figure 3**) onto the cylinder head nozzle. Secure the hose with the hose clamp.
19. Install the outlet hose onto the front cylinder head hose nozzle (**Figure 2**). Secure the hose with the hose clamp.
20. Refill the cooling system as described in Chapter Three.
21. Reconnect the spark plugs caps.
22. Reinstall the carburetors as described in Chapter Eight.

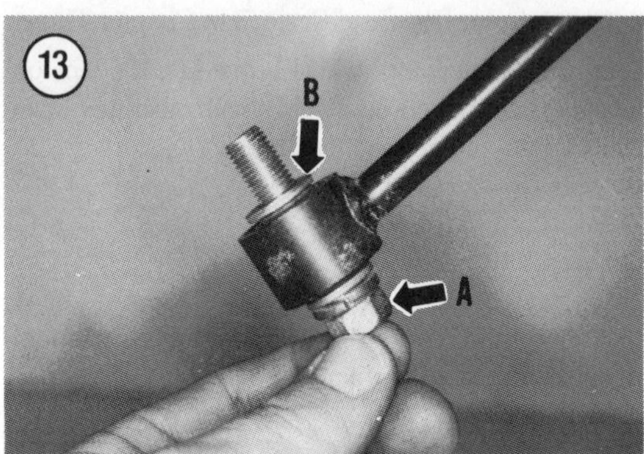

23. Install the exhaust system as described in Chapter Eight.

24. Install the front and rear fenders as described in Chapter Fourteen.

25. Install the fuel tank as described in Chapter Eight.

26. Install the radiator cover (**Figure 1**).

27. Install the seat as described in Chapter Fourteen.

28. Refill the clutch/transmission oil as described in Chapter Three.

29. Before starting the engine, check the following items as described in Chapter Three:
   a. Clutch/transmission oil level.
   b. Coolant level.
   c. Clutch adjustment.
   d. Throttle adjustment.
   e. Drive chain adjustment.

30. Start the engine and check for leaks.

DRIVE SPROCKET

The drive (countershaft) sprocket is mounted on the left end of the transmission countershaft (**Figure 14**). A lockwasher and nut secure the sprocket to the countershaft.

Removal/Installation

1. Remove the shift lever pinch bolt and shift lever.
2. Remove the left-hand side cover (**Figure 15**).
3. Shift the transmission into gear and set the parking brake.

NOTE
If the engine is not mounted in the frame, hold the sprocket with a sprocket holder or similar tool.

4. Flatten the bent-up lockwasher. Then loosen the sprocket nut (turn counterclockwise) and remove the nut, lockwasher and sprocket.
5. Remove the collar (A, **Figure 16**).
6. Install by reversing these steps. Note the following.
7. Check the collar (A, **Figure 16**) for any burrs or rough spots that could tear the oil seal when the spacer is installed.
8. Turn the collar (A, **Figure 16**) when passing it through the oil seal (B).
9. Install the sprocket so that the sprocket teeth number stamped in the sprocket faces out.
10. If you didn't disconnect the drive chain, fit the chain over the sprocket and slide the sprocket onto the countershaft.
11. Replace the lockwasher (**Figure 17**) if damaged.
12. Tighten the drive sprocket nut (**Figure 18**) to the torque specification in **Table 2**. Then bend the lockwasher so that one tab seats against one flat on the sprocket nut.

5

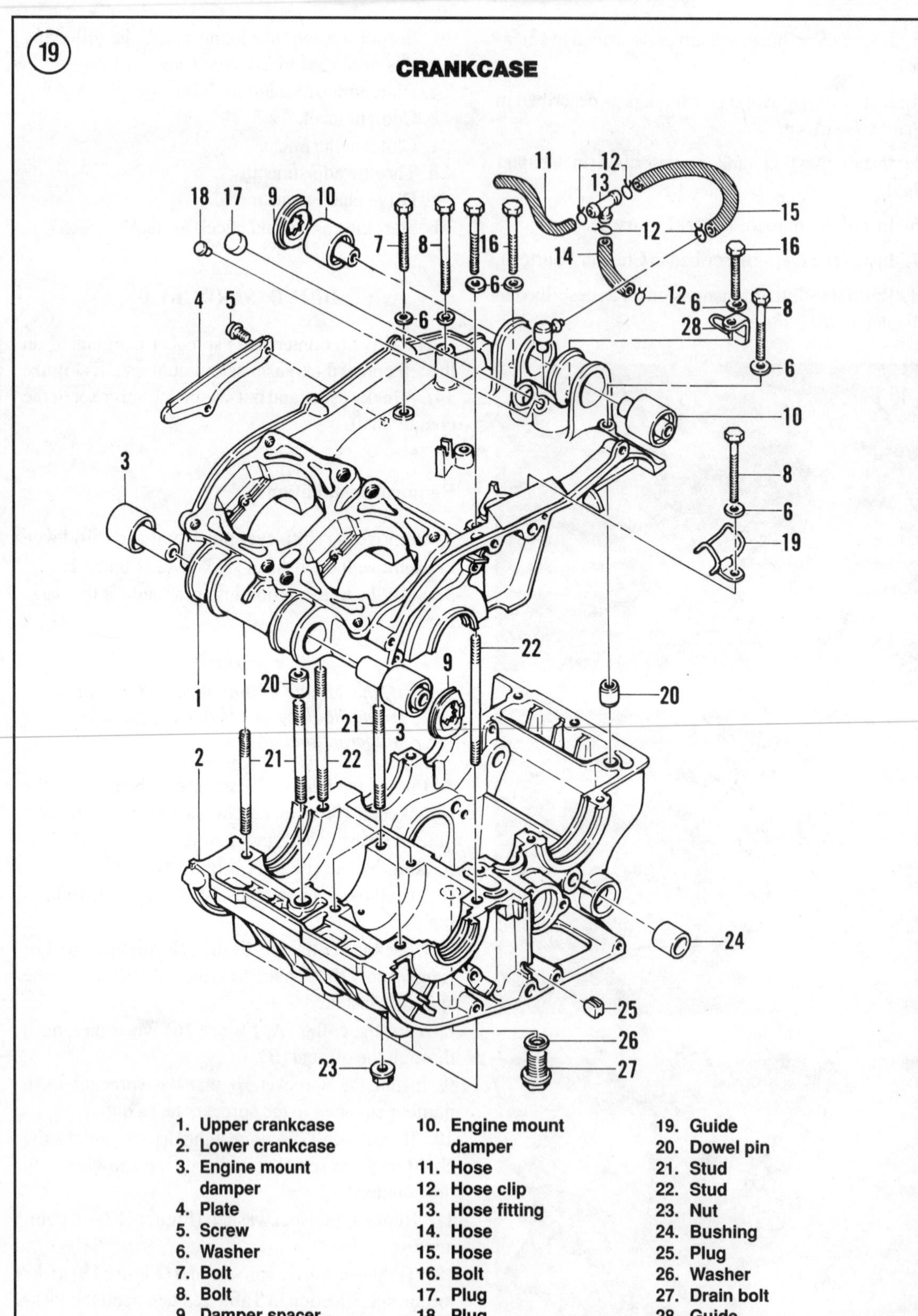

1. Upper crankcase
2. Lower crankcase
3. Engine mount damper
4. Plate
5. Screw
6. Washer
7. Bolt
8. Bolt
9. Damper spacer
10. Engine mount damper
11. Hose
12. Hose clip
13. Hose fitting
14. Hose
15. Hose
16. Bolt
17. Plug
18. Plug
19. Guide
20. Dowel pin
21. Stud
22. Stud
23. Nut
24. Bushing
25. Plug
26. Washer
27. Drain bolt
28. Guide

CRANKCASE AND CRANKSHAFT

Disassembly of the crankcase, splitting the cases, and removal of the crankshaft assembly require that the engine be removed from the frame. However, the cylinder head, cylinders and all other attached assemblies should be removed with the engine in the frame.

The crankcase (**Figure 19**) is made in 2 halves of precision diecast aluminum alloy and is of the "thin-walled" type. To avoid damage do not hammer or pry on any of the interior or exterior projected walls. These areas are easily damaged if stressed beyond the limit of their design. They are assembled without a gasket; only gasket sealer is used while dowel pins align the crankcase halves when they are bolted together. The crankcase halves are sold as a matched set only. If one crankcase half is damaged and cannot be repaired, both must be replaced.

Crankshaft components are available as individual parts. However crankshaft service—replacement of unsatisfactory parts or crankshaft alignment should be entrusted to a dealer or engine specialist. Special measuring and alignment tools, a hydraulic press and the experience to use them are necessary to disassemble, reassemble and accurately align the crankshaft assembly, which, in the case of the average twin cylinder engine, is made up of 7 pressed-together pieces, not counting the bearings, seals and connecting rods. You can save considerable expense by disassembling the engine and taking the crankshaft in for service.

The procedure which follows is presented as a complete, step-by-step major lower end overhaul that should be followed if the engine is to be completely reconditioned.

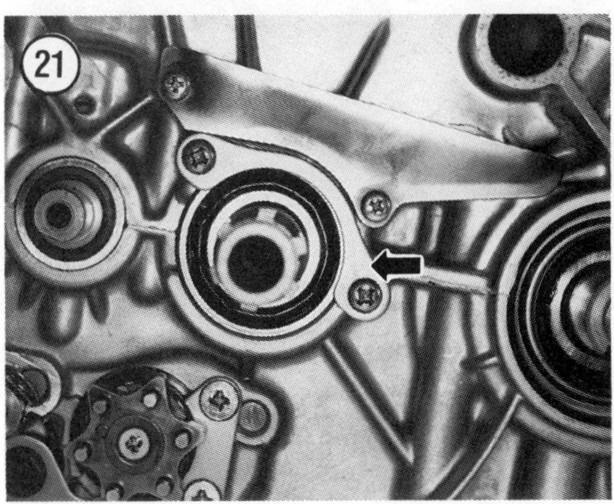

Crankcase Disassembly

This procedure describes disassembly of the crankcase halves and removal of the crankshaft, transmission and internal shift mechanism.

Refer to **Figure 19**.

1. Remove all exterior engine assemblies as follows:
   a. Engine top end (Chapter Four).
   b. Clutch (Chapter Six).
   c. Water pump drive gear and primary drive gear (Chapter Six).
   d. Kickstarter (Chapter Six).
   e. Idler gear (Chapter Six).
   f. External shift mechanism (Chapter Six).
   g. Flywheel and stator plate (Chapter Nine).
2. Remove the engine from the frame as described in this chapter.
3. Remove the shift drum plate screws. Then remove the plate and O-ring (**Figure 20**).
4. Remove the bearing stopper plate screws and remove the stopper plate (**Figure 21**).

CAUTION
Make sure to remove the entire external shift mechanism assembly as described in Chapter Six.

5. Turn the engine so that it rests upside-down on the workbench.
6. Loosen the lower crankcase nuts (**Figure 22**) 1/4 turn at a time in a crisscross pattern. Remove the nuts.
7. Turn the engine over so that the upper side faces up.

5

8. Loosen the upper crankcase bolts (**Figure 23**) 1/4 turn at a time in a crisscross pattern. Remove the bolts.

9. Remove the clutch release lever assembly (**Figure 24**).

10. Tap on the large bolt bosses with a soft mallet to separate the crankcase halves. Then remove the upper crankcase half (**Figure 25**).

11. Remove the 2 dowel pins (**Figure 26**).

12. Remove the countershaft (**Figure 27**) assembly.

13. Remove the mainshaft (**Figure 28**) assembly.

NOTE

If necessary, service the transmission assembly as described in Chapter Seven.

14. Remove the 2 countershaft bearing clips (**Figure 29**) from the lower crankcase grooves.

15. Lift the crankshaft (**Figure 30**) out of the lower crankcase and remove it.

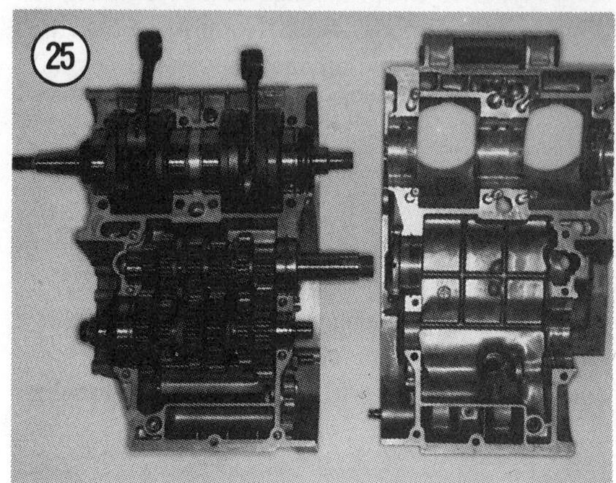

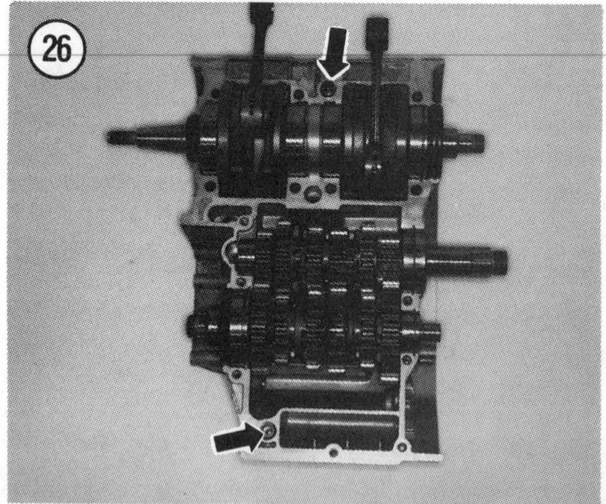

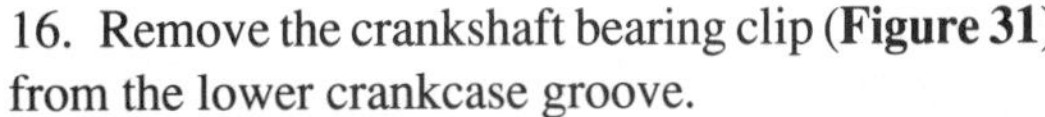

16. Remove the crankshaft bearing clip (**Figure 31**) from the lower crankcase groove.

17. Remove the internal shift mechanism (**Figure 32**) as follows:

   a. Straighten the lockwasher tab and loosen the adjust bolt locknut (A, **Figure 33**). Then remove the adjust bolt with a straight-tipped screwdriver.

   b. Remove the shift drum locating plate screws and remove the plate (B, **Figure 33**).

   c. Remove the E-clip from the groove in each shift fork shaft. See **Figure 34**.

NOTE
*Identify and store the shift forks and shafts (**Figure 35**) so that they can be reinstalled in their original position.*

d. Remove the shift fork shafts and remove the shift forks. See **Figure 36**, typical.
e. Remove the shift drum (**Figure 37**).

18. Clean and inspect the crankcase and crankshaft as described in this chapter.

19. Service the transmission and internal shift mechanism as described in Chapter Seven.

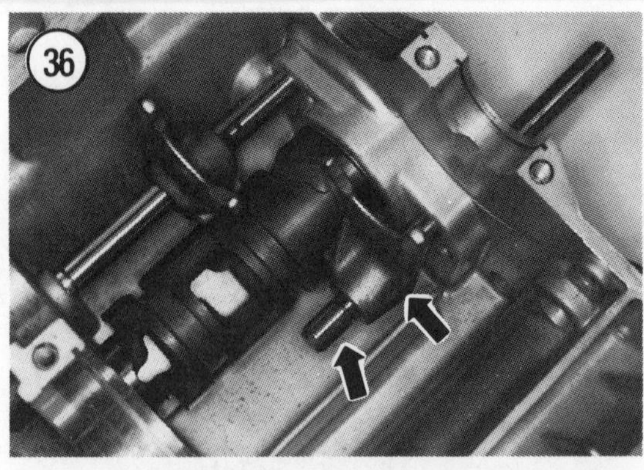

Crankcase Cleaning and Inspection

1. If necessary, replace the clutch release lever oil seal and bearing as described in this chapter.

2. Carefully remove all gasket and gasket residue from all mating surfaces.

3. Clean both crankcase halves in cleaning solvent. Dry with compressed air.

4. After cleaning in solvent, clean the cases in hot soapy water, then rinse thoroughly with clear water.

5. Dry the case halves and bearings with compressed air if available. Lubricate the clutch release needle bearing with clutch oil.

6. Carefully inspect the cases for cracks and fractures; see **Figure 38** and **Figure 39**. Also check the areas around the stiffening ribs, around bearing bosses and threaded holes. If any are found, have them repaired by a shop specializing in the welding and machining of precision aluminum castings. If the damaged cases cannot be repaired, they must be replaced as a set.

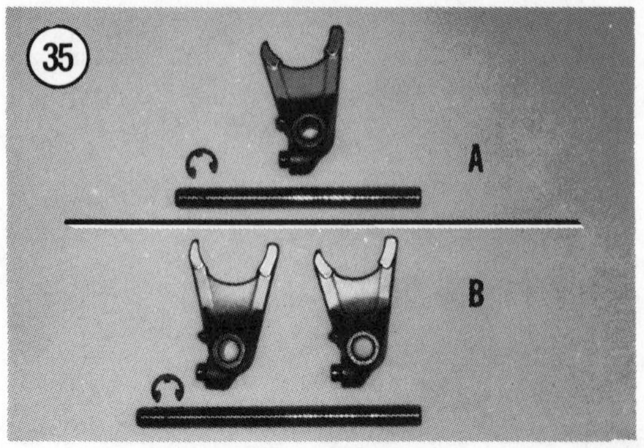

NOTE
Some crankcase repairs can be accomplished in the home workshop with a cold weld chemical, such as J-B Weld. However, if machining is required, and you are not equipped to do so, it is better to refer all repair to a qualified mechanic or machine shop.

7. Inspect machined surfaces for burrs, cracks or other damage. You may be able to repair minor damage with a fine-cut file or oilstone. Otherwise, the mating surface will have to be welded and then machined flat.

8. Inspect all of the bearing clip grooves (**Figure 40**) for cracks or other damage.

9. Inspect the front (**Figure 41**) and rear (**Figure 42**) engine mount damper assemblies. If the rubber dampers are severely worn, cracked or deteriorated, replace them. **Figure 19** shows the individual damper assemblies.

10. Where damper spacers are used, install them with their "UP" (**Figure 43**) mark facing up. See **Figure 44** and **Figure 45**.

11. Inspect the crankcase studs (**Figure 46**). If a stud(s) is bent, damaged or loose, replace or reinstall it as described under *Crankcase Stud Replacement* in this chapter.

12. Check all of the crankcase threaded holes for stripping, cross-threading or deposit buildup. Threaded holes should be blown out with compressed air as dirt and sealer in the bottom of the hole may prevent the screw from being torqued properly. If necessary, use a tap to true up threads and to remove deposits.

13. Replace damaged crankcase dowel pins (**Figure 47**).

Crankcase Stud Replacement

The upper crankcase is equipped with 8 studs (**Figure 46**). When purchasing replacement studs, make sure to order the correct stud as 2 different length studs are used. See **Figure 19**.

1. Measure the stud's installed height prior to removing it (A, **Figure 48**).

2. Thread 2 nuts (B, **Figure 48**) onto the stud to be removed and tighten them together. See **Figure 49**.

NOTE

If the stud threads are damaged, remove the stud(s) with a commercial type stud remover.

3. With a wrench on the lower nut, loosen and remove the stud (**Figure 50**).

4. Clean the crankcase threads with contact cleaner and dry with compressed air.

5. Apply Loctite 262 (red) onto the stud threads (longer end [**Figure 51**]) and hand-thread the stud into the crankcase. Install and tighten the 2 nuts onto

47

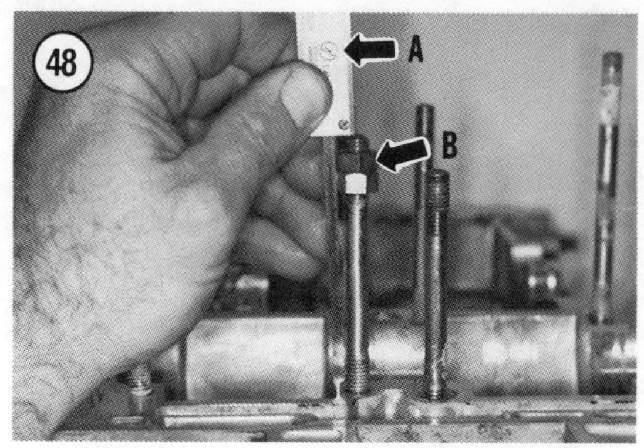

48

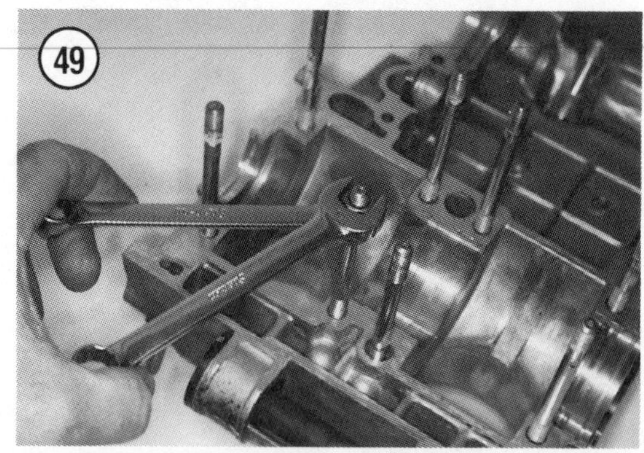
49

46

50

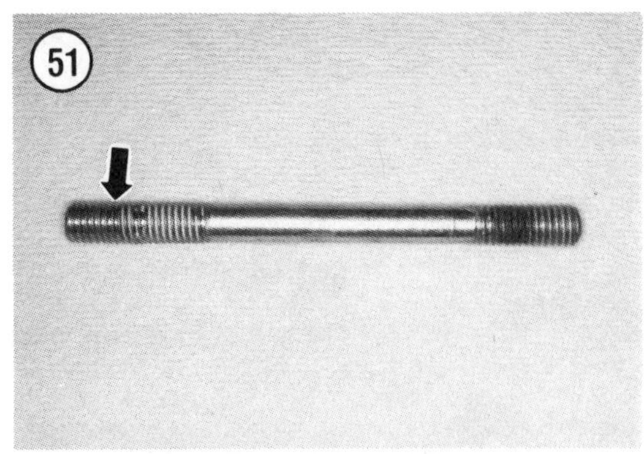

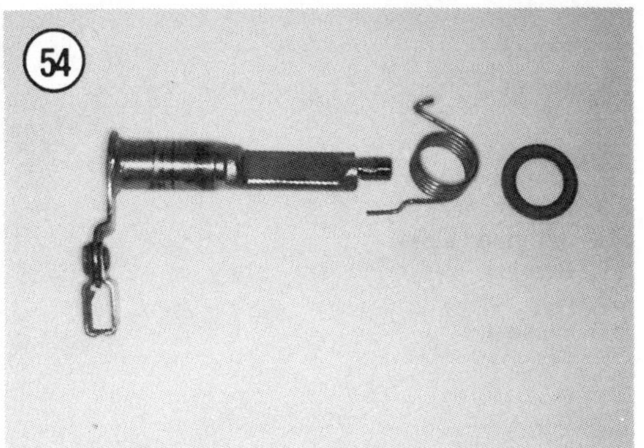

the stud and tighten the stud until its installed length is the same as that recorded prior to removal.

6. Remove the 2 nuts from the stud.
7. Repeat to install remaining studs.
8. After installing the stud(s), check their installed length by assembling the crankcase halves. Check that each stud has the same number of exposed threads; see **Figure 52**.

Clutch Release Lever Oil Seal and Bearing Inspection and Replacement

The clutch release lever needle bearing and oil seal are located in the upper crankcase. While the following procedures show the engine disassembled, the oil seal and bearing can be replaced with the engine assembled and mounted in the frame.

Because removing the oil seal and needle bearing destroys them, do not remove these parts for routine inspection and cleaning. When disassembling the engine, the oil seal should be replaced as part of engine reassembly. If the engine is assembled and the oil seal (**Figure 53**) is leaking, inspect the clutch release lever shaft (**Figure 54**) for burrs, scoring or other damage that could damage the oil seal. Recondition the shaft with emery cloth or a fine-cut file or replace the shaft.

1. Pry the oil seal out of the crankcase with a wide-blade screwdriver (**Figure 55**). Pad the screwdriver with a shop cloth to prevent the screwdriver from damaging the case.
2. Check the needle bearing. Because needle bearing wear is hard to determine, first inspect the bearing for visual damage. If any damage is noted, replace the bearing. If the bearing appears to be okay, install the clutch release lever through the bearing

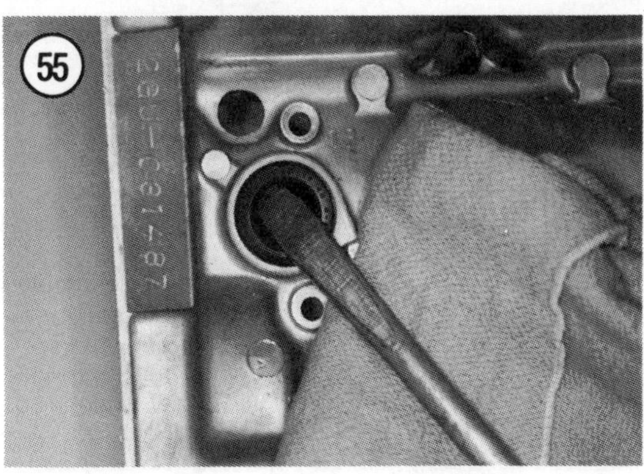

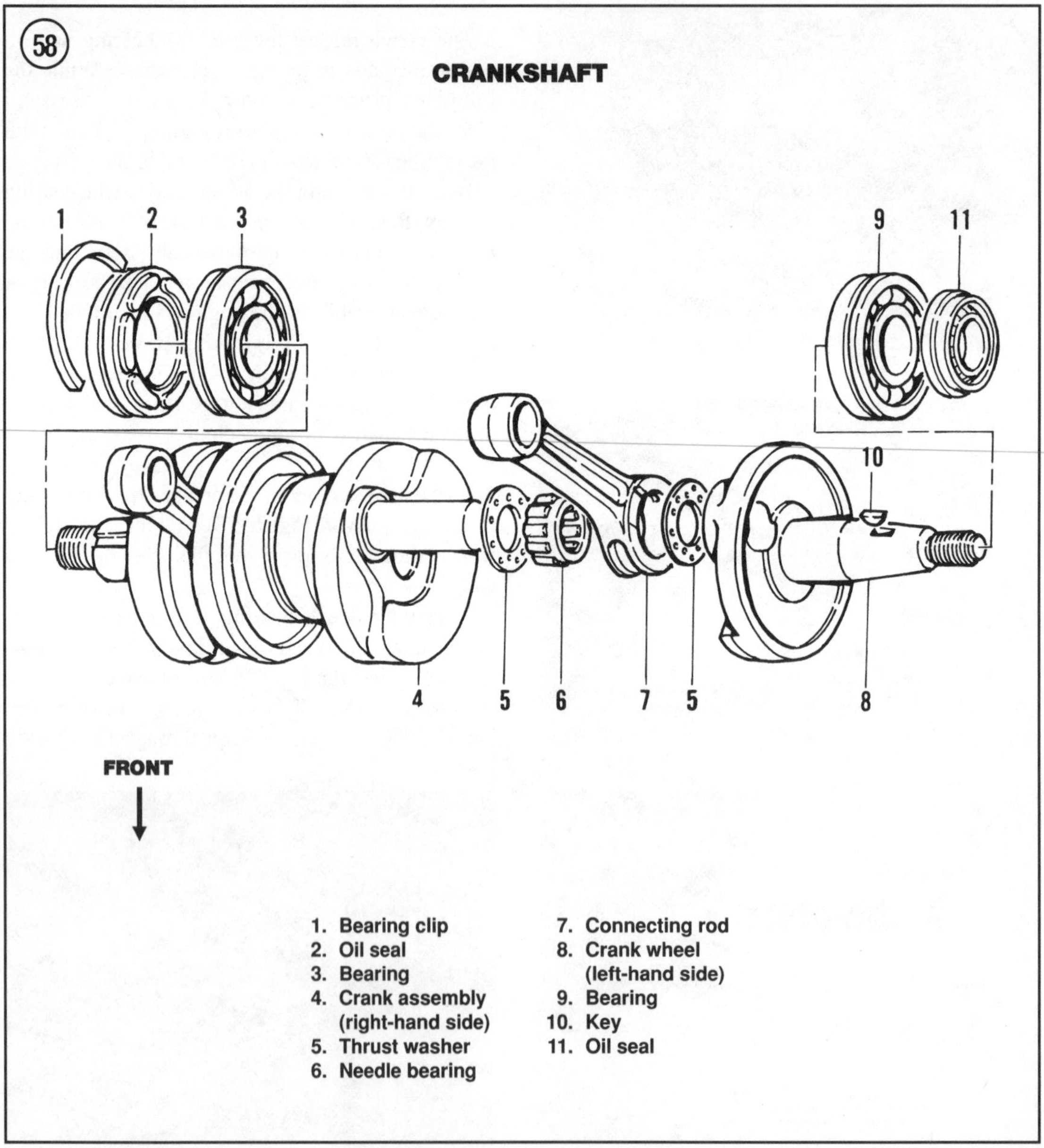

58

CRANKSHAFT

1 2 3 9 11 10 4 5 6 7 5 8

FRONT

1. Bearing clip
2. Oil seal
3. Bearing
4. Crank assembly (right-hand side)
5. Thrust washer
6. Needle bearing
7. Connecting rod
8. Crank wheel (left-hand side)
9. Bearing
10. Key
11. Oil seal

and turn the lever, checking for excessive play or other abnormal conditions. If necessary, replace the bearing as described in Step 3.

CAUTION
Removing the needle bearing will damage it. Do not remove the needle bearing for inspection or cleaning.

3. To replace the needle bearing (**Figure 56**), perform the following:
   a. Remove the needle bearing (**Figure 56**) with a suitable pilot bearing remover. If the engine is disassembled, support the upper crankcase carefully.
   b. Clean the needle bearing bore with solvent and dry with compressed air. Inspect the bore for cracks or other damage.
   c. Align the new needle bearing with the bearing bore so that its manufacturer's marks and size code faces up. Then press the bearing into the case until it bottoms out.
   d. After installing the bearing, check that the needles turn freely with no binding or other damage.
4. To install a new oil seal (**Figure 53**), perform the following:
   a. Pack the oil seal lip with a waterproof bearing grease.

   b. Place the oil seal into the bearing bore with its manufacturer's marks facing out. Then press in the oil seal until its outer surface is flush with the bearing bore inside surface as shown in **Figure 53**.

Shift Shaft Oil Seal Replacement

The shift shaft oil seal (**Figure 57**) is mounted in the lower crankcase and should be replaced prior to engine reassembly.

1. Pry the oil seal out of the crankcase with a wide-blade screwdriver. Pad the screwdriver with a shop cloth to prevent the screwdriver from damaging the case.
2. Clean the oil seal bore with solvent and dry thoroughly.
3. Pack the oil seal lip with a waterproof bearing grease.
4. Place the oil seal into the crankcase with its manufacturer's marks facing out. Then press in the oil seal until it bottoms out. See **Figure 57**.

Crankshaft Inspection

Because the crankshaft operates under severe stress, service tolerances are critical and must be maintained. Worn connecting rods, lower end bearings or an out-of-true crankshaft can cause severe engine damage if a failure occurs.

Table 1 lists tolerances and wear limits for the crankshaft. If you do not have all of the measuring tools as described in this section, take the crankshaft to a dealer and have them check it for you.

If you have disassembled the engine because of secondary damage that is not related to the crankshaft (e.g., piston seizure, piston skirt damage, etc.), the lower end bearings may have been damaged or contaminated. Check both connecting rods and lower end bearings carefully.

An exploded view of the crankshaft is shown in **Figure 58**.

1. Remove the left- (**Figure 59**) and right-hand (**Figure 60**) oil seals. Discard the oil seals.

NOTE
Even though the oil seals may appear okay, new seals should be installed when reassembling the engine. This will

5

help ensure that the crankcase is air tight during engine operation.

2. Install a dial indicator so that its stem is positioned against the connecting rod small end as shown in **Figure 61**. Zero the dial gauge. Then hold the connecting rod big end in place with one hand and attempt to rock the connecting rod back and forth with your other hand. The reading on the dial indicator is connecting rod small end free play. If the play meets or exceeds the service limit in **Table 1**, the connecting rods must be replaced and the crankshaft rebuilt.
3. Insert a flat feeler gauge between the crankshaft and connecting rod as shown in **Figure 62** and measure connecting rod side clearance. If the clearance exceeds the service specification in **Table 1**, the connecting rods must be replaced and the crankshaft rebuilt.
4. Repeat Steps 2 and 3 for the opposite connecting rod.
5. Basic crankshaft width specifications can be measured with a vernier caliper as shown in **Figure 63** (wheel width) and **Figure 64** (assembly width). Compare with the specifications listed in **Table 1**.
6. Turn each crankshaft bearing (**Figure 65**) by hand. The bearings should turn smoothly with no roughness, catching, binding or excessive noise. Some axial play (end play) is normal, but radial play should be negligible; see **Figure 66**. Severely worn or damaged bearings should be replaced.
7. Support the crankshaft by placing it on 2 V-blocks at the points (A, **Figure 65**). Then measure

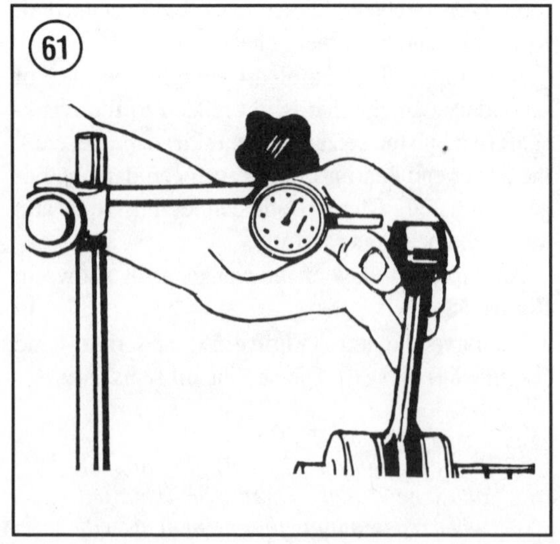
61

62

63

64

65

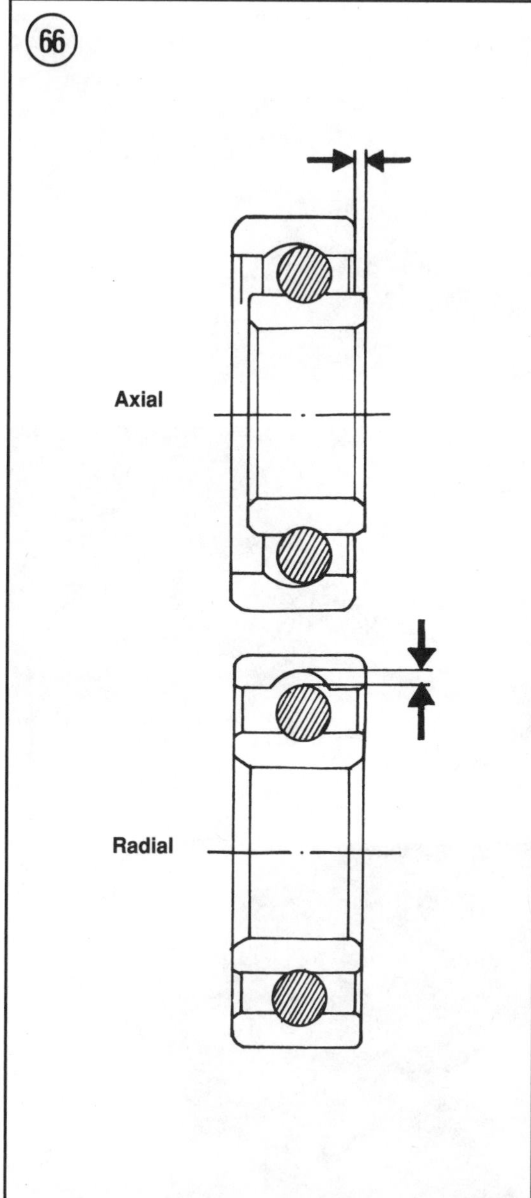

runout with a dial indicator at the points (B, **Figure 65**) shown in **Table 1**. Turn the crankshaft slowly and note the gauge reading. The maximum difference recorded is the crankshaft runout at that position. If the runout at any position exceeds the service limit in **Table 1**, the crankshaft should be trued by an experienced mechanic.

8. Check the left-hand crankshaft end (**Figure 67**) for:
   a. Damaged threads (A).
   b. Damaged crankshaft taper (B).
   c. Damaged keyway (C).
9. Check the right-hand crankshaft end (**Figure 68**) for:
   a. Damaged keyway (A).
   b. Damaged threads (B).
10. Refer all crankshaft repair and overhaul to a Yamaha dealer or qualified specialist.

Crankshaft Installation

Refer to **Figure 58** when performing this procedure.

1. Pack the lip of each crankshaft oil seal with a waterproof grease (**Figure 69**).

2. To install the left-hand oil seal (11, **Figure 58**):
   a. The left-hand oil seal has its manufacturer's marks imprinted on one side and a green mark on the other side.
   b. Install the oil seal (**Figure 70**) onto the crankshaft so that the side with the green mark faces toward the outside (away from crankshaft). See **Figure 71**.
3. To install the right-hand oil seal (2, **Figure 58**):
   a. The right-hand oil seal has notches on one side.
   b. Install the oil seal onto the crankshaft so that the notches face toward the inside (against crankshaft) as shown in **Figure 72**.
4. Support the lower crankcase on wooden blocks so that when the crankshaft is installed in the following steps, the connecting rods can hang down without contacting the workbench.
5. Install the bearing clip into the lower crankcase groove as shown in **Figure 73**.

NOTE

Step 6 describes crankshaft installation. However, because of the number of separate steps required, read Step 6 through first before actually installing the crankshaft.

6. Align the crankshaft with the lower crankcase half and install the crankshaft (**Figure 74**) while noting the following:
   a. Turn each bearing so that its pin is facing up; see **Figure 65**. Then, when installing the crankshaft, these pins will seat into the crankcase notches shown in A, **Figure 75**, **Figure 76** and A, **Figure 77**.
   b. Align the groove in the right-hand bearing with the bearing clip (B, **Figure 77**) when installing the crankshaft.
   c. Engage the outer ring on each oil seal with the corresponding groove in the crankcase. See B, **Figure 75** and C, **Figure 77**.
   d. Double check to make sure that all of the bearings and oil seals are seated properly.

Transmission Installation and Crankcase Assembly

This procedure describes complete assembly of the crankcase halves. If the transmission shafts were serviced, refer to Chapter Seven and check that all

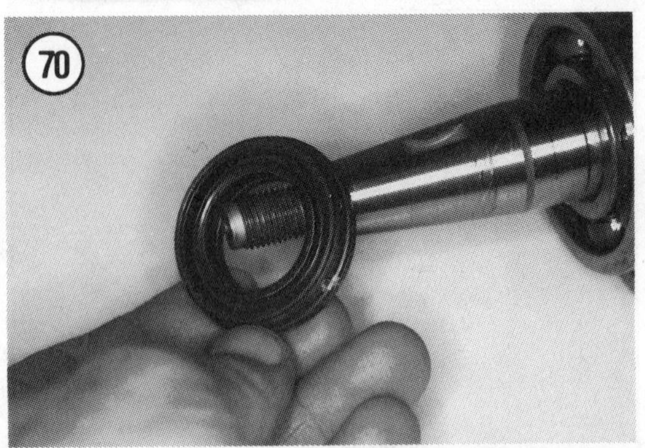

of the gears and circlips are properly installed on their respective shafts.

1. Install the crankshaft into the lower crankcase half as described in this chapter.

NOTE
*Refer to **Figure 78** when installing the internal shift mechanism in the following steps.*

2. Install the shift drum into the lower crankcase as shown in **Figure 79**.

NOTE
*Yamaha refers to the shift forks as shift fork No. 1 and shift fork No. 2. The No. 1 (A, **Figure 80**) shift fork (quantity 2) and No. 2 (B) shift fork (quantity 1) are identified in **Figure 78** and **Figure 80**.*

3. Install the No. 1 shift fork and shaft (A, **Figure 81**) as follows:
   a. Engage the No. 1 shift fork with the center shift drum groove as shown in A, **Figure 82**.
   b. Then install the short shift fork shaft, circlip groove facing inward, through the crankcase and shift fork as shown in B, **Figure 82**.

4. Install the No. 1 and No. 2 shift forks and shift fork shaft (B, **Figure 81**) as follows:
   a. Engage the No. 1 shift fork with the right-hand shift drum groove as shown in A, **Figure 83**.
   b. Install the long shift fork shaft, circlip groove facing inward, through the crankcase and shift fork as shown in B, **Figure 83**.
   c. Engage the No. 2 shift fork pin with the left-hand shift drum groove as shown in **Figure 84**. Then insert the shift fork shaft through the shift fork.

5. Install a new E-clip (**Figure 85**) into each shift fork shaft groove. Make sure the E-clips are fully seated in their shaft grooves (**Figure 86**).

NOTE
The lockwasher installed in Step 6 is also used locate the rear shift fork shaft in the crankcase. Replace the lockwasher if damaged.

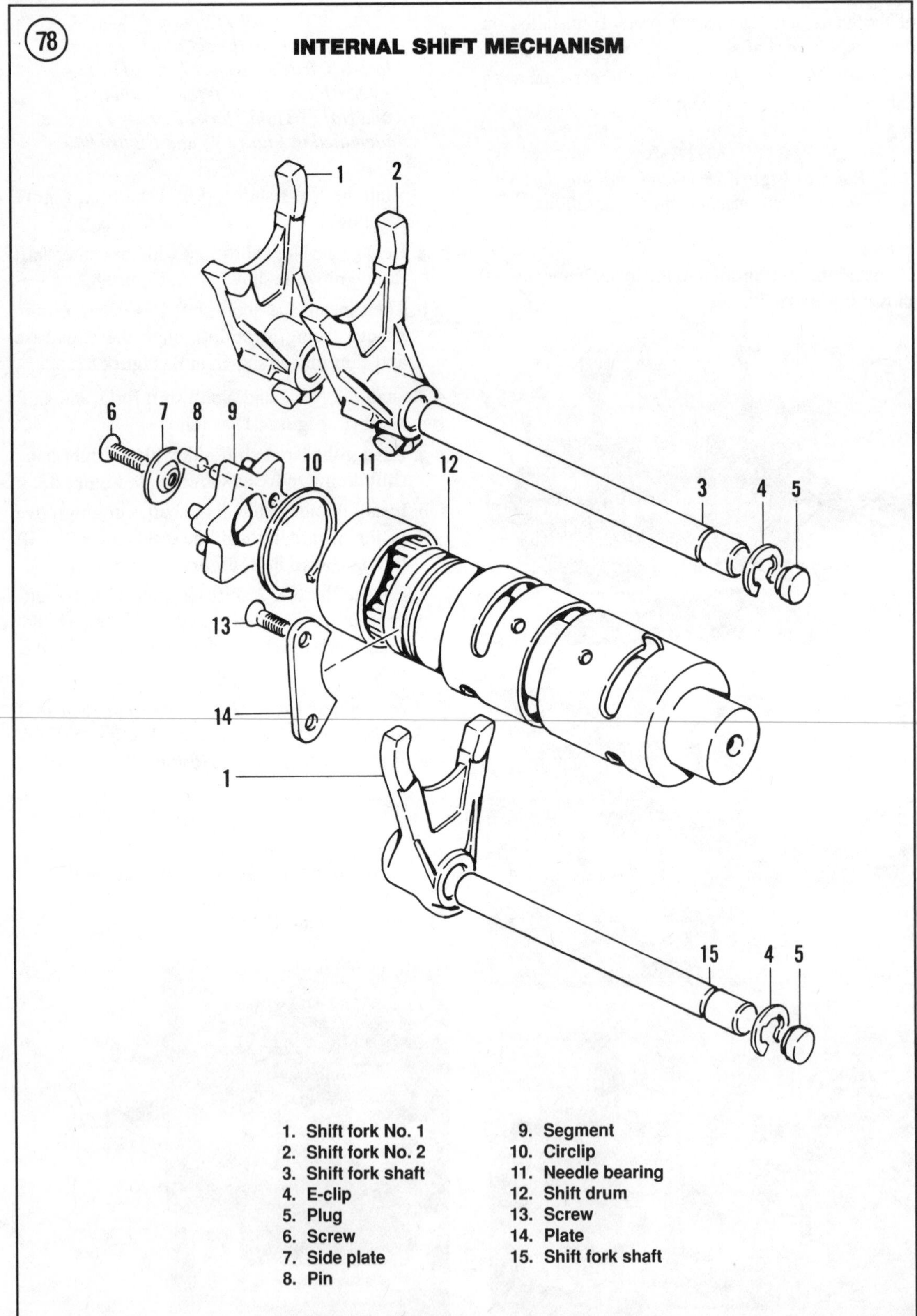

1. Shift fork No. 1
2. Shift fork No. 2
3. Shift fork shaft
4. E-clip
5. Plug
6. Screw
7. Side plate
8. Pin
9. Segment
10. Circlip
11. Needle bearing
12. Shift drum
13. Screw
14. Plate
15. Shift fork shaft

79

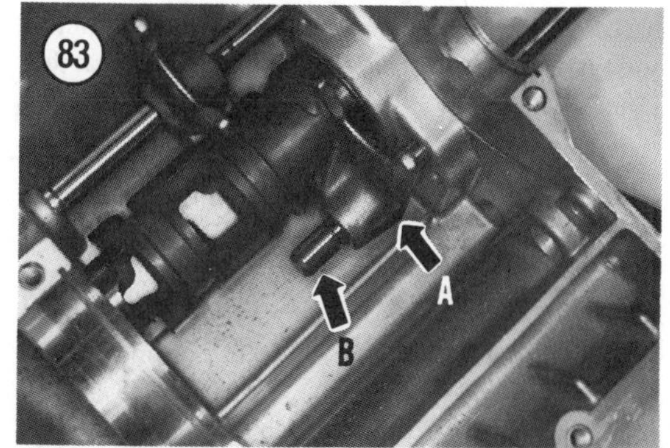
83
A
B

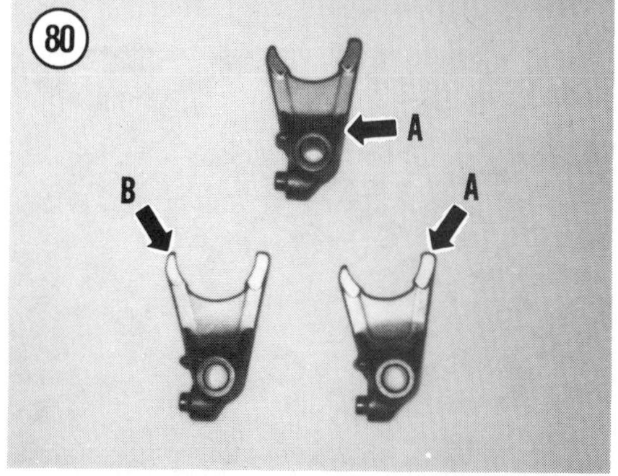
80
A
B
A

84

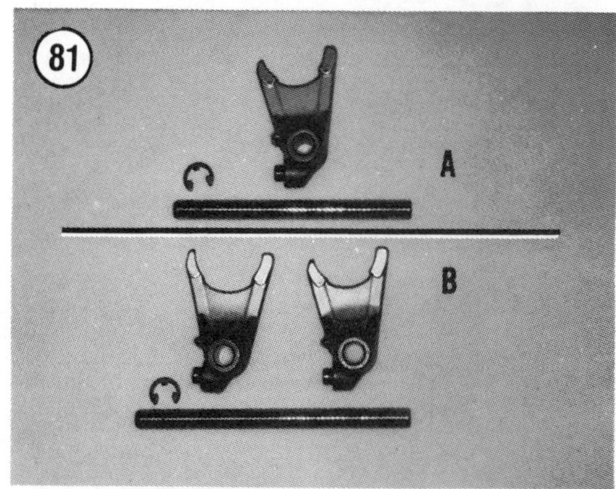
81
A
B

85

82
A
B

86

6. Install the lockwasher, adjust bolt and locknut as shown in **Figure 87**. Hand-tighten the locknut at this time.

7. Install the shift drum locating plate (**Figure 88**). Apply Loctite 242 (blue) to the mounting screws prior to installation. Then install the screws and tighten securely.

8. Turn the shift drum segment (**Figure 88**) by hand and check that the grooves in the shift drum slide the shift forks sideways on their shafts without any binding.

9. Install the 2 countershaft bearing clips (**Figure 89**) into the lower crankcase grooves.

10. Install the mainshaft as follows:

  a. Install the needle bearing onto the mainshaft as shown in A, **Figure 90**.
  b. Install the ball bearing onto the mainshaft as shown in **Figure B**, **Figure 90**. Make sure the circlip is fully seated in the bearing groove; see C, **Figure 90**.
  c. Install the mainshaft into the crankcase. Engage the shift fork with the mainshaft 3rd/4th gear groove as shown in A, **Figure 91**. Seat the ball bearing circlip into the crankcase groove as shown in B, **Figure 91**.

11. Install the countershaft as follows:

  a. Install the needle bearing, circlip groove outward, onto the countershaft as shown in A, **Figure 92**.
  b. Install the ball bearing, circlip groove inward, onto the countershaft as shown in B, **Figure 92**.
  c. Slide the collar onto the countershaft (A, **Figure 93**).
  d. Pack the countershaft oil seal lip (**Figure 94**) with a waterproof bearing grease prior to installation.
  e. Slide the oil seal over the collar with its closed side facing out; see B, **Figure 93**.
  f. Install the countershaft into the crankcase, meshing both gear sets together. Engage the shift forks with the countershaft 5th gear and 6th gear grooves as shown in A, **Figure 95**. Seat the 2 bearing clips (previously installed) in the grooves in the crankcase. See B, **Figure 95**.

12. Shift the transmission into NEUTRAL and spin the transmission shafts. Both shafts should turn smoothly.

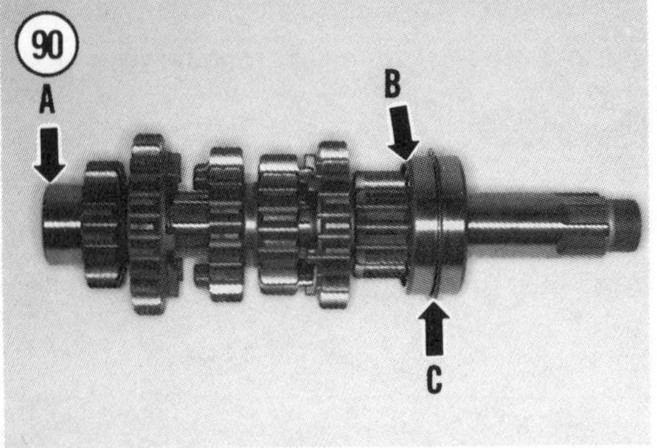

13. Perform the *Transmission Shifting Check and Adjustment* procedure in this chapter prior to installing the upper crankcase half.

NOTE
When the transmission shifts properly into all 6 gears, continue crankcase assembly with Step 14.

14. Install the 2 crankcase dowel pins (**Figure 96**).

15. Lightly oil the transmission gears with clutch oil.

16. Lightly oil the crankshaft lower end rod bearings with engine oil.

17. Make sure the crankcase mating surfaces are clean of all oil residue.

18. Apply a light coat of oil to the crankcase bolt threads.

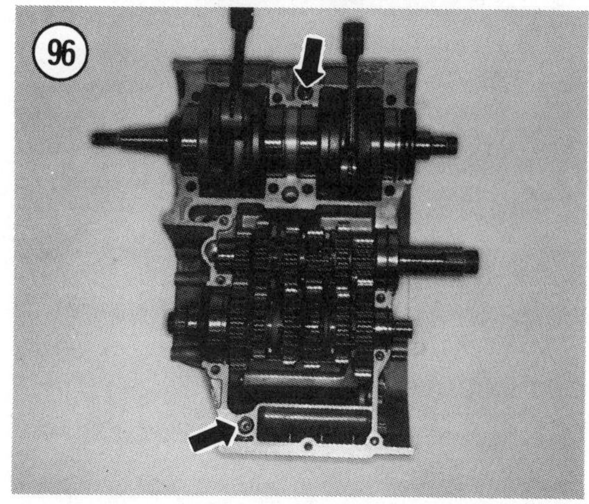

NOTE
Yamabond No. 4 is a semi-drying liquid gasket sealer. It dries semi-firm. Do not use a hard drying liquid gasket sealer.

19. Apply a thin layer of Yamabond No. 4 (or equivalent) to the mating surfaces of both case halves (**Figure 97**).
20. Slide the spring and washer onto the clutch release shaft as shown in **Figure 98**. Then slide the shaft into the upper crankcase (A, **Figure 99**) and set the spring against the case boss as shown in B, **Figure 99**.
21. Install the upper crankcase half (**Figure 100**) onto the lower half, making sure the connecting rods are installed through the crankcase cylinder openings. Check the mating surfaces all the way around the case halves to make sure they are even.
22. Install the upper crankcase bolts (**Figure 101**) and run them down hand-tight.
23. Turn the engine over so that the lower crankcase half faces up. Lightly oil the crankcase stud threads and install the nuts (**Figure 101**) finger-tight.
24. Tighten the crankcase bolts and nuts in the numerical order shown in **Figure 102**. Tighten the bolts and nuts as follows:

NOTE
When tightening the crankcase fasteners in the following steps, make frequent checks to ensure that the crankshaft and transmission shafts turn freely.

a. Tighten the crankcase nuts (No. 1-8) to 5 N•m (3.6 ft.-lb.).
b. Tighten the crankcase bolts (No. 9-16) to 5 N•m (3.6 ft.-lb.).
c. Tighten the crankcase nuts (No. 1-8) to 10 N•m (7.2 ft.-lb.).
d. Tighten the crankcase nuts (No. 1-8) to 25 N•m (18 ft.-lb.).
e. Tighten the crankcase bolts (No. 9-16) to 10 N•m (7.2 ft.-lb.).

25. Check that the crankshaft and transmission shafts turn freely. If there is any binding or roughness, loosen the crankcase bolts and nuts. Then

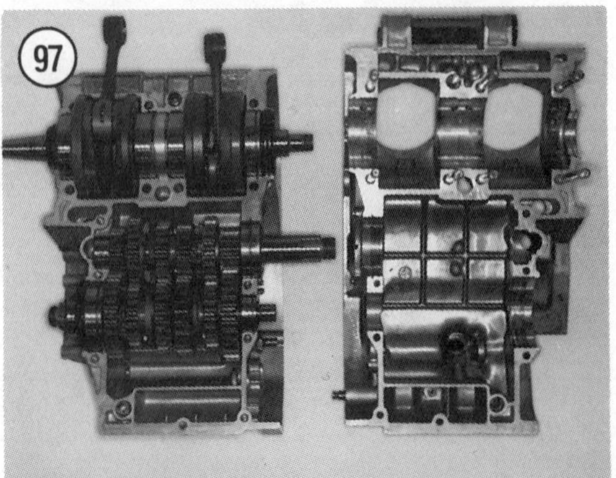
97

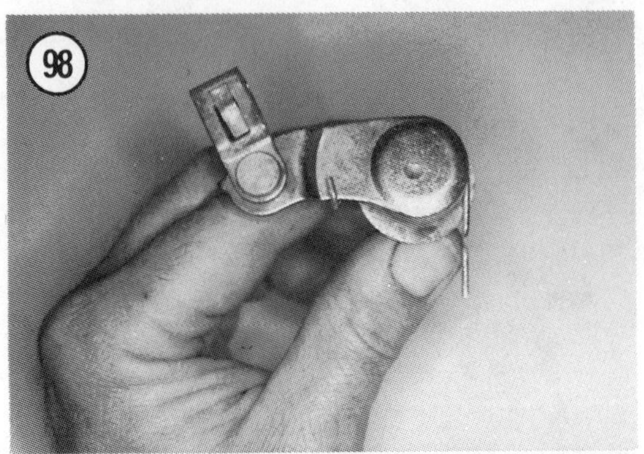
98

99

100

remove the upper crankcase and examine the parts to locate the problem.

26. Apply engine oil to the crank pin, bearing and oil delivery hole of both cylinders.

27. Install the bearing stopper plate as shown in **Figure 103**. Apply Loctite 242 (blue) to the mounting screws prior to installation. Then install the screws and tighten securely.

28. Install the shift drum plate, O-ring and screws. Tighten the screws securely.

29. Install the engine into the frame as described in this chapter.

30. Install all exterior engine assemblies as follows:
   a. Stator plate and flywheel (Chapter Nine).
   b. External shift mechanism (Chapter Six).
   c. Idler gear (Chapter Six).
   d. Kickstarter (Chapter Six).
   e. Primary drive gear and water pump drive gear (Chapter Six).
   f. Clutch (Chapter Six).

NOTE

After installing the clutch, reconnect the clutch cable at the clutch release lever and adjust the clutch release mechanism as described in Chapter Three. Then continue with sub-step g.

   g. Engine top end (Chapter Four).

31. Perform Steps 14-30 under *Engine Installation* in this chapter.

102

CRANKCASE TORQUE SEQUENCE

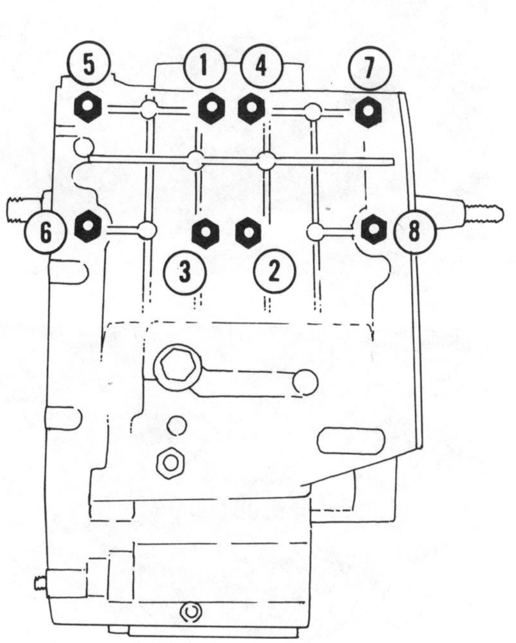

5 1 4 7 6 8 3 2 13 9 12 11 10 14 16 15

Transmission Shifting Check and Adjustment

Shifting should be checked and adjusted prior to reassembling the engine or whenever the external shift mechanism assembly requires adjustment. The following procedure can be performed with the engine mounted on the workbench (during engine reassembly) or with the engine installed in the frame (adjusting the shifting mechanism).

1. Install the stopper lever spring over the crankcase boss as shown in **Figure 104**. Then install the stopper lever and secure it with its shoulder bolt (**Figure 105**). Tighten the bolt securely.
2. If you are in the process of reassembling the engine, install the 2 dowel pins (**Figure 96**). Then install the upper crankcase half (without gasket sealer) and secure it with 3 or 4 mounting bolts. Tighten the bolts finger-tight.
3. Install the shift lever through the crankcase, making sure the centering spring grips the adjust bolt as shown in **Figure 106**.
4. Install the shift lever (**Figure 107**) onto the shift shaft and secure it with its pinch bolt.

NOTE

To hold the shift lever in place when checking shifting, mount a flat piece of aluminum onto the crankcase, centering it against the shift lever, and secure it with 2 bolts; see ***Figure 108****.*

5. Prior to checking the shifting, check and adjust the shift lever position as follows:
   a. Shift the transmission into any gear except NEUTRAL.
   b. Compare dimension A and B, as shown in **Figure 109**. Both dimensions must be equal. If not, loosen the locknut and turn the shifting mechanism adjust bolt as required. When dimension A and B are equal, hold the adjust bolt and tighten the locknut (**Figure 110**) to the torque specification in **Table 2**.
   c. Bend the lockwasher tab over the locknut.
6. To check shifting:
   a. Shift the transmission into NEUTRAL. **Figure 111** shows the shift drum/stopper arm assembly in its NEUTRAL position.
   b. Spin the mainshaft and move the shift lever down and then up to check transmission engagement of each gear.
7. If the transmission does not shift into each gear properly, recheck the shift lever adjustment position

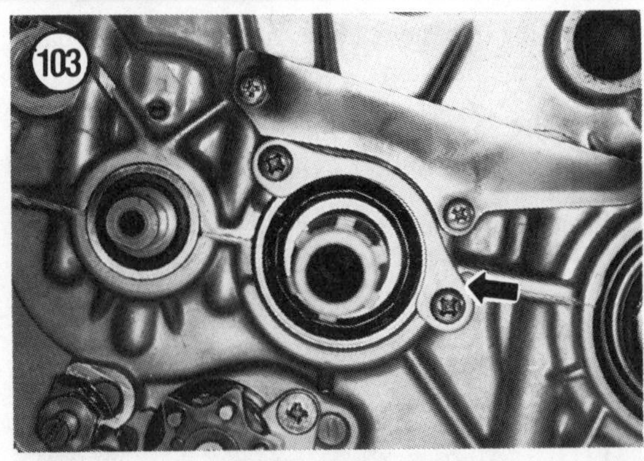

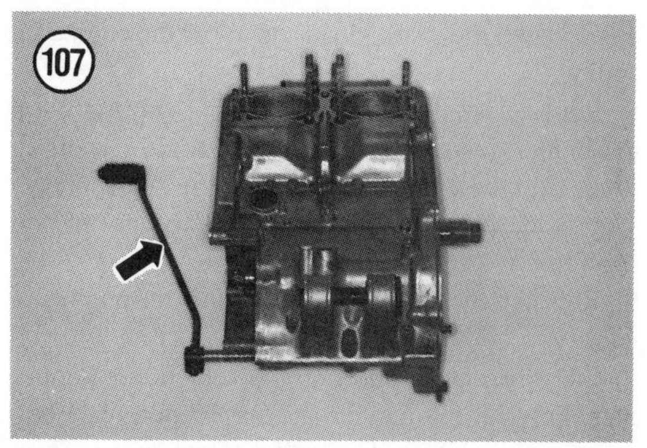

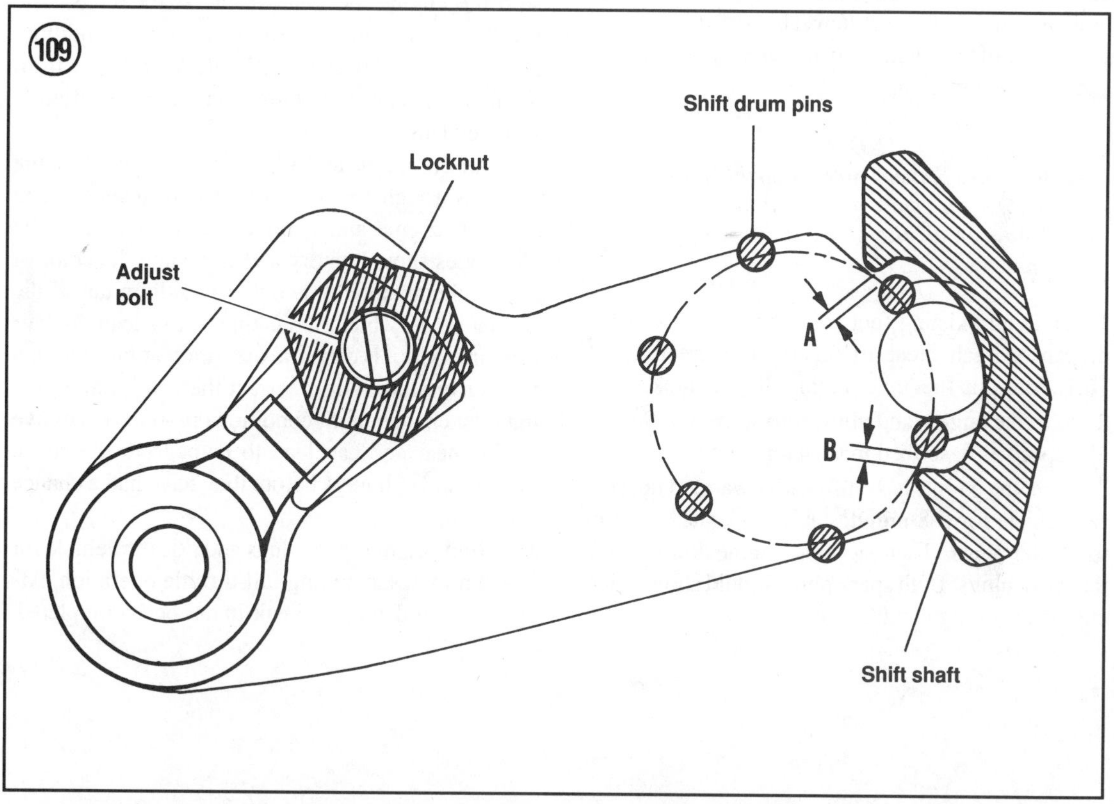

109

Shift drum pins

Locknut

Adjust bolt

A

B

Shift shaft

as described in Step 5. If the adjustment is correct, remove the transmission shafts and inspect the transmission gears and internal shift mechanism as described in Chapter Seven.

8. If the engine shifts into each gear correctly, remove parts previously installed and complete engine reassembly as described in this chapter.

ENGINE BREAK-IN

Following cylinder servicing (boring, honing, new pistons, new rings, etc.), the engine should be broken in just as if it were new. The performance and service life of the engine depends greatly on a careful and sensible break-in.

NOTE
Refer to Chapter Three for further information on spark plug reading and to Chapter Eight for carburetor jet changes.

1. Drain all existing fuel from the fuel tank. Then prepare a fresh break-in fuel/oil mixture ratio of 16:1. Pour this fuel mixture into the fuel tank.
2. Start the engine and allow it to warm up. Set the idle speed as described in Chapter Three.
3. After the engine has sufficiently warmed up, ride the vehicle for 5-8 minutes at a moderate speed in the lower gears. Then stop the engine and remove the spark plugs. Both spark plugs should show a rich engine operating condition.
4. Reinstall the spark plugs and allow the engine to cool.
5. Repeat Step 3 for 5 minutes then shift briefly to the higher gears while checking throttle response. Then stop the engine and remove the spark plugs. The spark plugs should not show a lean or hot condition.
6. Reinstall the spark plugs and allow the engine to cool.
7. Start the engine and ride the vehicle for 5 minutes. Full throttle may be used at higher gears but avoid prolonged steady running at one speed. Then stop the engine and remove the spark plugs. The spark plugs should not show a lean or hot condition.
8. Drain the left over break-in fuel/oil mixture from the fuel tank and refill with the mixture specified in Chapter Three.
9. Start the engine and allow it to warm up. Run the vehicle through its operating range in all gears. Then stop the engine and remove the spark plugs. The electrodes should be dry and clean and the color of the insulation should be light to medium tan. If the insulation is white (indicating a too lean fuel/air mixture) or if it is dark and oily (indicating a too rich fuel/air mixture ratio), correct the condition with a main jet change; both conditions produce excessive engine heat and can lead to damage to the rings, pistons and cylinders before they have had a chance to seat in.
10. Reinstall the spark plugs and ride the vehicle for 10-15 minutes, avoiding full-throttle operation. After this period, engine break-in has been completed.

Table 1 CRANKSHAFT SERVICE SPECIFICATIONS

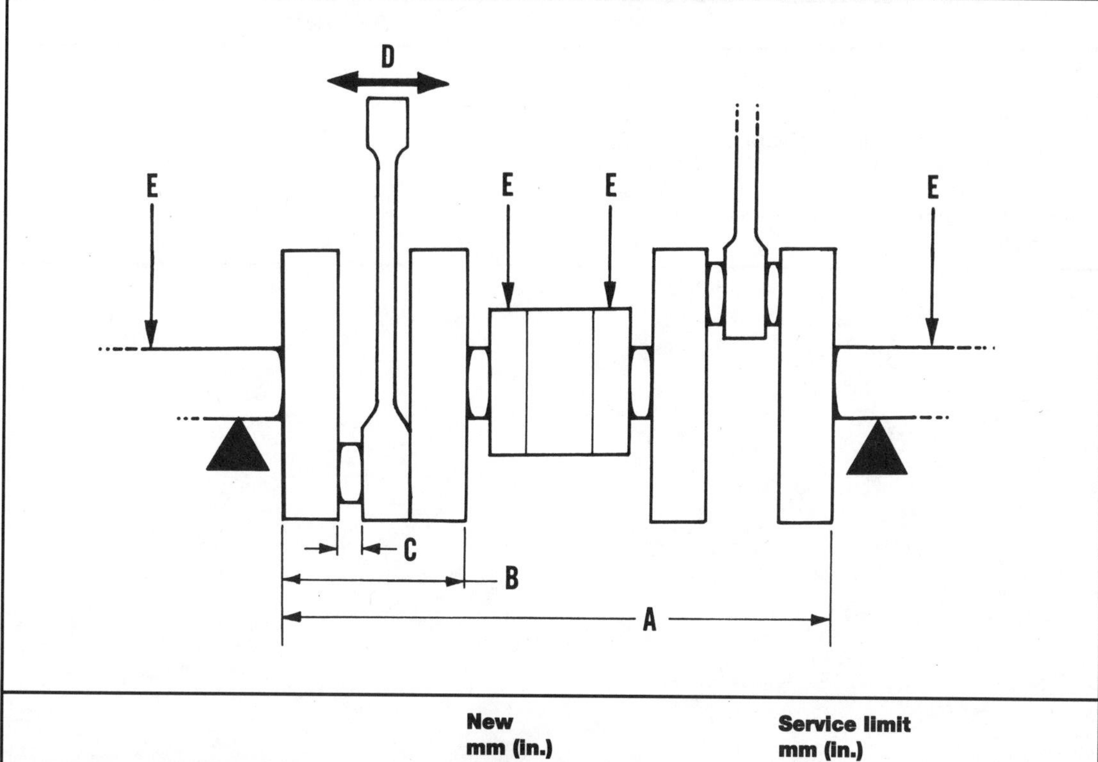

	New mm (in.)	Service limit mm (in.)
Crankshaft assembly width (A)	155.90-156.05 (6.138-6.144)	—
Crank wheel width (B)	53.95-54.00 (2.124-2.126)	—
Connecting rod side clearance (C)	0.25-0.75 (0.0098-0.0295)	—
Connecting rod small end free play (D)	0.36-0.98 (0.0142-0.0386)	2.0 (0.08)
Crankshaft runout limit (E)	—	0.05 (0.0021)

Table 2 ENGINE TIGHTENING TORQUES

	N•m	ft.-lb.
Bearing stopper plate	14	10
Clutch cover screws	7	5.1
Crankcase mounting bolts		
Upper case	10	7.4
Lower case	25	18
Drive sprocket nut	80	59
Flywheel cover screws	7	5.1
Flywheel nut	80	59
Shift cam stopper plate	14	10
Transmission drain plug	20	14
Engine mount bolts		
Front engine mount brackets	30	22
Front engine mount bolts	45	33
Rear engine mount bolt	45	33

(continued)

5

Table 2 ENGINE TIGHTENING TORQUES (continued)

	N•m	ft.-lb.
Engine mount bolts (continued)		
Rear tension rod mounting bolts	25	18
Tension rod bracket bolts	45	33
Front tension rod mounting bolts	45	33
Shift mechanism adjustment bolt locknut	30	22
Inlet hose nozzle Allen bolts	12	8

CHAPTER SIX

CLUTCH, PRIMARY DRIVE, KICKSTARTER AND EXTERNAL SHIFT MECHANISM

This chapter describes service procedures for the following sub-assemblies:

a. Clutch cover.
b. Clutch release lever.
c. Clutch.
d. Primary drive and water pump drive gears.
e. Kickstarter and idler gear.
f. External shift mechanism.
g. Clutch cable.

These sub-assemblies can be removed with the engine in the frame. General clutch specifications are listed in **Table 1**. **Tables 1-3** are found at the end of the chapter.

CLUTCH COVER

The water pump is mounted in the clutch cover. The clutch cover can be removed without having to remove the water pump. To service the water pump, refer to Chapter Ten.

An exploded view of the clutch cover assembly is shown in **Figure 1**.

Removal

1. Park the vehicle on a level surface and set the parking brake.
2. Drain the clutch/transmission oil as described in Chapter Three.
3. Drain the cooling system as described in Chapter Three.
4. Remove the kickstarter (**Figure 2**).
5. Remove the right-hand footpeg assembly (A, **Figure 3**).
6. Disconnect the brake pedal return spring (B, **Figure 3**).
7. Disconnect the master cylinder pushrod from the rear brake pedal (C, **Figure 3**). Then remove the E-clip and remove the brake pedal (D, **Figure 3**) from the frame.
8. Loosen the clutch cable adjuster at the handlebar (**Figure 4**).
9. Remove the inlet hose (A, **Figure 5**) at the clutch cover.

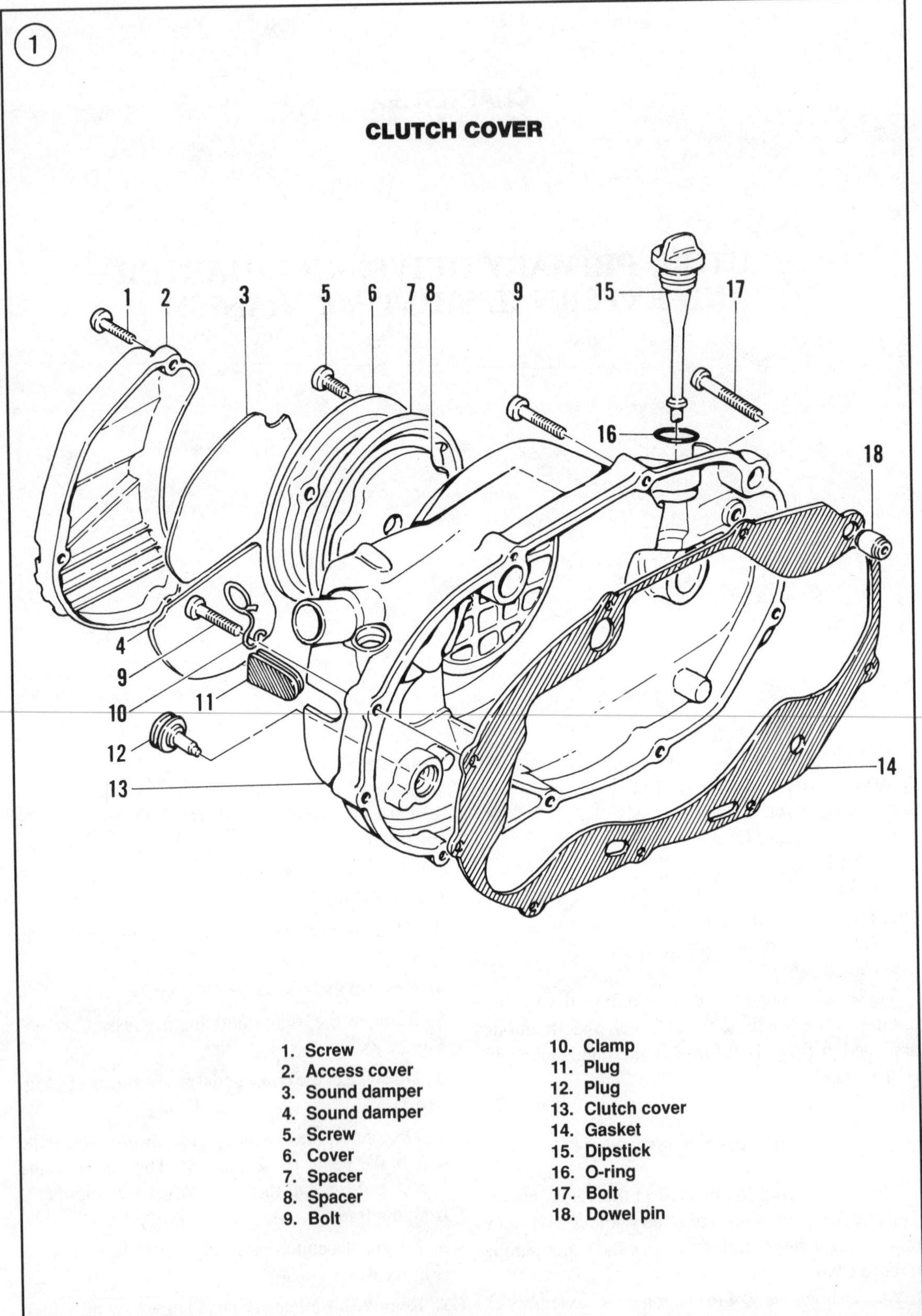
1
CLUTCH COVER
1
2
3
5
6
7
8
9
15
17
16
18
4
9
10
11
12
13
14
1. Screw
2. Access cover
3. Sound damper
4. Sound damper
5. Screw
6. Cover
7. Spacer
8. Spacer
9. Bolt
10. Clamp
11. Plug
12. Plug
13. Clutch cover
14. Gasket
15. Dipstick
16. O-ring
17. Bolt
18. Dowel pin

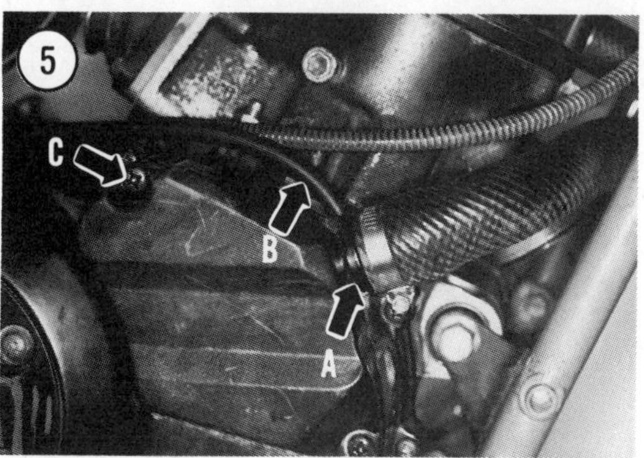

10. Disconnect the breather hose (B, **Figure 5**) from its junction outside of the clutch cover.

11. If necessary, remove the water pump cover screws and remove the cover (C, **Figure 5**).

12. Remove the screws securing the clutch cover to the engine. Then remove the clutch cover (A, **Figure 6**) and gasket. Discard the gasket if leaking or damaged.

13. Remove the dowel pin (**Figure 7**).

Installation

1. Remove all gasket residue from the clutch cover and crankcase gasket surfaces.

2. Apply a light coat of lithium soap base grease to the radiator hose joint O-ring shown in **Figure 8**. If

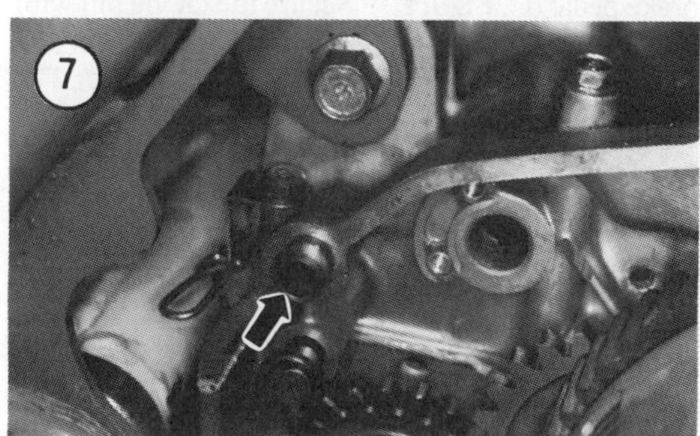

the O-ring is worn or damaged, replace it prior to installing the clutch cover.

3. Install the dowel pin (**Figure 7**).

4. Install the clutch cover gasket (**Figure 9**) and the clutch cover (A, **Figure 6**).

NOTE
*If the clutch cover will not seat all the way against the crankcase, turn the impeller (B, **Figure 6**) to engage the water pump drive and driven gears.*

5. Install the clutch cover mounting screws and tighten in a crisscross pattern to the torque specification in **Table 3**.

6. Reconnect the breather hose (B, **Figure 5**) to its junction outside of the clutch cover.

7. Reconnect the inlet hose (A, **Figure 5**) to the clutch cover.

8. Slide the brake pedal (D, **Figure 3**) onto the frame and install the flat washer and E-clip. Make sure the E-clip is fully seated in the groove.

NOTE
*Replace the E-clip (**Figure 10**) if weak or damaged.*

9. Reconnect the master cylinder pushrod to the rear brake pedal (C, **Figure 3**). Secure the clevis pin with a new cotter pin. Bend the cotter pin arms over to lock it.

10. Reconnect the brake pedal return spring (B, **Figure 3**).

11. Reinstall the right-hand footpeg assembly (A, **Figure 3**). Tighten the mounting bolt securely.

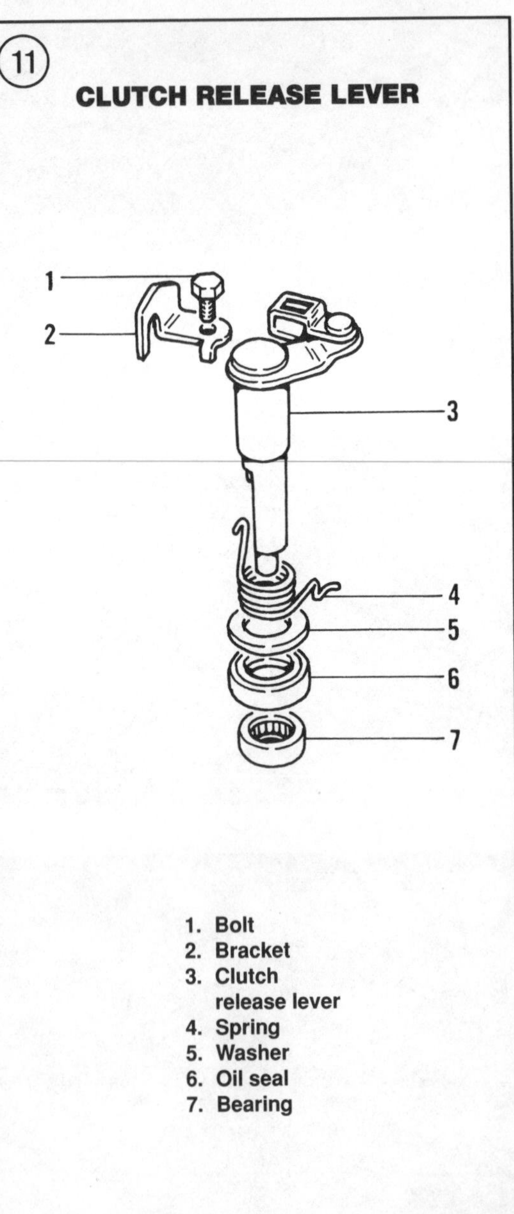

12. Install the kickstarter and its mounting bolt. Tighten the mounting bolt to the torque specification in **Table 3**.
13. Refill the cooling system as described in Chapter Three.
14. Check that the transmission drain plug is tightened to the torque specification in **Table 3**.

15. Refill the clutch/transmission oil as described in Chapter Three.
16. Adjust the clutch cable at handlebar adjuster (**Figure 4**) as described in Chapter Three.
17. Start the engine and check for engine oil and coolant leaks.

CLUTCH RELEASE LEVER

The clutch release lever assembly (**Figure 11**) is mounted in the upper crankcase.

Removal

1. Remove the left-hand carburetor as described in Chapter Eight.
2. Loosen the clutch cable adjuster at the handlebar (**Figure 4**).
3. Remove the clutch cover as described in this chapter.

NOTE
*The outer cover (**Figure 12**) mounted onto the clutch cover is not an access cover. Do not remove it.*

4. Loosen the adjuster locknut and turn the adjuster 1-2 turns counterclockwise with a Phillips screwdriver (**Figure 13**).
5. Remove the clutch cable holder bracket bolt and bracket (**Figure 14**). Then disconnect the clutch cable at the release lever.
6. Remove the bolt and bracket (**Figure 15**) holding the clutch release lever to the crankcase. Then lift

6

the clutch release lever assembly out of the crankcase and remove it (**Figure 16**).

Inspection

1. Clean all parts in solvent and dry thoroughly.
2. Inspect the clutch release shaft (**Figure 17**) for severe wear or damage.

NOTE
If there is an oil leak from the clutch release shaft oil seal, and you replaced the oil seal and it still leaks, the clutch release shaft is worn where it rides against the oil seal. Replace the oil seal and shaft during reassembly.

3. Replace the washer and/or spring if necessary.

NOTE
*The washer (**Figure 17**) prevents the spring from tearing into the oil seal and damaging it. If the washer is damaged, replace it during reassembly.*

4. To replace the clutch release lever oil seal and bearing, perform the *Clutch Release Lever Oil Seal and Bearing Inspection and Replacement* procedure in Chapter Five.

Installation

1. Fill the clutch release shaft oil seal lip with a waterproof bearing grease.
2. Install the spring and washer onto the release lever (**Figure 16**). Position the spring against the release lever arm as shown in **Figure 18**.
3. Place a dab of grease onto the release lever shaft where it contacts the clutch pushrod.
4. Insert the clutch release shaft (A, **Figure 19**) into the crankcase and position its arm and spring as shown in **Figure 19**. The spring arm should contact the crankcase boss as shown in B, **Figure 19**.
5. Install the bracket and bolt (**Figure 15**) that hold the clutch release lever to the crankcase. Tighten the bolt to 10 N•m (7.4 ft.-lb.).
6. Reconnect the clutch cable at the release lever (A, **Figure 20**). Then position the clutch cable housing shoulder so that the cable will pull against the crankcase boss arms as shown in B, **Figure 20**.
7. Install the bracket and bolt (**Figure 14**) that secures the clutch cable to the crankcase. Tighten the bolt securely.
8. Adjust the clutch as described in Chapter Three.
9. Reinstall the clutch cover as described in this chapter.
10. Reinstall the left-hand carburetor as described in Chapter Eight.

CLUTCH

The clutch is a wet multiplate type which operates immersed in the oil supply it shares with the transmission. The clutch boss is splined to the transmission mainshaft and the clutch housing can rotate freely on the mainshaft. The clutch housing is geared to the primary drive gear attached to the crankshaft.

The clutch can be removed with the engine in the frame.

Removal

Refer to **Figure 21** for this procedure.

16

17

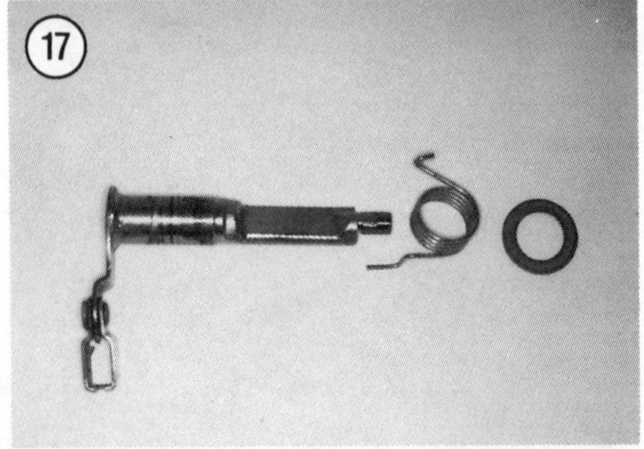

1. Remove the clutch cover as described in this chapter.
2. Loosen the 6 pressure plate bolts (**Figure 22**) a quarter turn at a time in a crisscross pattern. Continue until the clutch spring pressure is relieved. Then remove the bolts, springs and pressure plate (**Figure 23**).
3. Remove the steel ball and pushrod (**Figure 24**) from inside the mainshaft.
4. Referring to **Figure 21**, remove the clutch plates and stack them in order.

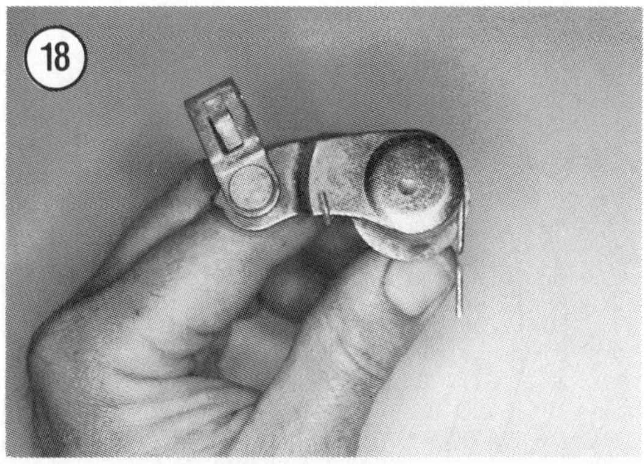

5. Pry the clutch nut lockwasher tab away from the clutch nut.
6. Hold the clutch boss with the Yamaha universal clutch holder (part No. YM-91042) or the Grabbit (same tool) (**Figure 25**). Then loosen the clutch nut by turning it counterclockwise.
7. Remove the clutch nut and lockwasher.
8. Remove the clutch boss.
9. Remove the thrust washer, clutch housing, thrust washer and spacer.

Inspection

Clutch service specifications and wear limits are listed in **Table 2**.

1. Clean all parts in solvent and dry with compressed air.
2. Measure the free length of each clutch spring (**Figure 26**) with a vernier caliper. Replace the springs as a set if any one spring is too short.
3. **Table 1** lists the number of cushion rings (A, **Figure 27**) used in the clutch assembly. Replace cushion rings that are cracked, broken, have flat spots or show other types of damage.
4. **Table 1** lists the number of friction plates (B, **Figure 27**) used in the stock clutch. The friction material is bonded onto an aluminum plate for warp resistance and durability. Measure the thickness of each friction plate at several places around the plate (**Figure 28**) with a vernier caliper. Replace all friction plates if any one is found too thin. Do not replace only 1 or 2 plates.
5. **Table 1** lists the number of clutch metal plates (C, **Figure 27**) used in the stock clutch. Place each clutch metal plate on a surface plate or a thick piece of glass and check for warpage with a feeler gauge (**Figure 29**). If any plate is warped more than specified, replace the entire set of plates. Do not replace only 1 or 2 plates.
6. The friction plates have tabs that slide in the clutch housing grooves (A, **Figure 30**). Inspect the tabs for cracks or galling in the grooves. The tabs must be smooth for chatter-free clutch operation. Light damage can be repaired with a fine-cut file or oilstone. Replace the clutch housing if damage is severe.
7. The metal clutch plate inner teeth mesh with the clutch boss splines (A, **Figure 31**). Check the splines for cracks or galling. They must be smooth for chatter-free clutch operation. Repair minor damage

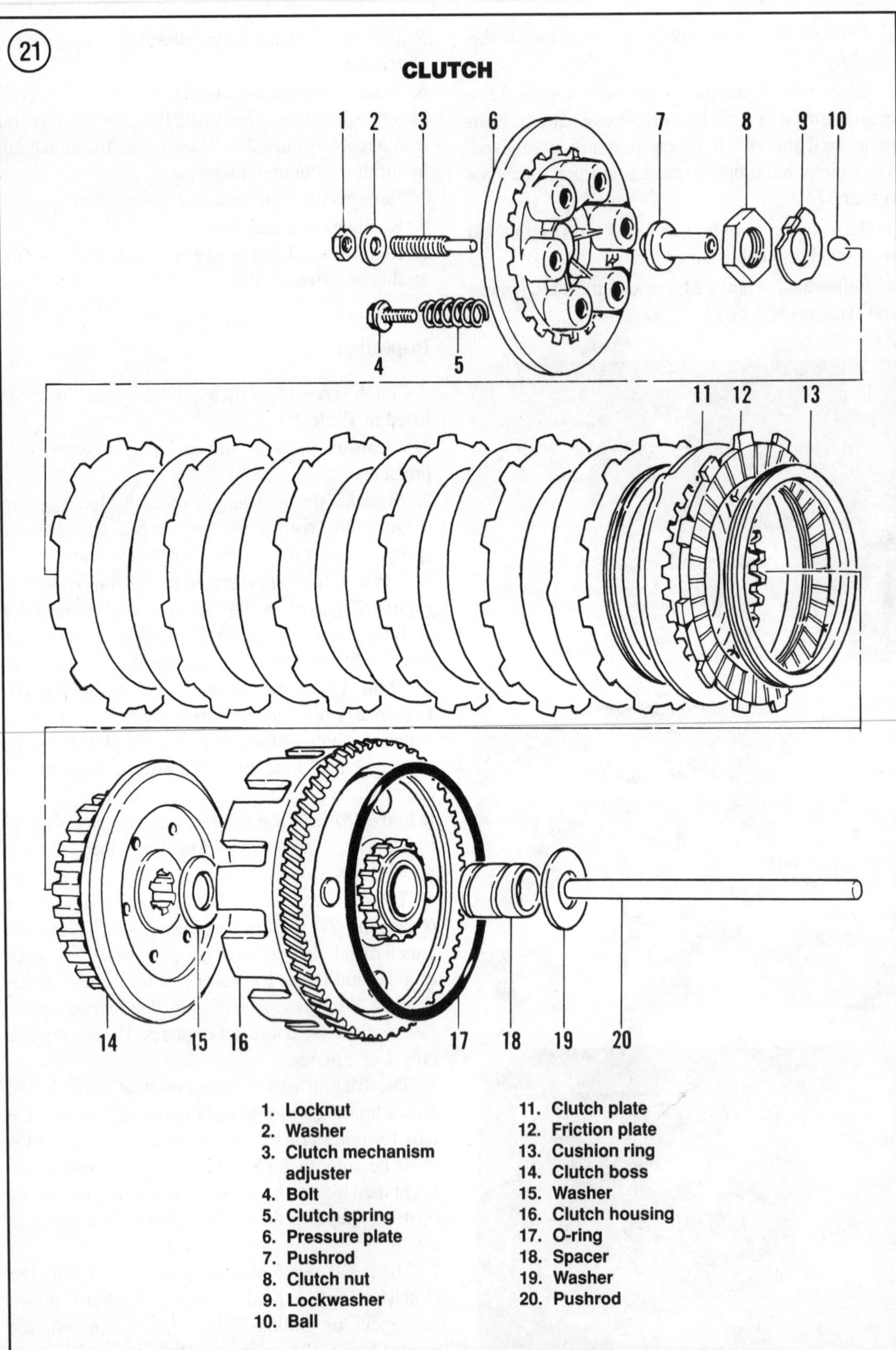
21
CLUTCH
1 2 3 6 7 8 9 10
4 5
11 12 13
14 15 16 17 18 19 20
1. Locknut
2. Washer
3. Clutch mechanism adjuster
4. Bolt
5. Clutch spring
6. Pressure plate
7. Pushrod
8. Clutch nut
9. Lockwasher
10. Ball
11. Clutch plate
12. Friction plate
13. Cushion ring
14. Clutch boss
15. Washer
16. Clutch housing
17. O-ring
18. Spacer
19. Washer
20. Pushrod

22

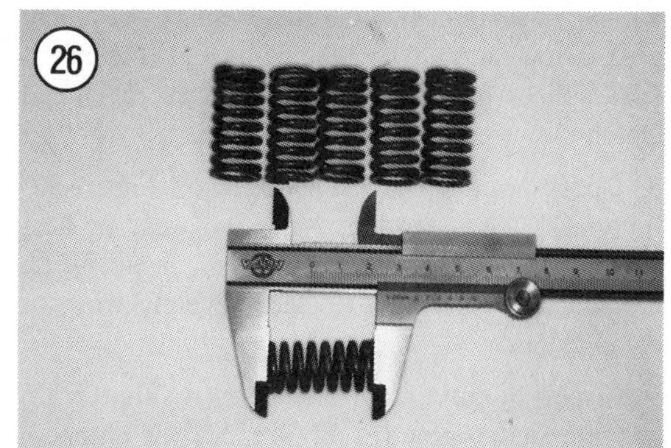
26

23

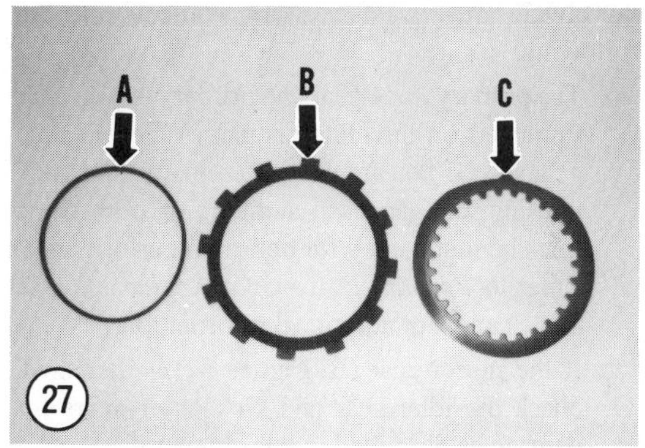
A
B
C
27

24
A
B

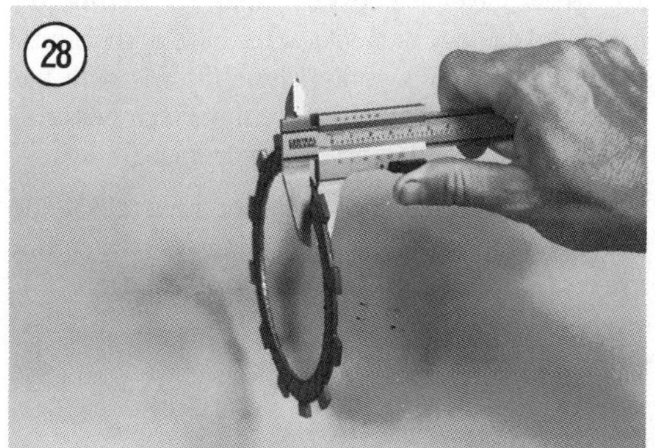
28

25

29

with an oilstone or fine-cut file. Replace the clutch boss if you cannot repair the damage. If the clutch boss splines are severely worn, check the metal clutch plate teeth for wear or damage.

8. Check the clutch housing bushing (B, **Figure 30**) for cracks, deep scoring, excessive wear or heat discoloration. If the bearing bore is damaged, check the spacer for damage. Replace severely worn or damaged parts.

9. Inspect the primary driven gear (A, **Figure 32**) and the starter gear (B, **Figure 32**) for chipped, missing or otherwise damaged gear teeth. Replace the clutch housing if necessary, while noting the following:

   a. The primary drive gear and primary driven gear (mounted on the clutch housing) are matched gear sets. If you are going to replace the clutch housing, the gear lash numbers on both gears must be maintained for optimum performance. Refer to *Primary Drive Gear Replacement* in this chapter for additional information.
   b. If the starter gear (B, **Figure 32**) is damaged, check the idler gear and kickstarter gears for damage as described in this chapter.

10. Check the clutch boss bolt studs (B, **Figure 31**) for thread damage or cracks at the base of the studs. If thread damage is minor, chase threads with the correct size metric tap. Replace the clutch boss if a bolt stud is cracked or otherwise damaged.

11. Inspect the pressure plate (A, **Figure 33**) for warpage, cracks or other damage. Inspect the spring towers (B, **Figure 33**) for cracks or breakage.

12. To service the pushrod/adjuster assembly (C, **Figure 33**), perform the following:

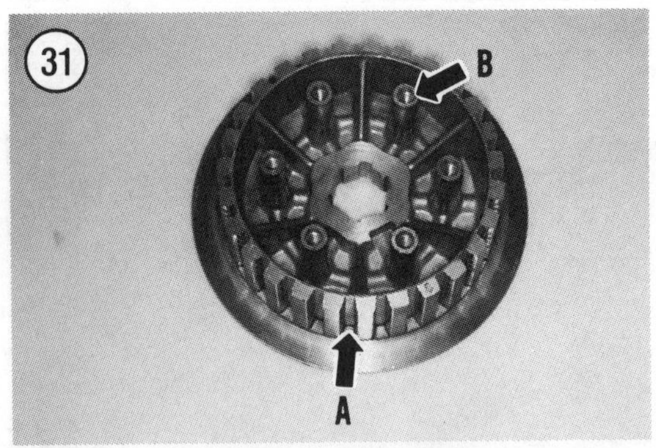

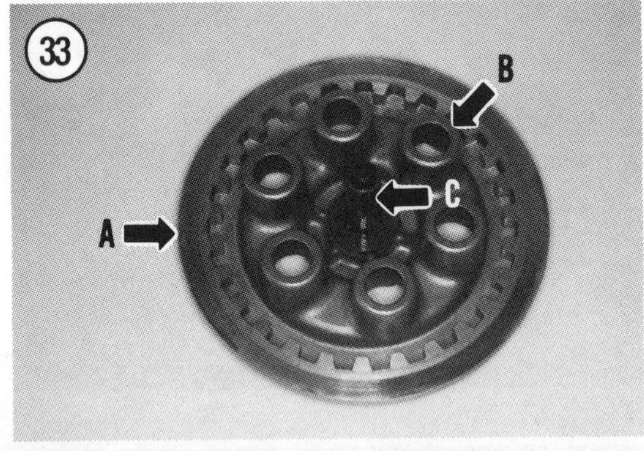

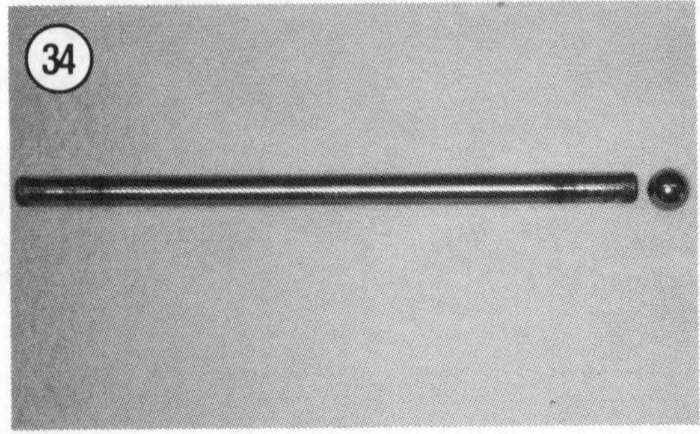

a. Remove the locknut, washer and adjuster (**Figure 21**). Then remove the pushrod assembly (C, **Figure 33**).

b. Clean parts thoroughly.

c. Replace severely worn or damaged parts. Replace the adjuster bolt if the Phillips end is stripped or severely worn.

d. Install the pushrod/adjuster assembly by reversing these steps.

13. Inspect the long pushrod and steel ball (**Figure 34**) for severe wear or damage. Check pushrod runout by rolling it on a flat surface or more accurately, place it on a set of V-blocks and measure runout with a dial indicator. Position the dial indicator stem against the center of the pushrod and zero the dial gauge. Turn the pushrod slowly by hand and read the runout on the dial gauge. If the runout exceeds the limit in **Table 2**, replace the pushrod. Do not attempt to straighten it.

14. If there is any doubt as to the condition of any part, replace it with a new one.

6

Assembly

Refer to **Figure 21** when installing the clutch assembly.

1. Coat all clutch parts and the mainshaft with transmission oil prior to assembly.

NOTE
*The 2 thrust washers (15 and 19, **Figure 21**) are identical.*

2. Slide the first thrust washer (A, **Figure 35**) onto the mainshaft.
3. Slide the spacer (B, **Figure 35**) onto the mainshaft and seat it against the thrust washer.
4. Slide the clutch housing onto the mainshaft and over the spacer, engaging the idler and starter gears and the primary drive and driven gears. See **Figure 36**.
5. Install the second thrust washer (**Figure 37**) and seat it next to the clutch housing.
6. Install the clutch boss (**Figure 38**) onto the mainshaft and seat it against the thrust washer.

NOTE
*The clutch nut lockwasher has 1 locking tab. Replace the washer if the locking tab is severely worn or broken off. Compare the used and new lockwashers in **Figure 39**.*

7. Install the lockwasher by engaging the flat tab on the lockwasher into the notch in the clutch boss; see **Figure 40**. Then install the clutch nut.

8. Secure the clutch boss with the same tool used during disassembly (**Figure 41**). Then tighten the clutch nut to the torque specification in **Table 3**.

9. Bend the lockwasher tab so that it seats against one flat of the clutch nut as shown in **Figure 42**.

10. Prior to installing the clutch plates, note the following:
   a. Thoroughly lubricate the clutch plates and cushion springs (**Figure 43**) with transmission oil.
   b. To help reduce clutch noise, each clutch plate has one part of its outer circumference machined away, leaving a round tab as shown in **Figure 44**. This allows the plates to be installed in a staggered fashion that will then allow the plates to move outward due to centrifugal force during engine and clutch operation.

11. Install the clutch plates as follows:
   a. Install a cushion ring (**Figure 45**) and seat it against the back of the clutch boss. Make sure the cushion ring seats squarely on the clutch boss.
   b. Slide the first friction plate (**Figure 46**) onto the clutch housing tabs and center it over the cushion ring.
   c. Slide the first clutch plate onto the clutch boss—align the clutch plate tab (A, **Figure 47**) with the arrow mark on the clutch boss (B, **Figure 47**).
   d. Repeat to install the remaining cushion rings, friction plates and clutch plates. When installing the remaining clutch plates (C, **Figure 43**), stagger each plate so that its plate tab is posi-

40

41

42

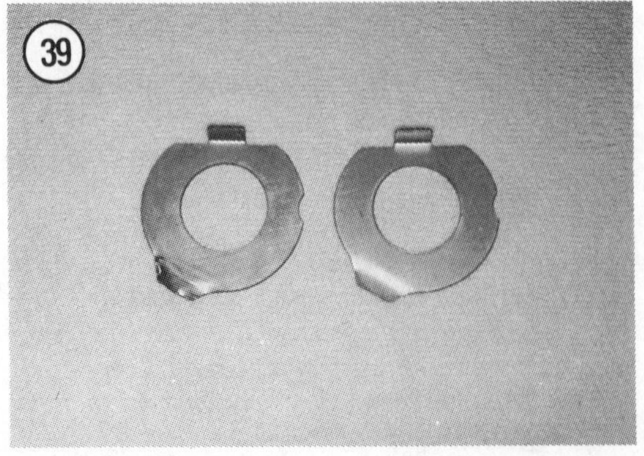
39

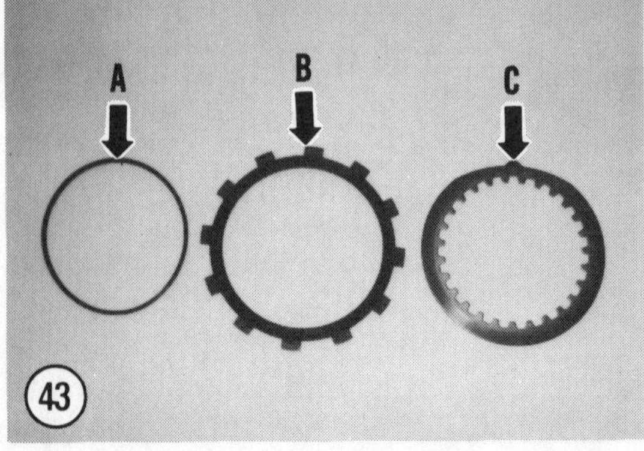

43

tioned 60° clockwise from the previously installed clutch plate tab; see **Figure 48**.

e. The last plate installed should be a friction plate (**Figure 49**).

12. Apply a dab of lithium soap base grease to both ends of the pushrod, then insert the pushrod (A, **Figure 50**) into the mainshaft.

13. Install the clutch ball (B, **Figure 50**) into the mainshaft and seat it against the pushrod.

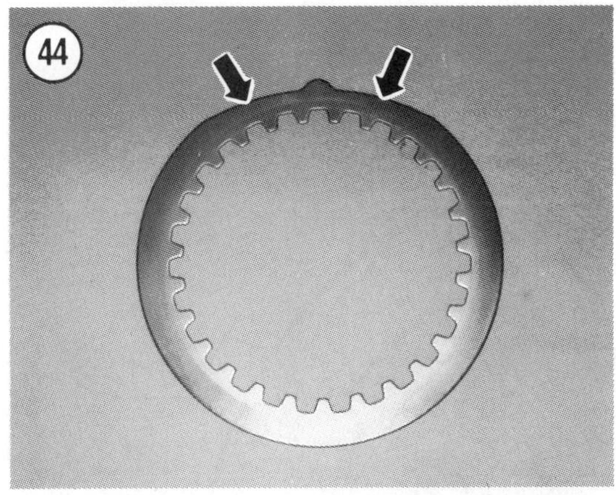

14. Slide the pressure plate onto the clutch boss—align the arrow on the pressure plate (A, **Figure 51**) with the arrow on the clutch boss (B, **Figure 51**). Make sure the pressure plate and clutch boss splines and grooves engage properly.

NOTE
When the pressure plate is properly installed, it will seat flush against the outer friction plate.

15. Install the clutch springs and bolts (**Figure 52**). Then tighten each of the 6 bolts 1/4 turn at a time in a crisscross pattern. Tighten the bolts to the torque specification in **Table 3**.

16. Check and adjust the clutch mechanism adjuster as described in Chapter Three.

17. Install the clutch cover as described in this chapter.

6

WATER PUMP AND PRIMARY DRIVE GEARS

The water pump and primary drive gears are mounted onto the right-hand end of the crankshaft. A square key engages the primary drive gear to the crankshaft. The water pump drive gear (A, **Figure 53**) can be removed without having to remove the clutch. The clutch will have to be removed to remove the primary drive gear (B, **Figure 53**).

Removal

1. Remove the clutch cover as described in this chapter.

2. If you are going to remove the primary drive gear, remove the clutch as described in this chapter.

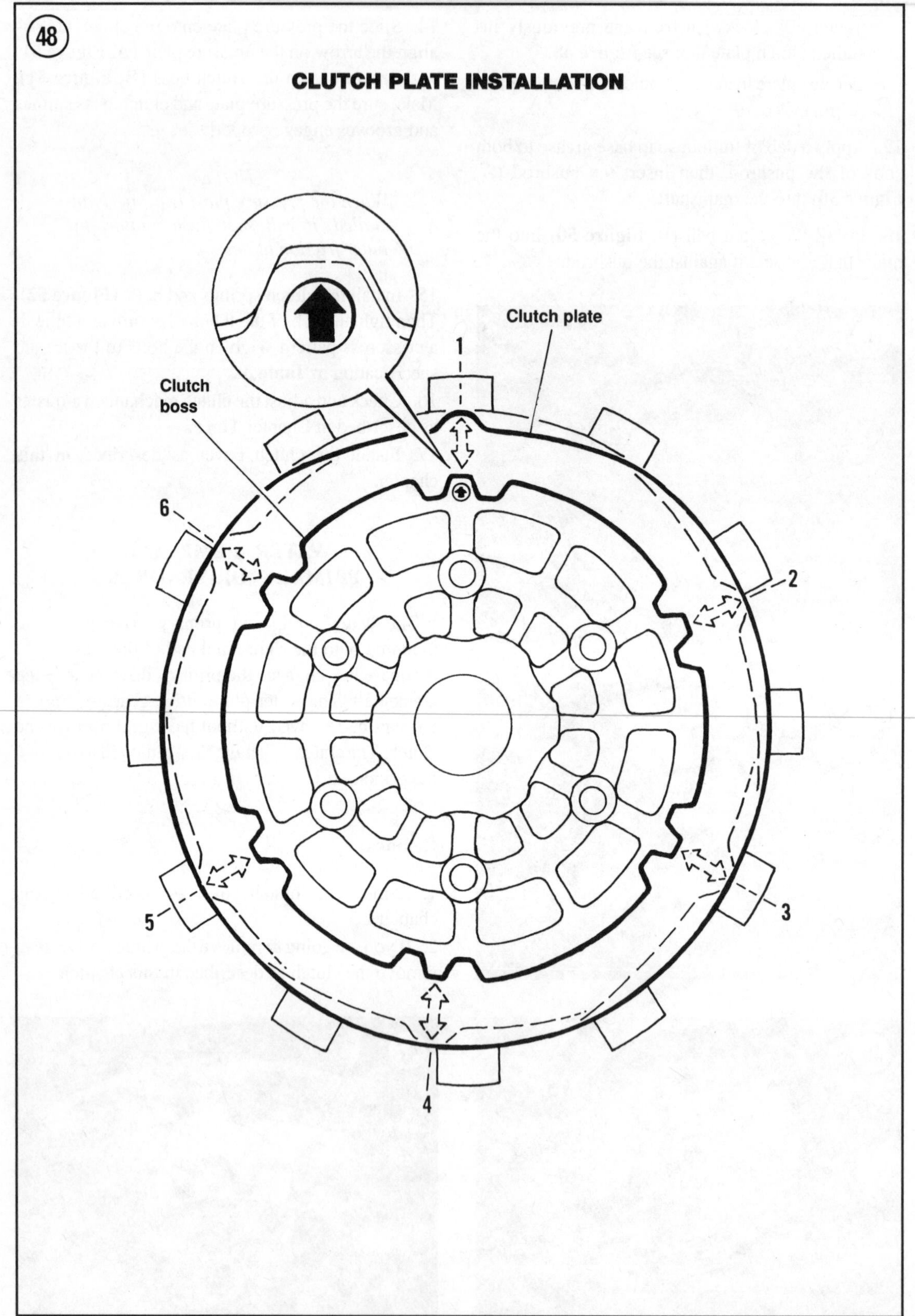
48
CLUTCH PLATE INSTALLATION
Clutch plate
Clutch boss
1
2
3
4
5
6

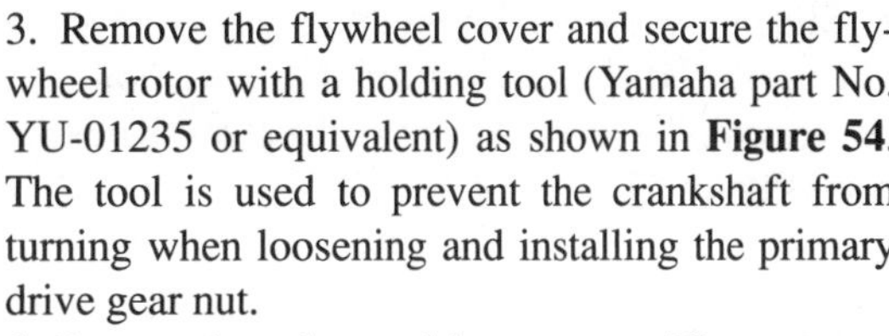
3. Remove the flywheel cover and secure the flywheel rotor with a holding tool (Yamaha part No. YU-01235 or equivalent) as shown in **Figure 54**. The tool is used to prevent the crankshaft from turning when loosening and installing the primary drive gear nut.

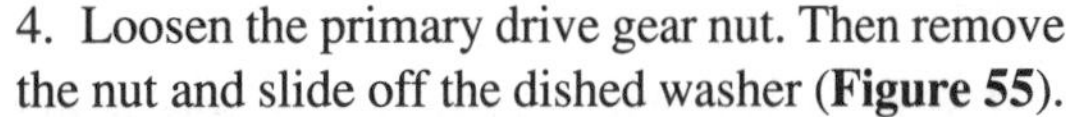
4. Loosen the primary drive gear nut. Then remove the nut and slide off the dished washer (**Figure 55**).

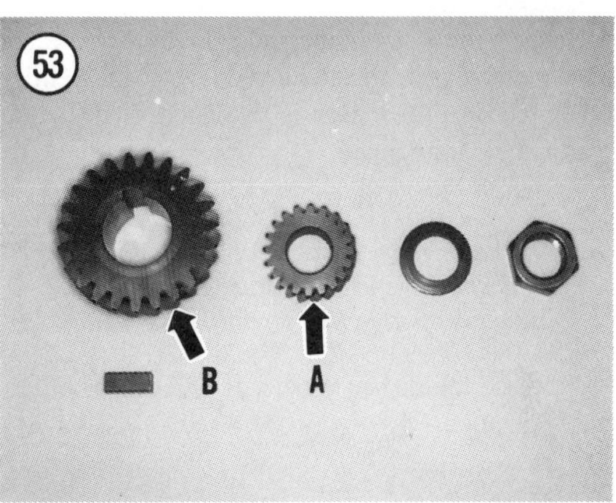

5. Slide off the water pump drive gear (A, **Figure 56**) and the primary drive gear (B, **Figure 56**).
6. Remove the square key from the crankshaft keyway (**Figure 57**).

Inspection

1. Clean the assembly (**Figure 53**) in solvent and dry thoroughly.
2. Inspect the water pump and primary drive gears for excessive gear wear, chipped or broken teeth or other damage. If a gear is damaged, inspect the mating gear for damage.

NOTE
If the primary drive gear requires replacement, refer to ***Primary Drive Gear Replacement*** *in this section.*

3. Replace the dished washer if cracked or otherwise damaged.

Primary Drive Gear Replacement

The primary drive gear and primary driven gear (mounted on the clutch housing) are matched gear sets. If you are going to replace the primary drive gear or clutch housing, the gear lash numbers on both gears must be maintained for optimum performance. **Figure 58** shows the location of the lash numbers for the primary drive and driven gears. See your Yamaha dealer for additional information.

Installation

1. Apply a light coat of grease onto the primary drive gear shoulder.
2. Align the primary drive gear and crankshaft keyways and slide the gear all the way onto the crankshaft (**Figure 59**). Then install the square key through the keyways until it bottoms out; see **Figure 60**.
3. With the primary drive gear fully seated, slide the water pump drive gear onto the crankshaft and seat it against the primary drive gear; see A, **Figure 56**.
4. Install the dished washer (**Figure 61**) so that its convex side is facing away from the water pump drive gear.
5. Thread the primary drive gear nut onto the crankshaft. Then use the same tool to hold the crankshaft (**Figure 54**) in place and torque the primary drive gear nut to the torque specification in **Table 3**.
6. Install the clutch, if removed, as described in this chapter.
7. Install the clutch cover as described in this chapter.

KICKSTARTER AND IDLER GEAR

A primary drive kickstarter system is used. The kickstarter is mounted on the right-hand side of the

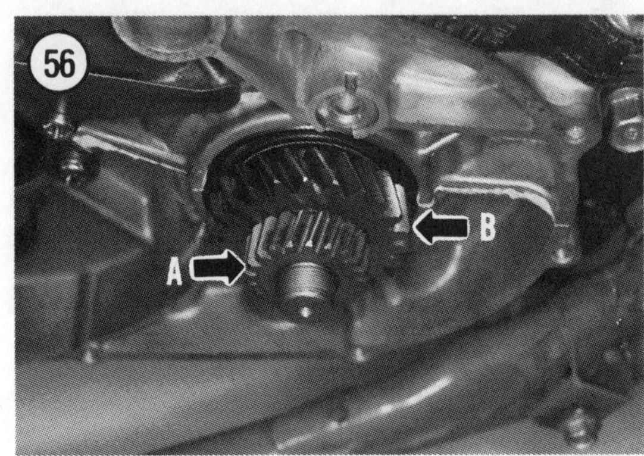

engine. An exploded view of the kickstarter is shown in **Figure 62**.

Removal

1. Remove the clutch as described in this chapter.
2. To remove the idler gear (**Figure 63**):
   a. Remove the circlip installed in the end of the countershaft (**Figure 64**).
   b. Remove the notched washer and slide the idler gear off the countershaft.

   c. Remove the small flat washer.
3. Using a pair of needlenose pliers, unhook the kickstarter return spring from the post shown in **Figure 65**. Then allow the spring to unwind and release it.
4. Slide the kickstarter assembly out of the engine and remove it.
5. If necessary, service the kickstarter assembly as described in this chapter.

Disassembly/Inspection

Refer to **Figure 62** when performing this procedure.

1. Slide the collar, return spring and kickstarter gear off of the kickstarter shaft (**Figure 66**).
2. Wash all of the parts in solvent and dry thoroughly.
3. Check the kickstarter shaft (**Figure 67**) as follows:
   a. Check the outer splines (A) for damage.
   b. Check the shaft bearing surface (B) for severe scoring, cracks or other damage.
   c. Check for a worn or damaged return spring mounting hole (C).
   d. Check the splines (D) for cracks or other damage. Install the kickstarter gear onto the shaft and work it back and forth. The gear should move smoothly with no binding or roughness.
   e. Check for a bent kickstarter shaft.

NOTE
If the kickstarter shaft is bent, check the kickstarter shaft bore in the clutch cover for damage.

4. Check the kickstarter and idler gears for chipped, broken or missing teeth. Check the kickstarter gear splines for damage.
5. Visually check the return spring (A, **Figure 68**) for weakness, cracks or other damage.
6. To measure the tension of the kick gear spring:
   a. Assemble the kickstarter gear and its spring onto the kickstarter shaft.
   b. Hook a spring tension scale onto the kickstarter gear spring as shown in **Figure 69**. Then hold the gear and pull the spring tension scale. Note the reading on the scale when the spring breaks free and slips on the gear. The standard tension range is 0.8-1.3 kg (1.8-2.9 lbs.). If the spring

6

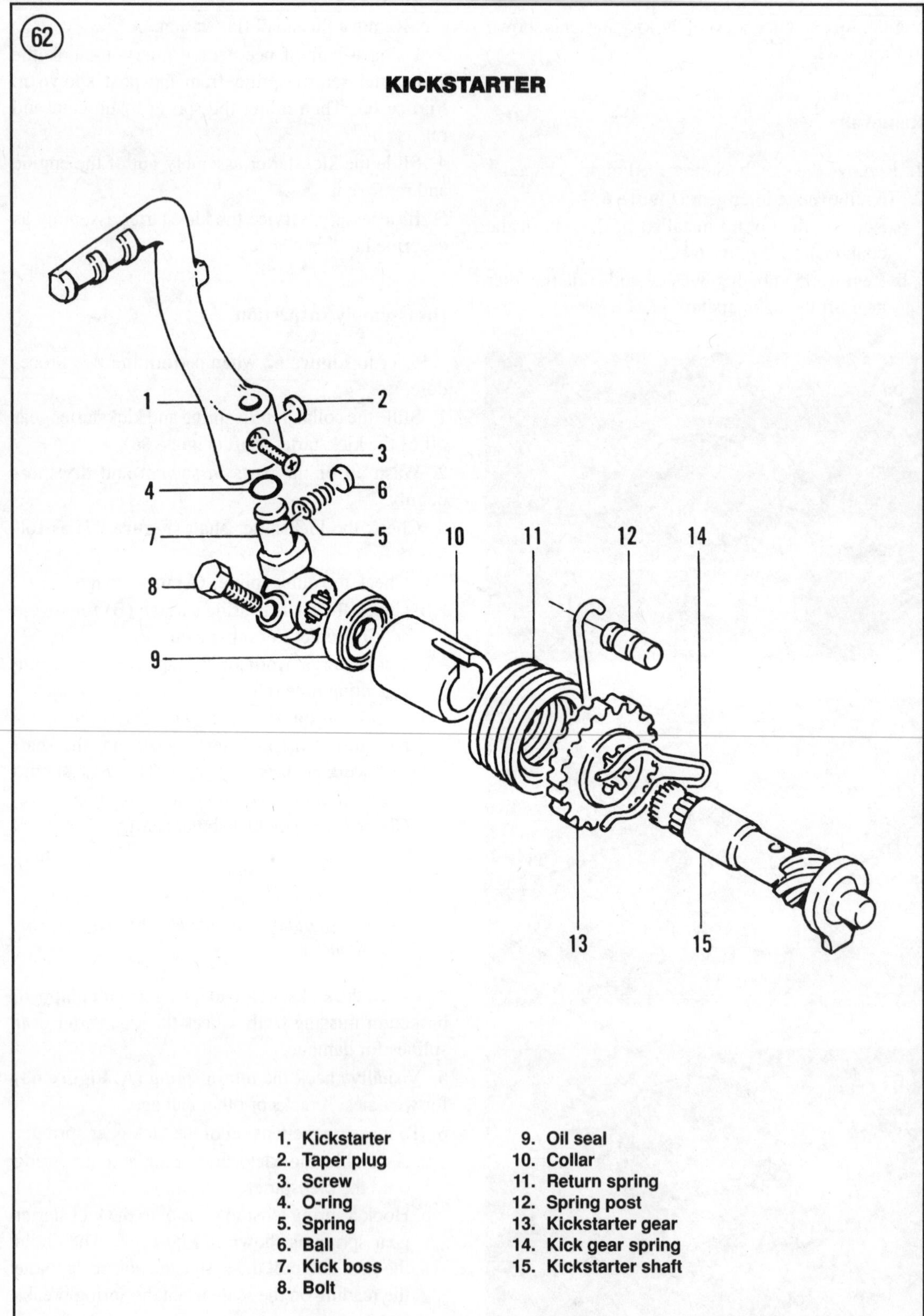

1. Kickstarter
2. Taper plug
3. Screw
4. O-ring
5. Spring
6. Ball
7. Kick boss
8. Bolt
9. Oil seal
10. Collar
11. Return spring
12. Spring post
13. Kickstarter gear
14. Kick gear spring
15. Kickstarter shaft

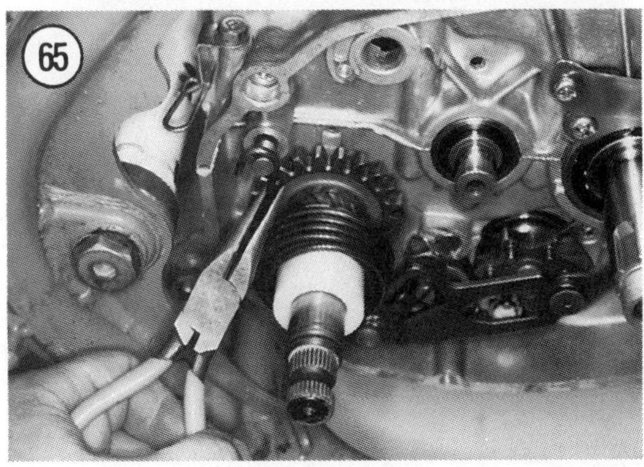

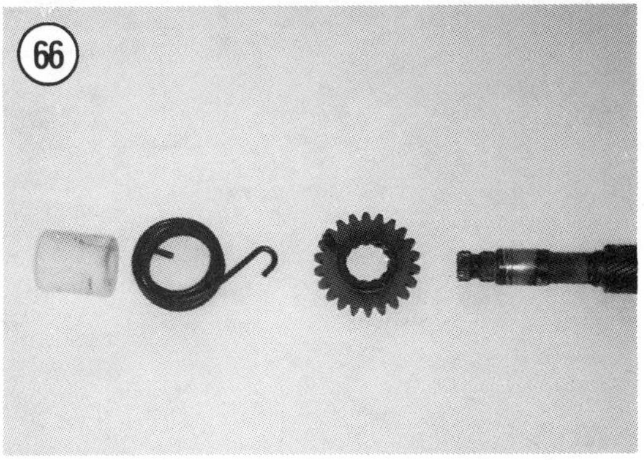

slips or moves before this tension range is reached, replace the kickstarter gear spring.

7. Replace questionable or damaged parts as required.

Reassembly

Refer to **Figure 62** when reassembling the kickstarter.

1. Slide the kickstarter gear onto the kickstarter shaft as shown in A, **Figure 70**.
2. If removed, install the kick gear spring onto the gear so that the angled part of the spring faces out as shown in B, **Figure 70**.
3. Install the return spring (A, **Figure 71**) onto the kickstarter shaft—insert the straight end of the spring into the kickstarter shaft hole as shown in B, **Figure 71**.
4. Slide the collar onto the kickstarter shaft so that the groove in the collar engages the spring end as shown in **Figure 72**.

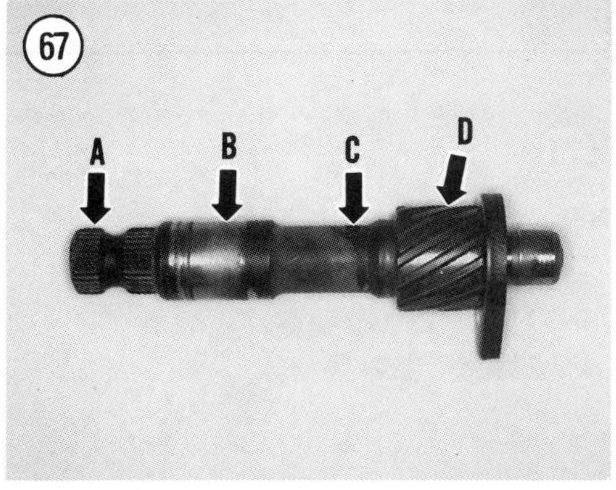

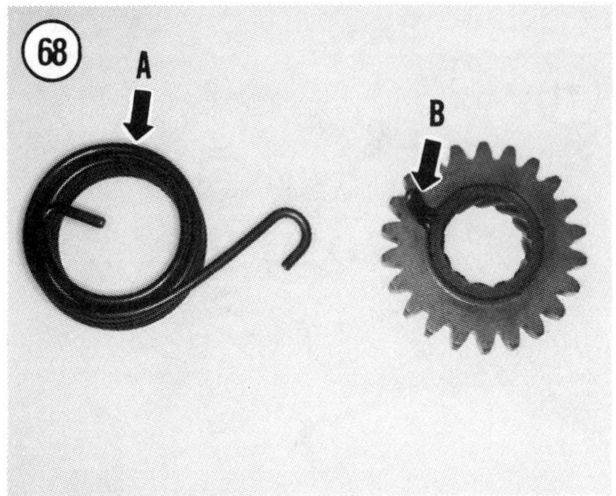

69

Kick gear spring
Spring scale

70

A
B

72

71

A
B

73

A
B

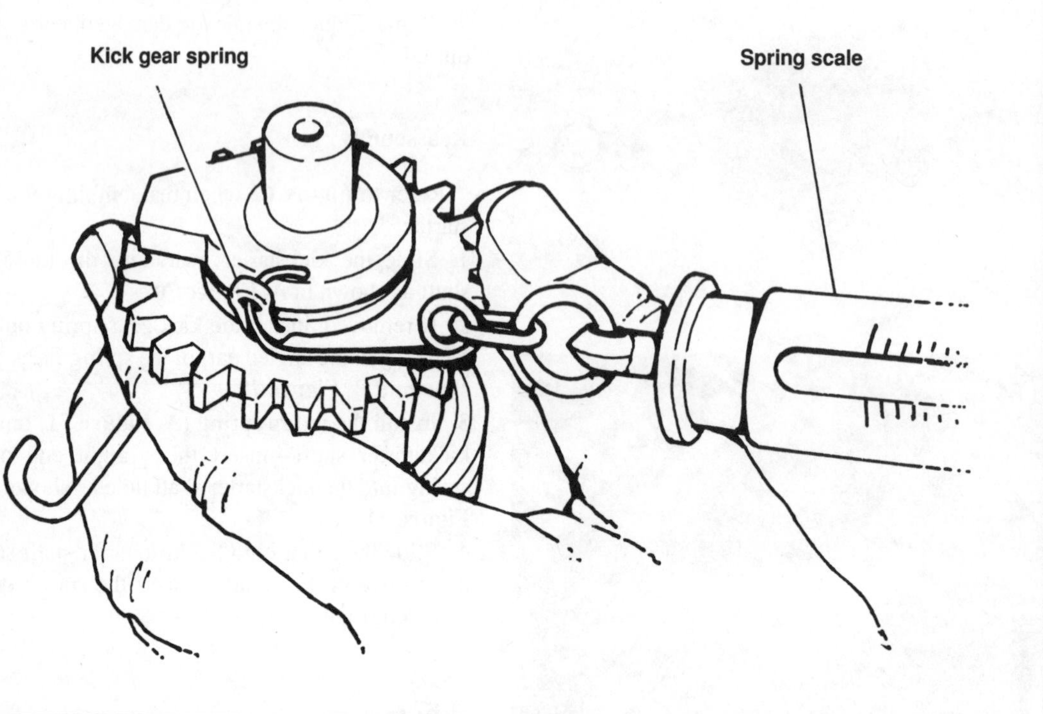

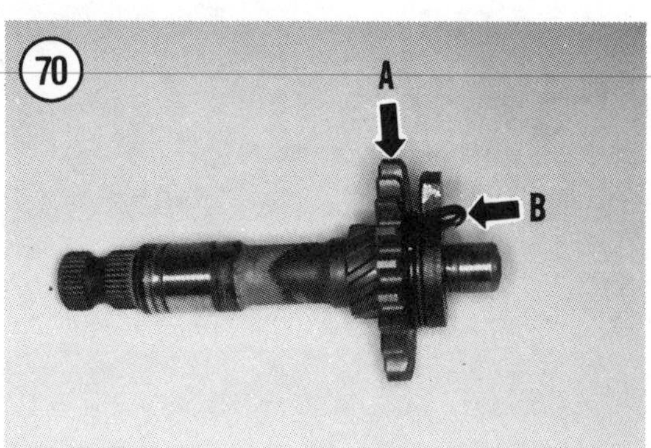

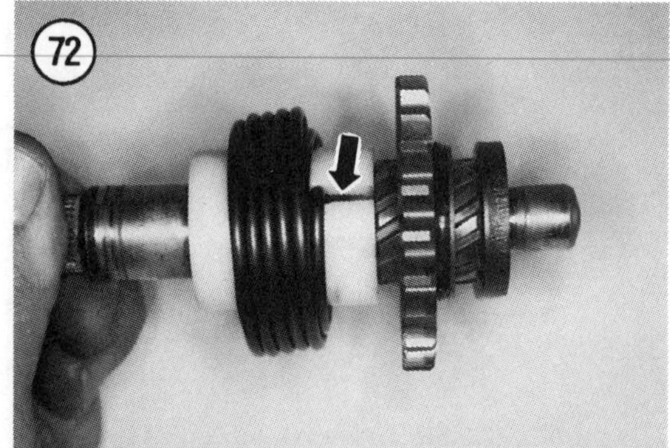

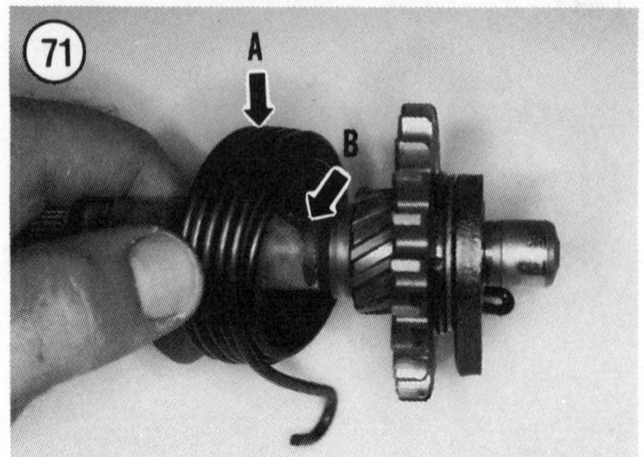

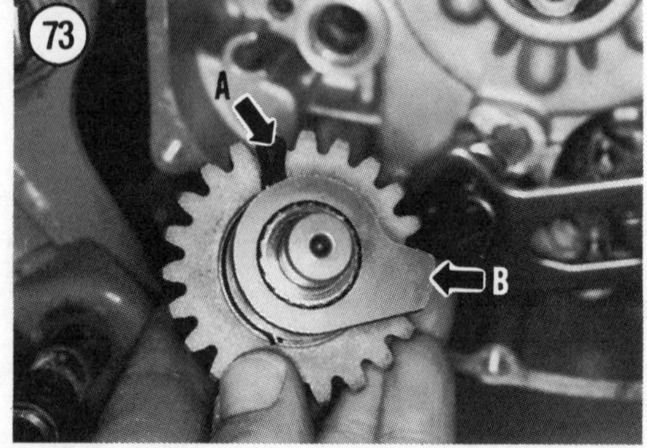

Installation

1. Apply transmission oil to all bearing surfaces on the kickstarter shaft.

2. Install the kickstarter into the crankcase, noting the following:

   a. Insert the kick gear spring end (A, **Figure 73**) into its mating crankcase groove (A, **Figure 74**).

   b. Seat the kick stop arm (B, **Figure 73**) against the case boss (B, **Figure 74**). See **Figure 75**.

3. Using a pair of needle nose pliers, turn the return spring clockwise (**Figure 76**) and hook the end of the spring onto the spring post as shown in **Figure 77**.

4. To install the idler gear assembly:

   a. Install the flat washer onto the countershaft (**Figure 78**).

   b. Install the idler gear, shoulder side facing in (**Figure 79**), onto the countershaft.

6

82

EXTERNAL SHIFT MECHANISM

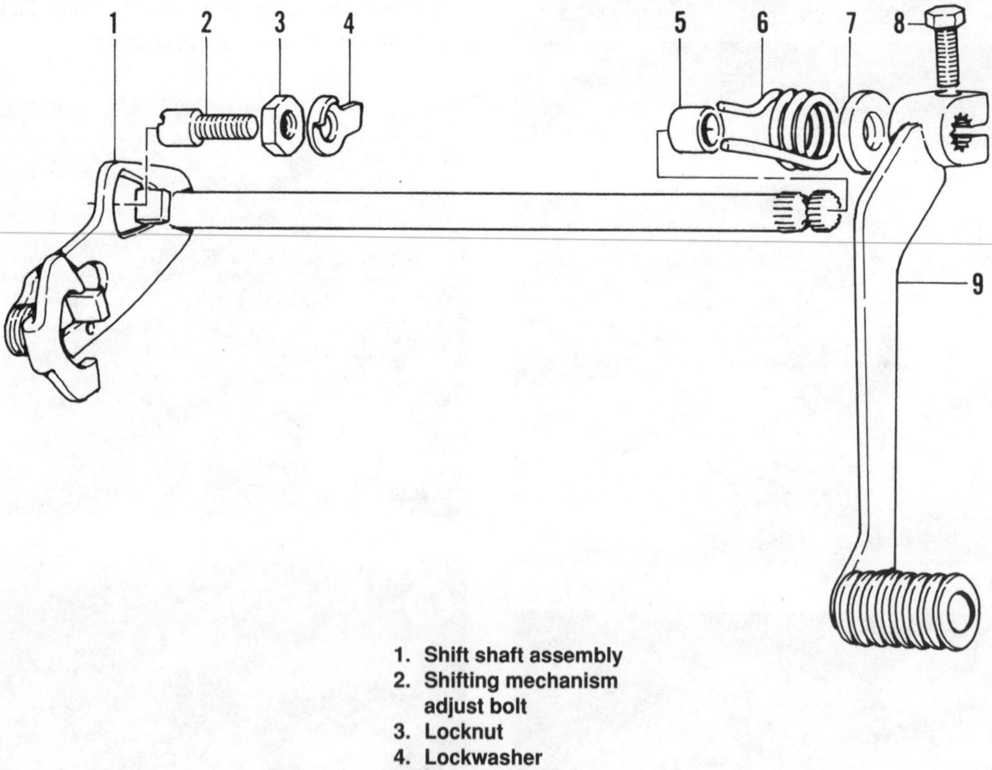

1 2 3 4 5 6 7 8 9

1. Shift shaft assembly
2. Shifting mechanism adjust bolt
3. Locknut
4. Lockwasher
5. Spacer
6. Return spring
7. Oil seal
8. Bolt
9. Shift lever

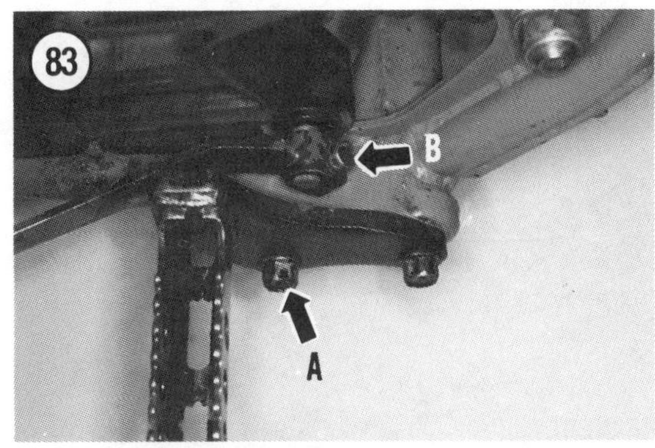

c. Install the notched washer as shown in **Figure 80**.

d. With the idler gear and washers fully seated, install a new circlip (**Figure 64**) into the countershaft groove. Make sure the circlip is fully seated in the groove. Now spin the idler gear by hand. It should turn smoothly with no roughness and it should not contact or engage the kickstarter gear.

5. To check kickstarter operation, perform the following:

a. Install the kickstarter lever (A, **Figure 81**) onto the kickstarter shaft.

b. Slowly push the kickstarter lever down by hand. When doing so, the kickstarter shaft will turn counterclockwise, forcing the kickstarter drive gear (B, **Figure 81**) outward where it meshes with the idler gear (C, **Figure 81**), turning it clockwise. Now slowly release the kickstarter lever and allow the kickstarter shaft to return to its normal position. As the shaft returns, the kickstarter gear will slide inward and disengage from the idler gear.

c. If the kickstarter did not operate as previously described, remove the kickstarter and inspect it for incorrect assembly or damaged parts.

6. Reinstall the clutch as described in this chapter.

6

EXTERNAL SHIFT MECHANISM

The external shift mechanism is located on the same side of the crankcase as the clutch assembly and can be removed with the engine in the frame. To remove the shift drum and shift forks it is necessary to remove the engine and split the crankcases (see Chapter Five).

Removal

Refer to **Figure 82** for this procedure.

1. Remove the clutch as described in this chapter.

2. Remove the left-hand footpeg (A, **Figure 83**) and the shift lever (B, **Figure 83**).

3. Pull the shift shaft (**Figure 84**) out of the engine and remove it.

4. Remove the shift drum stopper lever bolt (A, **Figure 85**) and remove the stopper lever (B, **Figure 85**) and spring (**Figure 86**).

Inspection

1. Clean all parts in solvent and dry thoroughly.
2. Check the shift shaft (**Figure 87**) for cracks or bending. Check the splines on the end of the shaft for damage.
3. Check the shift shaft return spring (A, **Figure 88**). The return spring arms should be centered on the shift shaft arm as shown in A, **Figure 88**. Replace the return spring if it shows signs of fatigue or is damaged.
4. Inspect the shift pawl spring (B, **Figure 87**). If the spring is severely damaged or missing, the shift shaft will have to be replaced as an assembly as replacement springs are not available.
5. Replace the spacer (5, **Figure 82**) if severely worn or damaged.
6. Check the stopper lever assembly (**Figure 89**) for the following:
   a. Weak or damaged spring.
   b. Bent or damaged stopper lever and roller.
   c. Damaged shoulder bolt.

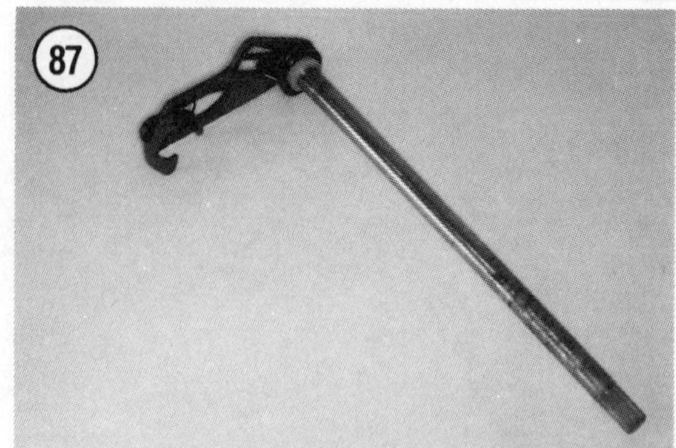
87

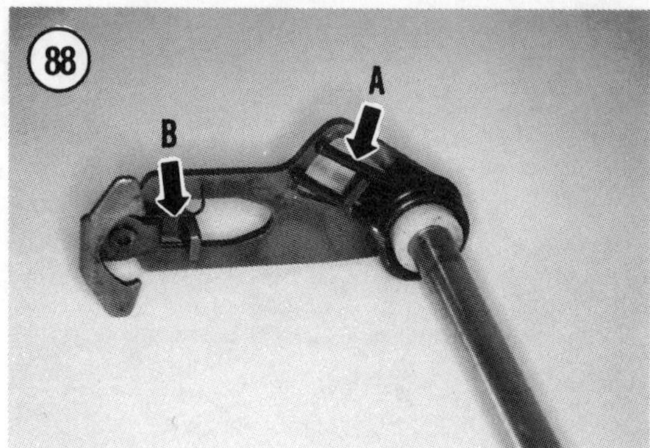

88

Installation

1. Apply Loctite 242 (blue) to the stopper lever mounting bolt prior to installation.
2. Install the stopper lever spring over the crankcase boss as shown in **Figure 86**. Then install the stopper lever (B, **Figure 85**) and secure it with its shoulder bolt (A, **Figure 85**). Tighten the bolt securely.
3. Slide the shift shaft into the crankcase, centering the return spring over the bolt stud as shown in **Figure 90**.

> *NOTE*
> *If the shift mechanism requires adjustment, refer to **Transmission Shifting Check and Adjustment** in Chapter Five.*

4. Install the shift lever (B, **Figure 83**) and left-hand footpeg (A, **Figure 83**).
5. Install the clutch as described in this chapter.

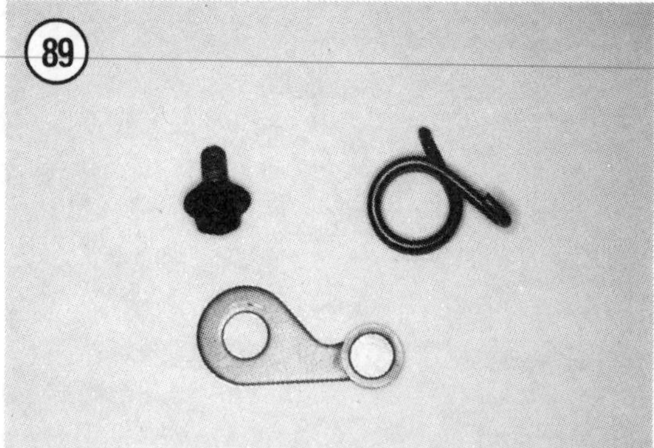
89

90

CLUTCH CABLE

Replacement

1. Remove the fuel tank as described in Chapter Eight.

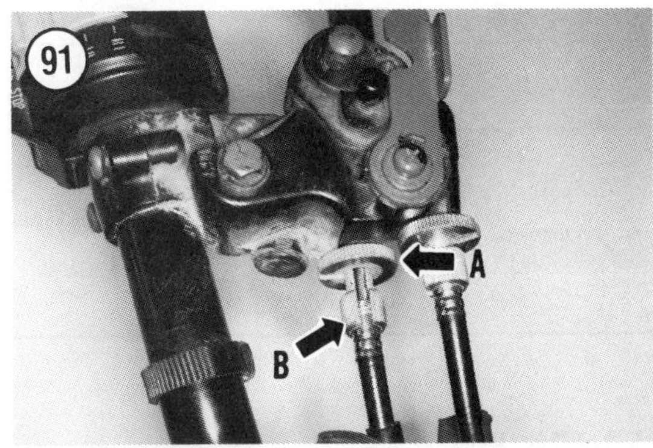

2. Pull the clutch/brake cable adjuster cover away from the handlebar cable adjusters.
3. Loosen the clutch cable adjuster locknut (A, **Figure 91**) and screw the adjuster (B, **Figure 91**) inward. Then release the clutch cable from the adjuster.
4. Disconnect the clutch cable at the release lever (**Figure 92**) as described under *Clutch Release Lever* in this chapter.

NOTE
Prior to removing the cable make a drawing of the cable routing through the frame. It is very easy to forget its routing after it has been removed. Reinstall the cable exactly as it was, avoiding any sharp turns.

5. Pull the cable out of any retaining clips on the frame.
6. Remove the clutch cable from the vehicle.
7. Lubricate the new cable as described in Chapter Three.
8. Install the new cable by reversing these removal steps. Make sure it is correctly routed with no sharp turns. Adjust the clutch cable as described in Chapter Three.

Table 1 GENERAL CLUTCH SPECIFICATIONS

Clutch type	Wet, multiple-disc
Clutch spring quantity	6
Friction plate quantity	7
Clutch plate quantity	6
Cushion ring quantity	7

Table 2 CLUTCH SERVICE SPECIFICATIONS

	New mm (in.)	Service limit mm (in.)
Friction plate thickness	3.0 (0.118)	2.7 (0.106)
Clutch plate		
Thickness	1.2 (0.047)	—
Warp limit	—	0.05 (0.002)
Clutch spring free length	36.4 (1.43)	34.4 (1.35)
Clutch pushrod runout limit	—	0.2 (0.008)

Table 3 TIGHTENING TORQUES

	N•m	ft.-lb.
Clutch cover screws	7	5.1
Clutch nut	90	66
Clutch spring bolts	10	7.4
Kickstarter bolt	25	18
Primary drive gear nut	65	47
Shift cam stopper plate	14	10
Shift lever adjust screw	30	22
Stopper lever bolt	10	7.4
Transmission drain plug	20	14

CHAPTER SEVEN

TRANSMISSION AND INTERNAL SHIFT MECHANISM

This chapter describes disassembly and reassembly of the transmission and internal shift mechanism (shift drum and forks) components. To gain access to the transmission and internal shift mechanism it is necessary to remove the engine and split the crankcase (Chapter Five). Once the crankcase has been split, removal of the transmission and shift drum and forks is a simple task of pulling the assemblies up and out of the crankcase.

Transmission ratios are listed in **Table 1**. Service specifications are listed in **Table 2**. Both tables are found at the end of the chapter.

NOTE
If disassembling a used, well run-in engine for the first time by yourself, pay particular attention to any additional shims that may have been added by a previous owner. These may have been added to take up the tolerance of worn components and must be reinstalled in the same position since the shims have developed a wear pattern. If new parts are going to be installed, these shims may be eliminated. This is something you will have to determine upon reassembly.

TRANSMISSION OPERATION

The basic transmission has 6 pairs of constantly meshed gears (**Figure 1**) on the mainshaft (A) and countershaft (B). Each pair of meshed gears gives one gear ratio. In each pair, one of the gears is locked to its shaft and always turns with it. The other gear is not locked to its shaft and can spin freely on it. Next to each free spinning gear is a third gear which is splined to the same shaft, always turning with it. This third gear can slide from side to side along the shaft splines. The side of the sliding gear and the free spinning gear have mating "dogs" and "slots." When the sliding gear moves up against the free spinning gear, the 2 gears are locked together, locking the free spinning gear to its shaft. Since both meshed mainshaft and countershaft gears are now locked to their shafts, power is transmitted at that gear ratio.

Shift Drum and Forks

Each sliding gear has a deep groove machined around its outside (**Figure 2**). The curved shift fork arm rides in this groove, controlling the side-to-side sliding of the gear, and therefore the selection of different gear ratios. Each shift fork (A, **Figure 3**) slides back and forth on a guide shaft, and has a peg (B, **Figure 3**) that rides in a groove machined in the shift drum. When the shift linkage rotates the shift drum, the zigzag grooves move the shift forks and sliding gears back and forth.

TRANSMISSION TROUBLESHOOTING

Refer to *Transmission* in Chapter Two.

TRANSMISSION

Removal/Installation

Remove and install the transmission and internal shift mechanism as described under *Crankcase Disassembly/Reassembly* in Chapter Five.

Transmission Service Notes

1. After removing the transmission shafts, place one of the shafts into a large can or plastic bucket and clean with solvent. Dry with compressed air or let sit on rags to drip dry. Repeat for the opposite shaft.
2. If you have intermixed gears from both shafts (mainshaft and countershaft), use the gear ratio information in **Table 1** and the transmission exploded view drawing (found in this chapter under *Transmission Overhaul*) to identify the gears.
3. A divided container such as an egg carton (**Figure 4**) can be used to help maintain correct alignment and position of the parts as they are removed from the transmission shafts.
4. Replace all of the transmission circlips during reassembly. Do not reuse circlips.

TRANSMISSION OVERHAUL

Figure 5 is an exploded view of the transmission assembly. Refer to it when performing the following service procedures.

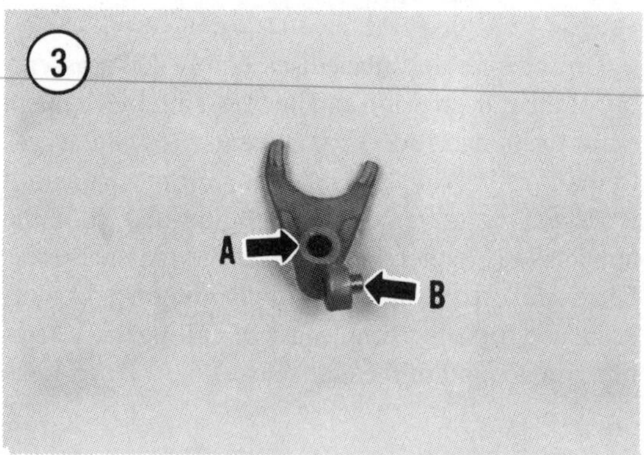

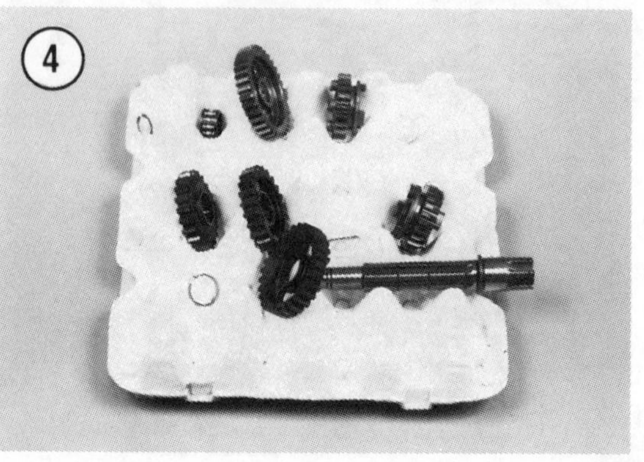

(5)

TRANSMISSION

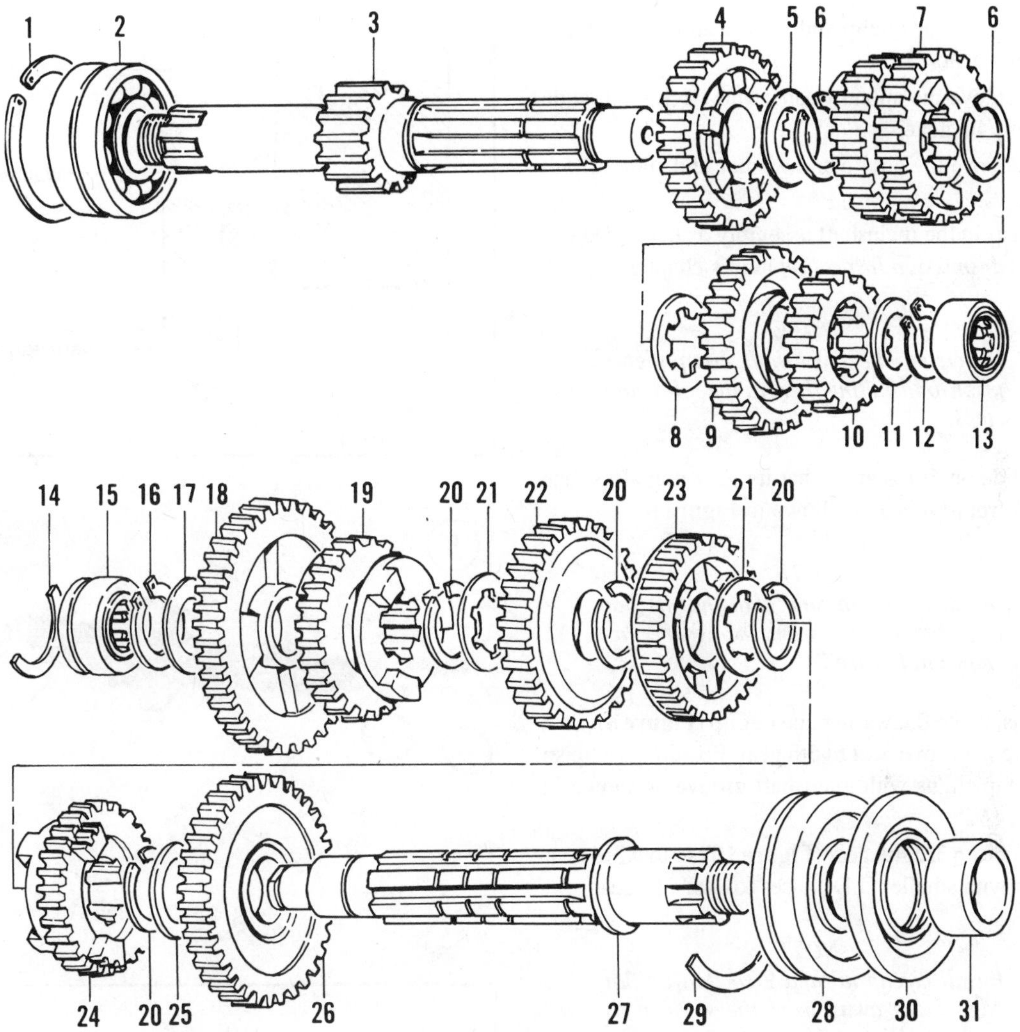

1. Circlip
2. Bearing
3. Mainshaft/1st gear
4. 5th gear
5. Washer
6. Circlip
7. 3rd/4th gear combination
8. Spline washer
9. 6th gear
10. 2nd gear
11. Washer
12. Circlip
13. Needle bearing
14. Bearing clip
15. Needle bearing
16. Circlip
17. Washer
18. 1st gear
19. 5th gear
20. Circlip
21. Spline washer
22. 3rd gear
23. 4th gear
24. 6th gear
25. Washer
26. 2nd gear
27. Countershaft
28. Bearing
29. Bearing clip
30. Oil seal
31. Collar

Mainshaft Disassembly/Assembly

1. Slide the 2 bearings off the mainshaft and remove them.
2. Remove the circlip and washer and slide off 2nd and 6th gears.
3. Remove the spline washer and circlip and slide off 3rd/4th gear.
4. Remove the circlip and washer and slide off 5th gear.
5. Inspect the mainshaft assembly as described under *Transmission Inspection* in this chapter.

NOTE
Lubricate the mainshaft components prior to installing them in the following steps.

6. Slide on 5th gear so that its gear dog slots face away from 1st gear as shown in **Figure 6**.

NOTE
*Install circlip in Step 7 so that its flat edge faces away from the washer as shown in **Figure 7**.*

7. Install the flat washer and circlip (**Figure 8**). Seat circlip in groove next to 5th gear. Position circlip so that gap aligns with mainshaft groove as shown in **Figure 9**.
8. Slide on 3rd/4th gear (**Figure 10**) so that 3rd gear (gear with smaller O.D.) faces toward 5th gear.

NOTE
*Install circlip in Step 9 so that its flat edge faces away from the washer as shown in **Figure 7**.*

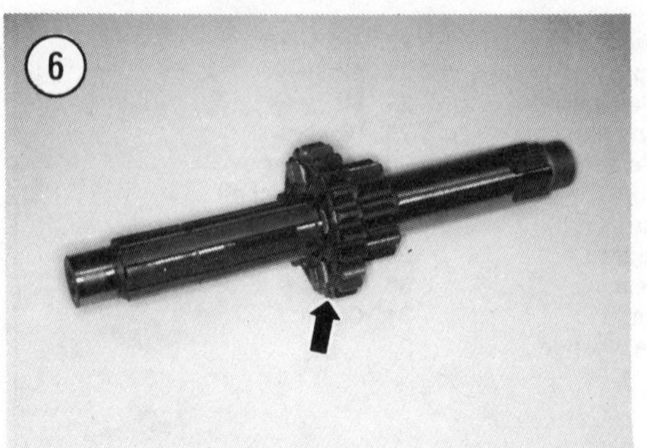

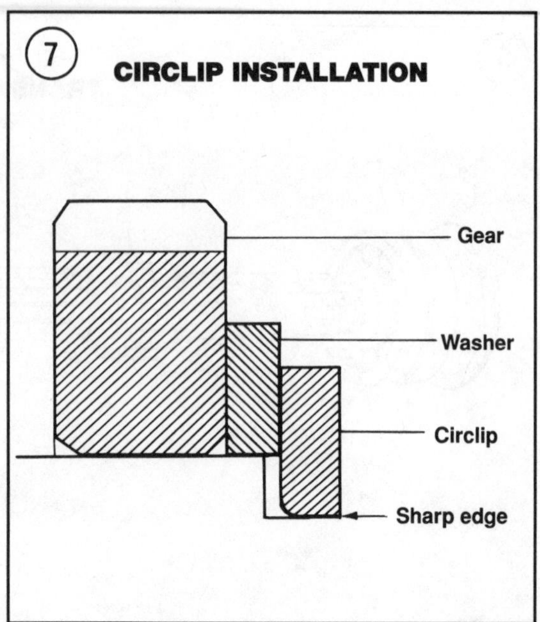

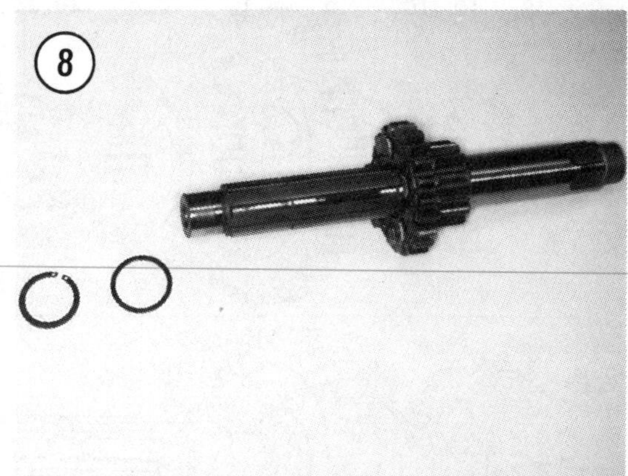

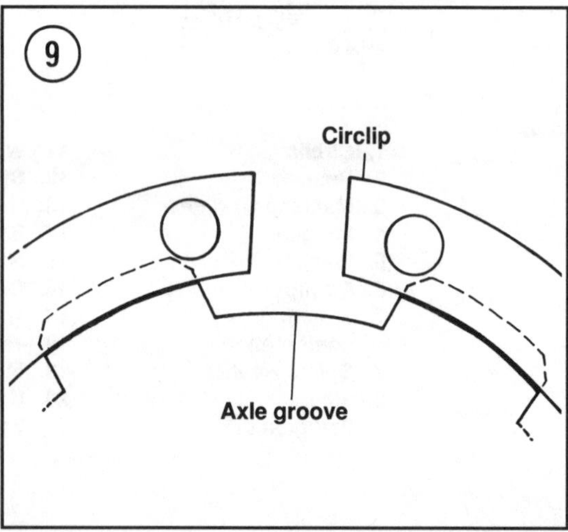

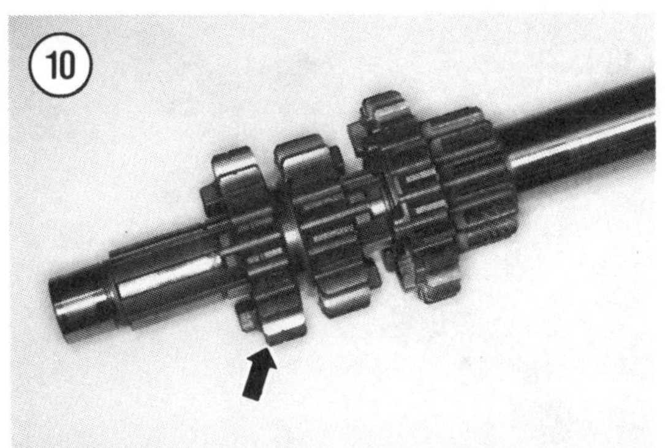

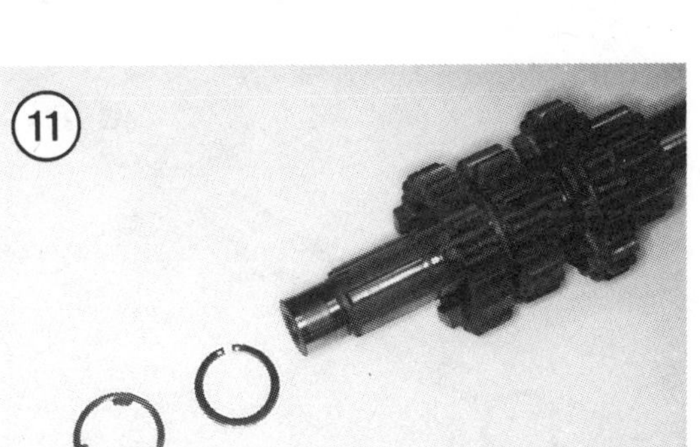

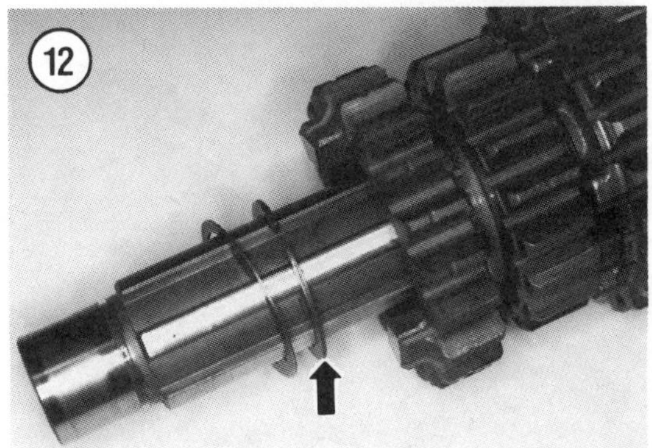

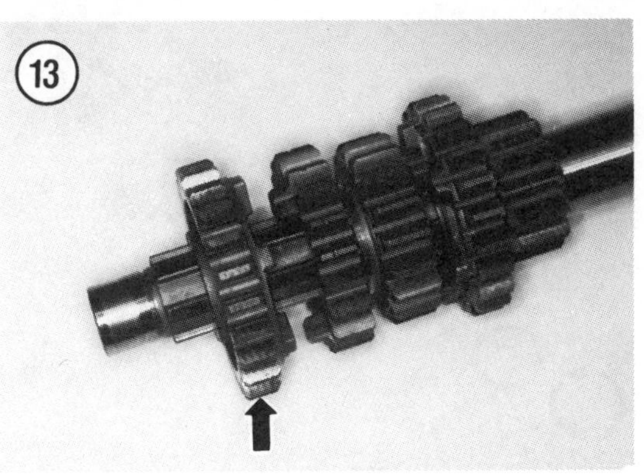

9. Install the circlip and spline washer (**Figure 11**). Seat circlip in mainshaft groove as shown in **Figure 12**. Position circlip so that gap aligns with mainshaft groove as shown in **Figure 9**.
10. Slide on 6th gear so that its gear dogs face toward 4th gear as shown in **Figure 13**.
11. Slide on 2nd gear so that its shoulder (**Figure 14**) faces toward 6th gear. See **Figure 15**.

NOTE
*Install circlip in Step 12 so that its flat edge faces away from the washer as shown in **Figure** 7.*

12. Install the flat washer and circlip (**Figure 16**). Seat circlip in groove next to 6th gear.

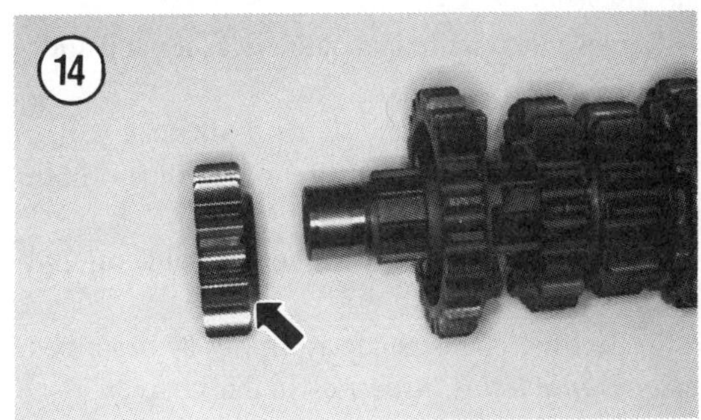

13. Install the needle bearing and ball bearing onto the mainshaft as shown in **Figure 17**. Install both bearings with their manufacturer's name and side code markings facing out.
14. After assembling mainshaft, refer to **Figure 5** and to **Figure 17** for the correct placement of all gears. Make sure all circlips are fully seated in mainshaft grooves.

Countershaft Disassembly/Assembly

1. Slide the 2 bearings off the countershaft and remove them.
2. Remove the circlip and washer and slide off 1st and 5th gears.
3. Remove the circlip and spline washer and slide off 3rd gear.
4. Remove the circlip and slide off 4th gear.
5. Remove the washer and circlip and slide off 6th gear.
6. Remove the circlip and washer and slide off 2nd gear.
7. Inspect the countershaft assembly as described under *Transmission Inspection* in this chapter.

NOTE
Lubricate the countershaft components prior to installing them in the following steps.

8. Slide on 2nd gear so that its gear dogs face inward as shown in **Figure 18**.

NOTE
*Install circlip in Step 9 so that its flat edge faces away from the washer as shown in **Figure 7**.*

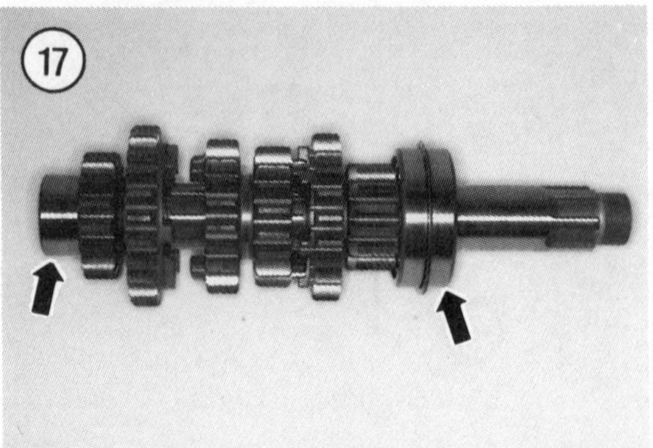

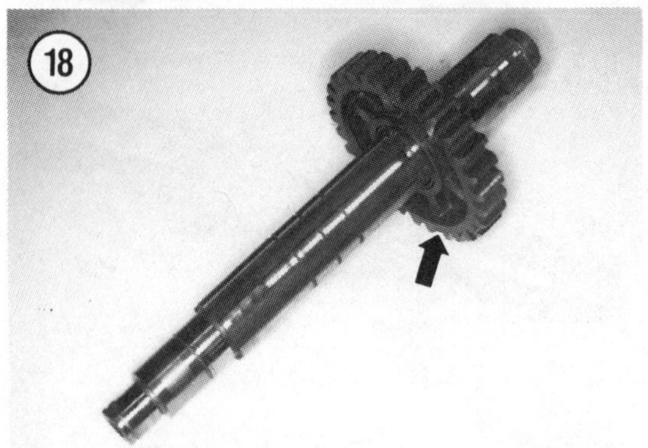

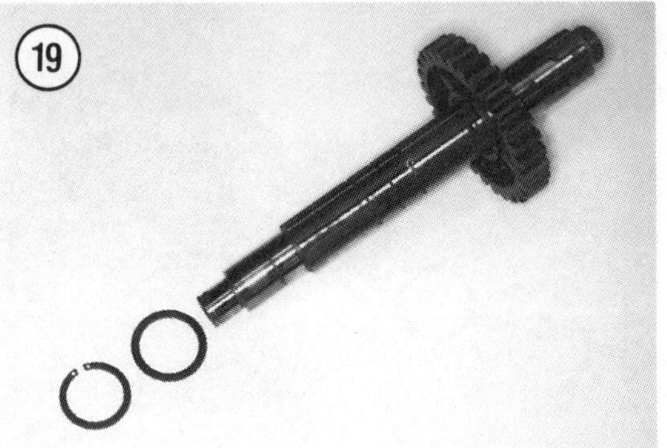

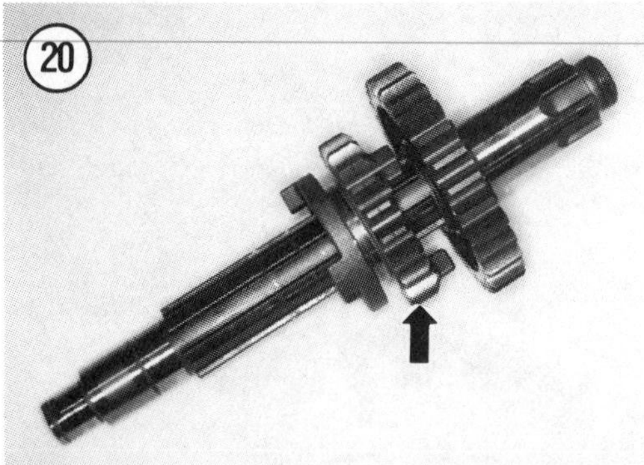

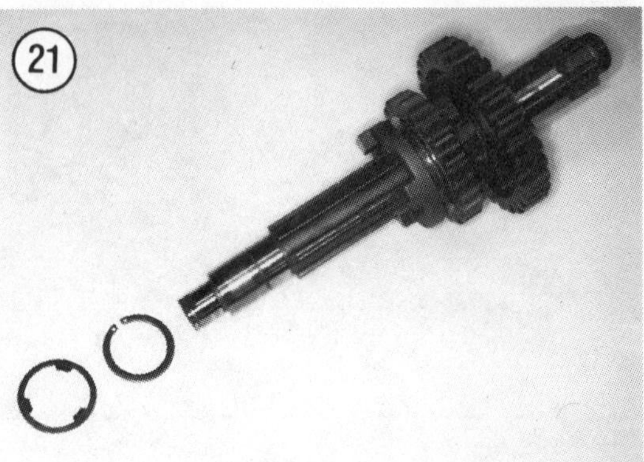

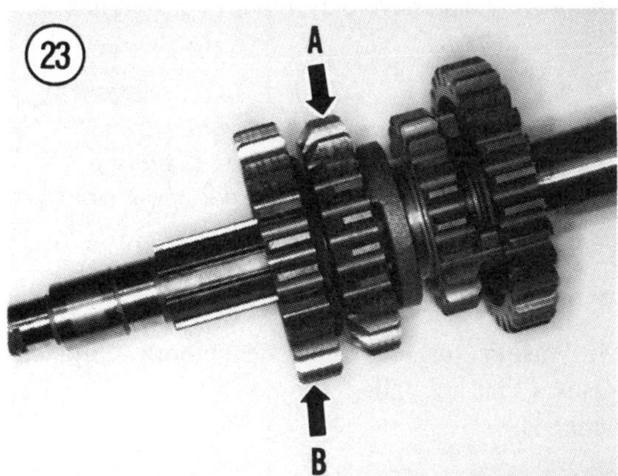

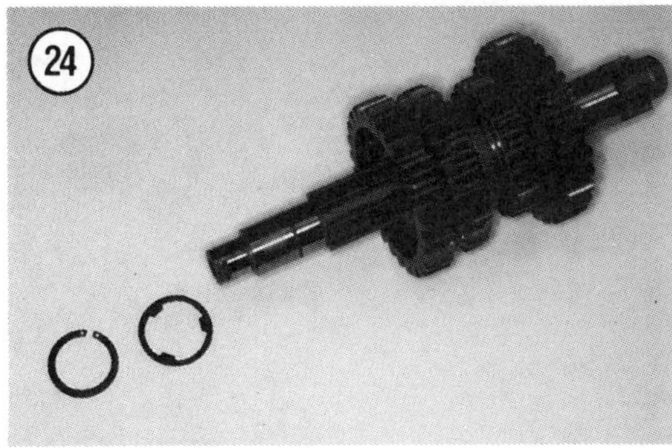

9. Install the flat washer and circlip (**Figure 19**). Seat circlip in groove next to 2nd gear. Position circlip so that gap aligns with countershaft groove as shown in **Figure 9**.

10. Slide on 6th gear so that its gear dogs face toward 2nd gear as shown in **Figure 20**.

NOTE
*Install circlip in Step 11 so that its flat edge faces away from the washer as shown in **Figure** 7.*

11. Install the circlip and spline washer (**Figure 21**). Seat circlip in countershaft groove as shown in **Figure 22**. Position circlip so that gap aligns with countershaft groove as shown in **Figure 9**.

12. Slide on 4th gear (A, **Figure 23**) so that its dog slots face toward 6th gear.

13. Slide on 3rd gear (B, **Figure 23**) so that its flat side faces toward 4th gear.

NOTE
*Install circlip in Step 14 so that its flat edge faces away from the washer as shown in **Figure** 7.*

14. Install the flat washer and circlip (**Figure 24**). Seat circlip in groove next to 3rd gear.

15. Slide on 5th gear so that its shift fork groove side faces toward 3rd gear as shown in **Figure 25**.

16. Slide on 1st gear (**Figure 26**) so that its gear dogs face toward 5th gear.

NOTE
*Install circlip in Step 17 so that its flat edge faces away from the washer as shown in **Figure** 7.*

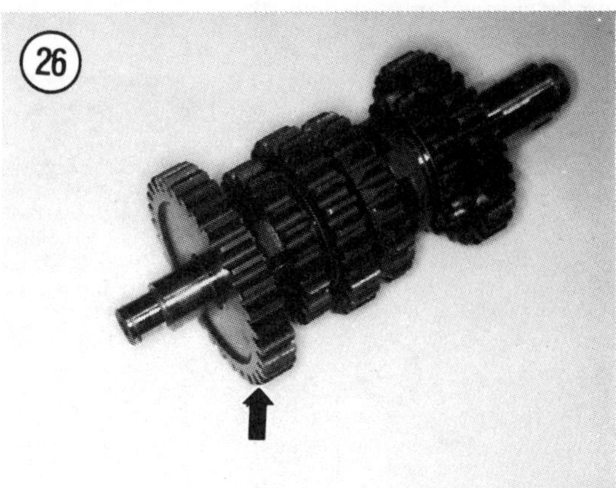

17. Install the flat washer and circlip (**Figure 27**). Seat the circlip in groove next to 1st gear.

18. Install the needle bearing onto the countershaft so that the circlip groove in the bearing faces away from 1st gear as shown in A, **Figure 28**.

19. Install the ball bearing onto the countershaft so that the circlip groove in the bearing faces toward 2nd gear as shown in B, **Figure 28**.

20. After assembling mainshaft, refer to **Figure 5** and to **Figure 28** for the correct placement of all gears. Make sure all circlips are fully seated in countershaft grooves.

Transmission Inspection

1. Clean all parts in solvent. Dry with compressed air.

NOTE
Maintain alignment of disassembled shafts, gears, circlips and washers when cleaning and drying them.

2. Check all shaft splines for wear, cracks or other damage. See **Figure 29** (mainshaft) and **Figure 30** (countershaft).

3. Check the mainshaft and countershaft circlip grooves. The grooves must have sharp square shoulders to prevent the circlips from coming out (**Figure 31**).

4. Check mainshaft 1st gear (**Figure 29**). If gear is damaged, replace mainshaft.

5. Place each shaft on V-blocks and check runout with a dial indicator. If runout exceeds service limit in **Table 2**, replace shaft.

6. Check each gear for excessive wear, burrs, pitting, or chipped or missing teeth.

7. Check each stationary gear bore (A, **Figure 32**) for scoring, cracks or other damage.

8. Check the gear dogs (B, **Figure 32**) for severe wear or damage.

9. Check each sliding gear groove (C, **Figure 32**) for severe wear, scoring or other damage.

10. Check that stationary gears (A, **Figure 32**) turn smoothly on their respective shafts without any excessive rocking.

11. Slide splined gears (C, **Figure 32**) onto their respective shafts. Gears should slide smoothly and without any excessive play, binding or roughness.

NOTE
Defective gears should be replaced, and it is a good idea to replace the mating gear even though it may not show as much wear or damage.

12. Replace all circlips during reassembly.

13. Washer surfaces must be smooth. Replace washers that are galled, scored, bent or otherwise damaged.

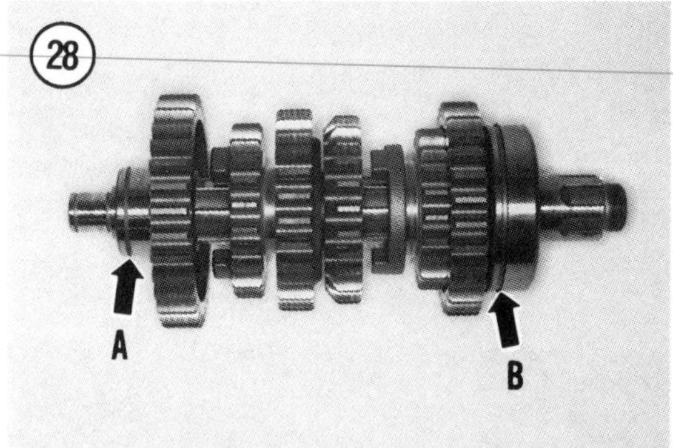

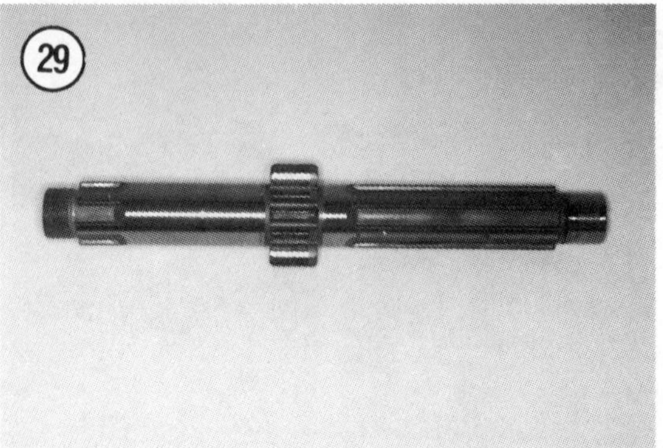

INTERNAL SHIFT MECHANISM

The internal shift mechanism is shown in **Figure 33**.

Removal/Installation

Remove and install the transmission assembly as described under *Crankcase Disassembly and Crankcase Assembly* in Chapter Five. **Figure 34** shows the internal shift mechanism assembly installed in the lower crankcase.

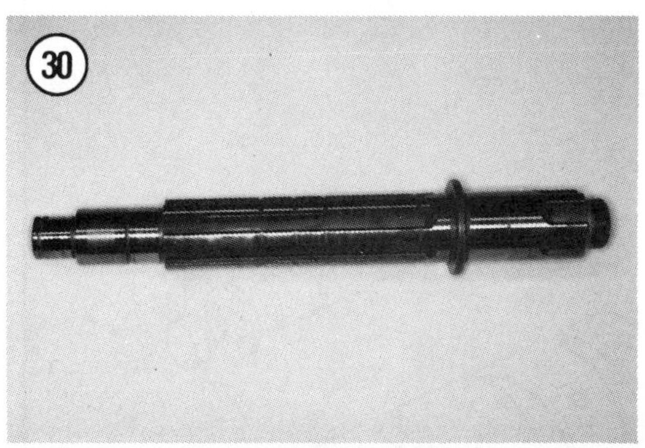

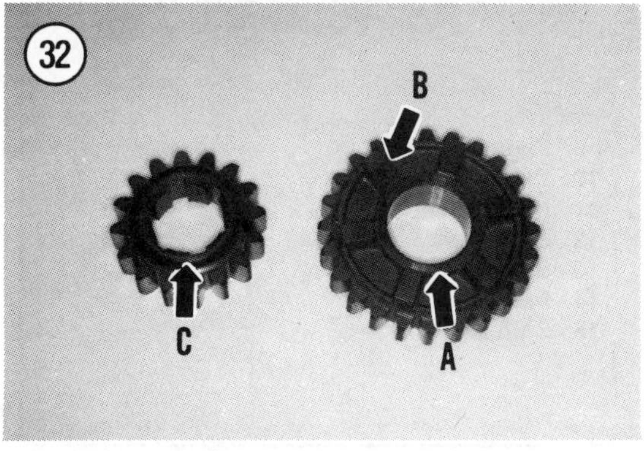

Shift Fork Inspection

Refer to **Figure 33** for this procedure.

1. Inspect each shift fork (**Figure 35**) for signs of wear or damage. Examine the shift forks at the points where they contact the slider gear A, **Figure 36**. This surface should be smooth with no signs of wear or damage.
2. Check for any arc-shaped wear or burn marks on the shift forks. This indicates that the shift fork has remained in contact with the gear. The shift fork fingers have become excessively worn and the shift fork must be replaced.
3. Check the shift fork pins (B, **Figure 36**) for galling, cracks or other damage.
4. Check the shaft bore (C, **Figure 36**) in each shift fork for galling or other damage.
5. Check the shift fork shafts (**Figure 35**) for bending or other damage. Check that each shift fork slides smoothly on its respective shaft.
6. Replace severely worn or damaged parts.

7

Shift Drum Inspection

Figure 37 shows a view of the shift drum assembly. The individual shift drum parts are available through Yamaha dealers.

1. Check the shift drum grooves (A, **Figure 37**) for severe wear or roughness.
2. Turn the bearing (B, **Figure 37**) by hand. The bearing should turn smoothly with no roughness, catching, binding or excessive noise. If bearing is damaged, refer to *Disassembly/Reassembly* in this chapter.
3. Check the shift drum segment pins for severe wear or damage.
4. Oil the bearing with new transmission oil.

Disassembly/Reassembly

1. Disassemble shift drum assembly (**Figure 38**) as follows:
   a. Loosen and remove the Phillips screw from the end of the shift drum.

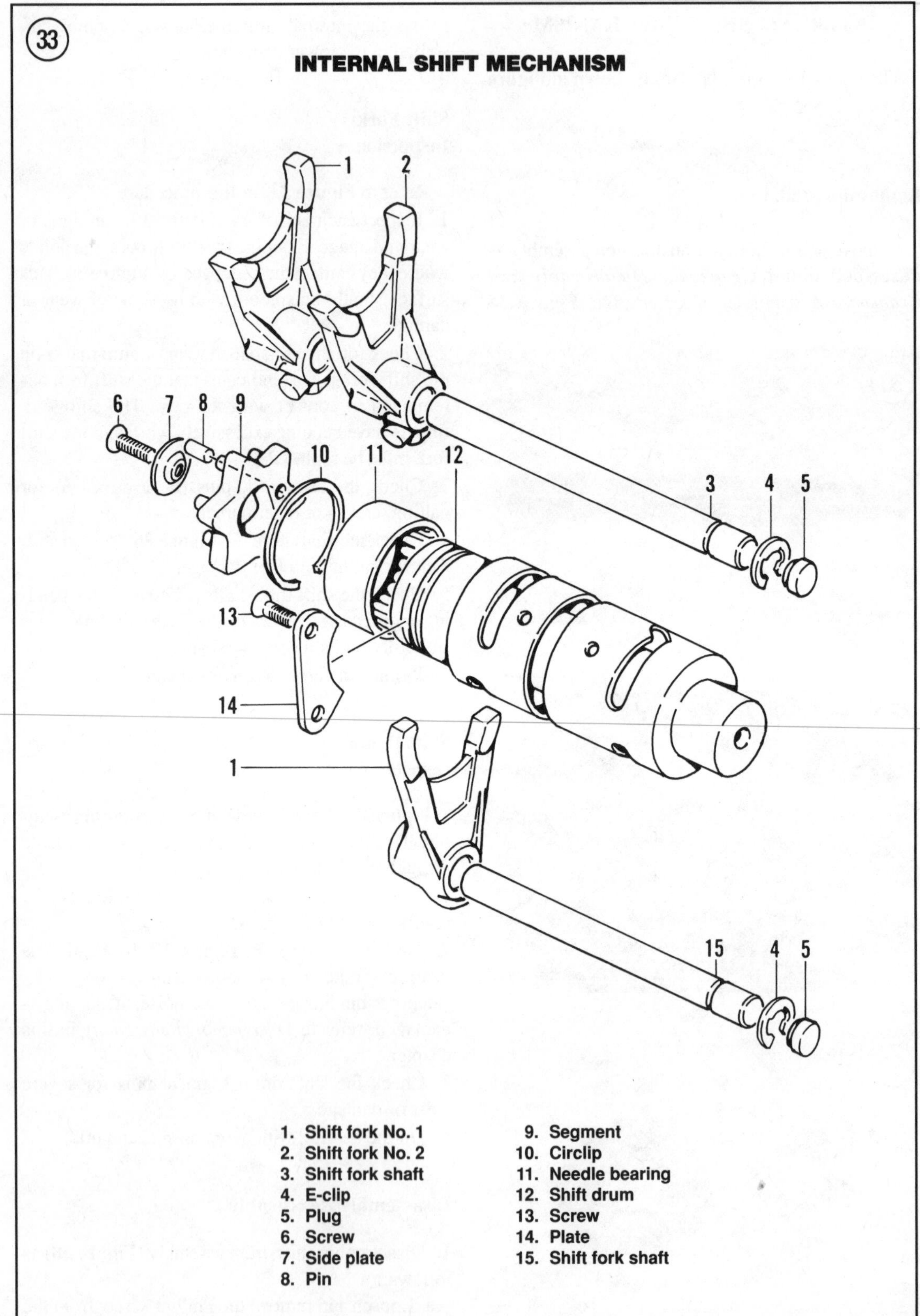

1. Shift fork No. 1
2. Shift fork No. 2
3. Shift fork shaft
4. E-clip
5. Plug
6. Screw
7. Side plate
8. Pin
9. Segment
10. Circlip
11. Needle bearing
12. Shift drum
13. Screw
14. Plate
15. Shift fork shaft

b. Remove the side plate and segment. Don't loose the side pin installed in the segment.

c. Remove the circlip and slide off the needle bearing.

2. Remove all thread sealer residue from the shift drum and Phillips screw threads.

3. Clean all parts in solvent. Dry with compressed air.

4. The shift drum circlip groove (A, **Figure 39**) must have sharp square shoulders.

5. Check the shift drum bearing surfaces (B, **Figure 39**) for scoring, galling or other damage.

6. Lubricate the needle bearing rollers with transmission oil, then install the bearing onto the shift drum with its manufacturers's name and size code markings facing out.

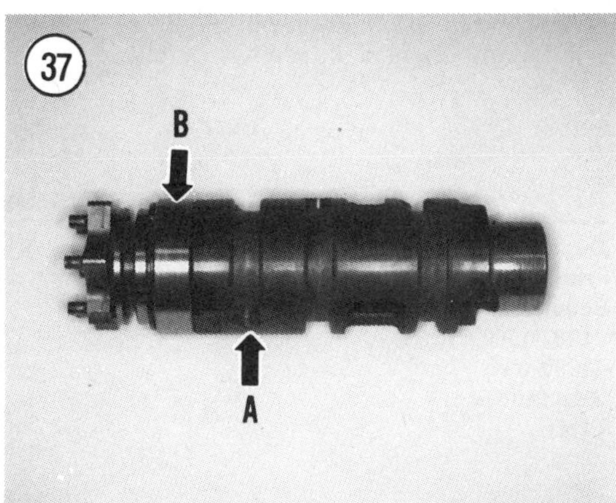

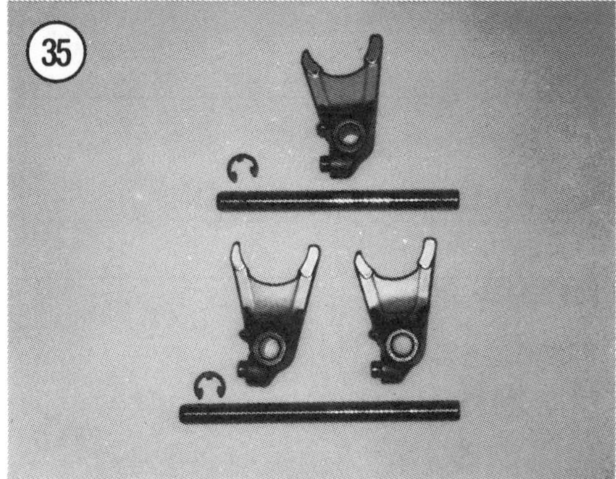

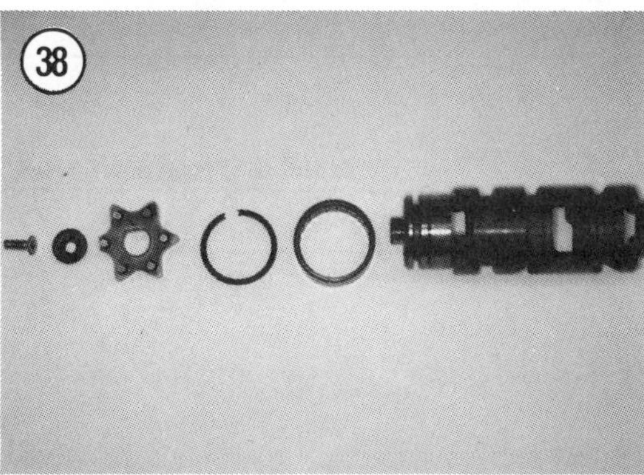

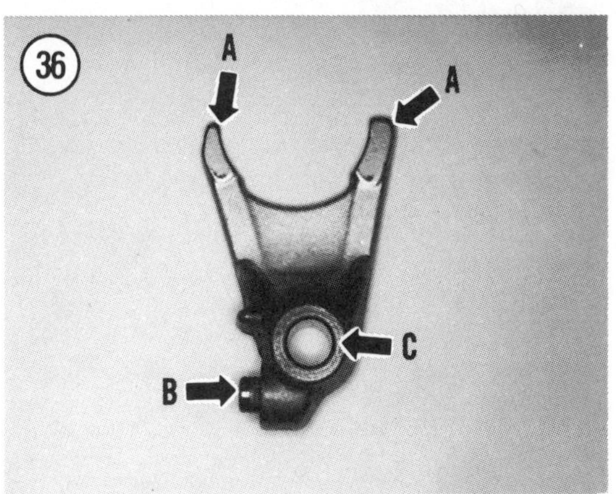

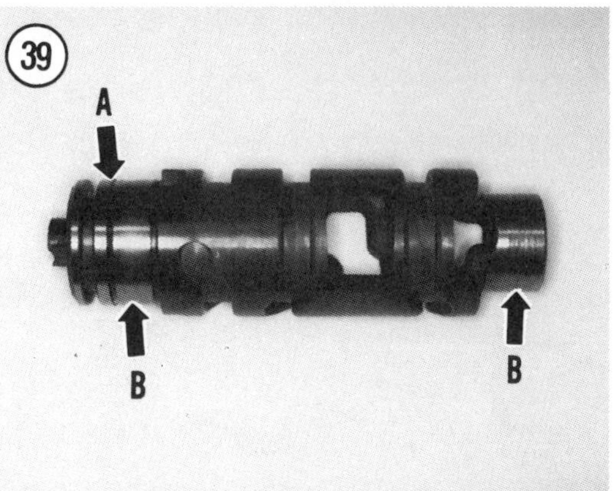

7

7. Install the circlip into the shift drum groove. Make sure the circlip is fully seated in the groove.
8. Install the pin into the segment pin hole (A, **Figure 40**). Then install the segment onto the shift drum making sure the pin properly engages the shift drum hole (B, **Figure 40**).
9. Install the side plate so that its dished side seats into the segment cone.
10. Apply a nonpermanent thread locking compound to the Phillips screw and install the screw into the shift drum. Tighten the screw securely.

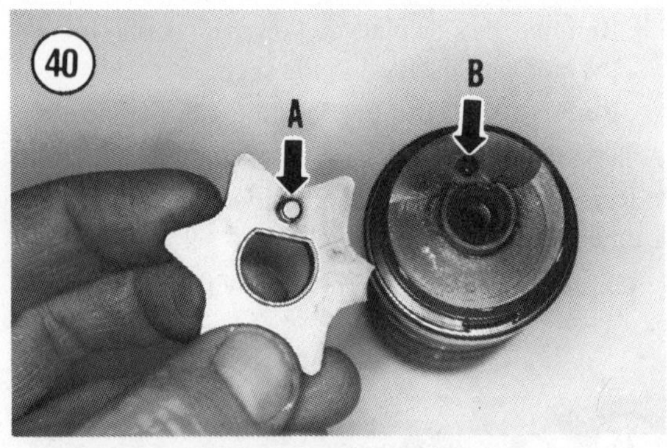

Table 1 TRANSMISSION GEAR RATIOS

Transmission type	Constant mesh, 6-speed
Primary reduction ratio	66:23 (2.869)
Secondary reduction ratio	
1987-1989	42:13 (3.230)
1990-on	41:14 (2.929)
Gear ratio	
1st	32:13 (2.461)
2nd	29:16 (1.812)
3rd	27:18 (1.500)
4th	25:20 (1.250)
5th	23:22 (1.045)
6th	21:24 (0.875)

Table 2 TRANSMISSION SERVICE SPECIFICATIONS

Shaft runout limit	0.08 mm (0.0031 in.)

CHAPTER EIGHT

FUEL AND EXHAUST SYSTEMS

The fuel system consists of the fuel tank, fuel shutoff valve, fuel lines, 2 carburetors and air filter.

The engine receives its lubrication from a gasoline and oil mixture (pre-mix). The engine is not equipped with an oil injection system. Refer to Chapter Three for fuel/oil mixture ratios.

The exhaust system consists of 2 expansion chambers and 2 silencers.

This chapter includes service procedures for all parts of the fuel system and exhaust system. Air filter service is covered in Chapter Three.

Carburetor specifications are covered in **Table 1**. **Tables 1-3** are at the end of the chapter.

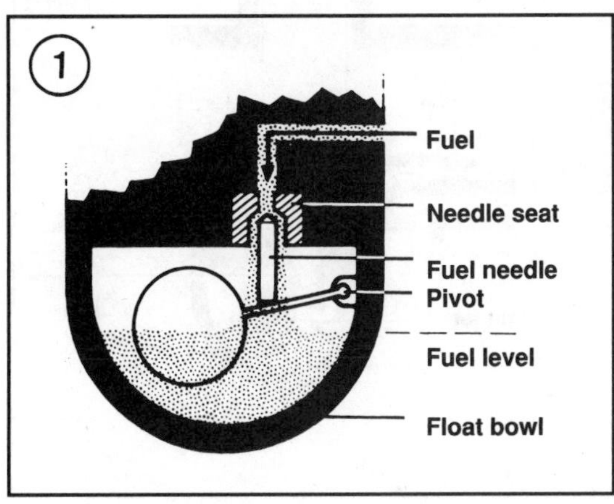

CARBURETOR OPERATION

For proper operation, a gasoline engine must be supplied with fuel and air mixed in proper proportions by weight. A mixture in which there is an excess of fuel is said to be rich. A lean mixture is one which contains insufficient fuel. A properly adjusted carburetor supplies the proper mixture to the engine under all operating conditions.

The carburetor consists of several major systems. A float and float valve mechanism maintain a constant fuel level in the float bowl. The pilot system supplies fuel at low speeds. The main fuel system supplies fuel at medium and high speeds. Finally, a starter (choke) system supplies a rich mixture needed to start a cold engine.

Float Mechanism

To ensure a steady supply of fuel, the carburetor is equipped with a float valve through which fuel flows by gravity from the fuel tank into the float bowls (**Figure 1**). Inside the bowl is a combined float assembly that moves up and down with the fuel level. Resting on the float arm is a fuel valve needle, which rides inside the fuel valve seat. The fuel valve regulates fuel flow into the float bowl. The fuel needle and seat valve contact surfaces are machined very accurately to insure correct fuel flow calibration. As the float rises, the fuel needle rises inside the fuel valve and blocks it, so that when the fuel has reached the required level in the float bowl, no more fuel can enter.

Pilot and Main Fuel Systems

The carburetor's purpose is to supply and atomize fuel and mix it in correct proportions with air that is drawn in through the air intake. At primary throttle openings (from idle to 1/8 throttle) a small amount of fuel is siphoned through the pilot jet by suction from the incoming air (**Figure 2**). As the throttle is opened further, the air stream begins to siphon fuel through the main jet and needle jet. The tapered needle increases the effective flow capacity of the needle jet as it rises with the throttle slide, in that it occupies decreasingly less of the area of the needle jet (**Figure 3**). In addition, the amount of cutaway in the leading edge of the throttle valve aids in controlling the air/fuel mixture during partial throttle openings.

At full throttle, the carburetor venturi is fully open and the needle is lifted far enough to permit the main jet to flow at full capacity. See **Figure 4** and **Figure 5**.

Starting System

The starting system consists of a choke plunger, mixing tube, starter jet and air passage (**Figure 6**). When the choke valve is pulled out, it opens the air passage permitting air to flow through the passage where it siphons fuel through the starter jet, into the mixing tube and then into the air passage where it is mixed (fuel-rich) and discharged into the throttle bore.

AIR BOX

The air box is mounted on the top frame rails, underneath the seat (**Figure 7**). The air filter element, mounted inside the air box, is a wet type element. A check hose is mounted in the bottom of the air box (**Figure 8**). When the check hose becomes contaminated with dirt and water, check the air box and air filter for contamination. Refer to Chapter Three for air filter service.

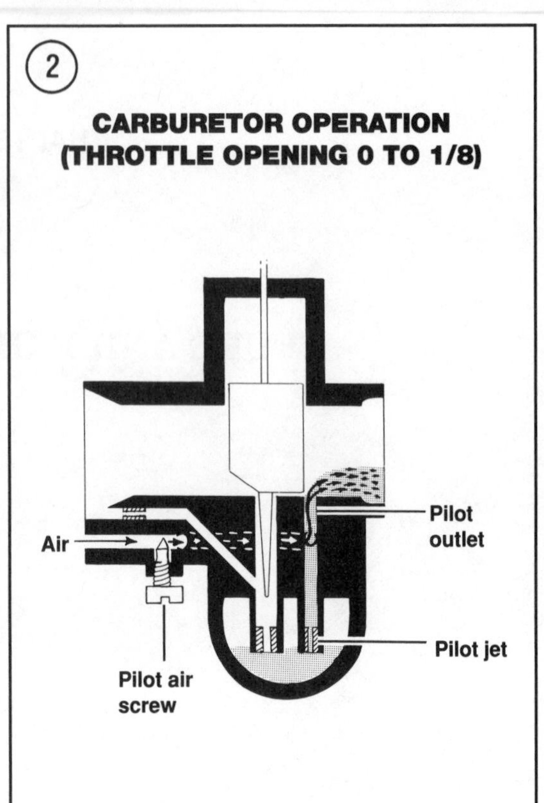

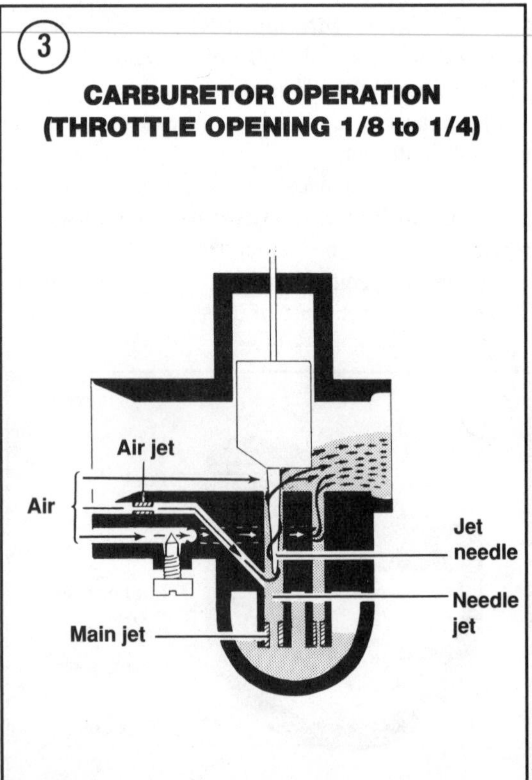

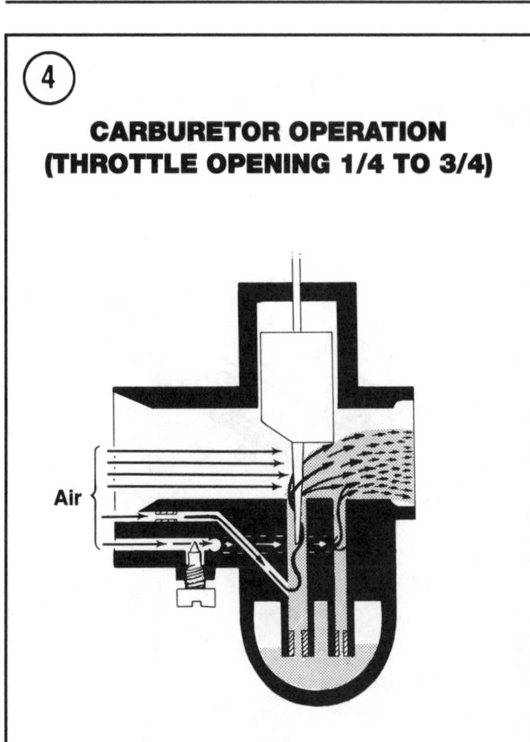

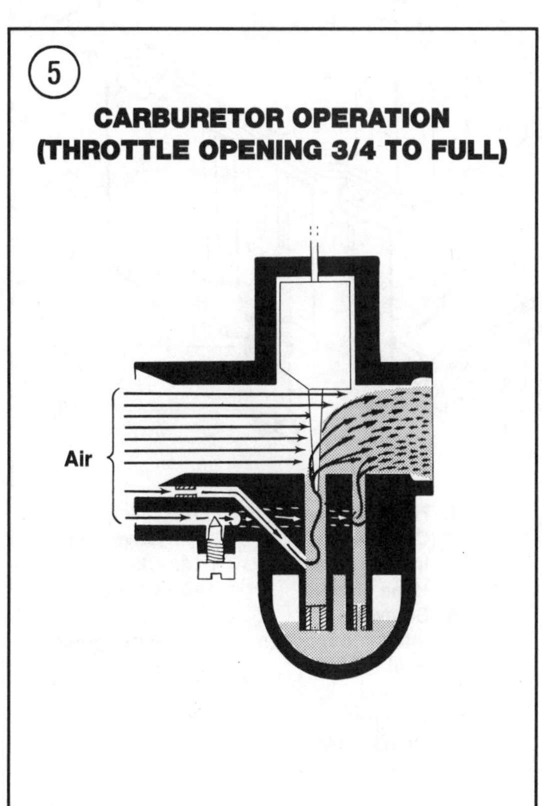

6

STARTING SYSTEM

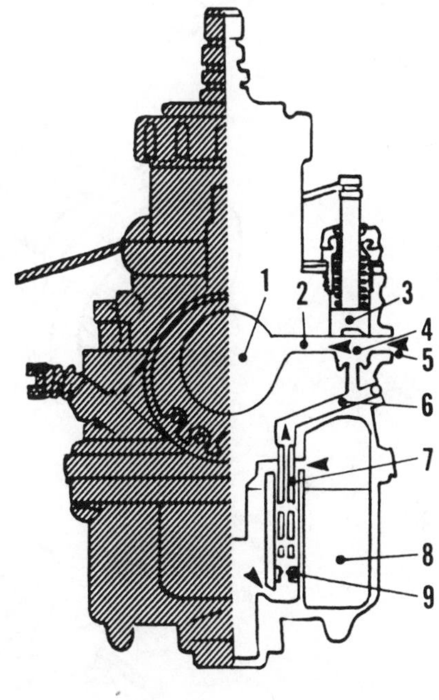

1. Carburetor bore
2. Mixture passage
3. Starter plunger
4. Plunger chamber
5. Air passage
6. Fuel passage
7. Mixing tube
8. Float chamber
9. Starter jet

8

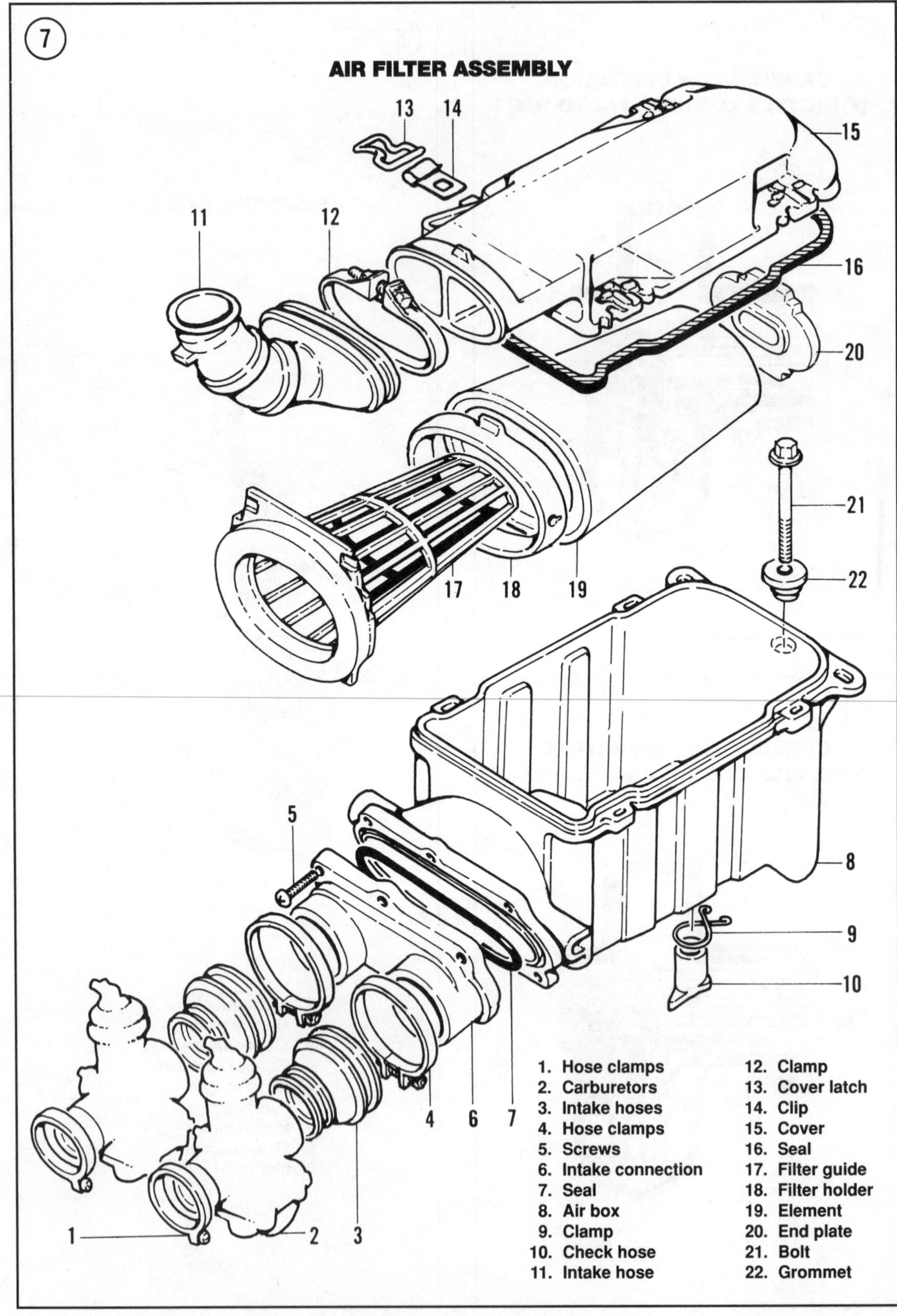
7
AIR FILTER ASSEMBLY
13
14
15
11
12
16
20
21
22
17
18
19
5
8
9
10
4
6
7
1
2
3
1. Hose clamps
2. Carburetors
3. Intake hoses
4. Hose clamps
5. Screws
6. Intake connection
7. Seal
8. Air box
9. Clamp
10. Check hose
11. Intake hose
12. Clamp
13. Cover latch
14. Clip
15. Cover
16. Seal
17. Filter guide
18. Filter holder
19. Element
20. End plate
21. Bolt
22. Grommet

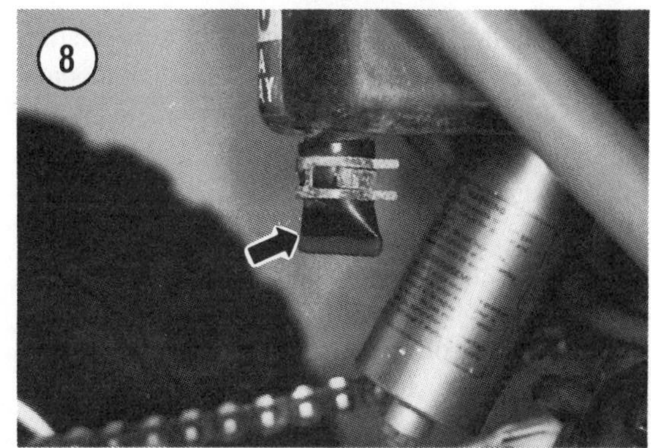

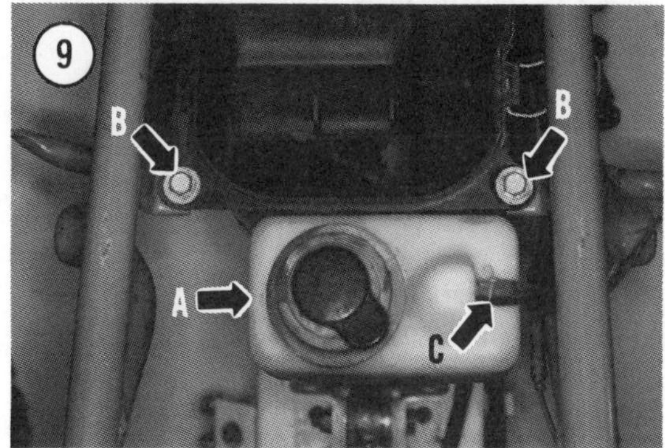

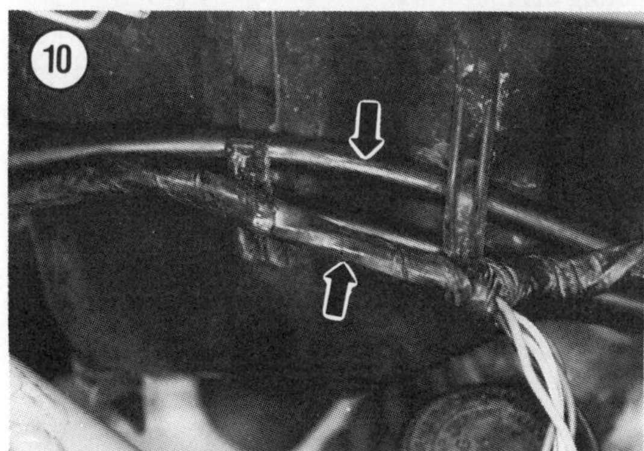

Removal/Installation

1. Park the vehicle on a level surface and set the parking brake.
2. Remove the seat and rear fender as described in Chapter Fourteen.
3. If necessary, remove the air filter element as described in Chapter Three.
4. Lift the coolant reserve tank (A, **Figure 9**) off of the air box and set it aside.
5. Remove the hoses and wiring harness from the guide tabs on the right-hand side of the air box (**Figure 10**).
6. Loosen the hose clamps securing the air boots to the carburetors (**Figure 11**).
7. Remove the 2 bolts (B, **Figure 9**) securing the air box to the frame.
8. Slide the air box forward to disconnect its front mounting cups (A, **Figure 12**) from the frame tabs, then lift and remove the air box from the rear of the frame.
9. Cover the carburetor openings to prevent abrasive dust and other debris from entering the carburetors.
10. Inspect the frame tab rubber dampers (B, **Figure 12**) for cracks or damage. Replace if necessary.
11. Inspect the air box (**Figure 13**) for cracks or other damage. Check for missing or damaged air box cover clamps and clips; replace as required.

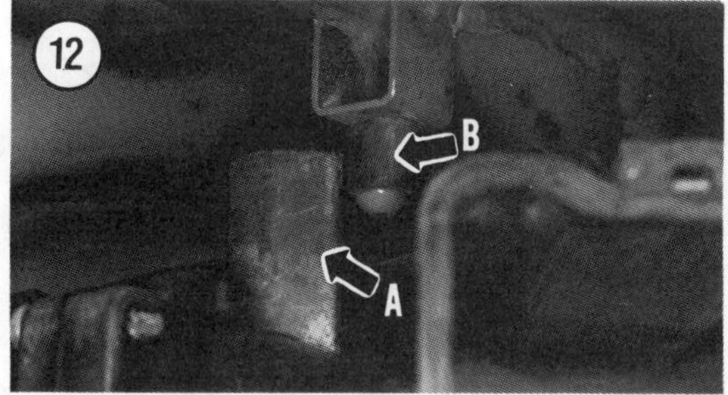

8

12. Check the air box cover rubber seal. If the seal is worn, twisted, flattened, cut or swollen, replace it.
13. Inspect intake boots for breaks, cracks or other damage. Replace if necessary.
14. Inspect intake boot hose clamps for damage. Replace if necessary.
15. Inspect the air box rubber dampers for cracks or damage. Replace if necessary.
16. Install by reversing these steps, plus the following.
17. Insert the coolant reserve tank arms into the air box rubber dampers as shown in **Figure 14**. The coolant hose should be on the vehicle's right-hand side; see C, **Figure 9**.

CARBURETOR

Two Mikuni round slide VM26SS carburetors are used on all YFZ350 models covered in this manual. The designation 26 indicates the carburetor size. A wide range of tuning components are available for the Mikuni VM carburetors.

Removal/Installation

Refer to **Figure 15** when removing and installing the carburetors.

1. Park the vehicle on level ground and set the parking brake.
2. Remove the seat as described in Chapter Fourteen.
3. Remove the fuel tank as described in this chapter.
4. If necessary, remove the exhaust pipes as described in this chapter.

NOTE
Using masking tape and a permanent type marking pen, label the hoses prior to disconnecting them.

5. Label, then disconnect the hoses at the carburetors. Plug the disconnected hoses with a golf tee or bolt. Don't forget to remove the choke hose connected to both carburetors.
6. Loosen the lock plate mounting screw and slide the lockplate (A, **Figure 16**) away from the carburetor cap.
7. Loosen, but do not remove, the carburetor cap (B, **Figure 16**).
8. Loosen the front and rear carburetor clamp screws and slide the clamps away from their mounting positions; see **Figure 17**.
9. Slide the carburetor back and free it from the intake manifold, then remove it from the air box boot.
10. Loosen the carburetor cap and pull the throttle valve (**Figure 18**) out of the carburetor. Set the throttle valve aside so that the jet needle is not damaged. Remove the carburetor assembly.

CAUTION
The jet needle tip is very fragile. Handle the throttle valve/jet needle carefully so that you don't nick the throttle valve or bend the needle.

11. Place a clean shop cloth into the intake manifold and air box boot openings to prevent the entry of foreign matter.
12. Repeat to remove the opposite carburetor.
13. To remove the throttle valve assembly, refer to *Throttle Valve/T.O.R.S. Housing Disassembly* in this chapter.
14. Install by reversing these removal steps, while noting the following.
15. If the throttle valve/T.O.R.S. housing switch assembly was removed, assemble these parts as described in this chapter.
16. To install the throttle valve and carburetor cap assembly:
   a. Install the throttle valve into the carburetor body—align the vertical slot in the side of the throttle valve with the pin in the carburetor while inserting the jet needle into the needle jet. The cutaway portion on the throttle valve

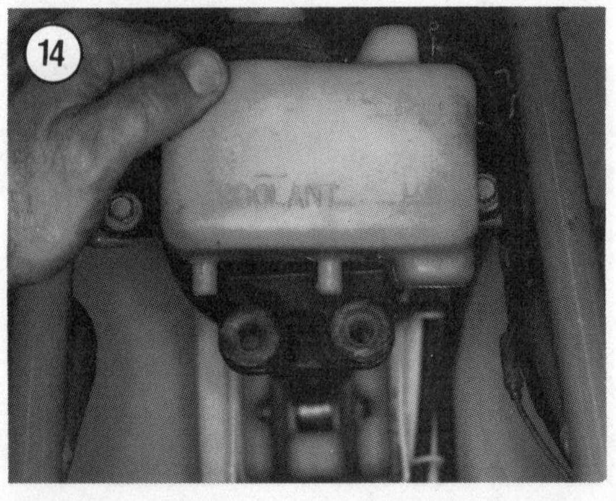

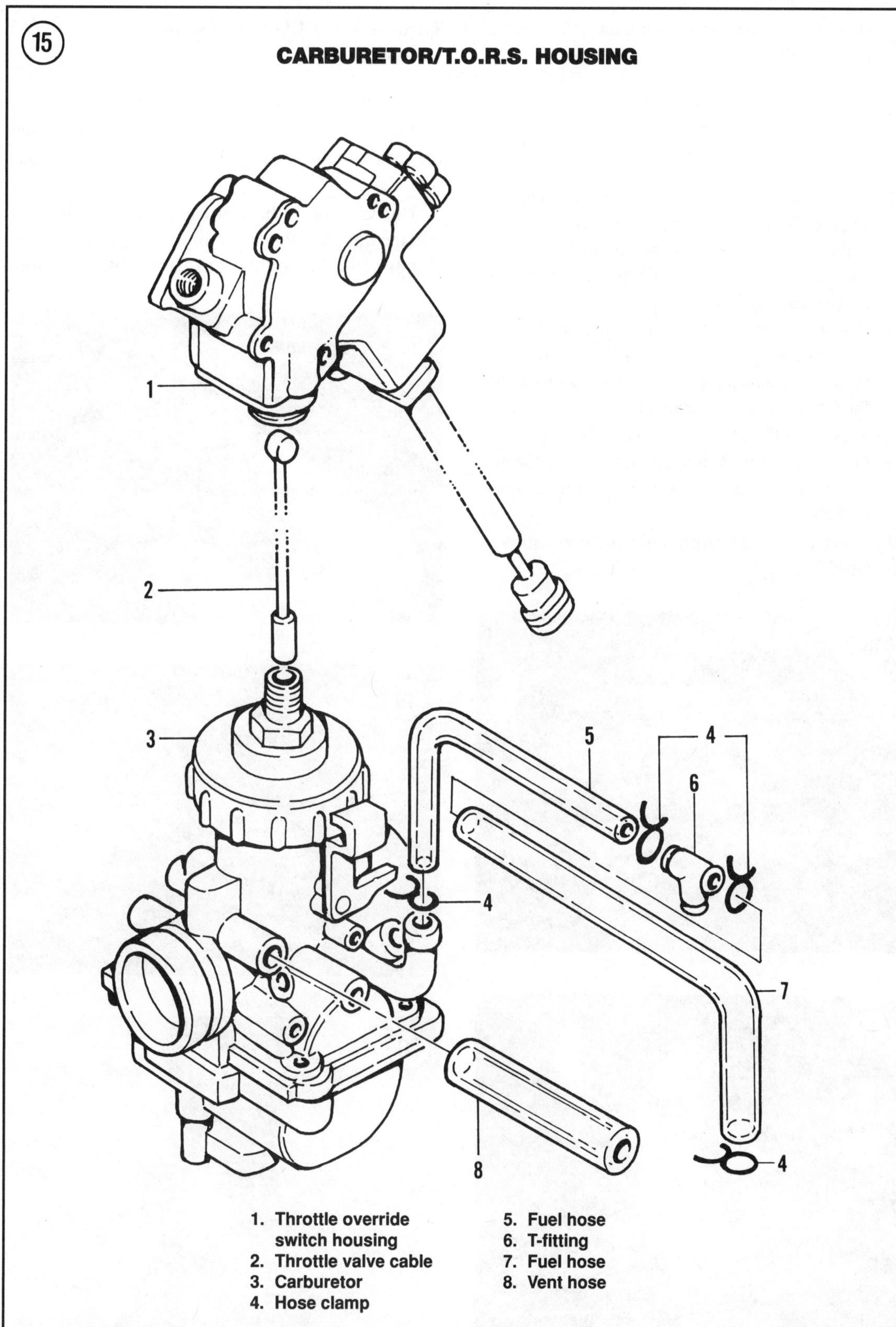
15
CARBURETOR/T.O.R.S. HOUSING
1
2
3
4
5
6
7
8
1. Throttle override switch housing
2. Throttle valve cable
3. Carburetor
4. Hose clamp
5. Fuel hose
6. T-fitting
7. Fuel hose
8. Vent hose

should be facing toward the back of the carburetor (intake side).

NOTE
***Figure 19** is shown with the carburetor partially disassembled for clarity.*

b. Align the tab on the inner carburetor cap (A, **Figure 19**) with the flat portion machined on the carburetor body (B, **Figure 19**) and install the carburetor cap assembly. Tighten the outer carburetor cap securely (**Figure 20**).
c. Position the lockplate so that one of its locking grooves clamps around one of the raised carburetor grip flanges (A, **Figure 16**). Then tighten the lockplate screw securely.
d. Repeat for the other carburetor.
e. Operate the throttle lever by hand. Both throttle valves should move smoothly with no binding or sticking.

17. Check and adjust carburetor synchronization as described in Chapter Three.

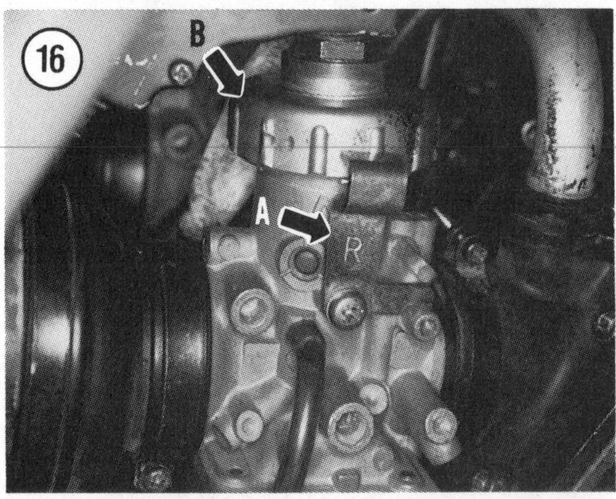

Throttle Valve/T.O.R.S. Housing Disassembly

Refer to **Figure 21**.

1. Loosen the lock plate mounting screw and slide the lockplate (A, **Figure 16**) away from the carburetor cap.
2. Unscrew the carburetor cap (B, **Figure 16**) and pull the throttle valve assembly out of the carburetor (**Figure 18**). Be careful not to damage the jet needle.

(21)

THROTTLE VALVE/T.O.R.S. HOUSING

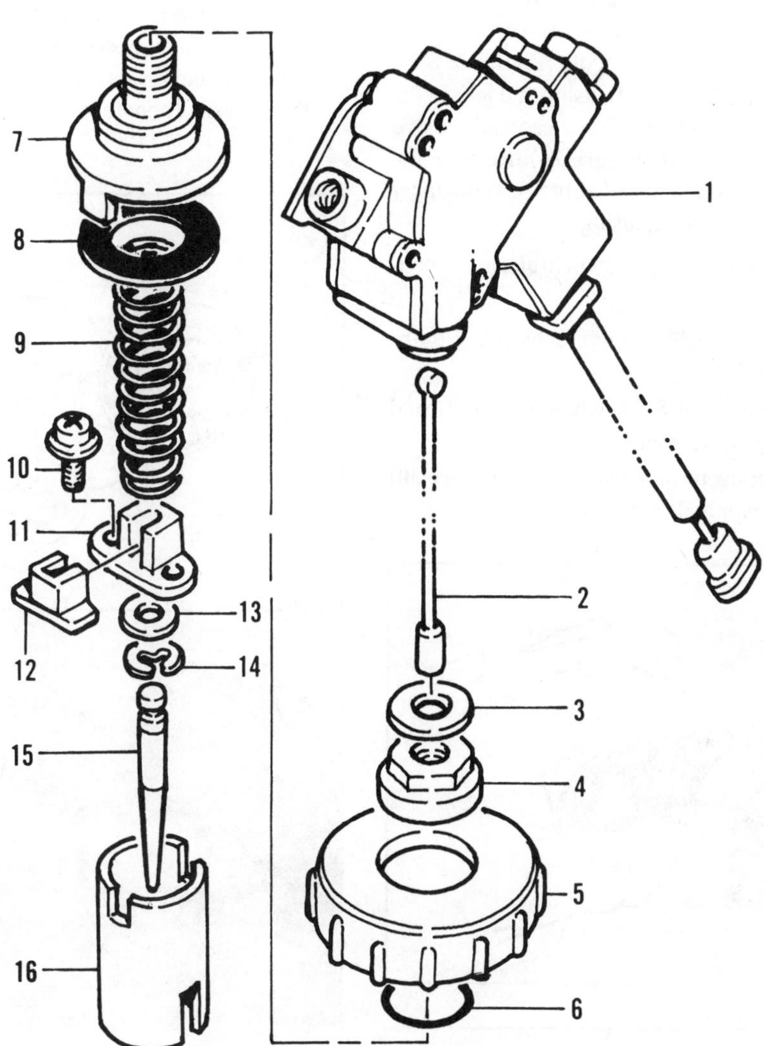

1. Throttle override switch housing
2. Throttle valve cable
3. Brass washer
4. Nut
5. Outer cap
6. O-ring
7. Inner cap
8. Rubber washer
9. Spring
10. Screw
11. Holder plate
12. Lock
13. Washer
14. E-clip
15. Jet needle
16. Throttle valve

3. Compress the throttle valve spring into the cap and remove the throttle cable lock (**Figure 22**).

4. Push down and then lift out the throttle cable (**Figure 23**).

5. Remove the 2 screws (**Figure 24**) securing the holder plate to the throttle valve. Remove the screws, holder plate, washer and jet needle (**Figure 25**).

6. Hold the T.O.R.S. switch housing and loosen the inner cap. Then unscrew the inner cap and remove the inner and outer caps (**Figure 26**). Remove the flat washer (**Figure 27**) installed between the inner cap and T.O.R.S. switch housing.

7. Disconnect the T.O.R.S. switch electrical connector (**Figure 28**).

8. To remove the throttle valve cable (A, **Figure 29**):

   a. Remove the T.O.R.S. switch housing left-hand cover screws and cover.
   b. Disconnect the throttle valve cable (**Figure 30**) from the lever and remove it.

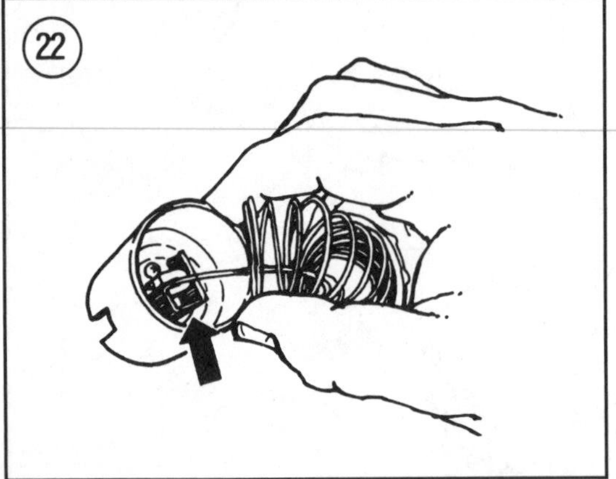

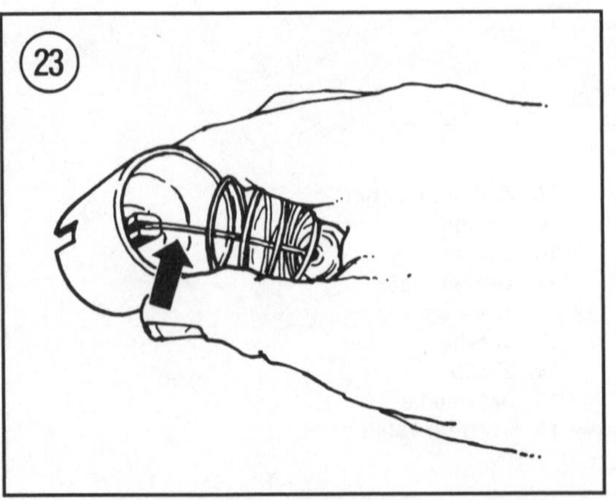

9. To replace the T.O.R.S. switch and/or disconnect the throttle cable from the T.O.R.S. housing:

   a. Remove the T.O.R.S. switch housing right-hand cover screws and cover (**Figure 31**).
   b. Pull the cover up and loosen the throttle cable adjuster locknut (A, **Figure 32**).
   c. Remove the adjuster (B, **Figure 32**) from the housing and disconnect the throttle cable from the lever. Then remove the T.O.R.S. switch housing.

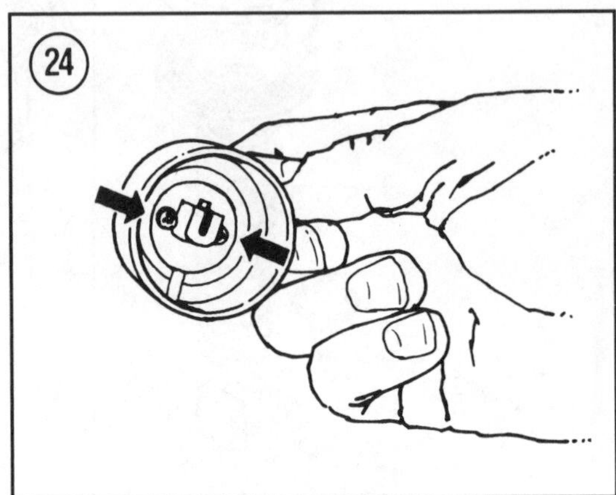

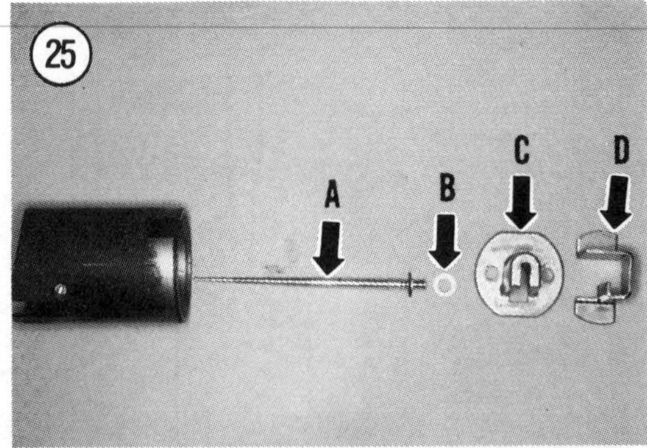

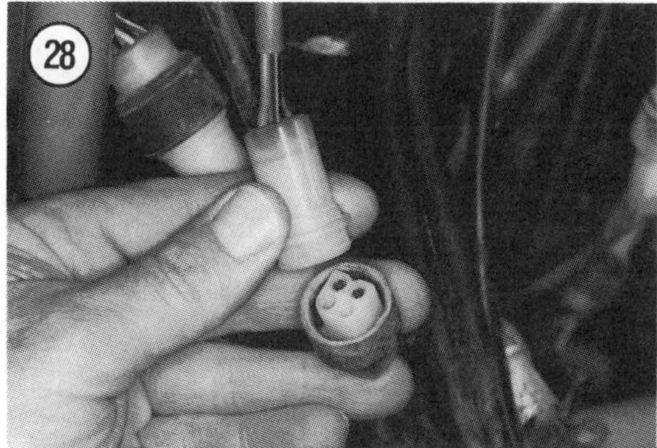

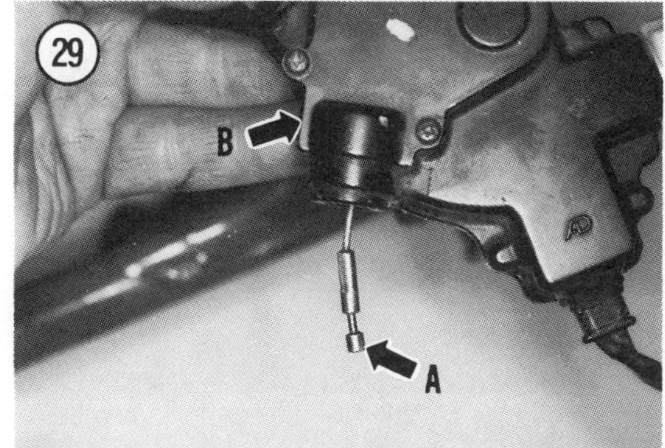

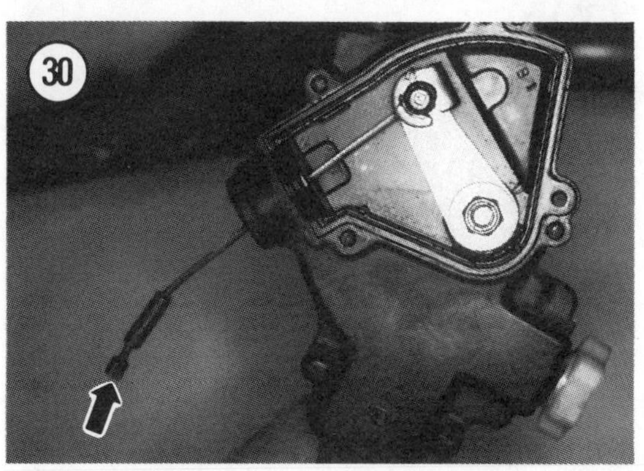

NOTE
*The T.O.R.S. switch (**Figure 33**) is an integral part of the switch housing. Do not remove the switch. If the switch is faulty, the T.O.R.S. switch housing assembly will have to be replaced.*

10. Inspect the inner cap/adjuster assembly (**Figure 34**). Replace severely worn or damaged parts.

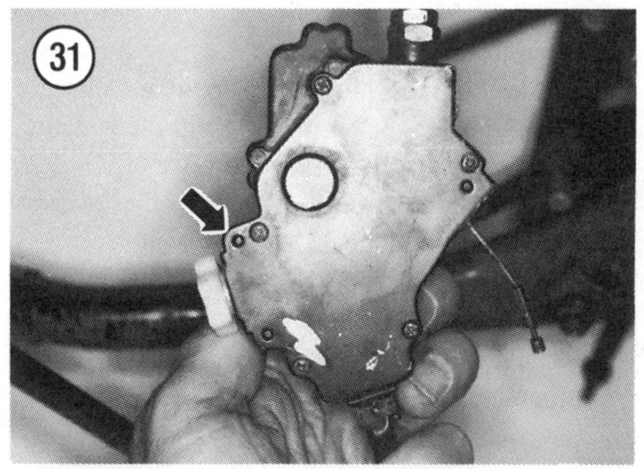

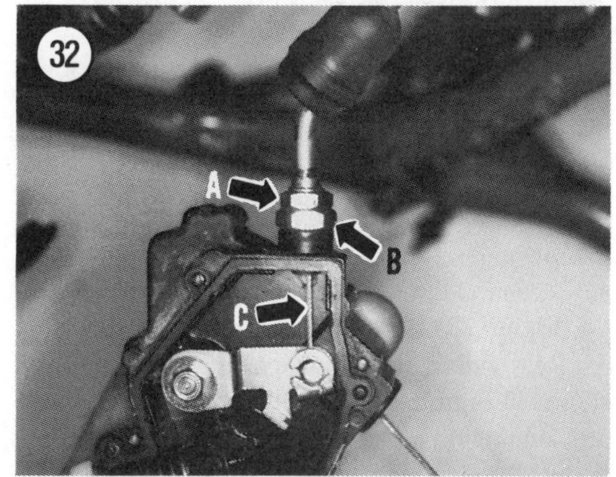

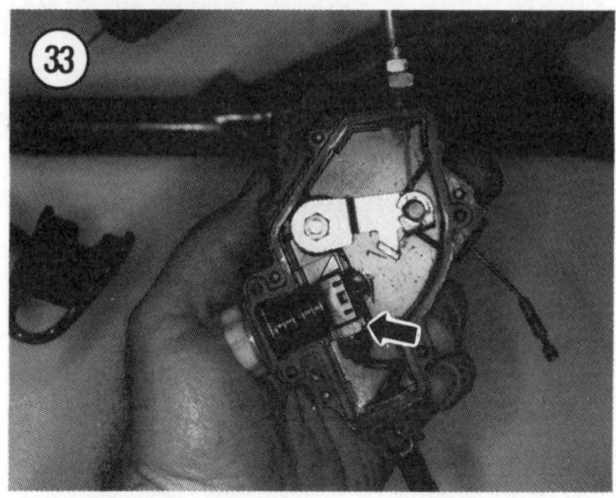

Throttle Valve/T.O.R.S. Housing Reassembly

Refer to **Figure 21**.

1. Clean the T.O.R.S. switch electrical connectors with contact cleaner. Allow to dry thoroughly.
2. To reconnect the throttle cable to the T.O.R.S. housing:
   a. Lightly grease the cable pivot on the end of the lever.
   b. Insert the throttle cable into the right-hand side of the T.O.R.S. housing. Thread the throttle cable adjuster (B, **Figure 32**) into the housing, then tighten the locknut (A, **Figure 32**).
   c. Reconnect the throttle cable onto the lever as shown in C, **Figure 32**.
   d. Make sure the rubber seal is installed into the outer groove in the T.O.R.S. housing. Then install the right-hand cover (**Figure 31**) and its mounting screws. Tighten the screws securely.
3. To reconnect the throttle valve cable (A, **Figure 29**):
   a. Lightly grease the cable pivot on the end of the lever.
   b. Reconnect the throttle valve cable onto the lever as shown in **Figure 30**.
   c. Make sure the rubber seal is installed into the outer groove in the T.O.R.S. housing. Then install the left-hand cover (B, **Figure 29**) and its mounting screws. Tighten the screws securely.
4. Reconnect the T.O.R.S. switch electrical connector (**Figure 28**).
5. Reassemble the inner cap/adjuster assembly as shown in **Figure 35**. Tighten the adjuster (**Figure 35**) hand-tight.
6. Install the washer onto the adjuster threads (**Figure 27**).
7. Install the outer cap over the inner cap/adjuster assembly and thread the adjuster into the T.O.R.S. housing as shown in **Figure 26**.
8. Align the inner cap with the carburetor body as follows:

NOTE
Figure 19 *is shown with the carburetor partially disassembled for clarity.*

   a. Align the tab on the inner carburetor cap (A, **Figure 19**) with the flat portion machined in the carburetor body (B, **Figure 19**) and install the carburetor cap assembly (**Figure 20**)
   b. If the tab does not align with the flat on the carburetor body, loosen the adjuster and until alignment is made, then tighten the adjuster securely.
   c. Remove the carburetor cap from the carburetor body.
9. Replace the carburetor inner cover gasket (**Figure 36**) if damaged. To install the new gasket, or to reapply a used gasket, apply Gasgacinch sealer to the top gasket surface and mount the gasket to the bottom of the inner cover as shown in **Figure 36**.
10. To install the jet needle assembly (**Figure 25**):
   a. Make sure the E-clip is positioned in the correct jet needle clip groove.
   b. Install the jet needle (A) into the center throttle valve hole. Install the small flat washer (B) on top of the jet needle.
   c. Install the holder plate (C) into the throttle valve and secure it with its 2 mounting screws and washers (**Figure 24**). Tighten the screws securely.

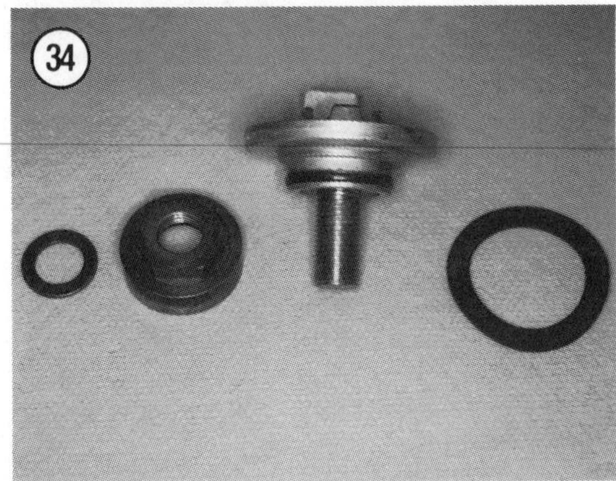

11. Slide the spring over the cable and compress it with your fingers.

12. Connect the throttle valve cable into the holder plate groove as shown in **Figure 23**.

13. Install the throttle cable lock so that it engages the holder plate groove as shown in **Figure 22**. Then release the spring (**Figure 37**), making sure that it seats against the throttle cable lock.

14. To install the throttle valve and carburetor cap assembly:

 a. Install the throttle valve into the carburetor body—align the vertical slot in the side of the throttle valve with the pin in the carburetor while inserting the jet needle into the needle jet. The cutaway portion on the throttle valve should be facing to the back of the carburetor (intake side).

NOTE
***Figure 19** is shown with the carburetor partially disassembled for clarity.*

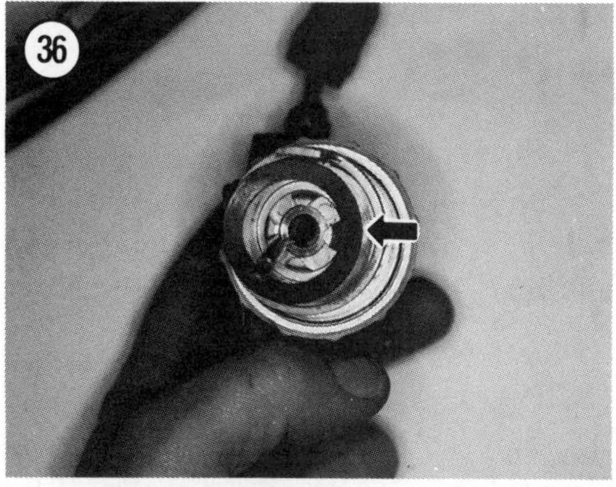

36

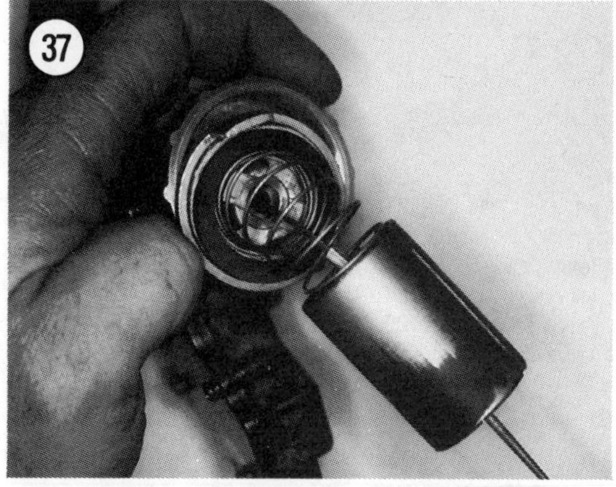

37

 b. Align the tab on the inner carburetor cap (A, **Figure 19**) with the flat portion machined on the carburetor body (B, **Figure 19**) and install the carburetor cap assembly. Tighten the outer carburetor cap securely (**Figure 20**).
 c. Position the lockplate so that one of its locking grooves clamps around one of the raised carburetor grip flanges (A, **Figure 16**). Then tighten the lockplate screw securely.
 d. Repeat for the other carburetor.
 e. Operate the throttle lever by hand. Both throttle valves should move smoothly with no binding or sticking.

15. Check and adjust carburetor synchronization as described in Chapter Three.

Carburetor Disassembly

Refer to **Figure 38** when servicing the carburetor.

1. Remove the fuel line and all drain and overflow tubes from the carburetor body.

2. Loosen the choke nut (**Figure 39**) and remove the choke (**Figure 40**).

NOTE
Before removing the pilot air screw, carefully screw it in until it lightly seats, counting the number of turns so it can be installed in the same position.

3. Remove the pilot air screw, O-ring and spring (**Figure 41**).

4. Remove the float bowl screws, hose guides, float bowl and gasket.

5. Remove the main jet ring (**Figure 42**).

6. Remove the float pivot pin (**Figure 43**) and remove the float and fuel valve assembly (**Figure 44**).

7. Remove the screw and plate (**Figure 45**), then remove the fuel valve and O-ring (**Figure 46**).

8. Unscrew and remove the main jet and washer (**Figure 47**).

9. Remove the needle jet through the top of the carburetor (**Figure 48**).

10. Unscrew and remove the pilot jet (**Figure 49**).

Cleaning and Inspection

1. Wash all of the carburetor parts with a solution of liquid detergent or a biodegradable soap cleaner and warm water. Rinse with clean water and dry

8

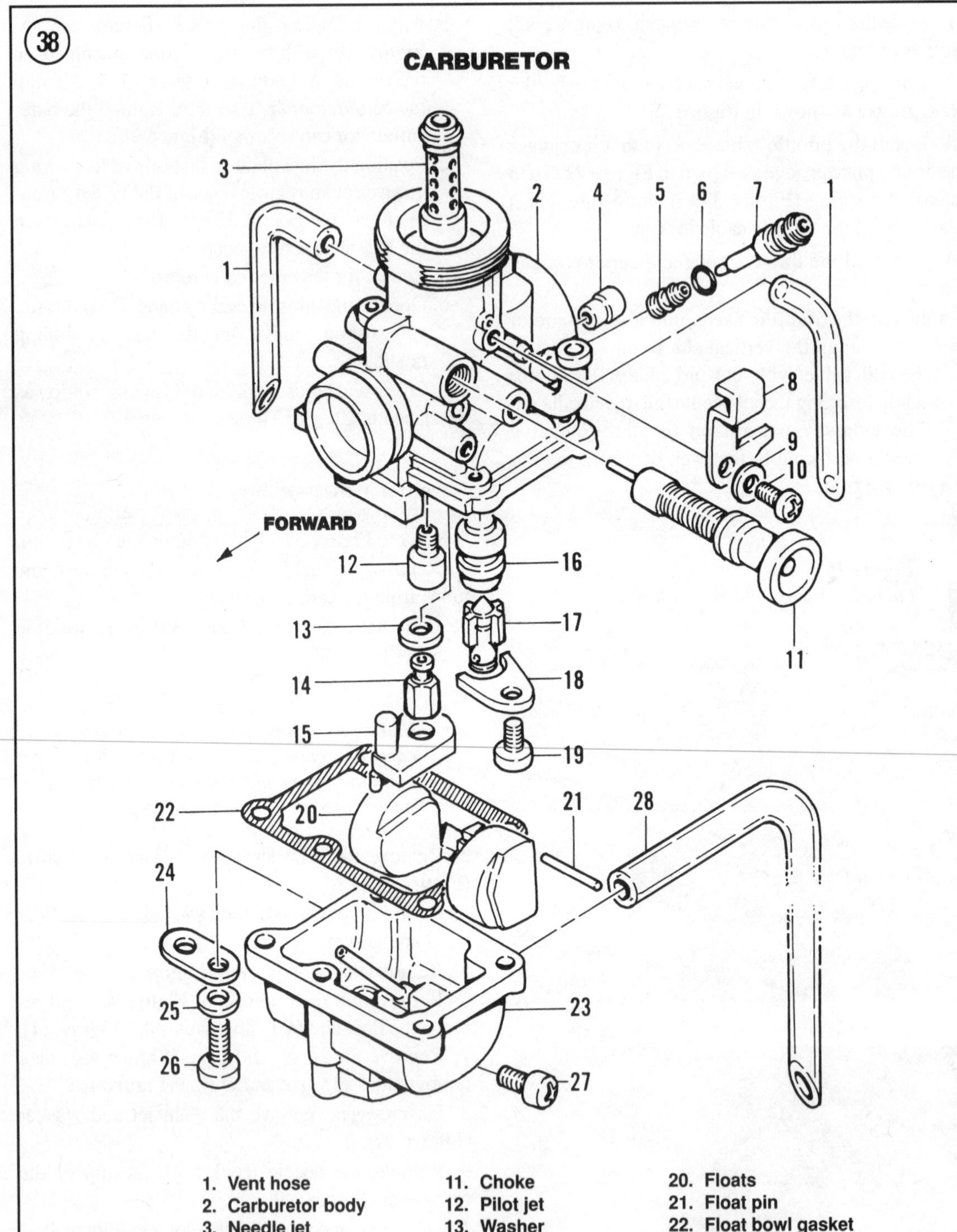

1. Vent hose
2. Carburetor body
3. Needle jet
4. Pilot air jet
5. Spring
6. O-ring
7. Pilot air screw
8. Clamp
9. Washer
10. Screw
11. Choke
12. Pilot jet
13. Washer
14. Main jet
15. Main jet ring
16. Fuel valve seat
17. Fuel valve
18. Plate
19. Screw
20. Floats
21. Float pin
22. Float bowl gasket
23. Float bowl
24. Hose guide
25. Lockwasher
26. Screw
27. Drain screw
28. Drain hose

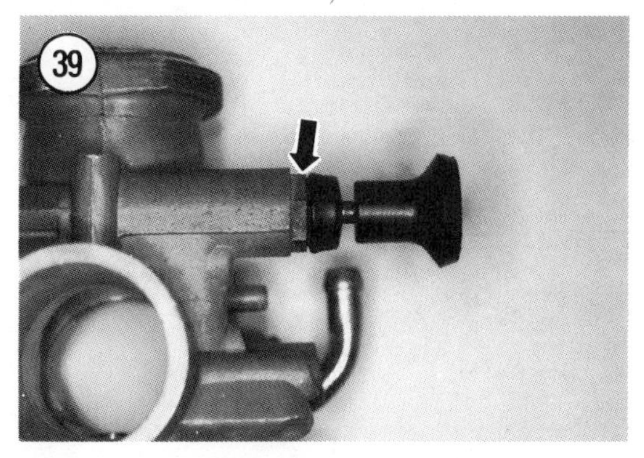
39

43

40

44

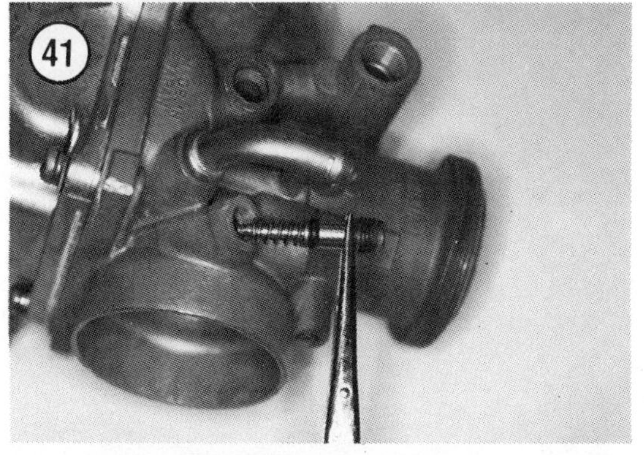
41

45

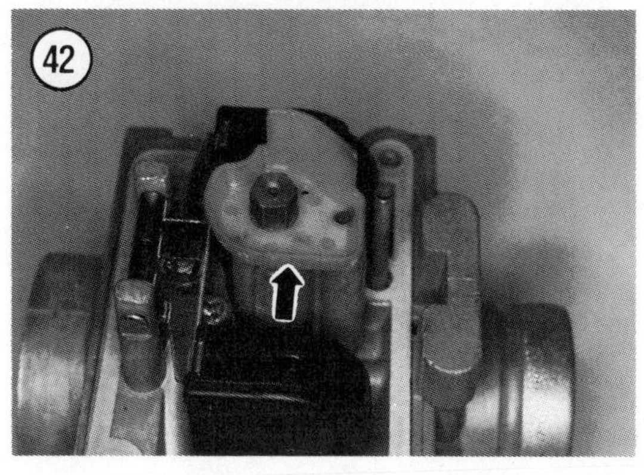
42

46

thoroughly with compressed air, if available. If not, allow the parts to air dry.

CAUTION
Cleaning rubber and plastic parts in carburetor cleaner will damage them.

2. If the carburetor has been sitting for some time with gasoline in the bowl, or if you cannot clean it thoroughly as described in Step 2, soak all of the parts, except rubber or plastic parts, in a good grade of carburetor cleaner. This solution is available at most automotive supply stores, in a small, resealable tank with a dip basket. If it is tightly sealed when not in use, the solution will last for several cleanings. Follow the manufacturer's instructions for correct soak time (usually about 1/2 hour). Remove all parts from the cleaner and wash thoroughly with soap and warm water. Rinse with clean water and dry thoroughly.
3. Blow out the jets with compressed air. *Do not* use a piece of wire to clean them as minor gouges in the jet can alter flow rate and upset the fuel/air mixture.
4. Blow out the float bowl overflow tube.
5. Inspect the tip of the fuel valve (**Figure 50**) and seat for wear or damage.

NOTE
A worn or damaged fuel valve and seat assembly will cause flooding, hard starting and a rich fuel mixture. Check the fuel valve and seat carefully if the engine is experiencing these types of operating conditions.

6. O-ring seals tend to become hardened after prolonged use and therefore lose their ability to seal properly. Inspect all O-rings and replace if necessary.

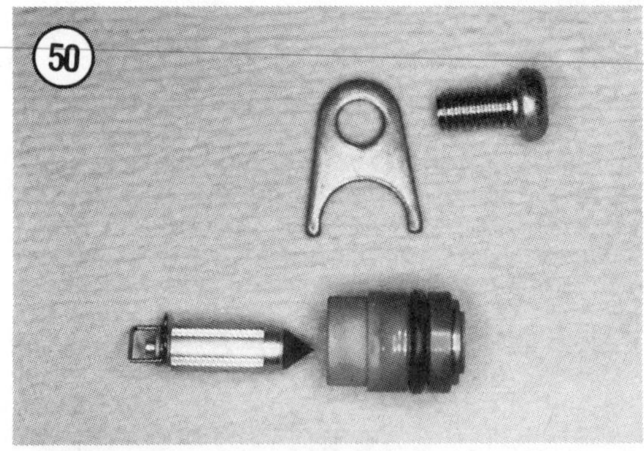

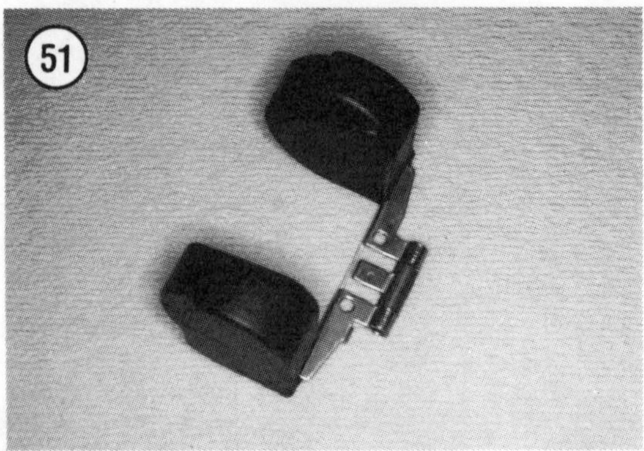

52

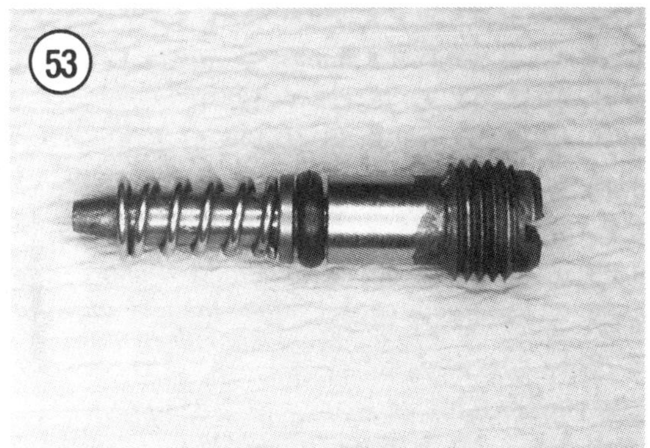

53

54

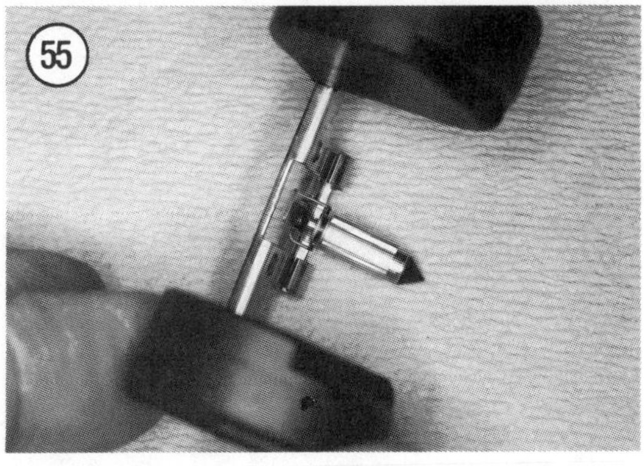

55

7. Check the float (**Figure 51**) for damage. Fill the float bowl or a container with water and push the float down. There should be no bubbles, indicating a leaking float. Replace the float if it leaks.

8. Check the choke valve assembly (**Figure 52**) for wear or damage. Check the plunger for deep scratches or other wear patterns. Replace the choke if necessary.

9. Check the end of the pilot air screw (**Figure 53**) for damage. Replace the pilot air screw if any grooves or roughness are present. A damaged end will prevent smooth low-end engine operation.

Assembly

1. Install and tighten the pilot jet (**Figure 49**).

2. Install the needle jet through the top of the carburetor (**Figure 48**)—align the slot in the side of the needle jet with the pin in the carburetor (**Figure 54**).

3. Install the main jet and washer (**Figure 47**). Tighten the main jet securely.

4. Install the fuel valve seat and its O-ring (**Figure 46**) into the carburetor. Push the valve seat into position until it bottoms out.

5. Install the plate around the fuel valve seat as shown in **Figure 45**. Then install the screw and tighten securely.

6. Hook the fuel valve onto the float as shown in **Figure 55**. Then install the fuel valve and float—insert the fuel valve into the fuel valve seat. See **Figure 44**.

7. Install the main jet ring over the main jet (**Figure 56**) and seat it in the carburetor. See **Figure 42**.

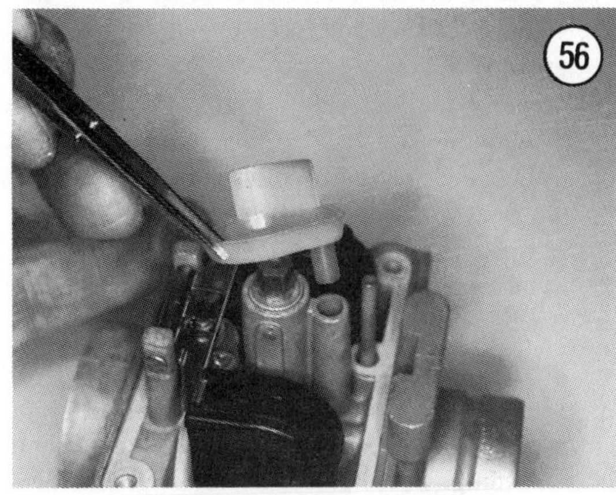

56

8. Install the float bowl gasket and float bowl (**Figure 57**). Install the screws and hose guides; tighten the screws securely.
9. Install the choke (**Figure 40**). Thread the choke nut (**Figure 39**) into the carburetor body and tighten securely.
10. Install the pilot air screw, O-ring and spring (**Figure 41**). Set the pilot air screw to the same number of turns noted during disassembly.
11. Install the drain hoses onto the carburetor body.

CARBURETOR FLOAT HEIGHT ADJUSTMENT

Float height specifications are listed in **Table 2**.
1. Remove the carburetors as described in this chapter.
2. Remove the float bowl mounting screws and remove the float bowl (**Figure 57**) and gasket.
3. Remove the main jet ring (**Figure 42**).
4. Hold the carburetor so that the float arm just contacts the fuel valve needle *without* compressing the needle. You may have to pivot the carburetor back and forth a few times to obtain the proper float arm to fuel valve needle contact pressure.
5. Measure the distance from the float bowl mating surface (without gasket) to the top of the float as shown in **Figure 58**. The correct float level specification is listed in **Table 2**. Continue with Step 6 or Step 7.

NOTE
Increasing the float height lowers the fuel level. Decreasing the float height raises the fuel level.

6. To adjust the float level:
   a. Remove the float pivot pin (**Figure 43**) and remove the float and fuel valve assembly (**Figure 44**).
   b. Remove the fuel valve (**Figure 55**) from the float.
   c. Adjust the float by bending the adjust tang on the float with a screwdriver. See **Figure 59**.
   d. Reverse to reinstall the float and float bowl.
7. Install by reversing these steps.

CARBURETOR REJETTING

Changes in altitude, temperature, humidity and track conditions can noticeably affect engine performance. To obtain maximum performance from your Yamaha, jetting changes may be necessary. Before attempting to rejet the engine, the engine should be in good running condition.

NOTE
If the engine is running poorly under the same weather, altitude and trail conditions where it once ran properly, it is unlikely the carburetor jetting is at fault. Attempting to tune the engine by rejetting the carburetors would only complicate matters.

NOTE
Changes in port shape and smoothness, or changing the expansion chamber, carburetor, etc., also requires jetting changes because these factors alter the engine's ability to breathe. When installing aftermarket equipment or when the engine has been modified, equipment manufacturers often include an instruction brochure or manual listing suitable jetting changes that correspond to their equipment or modification. This information should be taken

57

58

into account along with the altitude, temperature, humidity and trail conditions previously mentioned.

If your vehicle shows evidence of one of the following conditions, rejetting may be necessary:

a. Poor acceleration (too rich).
b. Excessive exhaust smoke (too rich).
c. Fouling spark plugs (too rich).
d. Engine misfire at low speeds (too rich).
e. Erratic acceleration (too lean).
f. Ping or rattle (too lean).

NOTE
Engine ping can also be caused by old gasoline or by using a gasoline with a too low octane rating. See Chapter Three.

g. Running hot (too lean).
h. Engine revs okay then cuts out like it is running out of fuel (too lean).

Before checking the carburetor for one of the previously listed operating conditions, consider the following maintenance procedures:

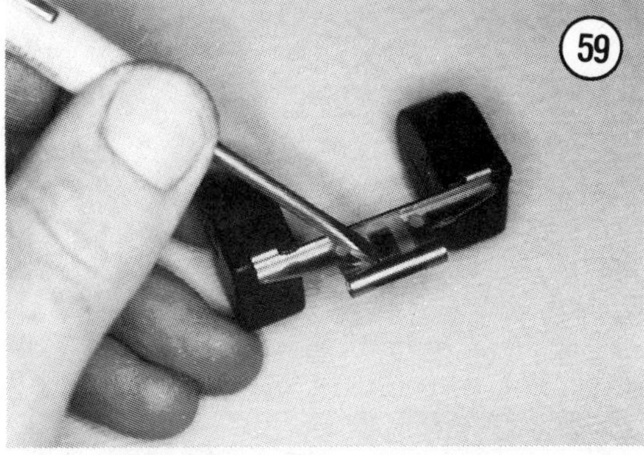
59

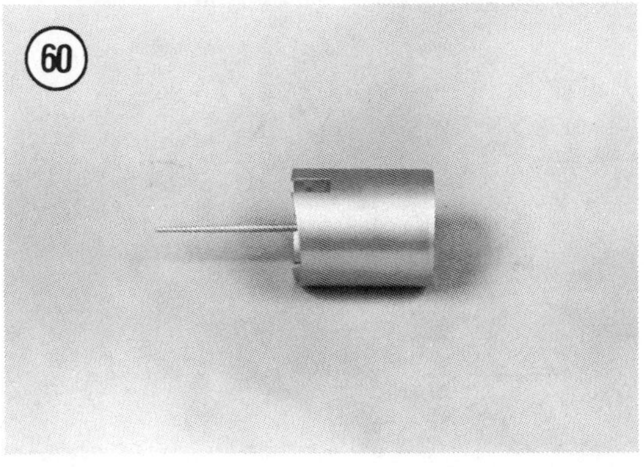
60

a. The float level in each carburetor must be properly adjusted. If the float level is incorrect, it will be difficult to jet the carburetor accurately.
b. The carburetors must be synchronized.
c. The air filter element should be clean. A dirty air filter element will cause the engine to run rich. Attempting to jet the engine with a dirty air filter element will only complicate engine tuning.
d. The ignition timing should be correct.
e. The engine top end should be routinely decarbonized.

If the previously mentioned service items are correctly performed, carburetor rejetting may be required if any of the following conditions hold true:

a. A nonstandard air filter element is being used.
b. A nonstandard exhaust system is being used.
c. Any of the top end parts (piston, porting, compression ratio, reed valve, etc.) have been modified or changed.
d. The vehicle is in use at considerably higher or lower altitudes, or in a markedly hotter or colder, or wetter or drier climate than in the past.
e. The vehicle is being operated at considerably higher speeds than before (faster track conditions) and changing to a colder spark plug does not solve the problem.
f. A previous owner changed the jetting or the jet needle clip positions.
g. The vehicle has never held a satisfactory engine tune.

The original jets, jet needle and throttle valve sizes are listed in **Table 1**.

Carburetor Variables

The following parts of the carburetor may be changed to vary the air/fuel mixture.

Pilot Jet

The pilot jet (**Figure 49**) and pilot air screw setting (**Figure 41**) control the fuel mixture from 0 to about 1/8 throttle. As the pilot numbers increase, the fuel mixture gets richer.

Throttle Valve

The throttle valve cutaway (**Figure 60**) affects airflow at small throttle openings. Cutaway sizes are numbered, and larger numbers result in a leaner mixture.

Jet Needle

The jet needle controls the mixture at medium speeds, from approximately 1/4 to 3/4 throttle. The jet needle has 2 operating ends. The top of the needle has 5 evenly spaced clip grooves (**Figure 61**). The bottom half of the needle is tapered (**Figure 62**); this portion extends into the needle jet. While the jet needle is fixed into position by the clip, fuel cannot flow through the space between the needle jet and jet needle until the throttle valve is raised approximately 1/4 open. As the throttle valve is raised, the jet needles tapered portion moves out of the needle jet. The grooves permit adjustment of the mixture ratio. If the clip is raised (thus dropping the needle deeper into the jet), the mixture will be leaner; lowering the clip (raising the needle) will richen the mixture.

If changing the jet needle clip position does not provide the desired results, it may be necessary to change to a smaller or larger needle jet.

Needle Jet

The needle jet (**Figure 48**) works in conjunction with the jet needle.

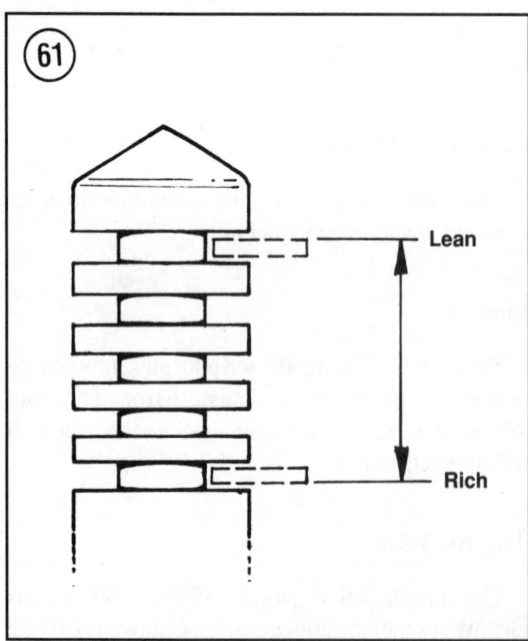

On Mikuni carburetors, the letter and number stamped on the side of the needle jet indicates the jet's inside diameter. The mixture gets richer in large steps as the letter increases (from "N" through "R"), and in small steps within the letter range as the number increases (from "0" through "9"). Some needle jets have a tab extending 2 to 8 mm into the throttle bore, indicated by "/2" through "/8" following the letter and number mark. This is called the primary choke, and it causes the mixture to be leaner at low speeds and richer at high speeds.

Main Jet

The main jet (**Figure 63**) controls the mixture from 3/4 to full throttle, and also has some effect at lesser throttle openings. Each main jet is stamped with a number. Larger numbers provide a richer mixture, smaller numbers a leaner mixture.

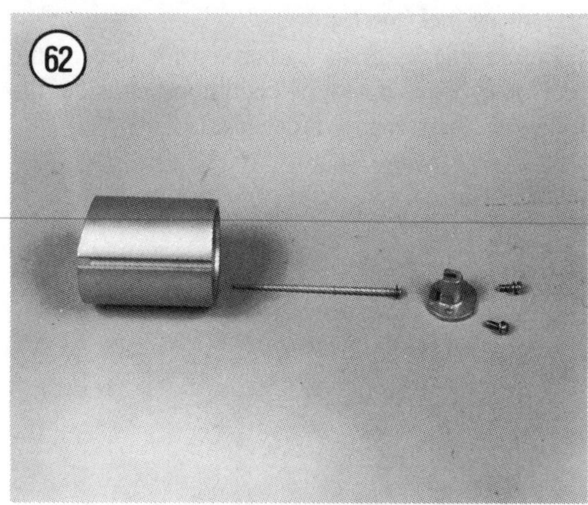

Rejetting

CAUTION
A too-lean mixture caused by running a too small main jet can cause serious engine damage in a matter of seconds. When determining proper jetting, always start out rich and progress toward a leaner mixture, one step at a time.

The engine must be at full operating temperature when checking jetting. Attempting to jet an engine not up to operating temperature can result in a too-lean mixture when the engine reaches full operating temperature.

When jetting a carburetor, basic procedures must be followed to ensure consistent results. Note the following before carburetor jetting:

a. Referring to **Figure 64**, note the different jetting circuits and how they overlap with each other in regard to throttle position. Then determine the throttle position at which the adjustment should be made. Too often, the main jet is changed when the adjustment calls for a jet needle adjustment.
b. When checking the jetting, the vehicle should be run on a track or on a private road where it can be run at top speed for a distance of 1/2 to 1 mile. Keep accurate records as to weather, altitude and track conditions.
c. The jetting should checked in the following order: Pilot air screw, main jet and jet needle.

1. Adjust the pilot air screw (if so equipped) and idle as described in Chapter Three.

2. Because the main jet controls the mixture from 3/4 to full throttle, the vehicle should be run a full throttle for a long distance. Stop the engine with the engine stop switch while the vehicle is still under full throttle. Pull in on the clutch lever and coast to a stop. Remove and examine the spark plugs after each test. The insulator should be a light tan color. If the insulator is soot black, the mixture is too rich; install a smaller main jet as described in this chapter.

8

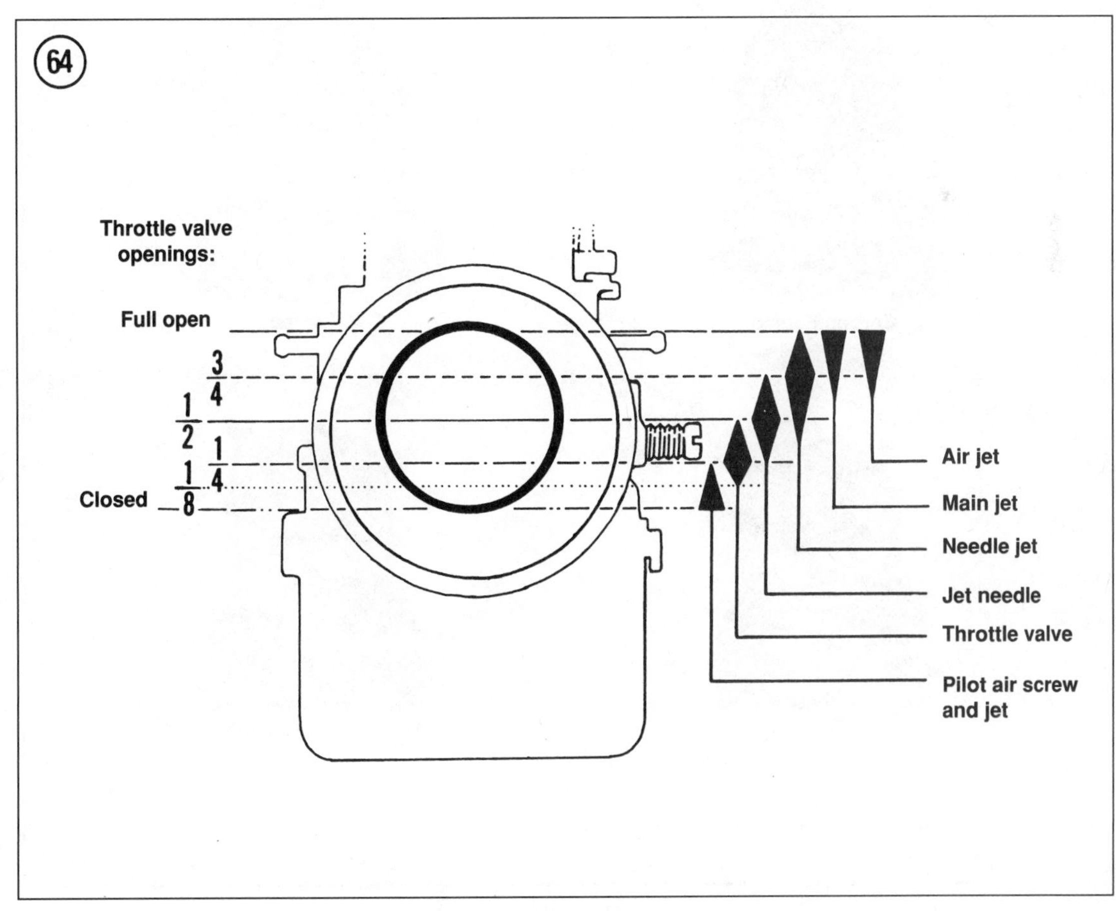

65

SPARK PLUG CONDITIONS

Normal

Gap Bridged

Carbon Fouled

Overheated

Oil Fouled

Sustained Preignition

If the insulator is white, or blistered, the mixture is too lean; install a larger main jet. See **Figure 65**.

3. Repeat the jetting check in Step 2 at different throttle positions. You may find that the full open throttle position is correct but that the 1/4 to 3/4 position is too rich or too lean. Refer to *Carburetor Variables*. If it is necessary to change the jet needle clip position, refer to *Jet Needle Adjustment* in this chapter.

Jet Needle Adjustment

1. Remove the throttle valve as described in this chapter.

2. Note the position of the clip. Raising the needle (lowering the clip) will enrich the mixture during mid-throttle opening, while lowering it (raising the clip) will lean the mixture. Refer to **Figure 61**.

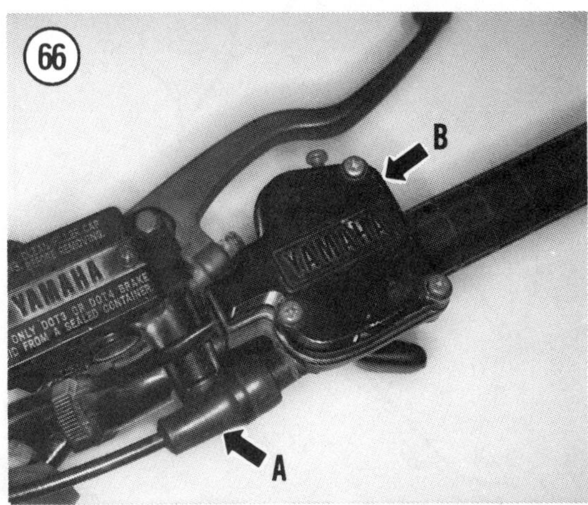

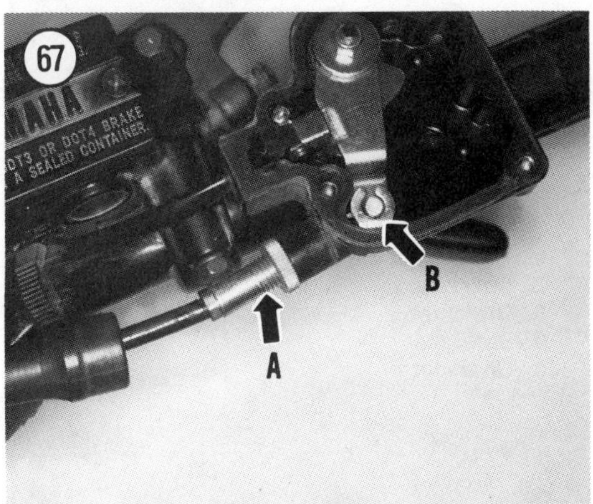

3. Refer to **Table 1** at the end of the chapter for standard clip positions.

4. Installation is the reverse of these steps.

THROTTLE CABLE REPLACEMENT

1. Place the vehicle on level ground and set the parking brake.
2. Remove the seat.
3. Remove the front fender as described in Chapter Fourteen.
4. Remove the fuel tank as described in this chapter.
5. Disconnect the throttle cable(s) from the carburetors as described under *Throttle Valve/T.O.R.S. Housing Disassembly* in this chapter.
6. Disconnect the throttle cable at the throttle lever as follows:
   a. Slide the rubber boot (A, **Figure 66**) off of the cable adjuster.
   b. Remove the throttle cover screws and remove the cover (B, **Figure 66**).
   c. Loosen the throttle cable adjuster (A, **Figure 67**) to provide as much cable slack as possible.
   d. Disconnect the throttle cable from the throttle arm (B, **Figure 67**). If you can't disconnect the cable end, remove the throttle arm nut, washer, lever and spring and disconnect the cable.
   e. Withdraw the throttle cable from the throttle housing.
7. Disconnect the throttle cable from any clips holding the cable to the frame.
8. Make a note of the cable routing path through the frame, then remove it.
9. Lubricate the new cable assembly as described in Chapter Three.
10. Reverse Steps 1-7 to install the new cable assembly, noting the following.
11. Reconnect throttle cables as described under *Throttle Valve/T.O.R.S. Housing Reassembly* in this chapter.
12. Apply grease to the cable end in the throttle lever housing.
13. Operate the throttle lever and make sure the carburetor throttle linkage is operating correctly and with no binding. If operation is incorrect or there is binding, carefully check that the cable is attached correctly and there are no tight bends in the cable.
14. Adjust carburetor synchronization as described in Chapter Three.

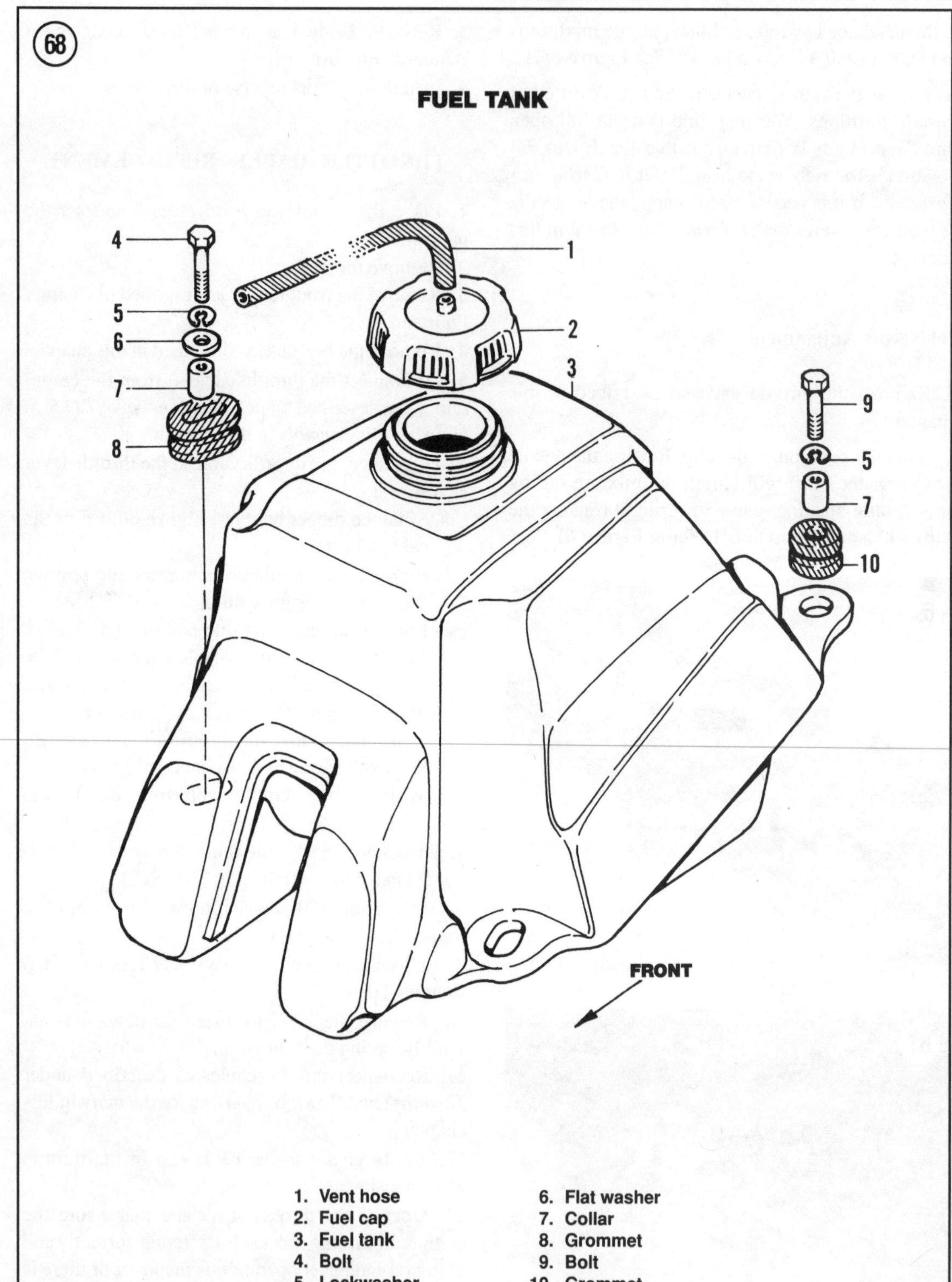

1. Vent hose
2. Fuel cap
3. Fuel tank
4. Bolt
5. Lockwasher
6. Flat washer
7. Collar
8. Grommet
9. Bolt
10. Grommet

15. Test ride the vehicle and make sure the throttle is operating correctly.

FUEL TANK

Removal/Installation

WARNING
Some fuel may spill from the fuel lines when performing this procedure. Because gasoline is extremely flammable and explosive, perform this procedure away from all open flames (including pilot lights) and sparks. Do not smoke or allow someone who is smoking in the work area. Wipe up any spills immediately.

Refer to **Figure 68** for this procedure.

69

1. Place the vehicle on level ground and set the parking brake.
2. Remove the seat.
3. Remove the front fender and side covers as described in Chapter Fourteen.
4. Turn the fuel shutoff valve (**Figure 69**) to the OFF position and disconnect the fuel line at the valve. Plug the open end of the fuel line with a golf tee or bolt.
5. Remove the front (A, **Figure 70**) and rear (B, **Figure 70**) fuel tank mounting bolts, washers and collars. Do not remove the rubber bushings installed in the fuel tank.
6. Pull the fuel tank (C, **Figure 70**) to the rear and remove it.
7. Inspect the rubber bushings on each side of the fuel tank where the tank is held in place. Replace if severely worn or damaged.
8. Replace the fuel line (**Figure 71**) if leaking or damaged.
9. Install by reversing these removal steps. Check for fuel leakage after installation is completed. Tighten fuel tank mounting bolts to the torque specification in **Table 3**.

8

FUEL SHUTOFF VALVE

The fuel shutoff valve is shown in **Figure 72** (1987-1989) and **Figure 73** (1990-on).

Removal/Installation

WARNING
Some fuel may spill from the fuel lines when performing this procedure. Be-

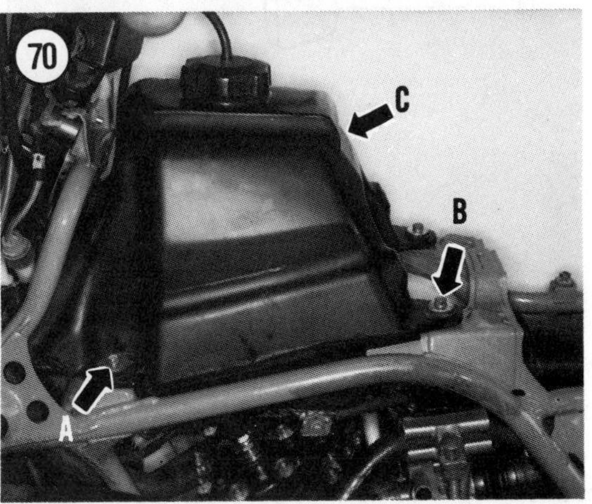
70

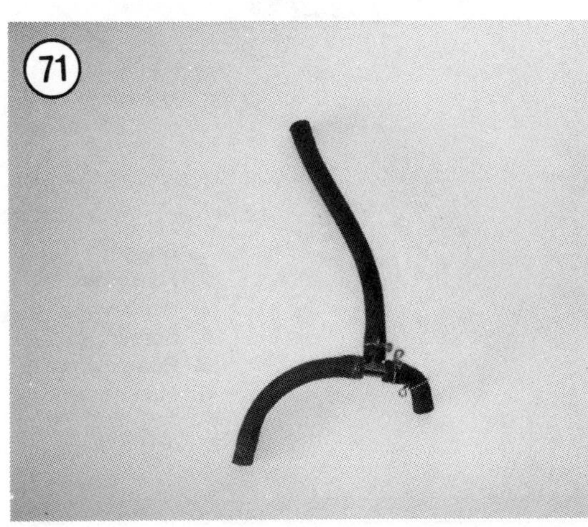
71

72

FUEL VALVE (1987-1989)

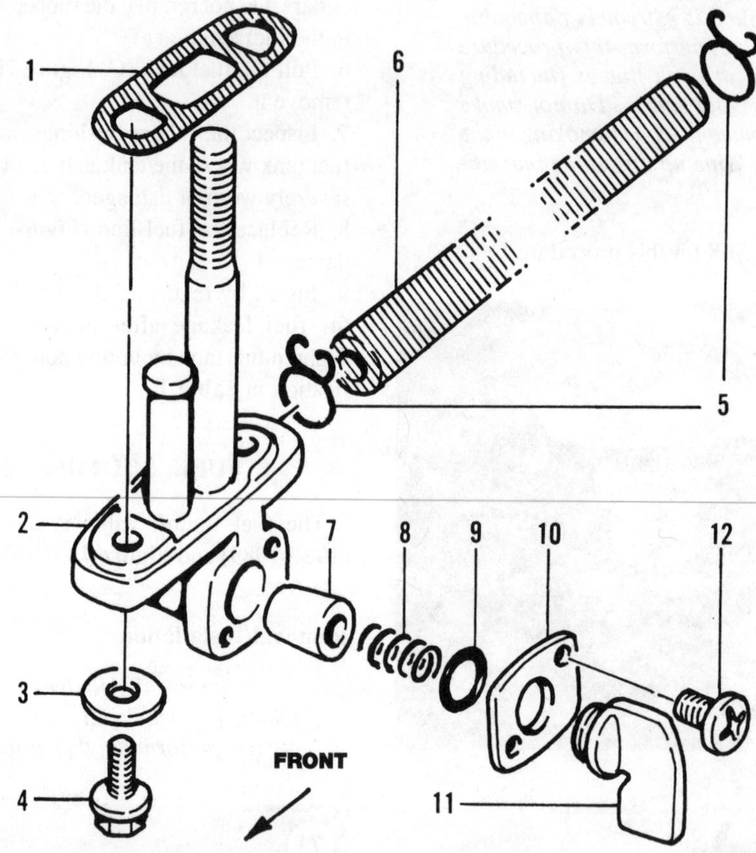

1. Gasket
2. Fuel valve
3. Washer
4. Screw
5. Hose clamp
6. Fuel hose
7. Valve
8. Spring
9. Seal
10. Plate
11. Handle
12. Screw

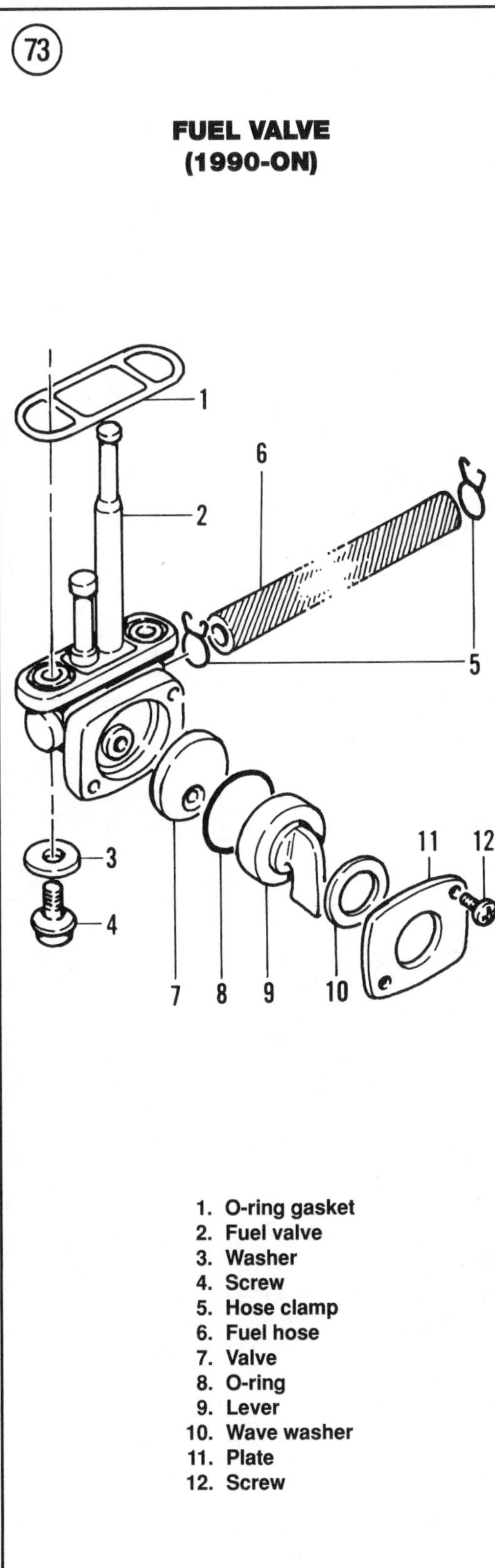

cause gasoline is extremely flammable and explosive, perform this procedure away from all open flames (including pilot lights) and sparks. Do not smoke or allow someone who is smoking in the work area. Wipe up any spills immediately.

1. Remove the fuel tank as described in this chapter.
2. Drain the fuel tank of all gas. Store the fuel in a can approved for gasoline storage.
3. Remove the screws securing the fuel shutoff valve to the fuel tank and remove the valve (**Figure 74**) and gasket.
4. To replace the fuel valve seal:
   a. Remove the 2 cover screws and disassemble the valve in the order shown in **Figure 72** or **Figure 73**.
   b. Replace the valve seal and reassemble the valve.
5. Install by reversing these steps. Install a new fuel shutoff valve O-ring gasket. Tighten the screws securely.
6. Check for fuel leakage after installation is completed.

8

EXHAUST SYSTEM

Check the exhaust system for deep dents and fractures and repair them or replace parts immediately. Check the silencer frame mounting flanges for fractures and loose bolts. Check the cylinder head mounting flange for tightness. A loose exhaust pipe connection will cause excessive exhaust noise and rob the engine of power.

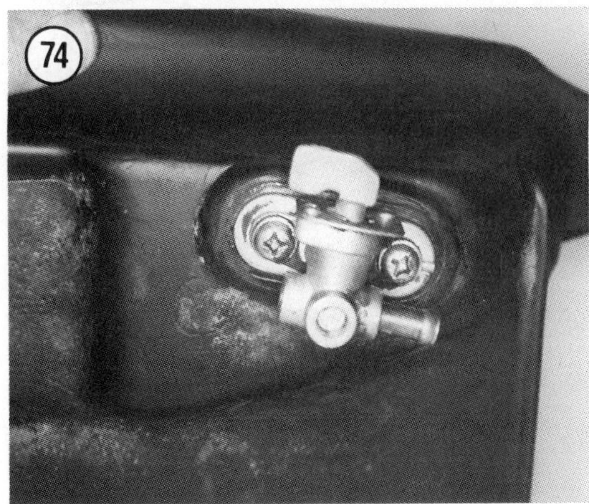

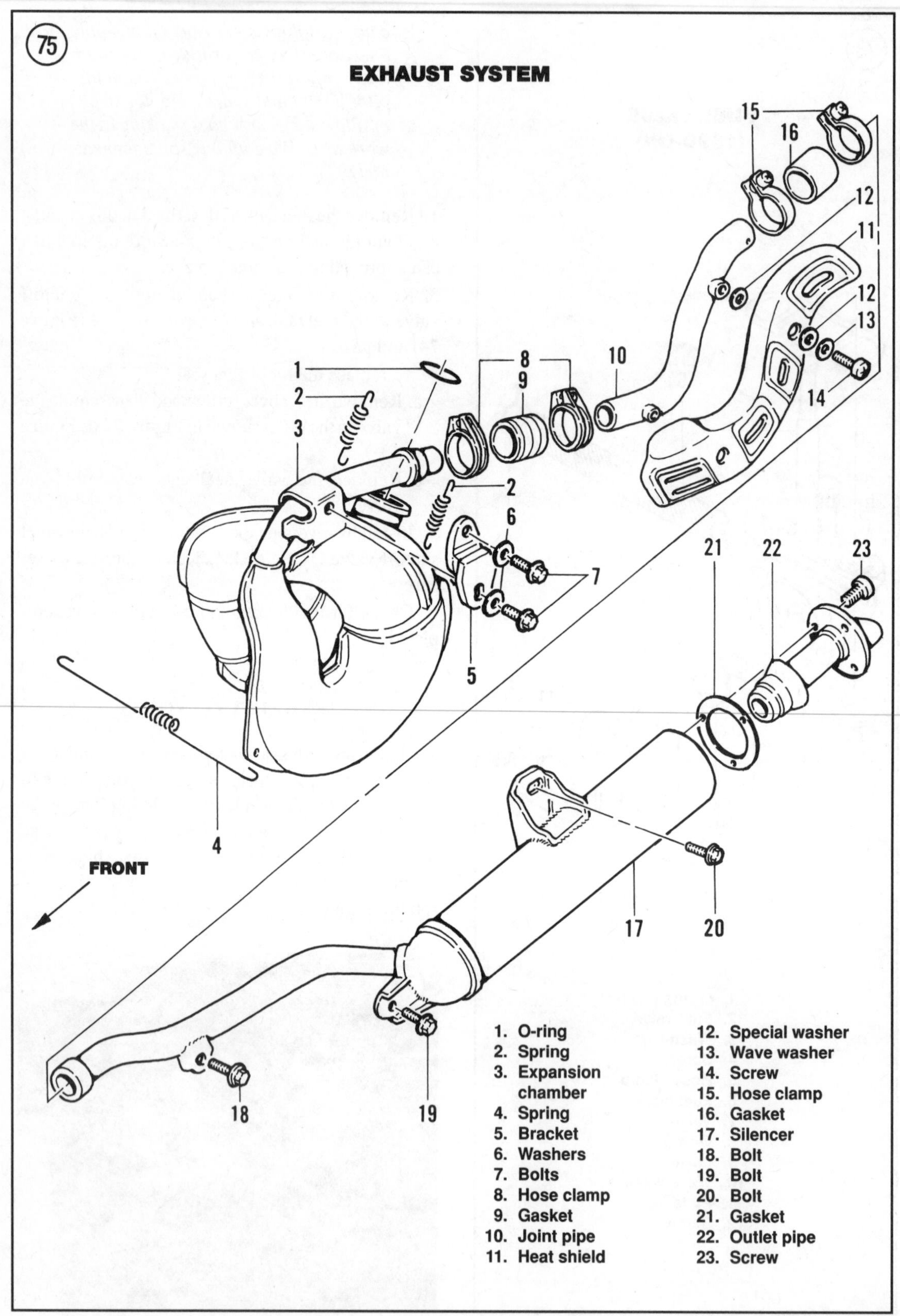
75
EXHAUST SYSTEM
FRONT
1
2
3
4
5
6
7
8
9
10
11
12
13
14
15
16
17
18
19
20
21
22
23
1. O-ring
2. Spring
3. Expansion chamber
4. Spring
5. Bracket
6. Washers
7. Bolts
8. Hose clamp
9. Gasket
10. Joint pipe
11. Heat shield
12. Special washer
13. Wave washer
14. Screw
15. Hose clamp
16. Gasket
17. Silencer
18. Bolt
19. Bolt
20. Bolt
21. Gasket
22. Outlet pipe
23. Screw

The stock exhaust system is shown in **Figure 75**.

Removal/Installation

1. Park the vehicle on level ground and set the parking brake.
2. Remove the seat and the rear fender as described in Chapter Fourteen.
3. Loosen the clamps securing the silencer to the expansion chamber.
4. Remove the silencer mounting bolts and remove the silencer (**Figure 76**).
5. Disconnect the springs at the front of the expansion chamber. See **Figure 77**, typical.
6. Remove the mounting brackets and remove the expansion chamber assembly. See **Figure 78**, typical.
7. Repeat for the opposite side.
8. Install by reversing these removal steps, noting the following.
9. Replace the front O-ring (**Figure 79**) if severely worn or damaged.
10. Replace the gasket (9, **Figure 75**) and gasket (16, **Figure 75**) if severely worn or damaged.
11. Tighten the expansion chamber and silencer mounting bolts to the torque specification in **Table 3**.
12. After installation is complete, start the engine and make sure there are no exhaust leaks.

Silencer Cleaning

1. Remove the screws securing the pipe outlet to the silencer. Then remove the pipe outlet and gasket.
2. Remove all carbon residue from the pipe outlet.
3. Replace the gasket if damaged.
4. Install by reversing these step. Install the pipe outlet so that the outlet nozzle faces down as shown in **Figure 76**.

76

78

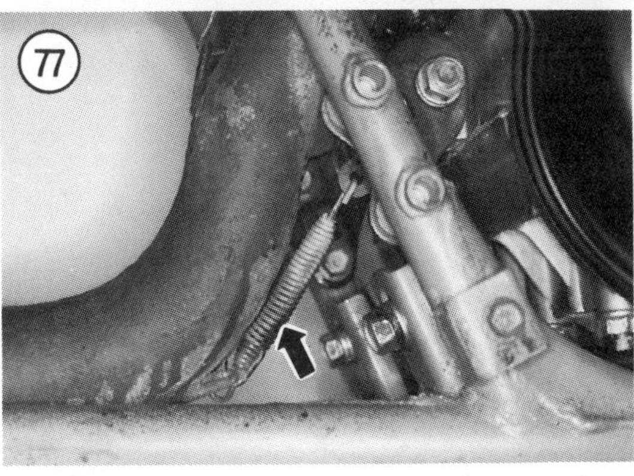
77

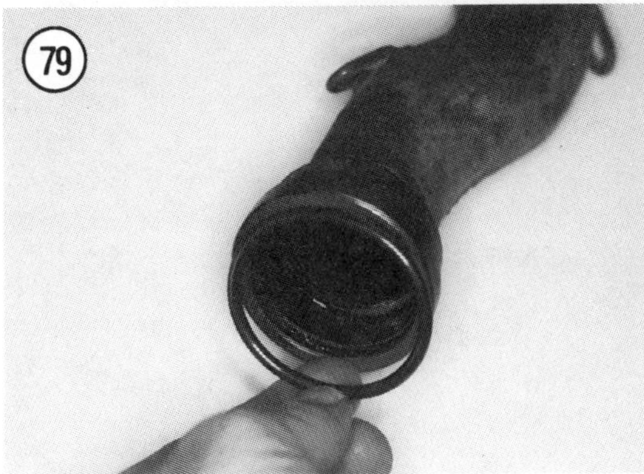
79

Tables 1-3 are on the following page.

8

Table 1 MIKUNI CARBURETOR SPECIFICATIONS

	1987-1989	1990-on
Type	VM26SS	VM26SS
Carburetor I.D. mark	2GU-00	2GU-01
Main jet	210	200
Main air jet	1.6	1.6
Jet needle/clip position	5N7/3	5N7/3
Needle jet	0-8	0-8
Pilot jet	25	25
Slide cutaway	2.0	2.0
Pilot outlet	0.6	0.6
Starter jet	1.4	1.4
Air screw (turns out)	2.0	2.0

Table 2 CARBURETOR FLOAT HEIGHT SPECIFICATIONS

	mm	in.
Float height	20-22	0.80-0.88

Table 3 TIGHTENING TORQUES

	N·m	ft.-lb.
Exhaust pipe	25	18
Silencer	35	25

CHAPTER NINE

ELECTRICAL SYSTEM

This chapter describes service procedures for the ignition and lighting systems.

General electrical system specifications are found in **Table 1**. **Tables 1-5** are at the end of the chapter.

COMPONENT TESTING/REPLACEMENT

An ohmmeter can be used for accurate testing of the ignition coil, stator plate coils, switches and wiring.

Resistance Testing

Resistance tests are performed after the component has been disconnected from the main wiring harness. You do not have to remove the part to test it, but instead, locate its wiring connectors and then disconnect them.

When using an ohmmeter, follow the manufacturer's instruction manual, while keeping the following guidelines in mind:

1. Make sure the test leads are connected properly. **Table 2** and **Table 3** list the specifications, test leads and wire connections for each test.
2. Perform when the engine is cold. Readings taken on a hot engine will show increased resistance caused by engine heat and may lead to inaccurate results.
3. When switching between ohmmeter scales on analog meters, always cross the test leads and zero the needle to assure a correct reading.

Replacement

Most motorcycle dealerships and parts suppliers will not accept the return of any electrical part. If you cannot determine the *exact* cause of any electrical system malfunction, have a Yamaha dealership retest that specific system to verify your test results. If you purchase a new electrical component(s), install it, and then find that the system still does not work properly, you will probably be unable to return the unit for a refund.

Consider any test results carefully before replacing a component that tests only *slightly* out of specification, especially resistance. A number of variables can affect test results dramatically. These include: the testing meter's internal circuitry, ambient temperature and conditions under which the machine has been operated. All instructions and specifications have been checked for accuracy; however, successful test results depend to a great degree upon individual accuracy.

CAPACITOR DISCHARGE IGNITION

All models are equipped with a capacitor discharge ignition (CDI) system. The system consists of the magneto assembly, CDI unit, ignition coil, main ignition switch, engine stop switch, T.O.R.S. control unit and the left and right carburetor

IGNITION SYSTEM*
(1987-2001 MODELS)

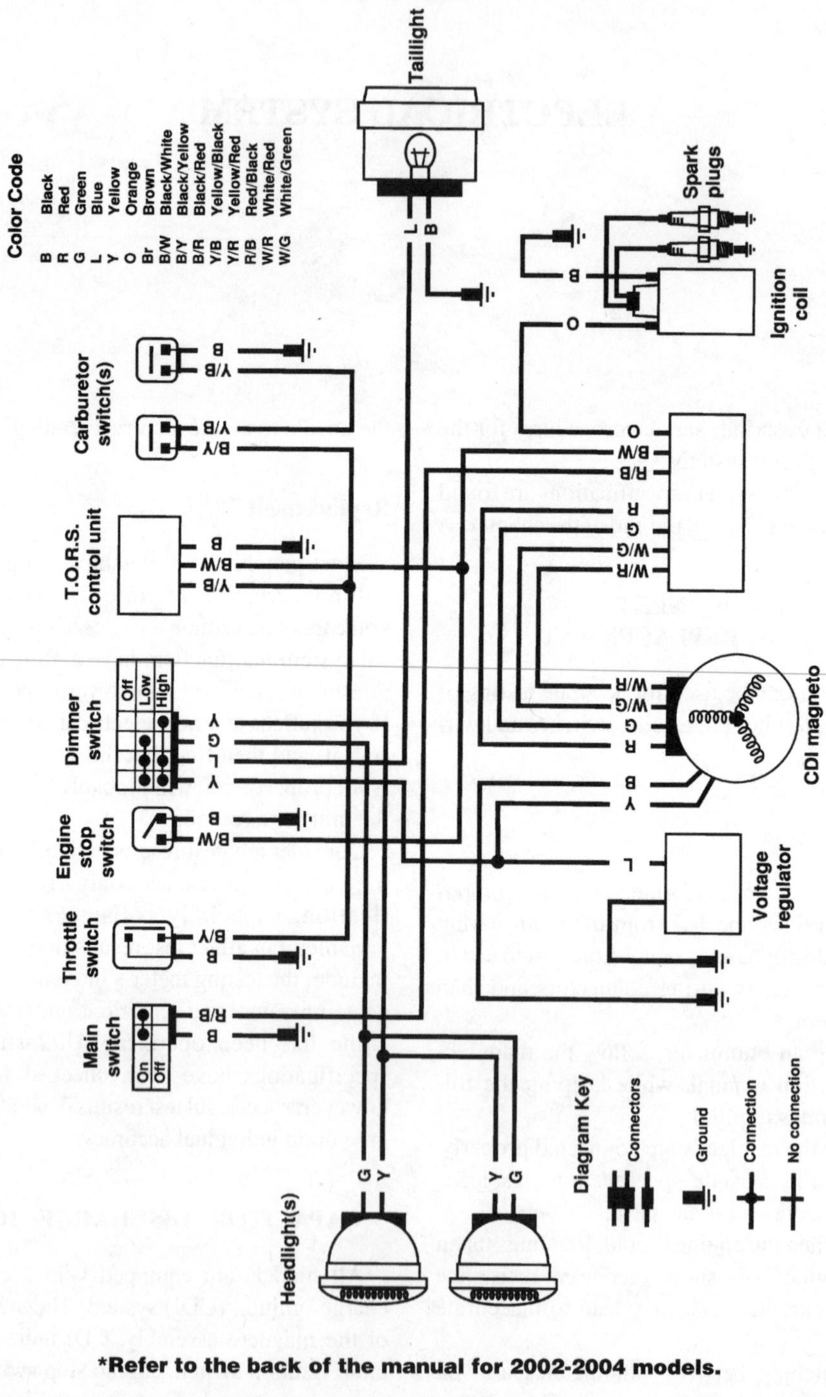

Color Code

B	Black
R	Red
G	Green
L	Blue
Y	Yellow
O	Orange
Br	Brown
B/W	Black/White
B/Y	Black/Yellow
B/R	Black/Red
Y/B	Yellow/Black
Y/R	Yellow/Red
R/B	Red/Black
W/R	White/Red
W/G	White/Green

Taillight

Spark plugs

Ignition coil

Carburetor switch(s)

T.O.R.S. control unit

Dimmer switch

Off Low High

Engine stop switch

Throttle switch

Main switch

On Off

CDI magneto

Voltage regulator

Headlight(s)

Diagram Key

Connectors

Ground

Connection

No connection

*Refer to the back of the manual for 2002-2004 models.

switches; see **Figure 1**. The magneto assembly consists of the flywheel and stator plate (**Figure 2**). The flywheel is equipped with magnets and is mounted on the crankshaft. The stator plate is mounted onto the engine. The flywheel and magnets revolve around the stator assembly. This solid state system, unlike a conventional ignition system, uses no contact breaker points or other moving parts.

Alternating current from the magneto is rectified and used to charge the capacitor. As the piston ap-

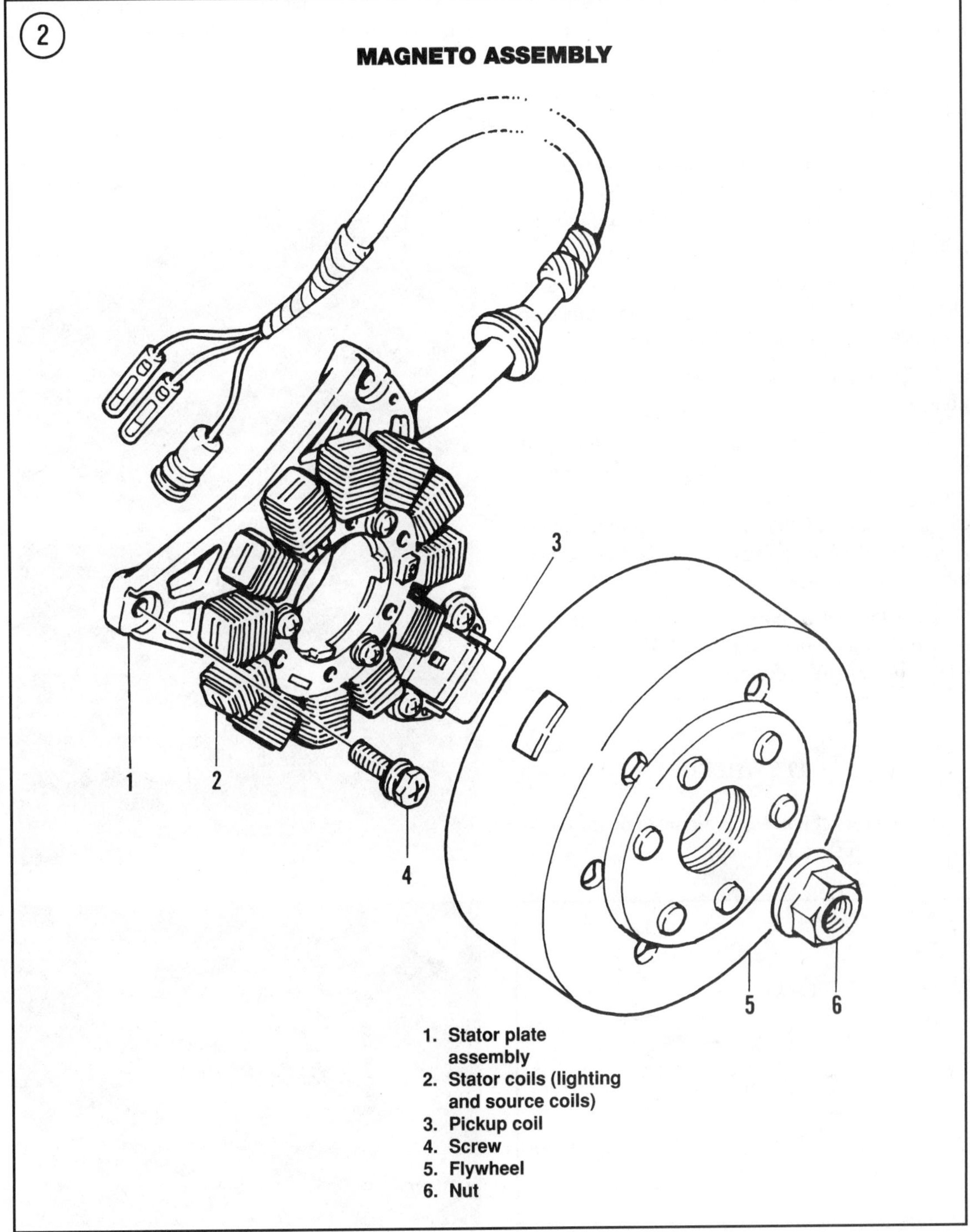

proaches the firing position, a pulse from the pulser (pickup) coil is rectified, shaped, and then used to trigger the silicone controlled rectifier. This in turn allows the capacitor to discharge quickly into the primary side of the high-voltage ignition coil where it is increased, or stepped up, to a high enough voltage to jump the gap between the spark plug electrodes.

CDI Cautions

Certain measures must be taken to protect the capacitor discharge system. Damage to the semiconductors in the system may occur if the following is not observed.

1. Keep all connections between the various units clean and tight. Be sure that the wiring connectors are pushed together firmly (**Figure 3**).
2. Never disconnect any of the electrical connections while the engine is running.
3. When kicking the engine over with the spark plugs removed, make sure the spark plugs are installed in the plug caps and grounded against the cylinder head (**Figure 4**) or the ignition switch turned off. If not, excessive resistance may damage the ignition system.
4. The CDI unit is mounted on a rubber vibration isolator or on rubber dampers. Make sure that the CDI unit is mounted correctly.

FLYWHEEL

The flywheel (**Figure 2**) is mounted on the end of the crankshaft (left-hand side).

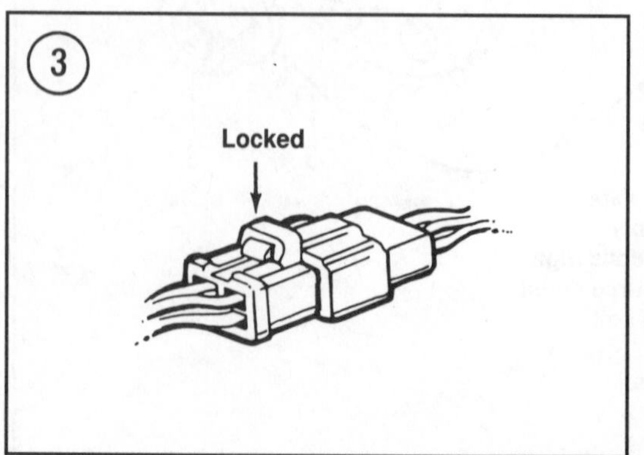

Removal/Installation

1. Park the vehicle on a level surface and set the parking brake.
2. Remove the shift lever.
3. Remove the left-hand side cover (**Figure 5**).
4. Secure the flywheel with a holding tool and loosen the flywheel nut (**Figure 6**). Remove the nut.

CAUTION
Flywheel removal requires a special flywheel puller. Do not pry or hammer on

the flywheel when removing it. Do not remove the flywheel with a different type of puller. Damage is sure to result, and you may destroy the flywheel's magnetism. Use the proper type of puller described.

NOTE
Yamaha flywheel puller (part No. YM-01189) will work on all models.

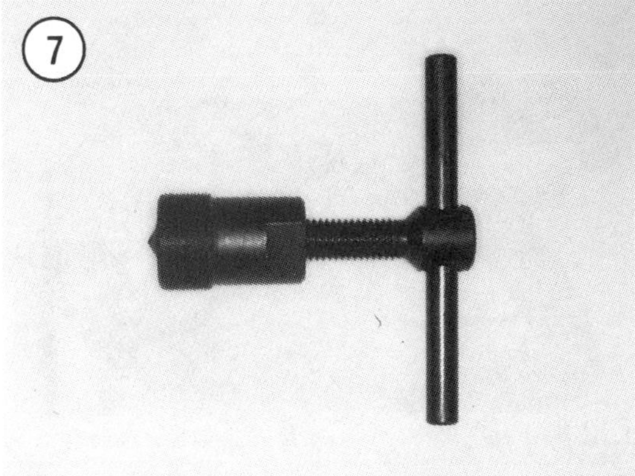

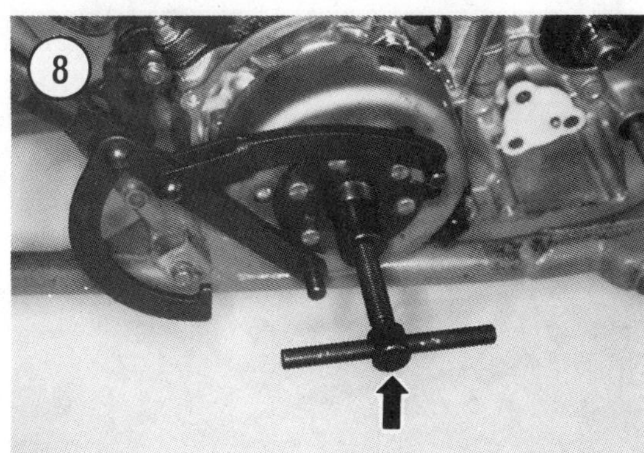

5. Apply a dab of grease onto the flywheel puller's pressure bolt where it will contact the crankshaft. Then thread the flywheel puller (**Figure 7**) into the flywheel. Screw the flywheel puller into the flywheel threads until its stops, then back out 1/2 turn (**Figure 8**).

CAUTION
Do not apply excessive force to the puller when removing the flywheel. Doing so can cause the puller to strip the threads in the flywheel or damage the end of the crankshaft. If necessary, take the engine to a dealer and have them remove the flywheel.

6. Turn the flywheel pressure bolt clockwise while holding the flywheel puller. When turning the pressure bolt, check the puller body to make sure that it has not started to pull out of the flywheel. Continue until the flywheel pops free.
7. Remove the flywheel and puller. Don't lose the Woodruff key (**Figure 9**) on the crankshaft.

CAUTION
*Inspect the inside of the flywheel (**Figure 10**) for small bolts, washers or other metal "trash" that may have been picked up by the magnets. These small metal bits can cause severe damage to the stator plate components.*

8. Install by reversing these removal steps, while noting the following:
   a. Make sure the Woodruff key (**Figure 9**) is in place on the crankshaft and align the keyway in the flywheel with the key during installation.

9

b. Install and tighten the flywheel nut (**Figure 11**) to the torque specification in **Table 5**. To keep the flywheel from turning, hold it with the same tool used during removal.

c. Replace the side cover gasket (**Figure 12**) if damaged.

Flywheel Inspection

The flywheel is permanently magnetized and cannot be tested except by replacement with a flywheel known to be good. A flywheel can lose magnetism from a sharp blow. If defective, the flywheel must be replaced; it cannot be remagnetized.

1. Check the flywheel (**Figure 10**) carefully for cracks or breaks.

2. Check the tapered bore of the flywheel and the crankshaft taper (**Figure 9**) for cracks or other abnormal conditions.

Stator Assembly Removal/Installation

Refer to **Figure 2**.

1. Remove the flywheel as described in this chapter.

2. Remove the fuel tank as described in Chapter Eight.

3. Disconnect the electrical wire connectors from the magneto to the CDI unit. See **Figure 1**.

4. Remove the screws (**Figure 13**) securing the stator plate to the engine.

5. Push the stator plate wiring harness grommet out of the crankcase as shown in **Figure 14**.

6. Carefully pull the wiring harness out of the hole in the crankcase and remove the stator plate assembly (**Figure 15**).

7. Install by reversing these removal steps, while noting the following.

8. Clean the wiring harness connectors with contact cleaner.

9. Route the electrical wires along their original path.

10. Insert the stator plate wiring harness grommet into the crankcase as shown in **Figure 16**. If the

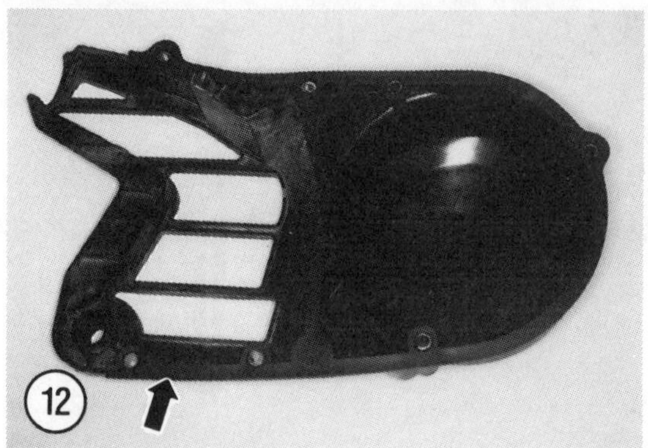

grommet is damaged, apply some RTV sealer onto the grommet before installing it.

11. Check the ignition timing as described in Chapter Three.

Stator Coil Testing

The stator coils (**Figure 13**, typical) can be inspected for continuity without removing the stator from the ATV. With the engine off, disconnect the stator plate electrical connectors (**Figure 1**) and measure the resistance between the pairs of leads listed in **Table 2**. **Figure 17** shows the stator plate connectors. If the resistance is zero (short circuit) or infinite (open circuit), check the wiring to the coils. Replace the stator plate if the wiring is okay.

On all models, the stator plate assembly (**Figure 15**) must be replaced as an assembly. Individual stator plate coils are not available from Yamaha.

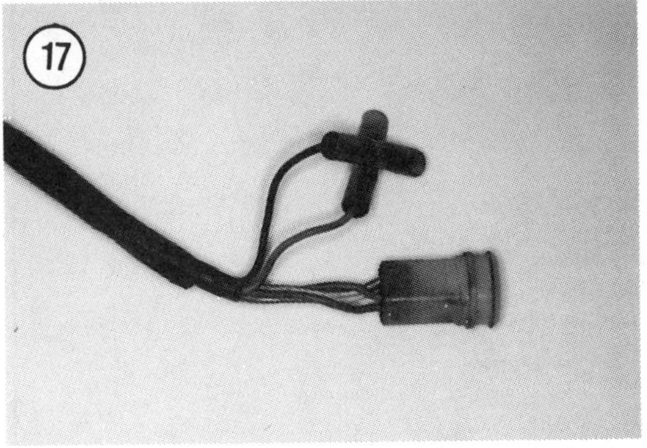

CDI UNIT

The CDI unit (A, **Figure 18**) is mounted underneath the rear fender.

Removal/Installation

1. Park the vehicle on a level surface and set the parking brake.
2. Disconnect the CDI electrical connectors (B, **Figure 18**).
3. Remove the bolts and washers securing the CDI unit to the frame and remove the CDI unit (A, **Figure 18**).
4. Install by reversing these steps, while noting the following.
5. Clean the connectors with contact cleaner.

Testing

Yamaha does not list test procedures or provide test equipment for testing the CDI unit (A, **Figure 18**).

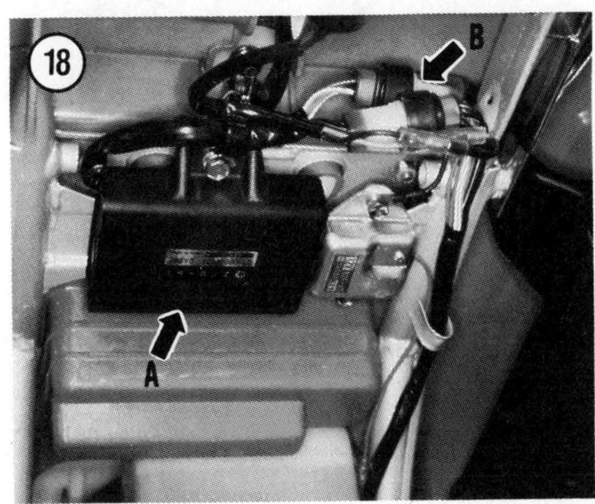

IGNITION COIL

The ignition coil (**Figure 19**) is mounted on the upper frame rail.

Removal/Installation

1. Park the vehicle on a level surface and set the parking brake.
2. Remove the front fender.
3. Disconnect the spark plug leads.
4. Disconnect the primary wires from the ignition coil.
5. Remove the screws securing the ignition coil to the frame and remove it (**Figure 19**).
6. Install by reversing these removal steps. Make sure all electrical connectors are tight and free of corrosion. Make sure the ground wire connection point on the frame is free of rust and corrosion.

Testing

If the functional condition of the coil is in doubt, there are several checks which should be made. Disconnect the coil wires before testing.

1. Disconnect the primary wires from the ignition coil. Disconnect the spark plug caps from the spark plugs.
2. Measure the coil primary resistance using an ohmmeter set at R × 1 (**Figure 20**). Measure the

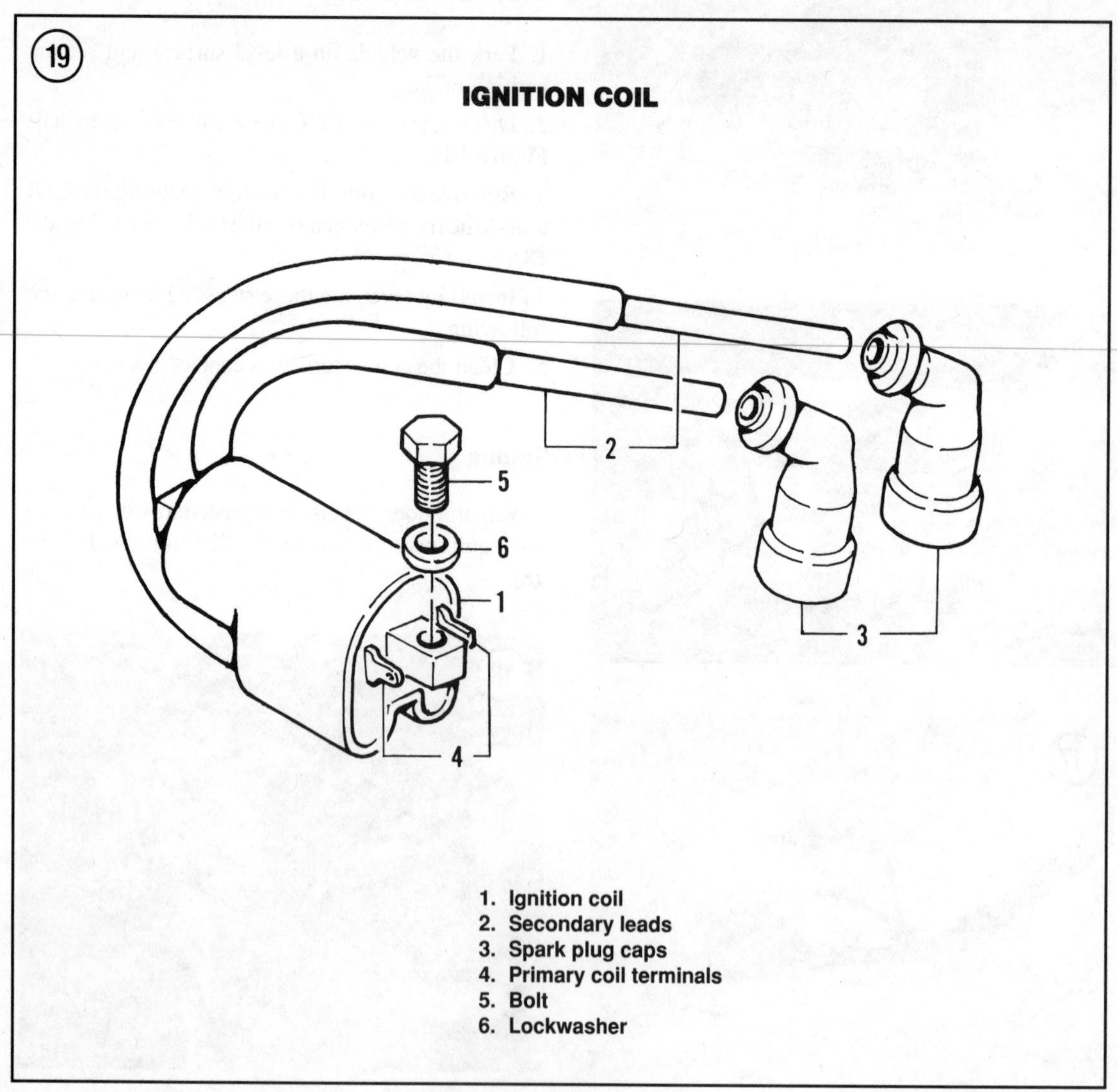

1. Ignition coil
2. Secondary leads
3. Spark plug caps
4. Primary coil terminals
5. Bolt
6. Lockwasher

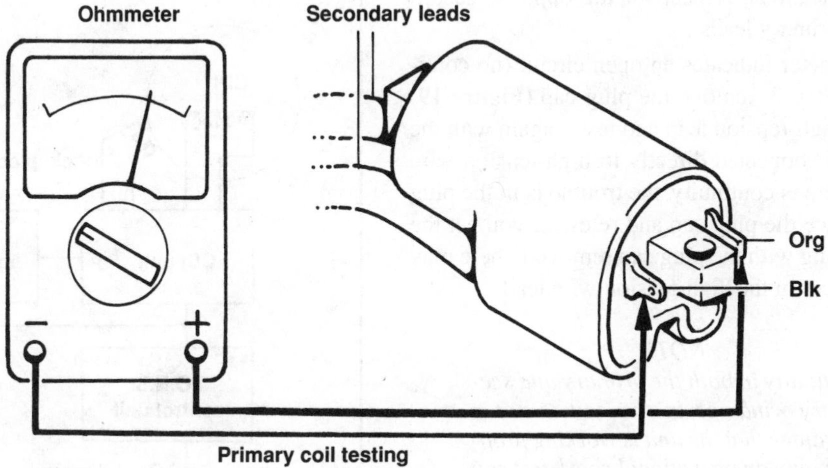
Ohmmeter
Secondary leads
Org
Blk
−
+
Primary coil testing

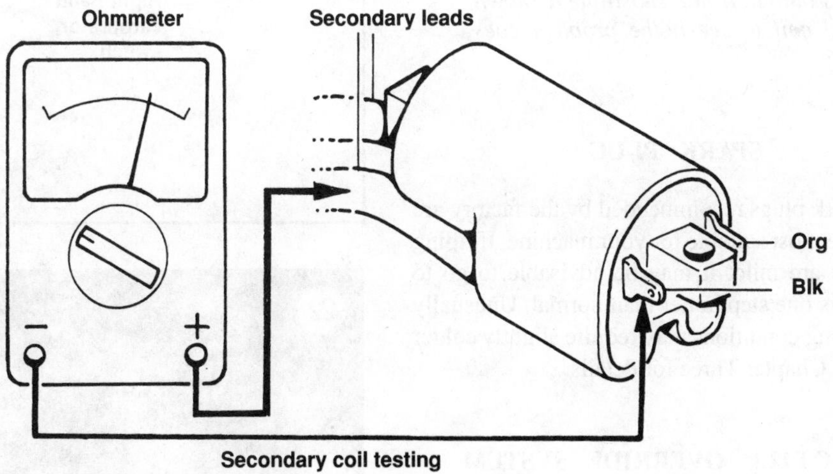
Ohmmeter
Secondary leads
Org
Blk
−
+
Secondary coil testing

9

resistance between the 2 ignition coil primary terminals shown in **Figure 20**. See **Table 3** for test specifications.

3. Measure the secondary resistance using an ohmmeter set at R × 1,000 (**Figure 20**). Measure the resistance between the secondary lead (spark plug lead) and the corresponding ignition coil primary coil terminal as shown in **Figure 20**. See **Table 3** for test specifications. Repeat for the opposite secondary and primary leads.

4. If the meter indicates an open circuit (no continuity) in Step 3, remove the plug cap (**Figure 19**) from the high-tension lead and test it again with the meter lead connected directly to high-tension wire lead. If there is continuity, the trouble is in the plug cap. Replace the plug cap and retest. If you get the same reading with the plug cap removed, there may be a problem in the high-tension wire lead.

NOTE

Continuity in both the primary and secondary windings in the coil is not a guarantee that the unit is working properly; only an operational spark test can tell if a coil is producing an adequate spark from the input voltage. Your motorcycle dealer or auto electrical repair shop may have the equipment to test the coil's output. If not, substitute a known good coil to see if the problem goes away.

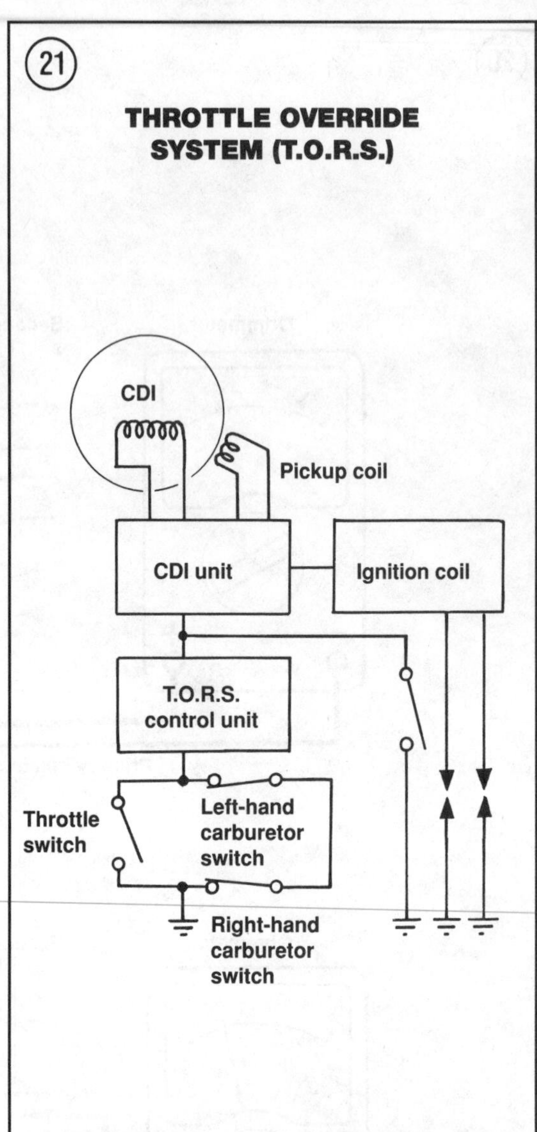

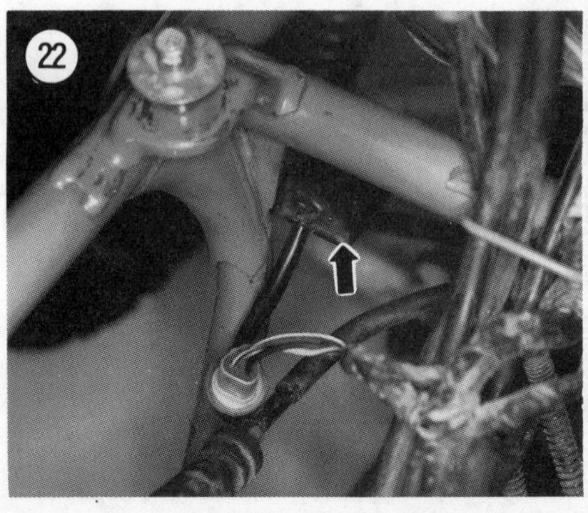

SPARK PLUG

The spark plugs recommended by the factory are usually the most suitable for your machine. If riding conditions are mild, it may be advisable to go to spark plugs one step hotter than normal. Unusually severe riding conditions may require slightly colder plugs. See Chapter Three for details.

THROTTLE OVERRIDE SYSTEM (T.O.R.S.)

On all models a throttle override system has been incorporated into the ignition system. The T.O.R.S. circuit is shown in **Figure 21**. The T.O.R.S. consists of a throttle switch, left and right-hand T.O.R.S. control units, left and right-hand carburetor switches and the T.O.R.S. control unit.

The T.O.R.S. system is a safety override system. If the carburetors stick open (throttle valves will not close) during engine operation, removing your thumb from the throttle lever will cause the T.O.R.S. system to shut off the ignition system immediately.

T.O.R.S. Troubleshooting

Refer to *Ignition System Troubleshooting* in Chapter Two.

T.O.R.S. Control Unit Removal/Installation

The T.O.R.S. control unit is mounted on the upper frame rail (**Figure 22**).

1. Remove the front fender as described in Chapter Fourteen.
2. Disconnect the electrical connector at the T.O.R.S. control unit.
3. Remove the bolt securing the T.O.R.S. control unit to the frame and remove the T.O.R.S. control unit. See **Figure 23**.
4. Install by reversing these removal steps.

T.O.R.S. Carburetor Switches Removal/Installation

The T.O.R.S. carburetor switches are mounted in the switch housings mounted on top of each carburetor (**Figure 24**). The carburetor switches (**Figure 25**) are an integral part of the switch housing. To access or replace the switch housings, refer to *Throttle Valve/T.O.R.S. Housing* disassembly and reassembly procedures in Chapter Eight. To test the carburetor switches, refer to *Switches* in this chapter.

T.O.R.S. Throttle Switch Removal/Installation

Refer to *Switches* in this chapter.

LIGHTING SYSTEM

The lighting system consists of a headlight and taillight. **Table 4** lists replacement bulbs for these components. **Figure 26** shows a circuit diagram of the lighting system.

Always use the correct wattage bulb as indicated in this section. The use of a larger wattage bulb will give a dim light and a smaller wattage bulb will burn out prematurely.

Headlight Bulb Replacement

Refer to **Figure 27** for this procedure.

CAUTION

*All models are equipped with quartz-halogen bulbs (**Figure 28**). Do not touch the bulb glass with your fingers because traces of oil on the bulb will drastically reduce the life of the bulb.*

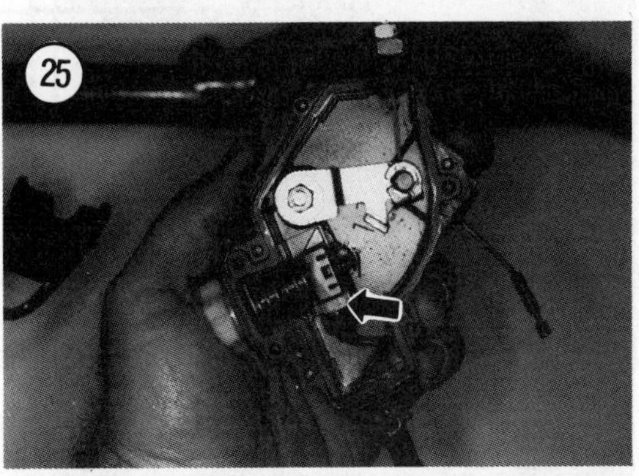

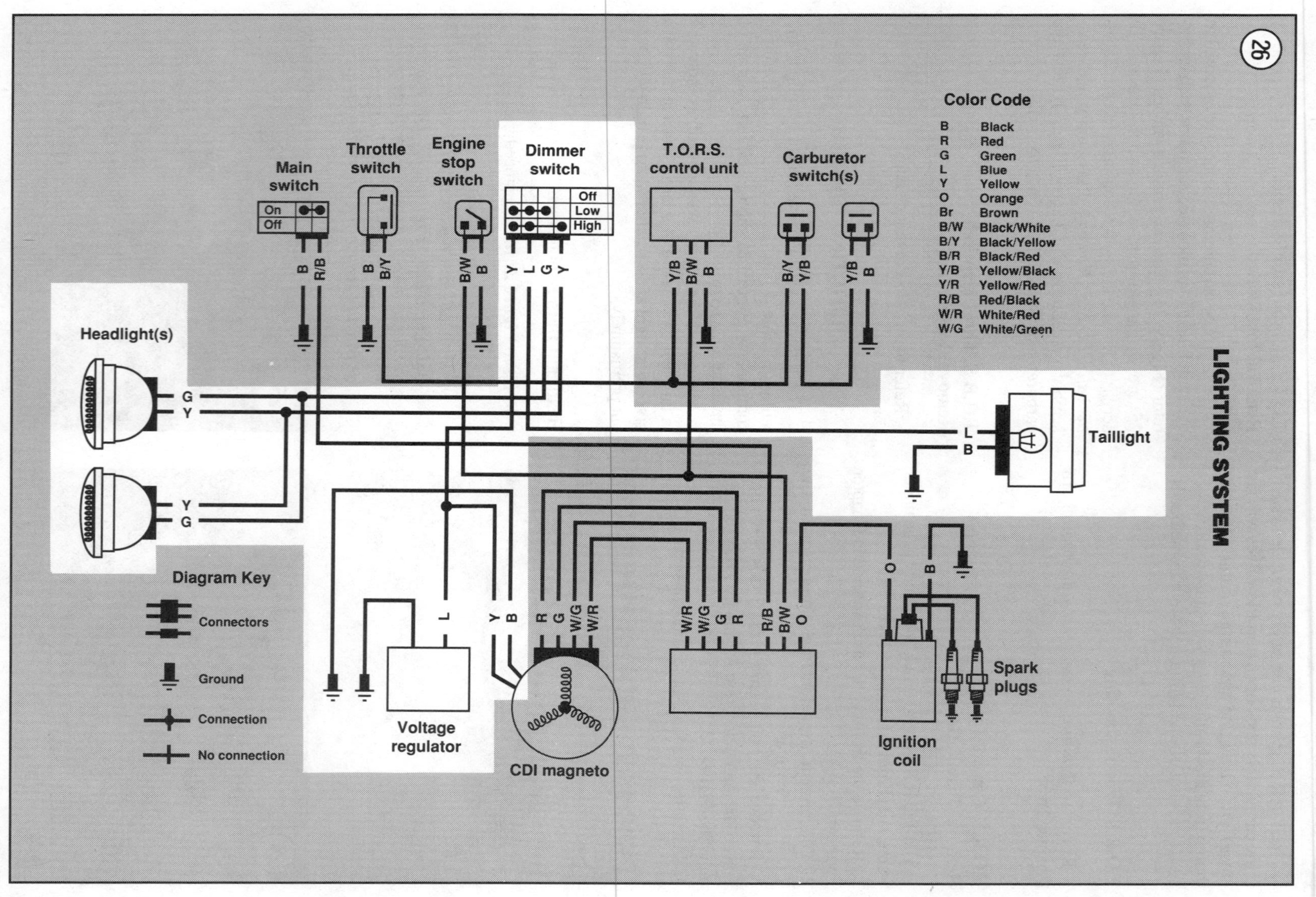
26
LIGHTING SYSTEM
Color Code
B Black
R Red
G Green
L Blue
Y Yellow
O Orange
Br Brown
B/W Black/White
B/Y Black/Yellow
B/R Black/Red
Y/B Yellow/Black
Y/R Yellow/Red
R/B Red/Black
W/R White/Red
W/G White/Green
Main switch
On
Off
Throttle switch
Engine stop switch
Dimmer switch
Off
Low
High
T.O.R.S. control unit
Carburetor switch(s)
Headlight(s)
Taillight
Diagram Key
Connectors
Ground
Connection
No connection
Voltage regulator
CDI magneto
Spark plugs
Ignition coil

HEADLIGHT

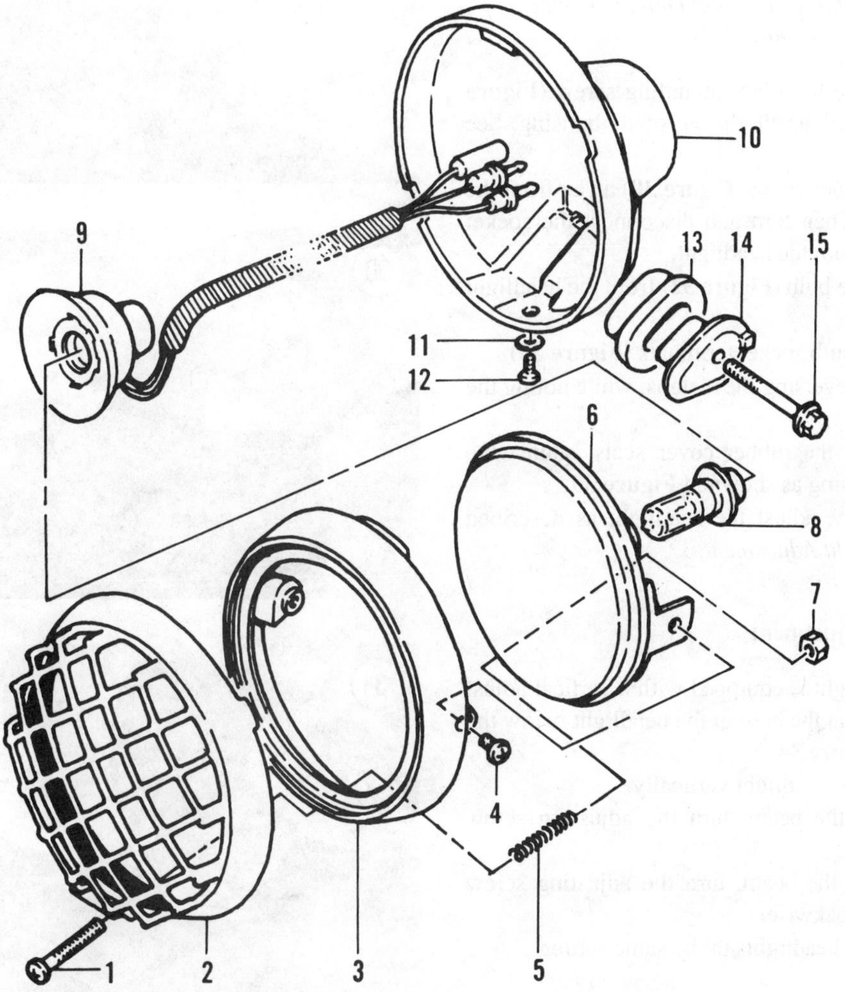

1. Screw
2. Cover
3. Rim
4. Screw
5. Spring
6. Lens assembly
7. Nut
8. Bulb
9. Connector
10. Housing
11. Washer
12. Screw
13. Grommet
14. Collar
15. Bolt

Clean any traces of oil or other chemicals from the bulb with a cloth moistened in alcohol or lacquer thinner.

WARNING

If the headlight has just burned out or turned off it will be hot! Don't touch the bulb until it cools off.

1. Remove the headlight mounting screw (**Figure 29**) and pull the headlight out of its housing. See **Figure 30**.
2. Pry the rubber cover (**Figure 30**) away from the bulb socket. Then turn and disconnect the socket (**Figure 31**) from the headlight.
3. Remove the bulb (**Figure 32**) from the headlight housing.
4. Clean the bulb socket terminals (**Figure 33**).
5. Install by reversing these steps, while noting the following.
6. Make sure the rubber cover seats against the headlight housing as shown in **Figure 30**.
7. If necessary, adjust the headlight as described under *Headlight Adjustment*.

Headlight Adjustment

Each headlight is equipped with a vertical adjust screw located at the base of the headlight below the grille. See **Figure 34**.

To adjust the headlight vertically:

a. To raise the beam, turn the adjusting screw clockwise.
b. To lower the beam, turn the adjusting screw counterclockwise.

Adjust both headlights to the same setting.

Taillight Bulb and Lens Replacement

Refer to **Figure 35** for this procedure.

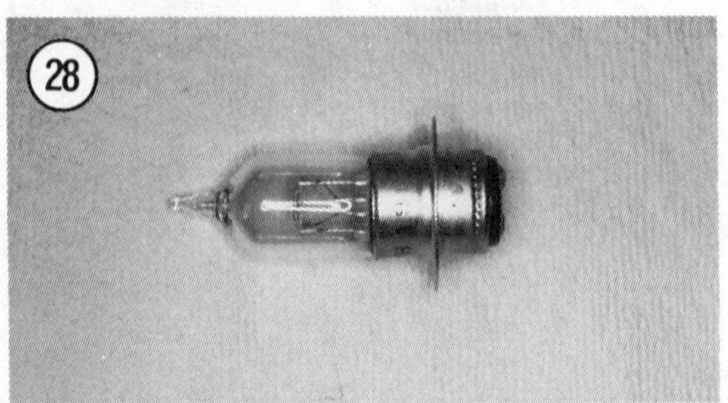

28

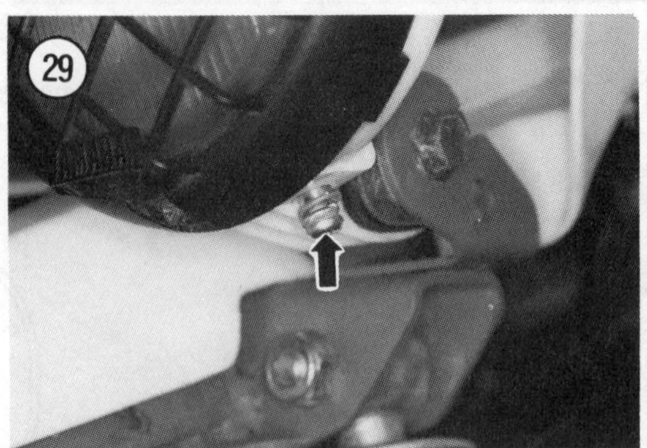

29

30

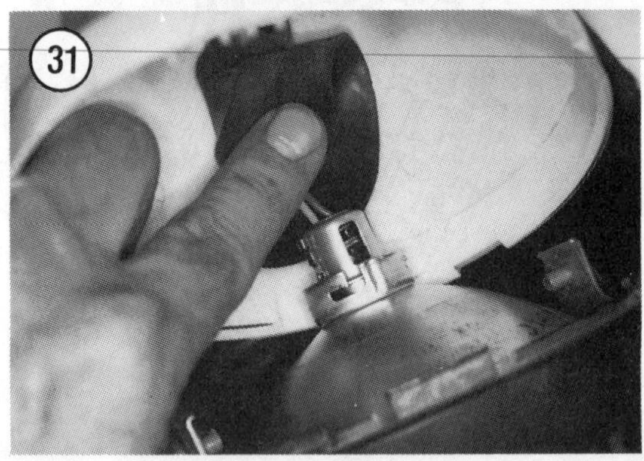

31

32

33

34

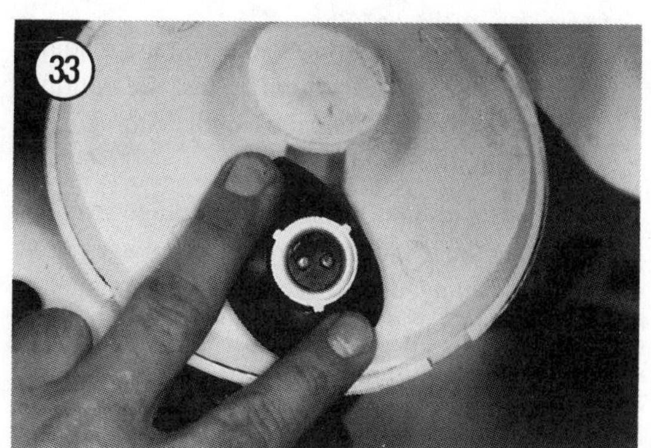

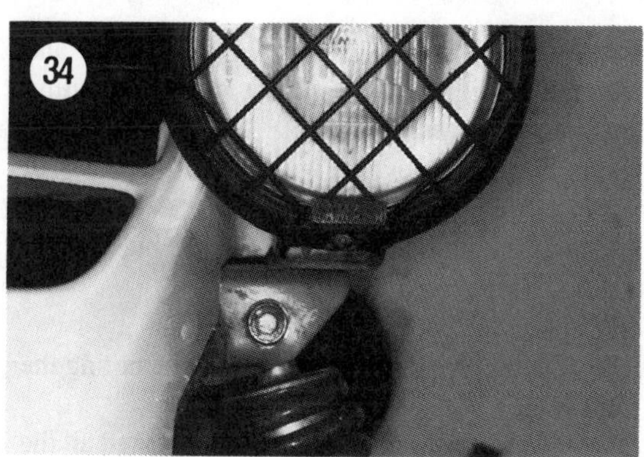

35

TAILLIGHT

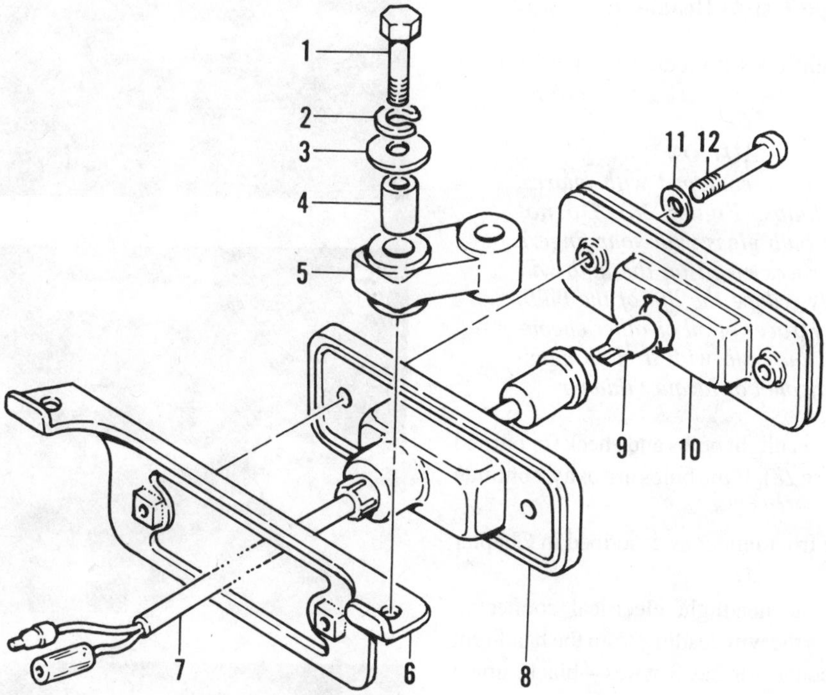
1
2
3
4
5
6
7
8
9
10
11
12

1. Bolt
2. Lockwasher
3. Washer
4. Collar
5. Bracket
6. Frame
7. Connector assembly
8. Housing
9. Bulb
10. Lens
11. Washer
12. Bolt

9

1. Remove the 2 Phillips screws (**Figure 36**) and pull the taillight assembly out of its mounting bracket on the frame.
2. Pry the rubber cover (**Figure 37**) off the back of the lens.
3. Turn the bulb holder and remove the bulb holder and bulb (**Figure 38**).
4. Replace the bulb.
5. Install by reversing these steps, while noting the following.
6. Make sure the rubber gasket seal is seated all the way around the lens when assembling the lens and bulb holder (**Figure 37**).

LIGHTING VOLTAGE TESTS

Lighting Voltage Test At Headlight

If the headlight does not come on, perform the following test.

CAUTION
*All models are equipped with quartz-halogen bulbs (**Figure 28**). Do not touch the bulb glass with your fingers because traces of oil on the bulb will drastically reduce the life of the bulb. Clean any traces of oil or other chemicals from the bulb with a cloth moistened in alcohol or lacquer thinner.*

1. Remove the headlight bulbs and check for burned out bulbs (**Figure 28**). If the bulbs are okay, continue with Step 2.
2. Remove the front fender as described in Chapter Fourteen.
3. Disconnect the headlight electrical connector. **Figure 39** shows the wire leading from the headlight housing. The connector has 3 wires—black, green and yellow.
4. Connect a tachometer to the engine following its manufacturer's instructions.
5. Connect a DC voltmeter to the headlight connector on the wiring harness side. Connect the negative voltmeter lead to the black wire and the positive voltmeter lead to the yellow wire.
6. Start and run the engine at approximately 2,500 rpm and then at 8,000 rpm. Record the voltmeter reading at both of the specified rpm speeds. The lighting voltage should be:
   a. 11.5 volts at 2,500 rpm. If the voltage reading is below the prescribed range, test the lighting coil resistance as described under *Stator Coil Testing* in this chapter.
   b. 16.3 volts at 8,000 rpm. If the voltage reading is above the prescribed range, the voltage regulator is damaged. Replace the voltage regulator as described in this chapter and retest.
   c. Repeat this test with the negative voltmeter lead connected to the green wire. The readings at both engine speeds should be the same.

36

37

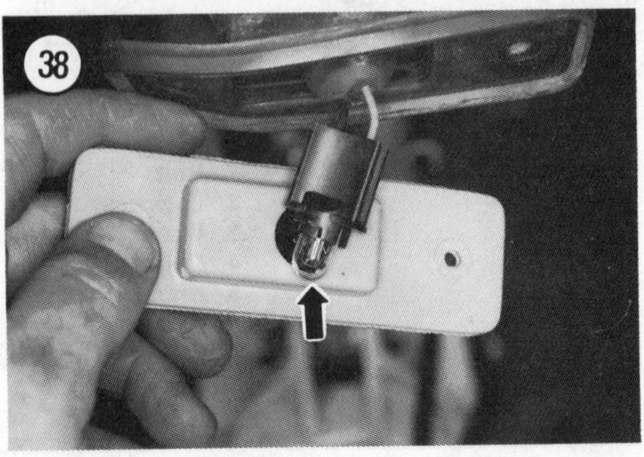
38

d. If the voltage readings are correct, proceed with Step 7.

7. Test the dimmer switch as described under *Switches* in this chapter.

8. If the dimmer switch is okay, check all of wiring and connectors for dirty or loose-fitting terminals; clean and repair as required.

9. Remove the voltmeter and tachometer. Reconnect the headlight connector.

Lighting Voltage Test At Taillight

If the taillight does not come on, perform the following test.

1. Remove the taillight bulb and check for a burned out bulb (**Figure 38**). If the bulb is okay, continue with Step 2.

2. Disconnect the taillight connector (A, **Figure 40**) in front of the taillight assembly. The connector has 2 wires—black and blue.

3. Connect a tachometer to the engine following its manufacturer's instructions.

4. Connect a DC voltmeter to the taillight connector on the wiring harness side. Connect the negative voltmeter lead to the black wire and the positive voltmeter lead to the blue wire.

5. Start and run the engine at approximately 2,500 rpm and then at 8,000 rpm. Record the voltmeter reading at both of the specified engine speeds. The correct lighting voltage should be:

   a. 11.5 volts at 2,500 rpm. If the voltage reading is below the prescribed range, test the lighting coil resistance as described under *Stator Coil Testing* in this chapter.

   b. 16.3 volts at 8,000 rpm. If the voltage reading is above the prescribed range, the voltage regulator is damaged. Replace the voltage regulator as described in this chapter and retest.

   c. If the lighting voltage readings are correct, proceed with Step 6.

6. Test the dimmer switch as described under *Switches* in this chapter.

7. If the dimmer switch is okay, check all wiring and connectors for dirty or loose-fitting terminals; clean and repair as required.

8. Remove the voltmeter and tachometer. Reconnect the taillight connector.

VOLTAGE REGULATOR

The voltage regulator is mounted underneath the rear fender. See B, **Figure 40**.

Testing

To test the voltage regulator, perform one of the tests listed under *Lighting Voltage Tests* in this chapter.

Removal/Installation

1. Disconnect the voltage regulator electrical connector.

2. Unbolt and remove the voltage regulator (B, **Figure 40**).

3. Install by reversing these steps. Make sure to reconnect the ground wire to one of the voltage regulator mounting bolts.

9

SWITCHES

Testing

Switches can be tested for continuity with an ohmmeter (see Chapter One) or a test light at the switch connector.

When testing switches, note the following:

a. After locating a defective circuit, check the connectors to make sure they are clean and properly connected. Check all wires going into a connector housing to make sure each wire is properly positioned and that the wire end is not loose.
b. To reconnect connectors properly, push them together until they click or snap into place.

Ignition Switch Testing/Replacement

The ignition switch (**Figure 41**) is mounted in front of the handlebar.

1. Remove the front fender as described in Chapter Fourteen.
2. Locate the main switch electrical connector and disconnect it. The ignition switch connector has 2 wires—black and black/red.
3. Use an ohmmeter set at R × 1 and connect the 2 ohmmeter leads to the ignition switch black and black/red wires.
4. Turn the ignition key to the OFF position. If the switch is good, there will be no continuity (infinite resistance).
5. Turn the ignition key to the ON position. If the switch is good, there will be continuity (very low resistance).
6. If the switch fails any of these tests, the switch is faulty and must be replaced.
7. To replace the ignition switch:
   a. Remove the plastic nut securing the ignition switch to its outer cover.
   b. Remove the 2 ignition switch mounting screws and remove the switch and its outer cover.
   c. Reverse to install. When installing the outer cover, align the outer cover notch with the ignition switch tab (**Figure 42**).
8. Reconnect the ignition switch electrical connector and reinstall the front fender.

Engine Stop Switch/Dimmer Switch Testing/Replacement

The switches mounted in the left-hand handlebar switch housing are not available separately. If one switch is damaged, the entire switch assembly must be replaced.

1. Remove the front fender assembly as described in Chapter Fourteen.
2. Disconnect the engine switch/dimmer switch electrical connectors.

41

42

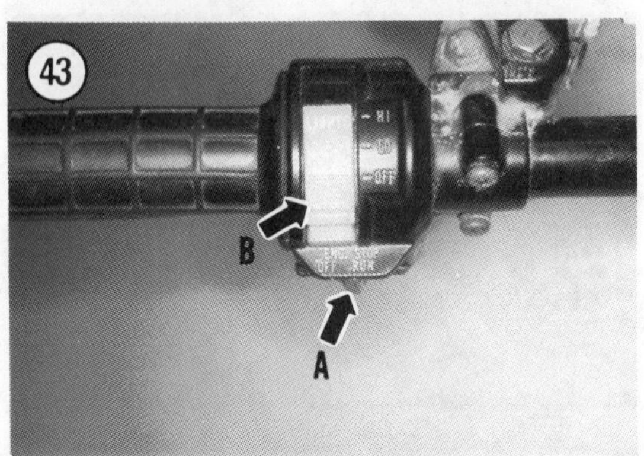

43

3. To test the engine stop switch (A, **Figure 43**), perform the following:
   a. Use an ohmmeter set at R × 1 and connect the 2 ohmmeter leads to the black/white and brown wires.
   b. Turn the engine stop switch to the OFF position. If the switch is good, there will be continuity (very low resistance).
   c. Turn the engine stop switch to the RUN position. If the switch is good, there will be no continuity (infinite resistance).
4. To test the dimmer switch (B, **Figure 43**), perform the following:
   a. Turn the dimmer switch to the HI position. Use an ohmmeter set at R × 1 and connect the 2 ohmmeter leads first to the yellow and blue wires, then to the blue and the second yellow wire. If the switch is good, there will be continuity (very low resistance).

44

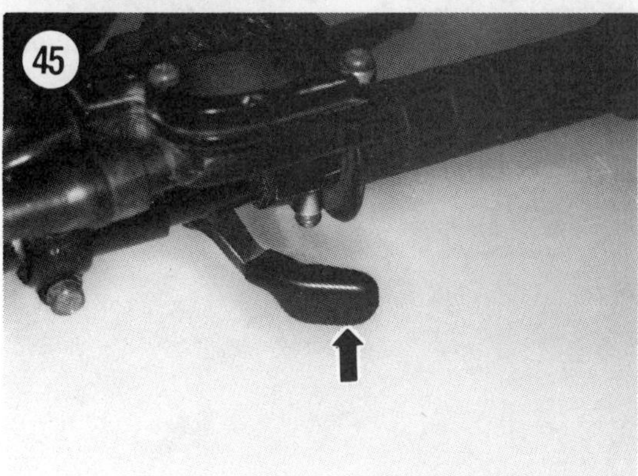
45

   b. Turn the dimmer switch to the LO position. Use an ohmmeter set at R × 1 and connect the 2 ohmmeter leads first to the yellow and blue wires, then to the blue and green wires. If the switch is good, there will be continuity (very low resistance).
   c. Turn the dimmer switch to the OFF position. Use an ohmmeter set at R × 1 and connect the 2 ohmmeter leads first to the yellow and blue wires, then to the green and second yellow wires. If the switch is good, there will be no continuity (infinite resistance).
5. If the switch fails any of these tests, the switch assembly is faulty and must be replaced.
6. Remove any cable straps securing the switch wiring harness to the handlebar and frame.
7. Remove the screws securing the switch housing to the handlebar and remove the switch housing.
8. Install by reversing these steps. Start the engine and check the switch in each of its operating positions.

Throttle Lever Switch Testing/Replacement

The throttle lever switch (**Figure 44**) is mounted in the throttle housing.

1. Check the throttle lever free play adjustment as described in Chapter Three. Adjust if necessary.
2. Remove the front fender as described in Chapter Fourteen.
3. Disconnect the throttle lever electrical connector. The connector has 2 wires—black and black/yellow.
4. Use an ohmmeter set at R × 1 and connect the red ohmmeter lead to the black/yellow wire and the black ohmmeter lead to the black wire.
5. Push the throttle lever (**Figure 45**) all the way in. If the switch is good, there will be continuity (very low resistance).
6. Release the throttle lever. If the switch is good, there will be no continuity (infinite resistance).
7. If the switch fails to pass any of these tests, the switch is faulty and must be replaced.
8. To replace the throttle lever switch:
   a. Remove the throttle lever housing cover and gasket.
   b. Remove the screw securing the switch to the throttle lever housing.

9

c. Lift the switch out of the housing and remove it (**Figure 46**).

d. Reverse to install the new switch. Push the grommet on the switch wiring harness into the throttle lever housing.

9. Reverse to reconnect the wiring harness connectors.

Carburetor Switches
Testing

A single carburetor switch is installed in each T.O.R.S. housing (**Figure 47**).

1. Check the throttle lever free play adjustment as described in Chapter Three. Adjust if necessary.
2. Remove the fuel tank as described in Chapter Eight.
3. Disconnect the carburetor switch electrical connector (**Figure 48**). The connector has 2 wires—black and black/yellow.
4. Use an ohmmeter set at R × 1 and connect the red ohmmeter lead to the black/yellow wire and the black ohmmeter lead to the black wire.
5. Push the throttle lever (**Figure 45**) all the way in. If the switch is good, there will be no continuity (infinite resistance).
6. Release the throttle lever. If the switch is good, there will be no continuity (very low resistance).
7. If the switch fails to pass any of these tests, the switch is faulty and must be replaced. To replace the carburetor switch, refer to the *Throttle Valve/T.O.R.S. Housing* disassembly and reassembly procedures in Chapter Eight.

NOTE

*The carburetor switch (**Figure 47**) is an integral part of the T.O.R.S. switch housing. Do not attempt to remove the switch from the housing. If the switch is faulty, the T.O.R.S. switch housing assembly will have to be replaced as described in Chapter Eight.*

WIRING DIAGRAMS

Wiring diagrams for all models are located at the end of this book.

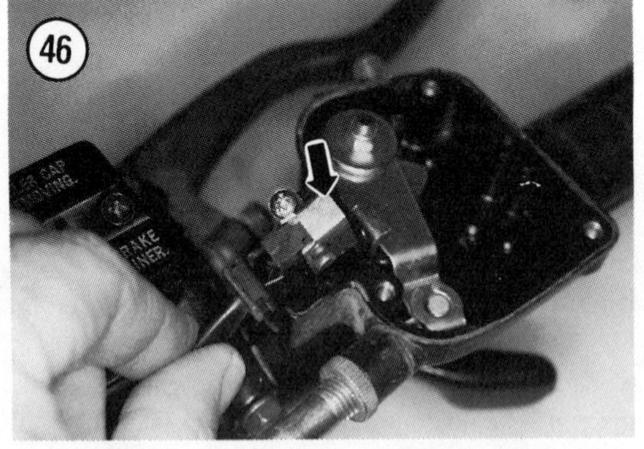

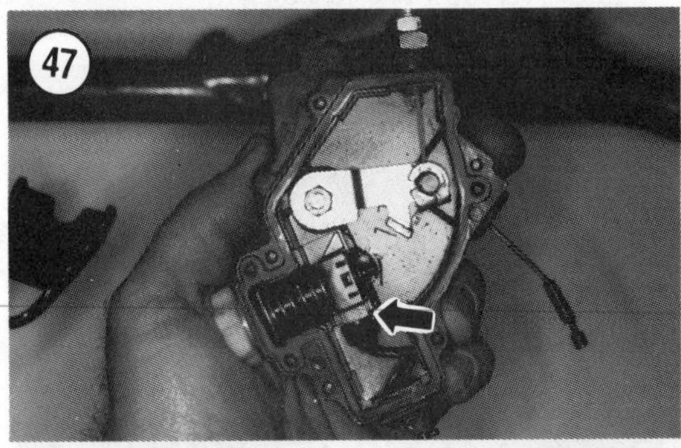

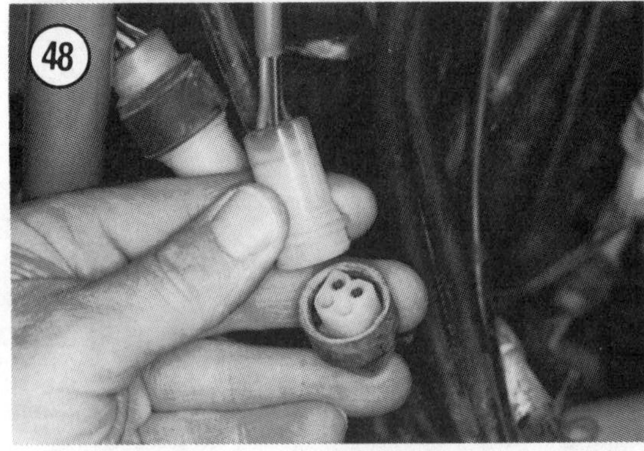

Table 1 ELECTRICAL SYSTEM SPECIFICATIONS

Ignition system	C.D.I.
Generator system	Flywheel magneto
Voltage regulator	
Model/manufacturer	TRIZ-50/Hitachi
Ignition coil	
Model/manufacturer	129700-146/Nippondenso
CDI	
Magneto model/manufacturer	032000-620/Nippondenso
Magneto	
Model/manufacturer	032000-620/Nippondenso
Lighting voltage	
Minimum	11.5 volts @ 2,500 rpm
Maximum	16.3 volts @ 8,000 rpm
Spark plug cap resistance	5,000 ohms
Minimum spark gap	6 mm (0.24 in.)

Table 2 STATOR COIL TEST SPECIFICATIONS

Test connection (wire to wire)	Resistance (ohms)*
Lighting coil resistance	
Yellow-to-black (1987-2001)	0.26-0.38
Yellow/red-to-black (2002)	0.26-0.38
Pickup coil resistance	
White/red to white/green	94-140
Charging coil resistance	
Green-to-red	13.7-20.5

* Tests should be made with component at a temperature of 20 C (68 F). Do not test when the engine is hot.

Table 3 IGNITION COIL TEST SPECIFICATIONS

	Resistance (ohms)*
Primary	0.28-0.38
Secondary	4,700-7,100

* Tests should be made with component at a temperature of 20 C (68 F). Do not test when the engine is hot.

Table 4 REPLACEMENT BULBS

Item	Voltage	Wattage
Headlight	12 volt	30W/30W
Tail/brake light	12 volt	3.8W

Table 5 TIGHTENING TORQUES

	N m	ft.-lb.
Flywheel nut	80	59

CHAPTER TEN

LIQUID COOLING SYSTEM

The liquid cooling system consists of a radiator, reservoir tank, crankshaft driven water pump, radiator cap and hoses. During operation, the coolant heats up and expands, thus pressurizing the system. The radiator cap is used to seal the system. Water cooled in the radiator is pumped down through the radiator and into the cylinder head where it passes through the cylinder water passages and back into the radiator at the top. The water then drains down through the radiator where it is cooled and the cycle is repeated.

The water pump requires no routine maintenance and can be overhauled (replacement parts are available) after removing the clutch cover. There is no thermostat or cooling fan and all cooling system service can be performed with the engine in the frame.

This chapter describes repair and replacement of cooling system components. Chapter Three describes maintenance of the system.

Cooling system specifications are listed in **Tables 1-3** at the end of the chapter.

SAFETY PRECAUTIONS

Certain safety precautions must be kept in mind to protect yourself from injury and the engine from damage. For your own safety, the cooling system must be cool before removing any part of the system, including the radiator cap (**Figure 1**).

WARNING

*Do not remove the radiator cap (**Figure 1**) when the engine is hot. The coolant* *is very hot and is under pressure. Severe scalding could result if the coolant comes in contact with your skin.*

To protect the engine and cooling system, drain and flush the cooling system at least once a year. When draining the cooling system, drain the coolant into a clean container so that you can reuse it. Because coolant deteriorates with age, replace it at least once a year or after rebuilding the engine. Refer to *Coolant Change* in Chapter Three. Refill with a mixture of ethylene-glycol antifreeze (formulated for aluminum engines) and distilled water.

CAUTION

Never operate the cooling system with water only, even in climates where antifreeze protection is not required. The all-aluminum engine will oxidize internally.

WARNING

Antifreeze has been classified as an environmental toxic waste by the EPA. Dispose of it according to local regulations. Antifreeze is poisonous and may attract animals. Do not store coolant where it is accessible to children or pets.

COOLING SYSTEM INSPECTION

1. Check the radiator (**Figure 2**) for clogged or damaged fins. If more than 20% of the radiator fin area is damaged, repair or replace the radiator.
2. To clean a clogged radiator, blow compressed air from the rear (engine side), keeping the air nozzle at least 0.5 m (20 in.) away from the radiator. Blow air directly through the radiator fins (perpendicular); never blow air at an angle against the fins.
3. Check all coolant hoses (**Figure 2**) for cracks or damage. Replace all questionable parts. Make sure the hose clamps are tight, but not so tight that they cut the hoses.
4. Pressure test the cooling system as described in Chapter Three.
5. If coolant loss is noted, the cylinder head gasket may be leaking or the cylinder head warped, allowing coolant to leak into the cylinder. If necessary, remove and service the cylinder head and gasket as described in Chapter Four.
6. Visually check the area underneath the water pump for signs of leakage or corrosion.

RADIATOR

Refer to **Figure 2** when servicing the radiator and hoses.

Removal/Installation

1. Park the vehicle on level ground and set the parking brake.
2. Remove the seat as described in Chapter Fourteen.
3. Remove the radiator cover screws and remove the radiator cover (**Figure 3**).
4. Remove the fuel tank as described in Chapter Eight.
5. If necessary, remove the front fender as described in Chapter Fourteen.
6. Drain the cooling system as described under *Coolant Change* in Chapter Three.
7. Disconnect the upper radiator hose from the hose nozzle on the clutch cover (**Figure 4**).
8. Disconnect the lower radiator hose from the hose nozzle on the cylinder head (**Figure 5**).
9. Disconnect the breather hose from the top of the radiator (A, **Figure 6**).
10. Disconnect the overflow hose from the top of the radiator, next to the radiator cap.
11. Remove the upper (B, **Figure 6**) and lower (**Figure 7**) radiator mounting bolts. Leave the rubber bushings attached to the radiator.
12. Note how the radiator hoses are routed from the radiator to the engine before removing the radiator.
13. Lift the radiator and remove it from the frame with the 2 hoses attached.

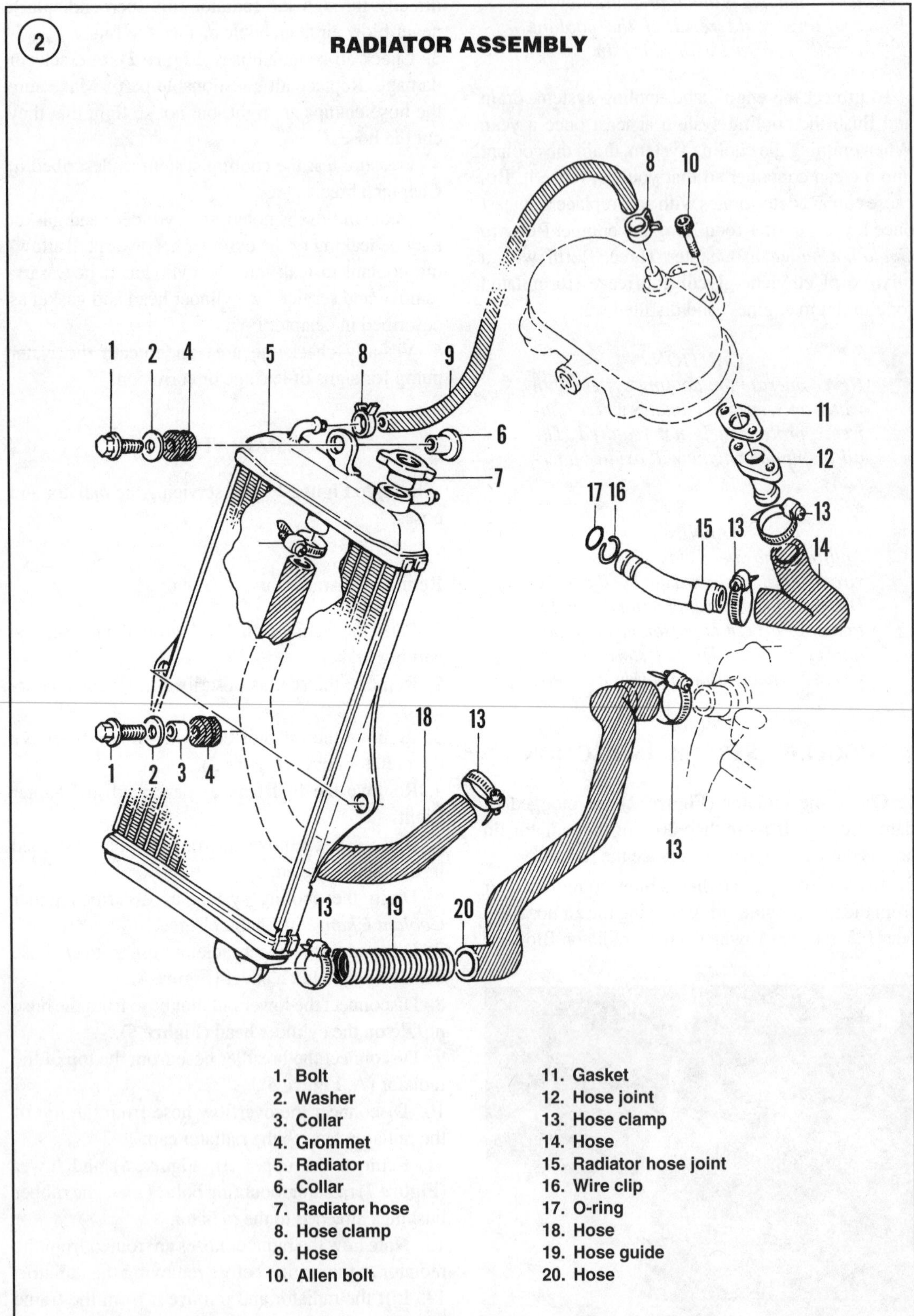
2
RADIATOR ASSEMBLY
1
2
4
5
8
9
6
7
8
10
11
12
17
16
15
13
13
14
1
2
3
4
18
13
13
13
19
20
1. Bolt
2. Washer
3. Collar
4. Grommet
5. Radiator
6. Collar
7. Radiator hose
8. Hose clamp
9. Hose
10. Allen bolt
11. Gasket
12. Hose joint
13. Hose clamp
14. Hose
15. Radiator hose joint
16. Wire clip
17. O-ring
18. Hose
19. Hose guide
20. Hose

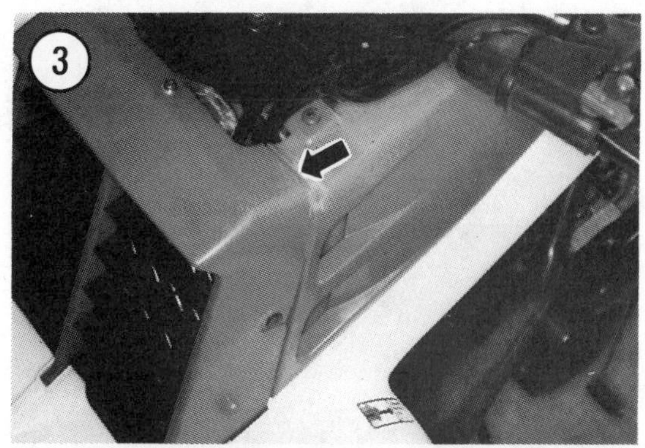

3

4

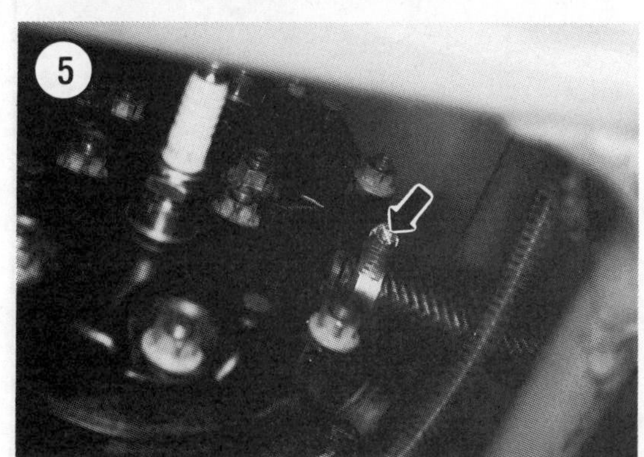

5

6

14. Prior to removing the radiator hoses, mark their position and alignment on the radiator for reference during reinstallation. Then, remove the upper and lower radiator hoses from the radiator.

15. Perform the *Inspection* procedures in this section.

16. Installation is the reverse of these steps, plus the following.

17. Referring to your alignment marks, reinstall the upper and lower radiator hoses onto the radiator.

18. Install the radiator onto the frame and its 3 mounting bolts (B, **Figure 6** and **Figure 7**). Guide the hoses through the frame and toward the engine when installing the radiator. Do not fully tighten the bolts at this time.

19. Reconnect the upper and lower radiator hoses at the engine; see **Figure 4** and **Figure 5**. Check that both hoses are routed properly. Then tighten the radiator mounting bolts securely. Tighten the radiator hose clamps securely.

20. Refill the cooling system as described in Chapter Three.

21. Start the engine and check for leaks.

Inspection

1. Flush off the exterior of the radiator with a low-pressure stream of water from a garden hose. Spray both the front and back to remove all dirt and debris. Carefully use a whisk broom or stiff paint brush to remove any stubborn dirt.

2. Examine the radiator cooling surface for damage. Also check along the sides. If the radiator is damaged, refer repair to a radiator repair shop. If damage is severe, replace the radiator.

3. Carefully straighten out any bent cooling fins with a wide-blade screwdriver. If the radiator has

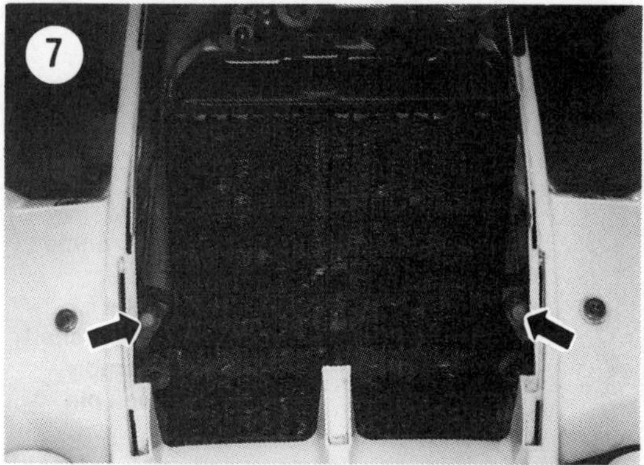

7

been damaged across approximately 20% or more of the frontal area, the radiator should be replaced.

4. Check for cracks or leakage (usually a moss-green colored residue) at the filler neck, the inlet and outlet hose fittings and the upper and lower tank seams.

5. Check for missing or damaged radiator bushings and collars (**Figure 2**). Replace if necessary.

6. Inspect the radiator cap (**Figure 8**). Check the rubber cap seal surfaces for tears or cracks. Check for a bent or distorted cap. Raise the vacuum valve

9

WATER PUMP

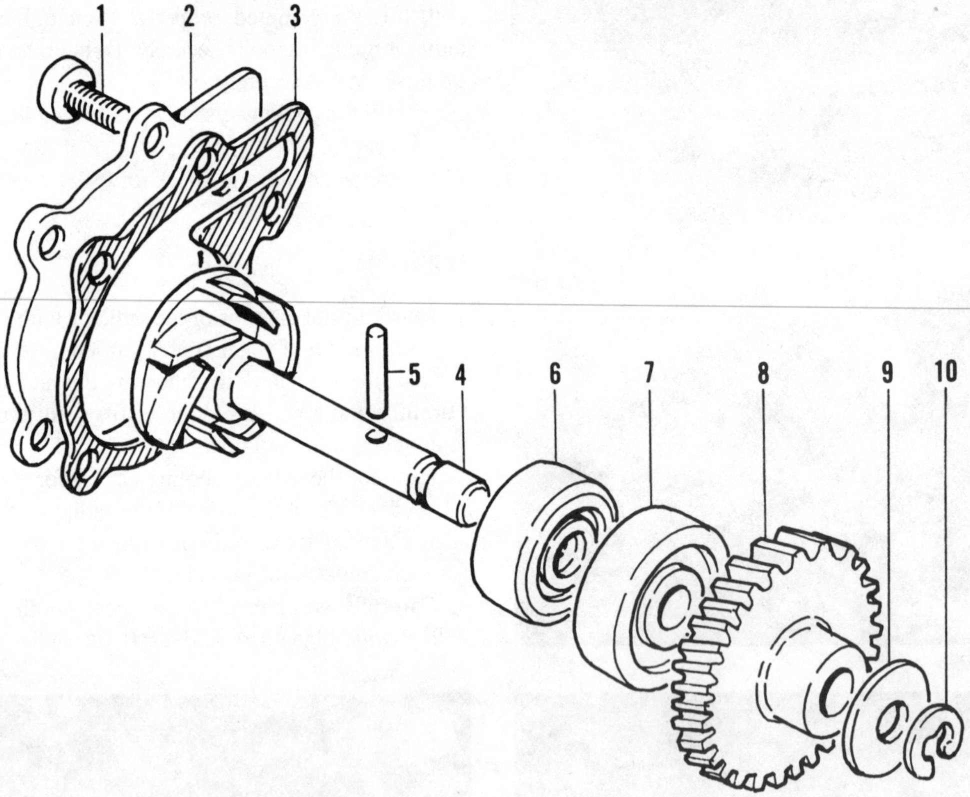

1. Screw
2. Water pump cover
3. Gasket
4. Impeller/shaft assembly
5. Knock pin
6. Oil seal
7. Bearing
8. Impeller shaft gear
9. Flat washer
10. E-clip

and rubber seal and rinse the cap under warm tap water to flush away any loose rust or dirt particles.

7. Check the coolant hoses for cracks, bulges or other damage and replace if necessary.

CAUTION

If the engine overheated, inspect the hoses carefully for damage. Excessive heat can damage the hoses and cause them to rupture.

8. Check for weak or damaged hose clamps; replace if necessary.

WATER PUMP

The water pump is mounted in the clutch cover on all models. Under normal operating conditions, disassembly of the water pump should not be necessary. However, if the engine overheats or if the coolant level changes, the water pump should be removed and examined.

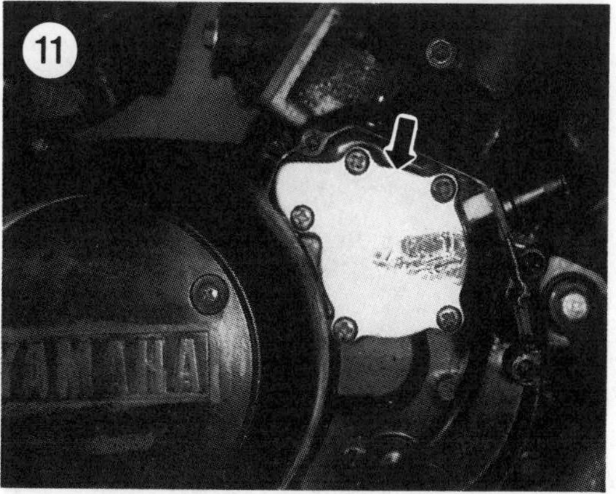

The water pump consists of an impeller, gear/shaft assembly, oil seal(s) and bearing(s).

Figure 9 is an exploded view of the water pump. The oil seal and bearing need be removed only if they require replacement. The impeller can be inspected without removing the clutch cover.

Water Pump Cover Removal/Installation

This procedure describes inspection of the impeller with the water pump/clutch cover assembly installed on the engine.

1. Drain the cooling system as described under *Coolant Change* in Chapter Three.

2. Remove the access cover screws and remove the access cover (**Figure 10**).

3. Remove the water pump cover screws and remove the water pump cover (**Figure 11**). Remove and discard the cover gasket.

4. Inspect the impeller (**Figure 12**) for cracked or broken vanes, severe corrosion buildup or other damage. If necessary, remove the water pump and service the impeller/water pump assembly as described in this chapter.

5. Remove all gasket residue from the water pump cover and clutch cover mating surfaces.

6. Clean the water pump cover in solvent and dry thoroughly.

7. Install the water pump cover (**Figure 11**) and a new gasket. Then install the mounting screws and tighten securely.

10

NOTE
*The access cover is fitted with 2 sound dampers (**Figure 13**). If the sound dampers are missing or damaged, replace them prior to installing the cover.*

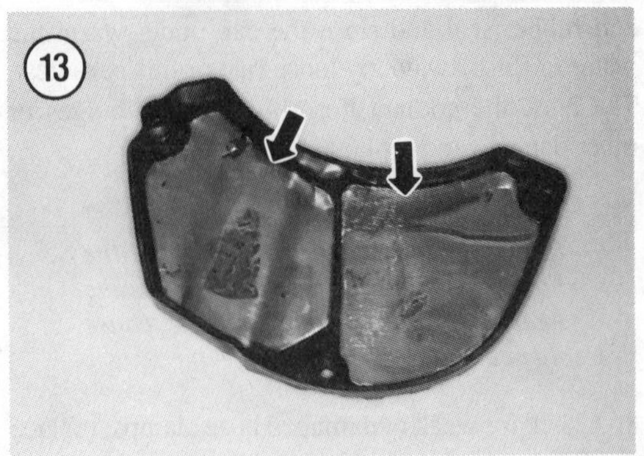

8. Install the access cover (**Figure 10**) and its mounting screws. Tighten the screws securely. Yamaha does not call for a gasket or sealer to be used with the access cover when installing it.

9. Refill the cooling system as described under *Coolant Change* in Chapter Three.

Impeller Removal

The impeller can be removed after removing the clutch cover. Refer to **Figure 9**.

1. Remove the access cover screws and remove the access cover (**Figure 10**).

2. Remove the clutch cover as described under *Clutch Cover Removal* in Chapter Six.

3. Remove the water pump cover screws and remove the water pump cover (**Figure 11**). Remove and discard the cover gasket.

4. Remove the E-clip (A, **Figure 14**) from the groove in the end of the impeller shaft. Then remove the flat washer (B, **Figure 14**).

5. Lift the impeller shaft gear off of the impeller shaft (**Figure 15**) and remove the knock pin (**Figure 16**).

CAUTION
To avoid damaging the water pump oil seal when removing the impeller, first remove any small burrs from the end of the shaft (at the E-clip groove) with a fine-cut file. Then wipe off the end of the shaft.

6. To remove the impeller, slowly turn the impeller and withdraw it from the bearing and oil seal (**Figure 17**). See **Figure 18**.

NOTE
After removing the impeller, check that the small garter spring installed in the outer end of the water pump oil seal did not pop out. If so, reinstall it into the oil seal.

17

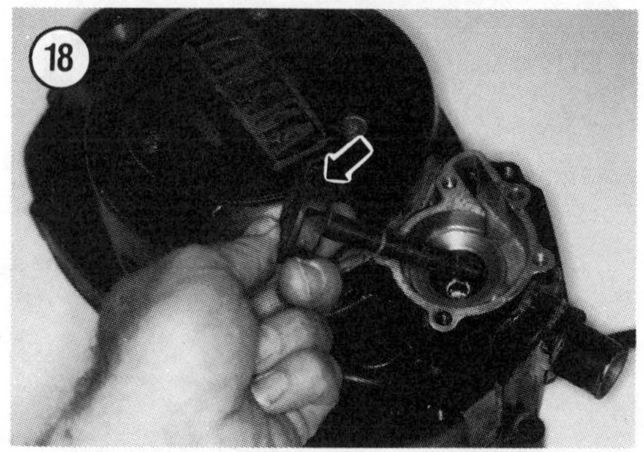
18

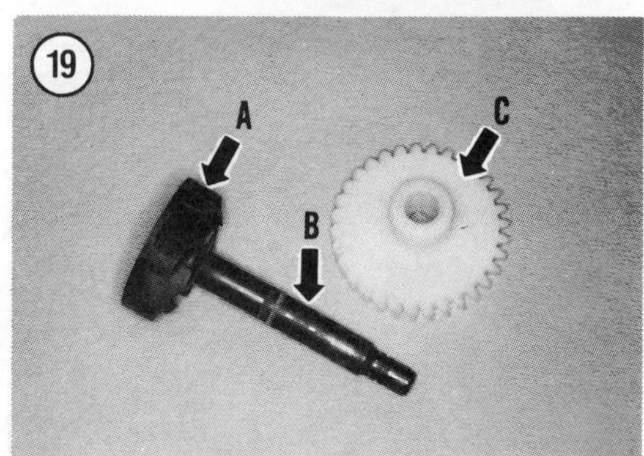

19

Inspection

1. Check the impeller (A, **Figure 19**) for broken or chipped impeller blades.
2. Check the impeller shaft (B, **Figure 19**) for scoring, galling, pitting or heat discoloration. Check the knock pin hole and the E-clip groove in the end of the shaft for wear or burring. Remove any burrs from the shaft with a fine-cut file.
3. Check the impeller gear (C, **Figure 19**) for broken or chipped teeth. Check the knock pin grooves in the back of the gear for wear, cracks or other damage.
4. Replace the E-clip, knock pin and flat washer if severely worn or damaged. Both sides of the washer should be smooth.
5. Visually inspect the oil seal (**Figure 20**) for severe wear, hardness, cracks or other damage. If damaged, replace the oil seal as described in this chapter.
6. Turn the inner bearing race (**Figure 21**) by hand. The bearing should turn smoothly with no roughness, catching, binding or excessive noise. If damaged, replace the bearing as described in this chapter.

Impeller Installation

1. If removed, install the oil seal and bearing as described in this chapter.
2. Apply a lightweight lithium base grease to the impeller shaft and to the oil seal lip (if not previously done).
3. Align the impeller shaft with the oil seal (**Figure 18**), then carefully turn the shaft (**Figure 17**) as it enters the oil seal. Continue turning the shaft until the impeller and shaft are installed all the way through the oil seal and bearing.

20

21

4. Insert the knock pin (**Figure 16**) through the hole in the end of the impeller shaft. Center the pin in the hole (**Figure 22**).
5. The impeller gear has 2 sets of grooves machined into the back of it (**Figure 23**). To install the impeller gear, slide the gear over the impeller shaft—grooved side facing down. Then align one set of grooves (**Figure 23**) with the knock pin and install the gear over the pin. If the gear is properly installed, the E-clip groove in the end of the shaft will be visible above the gear.
6. Install the flat washer (B, **Figure 14**) over the impeller shaft and seat against the gear. Then install the E-clip (A, **Figure 14**) into the shaft groove. Make sure the E-clip is fully seated in the groove.
7. Now turn the impeller slowly by hand. The shaft should turn smoothly with no roughness or binding.
8. Install the clutch cover as described under *Clutch Cover Installation* in Chapter Six.
9. Install the water pump cover (**Figure 11**) and a new gasket. Then install the mounting screws and tighten securely.

NOTE

*The access cover is fitted with 2 sound dampers (**Figure 13**). If the sound dampers are missing or damaged, replace them prior to installing the cover.*

10. Install the access cover (**Figure 10**) and its mounting screws. Tighten the screws securely. Yamaha does not call for a gasket or sealer to be used with the access cover when installing it.
11. Refill the cooling system as described under *Coolant Change* in Chapter Three.

Water Pump Bearing and Seal Replacement

Yamaha specifies that the oil seal and bearing be replaced as a set.

When removing the oil seal and bearing from the clutch cover, note and record the direction in which the manufacturer's marks or numbers on the seal and bearing face for proper reinstallation.

1. Remove the impeller as described in this chapter.
2. Place the clutch cover on wooden blocks. Then, using a socket or metal rod as shown in **Figure 24**, drive or press the bearing and oil seal out of the cover at the same time. See **Figure 25**.
3. Clean the cover in solvent and dry thoroughly.

22

23

24

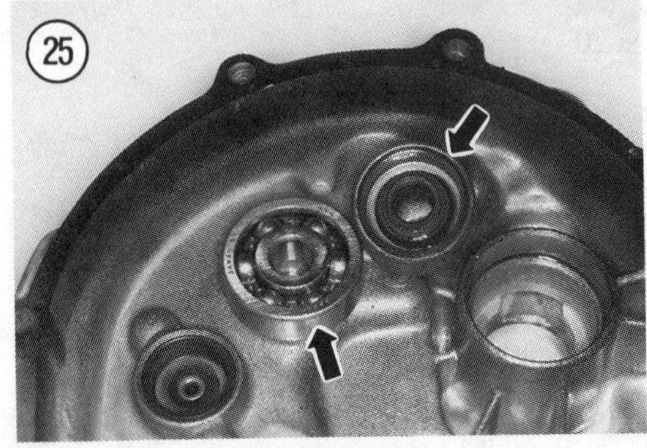
25

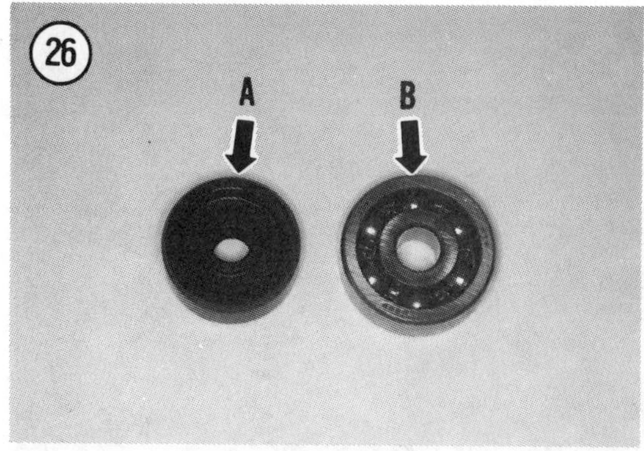

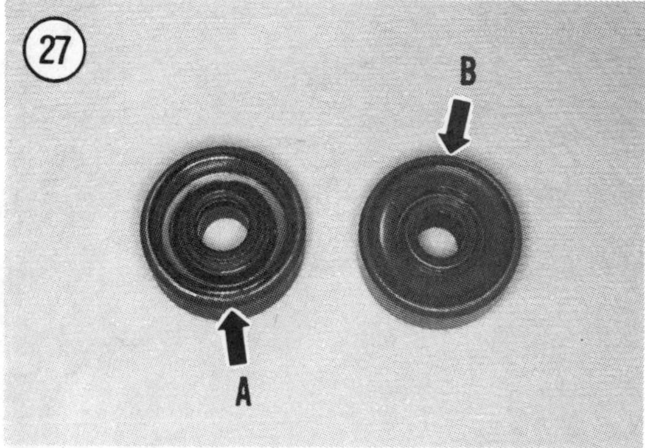

4. Apply a lightweight lithium base grease to the lips of the new oil seal (A, **Figure 26**).
5. Lubricate the ball bearing (B, **Figure 26**) with transmission oil.
6. To install the oil seal (A, **Figure 26**):
   a. A double lip mechanical oil seal is used. The outer side of the seal (A, **Figure 27**) prevents coolant from entering the primary side of the engine; this side of the seal is marked "WATER SIDE." The inner side (B, **Figure 27**) prevents transmission oil from entering the water pump side of the engine; this side is not marked.
   b. Position the oil seal into the bore so the side of the seal marked "WATER SIDE" is facing down (toward impeller).
   c. Drive or press the seal into position using a socket or bearing driver. Continue to apply force to the seal until it bottoms out. See **Figure 28**.
   d. Turn the clutch cover over (outer side facing up) and check that the garter spring installed behind the seal's outer lip (**Figure 20**) did not pop out. If so, reinstall it.
7. To install the bearing (B, **Figure 26**):
   a. Support the clutch cover on wooden blocks.
   b. Position the bearing into the bore so that the manufacturer's markings on the bearing are facing out.
   c. Press or drive the bearing into the bore until it bottoms out (**Figure 21**). Apply pressure against outer bearing race, not against the inner race.
   d. Turn the bearing inner race by hand. The bearing should turn smoothly with no roughness, catching, binding or excessive noise.

WATER PUMP DRIVE GEAR

The water pump drive gear is mounted on the right-hand end of the crankshaft; see **Figure 29**. This gear meshes with the impeller shaft gear. To service the water pump drive gear, refer to *Water Pump and Primary Drive Gears* in Chapter Six.

RADIATOR HOSE JOINT AND O-RING

A radiator hose joint and hose routes coolant from the water pump impeller to the cylinder head. An

10

O-ring, installed on the end of the hose joint, seats the joint connection in the clutch cover.

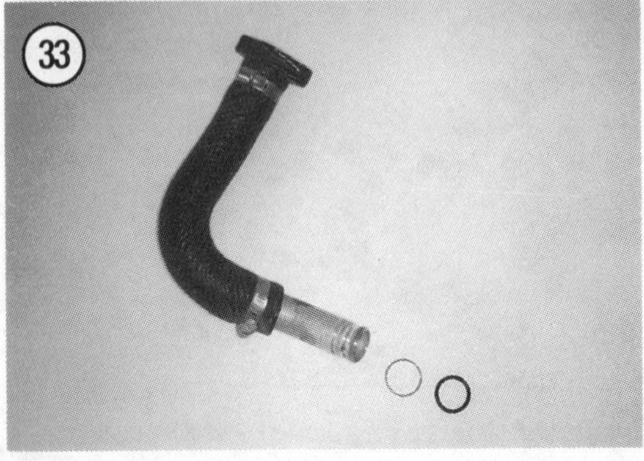

Removal/Installation

1. Drain the cooling system as described under *Coolant Change* in Chapter Three.
2. Remove the clutch cover as described under *Clutch Cover Removal* in Chapter Six.
3. Disconnect the coolant hose at the cylinder head (**Figure 30**).
4. Remove the wire clip (A, **Figure 31**) and O-ring (B, **Figure 31**) from the end of the radiator hose joint. Then pull the hose joint assembly (**Figure 32**) out of the crankcase and remove it.
5. To replace the hose or hose joint (**Figure 33**):
   a. Make a note of the hose and hose joint alignment positions before separating them.
   b. Remove the hose clamp(s) and separate the hose and hose joint.
   c. Insert the new hose onto the hose joint, following the alignment notes made prior to disassembly.
   d. Secure the hose to the hose joint with the hose clamp(s).
6. Inspect the hose joint O-ring. If the O-ring is severely worn or damaged, replace it.
7. Replace the wire clip if damaged.
8. Installation is the reverse of these steps, plus the following.
9. After installing the wire clip (A, **Figure 31**), make sure it is fully seated in the groove.
10. After installing the O-ring (B, **Figure 31**), lubricate it with a lightweight lithium base grease.

BREATHER HOSES

Inspect the cooling system breather hoses for cuts, loose connections or other damage. Replace or reconnect hoses as required. See **Figure 34** and **Figure 35**.

HOSES

Hoses deteriorate with age and should be replaced periodically or whenever they show signs of cracking or leakage. To be safe, replace the hoses every 2 years. The spray of hot coolant from a cracked hose can cause rider injury. Loss of coolant will also cause the engine to overheat and result in severe damage.

Whenever any component of the cooling system is removed, inspect the hoses(s) and determine if replacement is necessary.

Inspection

1. With the engine cool, check the cooling hoses for brittleness or hardness. A hose in this condition will usually show cracks and must be replaced.
2. With the engine hot, examine the hoses for swelling along the entire hose length. Eventually a hose will rupture at this point.
3. Check area around hose clamps. Signs of rust around clamps indicate possible hose leakage.

Replacement

Hose replacement should be performed when the engine is cool.

1. Drain the cooling system as described under *Coolant Change* in Chapter Three.
2. Loosen the hose clamps from the hose to be replaced. Slide the clamps along the hose and out of the way.
3. Twist the hose end to break the seal and remove from the connecting joint. If the hose has been on for some time, it may have become fused to the joint. If so, cut the hose parallel to the joint connections with a knife or razor. The hose then can be carefully pried loose with a screwdriver.

CAUTION
Excessive force applied to the hose during removal could damage the connecting joint.

4. Examine the connecting joint for cracks or other damage. Repair or replace parts as required. If the joint is okay, remove rust with sandpaper.
5. Inspect hose clamps and replace as necessary.
6. Slide hose clamps over outside of hose and install hose to inlet and outlet connecting joint. Make sure hose clears all obstructions and is routed properly.

NOTE
If it is difficult to install a hose on its joint, soak the end of the hose in hot water for approximately 2 minutes. This will soften the hose and ease installation.

7. With the hose positioned correctly on joint, position clamps back away from the end of hose slightly. Tighten clamps securely, but not so much that hose is damaged.
8. Refill cooling system as described under *Coolant Change* in Chapter Three. Start the engine and check for leaks. Retighten hose clamps as necessary.

Tables 1-3 are on the following page.

Table 1 COOLING SYSTEM SPECIFICATIONS

Water pump type	Single-suction centrifugal pump
Radiator core size	
Height	350 mm (13.8 in.)
Width	210 mm (8.27 in.)
Thickness	32 mm (1.26 in.)
Radiator cap opening pressure	93-123 kPa (13.5-17.8 psi)

Table 2 COOLANT CAPACITY*

	Liters	U.S. qt.	Imp. qt.
Total amount	2.5	2.64	2.20
Reservoir tank	0.28	0.30	0.25

* Mixing ratio is 50% coolant and 50% water.

Table 3 TIGHTENING TORQUES

	N•m	ft.-lb.
Water pump cover	8	5.8
Hose joint @ cylinder head	12	8

CHAPTER ELEVEN

FRONT SUSPENSION AND STEERING

This chapter describes repair and maintenance of the front wheels, hubs, front suspension arms and steering components.

Refer to **Table 1** for general front suspension and steering specifications. **Tables 2-4** list service specifications and torque specifications. **Tables 1-4** are located at the end of this chapter.

FRONT WHEEL

Removal/Installation

1. Place the vehicle on level ground and set the parking brake.

2. Mark the front tires with an "L" (left side) or "R" (right side) so that they can be installed onto the same side from which they were removed.
3. Loosen but do *not* remove the lug nuts (**Figure 1**) securing the wheel to the hub.
4. Jack up the front of the vehicle with a small hydraulic or scissor jack. Place the jack under the frame with a piece of wood between the jack and the frame.
5. Place wooden block(s) under the frame to support the vehicle securely with the front wheels off the ground.
6. Remove the lug nuts (loosened in Step 3) and washers and remove the front wheel.
7. Remove the outer disc cover (**Figure 2**), if required.

8. Clean the lug nuts in solvent and dry thoroughly.

9. Inspect the wheel for cracks, bending or other damage. If damage is severe, replace wheel as described under *Tires and Wheels* in this chapter.

10. Install the outer disc cover (**Figure 2**) and front wheel.

11. Install the washers and lug nuts (**Figure 1**). Finger tighten the nuts until the wheel is positioned squarely against the front hub.

WARNING
Always tighten the lug nuts to the correct torque specification or the nuts may work loose and the wheel could fall off.

12. Use a torque wrench and tighten the lug nuts in a crisscross pattern to the torque specification listed in **Table 4**.

13. After the wheel is installed completely, rotate it; apply the front brake several times to make sure that

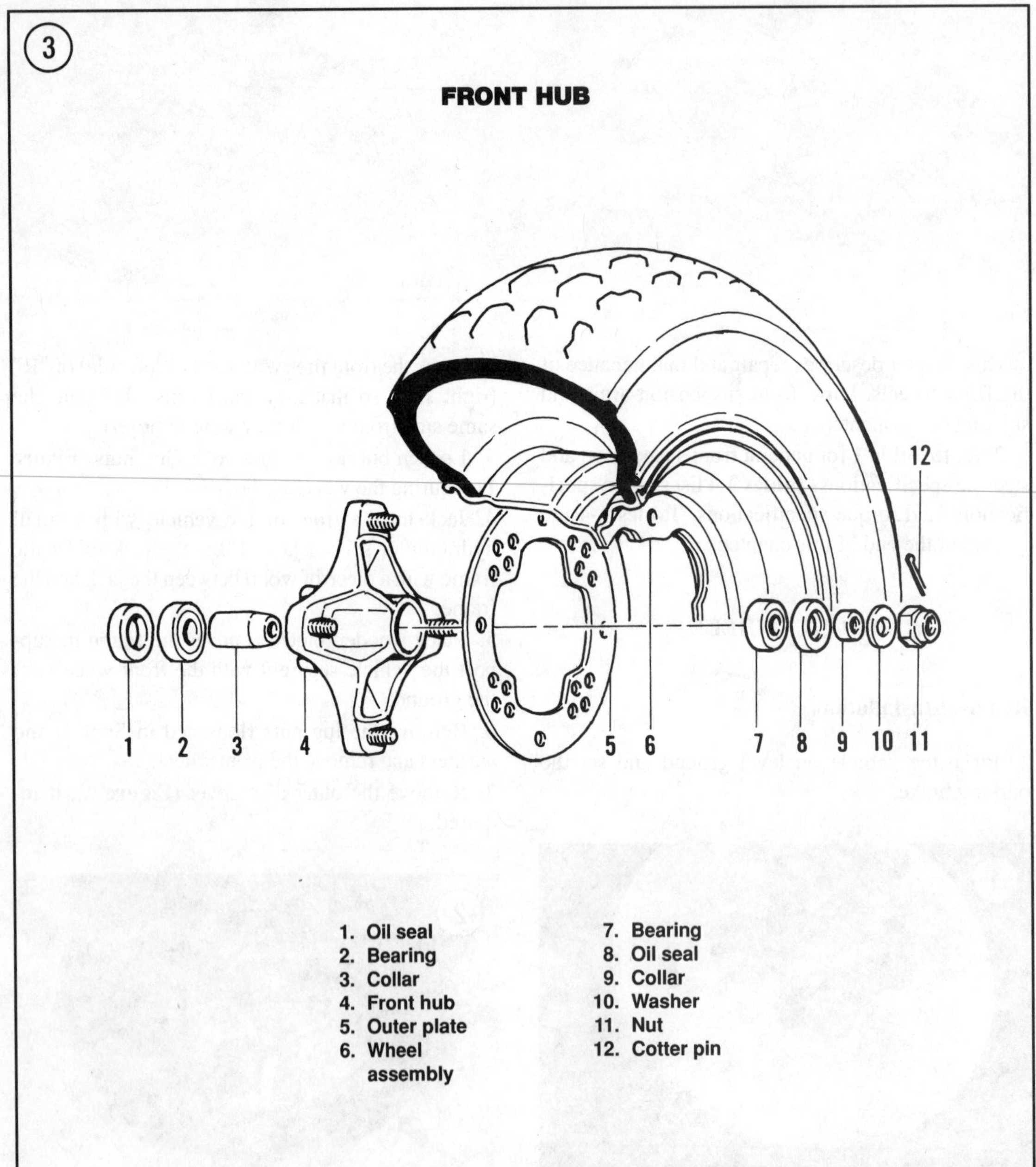

the wheel rotates freely and that the brake is operating correctly.

14. Measure wheel runout with a dial indicator as described under Front Hub in this chapter.

15. Jack up the front of the vehicle up a little and remove the wooden block(s).

16. Let the jack down and remove the jack and wooden block.

FRONT HUB

The front hub consists of 2 oil seals, 2 ball bearings and a tapered center hub spacer. The front brake disc is bolted to the front hub. Refer to **Figure 3** when servicing the front hub assembly in the following sections.

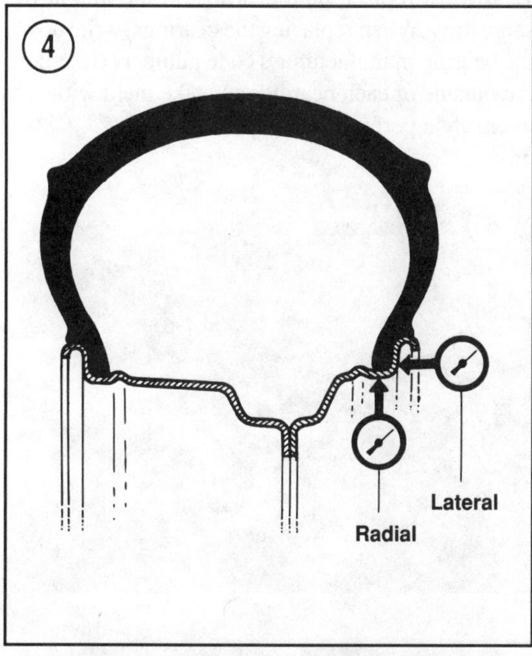

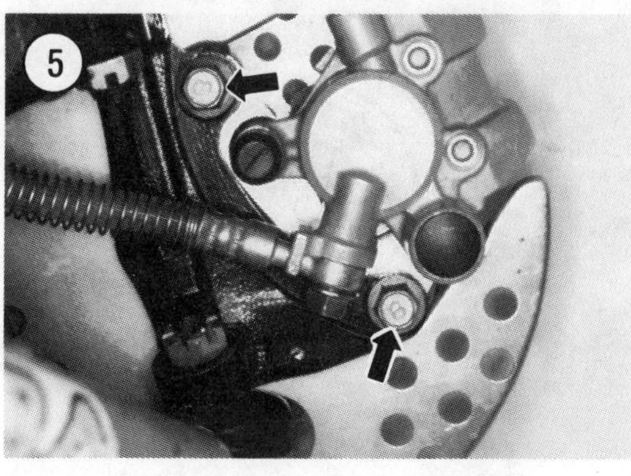

Inspection (Hub Installed)

Inspect each wheel bearing prior to removing it from the wheel hub.

CAUTION

Do not remove the wheel bearings for inspection purposes as they can be damaged during the removal process. Remove the wheel bearings only if they are to be replaced.

1. Check that wheel nuts (**Figure 1**) are tightened to the torque specification in **Table 4**.

2. Place the vehicle on level ground and set the parking brake. Block the rear wheels so the vehicle will not roll in either direction.

3. Jack up the front of the vehicle with a small hydraulic or scissor jack. Place the jack under the frame with a piece of wood between the jack and the frame.

4. Place wooden block(s) under the frame to support the vehicle securely with the front wheels off the ground.

5. Mount a dial indicator against the rim as shown in **Figure 4** to measure radial and lateral runout. Turn tire slowly by hand and read movement indicated on dial indicator. See **Table 2** for runout limits. Note the following:

   a. If runout limit is excessive, first check condition of wheel assembly. If wheel is bent or otherwise damaged, it may require replacement.

   b. If wheel condition is okay but runout is excessive, remove wheel and turn hub (**Figure 2**) by hand. Hub should turn smoothly with no sign of roughness, excessive play or other abnormal conditions. If hub does not turn smoothly, remove hub and check bearings.

6. Remove dial indicator and lower vehicle to ground, or proceed with following section.

Hub Removal

Refer to **Figure 3** for this procedure.

1. Remove the front wheel as described in this chapter.

2. Remove the 2 brake caliper mounting bolts (**Figure 5**, typical) and lift the caliper off of the brake

disc. Hang the caliper from the vehicle with a stiff wire hook.

NOTE

Insert a piece of vinyl tubing or plastic between the brake pads in the caliper, in place of the brake disc. That way if the brake lever is inadvertently squeezed, the piston will not be forced out of the cylinder. If this does happen, the caliper may have to be disassembled to reseat the piston. This will require bleeding of both front brakes. By blocking the brake pads, the piston cannot be forced out and bleeding the system should not be required.

3. Remove and discard the axle nut cotter pin.
4. Loosen and remove the axle nut (**Figure 6**).
5. Slide the front hub (**Figure 7**) off the steering knuckle and remove it.

Inspection (Hub Removed)

1. Remove the hub spacer (**Figure 8**) from the outer oil seal.
2. Inspect the oil seals. Replace if they are deteriorating or starting to harden.
3. Inspect the threaded studs on the front hub assembly.
4. If necessary, remove the oil seals as described under *Disassembly* in this chapter.
5. Turn each bearing inner race (**Figure 9**) with your fingers. The bearings should turn smoothly with no roughness, binding or excessive noise.
6. Inspect the play of the inner race (**Figure 10**) of each hub bearing. Check for excessive lateral and radial play. Replace the bearings if play is excessive.
7. Always replace both bearings in the hub at the same time. When replacing the bearings, write down the bearing manufacturer's code numbers (found on the outside of each bearing) and take them with you to ensure a perfect match up.

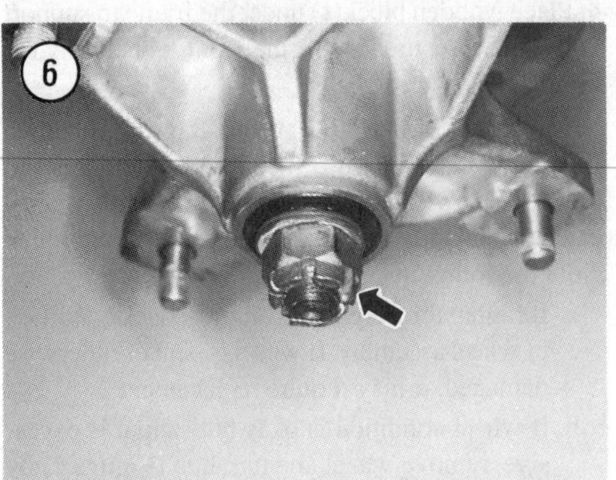
6

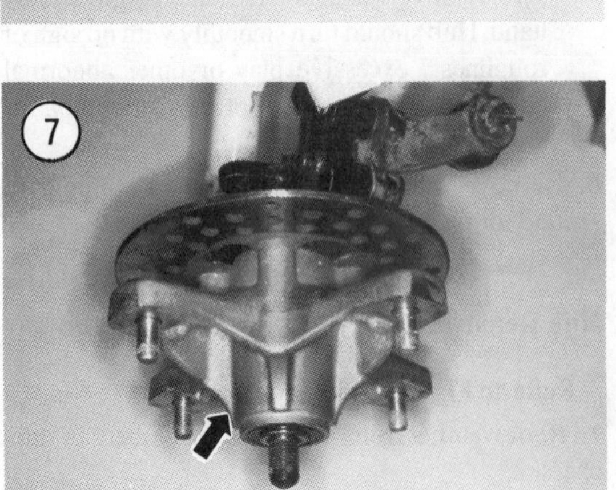
7

8

9

Disassembly

The steering hub bearings (**Figure 3**) are installed with a press fit and force is required to remove them.

This section describes 2 methods of removing the steering hub bearings. The first method (Step 2A) is recommended by Yamaha. However, because of the close fit between the bearings and hub spacer, this method can be difficult, as it is possible to damage the center hub spacer's machined surface when removing the first bearing. The second method (Step 2B), which is easier and decreases the chance of damaging the spacer, requires the use of a wheel bearing remover set.

Remove the bearings only if the bearings must be replaced. Note that the inner and outer bearings and the inner and outer oil seals are different. Prior to removing the oil seals and bearings, write down the size code on each part so that the correct replacement parts can be purchased.

1. Remove the oil seals by prying them out of the hub with a wide-blade screwdriver (**Figure 11**). Support the screwdriver with a rag to avoid damaging the hub or brake disc.

(10)

Axial

Radial

CAUTION

*When removing the bearings in the following steps, support the front hub carefully so that you do not damage the brake disc (**Figure 12**).*

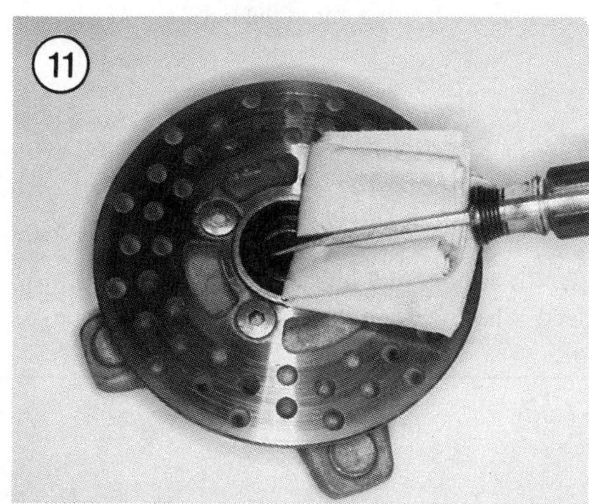

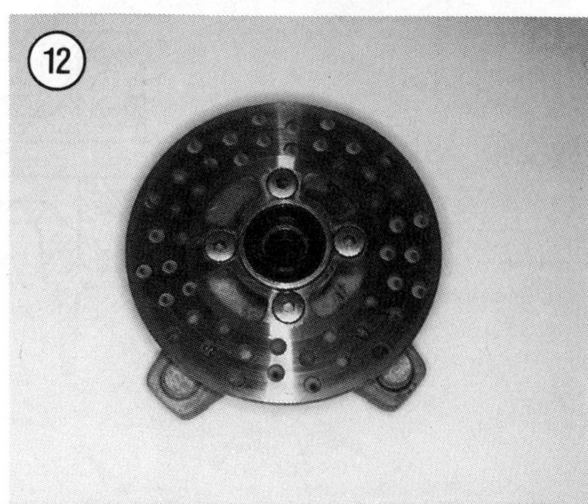

11

2A. To remove the steering hub bearings without special tools:

a. Using a long drift, tilt the center hub spacer away from one side of the outer bearing as shown in **Figure 13**.

NOTE

Do not damage the hub spacer's machined surface when positioning and driving against the long drift. You may have to grind a clearance groove in the drift to enable it to grab hold of the bearing while clearing the spacer.

b. Tap the bearing out of the hub with a hammer, working around the perimeter of the bearing's inner race.

c. Remove the center hub spacer from the hub, noting the direction in which the spacer is installed in the hub, for reassembly reference.

d. Using a large socket or bearing driver, drive the opposite bearing out of the hub.

NOTE

*The Kowa Seiki Wheel Bearing Remover set shown in **Figure 14** can be ordered by a Yamaha dealer through K & L Supply Co. in Santa Clara, CA.*

2B. To remove the hub bearings with the Kowa Seiki Wheel Bearing Remover set:

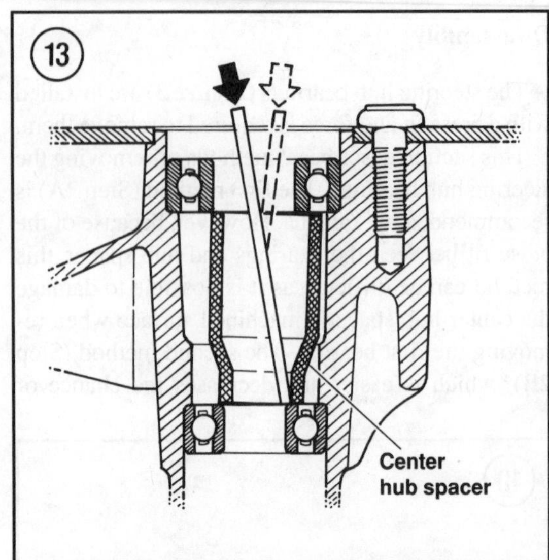

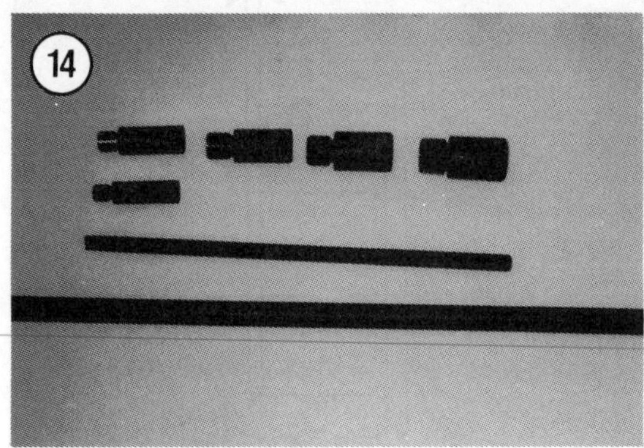

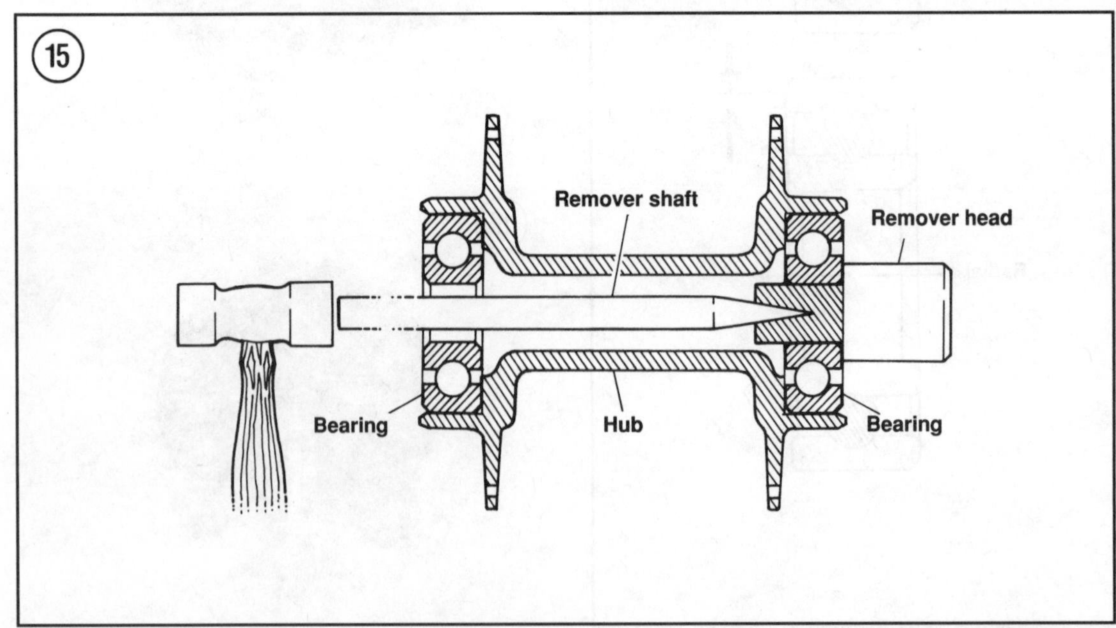

a. Select the correct size remover head tool and insert it into the outer bearing; see **Figure 15**.
b. From the opposite side of the hub, insert the remover shaft into the slot in the backside of the remover head; see **Figure 15**. Position the hub so that the remover head tool (**Figure 15**) is resting against a solid surface and tap the remover shaft to force it into the slit in the remover head. This will wedge the remover head against the inner bearing race.
c. Position the hub and tap on the end of the remover shaft with a hammer to drive the bearing out of the hub. Remove the bearing and tool. Tap on the remover head to release it from the bearing.
d. Remove the center hub spacer from the hub, noting the direction in which the spacer is installed in the hub, for reassembly reference.

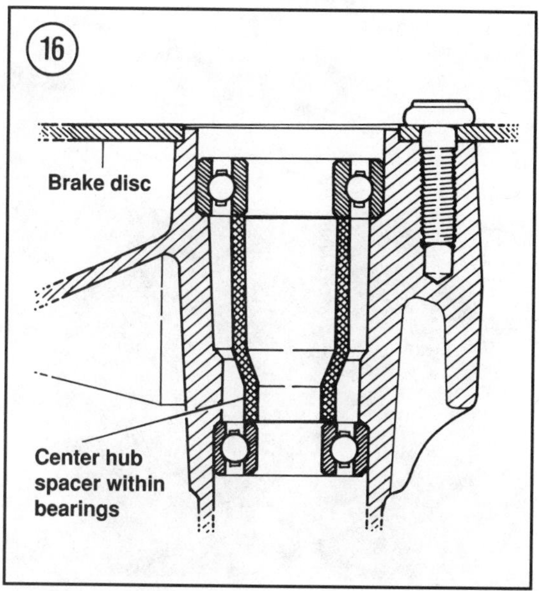

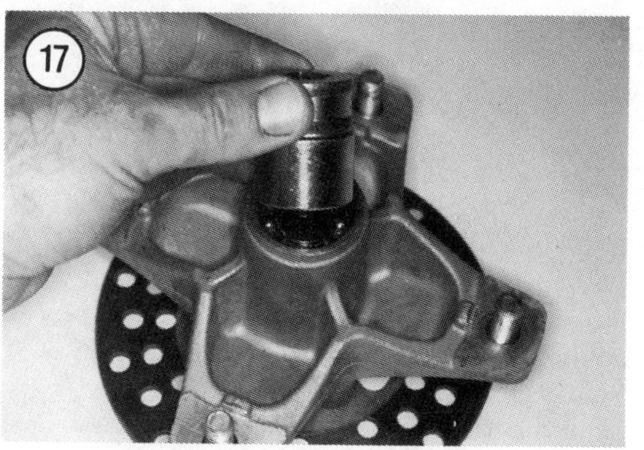

e. Using a large socket or bearing driver, drive the opposite bearing out of the hub.

3. Clean the hub and center hub spacer in solvent and dry thoroughly.

Assembly

Single row, deep-groove ball bearings are used in the front hub. Depending on model year, unshielded (open) or single shielded-bearings are used. Prior to installing new bearings and oil seals, note the following:

a. As noted during disassembly, the inner and outer oil seals and bearings are different. Refer to the drawing in **Figure 16** when assembling the front hub in the following steps.
b. When installing the bearings, install unshielded bearings so that the manufacturer's code marks and numbers face out. Install single-shielded bearings so that the open side faces out (**Figure 9**).
c. Install bearings by pressing them into hub with a socket or bearing driver that seats against the outer bearing race only (**Figure 17**).
d. Install oil seals with their closed side facing out.

1. Pack the bearings with a good quality bearing grease. Work the grease in between the balls thoroughly. Turn the bearing by hand to make sure the grease is seated evenly inside the bearing.
2. Blow any dirt or foreign matter out of the hub and out of the center hub spacer prior to installing the bearings.
3. Press in the inner bearing (**Figure 18**) until it bottoms in the hub bearing bore.

4. Turn the hub over and install the center hub spacer so that its larger inner diameter seats against the inner bearing as shown in **Figure 16**.
5. Press in the outer bearing (**Figure 19**) until it bottoms in the hub bearing bore.

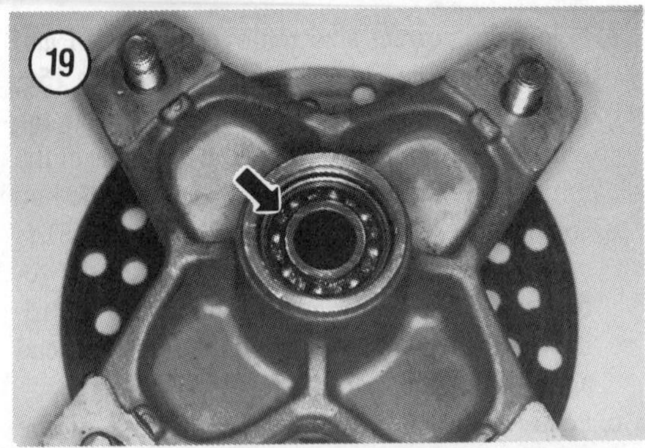

NOTE
Yamaha factory replacement front hub oil seals are pre-greased at the factory.

6. If the replacement oil seals are not pre-greased, pack the lip of each seal with a waterproof bearing grease.
7. Press in the inner oil seal (A, **Figure 20**) until its outer surface is flush with the oil seal bore as shown in **Figure 21**.
8. Press in the outer oil seal (B, **Figure 20**) until its outer surface is flush with the oil seal bore as shown in **Figure 22**.

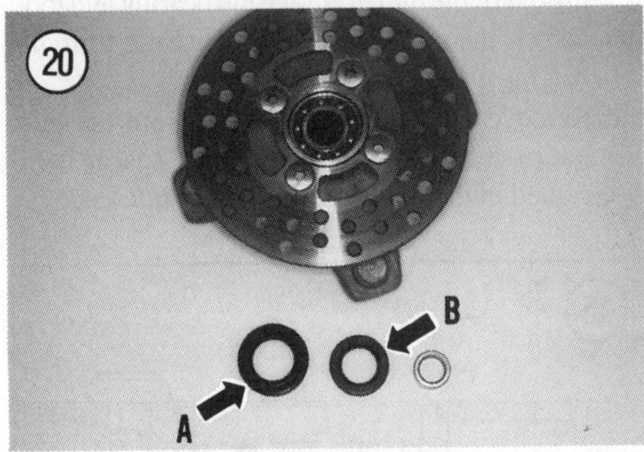

Installation

1. Clean the steering knuckle bearing surface, threads and axle nut with solvent or contact cleaner. Blow dry with compressed air.
2. Install the outer spacer into the front hub outer oil seal as shown in **Figure 8**.
3. Slide the front hub onto the steering knuckle (**Figure 23**).
4. Install the flat washer onto the steering knuckle.
5. Hand-thread the axle nut onto the steering knuckle. Then tighten the axle nut (**Figure 24**) to the torque specification in **Table 4**. Now check that one of the axle nut's grooves is aligned with the cotter pin hole in the steering knuckle. If not, align the groove by tightening the axle nut. Do not loosen the axle nut to align the groove.

WARNING
Always install a new cotter pin.

6. Insert the new cotter pin through the nut groove and steering knuckle hole and then bend its arms to lock it as shown in **Figure 25**.
7. Remove the spacer from between the brake pads and slide the brake caliper over the brake disc. Install the 2 brake caliper mounting bolts (**Figure 26**) and tighten to the torque specification in **Table 4**. Apply the front brake lever a few times to seat the pads against the disc.
8. Install the front wheel as described in this chapter.

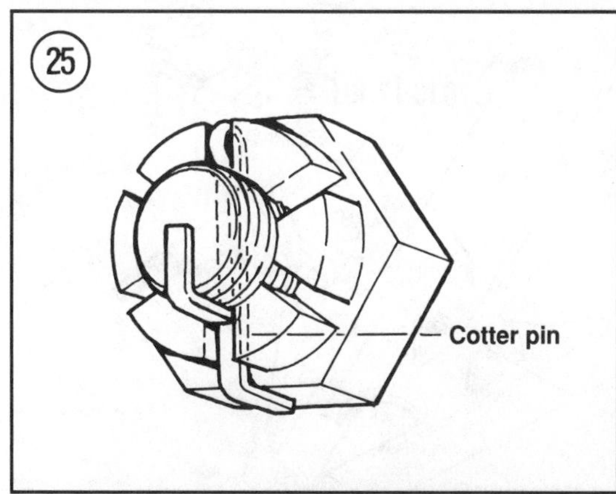

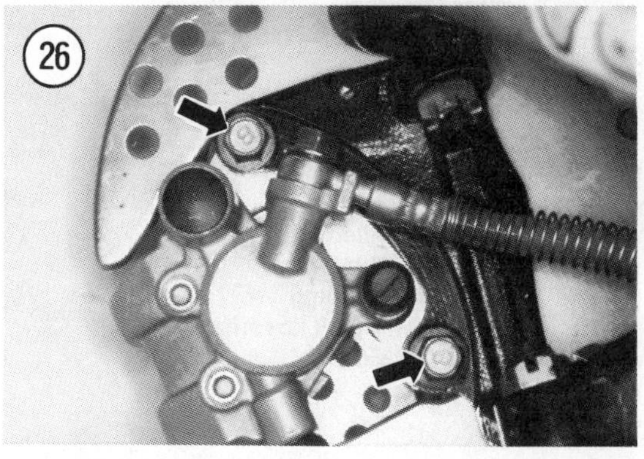

FRONT SUSPENSION

Figure 27 (1987) and **Figure 28** (1988-on) show the front suspension system. The control arms are bolted to mounting brackets welded to the frame. Ball joints connect both control arms to the steering knuckle. On all models, the ball joints are an integral part of the control arms and cannot be replaced separately.

Steering is controlled by tie rods connected to the steering shaft and steering knuckle.

Front Suspension Tools

Along with common hand tools, pullers are required to separate both control arms and tie rod from the steering knuckle. Likewise, a puller is required to separate the tie rod from the steering shaft. The pullers shown in **Figure 29** can be used to separate all of the ball joints on your Yamaha:

a. A universal 2-jaw puller (A, **Figure 29**) can be used to separate the tie rod from the steering knuckle and steering shaft.
b. Separating the control arms from the steering knuckle is a bit more difficult because of the confined working area. However, a special removal tool can be made quite easily. The tool shown in B, **Figure 29** was made from a discarded motorcycle flywheel puller, a 2 1/4 in. length of 1/2-13 threaded rod and two 1/2-13 nuts. The flywheel puller body was drilled and tapped to accept national coarse (USS) 1/2-13 threads. Basic dimensions for the tool are shown in **Figure 30**.

NOTE

*If you are going to machine the tool body (**Figure 30**) from a piece of steel, either machine it with hex or square stock or machine 2 opposite flats onto a round piece of metal so that you can hold it with a wrench when using it.*

SHOCK ABSORBER

Refer to **Figure 27** or **Figure 28** when servicing the shock absorbers.

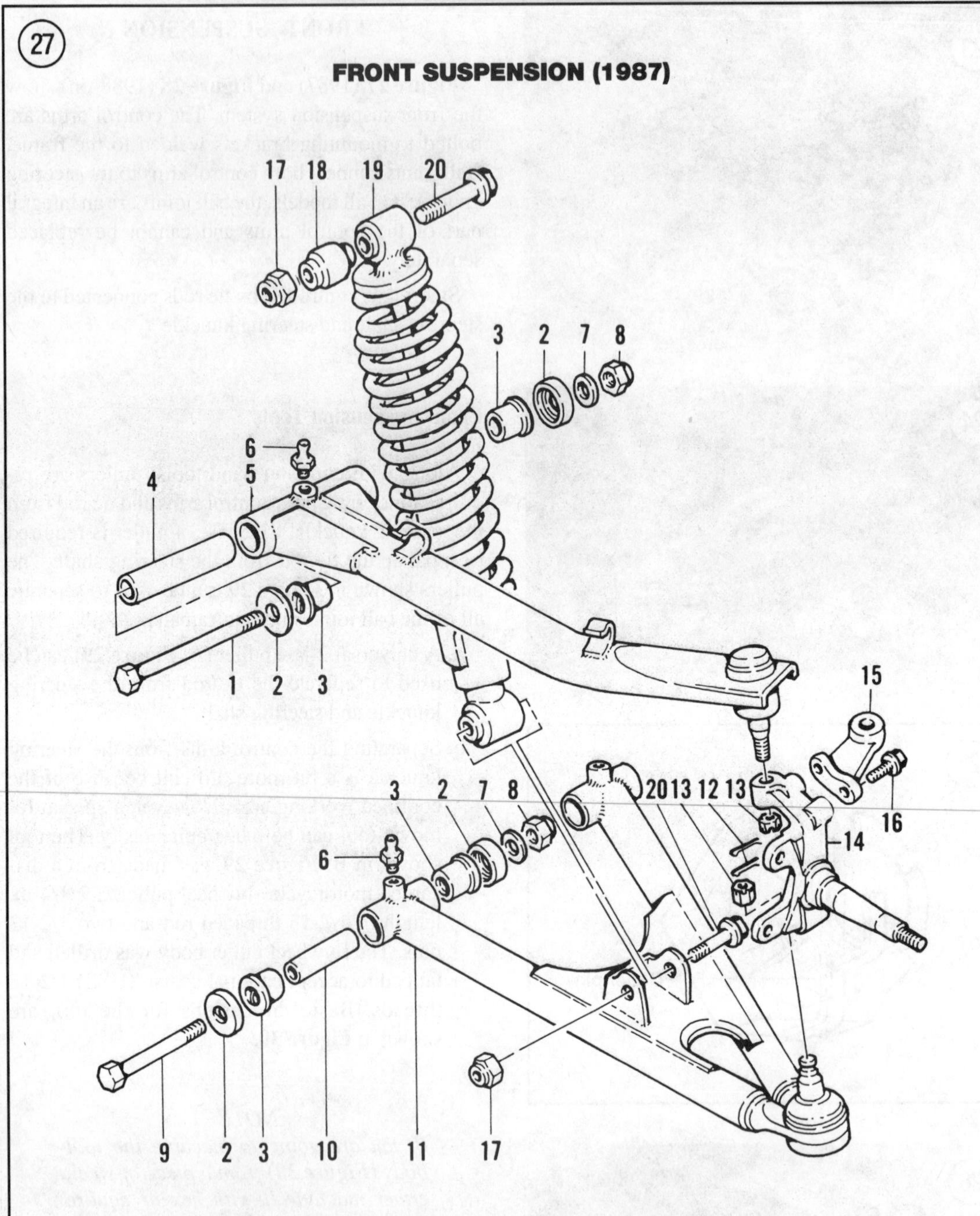

1. Pivot bolt
2. Thrust cover
3. Bushing
4. Collar
5. Upper arm
6. Grease fitting
7. Washer
8. Nut
9. Pivot bolt
10. Collar
11. Lower arm
12. Cotter pins
13. Nut
14. Steering knuckle
15. Steering knuckle arm
16. Allen bolts
17. Nut
18. Bushing
19. Shock absorber
20. Bolt

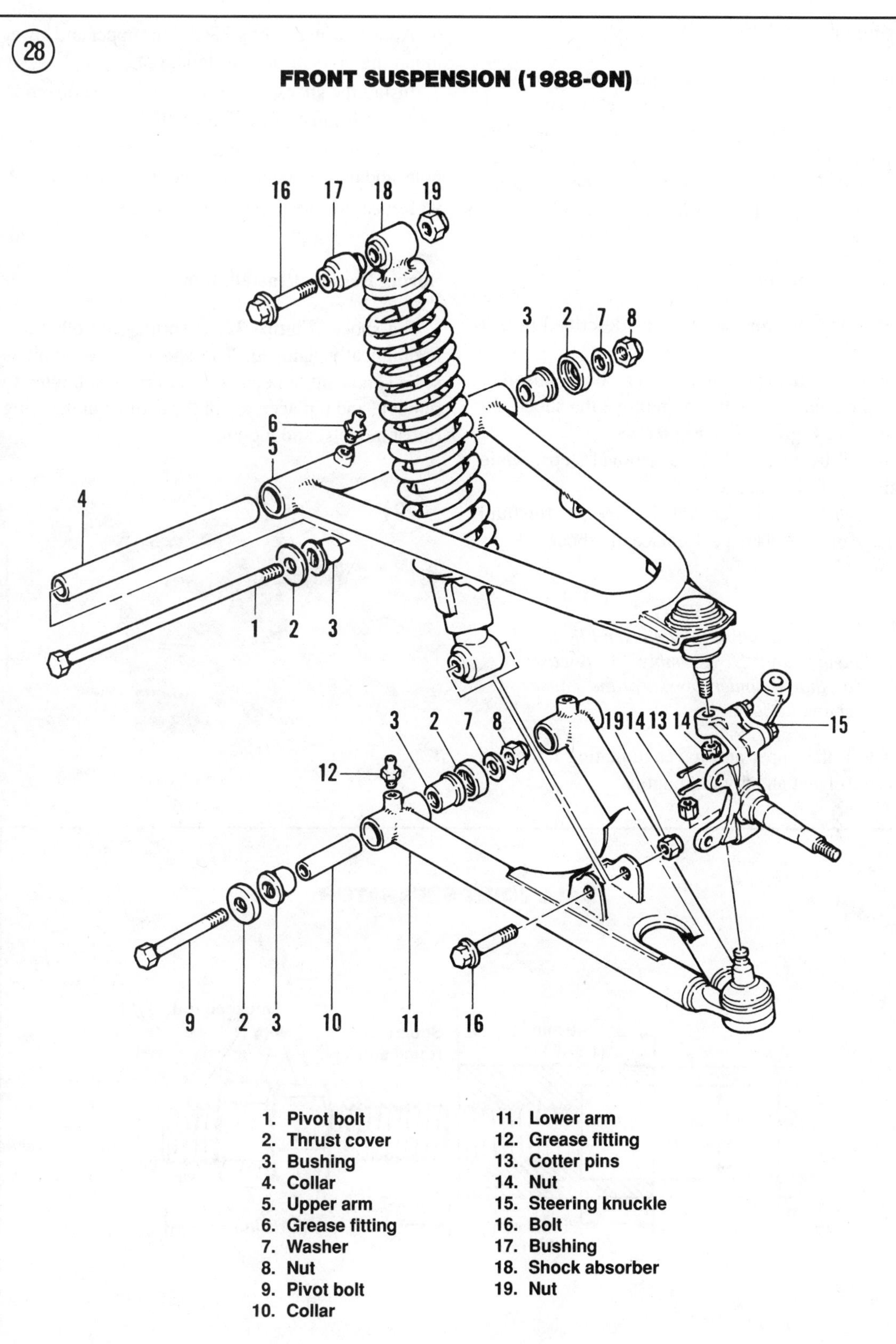

1. Pivot bolt
2. Thrust cover
3. Bushing
4. Collar
5. Upper arm
6. Grease fitting
7. Washer
8. Nut
9. Pivot bolt
10. Collar
11. Lower arm
12. Grease fitting
13. Cotter pins
14. Nut
15. Steering knuckle
16. Bolt
17. Bushing
18. Shock absorber
19. Nut

Spring Preload Adjustment

The front shock absorber springs are provided with 5 preload positions. See **Figure 31**. The No. 1 position is soft and the No. 5 position is hard. The spring preload can be changed by rotating the cam at the end of the spring. Set both front shock absorbers to the same preload position.

Removal/Installation

1. Remove the front wheel(s) as described in this chapter.
2. Remove the upper and lower shock absorber mounting nuts and bolts and remove the shock absorber. See **Figure 27 or Figure 28.**
3. Install by reversing these removal steps, while noting the following.
4. Inspect each damper unit (**Figure 32**) for fluid leakage or other damage. Replace the shock if leaks are found.

WARNING
Do not attempt to disassemble the damper unit. Disassembly can release gas that is under pressure and cause personal injury.

5. Clean the upper and lower mounting bolts and nuts in solvent and dry thoroughly.
6. Apply a waterproof grease to the upper and lower mounting bolts prior to installation.
7. Install the shock mounting bolts in the direction shown in **Figure 27** or **Figure 28**.
8. Tighten the upper and lower shock mounting bolts and nuts to the torque specification in **Table 4.**
9. Repeat for the other side as required.

Spring Removal/Installation

The shock (**Figure 32**) is spring-controlled and hydraulically damped. The shock damper unit is sealed and cannot be serviced. Service is limited to removal and replacement of the damper unit, spring (most models) and mounting bushings.

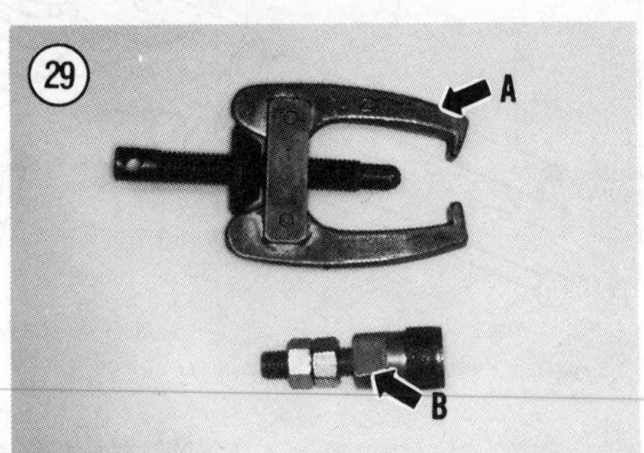

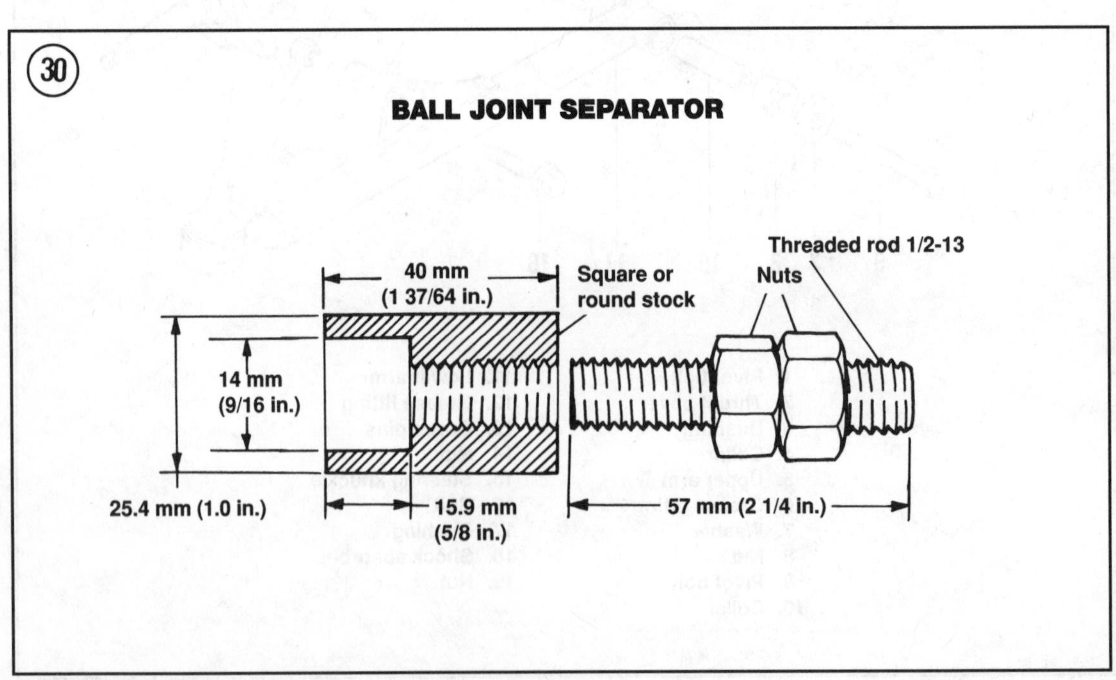

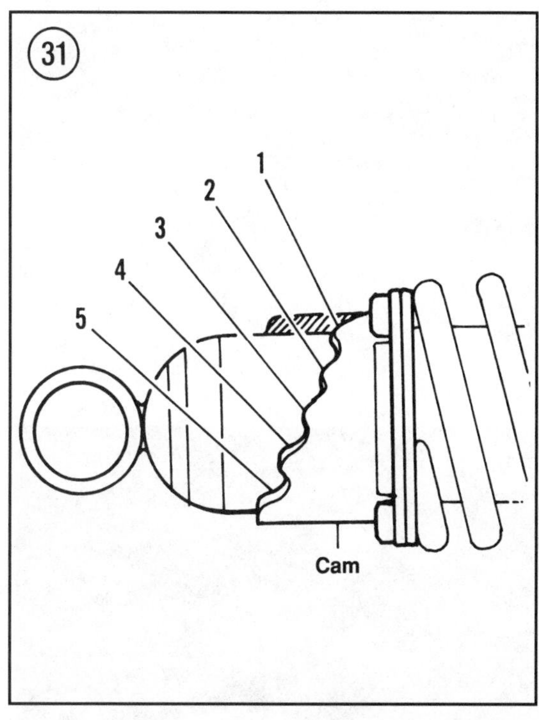

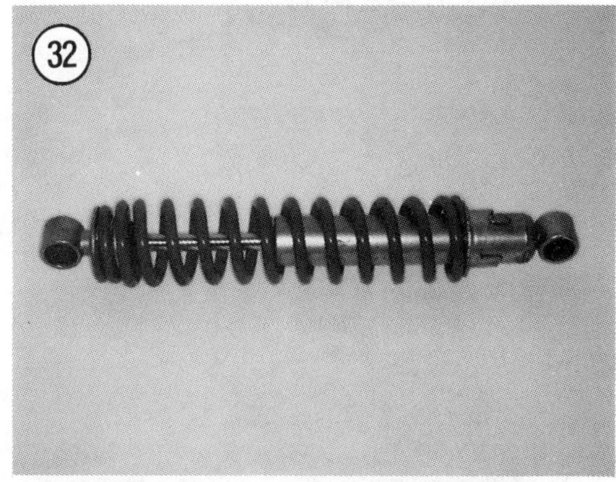

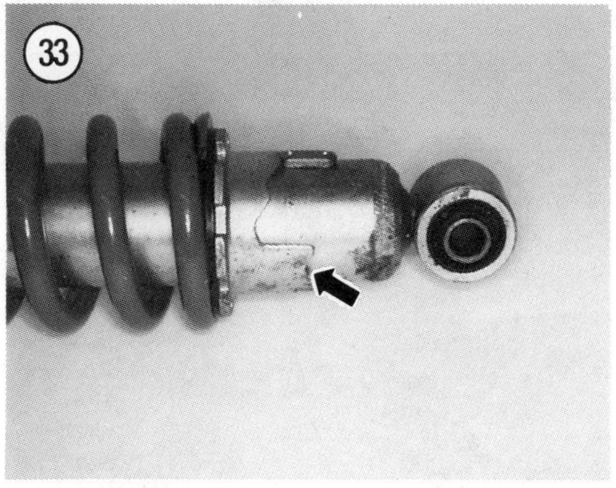

Table 1 lists stock spring rate specifications for all 1987-on stock shock absorbers.

NOTE

This procedure describes spring replacement procedures for shock absorbers that have removable spring seats. If the shocks on your model do not have removable spring seats, the stock shock springs cannot be removed.

1. Clamp the lower shock mount in a vise with soft jaws and turn the spring adjuster (**Figure 33**) to its softest position.

WARNING

Do not remove the spring without a spring compressor. The spring is under considerable pressure and may fly off and cause injury.

2. Mount a spring compressor onto the shock absorber and compress the spring. Then remove the upper spring seat and remove the spring.
3. Measure the spring free length (**Figure 34**). Replace the spring if its length is less than the standard spring length listed in **Table 1**. Yamaha does not list a service limit for spring length.

NOTE

The damper unit cannot be rebuilt; it must be replaced as a unit.

4. Check the damper unit for leakage and make sure the damper rod is straight. Replace the damper unit if necessary.

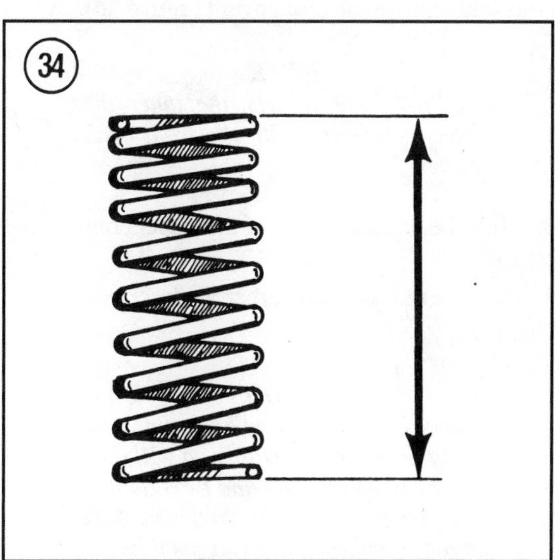

5. Check the shock bushings (**Figure 35**) for deterioration, severe wear or other damage. If necessary, replace bushings as follows:
   a. Support damper unit in a press and press out damaged bushing.
   b. Clean shock bushing bore to remove dirt, rust and other debris.
   c. Press in the new bushing until its outer surface is flush with the bushing bore inside surface as shown in **Figure 35**.
6. Assemble the shock by reversing these steps, while noting the following.
7. If installing progressive rate springs, install spring with closer wound coils toward top of shock.
8. Make sure the spring is properly seated in the spring seat (**Figure 33**).
9. Turn the spring adjuster to adjust spring preload (**Figure 31**).

NOTE
Adjust both shocks to the same spring preload setting.

35

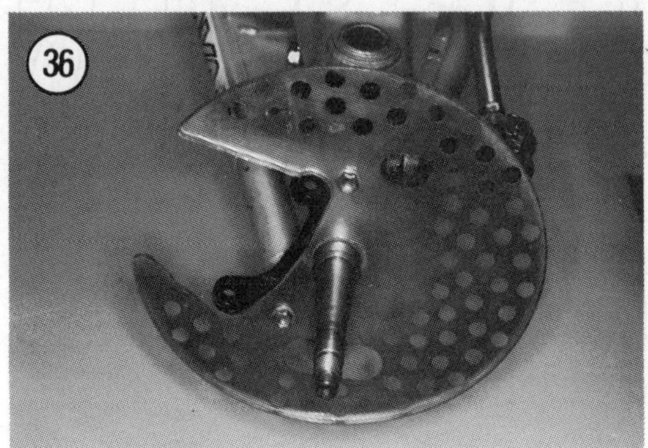
36

STEERING KNUCKLE

Refer to **Figure 27** or **Figure 28** when servicing the steering knuckle.

Removal

1. Remove the front hub as described in this chapter.
2. On 1990-on models, remove the inner disc cover bolts and remove the disc cover (**Figure 36**).

NOTE
On 1987-1989 models, the inner disc cover is removed with the front brake caliper.

3. Slide the brake hose out of the upper control arm clamp.
4. Remove the shock absorber as described in this chapter.

CAUTION
Do not hammer on any ball joint when trying to remove it. Doing so will damage the ball joint stud and threads. This will require complete replacement of the tie rod or control arm(s) assembly.

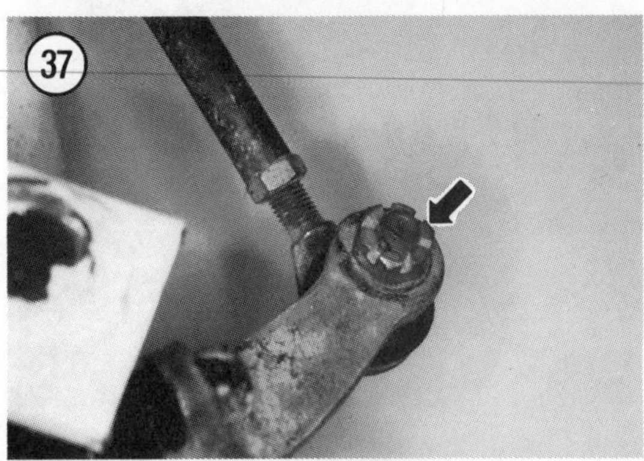
37

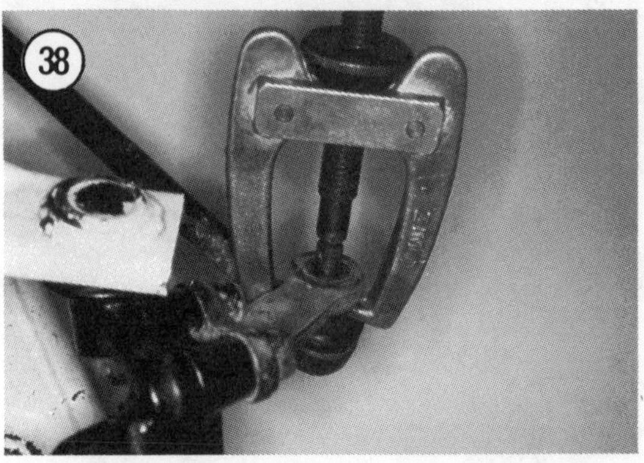
38

5. To disconnect the tie rod ball joint from the steering knuckle:
   a. Remove the cotter pin from the tie rod ball joint stud nut. Discard the cotter pin.
   b. Remove the castellated nut from the ball joint stud (**Figure 37**).

NOTE
When installing the puller, make sure you do not damage the ball joint rubber seal. If the angled arms on the puller are too thick, they can damage the seal.

   c. Attach a 2-jaw puller to the steering knuckle and center the puller's pressure bolt against the ball joint stud as shown in **Figure 38**.
   d. Operate the puller to apply pressure against the ball joint stud, checking that the puller is not cocked to one side. When the ball joint stud is under pressure, strike the top of the puller with a hammer to free the ball joint from the steering knuckle (**Figure 39**).

6. To disconnect the upper and lower control arm ball joints from the steering knuckle:
   a. Remove the cotter pins from the upper (A, **Figure 40**) and lower (B, **Figure 40**) control arm ball joint stud nuts. Discard the cotter pins.
   b. Remove the castellated nuts that hold the ball joint in each control arm to the steering knuckle.

NOTE
*Refer to **Front Suspension Tools** under **Front Suspension** in this chapter for a description of the tool used to separate the control arm ball joints from the steering knuckle.*

   c. To separate the lower control arm, install the special tool between upper and lower control arm ball joint studs as shown in **Figure 41**; center the tool's pressure bolt against the lower control arm stud. Tighten the tool's pressure bolt (**Figure 42**) to apply pressure against the ball joint stud. Continue until the ball joint pops free.
   d. To separate the upper control arm, attach the special tool between the control arm ball joint

39

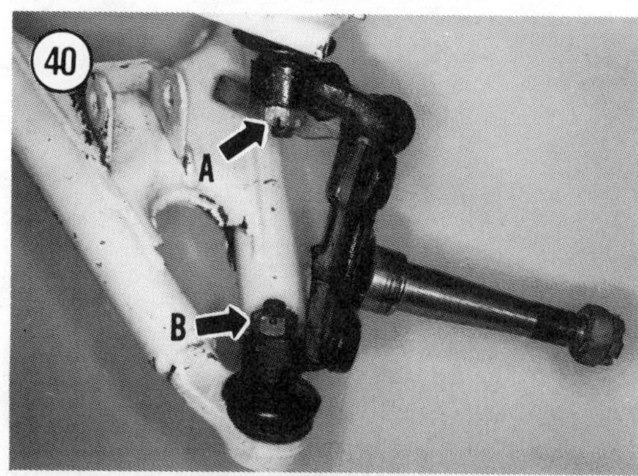

40

41

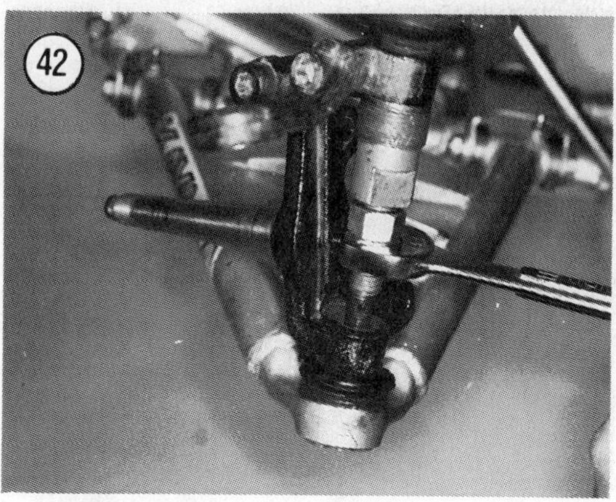
42

11

stud and steering knuckle arm as shown in **Figure 43**; center the tool's pressure bolt against the upper control arm stud. Tighten the tool's pressure bolt (**Figure 44**) to apply pressure against the ball joint stud. Continue until the ball joint pops free.

7. Lower the upper control arm and remove the steering knuckle.

Inspection

1. Clean the steering knuckle in solvent and dry with compressed air.

NOTE

*On 1987 models, the knuckle arm bolts and arm (15, **Figure 27**) can be removed from the knuckle assembly. On 1988-on models, the knuckle arm bolts (A, **Figure 45**) are spot welded to the knuckle assembly; do not attempt to separate the knuckle arm (B, **Figure 45**) from the knuckle assembly.*

2. Inspect the steering knuckle (**C, Figure 45**) for bending, thread damage, cracks or other damage.

3. Inspect the spindle portion where the front wheel bearings ride for wear or damage. A hard spill or collision may cause the spindle portion to bend or fracture. If the spindle is damaged in any way, replace the steering knuckle.

4. Check the hole at the end of the spindle where the cotter pin fits. Make sure there are no fractures or cracks leading out toward the end of the steering knuckle. If any are present, replace the steering knuckle.

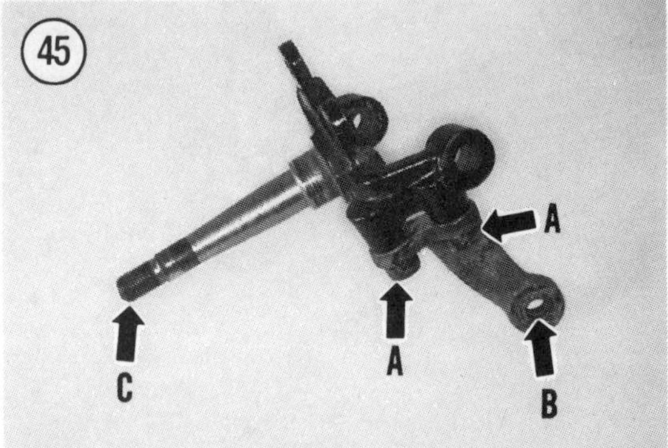

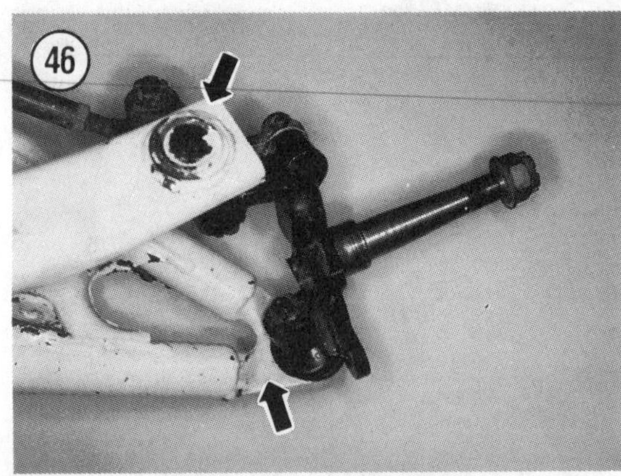

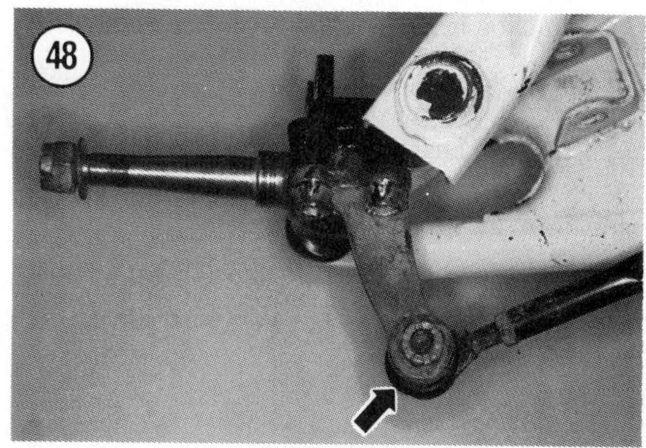

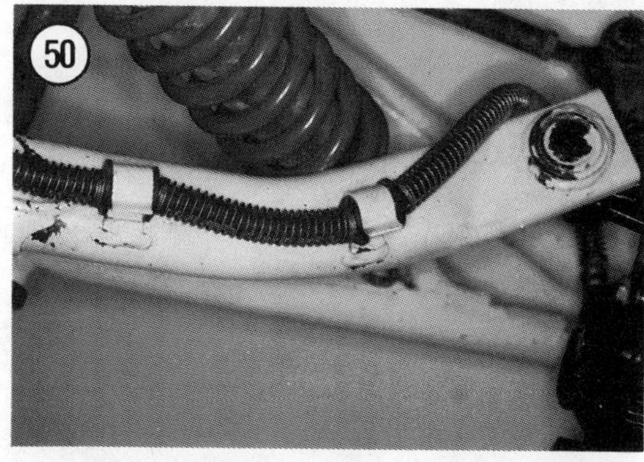

5. If replacing the knuckle arm (15, **Figure 27**) on 1987 models, tighten the knuckle arm Allen bolts to 38 N•m (27 ft.-lb.).

Installation

1. Position the steering knuckle between the control arms. Then install the upper and lower control arm ball joint studs through the steering knuckle. See **Figure 40** and **Figure 46.**
2. Thread the castellated nuts onto the upper and lower ball joint studs (**Figure 40**). Then tighten both nuts to the torque specification in **Table 4**. Tighten the nuts (do not loosen), if necessary, to align the cotter pin hole with the nut slot. Then check that the ball joint boot seats against the steering knuckle (**Figure 47**).
3. Install the tie rod ball joint through the steering knuckle as shown in **Figure 48**. Install the castellated nut and tighten to the torque specification in **Table 4**. Tighten the nut, if necessary, to align the cotter pin hole with the nut slot.
4. Install new cotter pins through all ball joint studs. Open the arms of the cotter pins to lock them in place.
5. Install the shock absorber as described in this chapter.
6. Turn handlebar from side to side, check that steering knuckle (**Figure 49**) moves smoothly with no binding or roughness.
7. On 1990-on models, install inner disc brake cover (**Figure 36**) and its mounting bolts. Tighten bolts securely.
8. Install front hub as described in this chapter.
9. Reposition the front brake hose into the control arm clamps. See **Figure 50** (1987-1989) or **Figure 51** (1990-on).

WARNING
Make sure the brake hoses are not twisted or damaged.

CONTROL ARMS

Refer to **Figure 27** or **Figure 28** when servicing the upper and lower control arms.

Removal

1. Disconnect the control arm(s) from the steering knuckle as described under Steering Knuckle in this chapter.
2. Loosen the upper front bumper bolts. Then remove the lower front bumper bolts and pivot the front bumper (A, **Figure 52**) forward.
3. Remove the nut from the pivot bolt that secures the upper control arm to the frame. Remove the pivot bolt, control arm, thrust covers and bushings. See B, **Figure 52** (1987-1990) or **Figure 53** (1991-on).
4. Remove the nut from each pivot bolt that secures the lower control arm to the frame. Remove the pivot bolt, control arm, thrust covers and bushings. See **Figure 54**, typical.

Control Arm Cleaning and Inspection

NOTE

Do not intermix the pivot bolts, nuts, bushings and thrust covers when disassembling and cleaning the upper and lower control arms. Separate the parts so that they can be installed in their original mounting positions.

1. Remove the thrust covers and collars from the upper (**Figure 55,** typical) and lower (**Figure 56**) control arms.

NOTE

*When cleaning the control arms, do not wash the ball joints (**Figure 57**) in solvent. Handle the ball joints carefully to avoid contaminating the grease or damaging the outer cover.*

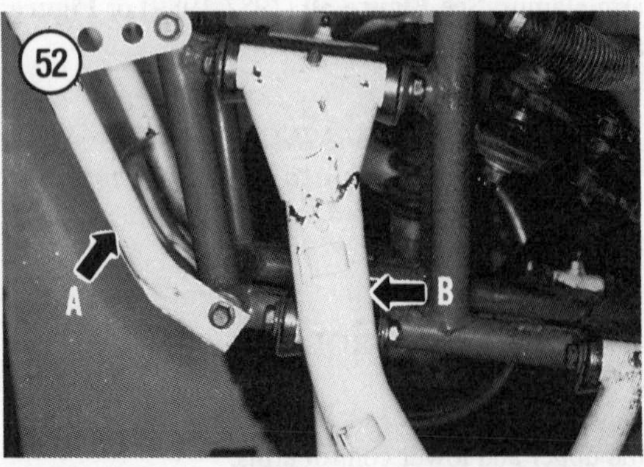

2. Clean parts in solvent and dry with compressed air.
3. Inspect both control arms for cracks, fractures and dents. If damage is severe, replace the control arm. Never try to straighten a damaged or dented control arm as it cannot be straightened properly.
4. Inspect each bushing (A, **Figure 58**) and collar (B, **Figure 58**) set for severe wear or damage. Replace damaged parts.
5. To replace the control arm bushings (A, **Figure 58**):
   a. Support the control arm and drive or press out the bushing. Repeat this step for each bushing.
   b. Clean the control arm bushing bores in solvent and dry thoroughly. Remove all rust and dirt residue.
   c. Support control arm and press bushing into bore until bushing shoulder bottoms.
6. Inspect the rubber seal in each thrust cover for severe wear or damage. Replace the thrust cover if damage is severe.
7. Inspect pivot bolts for bending or other damage. Replace damaged bolts.

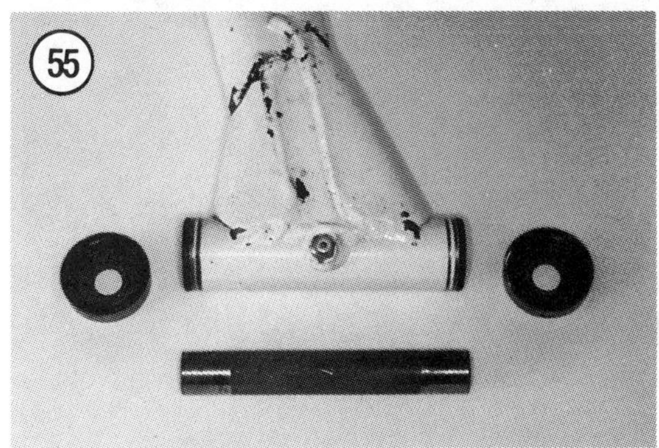

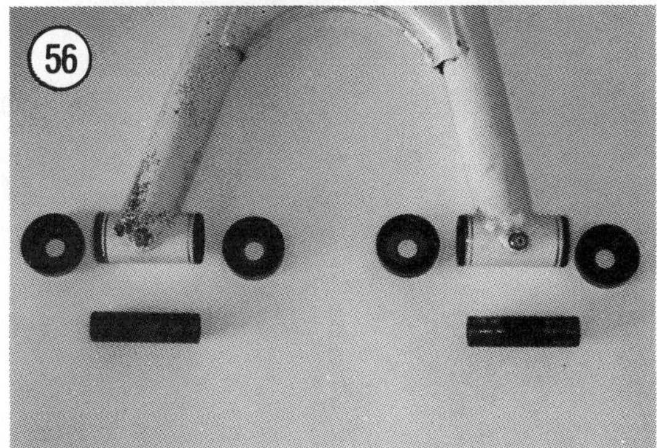

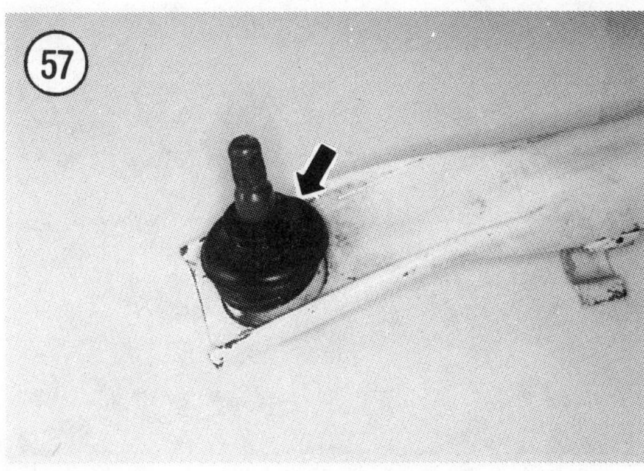

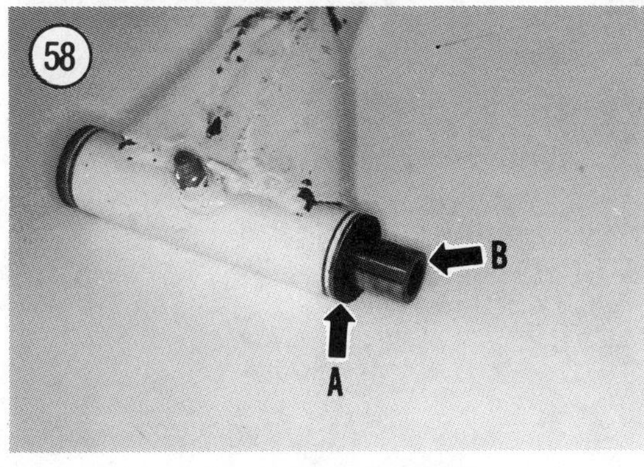

8. Inspect ball joints (**Figure 57**) as described under *Ball Joints Inspection and Replacement* in this chapter.

Ball Joints Inspection and Replacement

A single ball joint (**Figure 57**) is mounted on each control arm. The ball joints on these models are an integral part of the control arm and cannot be replaced separately.

Inspect the ball joint rubber boot. The swivel joint is packed with grease. If the rubber boot or ball joint is damaged, replace control arm as the ball joint cannot be replaced.

Installation

1. Prior to installation, apply a waterproof grease to each of the following components (**Figure 55** and **Figure 56**):
   a. Collar outer diameter.
   b. Thrust cover rubber seal.
   c. Pivot bolts.
2. Install the collars and thrust covers; see **Figure 55** and **Figure 56**.
3. Position the lower control arm between its mounting brackets and install the pivot bolts, washers and nuts (**Figure 54**). Tighten both nuts to the torque specification in **Table 4**.
4. Position the upper control arm between its mounting brackets and install the pivot bolt, washers and nuts (B, **Figure 52**). Also see **Figure 53**. Tighten the nut to the torque specification in **Table 4**.
5. Raise and lower both control arms by hand. Control arms should pivot smoothly with no roughness or binding.
6. Connect control arm ball joints to steering knuckle as described under *Steering Knuckle* in this chapter.
7. Install lower front bumper mounting bolts. Then tighten all front bumper mounting bolts securely.

HANDLEBAR

Removal

CAUTION
Cover the seat, fuel tank and front fender with a heavy cloth or plastic tarp

to protect them from the accidental spilling of brake fluid. Wash any spilled brake fluid off any painted or plated surface immediately as it will destroy the finish. Use soapy water and rinse thoroughly.

1. Remove the bolts (A, **Figure 59**) securing the front master cylinder to the handlebar and rest it on the front fender. Keep the reservoir in the upright position to keep air from entering the brake system. Do not remove the brake line from the master cylinder unless you are going to remove the master cylinder from the vehicle.

CAUTION

Do not allow the master cylinder to hang by its hose. This could damage the hose.

2. Remove the screws and clamp securing the throttle assembly (B, **Figure 59**) to the handlebar and remove the assembly. Lay the assembly over the front fender. Be careful that the cable does not get crimped or damaged.
3. Remove all wire bands holding the left-hand switch housing wires to the handlebar.
4. Remove the screws securing the left-hand switch housing (A, **Figure 60**). Then separate the switch housing and remove from the handlebar.
5. Remove the screws and clamp (B, **Figure 60**) securing the left-hand clutch and parking brake assembly to the handlebar and remove the assembly. Position the assembly so that the cables do not get crimped or damaged.
6. Remove the ignition switch screws and lift off the ignition switch assembly (**Figure 61**). Set the ignition switch aside.
7. Remove the bolts securing the handlebar upper holders and remove the holders (A, **Figure 62**) and the ignition switch mounting bracket (B, **Figure 62**).
8. Remove the handlebar.
9. To maintain a good grip on the handlebar and to prevent it from slipping down, clean the knurled section of the handlebar with a wire brush. It should be kept rough so it will be held securely by the holders. The holders should also be kept clean and free of any metal that may have been gouged loose by handlebar slippage.
10. Inspect the holders, bolts and ignition switch bracket (**Figure 63**) for damage.

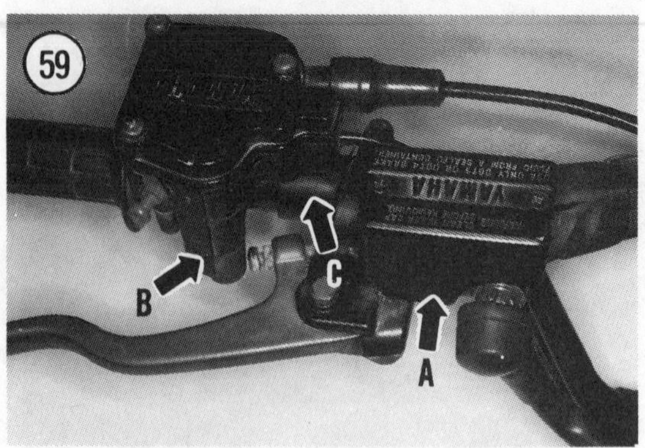

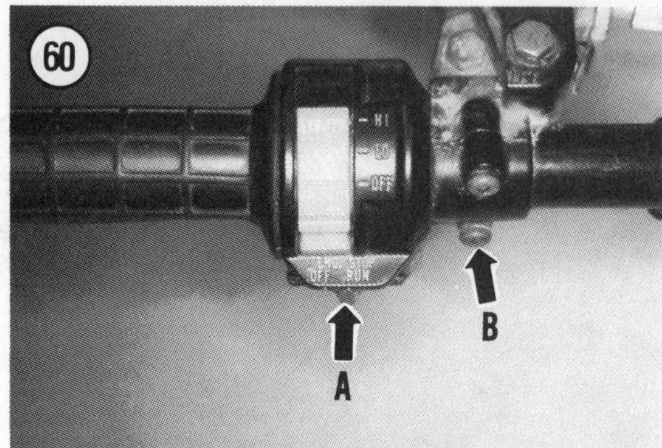

Installation

1. Position the handlebar on the lower handlebar holders and hold it in place.
2. Install ignition switch bracket between the handlebar holders as shown in B, **Figure 62**.

NOTE
*The upper handlebar holders are directional; they are machined with one side offset from the other (A, **Figure 64**). The front side is marked with a punch mark (B, **Figure 64**). To ensure correct handlebar installation, the upper holders must be installed as described in Step 3.*

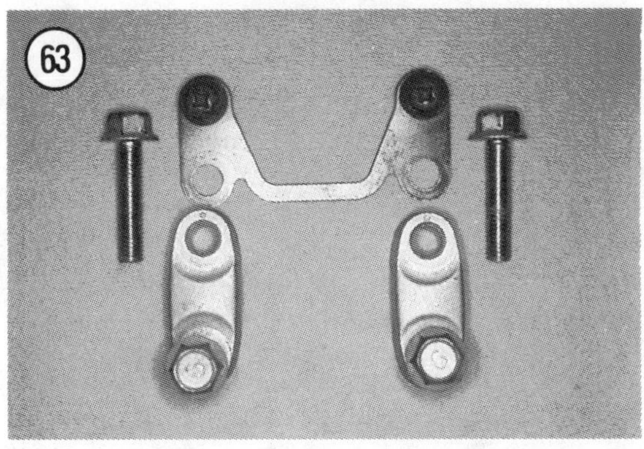
63

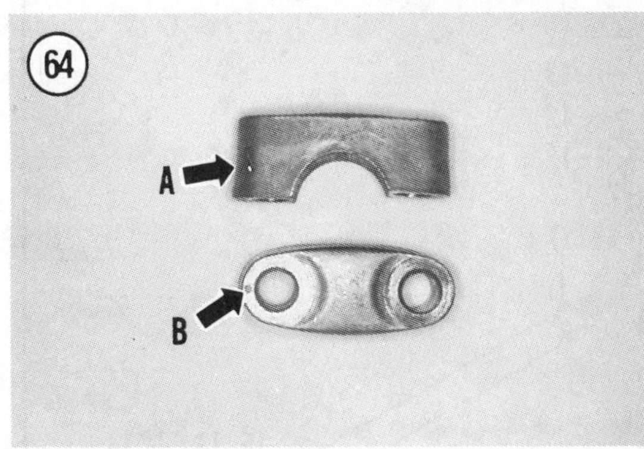

64

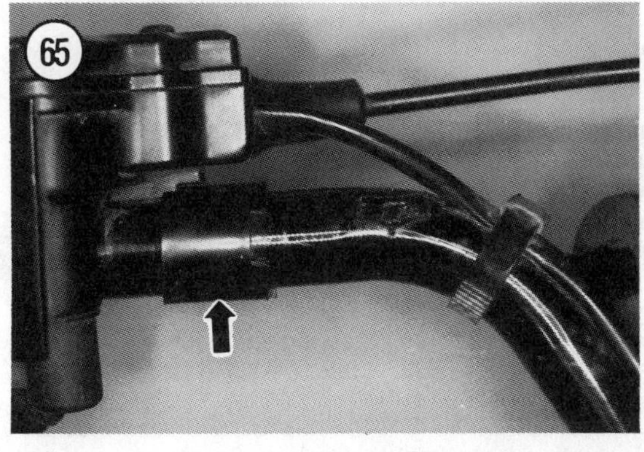
65

3. Install the upper handlebar holders with their punch mark (B, **Figure 64**) facing toward the front.
4. Install the handlebar holder bolts. Tighten the forward bolts first and then the rear bolts; tighten to the torque specification listed in **Table 4**.
5. Position the ignition switch (**Figure 61**) over the handlebar and secure it with its 2 mounting screws. Tighten the screws securely.

NOTE
*If you are installing a new handlebar, do not forget to install the master cylinder spacer (**Figure 65**) onto the handlebar before installing the right-hand grip.*

6. If you installed a new handlebar, install new grips now. Follow grip manufacturer's directions for installing and sealing grips to handlebar.
7. Position the left-hand switch housing (A, **Figure 60**) onto the handlebar and seat it next to the grip as shown in A, **Figure 60**. Tighten the switch screws securely.
8. Secure housing wiring harness to handlebar with clamps. Make sure harness is routed with no sharp bends.
9. Position left-hand clutch and parking brake assembly on handlebar and install clamp and 2 screws (B, **Figure 60**). Check clutch lever position while sitting on seat, then tighten 2 clamp screws securely.
10. Position throttle assembly (B, **Figure 59**) onto handlebar and secure with clamp and 2 screws.
11. Slide master cylinder spacer along handlebar and seat groove in spacer into notch on throttle housing; see C, **Figure 59**.
12. Install master cylinder onto handlebar and secure with clamp and 2 bolts (A, **Figure 59**). Install clamp so that arrow faces up. Slide master cylinder toward throttle housing until it contacts master cylinder spacer (C, **Figure 59**). Then check front brake lever position while sitting on seat and tighten master cylinder mounting bolts to torque specification in **Table 4**.
13. Install handlebar crossover bar pad.
14. After all assemblies have been installed, test each one to make sure it operates correctly. Correct any problem at this time.

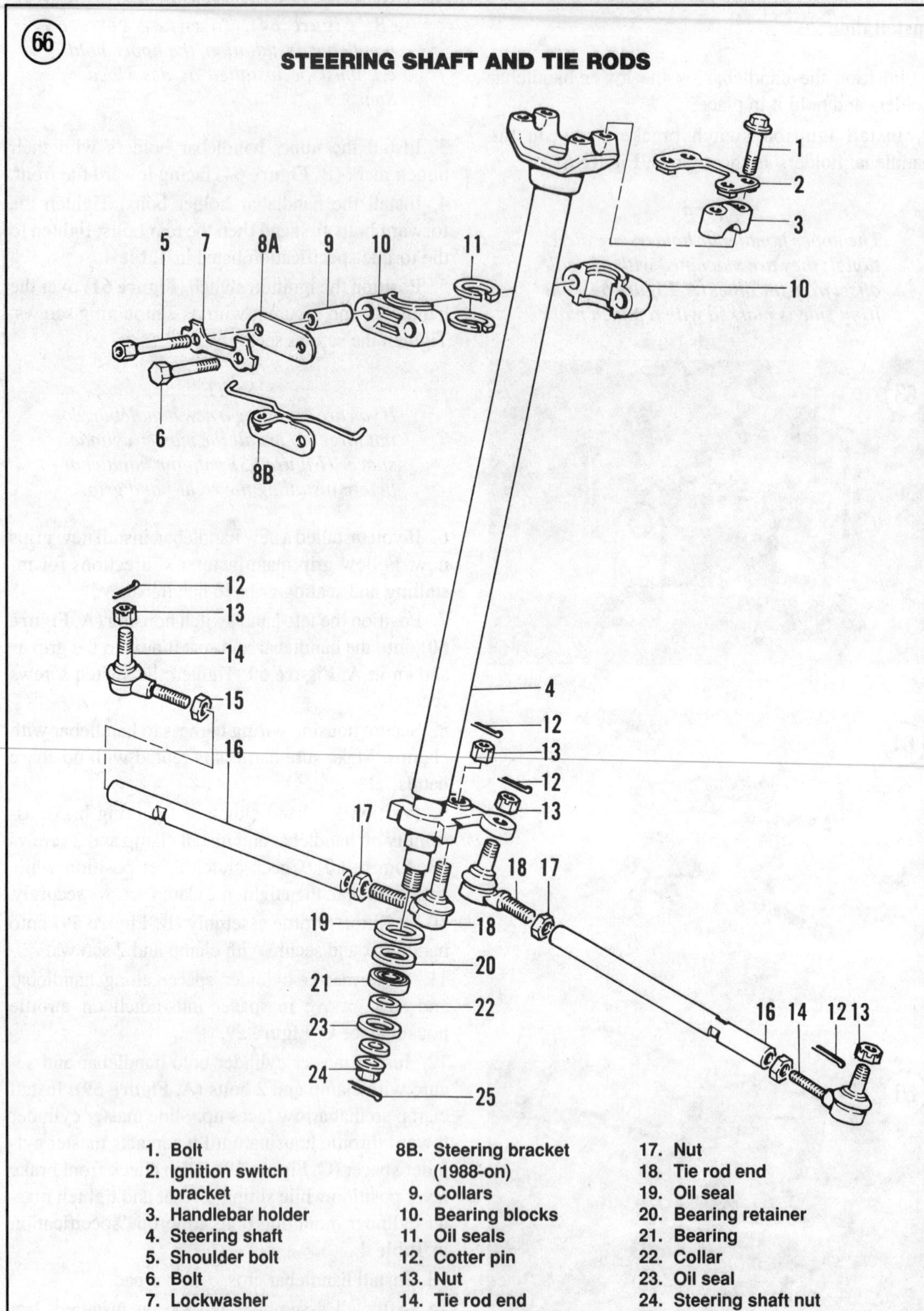

66

STEERING SHAFT AND TIE RODS

1. Bolt
2. Ignition switch bracket
3. Handlebar holder
4. Steering shaft
5. Shoulder bolt
6. Bolt
7. Lockwasher

8A. Steering bracket (1987)

8B. Steering bracket (1988-on)

9. Collars
10. Bearing blocks
11. Oil seals
12. Cotter pin
13. Nut
14. Tie rod end
15. Nut
16. Tie rod shaft
17. Nut
18. Tie rod end
19. Oil seal
20. Bearing retainer
21. Bearing
22. Collar
23. Oil seal
24. Steering shaft nut
25. Cotter pin

TIE RODS

Figure 66 is an exploded view of the steering shaft and tie rod assemblies. The tie rods are comprised of an inner end and outer end. All of the individual parts that make up the tie rod can be replaced separately.

A 2-jaw puller (**Figure 67**) is required to separate the tie rod from the steering knuckle and steering shaft.

Removal

You can replace the outer tie rod ball joint (**Figure 68**) without having to disconnect the tie rod from the steering shaft.

When replacing the inner tie rod ball joint (**Figure 69**), it is best to remove the tie rod from the vehicle so that the inner tie rod can be properly adjusted.

1. Support the vehicle and remove the front wheel(s) as described in this chapter.

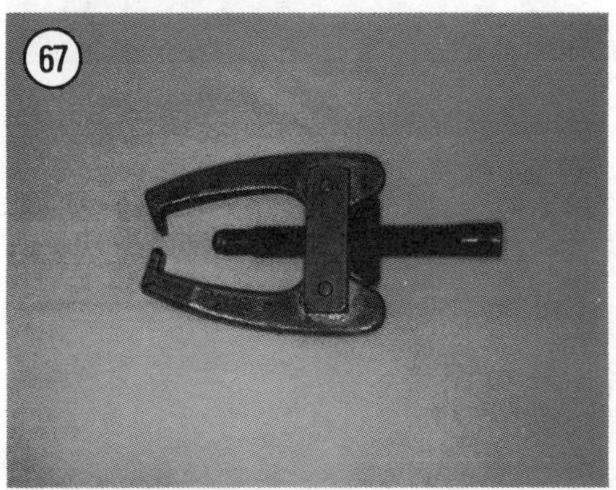
67

68

CAUTION

Do not hammer on any ball joint when trying to remove it. Doing so will damage the ball joint stud and threads. This will require a new ball joint.

2. To disconnect the tie rod ball joint from the steering knuckle:
   a. Remove the cotter pin from the tie rod ball joint stud nut. Discard the cotter pin.
   b. Remove the castellated nut from the ball joint stud (**Figure 68**).

NOTE

When installing the puller, make sure you do not damage the ball joint rubber seal. If the angled arms on the puller are too thick, they can damage the seal.

   c. Attach a 2-jaw puller to the steering knuckle and center the puller's pressure bolt against the ball joint stud as shown in **Figure 70**.
   d. Tighten the puller to apply pressure against the ball joint stud, checking that the puller is not cocked to one side. When the ball joint stud is under pressure, strike the top of the puller with

69

70

a hammer to free the ball joint from the steering knuckle (**Figure 71**).

NOTE
*If you are going to replace the outer tie rod ball joint, refer to **Tie Rod Disassembly/Reassembly** in this chapter.*

3. To disconnect the tie rod ball joint from the steering shaft:
   a. Remove the cotter pin from the tie rod ball joint stud nut. Discard the cotter pin.
   b. Remove the castellated nut from the ball joint stud (**Figure 69**).

NOTE
When installing the puller, make sure you do not damage the ball joint rubber seal. If the angled arms on the puller are too thick, they can damage the seal.

   c. Attach a 2-jaw puller to the steering knuckle and center the puller's pressure bolt against the ball joint stud as shown in **Figure 72**.
   d. Tighten the puller to apply pressure against the ball joint stud, checking that the puller is not cocked to one side. Continue to apply pressure with the puller until the ball joint pops free from the steering shaft.
4. Remove the tie rod.

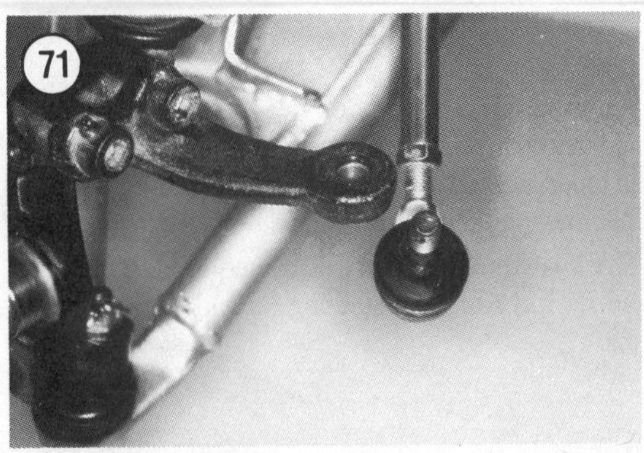
71

72

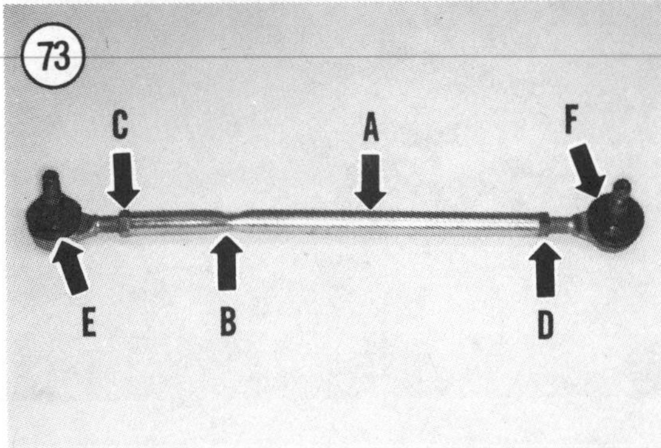

73

Inspection

NOTE
If you clean the tie rod with solvent, work carefully to prevent the solvent from contaminating the grease in the rubber boot.

1. Inspect the tie rod shaft (A, **Figure 73**) for damage. There should be no creases or bends along the shaft. Check with a straightedge placed against the tie rod shaft.
2. Inspect the rubber boot at each end of the tie rod end ball joint (**Figure 74**). The ball joints are permanently packed with grease. If the rubber boot is damaged, dirt and moisture can enter the ball joint and destroy it. If the boot is damaged in any way, disassemble the tie rod and replace the tie rod end(s). Refer to *Tie Rod Disassembly/Reassembly* in the following procedure.
3. Pivot the tie rod end (**Figure 74**) back and forth by hand. If the tie rod end moves roughly or with

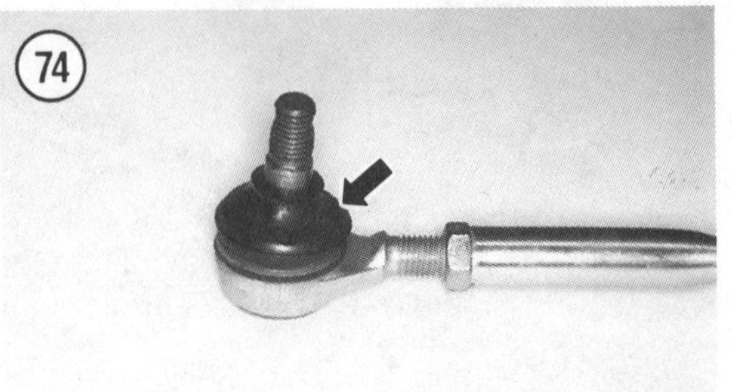
74

excessive play, replace it as described in the following procedure.

Tie Rod Disassembly/Reassembly

Refer to **Figure 75** when performing this procedure.

1. Hold the tie rod with a wrench across the shaft flat (B, **Figure 73**) and loosen the locknut for the ball joint being replaced.

NOTE

*The locknut securing the outside tie rod end (C, **Figure 73**) has left-hand threads. The inside tie rod end locknut (D, **Figure 73**) has right-hand threads.*

2. Unscrew and remove the damaged tie rod end(s).
3. Clean mating shaft and tie rod end threads with contact cleaner.
4. Identify the new tie rod end with the drawing in **Figure 75**. The outside (E, **Figure 73**) and inside (F, **Figure 73**) tie rods are different. Likewise, the left- and right-hand tie rod shafts are different; the right-hand tie rod shaft is marked with a white paint mark as shown in **Figure 75**.
5. Thread the tie rod (with locknut) into the tie rod shaft.
6. Adjust the tie rod length and position the ball joints as follows, referring to **Figure 75**:
   a. Adjust the tie rod ball joints to obtain the tie rod length measurement shown in **Figure 75**.

NOTE

*When adjusting the ball joints in the following steps, note that dimension A in **Figure 75** must be equal for both ends.*

   b. Align both ball joints, then continue with substep c.
   c. Turn the inner ball joint (F, **Figure 73**) 20.5° counterclockwise from the center position. Then turn the outer ball joint (E, **Figure 73**) 20.5° clockwise from the center position. See insert in **Figure 75**.
   d. Tighten the locknuts securely. Then check that dimension A in **Figure 75** is equal for both sides.

Installation

NOTE

*The left- and right-hand tie rod assemblies are different. The right-hand tie rod assembly has a white dot mark painted onto its shaft; see **Figure 75**.*

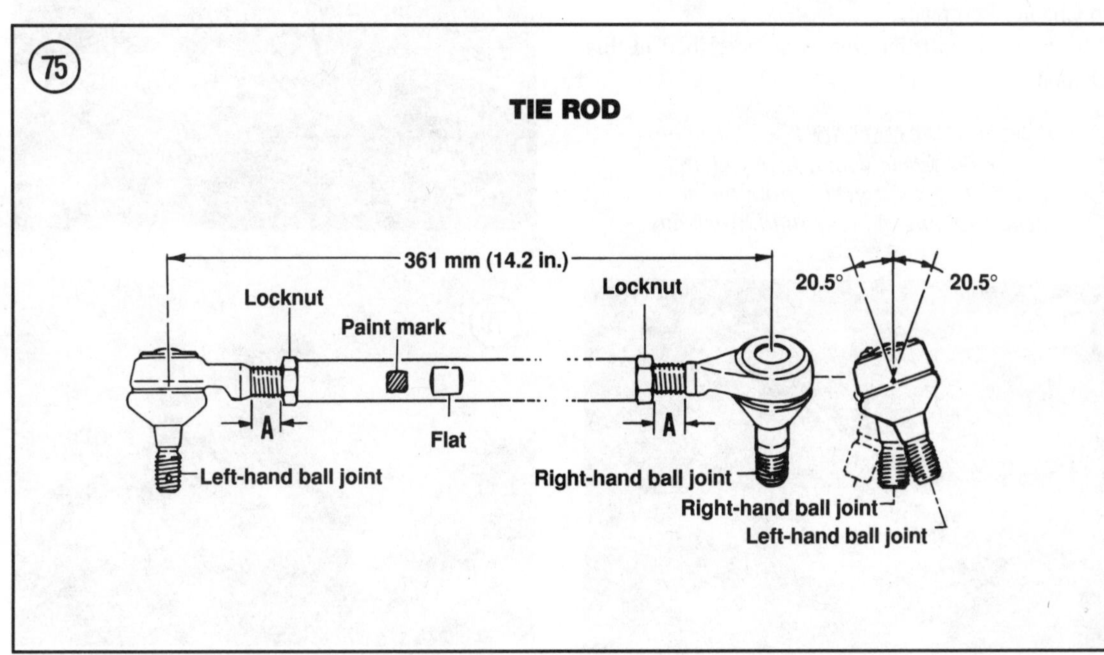

1. Position the tie rod assembly so the end with the flat on the shaft (**Figure 76**) is attached to the steering knuckle.
2. Attach the tie rod assembly to the steering shaft (**Figure 69**) and to the steering knuckle (**Figure 68**).
3. Thread the castellated nut onto each ball joint stud and tighten to the torque specification in **Table 4**. Tighten the nut(s), if necessary, to align the cotter pin hole with the nut slot.
4. Install new cotter pins through all ball joint studs. Open and bend the cotter pin arms to lock them in place.
5. Install the front wheels as described in this chapter.
6. Check the toe-in adjustment, and adjust if necessary, as described in Chapter Three.

STEERING SHAFT

Figure 66 is an exploded view of the steering shaft and the components that are connected to it. The steering shaft pivots on split bearing halves at the top and a ball bearing at the lower end. Adjustable tie rods connect the steering shaft to the steering knuckle.

Removal

1. Remove the front fender assembly as described in Chapter Fourteen.
2. Remove both front wheels as described in this chapter.

CAUTION
Cover the frame with a heavy cloth or plastic tarp to protect it from the accidental spilling of brake fluid. Wash any spilled brake fluid off any painted or plated surface immediately as it will destroy the finish. Use soapy water and rinse thoroughly.

3. Reposition the handlebar as follows:
   a. Remove the ignition switch screws and lift off the ignition switch assembly (**Figure 61**). Set the ignition switch aside.
   b. Remove the bolts securing the handlebar upper holders and remove the holders (A, **Figure 62**)

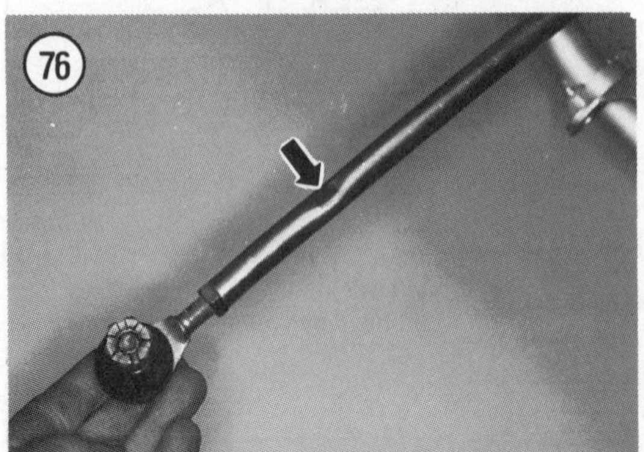
76

77

78

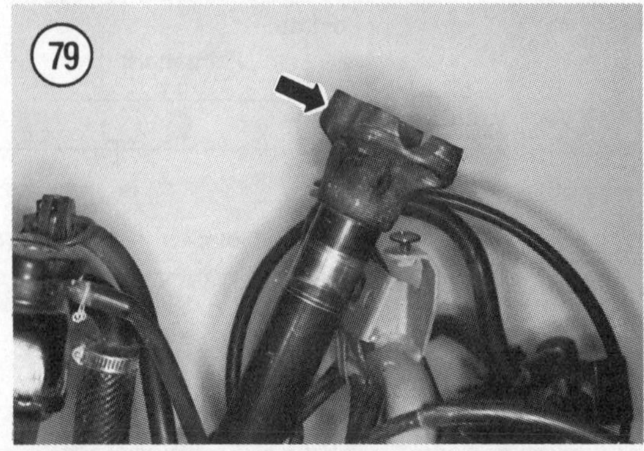
79

and the ignition switch mounting bracket (B, **Figure 62**).

c. Move the handlebar assembly back and off the steering shaft and place it on the frame. Keep the master cylinder in an upright position to minimize loss of brake fluid and to keep air from entering the brake system. It is not necessary to remove the hydraulic brake line from the master cylinder.

NOTE
It is not necessary to drain and remove the radiator prior to removing the steering shaft.

4. Remove the radiator mounting bolts. Support the radiator with a Bunjee cord.
5. Disconnect both tie rods from the steering shaft as described under *Tie Rods* in this chapter.
6. Remove the cotter pin, nut and washer that secure the bottom of the steering shaft to the frame. See **Figure 77.**
7. Make a diagram of the cables and wiring harnesses as they pass around the steering shaft for reassembly reference.
8. Pry the lockwasher tabs away from the bolts securing the upper bearing blocks to the frame.
9. Remove the bolts (**Figure 78**) that hold the upper bearing blocks to the frame. Then remove the outer block, collars, split dust seals and inner block assembly.
10. Carefully lift the steering shaft (**Figure 79**) out of the lower frame mount and remove it from the frame.

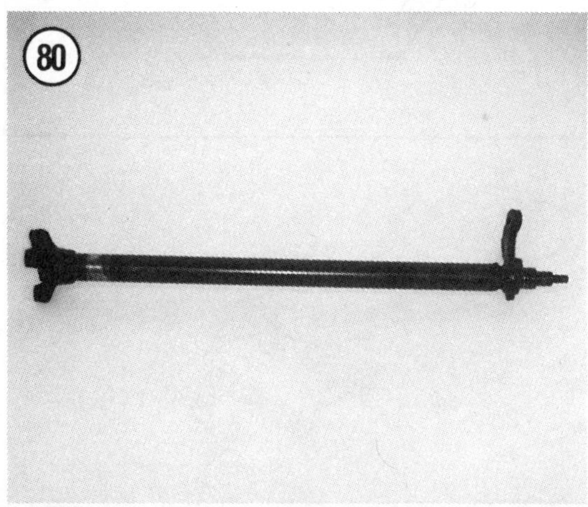

Inspection

1. Wash all parts in solvent and dry thoroughly.
2. Inspect the steering shaft (**Figure 80**), especially if the vehicle has been involved in a collision or spill. If the shaft is bent or twisted in any way it must be replaced. If a damaged shaft is installed in the vehicle, it will cause rapid and excessive wear to the bearings as well as place undue stress on other components in the frame and steering system. If shaft straightness is questionable, check with set of V-blocks and dial indicator (**Figure 81**). Yamaha does not provide runout limits.

NOTE
***Figure 82** shows the type of damage that can occur to a bent steering shaft. The area where the upper bearing block rides (see arrow in **Figure 82**) is severely worn.*

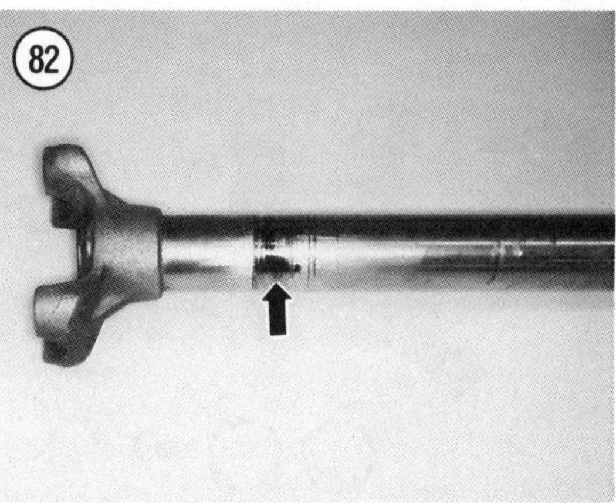

11

3. Inspect the tie rod attachment holes (A, **Figure 83**) in the lower section of the steering shaft. Check for hole elongation, cracks or wear. Replace the steering shaft if necessary.

4. Inspect the upper bearing assembly (**Figure 84**) for:
   a. Severely worn or damaged dust seals (A, **Figure 84**).
   b. Worn or damaged bearing block halves (B, **Figure 84**).
   c. Bent or damaged bolts and collars.

5. Inspect the lower steering shaft bearing and oil seal surfaces (B, **Figure 83**). If the machined surfaces are severely scored or damaged, replace the steering shaft and the lower bearing assembly.

6. Inspect the steering bearing oil seals (**Figure 66**). If the oil seals are severely worn, leaking or damaged, replace both oil seals as described in this chapter.

7. Inspect the steering bearing (**Figure 66**) by turning its inner race with your finger. If the bearing turns roughly or has excessive play, replace the bearing as described in this chapter.

Steering Shaft Oil Seal and Bearing Replacement

A 30 mm hex driver will be required to remove and install the bearing retainer in the following steps. You can use the Yamaha fork damper rod holder (part No. YM-01327 [**Figure 85**]) along with a

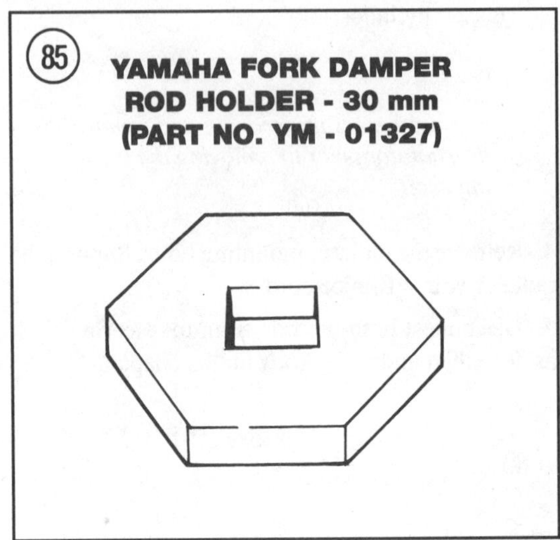

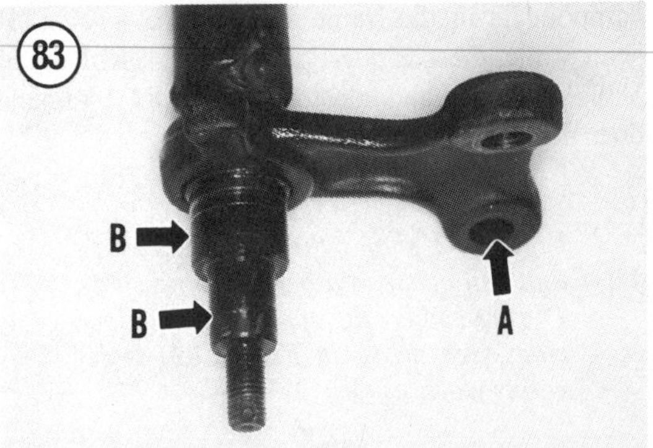

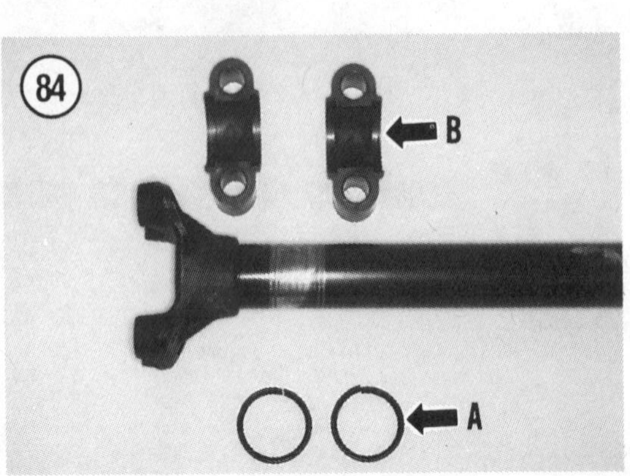

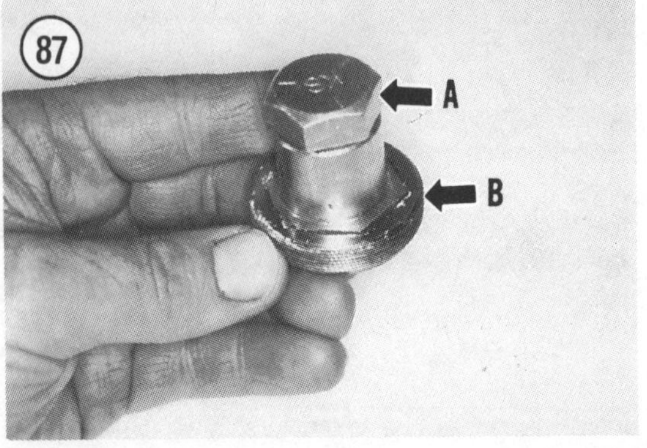

88

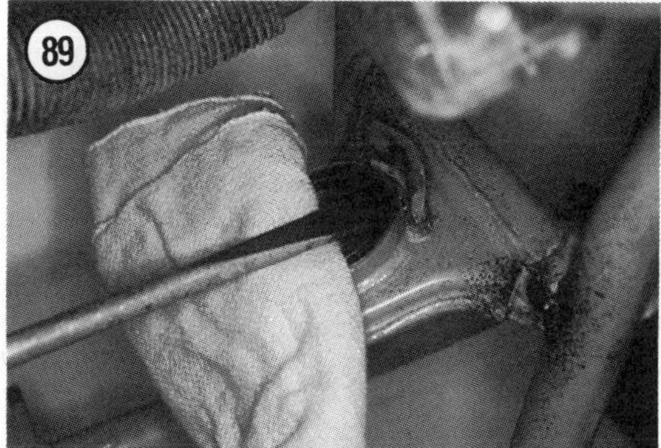

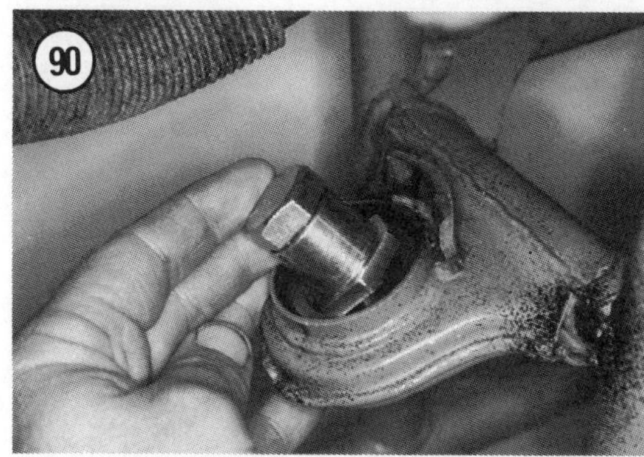

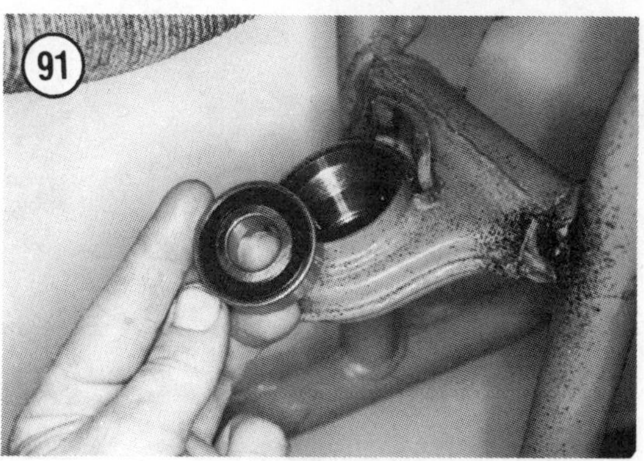

ratchet and extension or you can make a tool with a 30 mm bolt or nut similar to the one shown in **Figure 86. Figure 87** shows how the tool (A) fits into the bearing retainer (B).

1. Remove the collar from the lower oil seal (**Figure 88**).

2. Pry the upper and lower oil seals out of the frame tube with a wide-blade screwdriver. Pad the screwdriver to avoid damaging the frame. See **Figure 89**. Discard both oil seals.

3. Use the 30 mm hex driver (**Figure 90**) and remove the bearing retainer that holds the bearing in the frame. Then remove the tool and bearing retainer and lift out the bearing (**Figure 91**).

4. Clean the bearing retainer and collar in solvent and dry thoroughly.

5. Clean bearing retainer threads (**Figure 92**) in frame.

6. Place bearing in frame with manufacturer's name and size code facing up (**Figure 91**). Make sure bearing seats squarely in bore (**Figure 93**).

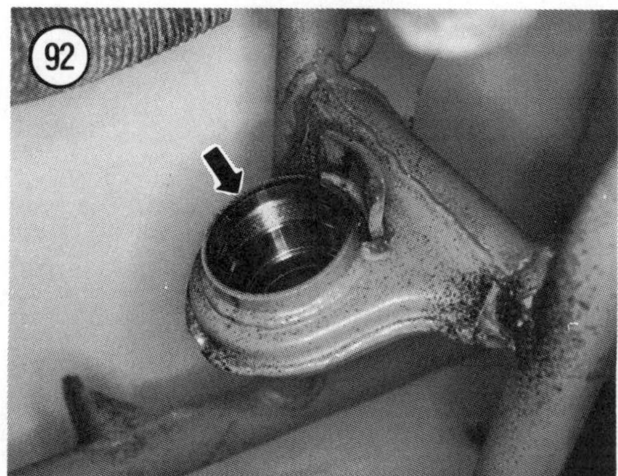

7. Thread the bearing retainer, with its shoulder side facing down (**Figure 94**), into the frame. Hand tighten retainer against bearing (**Figure 95**). Torque bearing retainer to specification in **Table 4**.

8. Install upper and lower oil seals as follows:
   a. Upper oil seal (A, **Figure 96**) is larger than lower oil seal (B, **Figure 96**).
   b. Install both oil seals so that closed side faces out (away from bearing). See **Figure 97** and **Figure 98**.
   c. Pack the lip of each oil seal with a waterproof grease prior to installation.
   d. Drive in the lower oil seal until its outer surface is flush with or slightly below the oil seal bore inside surface as shown in **Figure 99**. A socket and extension (**Figure 100**) can be used to install the oil seal.
   e. Drive in the upper oil seal until its outer surface is flush with the oil seal bore inside surface as shown in **Figure 101**. A socket and extension can be used to install the oil seal.

9. Insert the collar (**Figure 88**) into the lower oil seal.

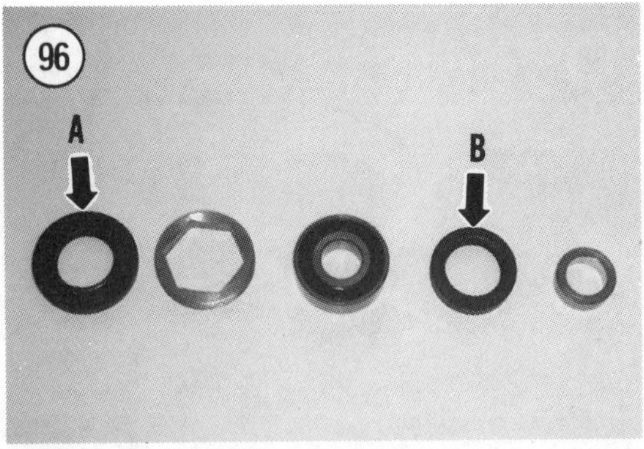

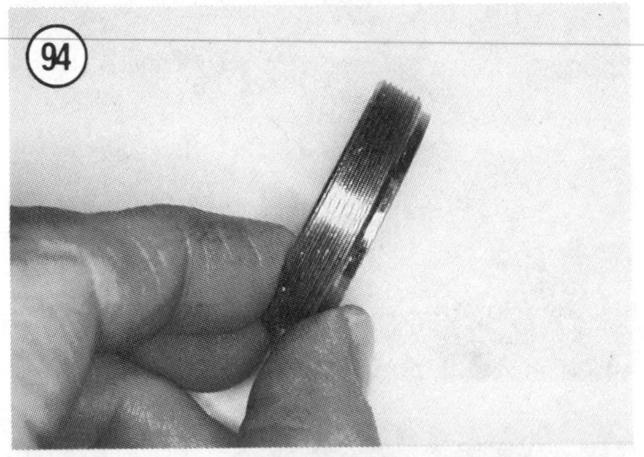

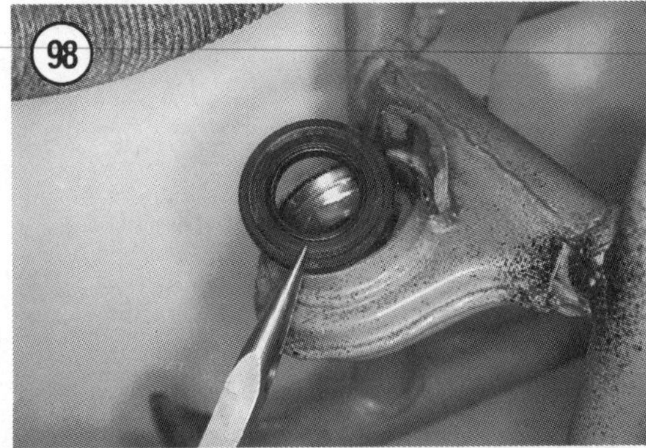

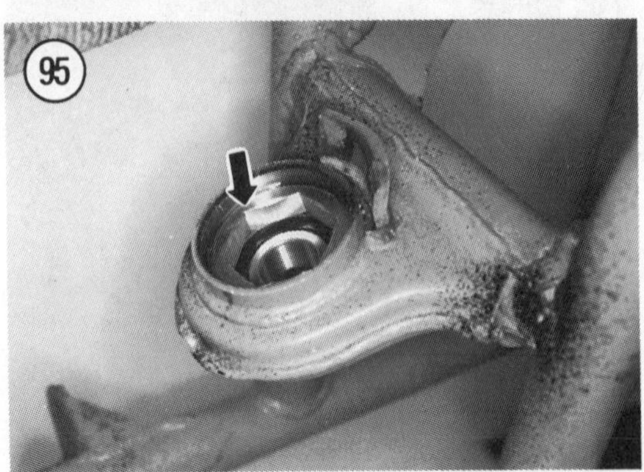

100

Installation

1. Apply a coat of grease to the steering shaft where it fits into the lower bearing assembly; see B, **Figure 83**.

2. Install the steering shaft into the frame with the tie rod brackets toward the back, and carefully align it with the lower bearing assembly. Then turn steering shaft and insert into bearing until shaft bottoms (**Figure 102**). Check that the collar is in place and did not drop out.

3. Loosely install the washer and nut (**Figure 103**) that holds the steering shaft to the frame.

4. Assemble and install the upper bearing assembly (**Figure 104**) as follows:

   a. Grease the inner diameter of both bearing block halves.

   b. Grease the dust seals and install them into one of the bearing block halves (**Figure 105**).

NOTE
The inner and outer bearing block halves are identical.

101

102

104

103

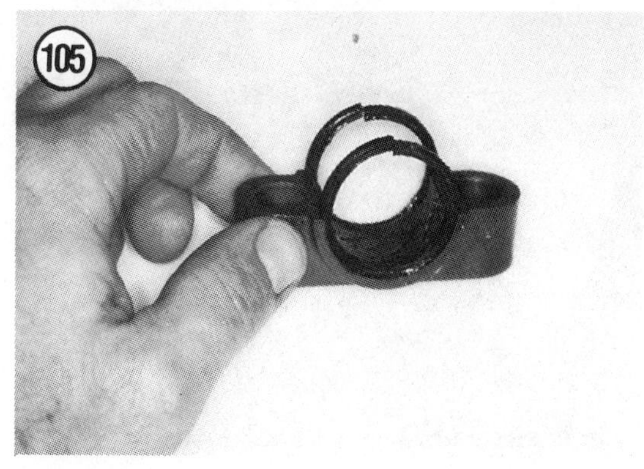

105

c. Install the inner bearing block between the frame and steering shaft, along with the dust seals, and align with the 2 frame mounting holes (**Figure 106**). Reposition the dust seals, if necessary, so that they sit flush in the bearing block grooves.
d. Install the outer bearing block (A, **Figure 107**), engaging the block grooves with the dust seals. Then align and install the 2 collars (B**, Figure 107**) through both bearing block halves until flush with the outer block.
e. Install the steering bracket, lockwasher and 2 bolts. Install the shoulder bolt (**Figure 108**) on the right-hand side. Install the bolts finger-tight.
f. Torque the steering shaft nut (**Figure 103**) to the specification in **Table 4**. Install a new cotter pin through the steering shaft hole. Bend the cotter pin arms around the steering shaft to lock it in place. After bending the cotter pin arms, make sure the cotter pin is a tight fit.
g. Torque the 2 steering shaft bearing block bolts to the specification in **Table 4**.

6. Turn the steering shaft from side to side. The steering shaft should turn smoothly with no binding, roughness or excessive play.
7. Bend the lockwasher tabs that secure the bearing block bolts around the bolt heads (**Figure 109**).
8. Install the handlebar assembly onto the steering shaft and tighten as described under *Handlebar* in this chapter.
9. Connect both tie rods onto the steering shaft lower end as described in this chapter.
10. Install the front fender and seat as described in Chapter Fourteen.
11. Check toe-in as described in Chapter Three.

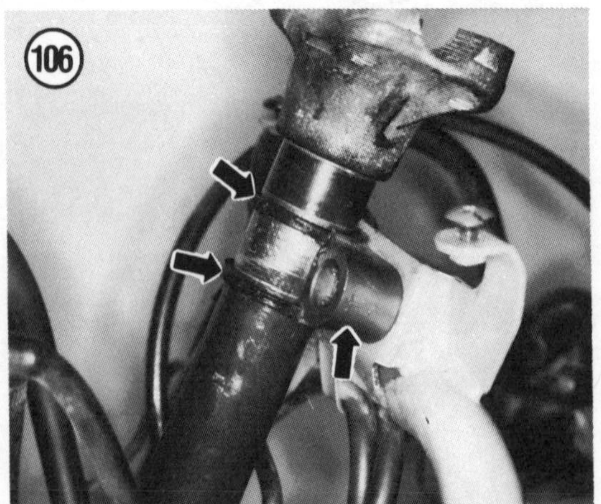

TIRES AND WHEELS

The vehicle is equipped with tubeless, low pressure tires designed specifically for off-road use only. Rapid tire wear will occur if the vehicle is ridden on paved surfaces. Due to their low pressure requirements, they should be inflated only with a hand-op-

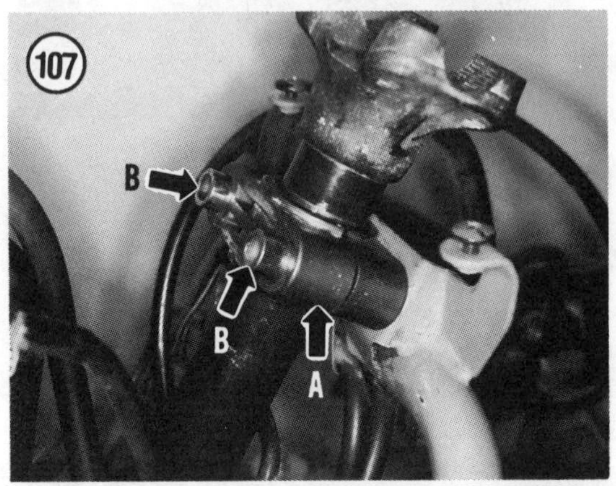

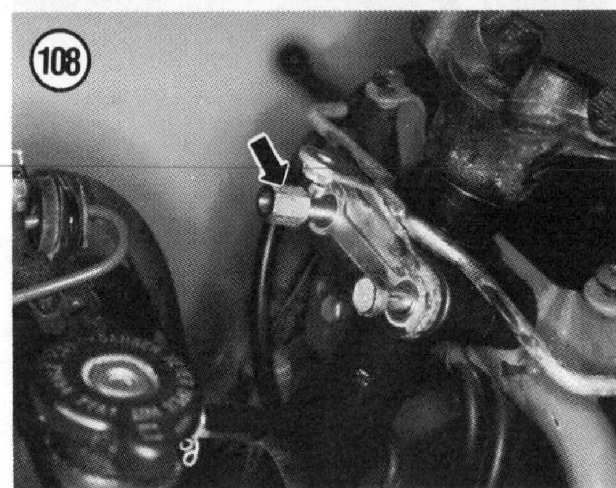

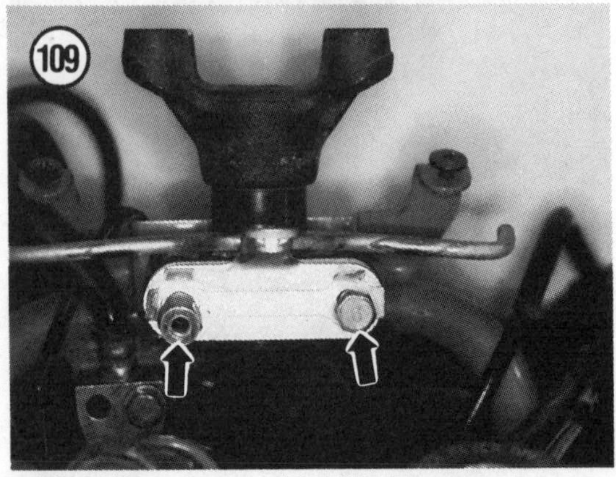

erated air pump instead of using an air compressor or the compressed air available at service stations.

CAUTION
Do not overinflate the stock tires as they will be permanently distorted and damaged. If overinflated they will bulge out similar to an inner tube that is not within the constraints of a tire and ***will not*** *return to their original contour.*

NOTE
Additional inflation pressure in the stock tires will not improve the ride or the handling characteristics of the vehicle. For improved handling, aftermarket tires will have to be installed.

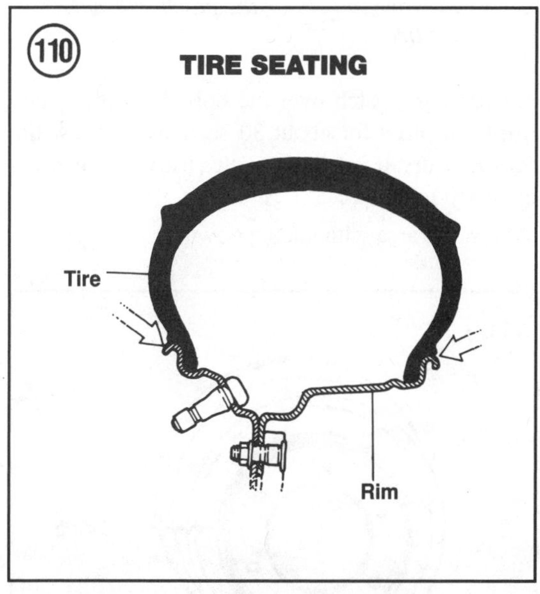

It's a good idea to carry a cold patch tire repair kit and hand held pump in the tow vehicle. Removing the tire from the rims is different than on a motorcycle or automobile wheel.

CAUTION
Do not *use conventional motorcycle tire irons for tire removal as the tire sealing bead will be damaged when forced away from the rim flange.*

Tire Changing

The front and rear tire rims used on all models are of the 2-piece type and have a very deep built-in ridge (**Figure 110**) to keep the tire bead seated on the rim under severe riding conditions. Unfortunately it also tends to keep the tire on the rim during tire removal as well.

A special tool is required for tire changing on these models. A typical tool is shown in **Figure 111**.

1. Remove the valve stem cap and core and deflate the tire. Do not reinstall the core at this time.
2. Lubricate the tire bead and rim flanges with a liquid dish detergent or any rubber lubricant. Press the tire sidewall/bead down to allow the liquid to run into and around the bead area. Also apply lubricant to the area where the bead breaker arm will come in contact with the tire sidewall.
3. Position the wheel into the tire removal tool (**Figure 111**).
4. Slowly work the tire tool, making sure the tool is up against the inside of the rim, and break the tire bead away from the rim.
5. Using your hands, press down on the tire on either side of the tool and try to break the rest of the bead free from the rim.
6. If the rest of the tire bead cannot be broken loose, raise the tool, rotate the tire/rim assembly and repeat Steps 4 and 5 until the entire bead is broken loose from the rim.
7. Turn the wheel over and repeat to break the opposite loose.
8. Remove the tire rims from the tire.
9. Inspect the rim sealing surface of the rim. If the rim has been severely hit, it will probably cause an air leak. Repair or replace the rim as required.
10. Inspect the tire for cuts, tears, abrasions or any other defects.
11. Clean the rims and tire sealing surfaces.

12. Inspect the large O-ring seal (**Figure 112**), if so equipped. If it is starting to harden or deteriorate replace it with a new one.
13. Set the tire into position on the outer rim.
14. Apply a light coat of grease to the large O-ring seal and place it in the groove in the rim (**Figure 112**).
15. Install the inner rim into the tire and onto the outer rim. Align the bolt holes.
16. Install the wheel onto its hub and install the wheel lug nuts and washers. Tighten the wheel lug nuts to the torque specification in **Table 4**.
17. Install the valve stem core.
18. Apply tire mounting lubricant to the tire bead and inflate the tire to the pressure valve listed in **Table 3**.
19. Deflate the tire and let it sit for about one hour.
20. Inflate the tire to the recommended air pressure, refer to **Table 3**.
21. Check the rim line molded into the tire around the edge of the rim. It must be equally spaced all the way around. If the rim line spacing is not equal, the tire bead is not properly seated. Deflate the tire and unseat the bead completely. Lubricate the bead and reinflate the tire.
22. Check for air leaks and install the valve cap.

Cold Patch Repair

This is the preferred method of patching a tire. The rubber plug type of repair is recommended only for an emergency repair, or until the tire can be patched correctly with the cold patch method.

Use the manufacturer's instructions for the tire repair kit you are going to use. If there are no instructions, use the following procedure.

1. Remove the tire as described in this chapter.
2. Prior to removing the object that punctured the tire, mark the location of the puncture with chalk or crayon on the outside of the tire.
3. On the inside of the tire, roughen the area around the hole slightly larger than the patch. Use the cap from the tire repair kit or pocket knife. Do not scrape too vigorously or you may cause additional damage.
4. Clean the area with a non-flammable solvent. Do not use an oil base solvent as it will leave a residue rendering the patch useless.
5. Apply a small amount of special cement to the puncture and spread it with your finger.
6. Allow the cement to dry until tacky—usually 30 seconds or so is sufficient.
7. Remove the backing from the patch.

CAUTION
Do not touch the newly exposed rubber with your fingers or the patch will not stick firmly.

8. Center the patch over the hole. Hold the patch firmly in place for about 30 seconds to allow the cement to dry. If you have a roller, use it to help press the patch into place.
9. Dust the area with talcum powder.

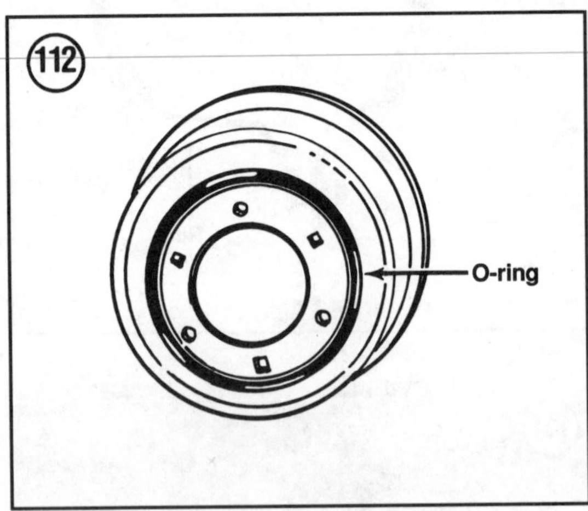

Table 1 FRONT SUSPENSION AND STEERING GENERAL SPECIFICATIONS

Caster angle	9°
Trail	40 mm (1.57 in.)
Tread (standard)	
Front	900 mm (35.4 in.)
Rear	
1987-1989 and 1991-on	840 mm (33.1 in.)
1990	870 mm (34.2 in.)
Toe-in	0-10 mm (0-0.39 in.)
Front suspension type	Double wishbone
Front wheel travel	
1987-1990	220 mm (8.66 in.)
1991-on	230 mm (9.1 in.)
Steering lock-to-lock angle	38°
Front shock absorbers	
Cushion stroke	110 mm (4.33 in.)
Spring free length	
1987-1989	279.5 mm (11.0 in.)
1990	282 mm (11.1 in.)
1991-on	286.5 mm (11.3 in.)
Spring rate	
1987-1989	
K1	3.5 kg/mm (7.7 lb./in.)
K2	4.0 kg/mm (8.8 lb./in.)
1990	
K1	2.9 kg/mm (6.4 lb./in.)
K2	3.4 kg/mm (7.5 lb./in.)
1991-on	
K1	2.7 kg/mm (5.9 lb./in.)
K2	3.4 kg/mm (7.5 lb./in.)
Shock stroke	
1987-1989	
K1	0-59.5 mm (0-2.34 in.)
K2	59.5-127.0 mm (2.34-5.00 in.)
1990	
K1	0-65 mm (0-2.56 in.)
K2	65-135.5 mm (2.56-5.33 in.)
1991-on	
K1	0-93 mm (0-3.66 in.)
K2	93-133 mm (3.66-5.24 in.)

Table 2 TIRE AND WHEEL SPECIFICATIONS

Tires	
Type	Tubeless
Size	
Front	AT21 × 7-10
Rear	
1987-1989	AT22 × 10-9
1990	AT20 × 11-10
1991-on	AT20 × 10-9
Wheels	
Type	Panel wheel
Material	Aluminum
Front rim size	10 × 6
Rear rim size	9 × 8.5
Rim runout	
Radial and lateral limit	2.0 mm (0.08 in.)

Table 3 TIRE INFLATION PRESSURE

	Standard psi (kPa)	Minimum psi (kPa)
Front		
1987-1990	4.3 (30)	3.8 (27)
1991-on	4.3 (30)	3.8 (27)
Rear		
1987-1990	3.6 (25)	3.1 (22)
1991-on	4.3 (30)	3.1 (22)

Table 4 TIGHTENING TORQUES

	N·m	ft.-lb.
Front axle nut (steering knuckle)	85	62
Front wheel lug nuts	45	33
Front brake caliper	28	20
Steering knuckle		
At knuckle arm	38	28
At ball joint	25	18
Tie rod ball joint at steering knuckle	25	18
Tie rod ball joint at steering shaft	25	18
Ball joint at tie rod	30	22
Steering shaft nut	30	22
Steering shaft bearing block bolts	23	17
Handlebar holder	20	14
Bearing retainer (steering shaft)	40	29
Upper arm at frame		
1987-1990	30	22
1991-on	38	28
Lower arm at frame		
1987-1990	30	22
1991-on	32	23
Front shock absorber bolts	45	33
Front master cylinder bolts	10	7.4

CHAPTER TWELVE

REAR SUSPENSION

This chapter contains repair and replacement procedures for the rear wheels, rear axle, axle housing and rear suspension components. Service to the rear suspension consists of periodically checking bolt tightness, lubrication of all pivot points, swing arm bushing replacement and rear shock service.

Rear suspension specifications are listed in **Table 1**. Drive chain size and link numbers are listed in **Table 2**. Tightening torques are listed in **Table 3**. **Tables 1-4** are found at the end of this chapter.

REAR WHEELS

Refer to **Figure 1** (1987-1988) or **Figure 2** (1989-on) when servicing the rear wheel.

Removal

1. Park the vehicle on level ground and set the parking brake. Block the front wheels so that the vehicle will not roll in either direction.

2. Lift the vehicle so that both rear wheels are off the ground. Support the vehicle with jackstands or wooden blocks.

3A. To remove the tire/wheel assembly only:

a. Remove the lug nuts (A, **Figure 3**) and washers that hold the rear wheel to the axle hub.
b. Remove the tire/wheel assembly from the rear axle hub.

3B. To remove the tire/wheel and axle hub at the same time:

a. Remove the cotter pin, axle nut (B, **Figure 3**) and washer that hold the axle hub to the rear axle.
b. Remove the tire/wheel and axle hub assembly from the rear axle.

4. Install by reversing these removal steps, noting the following.

5A. If only the tire/wheel reassembly was removed, perform the following:

a. Place the tire/wheel assembly onto the rear axle hub studs.

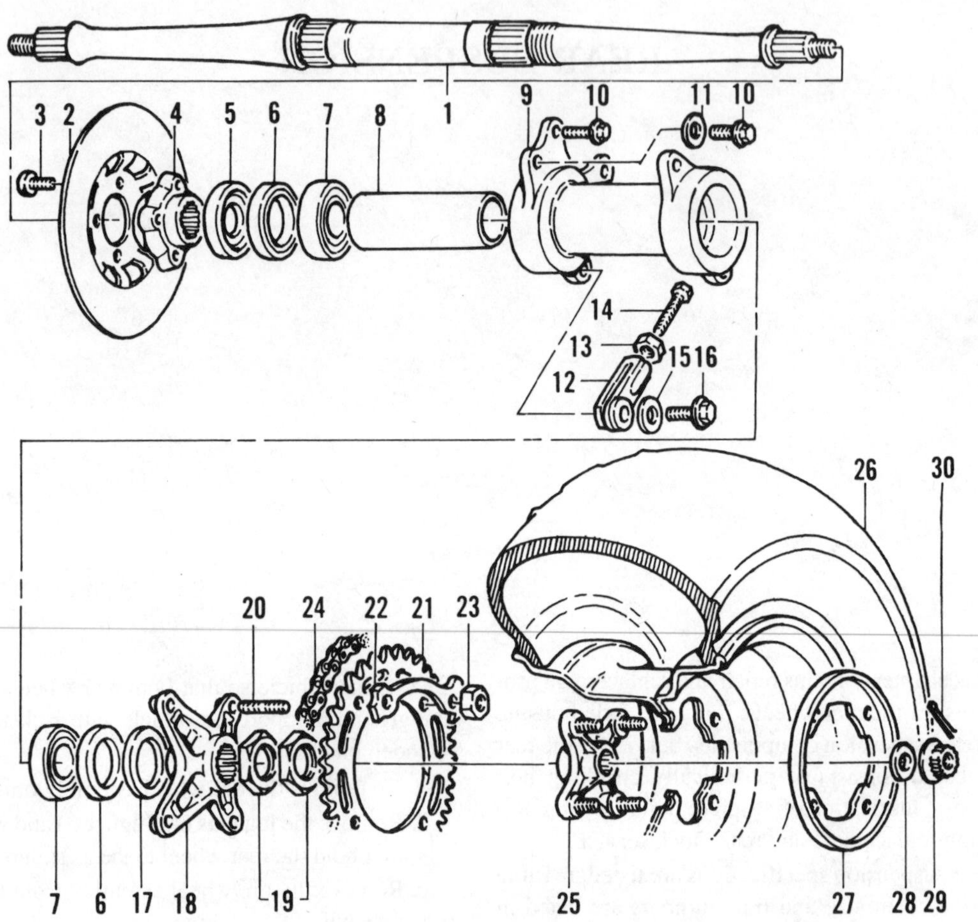

1. Rear axle
2. Brake disc
3. Bolt
4. Disc hub
5. Hub dust cover (1987)
6. Oil seal
7. Bearing
8. Spacer
9. Axle housing
10. Bolt
11. Washer
12. Chain adjuster
13. Locknut
14. Adjust bolt
15. Washer
16. Bolt
17. Hub dust cover
18. Sprocket hub
19. Axle nuts
20. Sprocket studs
21. Driven sprocket
22. Lockwasher
23. Nut
24. Drive chain
25. Axle hub
26. Rear wheel
27. Reinforcement plate (1987)
28. Washer
29. Axle nut
30. Cotter pin

(2)

REAR AXLE (1989-ON)

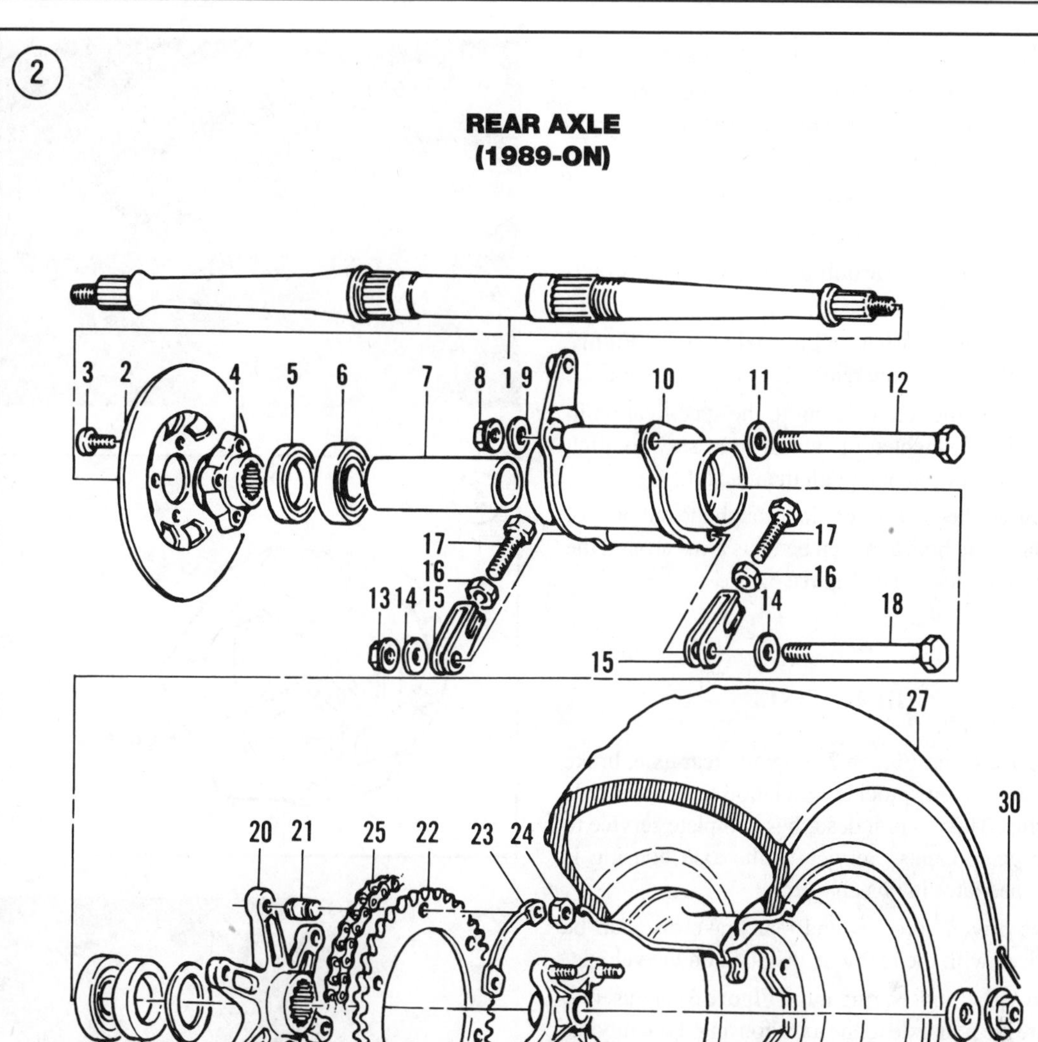

1. Rear axle
2. Brake disc
3. Bolt
4. Disc hub
5. Oil seal
6. Bearing
7. Spacer
8. Nut
9. Washer
10. Axle housing
11. Washer
12. Bolt
13. Nut
14. Lockwasher
15. Chain adjuster
16. Locknut
17. Adjust bolt
18. Bolt
19. Dust hub cover
20. Sprocket hub
21. Stud
22. Driven sprocket
23. Lockwasher
24. Nut
25. Drive chain
26. Axle hub
27. Tire/wheel assembly
28. Washer
29. Axle nut
30. Cotter pin

b. Install the washers and lug nuts (A, **Figure 3**) that secure the rear wheel to the rear axle hub. Finger tighten the lug nuts at first. Then torque to the specification in **Table 3**.

5B. If the tire/wheel assembly and the rear axle hub were removed, perform the following:

a. Slide the rear axle hub and wheel assembly onto the rear axle splines.

b. Install the washer and the axle nut (B, **Figure 3**) that secure the rear axle hub to the rear axle.

c. Torque the rear axle nut to the specification in **Table 3**. Tighten the nut, if necessary, to align the cotter pin hole with the nut slot.

d. Insert the new cotter pin through the nut groove and axle hole and then bend its arms around the nut to lock it; see **Figure 4**.

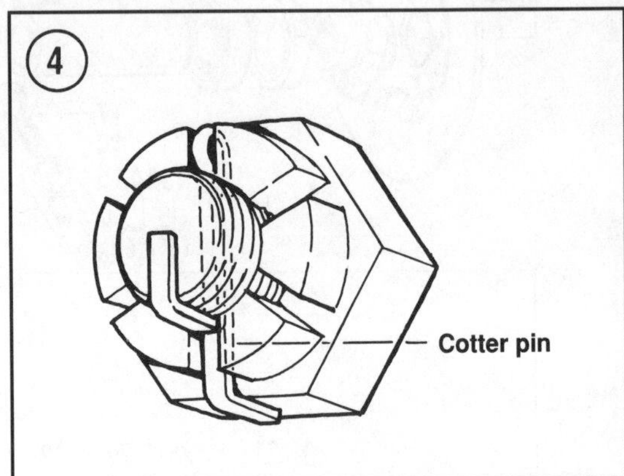

REAR AXLE

Figure 1 and **Figure 2** show the rear axle, brake disc and driven sprocket in relation to the rear axle housing. This section describes complete service to these components. Service to the axle housing is described later in this chapter.

The driven sprocket and rear brake disc can be removed with the rear axle installed on the vehicle.

On early models, ring nuts (**Figure 5**) are used to secure the rear axle to the axle housing. Late models are equipped with hex nuts (**Figure 6**). Replacement ring nuts are no longer available through Yamaha dealers. If ring nuts are ordered, the part number will be superseded and you will receive hex nuts. Because the ring nuts are difficult to remove and tighten, it is suggested that you discard the ring nuts and install hex nuts during reassembly.

When removing and installing the rear axle, a special wrench is required to loosen and tighten the axle housing nuts. Use the Yamaha axle nut wrench (part No. YM-37132 [**Figure 7**]) or an equivalent wrench that can be used with a torque wrench. Proper tightening of the axle housing nuts is critical in preventing the nuts from backing off and the axle from loosening in the housing.

To avoid starting a procedure that you may be unable to complete, read the following sections through before starting work. Note any tool that you may need and acquire it before starting.

7

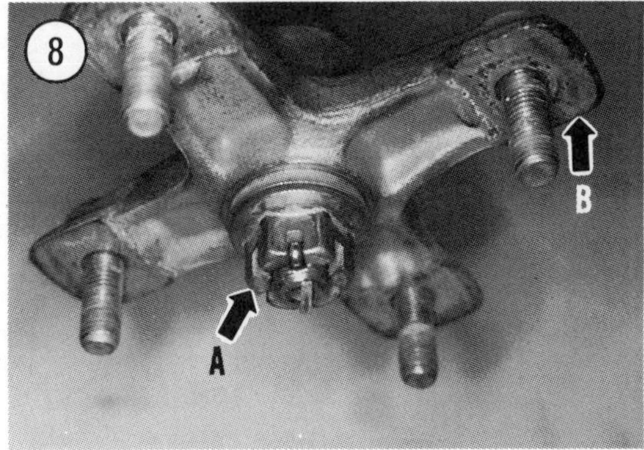

8

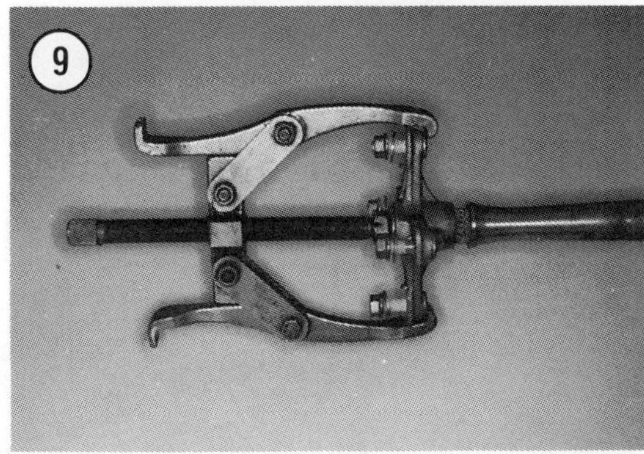
9

10

Removal

1. Park the vehicle on level ground and set the parking brake.
2. Support the vehicle and remove both rear wheels as described in this chapter.
3. Remove the axle hub from the axle as follows:
   a. Remove and discard the axle nut cotter pin.
   b. Loosen the nut (A, **Figure 8**) securing the axle hub to the rear axle. Then remove the nut and washer.
   c. Slide the axle hub (B, **Figure 8**) off the axle and remove it. If the axle hub is stuck on the axle, remove it with a puller as shown in **Figure 9**.

CAUTION
*The axle hub is designed to be a sliding fit on the axle. However, corrosion built up on the mating hub and axle splines (**Figure 10**) can make axle hub removal difficult. Do not drive the axle hub off of the axle with a hammer as the force may bend one of the axle hub arms. Use a puller as previously described.*

4. Remove the axle nuts from the axle as follows:

CAUTION
The inner and outer axle nuts have had a thread locking compound applied to their threads during assembly and are tightened to a high torque valve (240 N•m [170 ft.-lb.]). The ring nuts are difficult to remove. Do not heat the axle nuts in order to remove them, as the heat may ruin the heat-treated hardness of the axle.

   a. Clean the exposed axle threads with contact cleaner and dry with compressed air.

NOTE
Because the thread sealing compound applied to the axle nuts may spread to the sides of the nuts when they are tightened, hold the inner axle nut when loosening the outer axle nut.

WARNING
Safety glasses must be worn when removing the ring nuts with a punch and hammer.

   b. On models with ring nuts, loosen and remove the outer ring nut with a large punch and hammer. Clean the exposed axle threads and then spray the axle threads with a penetrating lubricant (**Figure 11**).

c. On models with hex nuts, loosen and remove the outer nut with the Yamaha rear axle nut wrench (**Figure 12**) and a breaker bar. Clean the exposed axle threads (**Figure 13**) and then spray the axle threads with a penetrating lubricant.
d. Loosen and remove the inside axle nut.

5. Remove the drive chain, if you have not already done so, as described in this chapter.

6. Release the parking brake at the handlebar.

7. Remove the bolts (A, **Figure 14**) holding the rear brake caliper to the axle housing. Then slide the brake caliper (B, **Figure 14**) off the brake disc. Make a hook out of a piece of stiff wire and hang the caliper from it so that weight is not placed on the brake hose.

NOTE
Insert a wooden or plastic spacer in the caliper between the brake pads. That way, if the brake lever is inadvertently pressed, the piston will not be forced out of the caliper bore. If this does happen, the caliper will probably have to be disassembled to reseat the piston and the rear brake will have to be bled.

8. Slide the driven sprocket and its collar (**Figure 15**) off of the axle and remove it.

9. Drive the rear axle out of the axle housing as follows:

a. Make sure the vehicle is secured on a stand.
b. Slide the left-hand axle hub (A, **Figure 16**) onto the axle.

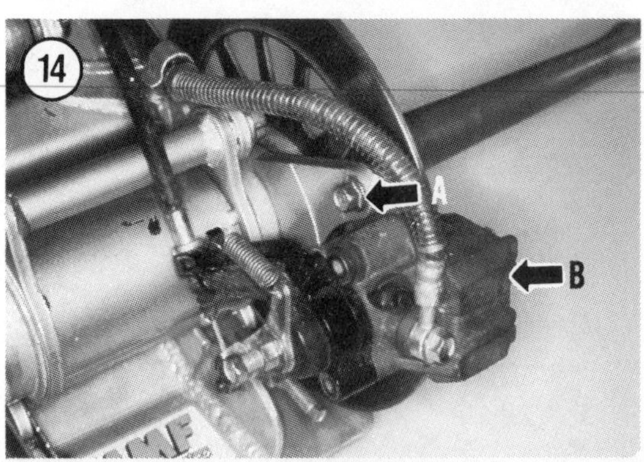

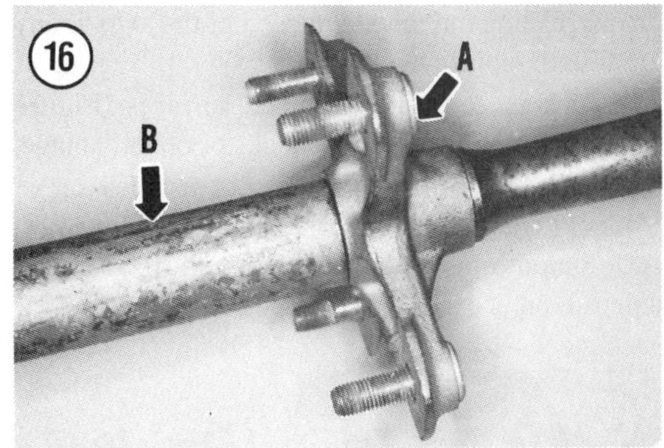

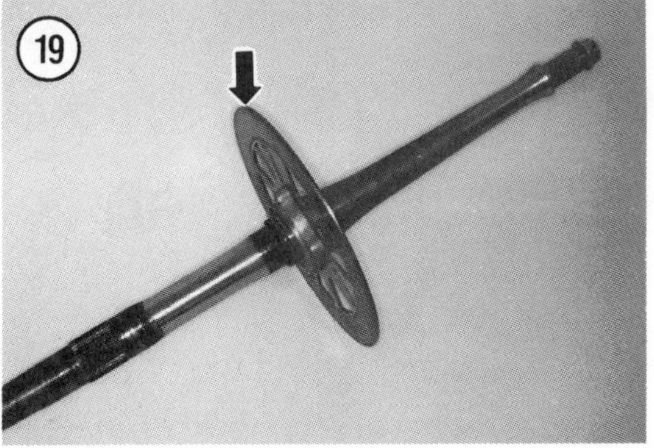

WARNING

Safety glasses must be worn when driving the axle out of the axle housing in the following steps.

CAUTION

When removing the rear axle, never hit directly against the axle with a hammer as this will damage the axle. Use a piece of pipe as described in the following procedure.

c. Center a piece of pipe against the axle hub as shown in B, **Figure 16**. Hit the pipe with a hammer and remove the axle from the right-hand side.

NOTE

*If the axle housing oil seals and bearings have not been properly serviced, the axle may be difficult to remove. What normally happens is that the axle housing spacer (8, **Figure 1** or 7, **Figure 2**) becomes rusted to the axle shaft. Then, when removing the axle, the spacer forces the right-hand bearing and oil seal out of the axle housing as the axle is driven out. See **Figure 17**. If this happens, refer to **Axle Disassembly** to remove the spacer, bearing, oil seal and brake disc.*

d. When the axle is free of the axle housing, remove the left-hand axle hub (A, **Figure 16**) and carefully slide the axle out of the axle housing and remove it. See **Figure 18**.

e. Slide the brake disc assembly (**Figure 19**) off of the axle and remove it.

10. Inspect the axle housing oil seal (**Figure 20**) and bearings as described under *Inspection* in this chapter.

11. Inspect the axle as described in this chapter.

Axle Disassembly

If the axle housing spacer, right-hand bearing and right-hand oil seal (**Figure 17**) came off with the axle when the axle was removed, remove them as follows:

1. Assemble a bearing splitter and puller onto the axle as shown in **Figure 21**. Then tighten the puller to pull the spacer (**Figure 22**) off of the axle and remove it.

CAUTION

When pressing out the axle in Step 2, it will fall to the floor when the right-hand bearing is free of the axle. Support the axle so that it does not fall.

2. Support the axle assembly in a press (**Figure 23**) and press the axle off of the right-hand bearing and the right-hand oil seal.
3. Remove the axle from the press and slide off the brake disc assembly.

Inspection

1. Wash the axle in solvent and dry thoroughly. Handle the axle carefully to avoid scoring the bearing surfaces and splines on the axle.
2. Inspect the axle for signs of fatigue, fractures and other damage. Inspect the splines (**Figure 24**) for wear or damage.
3. Check the hole at each end of the axle where the cotter pin fits. Make sure there are no fractures or cracks leading out toward the end of the axle. If any are found, replace the axle.
4. Check the bearing machined surfaces (**Figure 25**) on the axle for scoring, cracks or other damage.
5. Check the axle for straightness using a set of V-blocks and a dial indicator as shown in **Figure 26**. Axle runout must not exceed 1.5 mm (0.06 in.). If axle runout is excessive, replace the axle.

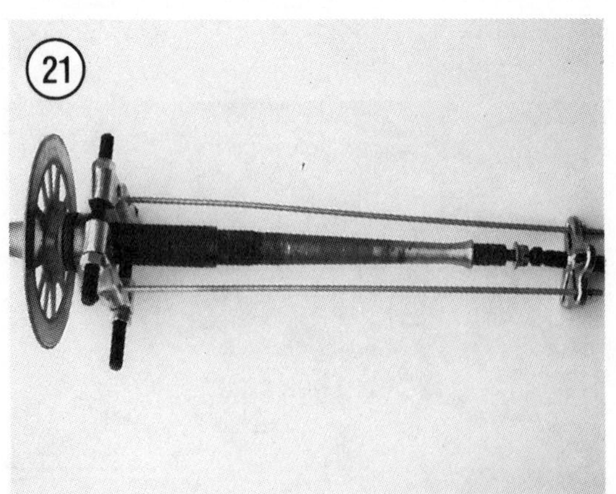

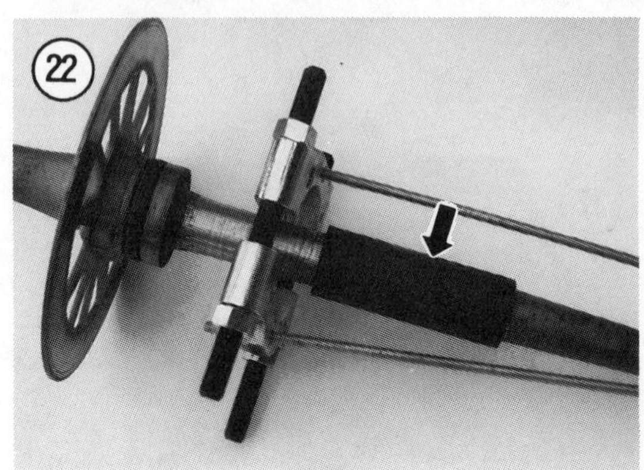

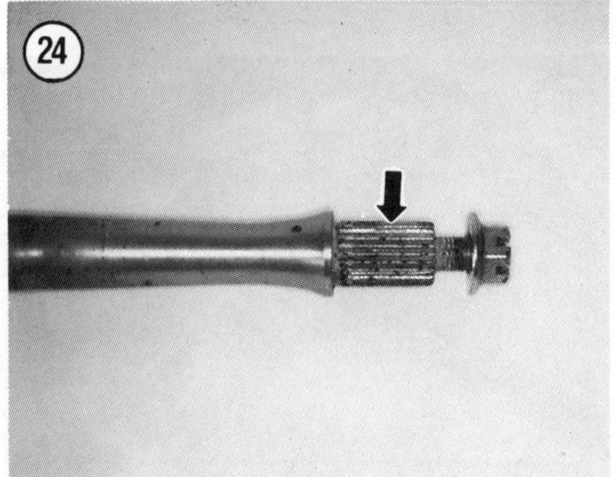

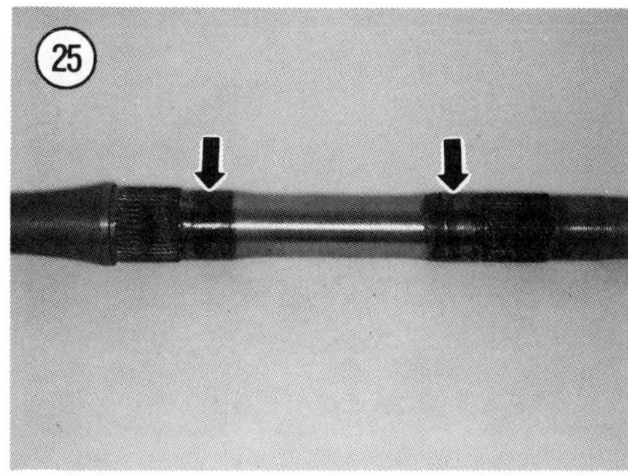

WARNING
Do not attempt to straighten a bent axle. Axle failure may occur during riding and cause loss of control and severe personal injury.

6. Inspect the axle nuts (**Figure 27**) for wear or damage. Replace the axle nuts if the threads are damaged or if the hex portion of the nut is rounded over or damaged.

7. Inspect the driven sprocket hub (**Figure 28**) and brake disc hub (A, **Figure 29**) splines for severe wear or damage. Replace the hub(s) if necessary.

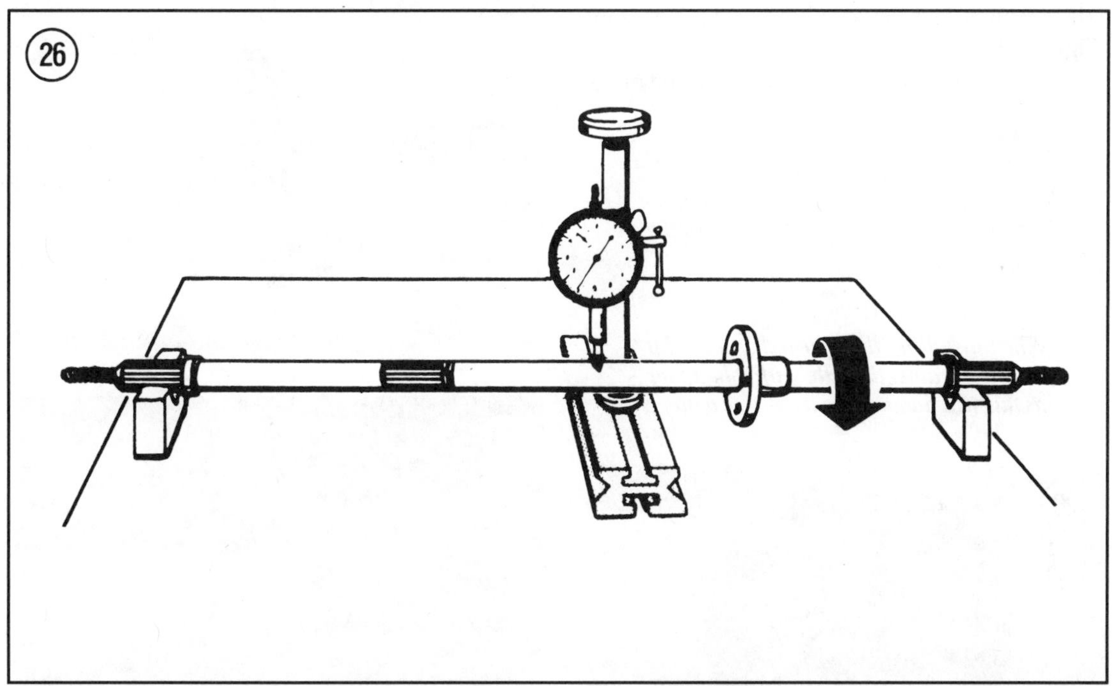

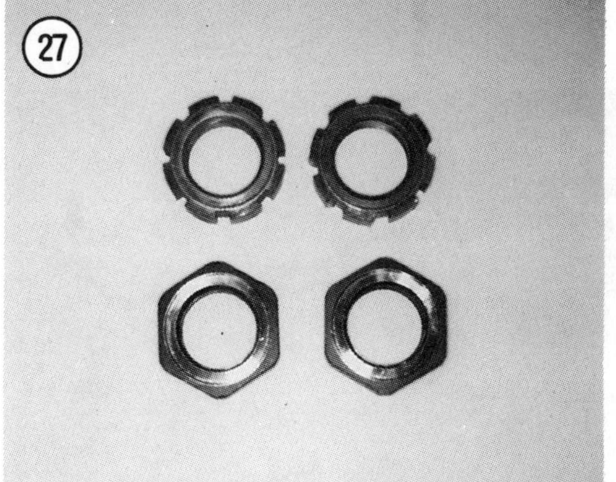

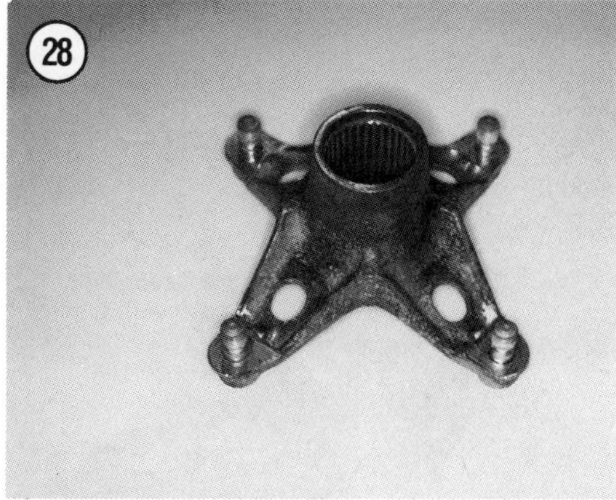

8. Inspect the oil seal surfaces on the driven sprocket hub (**Figure 30**) and brake disc hub for severe wear, scoring or other damage.

Installation

1. Apply a light coat of wheel bearing grease to the lips of both axle housing oil seals (**Figure 31**).
2. Apply a light coat of grease onto the brake disc hub shoulder (B, **Figure 29**). Then slide the brake disc hub onto the axle and seat it against the right-hand axle shoulder as shown in **Figure 32**.
3. Working from the right-hand side, slide the rear axle assembly into the axle housing until it stops (**Figure 33**).
4. Slide the right-hand axle hub onto the end of the axle as shown in **Figure 34**.

WARNING
Safety glasses must be worn when driving the axle into the axle housing in the following steps.

CAUTION
When installing the rear axle, never hit directly against the axle with a hammer as this will damage the axle. Use a piece

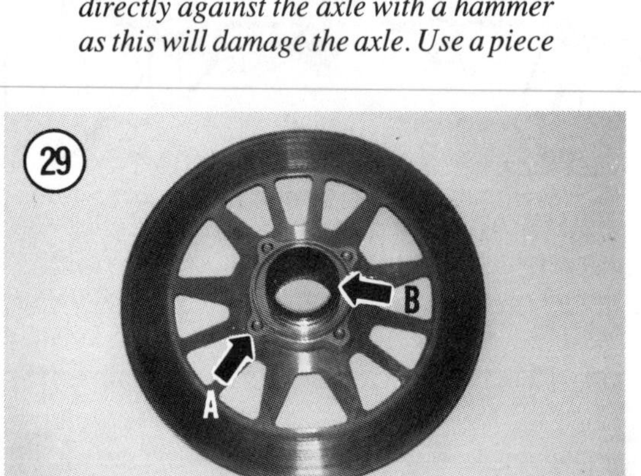

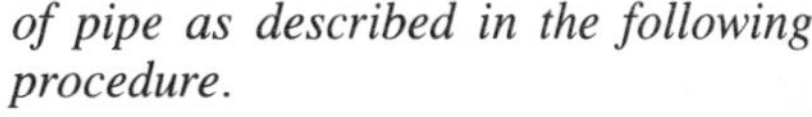

of pipe as described in the following procedure.

5. Center a piece of pipe against the axle hub as shown in **Figure 35**. Hit the pipe with a hammer and drive the axle through the right-hand bearing until the left-hand axle bearing race passes through the right-hand bearing. Then stop and slide the axle inward until the right-hand bearing race (**Figure 36**) contacts the right-hand bearing. Hit the pipe with a hammer once again and continue to drive the axle into the left- and right-hand bearings until it stops when the shoulder on the brake disc hub bottoms against the right-hand bearing. See **Figure 37**.
6. Spin the axle by hand. It should turn smoothly with no roughness, binding or excessive noise.
7. Apply a light coat of wheel bearing grease onto the driven sprocket hub shoulder (**Figure 30**). Then slide the driven sprocket hub onto the axle splines (**Figure 38**) and push it into the axle housing until it bottoms. See **Figure 39**.
8. Remove the plastic spacer from between the brake pads in the brake caliper.
9. Slide the brake caliper (**Figure 40**) over the brake disc. Install the 2 bolts holding the brake caliper to

the axle housing. Torque the brake caliper bolts to the specification in **Table 3**.

NOTE
To make sure the brake pads are seated against the brake disc, depress the brake pedal several times.

10. Set the parking brake.
11. Using the Yamaha rear axle nut wrench (YM-37132) and a torque wrench, tighten the rear axle nuts as follows:
  a. Apply Loctite 271 (red) to the threads on the rear axle.
  b. Install the inside nut (**Figure 41**) and tighten hand tight.

NOTE
The Yamaha rear axle nut wrench (YM-37132) or an equivalent tool is required to tighten the rear axle nuts. Because the rear axle nut wrench is a horizontal adapter, it effectively lengthens the torque wrench; the torque value indicated on the torque wrench will not be the same amount of torque actually applied to the axle nuts. When using a torque wrench with a horizontal adapter, it is necessary to recalculate the torque readings. To calculate the amount of torque indicated at the torque wrench when applying a specific amount of torque to the axle nuts, you must know: The lever length of the torque wrench, the center-to-center length of the torque adapter, and the correct amount of actual torque desired at the axle nuts. ***Figure 42*** *shows how to do this. The actual torque readings for the inside and outside axle nuts are listed in the following steps.*

  c. Using the information in **Figure 42**, determine the indicated torque valves for the following 3 torque specifications: (1) 55 N•m (40 ft.-lb.); (2) 190 N•m (140 ft.-lb.); and (3) 240 N•m (177 ft.-lb.).

41

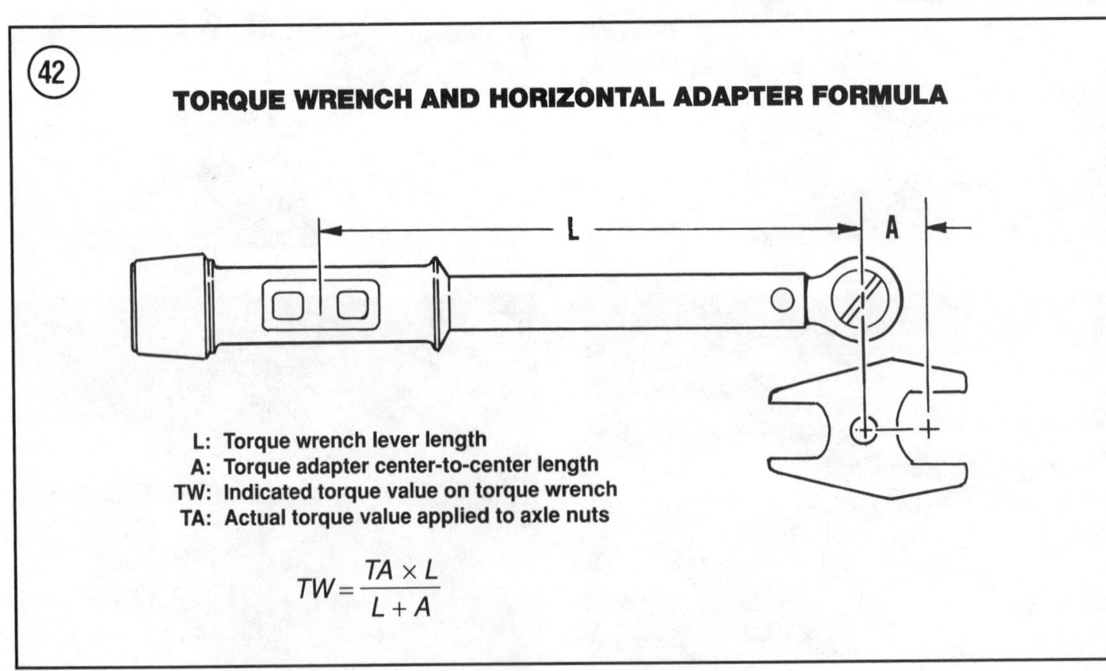

$$TW = \frac{TA \times L}{L + A}$$

d. Mount the rear axle nut wrench onto a torque wrench.

e. Tighten the inside axle nut to 55 N•m (40 ft.-lb.). See **Figure 43**.

NOTE

*In **Figure 43**, note how the axle nut wrench extends straight from the end of the torque wrench. This position is critical to ensuring the accuracy of the computed torque reading. If the axle nut wrench is angled on the torque wrench, the torque applied to the nut will be incorrect.*

f. Install the outside axle nut (A, **Figure 44**) and hand tighten it against the inside axle nut (B, **Figure 44**).

g. Hold the inside nut (B, **Figure 44**) and tighten the outside nut (A, **Figure 44**) to 190 N•m (140 ft.-lb.).

h. Draw a straight line across the inside and outside axle nuts as shown in **Figure 45**.

i. Hold the outside axle nut (A, **Figure 44**) and turn the inside axle nut (B, **Figure 44**) back (turn torque wrench clockwise) against the outside nut to a torque reading of 240 N•m (177 ft.-lb.).

j. Now measure the distance between the 2 straight lines made in sub-step h; see **Figure 46**. If the measured distance is less than 3 mm (0.12 in.), retighten the inside nut against the outside nut as described in sub-step i. Then remeasure the distance once again, and retorque as required to obtain a minimum distance of 3 mm (0.12 in.). See **Figure 47**.

12. Install the drive chain as described in this chapter.
13. Slide the axle hub (**Figure 48**) onto the axle.
14. Install the large flat washer onto the axle shaft.
15. Hand-thread the axle nut onto the axle. Then tighten the axle nut (**Figure 48**) to the torque specification in **Table 3**. Tighten the axle nut, if necessary, to align the cotter pin hole with the nut slot.

WARNING
Always install a new cotter pin.

16. Insert the new cotter pin through the nut groove and rear axle hole and then bend its arms to lock it as shown in **Figure 49**.
17. Install the rear wheels as described in this chapter.

REAR AXLE HOUSING

The rear axle housing is bolted to the rear swing arm. Four bolts are used on 1987-1988 models. On 1989 and later models, 2 long bolts are used. These bolts are loosened during chain adjustment and should be checked periodically for looseness or damage.

The rear axle housing is equipped with 2 ball bearings, 2 oil seals and an axle housing spacer. The bearings are pressed into the rear axle housing and should be installed with a hydraulic press and suitable bearing drivers.

Figure 50 and **Figure 51** shows the axle housing and its components in relationship to the rear axle and axle hub components.

Bearing Preliminary Inspection

Before removing the rear axle housing, check the bearings as follows:

1. Remove the rear axle as described in this chapter.
2. Wipe off all excessive grease from both bearings.
3. Inspect each bearing (**Figure 52**) for visual damage. Check for overheating, a broken or cracked cage and corrosion. If the oil seals are damaged, moisture will have entered the axle housing, producing corrosion on the bearing, axle and spacer.
4. Turn each bearing (**Figure 52**) by hand. The bearings should turn smoothly with no roughness, catching, binding or excessive noise. Some axial play (end play) is normal, but radial play should be negligible; see **Figure 53**.
5. Replace the bearings, if necessary, as described in this chapter.

Removal

1. Remove the rear axle as described in this chapter.
2. Remove the bolts and the washers that hold the rear axle housing to the rear swing arm; see **Figure 50** or **Figure 51**.
3. Slide the rear axle housing (**Figure 54**) away from the swing arm and remove it. Remove the 2 chain adjusters.

CAUTION
Double shielded bearings are used. Do not wash these bearings in solvent or any other chemical as the chemical may enter the bearing and contaminate the grease.

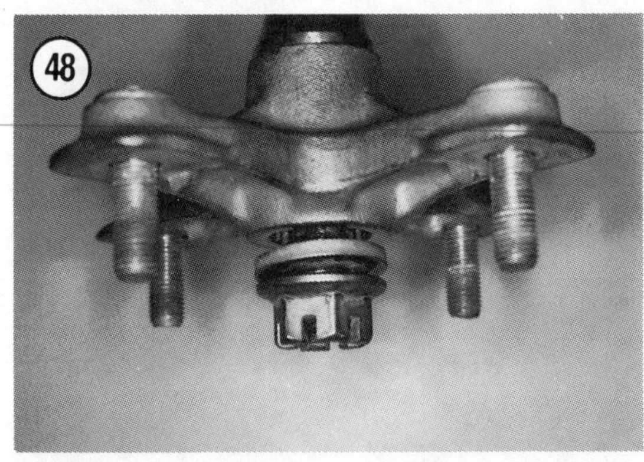

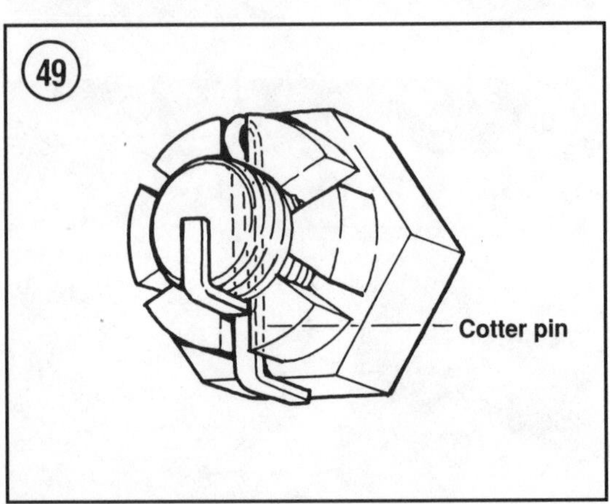

REAR AXLE (1987-1988)

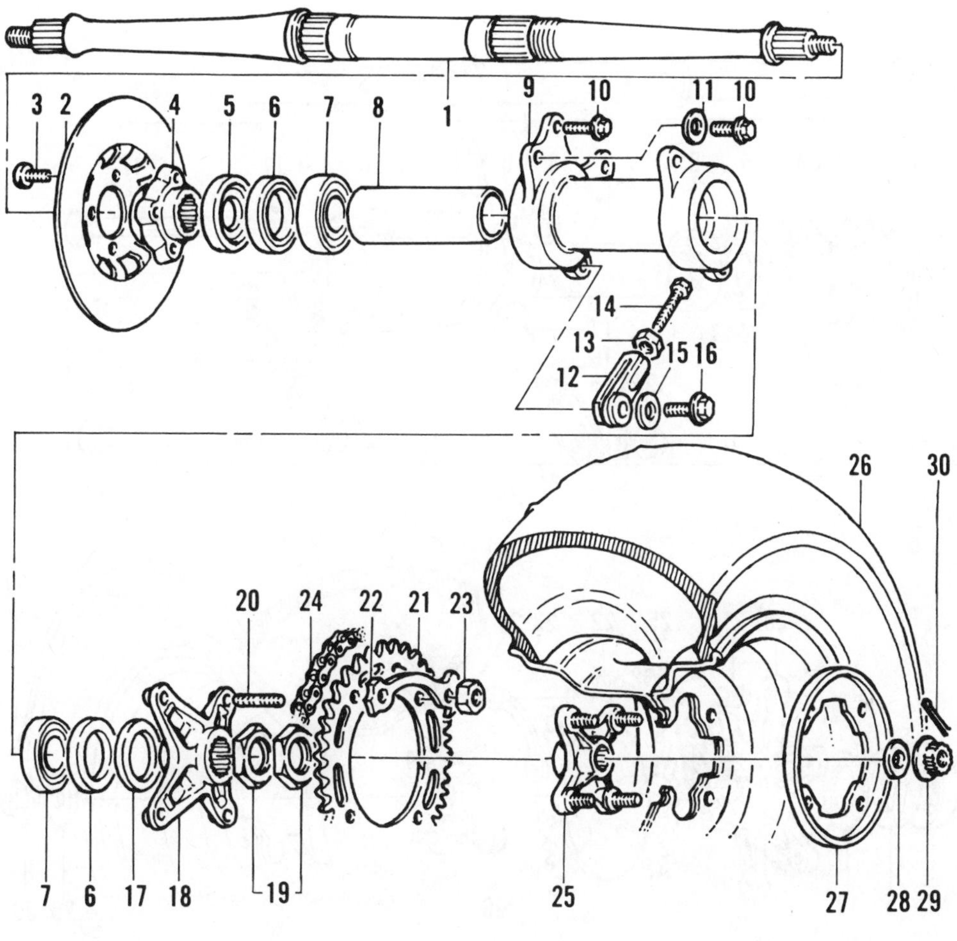

1. Rear axle
2. Brake disc
3. Bolt
4. Disc hub
5. Hub dust cover (1987)
6. Oil seal
7. Bearing
8. Spacer
9. Axle housing
10. Bolt
11. Washer
12. Chain adjuster
13. Locknut
14. Adjust bolt
15. Washer
16. Bolt
17. Hub dust cover
18. Sprocket hub
19. Axle nuts
20. Sprocket studs
21. Driven sprocket
22. Lockwasher
23. Nut
24. Drive chain
25. Axle hub
26. Rear wheel
27. Reinforcement plate (1987)
28. Washer
29. Axle nut
30. Cotter pin

(51)

REAR AXLE (1989-ON)

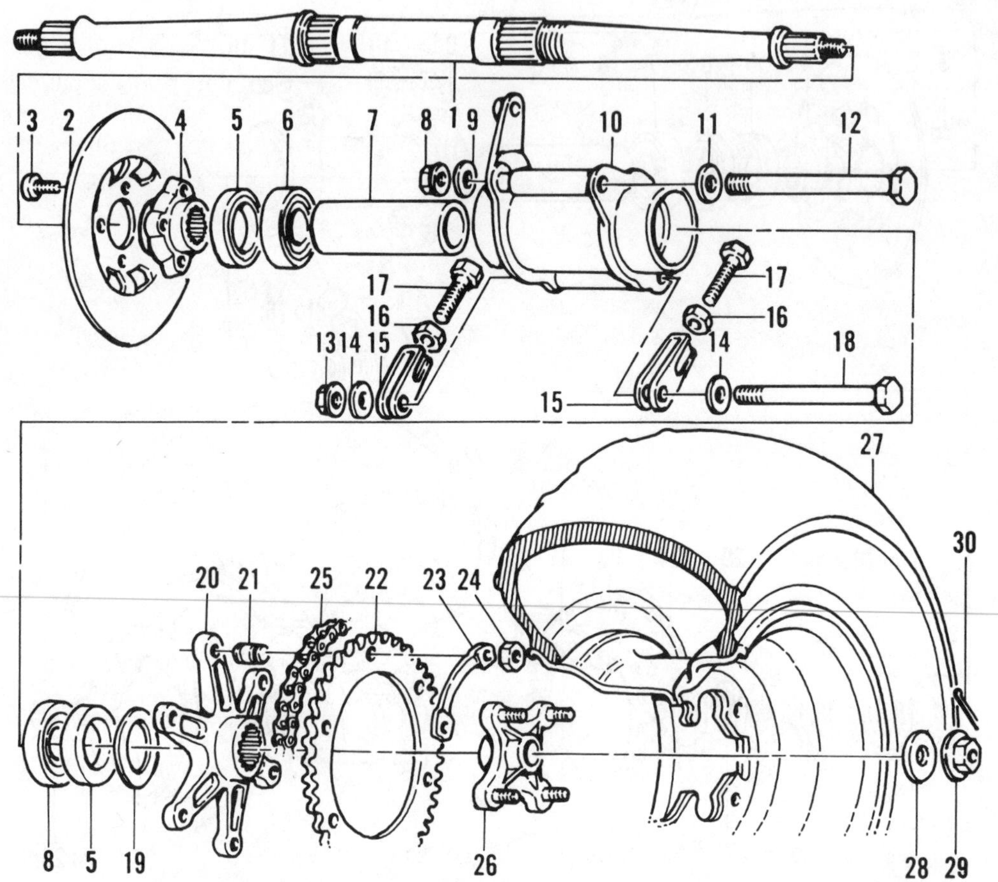

1. Rear axle
2. Brake disc
3. Bolt
4. Disc hub
5. Oil seal
6. Bearing
7. Spacer
8. Nut
9. Washer
10. Axle housing
11. Washer
12. Bolt
13. Nut
14. Lockwasher
15. Chain adjuster
16. Locknut
17. Adjust bolt
18. Bolt
19. Dust hub cover
20. Sprocket hub
21. Stud
22. Driven sprocket
23. Lockwasher
24. Nut
25. Drive chain
26. Axle hub
27. Tire/wheel assembly
28. Washer
29. Axle nut
30. Cotter pin

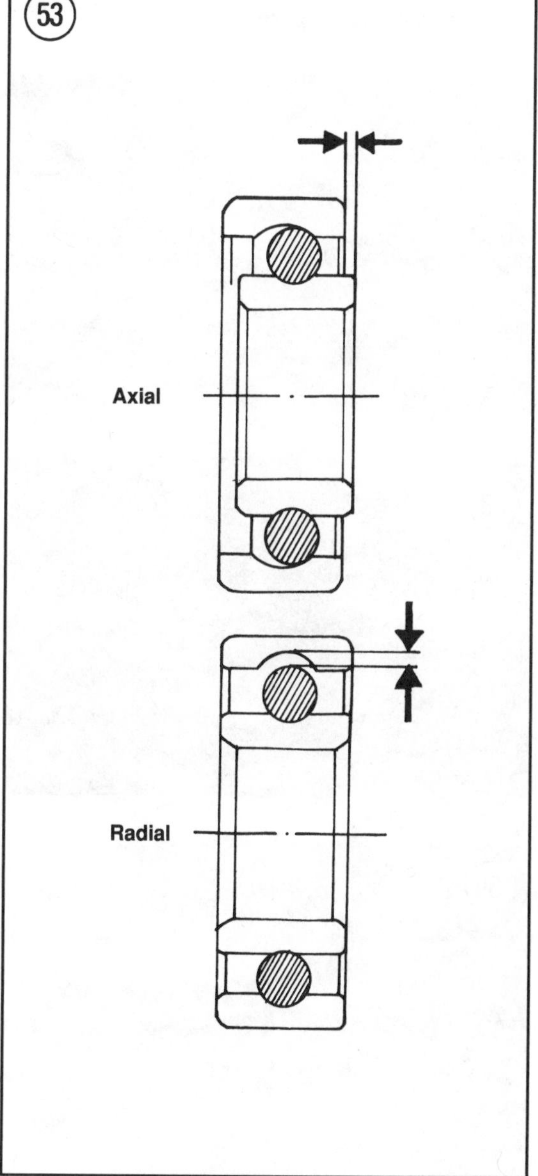

Disassembly

NOTE
*If the right-hand bearing and spacer came off with the rear axle (**Figure 17**), remove them as described under **Axle Disassembly**; see **Rear Axle** in this chapter.*

1. Pry the oil seals out of the axle housing with a wide-blade screwdriver as shown in **Figure 55**. Pad the screwdriver to prevent it from damaging the axle housing bore.
2. Insert a drift into one side of the axle housing.
3. Push the spacer over to one side and place the drift on the inner race of the opposite bearing.
4. Tap the bearing out of the hub with a hammer, working around the perimeter of the bearing's inner race to prevent the bearing from binding in the housing bore.
5. Remove the bearing and spacer.
6. Tap out the opposite bearing with a suitable driver inserted through the axle housing.

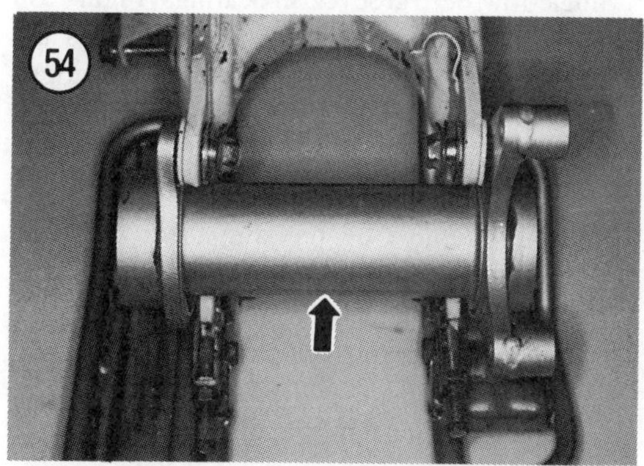

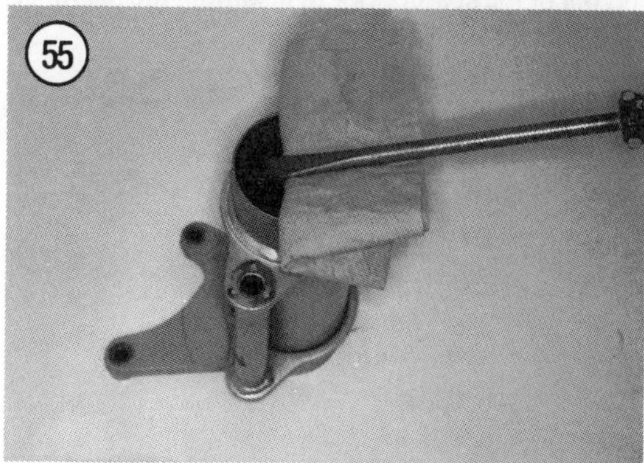

Inspection

1. Clean the axle housing in solvent and dry with compressed air.
2. Remove all corrosion and rust from the spacer with a steel brush or a wire wheel mounted in a drill. Then clean the spacer and dry with compressed air.
3. Check the center spacer for cracks, distortion or other damage. Replace if necessary.
4. Check the axle housing bores (**Figure 56**) for cracks or other damage. Remove any burrs or nicks with a file or fine sandpaper.

NOTE

If one or both bearings are loose in their respective housing bore, do not center punch or rough up the area to increase its bore size. Installing the bearing will flatten these areas, causing the bearing to run loose once again. If the axle housing bearing bores are severely worn or damaged, replace the axle housing.

Reassembly

Single-row, deep groove ball bearings (**Figure 57**) are used in the axle housing. Both bearings are double-shielded. Prior to installing new bearings and oil seals, note the following:

a. Install bearings with their manufacturer's code marks and numbers facing out.
b. Install bearings by pressing them into axle housing with a socket or bearing driver that seats against the outer bearing race only.
c. Install oil seals with their closed side facing out.
d. Refer to *Ball Bearing Replacement* in Chapter One for additional information.

1. Blow any dirt or foreign matter out of the housing and out of the spacer prior to installing the bearings.

56

2. Press in the first bearing until it bottoms in the axle housing bearing bore (**Figure 58**).
3. Turn the axle housing over and install the spacer (A, **Figure 59**).
4. Press in the second bearing (B, **Figure 59**) until it bottoms in the axle housing bearing bore or just contacts the spacer.
5. Remove the axle housing and check that both bearings (**Figure 60**) turn smoothly.
6. Pack the lip of each oil seal with a waterproof bearing grease.
7. Press in the first oil seal until its outer surface is flush with or slightly below the oil seal bore inside surface as shown in **Figure 61**.

57

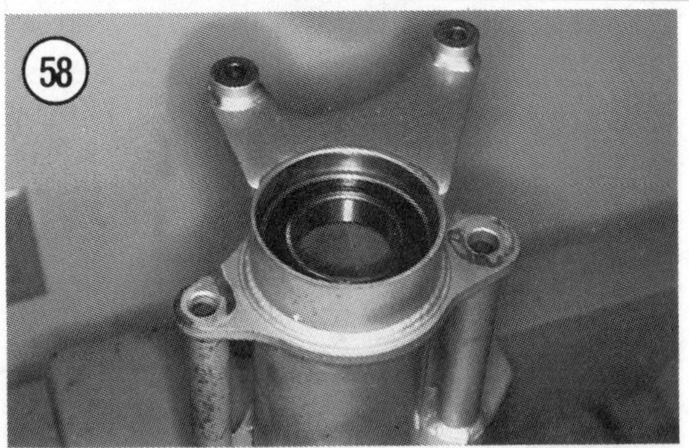
58

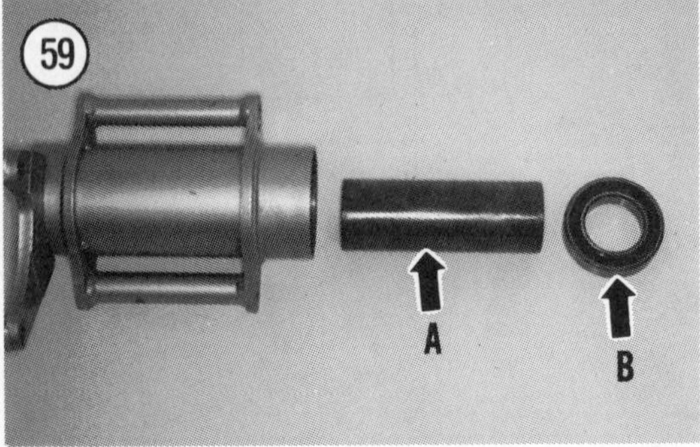
59

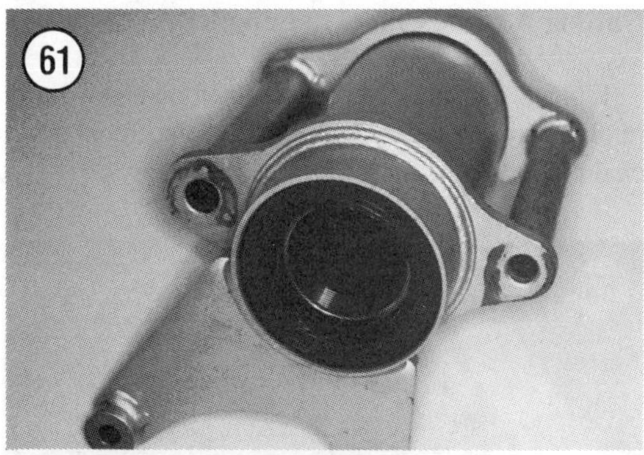

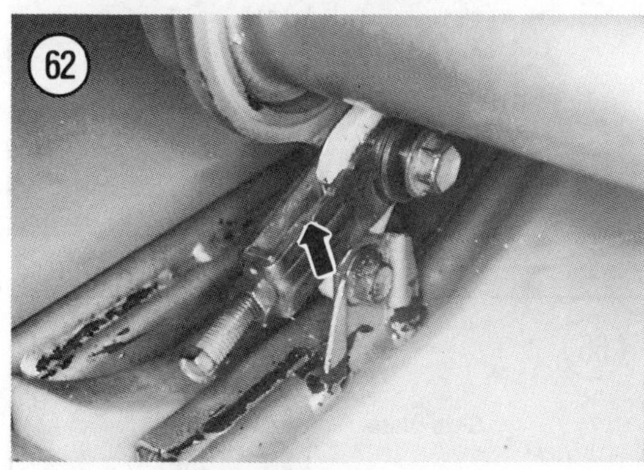

8. Repeat Step 7 to install the second oil seal.

Installation

1. Install the axle housing (**Figure 54**) into the swing arm.
2. Install the chain adjusters so that they are positioned between the swing arm and axle housing. Adjustment marks on chain adjusters must be facing up as shown in **Figure 62**.

3A. On 1987-1988 models, install the bolts and washers securing the axle housing to the swing arm as shown in **Figure 50**.

3B. On 1989-on models, install the 2 bolts, washers and nuts securing the axle housing to the swing arm. Install the bolts from the left-hand side (**Figure 63**).

4. Install the rear axle as described in this chapter.
5. Install the drive chain as described in this chapter.
6. Adjust the drive chain as described in Chapter Three. Then tighten the upper and lower bolts/nuts that secure the axle housing to the swing arm to the torque specification listed in **Table 3**.

DRIVE CHAIN

A 520 O-ring drive chain was originally installed on all models. O-ring drive chains are equipped with rubber O-rings between each side plate. The master link is equipped with 4 removable O-rings (**Figure 64**). O-ring chains are internally lubricated at the

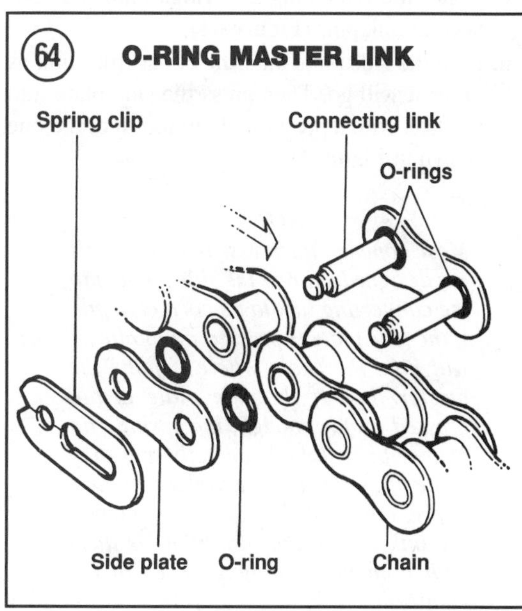

time of manufacture and assembly. The O-rings are designed to seal in the chains lubricant while keeping dirt and moisture out.

Table 2 lists drive chain specifications.

Removal/Installation

1. Support the vehicle with both rear wheels off the ground.
2. Turn the rear axle and drive chain until the master link is accessible.
3. Remove the master link spring clip with a pair of pliers.
4. Use a chain breaker to separate the side plate from the master link (**Figure 65**). Then remove the side plate and the 2 outside O-rings (**Figure 64**).
5. Push out the connecting link and remove the 2 inside O-rings (**Figure 64**).
6. Pull the drive chain off of the drive sprocket and remove it.
7. Install by reversing these removal steps while noting the following.
8. Assemble the drive chain and install the master link as follows:
   a. Install an O-ring on each connecting link pin (**Figure 64**).
   b. Insert the connecting link through the chain to join it together.
   c. Install the remaining 2 O-rings onto the connecting link pins (**Figure 64**).
   d. Push the side plate onto the connecting link as far as it will go. Then press the side plate into position with a press-fit chain tool like the one shown in **Figure 66**.

NOTE

Most commercial press-fit chain tools are designed to press the side plate onto the connecting link to its correct depth. If the side plate is pressed on too far, it will bind the chain where it joins the master link. If the side plate is not pressed on far enough, the spring clip cannot be installed correctly and may come off. What you are looking to do is to press the side plate onto the connecting link so that the slide plate is flush with both pin seating grooves in the connecting link.

CAUTION

Attempting to install a press-fit master link without the proper tools may cause you to damage the master link and drive chain.

   e. Install the spring clip on the master link so that the closed end of the clip is facing the direction of chain travel (**Figure 67**).

9. Adjust the drive chain as described in Chapter Three.

Cutting A Drive Chain To Length

Table 2 lists the correct number of chain links required for stock gearing. If your replacement drive chain is too long, cut it to length as follows.

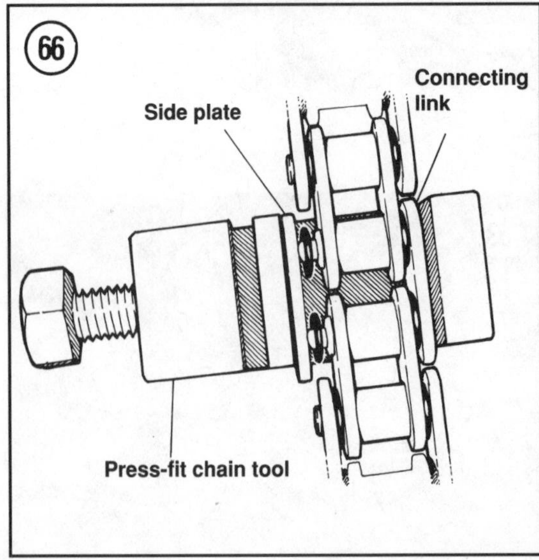

1. Remove the new chain from its box and stretch it out on your workbench. Set the master link aside for now.
2. Refer to **Table 2** for the correct number of links for your chain, then count the links out on the new chain. Make a chalk mark on the 2 chain pins where you want to cut it. Count the chain links one more time just to make sure you are correct.

WARNING
A bench grinder or hand-operated high-speed grinding tool is required to grind the chain pins when cutting the chain. When using this equipment, safety glasses must be worn.

3. Grind the head of two pins flush with the face of the side plate with a grinder or suitable grinding tool.
4. Next, use a chain breaker or a punch and hammer and lightly tap the pins out of the side plate; support the chain carefully when doing this. If the pins are still tight, grind more material from the end of the pins and then try again.
5. Remove the side plate and push out the connecting link.

Drive Chain Cleaning/Lubrication

CAUTION
The O-rings can be easily damaged by improper cleaning and handling of the drive chain. Do not use a steam cleaner, a high-pressure washer or any solvent that may damage the rubber O-rings.

1. Remove the drive chain as described in this chapter.

2. Immerse the chain in a pan of kerosene and allow it to soak for about half an hour. Move it around and flex it during this period so that the dirt between the links, pins, rollers and O-rings can work its way out.

CAUTION
In the next step, do not use a wire brush to clean the chain or the O-rings will be damaged and the drive chain must be replaced.

3. Lightly scrub the rollers with a soft brush and rinse away loosened dirt. Do not scrub hard or use a hard brush as the O-rings may be damaged. Rinse the chain a couple of times in kerosene to make sure all dirt and grit are washed out. Hang the chain up over a pan and allow the chain to dry thoroughly.

4. After cleaning the chain, examine it carefully for wear or damage. Check the O-rings for damage. Replace the chain if necessary.

5. Externally lubricate the chain with SAE 30-50 weight motor oil or a good grade of chain lubricant (non-tacky) specifically formulated for O-ring chains, following the manufacturer's instructions.

CAUTION
Do not use a tacky chain lubricant on O-ring chains. Dirt and other abrasive materials that stick to the lubricant will grind away at the O-rings and damage them. Remember, an O-ring chain is pre-lubricated during its assembly at the factory. External oiling is only required to prevent chain rust and to keep the O-rings pliable.

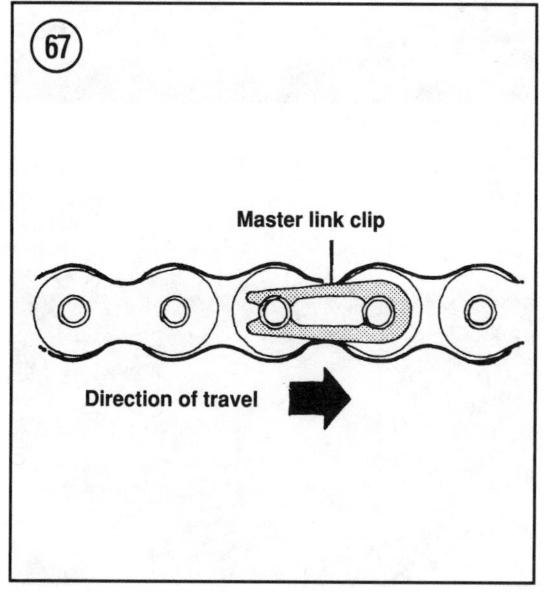

DRIVEN SPROCKET

The driven sprocket rides on a hub that is mounted on the rear axle. The driven sprocket can be removed without having to remove the rear axle from the vehicle. See **Figure 50** or **Figure 51**.

Inspection

Check the sprocket teeth for severe wear, undercutting or other damage. If the sprocket is damaged, replace both sprockets and chain at the same time. Installing a new chain over severely worn or damaged sprockets will cause rapid chain wear.

Removal/Installation

1. Remove the left-hand rear axle hub as described under *Rear Axle* in this chapter.
2. Remove the drive chain as described under *Drive Chain* in this chapter.
3. Pry the lockwasher tabs away from the sprocket nuts. Then remove the nuts that hold the sprocket to the hub and remove the sprocket (**Figure 68**).
4. Install by reversing these steps, while noting the following.
5. Replace weak or damaged lockwashers.
6. One side of the sprocket is stamped with the number of teeth on the sprocket. Install the sprocket with the stamped side facing out.
7. Tighten the sprocket nuts securely. Then bend the lockwasher tabs over one nut flat to lock the nuts in position.

TIRE CHANGING AND TIRE REPAIRS

Refer to Chapter Eleven.

SHOCK ABSORBER

All models use a single rear shock absorber and spring unit with a nitrogen gas/oil reservoir for better fade resistance.

Table 1 lists shock and spring specifications.

Rebound Damping Adjustment

Rebound damping affects the rate of speed at which the shock absorber is able to return to the fully extended position after compression. This adjustment will not affect the action of the shock absorber on compression. But if the rebound is too slow, the rear wheels may bottom on subsequent bumps.

Rebound damping can be adjusted to 20 different settings. The adjuster screw is located at the bottom of the shock absorber (A, **Figure 69**). A clicker

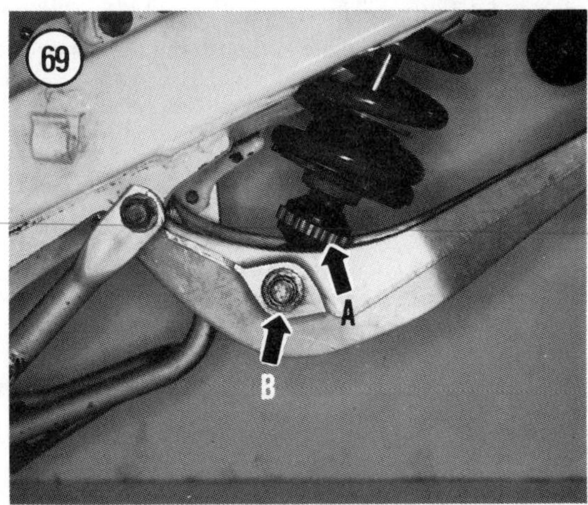

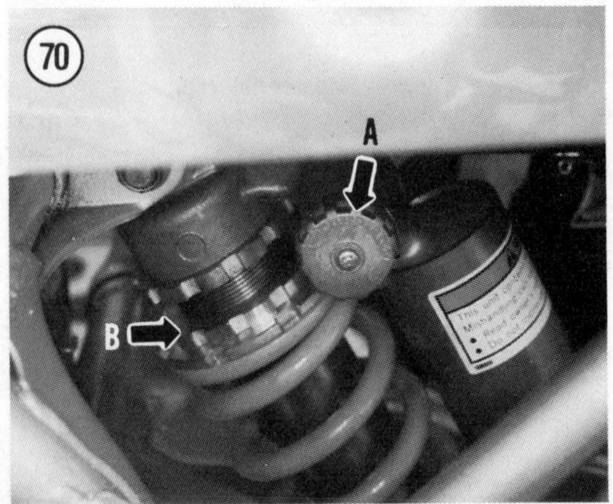

adjuster is used; each click of the adjuster screw represents one adjustment change.

For the standard setting, turn the adjuster screw clockwise until it stops, then turn it counterclockwise the number of clicks (standard) listed in **Table 4**. When the standard setting has been set, the 2 index marks on the adjuster will line up.

For the minimum setting, turn the adjuster screw 8 clicks counterclockwise from the standard setting.

CAUTION

Do not turn the adjuster screw more than 20 clicks counterclockwise from its fully turned in position.

For the maximum setting, turn the adjuster screw 12 clicks clockwise from the standard setting.

To increase the rebound damping, turn the adjuster screw clockwise.

To decrease the rebound damping, turn the adjuster screw counterclockwise.

The rebound setting should be adjusted to personal preference to accommodate rider weight and track conditions. Make sure the adjuster wheel is located in one of the detent positions and not in between any 2 settings.

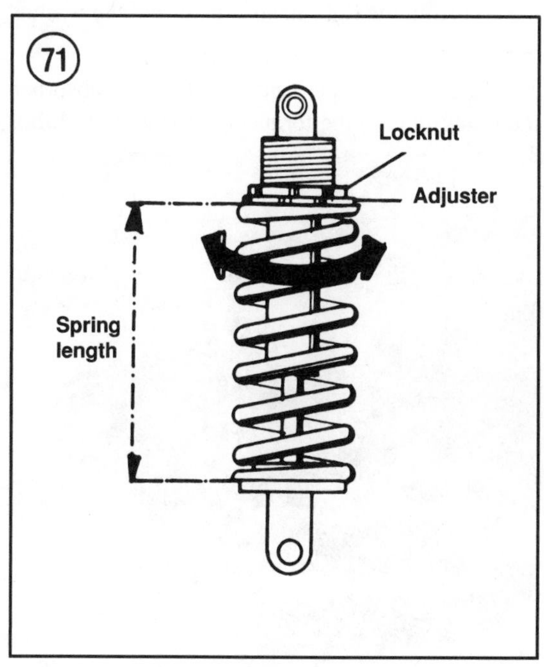

Compression Damping Adjustment

Compression damping affects the rate of speed that the shock compresses. This adjustment will not affect the action of the shock absorber on rebound.

Compression damping can be adjusted to 20 different settings. The adjuster screw is located at the top of the shock absorber (A, **Figure 70**). A clicker adjuster is used; each click of the adjuster screw represents one adjustment change.

For the standard setting, turn the adjuster screw counterclockwise until it stops, then turn it clockwise 11 clicks. When the standard setting has been set, the 2 index marks on the adjuster will line up.

For the minimum setting, turn the adjuster screw 11 clicks counterclockwise from the standard setting.

CAUTION

Do not turn the adjuster screw more than 20 clicks counterclockwise from its fully turned in position.

For the maximum setting, turn the adjuster screw 9 clicks clockwise from the standard setting.

To increase the compression damping, turn the adjuster screw clockwise.

To decrease the compression damping, turn the adjuster screw counterclockwise.

The compression setting should be adjusted to personal preference to accommodate rider weight and track conditions. Make sure the adjuster wheel is located in one of the detent positions and not in between any 2 settings.

Shock Spring Preload Adjustment

By varying the position of the spring adjuster on the shock body (B, **Figure 70**), spring preload can be changed to best suit rider weight and riding conditions.

Spring preload can be adjusted on all models. Initially, remove the shock as described in this chapter and measure the spring's installed length (**Figure 71**) on the shock absorber, then reinstall the shock. Write down the spring's installed length measurement so that you can refer to it when adjusting spring preload with the shock mounted on the vehicle.

1. Support the vehicle with both rear wheels off the ground.

2. Clean the threads at the top of the shock absorber (A, **Figure 72**).

NOTE
Shock preload is adjusted by changing the position of the adjuster on the shock absorber.

3. Measure the existing spring length (**Figure 71**) with a tape measure.

NOTE
Use the spanner wrench provided in your owner's tool kit or a similar tool to turn the locknut and adjuster on the shock absorber.

4. To adjust, loosen the locknut (B, **Figure 72**) and turn the adjuster (C, **Figure 72**) in the desired direction, making sure to maintain the spring length within the dimensions listed in **Table 1**. Tightening the adjuster increases spring preload and loosening it decreases preload. One complete turn (360°) of the adjuster moves the spring 1.5 mm (1/16 in.).

CAUTION
*Remember, the spring preload adjustment must be maintained between the minimum and maximum dimensions listed in **Table 1**.*

5. After the desired spring preload is achieved, tighten the locknut to 70 N•m (50 ft.-lb.).

Nitrogen Pressure Adjustment

Yamaha does not list nitrogen pressure ranges or limits for the stock shock absorber. Refer all nitrogen pressure adjustment to a Yamaha dealer or suspension specialist.

Shock Absorber Removal/Installation

Refer to **Figure 73**.

1. Support the vehicle with both rear wheels off the ground.
2. Remove the nut, washers and bolt (B, **Figure 69**) that hold the lower end of the shock absorber to the relay arm.
3. Remove the nut, washer and bolt (**Figure 74**) that hold the connecting rod to the swing arm.
4. Remove the nut, washer and bolt (**Figure 75**) that hold the upper end of the shock absorber to the frame.
5. Remove the shock absorber assembly from the vehicle.
6. Remove the collars (**Figure 76**) that are located on each side of the shock absorber bearings. Note that the upper and lower collars are different sizes.
7. Install by reversing these steps. Note the following.
8. Clean the shock bolts, nuts, washers and collars in solvent. Dry thoroughly.
9. Inspect and service the dust seals and shock bearings as described in this section.
10. Apply bearing grease to the shock bearings and collars. Then install a collar into each shock absorber oil seal.
11. Apply a light coat of bearing grease onto each shock absorber mounting bolt.
12. Position the upper end of the shock absorber in the frame. Then install the upper shock mounting bolt from the right-hand side. Install the washer and nut (**Figure 75**).
13. Position the lower end of the shock absorber in the relay arm (B, **Figure 69**). Then install the large washer on the lower shock mounting bolt and install the bolt from the right-hand side. Install the washer and nut.
14. Torque the upper and lower shock absorber mounting nuts to the torque specification in **Table 3**.

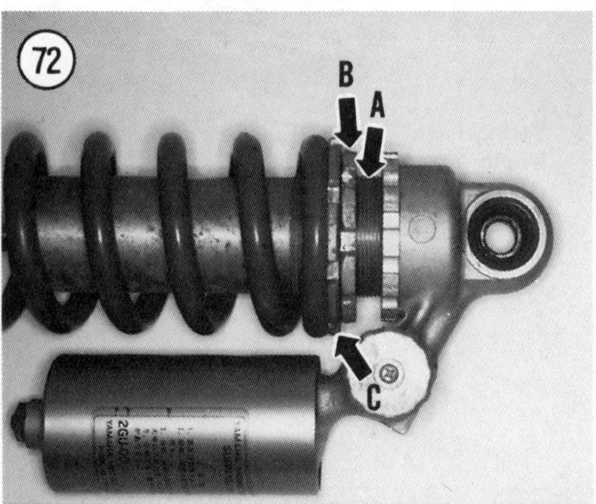

(73)

REAR SHOCK ABSORBER

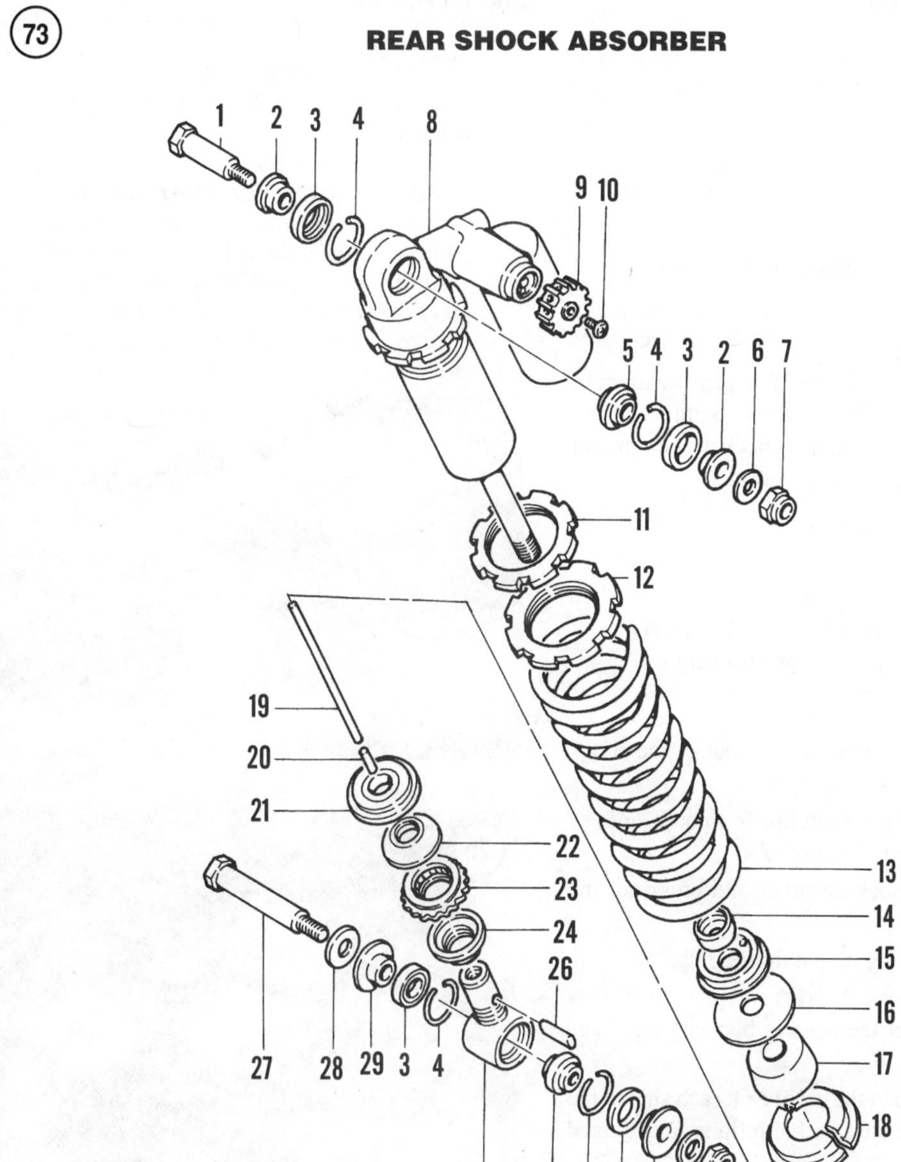

1. Bolt
2. Collar
3. Oil seal
4. Clip
5. Bushing
6. Washer
7. Nut
8. Shock body
9. Adjuster knob
10. Screw
11. Locknut
12. Spring adjuster
13. Spring
14. Ring
15. Cover
16. Washer
17. Bumper
18. Spring seats
19. Rod
20. Pin
21. Seal
22. Cover
23. Adjuster
24. boot
25. Shock boss
26. Pin
27. Pin
28. Washer
29. Collar
30. Washer

Dust Seal and Bearing Inspection/Replacement

The bearings are centered in the shock mounts and secured with a circlip on each side. Oil seals are installed on both sides of each bearing to protect the bearings from damage and dirt contamination. See **Figure 73**.

1. Remove the collar (**Figure 76**) from each oil seal.
2. Inspect the dust seals (**Figure 77**) for cracks, age deterioration or other damage. Replace if necessary.
3. Pivot the bearing (**Figure 77**, typical) with your hand. The bearing should pivot smoothly with no roughness or binding. Visually check the bearing for rust or other types of contamination.
4. To replace the bearing(s):

WARNING
Safety glasses should be worn when removing and installing the bearing circlips in the following steps.

   a. Pry the oil seals (**Figure 77**) out of the shock absorber.
   b. Remove the bearing circlips from both sides of the bearing. See 4, **Figure 73**.
   c. Support the shock absorber and press out the bearing.
   d. Clean the bearing mount thoroughly.
   e. Support the shock absorber and press in the new bearing. Center the bearing between the 2 circlip grooves.
   f. Install a circlip in the groove on each side of the bearing. Make sure each circlip is fully seated in its groove.
   g. Lubricate the bearing with bearing grease.
   h. Check that the bearing pivots smoothly.
   i. Repeat for the opposite bearing if necessary.
5. To install the rear shock absorber oil seals (**Figure 77**):
   a. Pack the lip of each oil seal with bearing grease prior to installation.
   b. Install the oil seals with their closed side facing out.
   c. Press in the oil seal until its outer surface is flush with the bearing bore inside surface as shown in **Figure 77**.

Shock Inspection

WARNING
The shock absorber damper unit and remote reservoir contain nitrogen gas. Do not tamper with or attempt to open the damper unit or disconnect the reservoir hose from either unit. Do not place it near an open flame or other extreme heat. Do not dispose of the damper assembly yourself. Take it to a dealer where it can be deactivated and dis-

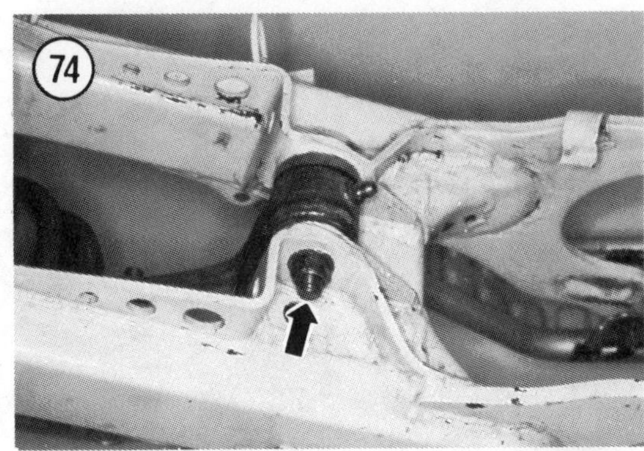

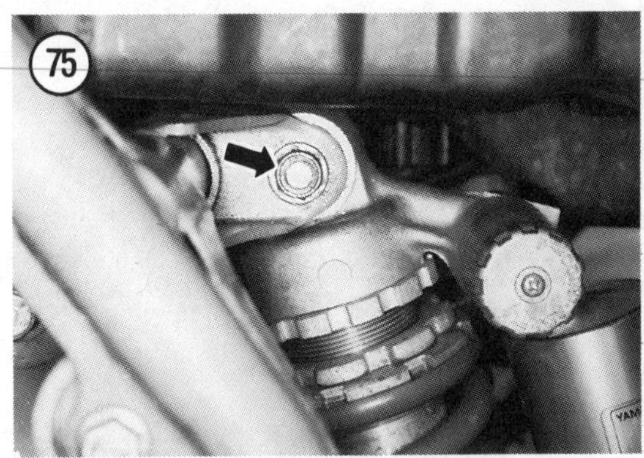

*posed of properly. Never attempt to remove the valve core from the base of the reservoir. Read the WARNING label fixed to the reservoir (**Figure 78**).*

1. Inspect the shock absorber (**Figure 79**) for gas and oil leaks.
2. Check the damper rod for bending, rust or other damage.
3. Check the reservoir for dents or other damage.
4. Remove and inspect the spring as described in the following procedure.

Spring Removal/Installation

In addition to the standard shock spring, you can purchase replacement shock springs, from aftermarket suspension specialists, in a variety of spring rates. To replace a spring, perform the following.

1. Remove the shock absorber as described in this chapter.
2. If you are satisfied with the existing spring preload setting and want to maintain it, measure and record the spring preload position as described under *Shock Spring Preload Adjustment* in this chapter.
3. Clean the shock threads (A, **Figure 72**).
4. Secure the shock absorber upper mount in a vise with soft jaws.
5. Loosen the spring locknut (B, **Figure 72**) with a spanner wrench and turn it all the way down. Then do the same for the adjuster (C, **Figure 72**) to reduce spring preload. There should be no preload on the spring.
6. Slide the rubber shock bumper down the shock shaft.
7. Secure the spring with a shock spring tool and remove the spring retainer, spring seat and spring from the shock.
8. Measure spring free length with a tape measure or caliper (**Figure 80**). Replace the spring if it is appreciably shorter than the free length listed in **Table 1**. Yamaha does not list wear limits for spring free length.

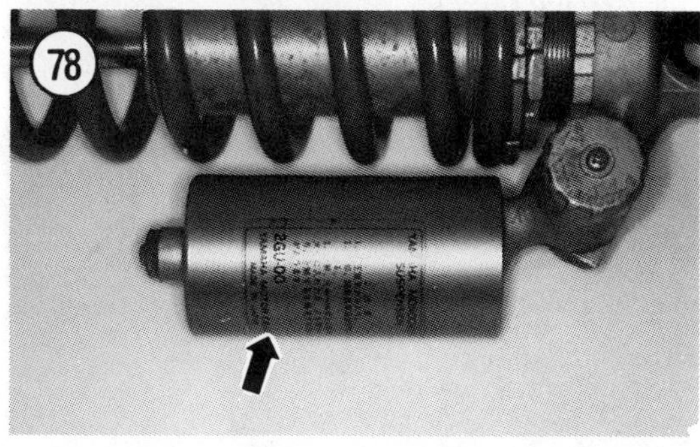

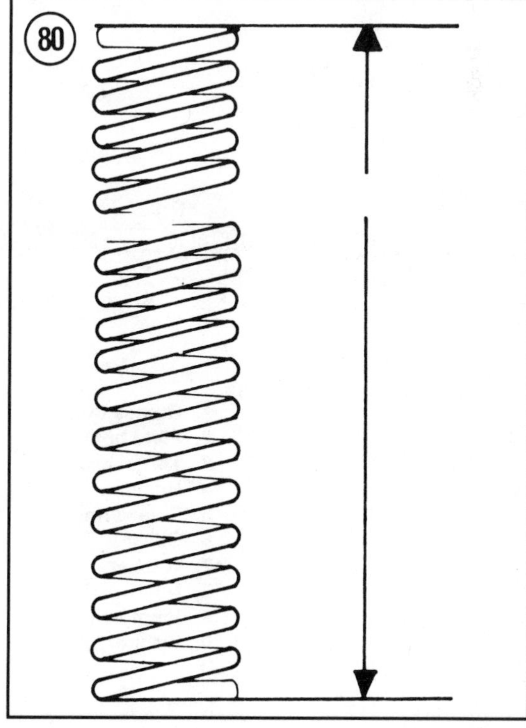

81

REAR SUSPENSION

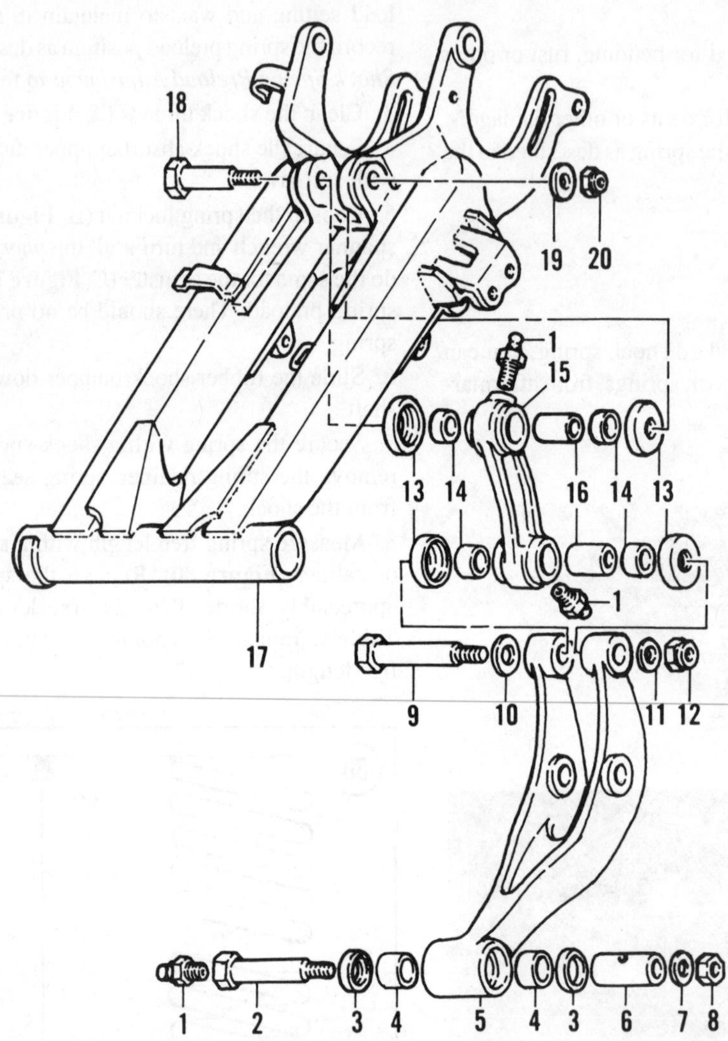

1. Grease fitting
2. Pivot bolt
3. Thrust cover
4. Bushing
5. Relay arm
6. Collar
7. Washer
8. Nut
9. Pivot bolt
10. Washer
11. Washer
12. Nut
13. Thrust cover
14. Bushing
15. Connecting rod
16. Collar
17. Swing arm
18. Pivot bolt
19. Washer
20. Nut

9. Install by reversing these steps, while noting the following.
10. Install the spring, spring guide and spring retainer. Check that the spring guide and spring retainer seat flush against the spring.
11. Adjust the spring preload as described under *Shock Preload Adjustment* in this chapter.

SUSPENSION LINKAGE

Figure 81 shows the rear suspension linkage assembly. The relay arm is bolted to the frame, rear shock absorber and connecting rod. The connecting rod is bolted to the rear swing arm and relay arm. The relay arm and connecting rod pivot on solid bushings, steel collars and pivot bolts. Dust seals are mounted outside of each bushing to prevent the entry of dirt and moisture. Grease fittings are installed at each bushing position. For the rear swing arm and linkage assembly to operate properly, all pivot areas must be removed, cleaned and lubricated periodically.

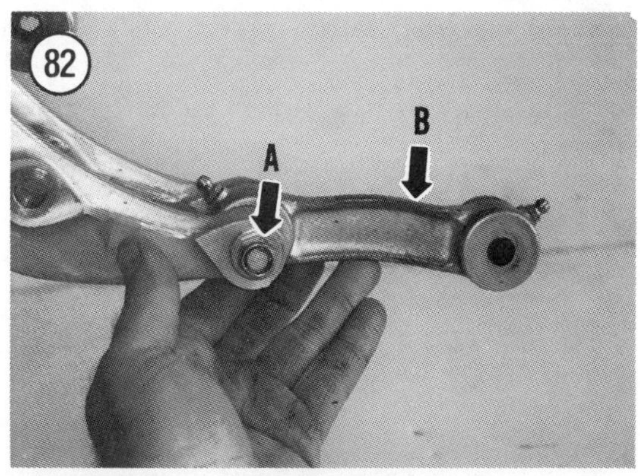

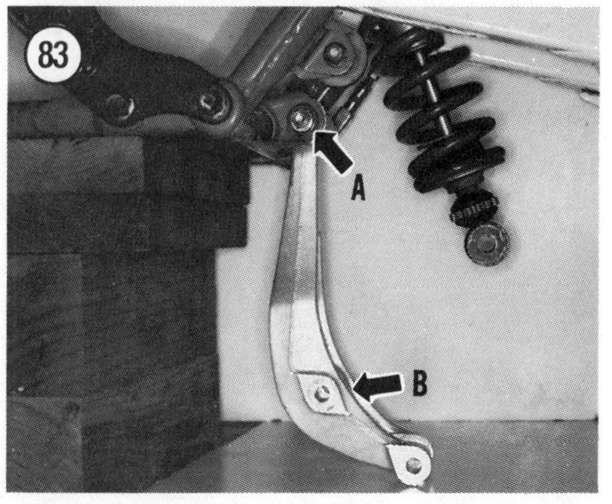

Removal

1. Support the vehicle with both rear wheels off the ground.
2. Remove the nut, washers and bolt (B, **Figure 69**) that hold the lower end of the shock absorber to the relay arm.
3. Remove the nut, washer and bolt (**Figure 74**) that hold the connecting rod to the rear swing arm. Then pull the connecting rod out of the rear swing arm mounting brackets.
4. Suspend the rear swing arm to the frame with a stiff wire hook or prop it up with wood blocks.
5. Remove the nut, washers and bolt (A, **Figure 82**) that hold the connecting rod to the relay arm. Then remove the connecting rod (B, **Figure 82**).
6. Remove the nut, washer and bolt (A, **Figure 83**) that hold the relay arm to the frame. Then remove the relay arm (B, **Figure 83**) from the frame.
7. Remove the rear swing arm, if necessary, as described later in this chapter.

Connecting Rod and Relay Arm Disassembly/Inspection/Reassembly

Store the connecting rod and relay arm collars, bushings and pivot bolt assemblies in separate containers so that they can be installed in their original locations. See **Figure 81** and **Figure 84**.
1. Remove the dust seals from the connecting rod.
2. Prior to removing the collars from their bushings, turn each collar slowly with your fingers. Each collar should turn smoothly with no roughness or binding. If any roughness or binding is noted, examine the bushing and collars as described in the following steps.

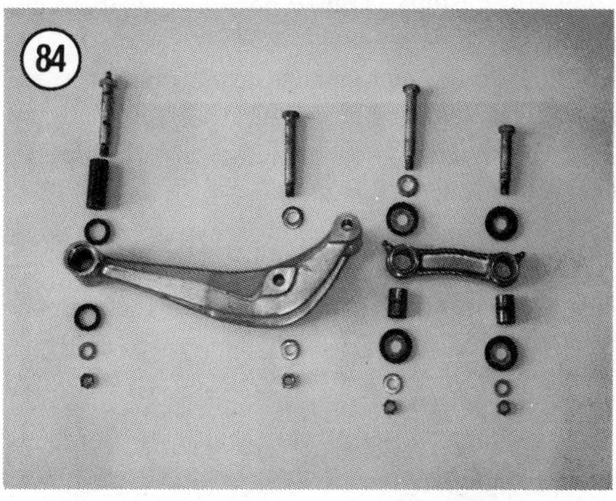

3. Remove the connecting rod and relay arm collars. See **Figure 85**, typical.
4. Pry the oil seals out of the relay arm with a wide-blade screwdriver as shown in **Figure 86**. Pad the screwdriver to avoid damaging the relay arm bushing bore.
5. Wash parts in solvent and dry thoroughly with compressed air.
6. Check the pivot bolts and collars for scoring, cracks or severe wear. If the collars are severely worn or damaged, they should be replaced along with the bushings. Rusted pivot bolts can be cleaned with a wire wheel mounted in a drill. Replace scored or excessively worn pivot bolts.
7. Visually check the connecting rod (**Figure 87**) and relay arm (**Figure 88**) bushings for severe wear, looseness, cracks or other damage. Refer to *Bushing Replacement* in the following section.
8. Inspect the relay arm (**Figure 89**) for cracks, distortion or other damage. Check the rear shock absorber and connecting rod pivot holes for cracks or other damage.
9. Inspect the connecting rod (**Figure 87**) for severe wear or damage.
10. To install the relay arm oil seals:
   a. Pack the lip of each oil seal with bearing grease prior to installation.
   b. Install the oil seals with their closed side facing out.
   c. Press in the oil seal until its outer surface is flush with the bushing bore inside surface as shown in **Figure 90**.

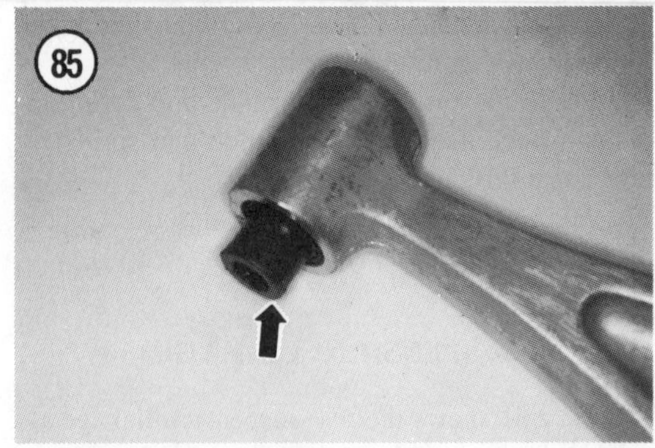

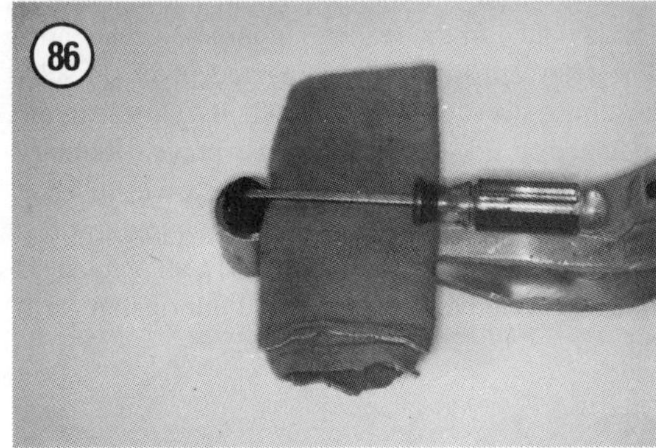

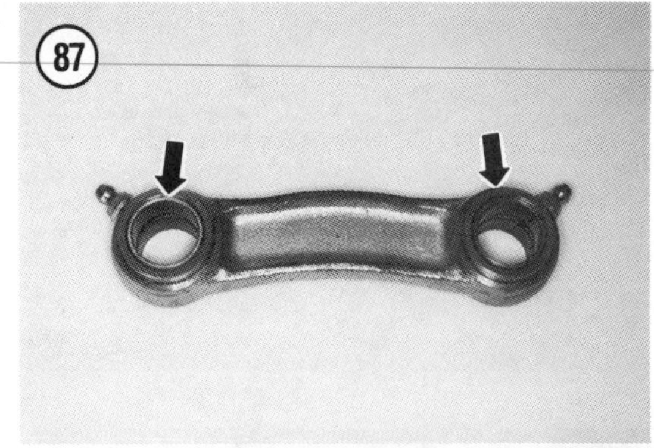

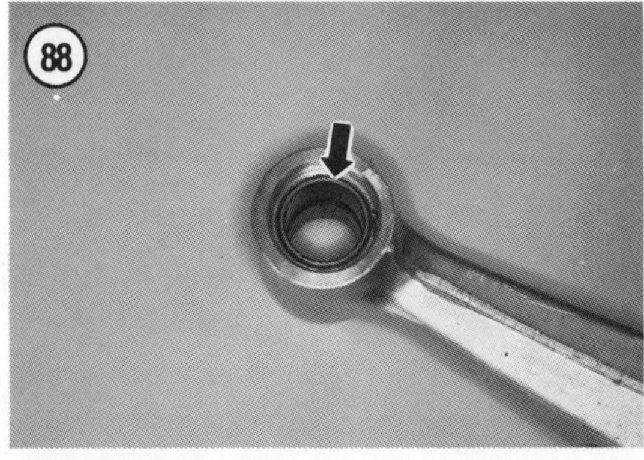

Bushing Replacement

If the connecting rod bushings (**Figure 87**) or the relay arm bushing (**Figure 88**) must be replaced, perform the following.

1. Purchase the replacement bushings prior to removing the damaged bushing(s).
2. Remove the 2 grease fittings installed in the connecting rod; see **Figure 87**.
3. Support the connecting rod or relay arm in a press and press out the old bushing.
4. Clean the bushing bores and the replacement bushings in solvent. Dry with compressed air.

NOTE

When replacing the connecting rod bushings, align the grease hole in the bushing with the hole in the connecting rod.

5A. Press in the connecting rod bushing until its outer surface is flush with the connecting rod bushing bore inside surface as shown in **Figure 87**. Repeat for the other bushing.

5B. Press in the relay arm bushing until its outer surface is flush with the relay arm bushing bore inside surface as shown in **Figure 88**.

6. Install the 2 connecting rod grease fittings (**Figure 87**).

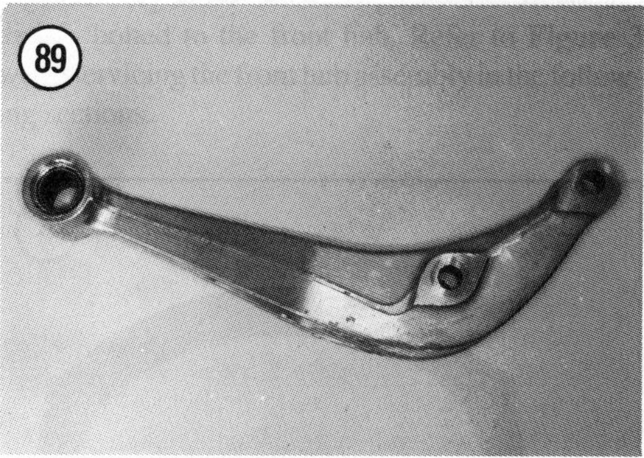

89

90

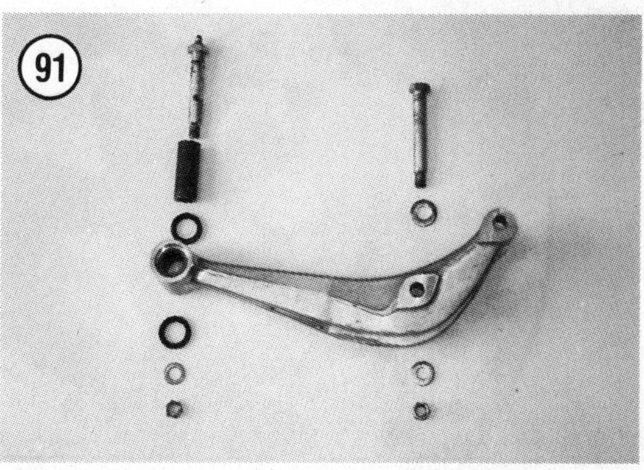

91

7. Install the relay arm oil seals as described in the previous section.

Installation

1. Lubricate the following components with bearing grease:
   a. Bushing inside diameters.
   b. Collars.
   c. Pivot bolt shafts.
2. Install the relay arm assembly (**Figure 91**) as follows:
   a. Install the collar into the relay arm bushing.
   b. Position the relay arm between the frame mounting brackets as shown in B, **Figure 83**.
   c. Install the front pivot bolt through the relay arm from the right-hand side. Then install the flat washer and nut. Torque the relay arm nut to the specification in **Table 3**.
   d. Check that the relay arm pivots up and down smoothly.
3. Install the connecting rod assembly (**Figure 92**) onto the relay arm as follows:
   a. Install the collars and dust seals onto the connecting rod.
   b. Position the connecting rod between the relay arm as shown in **Figure 82**—the grease fittings must be facing up.
   c. Install the pivot bolt and washer through the connecting rod from the right-hand side (**Figure 82**). Then install the flat washer and nut. Torque the connecting rod-to-relay arm pivot bolt to the specification in **Table 3**.
4. Install the 2 collars into the lower shock absorber oil seals.

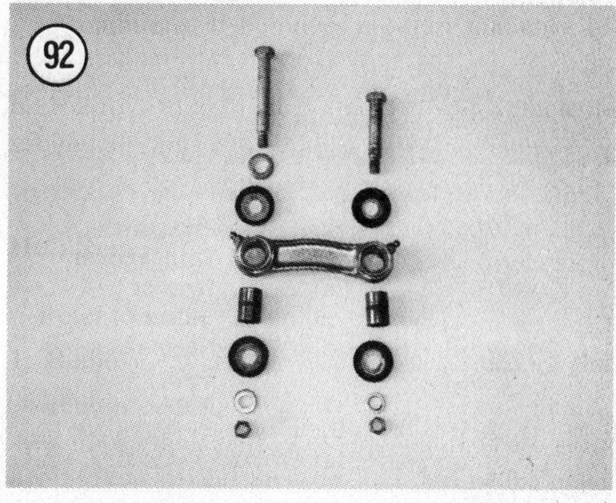

92

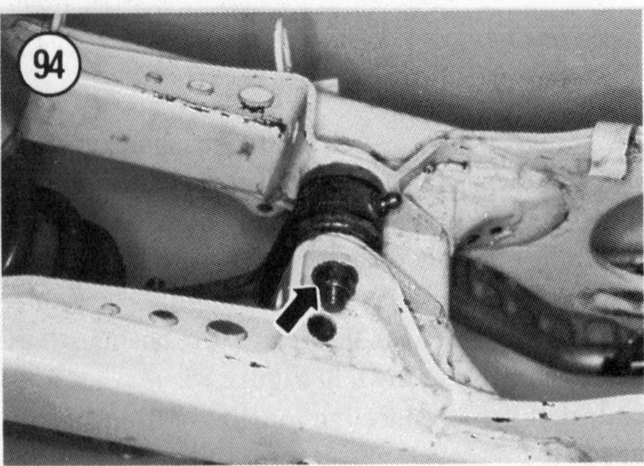

95

REAR SWING ARM

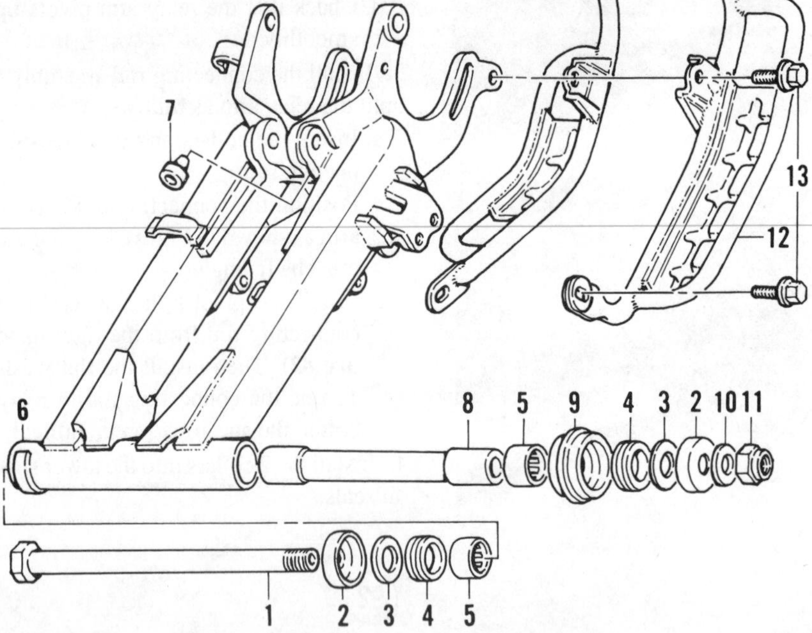

1. Pivot shaft
2. Thrust cover
3. Washer
4. Oil seal
5. Needle bearing
6. Swing arm
7. Rubber stopper
8. Collar
9. Chain guard
10. Washer
11. Nut
12. Guard
13. Bolt

5. Pivot the rear swing arm up and install the shock absorber lower end into the relay arm (**Figure 93**). Install the large washer on the lower shock pivot bolt and install the bolt from the right-hand side. Install the washer and nut and torque to the specification in **Table 3**.

6. Pivot the connecting rod up and install it between the swing arm mounting brackets as shown in **Figure 94**. Install the pivot bolt through the connecting rod from the right-hand side. Then install the flat washer and nut. Torque the connecting rod-to-rear swing arm pivot bolt to the specification in **Table 3**.

7. Lower the vehicle so that both rear wheels contact the ground.

REAR SWING ARM

Figure 95 is an exploded view of the rear swing arm. Needle bearings are pressed into both sides of the swing arm. A center collar is installed through the needle bearings. Oil seals are installed on the outside of each needle bearing to prevent dirt and moisture from entering the bearings. Steel thrust covers are installed on the outside of each oil seal. A nylon chain roller is installed on the swing arm right-hand side to prevent the chain from damaging the swing arm. The hollow pivot shaft is installed through the swing arm from the right-hand side. Plate washers, 2.05 mm (0.081 in.) thick, are installed between the outer thrust covers and oil seals to maintain swing arm side play. Yamaha does not provide swing arm side play specifications or provide procedures on adjusting side play.

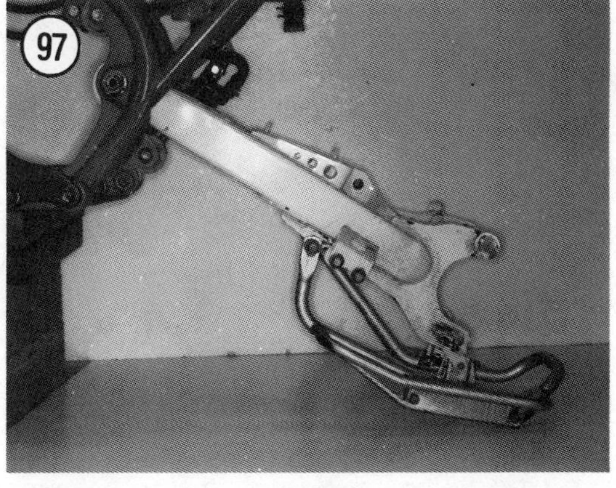

Swing Arm Bearing Inspection

The swing arm needle bearings and bushings should be inspected periodically for excessive play, roughness or damage.

1. Remove the rear axle as described in this chapter.
2. Remove the nut, washer and bolt (**Figure 94**) that hold the connecting rod to the rear swing arm. Then lower the rear shock absorber and connecting rod assembly (**Figure 93**).
3. Loosen the swing arm pivot shaft nut (**Figure 96**), then retorque the nut to the specification in **Table 3**.

NOTE
Have an assistant steady the vehicle when performing Step 4.

4. Grasp the rear end of the swing arm (**Figure 97**) and try to move it from side to side in a horizontal arc. There should be no noticeable side play.
5. Grasp the rear of the swing arm once again and pivot it up and down through its full travel. The swing arm should pivot smoothly with no roughness or binding.
6. If play is evident and the pivot shaft nut is tightened correctly, remove the swing arm and inspect the needle bearings as described in the following sections.
7. Reverse Steps 1-3 if you are not going to remove the swing arm. See **Table 3** for tightening torques.

Removal

1. Support the vehicle with both rear wheels off the ground.
2. Remove the drive sprocket cover.

NOTE
You do not have to remove the rear axle from the axle housing when performing Step 3.

3. Remove the rear axle housing as described in this chapter.
4. If necessary, remove the bolts that hold the wheel hub cover to the rear swing arm. Then remove the wheel hub cover.
5. Remove the nut, washer and bolt (**Figure 94**) that hold the connecting rod to the rear swing arm. Then lower the rear shock absorber and connecting rod assembly (**Figure 93**).
6. Suspend the rear swing arm to the frame with a stiff wire hook or prop it up with wood blocks.
7. Remove the nut, washers and bolt (A, **Figure 82**) that hold the connecting rod to the relay arm. Then remove the connecting rod (B, **Figure 82**).
8. Remove the nut, washer and bolt (A, **Figure 83**) that hold the relay arm to the frame. Then remove the relay arm (B, **Figure 83**) from the frame.
9. Remove the brake hose from its guide clamps on the swing arm. Support the brake caliper with a heavy wire hook.
10. Loosen the swing arm pivot shaft nut (**Figure 96**). Then remove the nut and washer.
11. Remove the pivot shaft (1, **Figure 95**) from the right-hand side. If the pivot shaft is tight, tap it out with a brass or aluminum drift. Tap on the pivot shaft carefully, however, as you may damage the threads on the end of the shaft.
12. Pull back on the swing arm (**Figure 97**), free it from the frame and remove it.
13. If you are not going to remove the swing arm thrust cover and bearing assemblies, cover the left- and right-hand bearing assemblies with plastic bags. Secure the plastic bags with tape or lock ties. The bags will prevent the bearing assemblies from falling out.

Swing Arm Disassembly/Inspection/Reassembly

Store the left- and right-hand bearing assemblies in separate containers so that they can be installed in their original locations. Refer to **Figure 95**.

1. Remove the chain guide mounting bolts and remove the chain guide from the swing arm.
2. Remove the dust seals, plate washers and collar from the swing arm as shown in **Figure 98**. Do not remove the needle bearings from the swing arm.
3. Wash parts in solvent and dry thoroughly with compressed air.
4. Wipe off any excess grease from the needle bearings at each end of the swing arm. Needle bearing wear is difficult to measure. Turn each bearing (**Fig-**

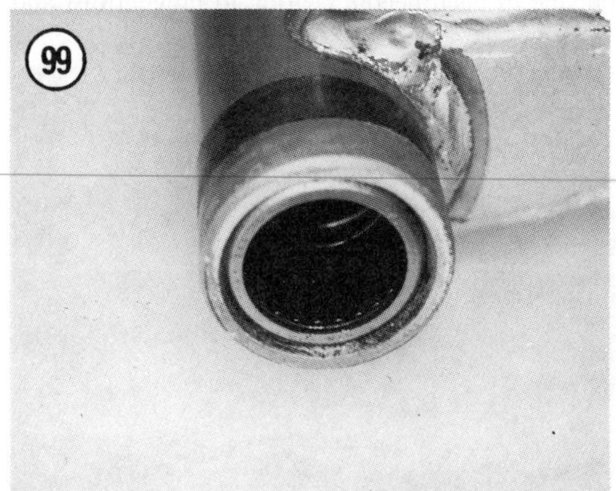
99

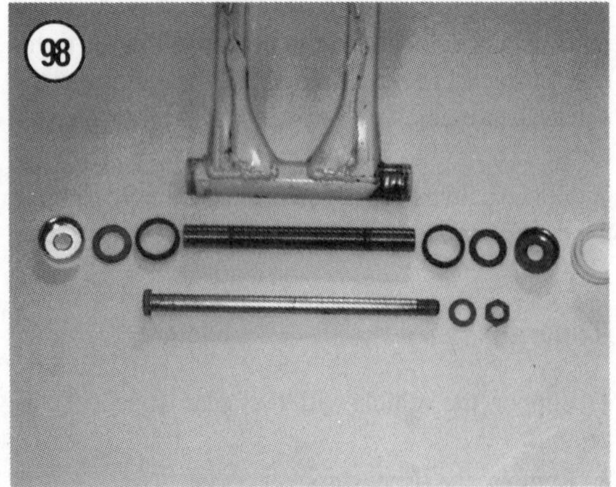
98

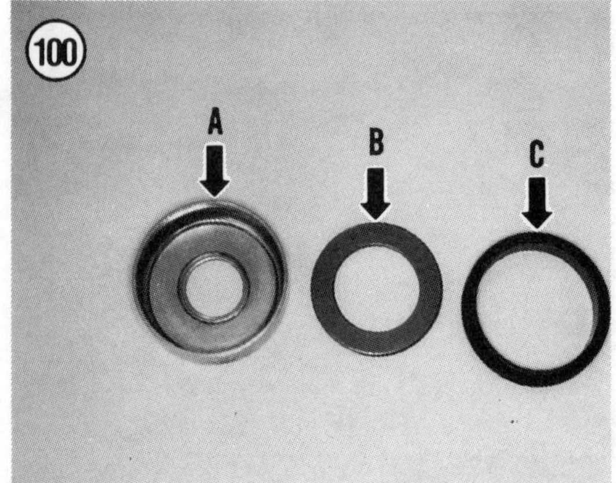

100

ure 99) with your finger. The bearings should turn smoothly with no roughness or excessive play. Check the rollers for evidence of wear, pitting or rust. Then repeat with the collar installed in the swing arm.

5. Check the collar (8, **Figure 95**) for scoring, cracks or severe wear. If the collar is severely worn, replace the collar and bearings as a set.

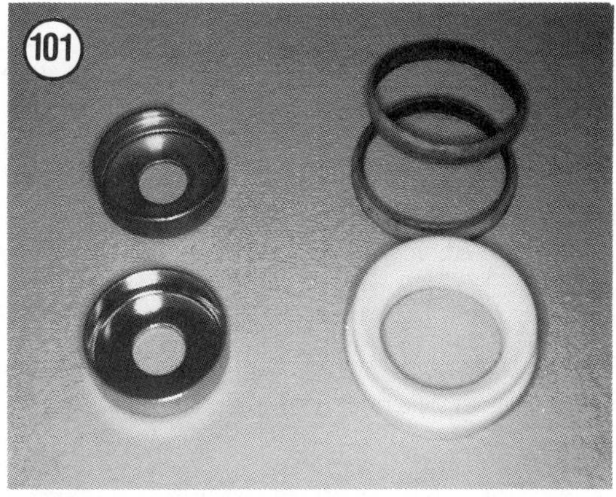

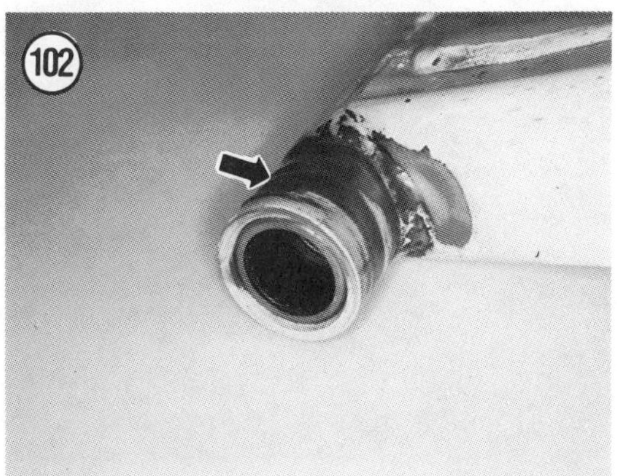

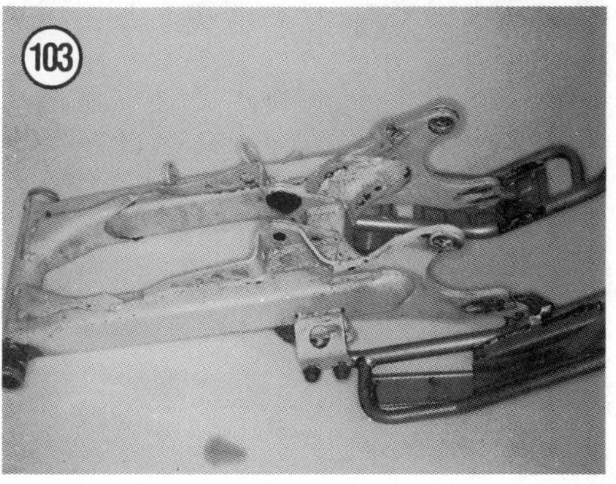

6. Replace severely worn or damaged needle bearings as described under *Bearing Replacement* in this chapter.

7. Check the outer dust covers and oil seals (**Figure 100**) for severe wear or damage.

8. Check the plate washers (3, **Figure 95**) for galling, cracks or other damage.

9. Replace the oil seals if severely worn or damaged. Install new seals when replacing bearings.

10. Replace the chain slider if severely worn or damaged. Compare the new and damaged chain slider in **Figure 101**.

NOTE

*A damaged chain slider will cause swing arm damage like that shown in **Figure 102**. Replace the chain slider before it allows the drive chain to run against the swing arm.*

11. Check the swing arm (**Figure 103**) for cracks, bending or other damage. Check the axle housing mounts for damage. Refer repair to a Yamaha dealer or welding shop or replace the swing arm.

12. Check for a bent, cracked or scored pivot shaft. Replace if necessary.

13. Lubricate the following parts with bearing grease prior to assembly:

   a. Needle bearings (**Figure 99**).
   b. Plate washers (3, **Figure 95**).
   c. Collar (8, **Figure 95**).
   d. Oil seals.

14. Slide the collar through the needle bearings in the swing arm.

15. Install a plate washer (B, **Figure 100**) and oil seal (C, **Figure 100**) in its dust cover (A, **Figure 100**). See **Figure 104**. Repeat for the other side.

12

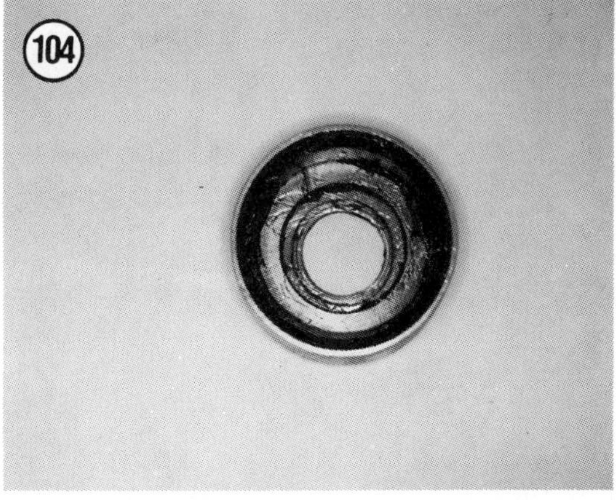

16. Install the left-hand dust cover assembly onto the swing arm; see A, **Figure 105**.
17. Install the chain guide with its tapered bore facing inside (**Figure 106**), onto the swing arm. See B, **Figure 105**.
18. Install the right-hand dust cover assembly onto the swing arm; see **Figure 107**.
19. Install the swing arm as described in this chapter.

Swing Arm Needle Bearing Replacement

The swing arm needle bearings (**Figure 99**) should not be removed unless replacement is required. When replacing the bearings, refer to **Figure 95.**

Replace both needle bearings at the same time.

1. Remove the collar (8, **Figure 95**) from the swing arm.
2. Support the swing arm and press out the old bearing.
3. Clean the bearing bore in solvent and dry thoroughly. Remove all corrosion from the bore as required.
4. Pack the bearings with a waterproof bearing grease prior to installation.
5. Wipe the outside of the bearing with grease prior to installation.
6. To install the needle bearings:
   a. Install bearings with their manufacturer's name and size code facing out.
   b. Press in the bearing until it bottoms in the bearing bore.
7. Apply grease onto the collar and slide it into the swing arm.

Installation

1. Assemble the swing arm collar and dust cover assemblies as described in the previous section.
2. Lubricate the pivot shaft with waterproof grease.
3. Position the swing arm between the frame and engine. Then install the pivot shaft from the left-hand side.
4. Install the swing arm washer and nut. Torque the pivot shaft nut to the specification in **Table 3**.
5. Perform the *Swing Arm Bearing Inspection* check in this chapter.
6. If removed, install the hub cover onto the swing arm. Then install and tighten the hub cover mounting bolts securely.
7. Install the relay arm and connecting rod onto the swing arm as described under *Suspension Linkage* in this chapter.

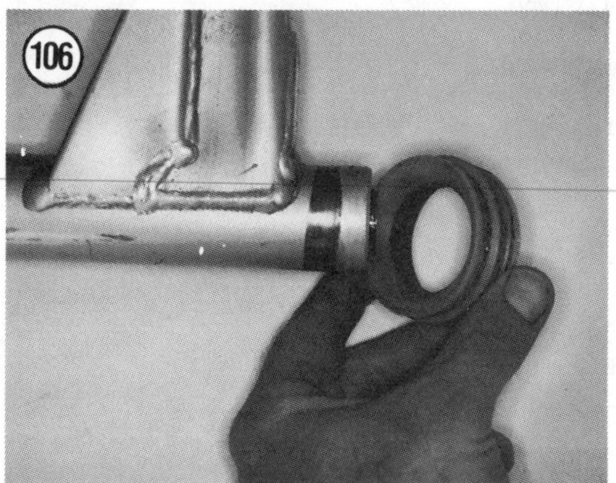

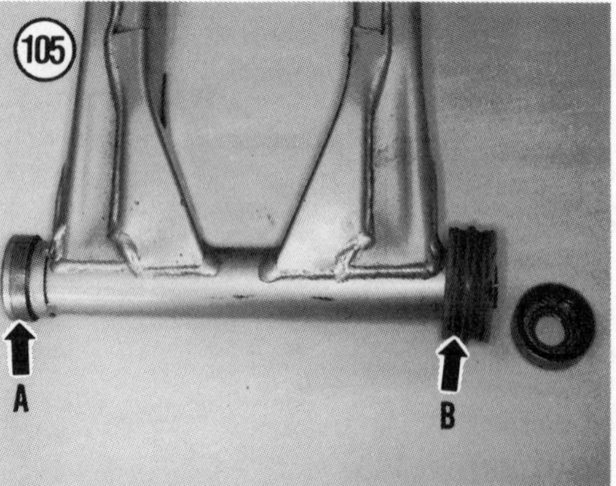

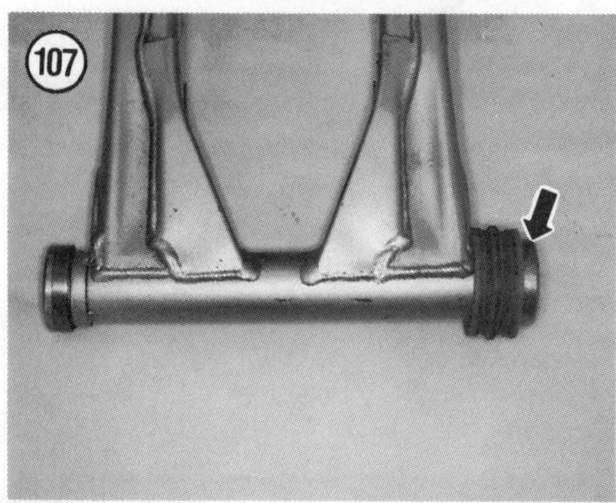

8. Install the rear shock absorber lower end onto the relay arm as described under *Suspension Linkage* in this chapter.
9. Install the rear axle housing onto the rear swing arm as described in this chapter.
10. Reconnect the drive chain as described in this chapter.
11. Adjust the drive chain as described in Chapter Three.
12. Install the drive sprocket cover onto the engine.
13. Install the rear brake hose onto the rear swing arm.
14. Install the rear brake caliper as described in Chapter Thirteen.

Table 1 REAR SUSPENSION GENERAL SPECIFICATIONS

Rear suspension	Swing arm
Rear wheel travel	220 mm (8.66 in.)
Rear shock absorber	
Type	Coil spring, gas/oil damper type
Stroke	
1987-1989	86 mm (3.39 in.)
1990-on	89 mm (3.50 in.)
Enclosed gas pressure	Not specified
Spring free length	
1987-1990	234.5 mm (9.23 in.)
1991-on	240.5 mm (9.47 in.)
Spring installed length	
1987-1989	
Standard	218.5 mm (8.6 in.)
Minimum	210.5 mm (8.3 in.)
Maximum	225.5 mm (8.8 in.)
1990-on	
Standard (1990-2001)	218.5 mm (8.6 in.)
Standard (2002)	220.5 mm (8.68 in.)
Minimum	213.5 mm (8.4 in.)
Maximum	228.5 mm (9.0 in.)
Spring rate	
1987-1990	6.5 kg/mm (364 in.-lb.)
1991-on	5.5 kg/mm (308 in.-lb.)
Stroke	
1987-1989	0-124.5 mm (0-4.90 in.)
1990	0-110 mm (0-4.3 in.)
1991-on	0-109 mm (0-4.29 in.)

Table 2 DRIVE CHAIN SPECIFICATIONS

Size	520
Number of links	
1987-1989	103
1990-on	104
Chain free play	15-20 mm (0.6-0.78 in.)

12

Table 3 TIGHTENING TORQUES

	N•m	ft.-lb.
Rear wheel lug nuts	45	33
Rear axle nut	120	88
Pivot shaft		
1987-1990	85	62
1991-on	95	70
Rear shock absorber	30	22
Relay arm		
At frame	30	22
At connecting rod	30	22
Connecting rod at swing arm	30	22
Rear brake caliper	23	17
Rear axle nuts at axle housing	*	*
Rear axle housing at swing arm		
Upper bolts/nuts	120	88
Lower bolts/nuts	60	44
Driven sprocket bolts	60	44
Swing arm guard		
1987-1989	23	17
1990-on	28	20

* See text for tightening torques and service procedures.

Table 4 REAR SHOCK DAMPING ADJUSTMENT

	Clicks
Rebound damping adjuster	
Standard	12 clicks out [1]
Minimum	8 clicks out [2]
Maximum	12 clicks in [2]
Compression damping adjuster	
Standard	11 clicks in [3]
Minimum	11 clicks out [2]
Maximum	9 clicks in [2]

[1] From the fully turned-in position.
[2] From the standard position.
[3] From the fully turned-out position.

CHAPTER THIRTEEN

BRAKES

This chapter describes service procedures for the front and rear disc brakes.

Brake specifications are listed in **Tables 1-3** at the end of this chapter.

DISC BRAKE

The front and rear disc brakes are actuated by hydraulic fluid and controlled by a hand or foot lever on the master cylinder. As the brake pads wear, the brake fluid level drops in the reservoir and the calipers automatically adjust for wear.

When working on hydraulic brake systems, it is necessary that the work area and all tools be absolutely clean. Any tiny particles of foreign matter and grit in the caliper assembly or master cylinder can damage the components.

Consider the following when servicing the front disc brake.

1. Use only DOT 4 brake fluid from a sealed container.
2. Do not allow disc brake fluid to contact any plastic parts or painted surfaces as damage will result.
3. Always keep the master cylinder reservoir and spare cans of brake fluid closed to prevent dust or moisture from entering. This would result in brake fluid contamination and brake problems.
4. Use only disc brake fluid (DOT 4) to wash parts. Never clean any internal brake components with solvent or any other petroleum base cleaners.
5. Whenever any component has been removed from the brake system, the system is considered "opened" and must be bled to remove air bubbles. Also, if the brake feels "spongy," this usually means there are air bubbles in the system and it must be bled. For safe brake operation, refer to *Brake Bleeding* in this chapter for complete details.

CAUTION

Disc brake components rarely require disassembly, so do not disassemble unless absolutely necessary. Do not use solvents of any kind on the brake system's internal components. Solvents will cause the seals to swell and distort. When disassembling and cleaning brake components (except brake pads) use new DOT 4 brake fluid.

CAUTION
Never reuse brake fluid. Contaminated brake fluid can cause brake failure. Dispose of brake fluid according to local EPA regulations.

FRONT BRAKE CALIPER (1987-1989)

Refer to **Figure 1** when replacing the front brake pads or servicing the front brake caliper.

Front Brake Pad Replacement

There is no recommended time interval for changing the friction pads in the front brakes. Pad wear depends greatly on riding habits and conditions.

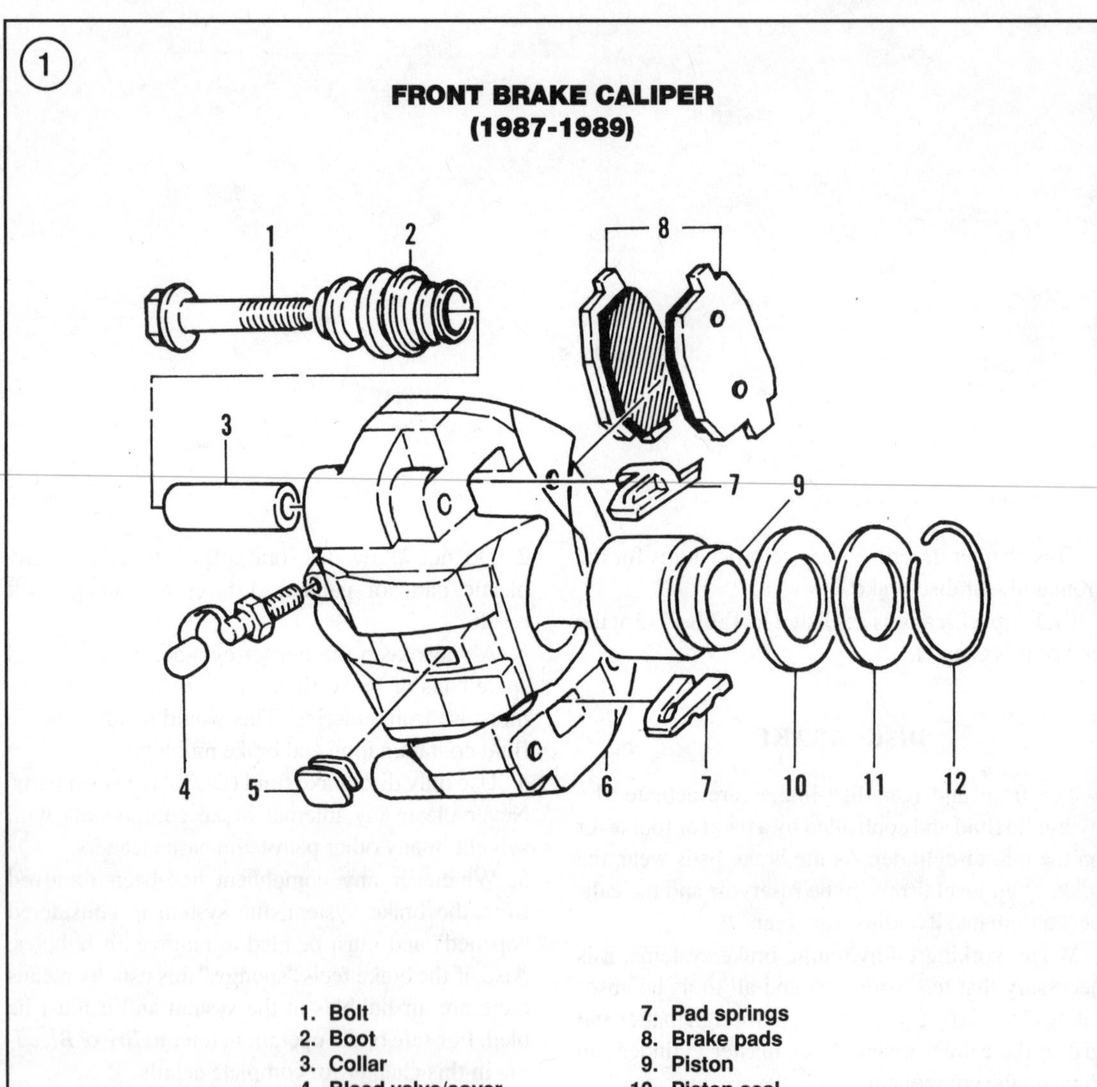

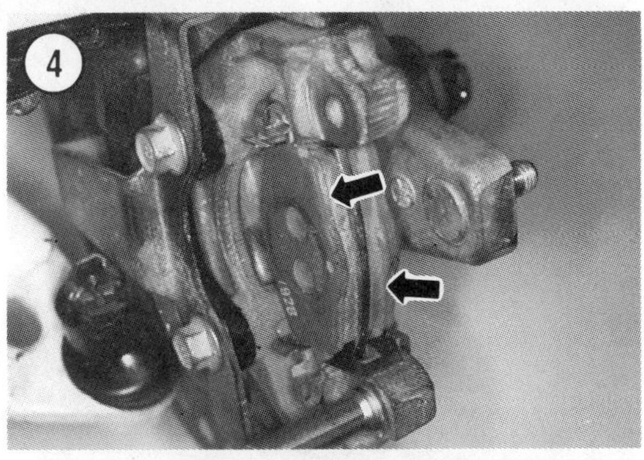

To maintain an even brake pressure on the disc always replace both pads in both calipers at the same time.

1. Read the information listed under *Disc Brake* in this chapter.
2. Remove the front wheel as described in Chapter Eleven.
3. Remove the brake caliper mounting bolt (**Figure 2**) and pivot the caliper housing off of the brake pads (**Figure 3**). Slide the caliper off of its pivot bolt and secure it with a Bunjee cord.

NOTE

If the pads are to be reused, handle them carefully to prevent grease contamination.

4. Slide each brake pad (**Figure 4**) outward and remove them from the caliper.
5. Check the upper and lower pad springs (**Figure 5**), mounted on the caliper arm, for damage. Replace the pad springs, if necessary.
6. Measure the thickness of each brake pad (**Figure 6**). Replace the brake pads if the thickness of any one pad meets or is less than the service limit in **Table 1**. Replace both brake pads as a set.
7. Inspect the brake pads for uneven wear, damage or grease contamination. Replace the pads as a set, if necessary.
8. Check the piston and seals as follows:
   a. Check the dust seal (**Figure 3**) for severe wear or damage.
   b. Check the end of the piston for fluid leakage. If the dust seal is damaged and/or if there is fluid leakage, overhaul the brake caliper as described in this chapter.
9. Check the brake disc for wear as described in this chapter.
10. To make room for the new pads, the piston (**Figure 3**) must be pushed back into the caliper. This will force brake fluid to backup through the hose and

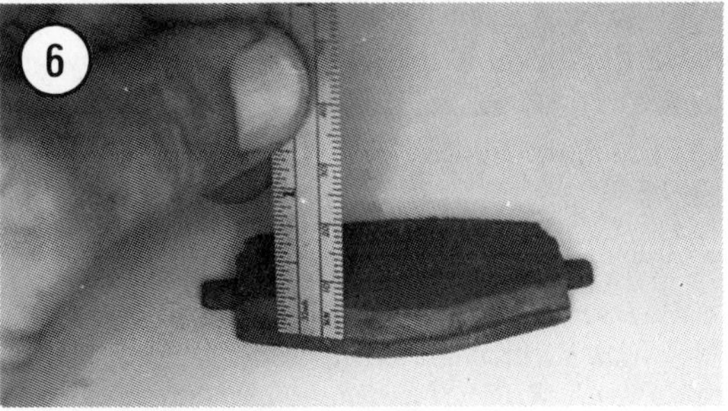

fill the master cylinder reservoir. To prevent the reservoir from overflowing, remove some of the brake fluid as follows:

a. Clean the top of the master cylinder of all dirt.
b. Remove the cap and diaphragm from the master cylinder.
c. Slowly push the piston back into the caliper.
d. Constantly check the reservoir to make sure brake fluid does not overflow. Siphon fluid, if necessary, before it overflows.

WARNING
Brake fluid is poisonous. Do not siphon with your mouth.

e. The caliper piston should move freely. If not, the caliper should be removed and overhauled as described in this chapter.
f. Push the caliper piston in all the way to allow room for the new pads.

11. Install the upper and lower pad springs (**Figure 5**) onto the caliper bracket.
12. Install the brake pads as follows:
  a. Install both brake pads with their round side (**Figure 7**) facing forward.
  b. Align the brake pads with the caliper bracket slots and push the pads into place (**Figure 4**).
  c. Check that the pads seat against the pad springs as shown in **Figure 8**.
13. Slide the caliper onto the pivot bolt (**Figure 3**), then pivot the caliper over the brake pads.
14. Install the caliper mounting bolt (**Figure 2**) and tighten to the torque specification in **Table 3**.
15. Repeat for the other brake caliper.

WARNING
Use new brake fluid clearly marked DOT 4 from a sealed container.

16. Install the master cylinder reservoir diaphragm and top cover. Tighten the cover screws securely.
17. Pull and release the brake lever a few times to seat the pads against each disc, then recheck the brake fluid level in the reservoir. If necessary, add fresh DOT 4 brake fluid.
18. Install the front wheels as described in Chapter Eleven.

WARNING
Do not ride the vehicle until you are sure that both front brakes are operating correctly with full hydraulic advantage. If necessary, bleed the front brakes as described in this chapter.

Removal/Installation (Caliper Will Not Be Disassembled)

If the brake caliper is to be removed without disassembling it, perform this procedure. If the caliper is to be disassembled, refer to *Caliper Removal/Piston Removal* in this section.

1. Remove the front wheel(s) as described in Chapter Eleven.

2A. If the caliper is to be completely removed from the vehicle, perform the following:
  a. Loosen the brake hose at the caliper.
  b. Remove the brake caliper mounting bolt (**Figure 2**) and pivot the caliper housing off of the brake pads (**Figure 3**). Slide the caliper off of its pivot bolt and secure it with a Bunjee cord.

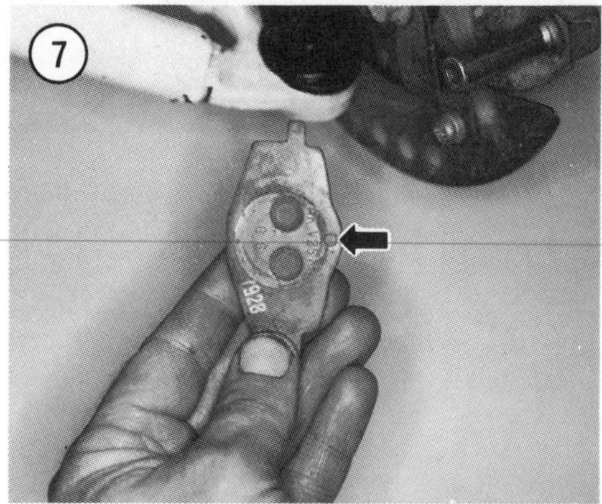

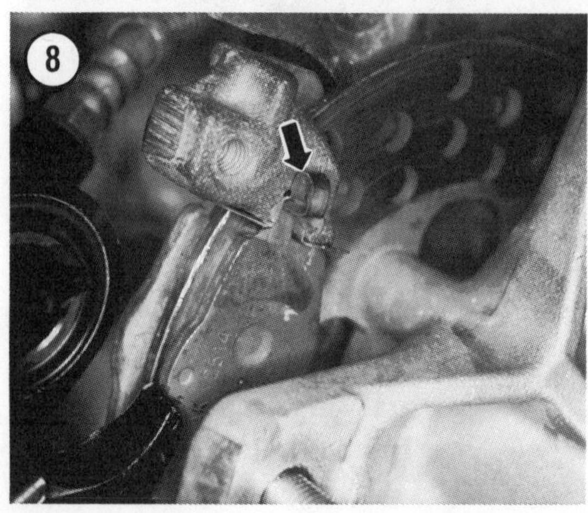

c. Hold the brake hose and turn the caliper to remove it from the brake hose (**Figure 9**). Remove the washer (**Figure 10**).

d. Place the end of the brake hose in a container to prevent brake fluid from dripping onto the vehicle.

e. Place the caliper in a plastic bag and tie the bag closed. Position the caliper so that brake fluid cannot run down the side of the caliper and contaminate the pads.

2B. If the caliper is only being partially removed and it is not necessary to disconnect the brake line at the caliper, perform the following:

a. Remove the brake caliper mounting bolt (**Figure 2**) and pivot the caliper housing off of the brake pads (**Figure 3**). Slide the caliper off of its pivot bolt and secure it with a Bunjee cord.

b. Insert a wooden or plastic spacer block in the caliper between the brake pads.

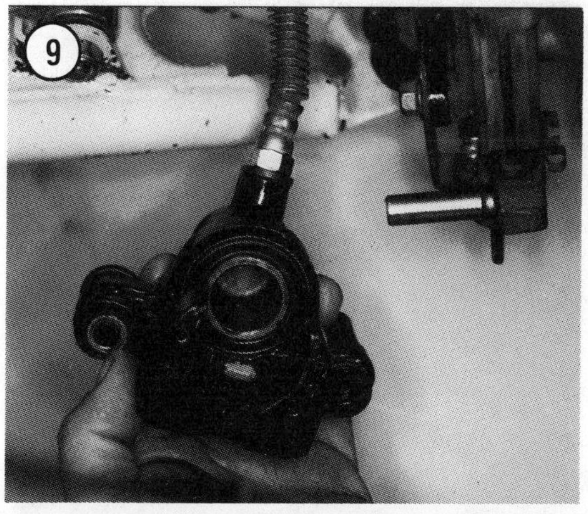

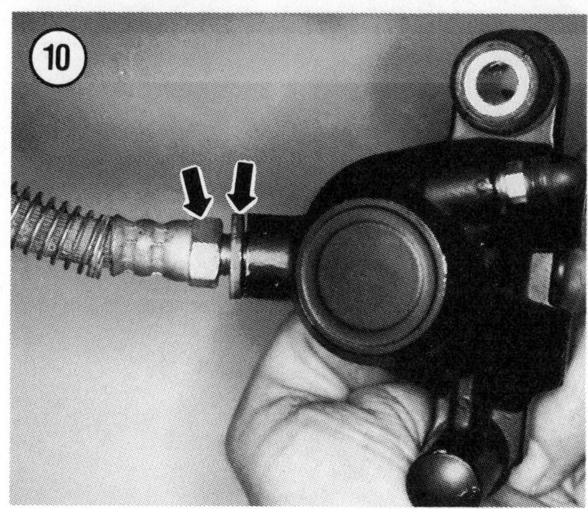

NOTE

The spacer block prevents the piston from being forced out of the caliper if the brake lever is squeezed while the caliper is removed from the brake disc. If the brake lever is squeezed, the piston will be forced out. If this happens, the caliper will have to be disassembled and then reassembled to properly reseat the piston. Bleeding the system will also be required.

c. Support the caliper with a Bunjee cord or a wire hook. Do not allow the caliper to hang by its hose.

3. Install the caliper by reversing these steps, while noting the following.

4A. If the caliper was removed from the vehicle:

a. Remove the caliper from the bag and check that the brake pads were not contaminated with brake fluid.

b. Install the washer (**Figure 10**) onto the brake hose. Then hold the brake hose and thread the caliper onto it. Tighten the caliper hand-tight.

c. Slide the caliper onto pivot bolt (**Figure 3**), then pivot the caliper over the brake pads.

d. Install the caliper mounting bolt (**Figure 2**) and tighten to the torque specification in **Table 3**.

e. Tighten the brake hose securely.

f. Refill the master cylinder and bleed both front brakes as described in this chapter.

4B. If the caliper was only partially removed from the vehicle:

a. Remove the spacer block from between the brake pads.

b. Disconnect the caliper from its hanger.

c. Slide the caliper onto pivot bolt (**Figure 3**), then pivot the caliper over the brake pads.

d. Install the caliper mounting bolt (**Figure 2**) and tighten to the torque specification in **Table 3**.

e. Operate the brake lever a few times to seat the pads against the brake disc.

WARNING

Do not ride the vehicle until you are sure that both front brakes are operating correctly with full hydraulic advantage. If necessary, bleed the front brakes as described in this chapter.

Caliper Removal/Piston Removal (Caliper Will Be Disassembled)

If the caliper is to be completely disassembled, force will be required to remove the piston from the caliper. This can be either the hydraulic pressure in the brake system itself, or compressed air. If you are going to use hydraulic pressure, you must do so before disconnecting the brake hose from the caliper. This procedure describes how to remove the piston while the caliper is still mounted on the vehicle.

1. Remove the brake pads as described in this chapter.
2. Operate the front brake lever to force the piston out of the caliper bore (**Figure 11**).

NOTE
*If the piston will not come out, you will have to use compressed air. Refer to **Disassembly** in this chapter.*

3. Support the caliper and loosen the caliper brake hose. Then hold the hose and turn the caliper to remove it and the washer from the brake hose. Place the end of the brake hose in a container to prevent brake fluid from dripping onto the vehicle.
4. Take the caliper to a workbench for further disassembly.

Disassembly

1. Remove the caliper as described in this chapter.

NOTE
If you have removed the piston, proceed to Step 3.

WARNING
The piston will be forced out of the caliper with considerable force. Do not try to cushion the piston with your fingers, as injury could result.

2. Cushion the piston with a shop rag. Do not place your hand or fingers in the piston area. Then apply compressed air through the brake line port to force the piston out.
3. Remove the retaining ring (if so equipped) and the dust seal.
4. Pry the piston seal from the caliper bore. Do not damage the bore.
5. Remove the bleed valve from the caliper.
6. Remove the caliper friction and dust boots.

Inspection

1. Clean the outside of the caliper housing with alcohol-based solvent and dry thoroughly. Clean the

dust and piston seal grooves with a soft-faced tool to avoid damaging the bore.

2. Discard the piston and dust seals. Discard the retaining ring on 1988-1989 models. Yamaha specifies to replace these parts whenever the caliper is disassembled.

3. Clean the piston in clean DOT 4 brake fluid.

4. Inspect the piston and the caliper piston bore (**Figure 12**) for deep scratches or other wear marks. Do not hone the piston bore. Replace if questionable.

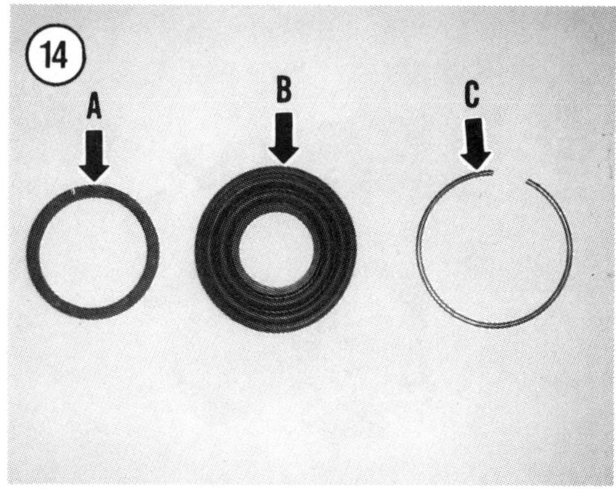

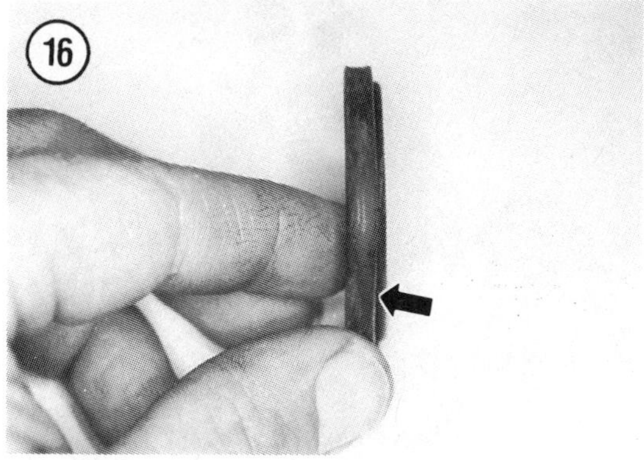

5. Clean the bleed valve with compressed air. Check the valve threads for damage. Replace the dust cap if missing or damaged.

6. Replace the brake hose washer if cracked or otherwise damaged.

7. Replace missing or damaged caliper boots (**Figure 13**).

8. Measure the thickness of each brake pad with a vernier caliper or ruler and compare to the specification listed in **Table 1**. If the pad thickness is equal to or less than the wear limit, replace all 4 brake pads at the same time.

Assembly

Install a new caliper seal kit (**Figure 14**) during reassembly:

a. Piston seal (A).
b. Dust seal (B).
c. Retaining ring (C) (used on 1988-1989 models only).

NOTE
Use new, DOT 4 brake fluid when brake fluid is called for in the following steps.

1. Soak the piston seal (A, **Figure 14**) in brake fluid for approximately 5 minutes.

2. Lightly coat the caliper bore with brake fluid.

3. Install the new piston seal into the caliper bore groove as shown in **Figure 15**.

4. Remove the new dust seal from its package and note the shoulder on one side of the seal (**Figure 16**). Then install the dust seal into the piston groove so that the shoulder on the seal faces away from the piston body as shown in **Figure 17**.

5. Lightly wipe the piston O.D. with brake fluid.

6. Insert the piston partway into the caliper bore (**Figure 18**).

7. Pull the dust seal back and seat it in the caliper bore groove (**Figure 19**).

8. On 1988-1989 models, install the retaining ring into the caliper bore ring groove (**Figure 20**). Then check that the dust seal seats squarely around the caliper bore (**Figure 21**).

9. Install and tighten the bleed screw.

10. Install the brake pads as described in this chapter.

18

19

Caliper Bracket Removal/Inspection/Installation

1. Remove the brake caliper as described in this chapter.

2. Remove the caliper bracket mounting bolts (**Figure 22**) and remove the caliper bracket.

3. Inspect the bracket (**Figure 23**) for cracks or other damage.

4. Install by reversing these steps. Tighten the caliper bracket mounting bolts (**Figure 22**) securely.

20

FRONT CALIPER (1990-ON)

Refer to **Figure 24** when replacing the front brake pads or servicing the front brake caliper.

Brake Pad Inspection

You can measure brake pad wear with the brake caliper installed on the vehicle as follows.

1. Remove the front wheels as described in Chapter Eleven.

2. Measure the distance from the disc surface to the back of the pad's friction material with a small ruler as shown in **Figure 25**. The brake pads should be replaced when the friction material thickness is equal to or less than the service limit specification in **Table 1**.

3. Install the front wheels as described in Chapter Eleven, or replace the brake pads as described in the following section.

21

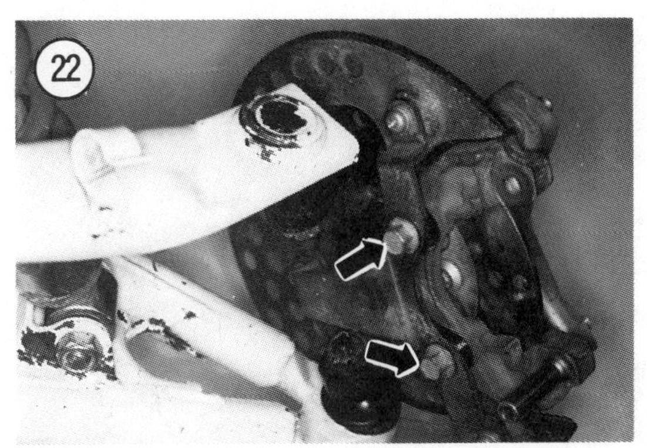

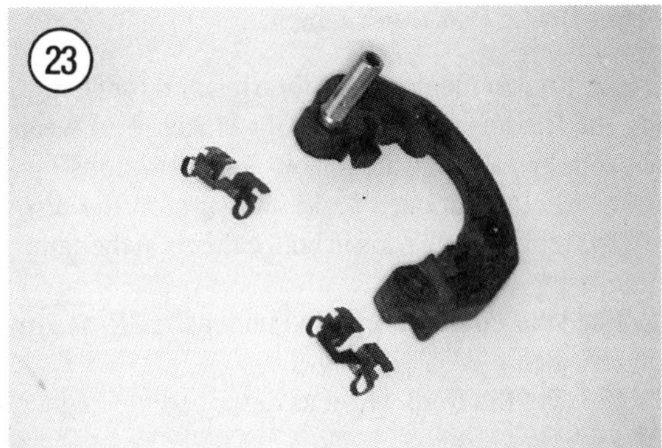

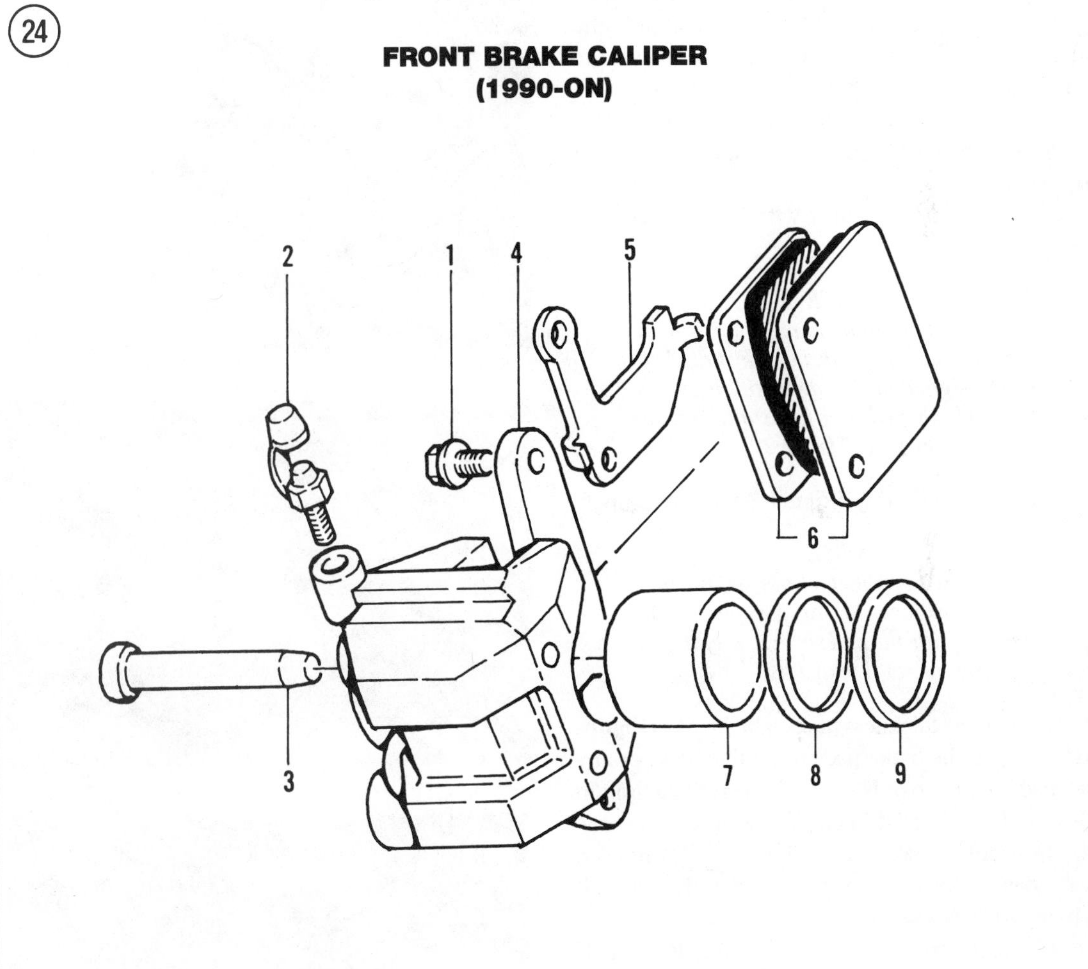

24
FRONT BRAKE CALIPER
(1990-ON)
1
2
3
4
5
6
7
8
9

1. Bolt
2. Bleed valve/cover
3. Pad pin bolts
4. Caliper housing
5. Shim
6. Brake pads
7. Piston
8. Piston seal
9. Dust seal

Front Brake Pad Replacement

There is no recommended time interval for changing the friction pads in the front brakes. Pad wear depends greatly on riding habits and conditions.

To maintain an even brake pressure on the disc always replace both pads in both calipers at the same time.

1. Read the information listed under *Disc Brake* in this chapter.
2. Remove the front wheel as described in Chapter Eleven.
3. Loosen, but do not remove, the 2 pad pin bolts (A, **Figure 26**) that hold the brake pads to the caliper.
4. Remove the 2 bolts (B, **Figure 26**) that hold the brake caliper to the steering knuckle. Then slide the brake caliper off of the brake disc.
5. Remove the 2 brake pad pin bolts (**Figure 27**).
6. Lift the brake pads out of the caliper as shown in **Figure 28**.
7. Support the brake caliper with a Bunjee cord or heavy wire hook.

NOTE

*If the pads are to be reused, mark each pad so that they can be reinstalled in their original mounting positions. Note that an L-shaped shim is installed on the inside brake pad (**Figure 29**).*

8. Check the pad spring (**Figure 30**) in the caliper.

NOTE

*Currently, Yamaha does not sell the pad spring (**Figure 30**) as a replacement item. Handle the pad spring carefully so that you do not damage it.*

9. Measure the thickness of each brake pad (**Figure 31**). Replace the brake pads if the thickness of any one pad is equal to or is less than the service limit in **Table 1**. Replace all 4 brake pads as a set.
10. Inspect the brake pads (**Figure 32**) for uneven wear, damage or grease contamination. Replace all 4 brake pads as a set.
11. Check the end of the piston for fluid leakage. If the dust seal is damaged and/or if there is fluid leaking from the caliper, overhaul the brake caliper as described in this chapter.
12. Check the pad pin bolts for corrosion, bending or other damage.
13. Check the brake disc for wear as described in this chapter.

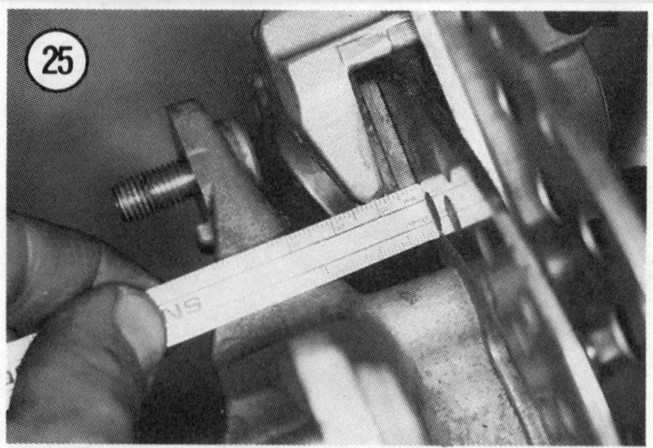

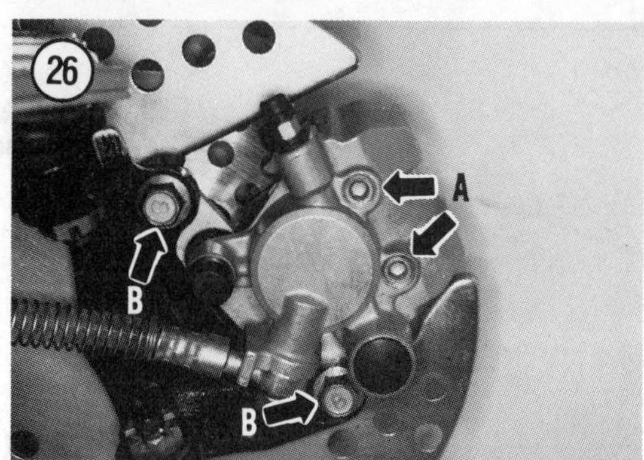

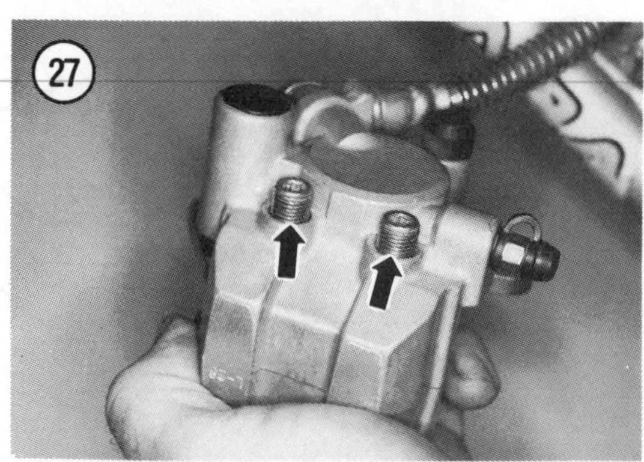

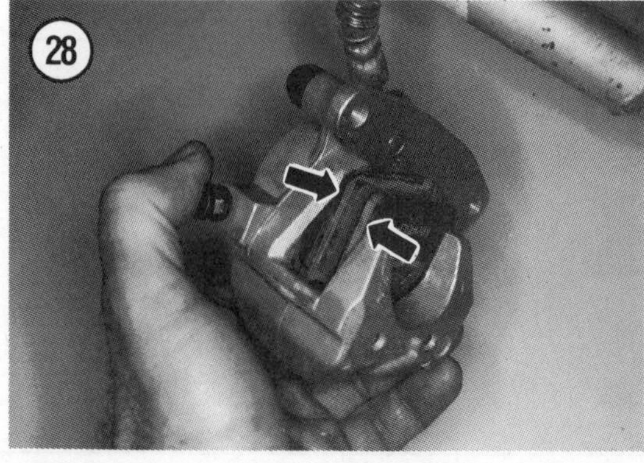

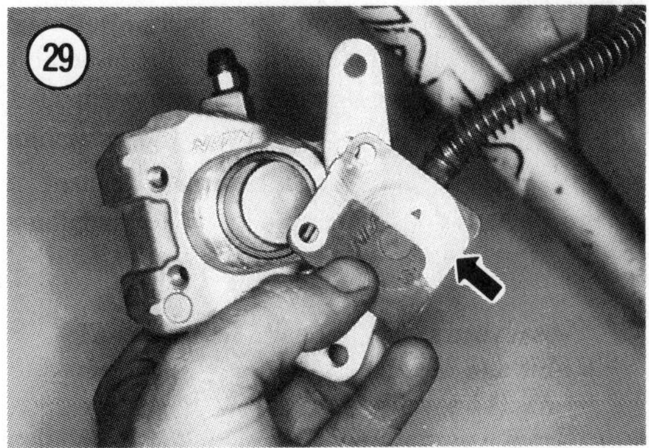

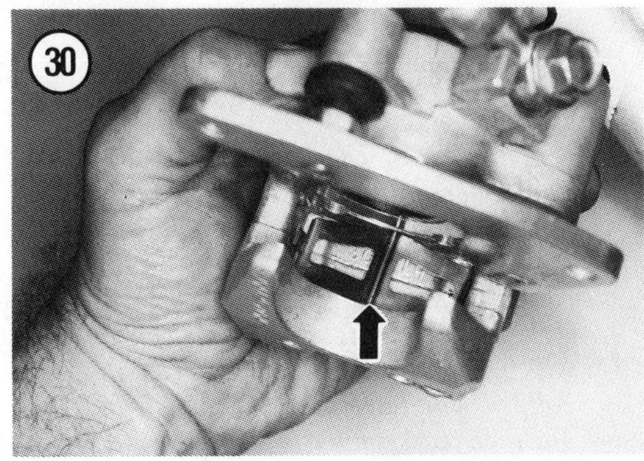

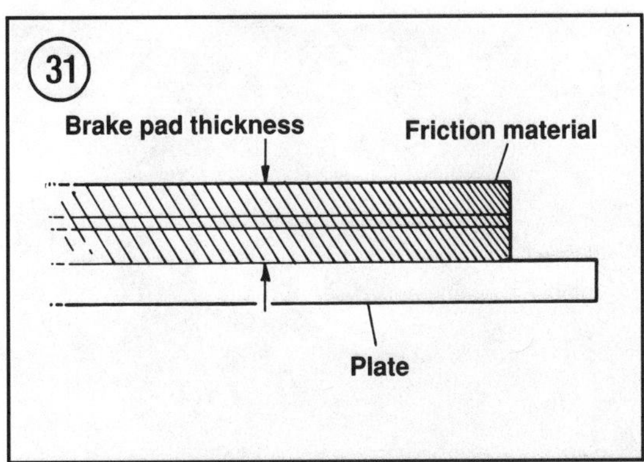

14. To make room for the new pads, the piston must be pushed back into the caliper. This will force brake fluid to backup through the hose and fill the master cylinder reservoir. To prevent the reservoir from overflowing, remove some of the brake fluid as follows:
   a. Clean the top of the master cylinder of all dirt.
   b. Remove the cap and diaphragm from the master cylinder.
   c. Temporarily install the inside brake pad into the caliper and slowly push the piston back into the caliper.
   d. Constantly check the reservoir to make sure brake fluid does not overflow. Siphon fluid, if necessary, before it overflows.

WARNING
Brake fluid is poisonous. Do not siphon with your mouth.

   e. The caliper piston should move freely. If not, the caliper should be removed and overhauled as described in this chapter.
   f. Push the caliper piston in all the way to allow room for the new pads.
   g. Remove the inside pad.
15. Install the brake pads as follows:
   a. If you are installing new brake pads, hook the pad shim onto one of the brake pads as shown in **Figure 33**. This pad is now the inside pad.

WARNING
Do not use grease on the pad shim to hold it in place. Heat produced during braking will melt the grease and cause it to run onto the brake pads and contaminate them and the brake disc.

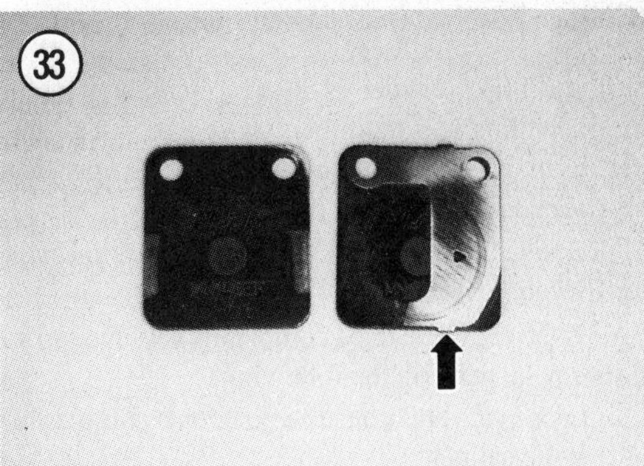

b. Install the inside brake pad (with pad shim) into the caliper so that the pad shim faces against the caliper piston; see **Figure 29** and **Figure 34**.

c. Install the outside brake pad (**Figure 35**) into the caliper. The friction material on both brake pads must face toward each other.

16. Compress both brake pads and install the 2 pad pin bolts (**Figure 27**) through the brake pads. Using an Allen wrench, tighten the pad pin bolts hand-tight.

17. Slide the brake caliper over the brake disc. Then install the brake caliper mounting bolts (B, **Figure 26**) and torque to the specification in **Table 3**.

18. Torque the brake pad pin bolts (A, **Figure 26**) to the specification in **Table 3**.

19. Repeat for the other brake caliper.

WARNING
Use new brake fluid clearly marked DOT 4 from a sealed container.

20. Install the master cylinder reservoir diaphragm and top cover. Tighten the cover screws securely.

21. Pull and release the brake lever a few times to seat the pads against each disc, then recheck the brake fluid level in the reservoir. If necessary, add fresh DOT 4 brake fluid.

22. Install the front wheels as described in Chapter Eleven.

WARNING
Do not ride the vehicle until you are sure that both front brakes are operating correctly with full hydraulic advantage. If necessary, bleed the front brakes as described in this chapter.

Removal/Installation (Caliper Will Not Be Disassembled)

If the brake caliper is to be removed without disassembling it, perform this procedure. If the caliper is to be disassembled, refer to *Caliper Removal/Piston Removal* in this chapter.

1. Remove the front wheel(s) as described in Chapter Eleven.

2A. If the caliper is to be completely removed from the vehicle, perform the following:

a. Loosen the brake hose banjo bolt (A, **Figure 36**) at the caliper.

b. Remove the bolts (B, **Figure 36**) that hold the brake caliper to the steering knuckle. Then lift the caliper off the brake disc.

c. Remove the banjo bolt and the 2 washers and remove the brake caliper. Seal the hose so that brake fluid does not drip out.

2B. If the caliper is only being partially removed, and it is not necessary to disconnect the brake line at the caliper, perform the following:

a. Remove the bolts (B, **Figure 36**) that hold the brake caliper to the steering knuckle. Then lift the caliper off the brake disc.

b. Insert a wooden or plastic spacer block in the caliper between the brake pads.

NOTE
The spacer block prevents the piston from being forced out of the caliper if the brake lever is squeezed while the caliper is removed from the brake disc. If the brake lever is squeezed, the piston will be forced out. If this happens, the caliper will have to be disassembled and then reassembled to properly reseat

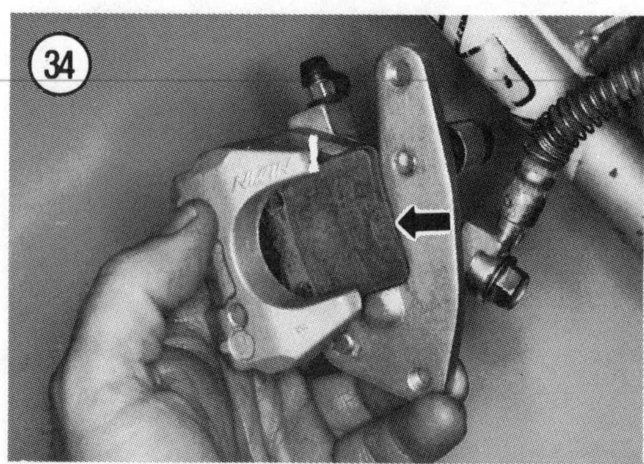
34

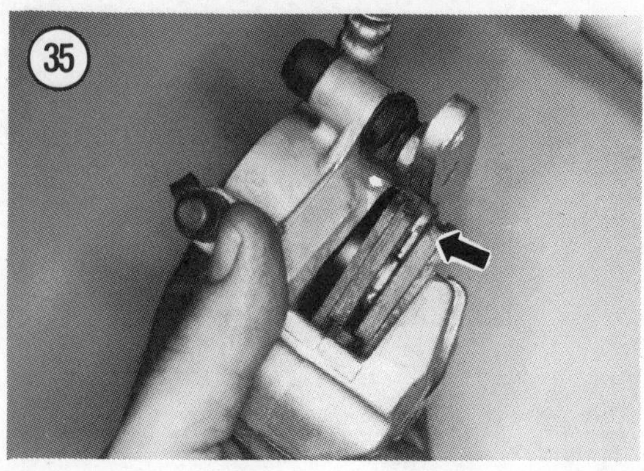
35

the piston. Bleeding the system will also be required.

c. Support the caliper with a Bunjee cord or a wire hook. Do not allow the caliper to hang by its hose.

3. Install the caliper by reversing these steps, while noting the following.

4A. If the caliper was completely removed from the vehicle:

a. Check that the brake pads are not contaminated with brake fluid. Wipe the caliper housing off with a clean rag.
b. Route the brake hose through the 2 raised tabs on the brake caliper as shown in **Figure 37**.
c. Place a washer on each side of the brake hose. Then install the bolt into the caliper (**Figure 38**). Tighten the banjo bolt finger-tight at this time.
d. Carefully install the caliper assembly over the brake disc. Be careful not to damage the leading edge of the pads during installation.
e. Install the 2 bolts that hold the brake caliper to the steering knuckle. Then torque the bolts to the specification in **Table 3**.
f. Torque the brake hose banjo bolt to the specification in **Table 3**.
g. Refill the master cylinder and bleed the front brake as described in this chapter.

4B. If the caliper was only partially removed from the vehicle:

a. Remove the spacer block from between the brake pads.
b. Disconnect the caliper from its hanger and carefully install the caliper over the brake disc. Be careful not to damage the leading edge of the pads during installation.
c. Install the 2 bolts that hold the brake caliper to the steering knuckle. Then torque the bolts to the specification in **Table 3**.
d. Operate the brake lever a few times to seat the pads against the brake disc.

WARNING

Do not ride the vehicle until you are sure that both front brakes are operating correctly with full hydraulic advantage. If necessary, bleed the front brakes as described in this chapter.

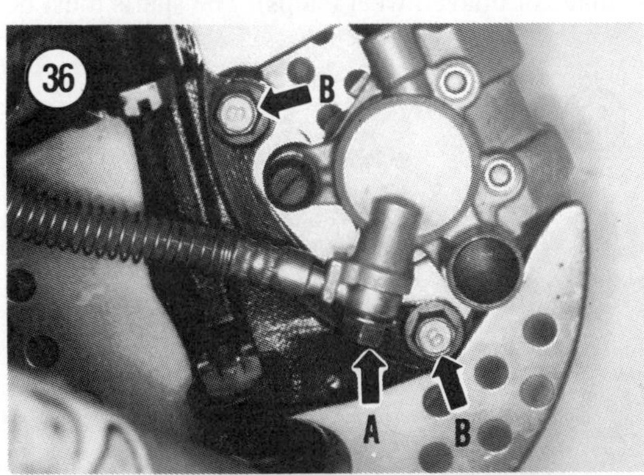

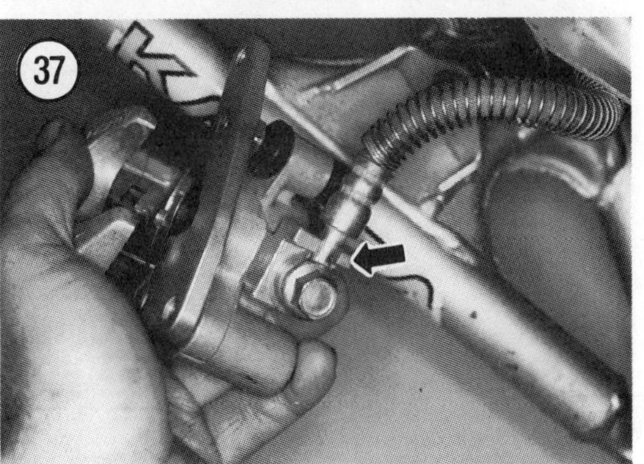

Caliper Removal/Piston Removal (Caliper Will Be Disassembled)

If the caliper is to be completely disassembled, force will be required to remove the piston from the caliper. Force can be supplied by hydraulic pressure in the brake system itself, or compressed air. If you are going to use hydraulic pressure, you must do so before the brake hose is disconnected from the caliper. This procedure describes how to remove the piston while the caliper is still mounted on the vehicle.

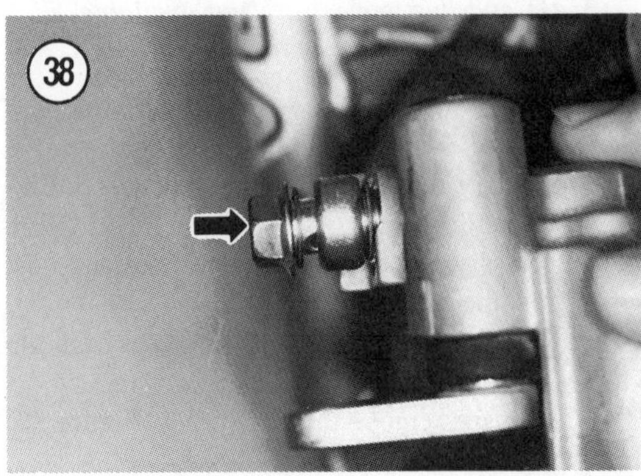

1. Remove the brake pads as described in this chapter.
2. Slide the support bracket out of the caliper.
3. Wrap a large cloth around the brake caliper.
4. Hold the caliper so that your hand and fingers are placed away from the piston and brake pad areas.
5. Operate the front brake lever to force the piston out of the caliper cylinder. Remove the piston.

NOTE

If the piston will not come out, you will have to use compressed air to remove it. Refer to Disassembly in this chapter.

6. Support the caliper. Then loosen the caliper banjo bolt (**Figure 37**) and remove the bolt and its 2 washers (**Figure 38**) from the caliper. Seal the brake hose to prevent brake fluid from dripping out.
7. Take the caliper to a workbench for further disassembly.

Disassembly

1. Remove the caliper as described in this chapter.

WARNING

The piston will be forced out of the caliper with considerable force. Do not try to cushion the piston with your fingers, as injury could result.

2. Cushion the caliper piston with a shop rag, making sure to keep your fingers and hand away from the piston area. Then apply compressed air through the brake line port (**Figure 39**) to remove the piston.
3. Remove the dust seal (A, **Figure 40**) and piston seal (B, **Figure 40**) from the inside of the cylinder.

NOTE

*Replacement friction boots (A, **Figure 41**) and dust covers are not available from Yamaha. Handle the caliper carefully so that you do not damage them in the following steps.*

4. If necessary, remove the support bracket (B, **Figure 41**) from the caliper.
5. If necessary, remove the friction boot and dust cover from the caliper body.
6. Remove the bleed valve and its cover from the caliper.
7. If necessary, remove the pad spring (**Figure 30**) from the caliper.

Inspection

1. Clean the outside of the caliper housing in alcohol-based solvent. Remove stubborn dirt with a soft brush, but do not brush the cylinder bores as this may damage them. Clean the dust and piston seal grooves with a plastic tipped tool so that you do not damage them or the cylinder bore. Then clean the caliper in hot soapy water and rinse in clear, cold water. Dry with compressed air.
2. Clean the piston in clean DOT 4 brake fluid.
3. Check the piston and cylinder bore for deep scratches or other obvious wear marks. Do not hone the cylinder. If the piston or cylinder is damaged, replace the caliper assembly.
4. Clean the bleed valve with compressed air. Check the valve threads for damage. Replace the dust cap if missing or damaged.
5. Clean the banjo bolt (**Figure 42**) with compressed air. Check the threads for damage. Replace worn or damaged washers.
6. Check the friction boot and dust cover. If swollen, cracked or severely worn, the entire brake caliper will have to be replaced.
7. Check the support bracket shafts for severe wear, damage or uneven wear (steps). The shafts must be

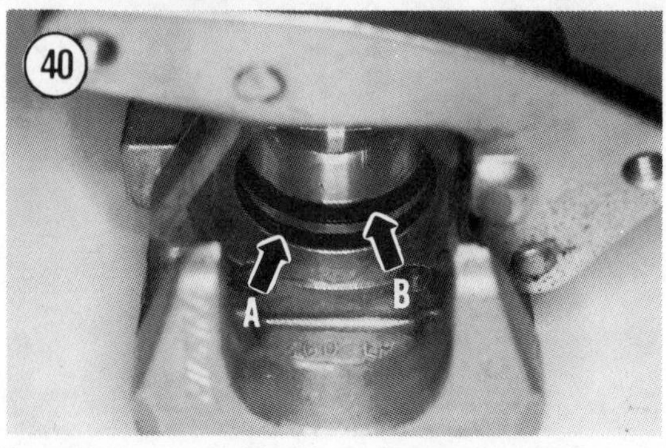

in good condition for the caliper to slide back and forth. Remove all grease residue from the bracket. If the support bracket is damaged, the entire brake caliper will have to be replaced.

8. Measure the thickness of each brake pad with a vernier caliper or ruler and compare to the specification listed in **Table 1**. If the pad thickness is equal to or less than the wear limit, replace the pads.

9. Inspect the brake pads (**Figure 32**) for uneven wear, damage or grease contamination. Replace the pads as a set, if necessary.

10. Replace the piston seal and dust seal as a set.

NOTE
Yamaha states that the piston seal and dust seal must be replaced whenever the caliper is disassembled.

Assembly

NOTE
Use new, DOT 4 brake fluid when brake fluid is called for in the following steps.

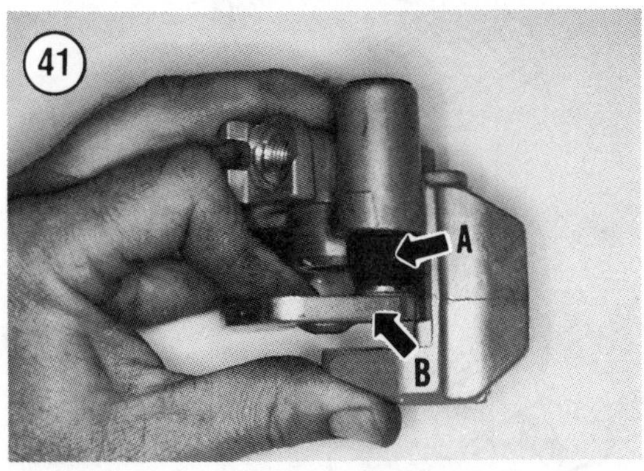

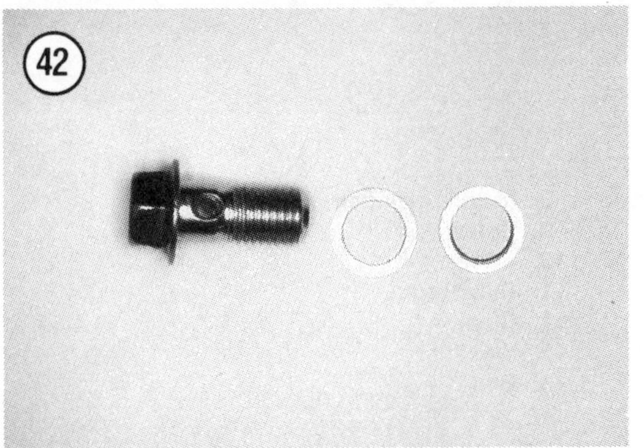

1. Soak the piston seal and dust seal in brake fluid for approximately 5 minutes.

2. Lightly coat the piston and cylinder bore with brake fluid.

3. Install a new piston seal (B, **Figure 40**) into the second groove in the cylinder bore.

4. Install a new dust seal (A, **Figure 40**) into the front groove in the cylinder bore.

NOTE
Check that both seals fit squarely into their respective cylinder bore grooves. If a seal is not installed properly, the caliper assembly will leak and braking performance will be reduced.

5. Install the closed end of the piston into the cylinder bore first. See **Figure 43**.

6. If the support bracket was removed, perform the following:

   a. Apply a thin coat of PBC (Poly Butyl Cuprysil) grease (or equivalent) to the caliper bracket shafts.

CAUTION
PBC grease (or equivalent) is a special high temperature, water-resistant grease that can be used in braking systems. Do not use any other kind of lubricant as it may thin out and contaminate the brake pads.

   b. Slide the support bracket shafts into the caliper (B, **Figure 41**). Slide the bracket back and forth, without removing it, to distribute the grease and to check the shafts for binding. The bracket must move smoothly; if any binding is noted, remove the bracket and inspect the shafts for

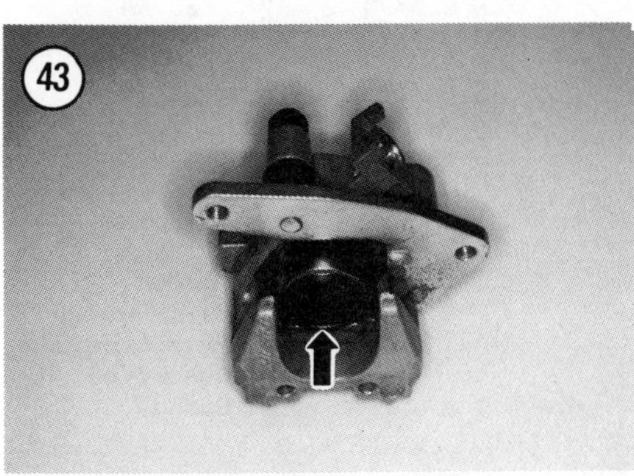

damage. Wipe off any excess grease from the outside of the caliper or bracket.

7. If necessary, install the bleed screw and its dust cover. Tighten securely.
8. If necessary, install the pad spring (**Figure 30**) into the brake caliper.
9. Install the brake caliper assembly and brake pads as described in this chapter.

FRONT MASTER CYLINDER

The front master cylinder is bolted to the handlebar with 2 bolts and a removable clamp. A spacer positions the master cylinder a specified distance away from the throttle housing assembly.

Figure 44 is an exploded view of the front master cylinder. Refer to it when servicing the master cylinder in the following sections.

Read the information listed under *Disc Brake* in this chapter before servicing the front master cylinder.

Removal/Installation

1. Park the vehicle on level ground and set the parking brake.

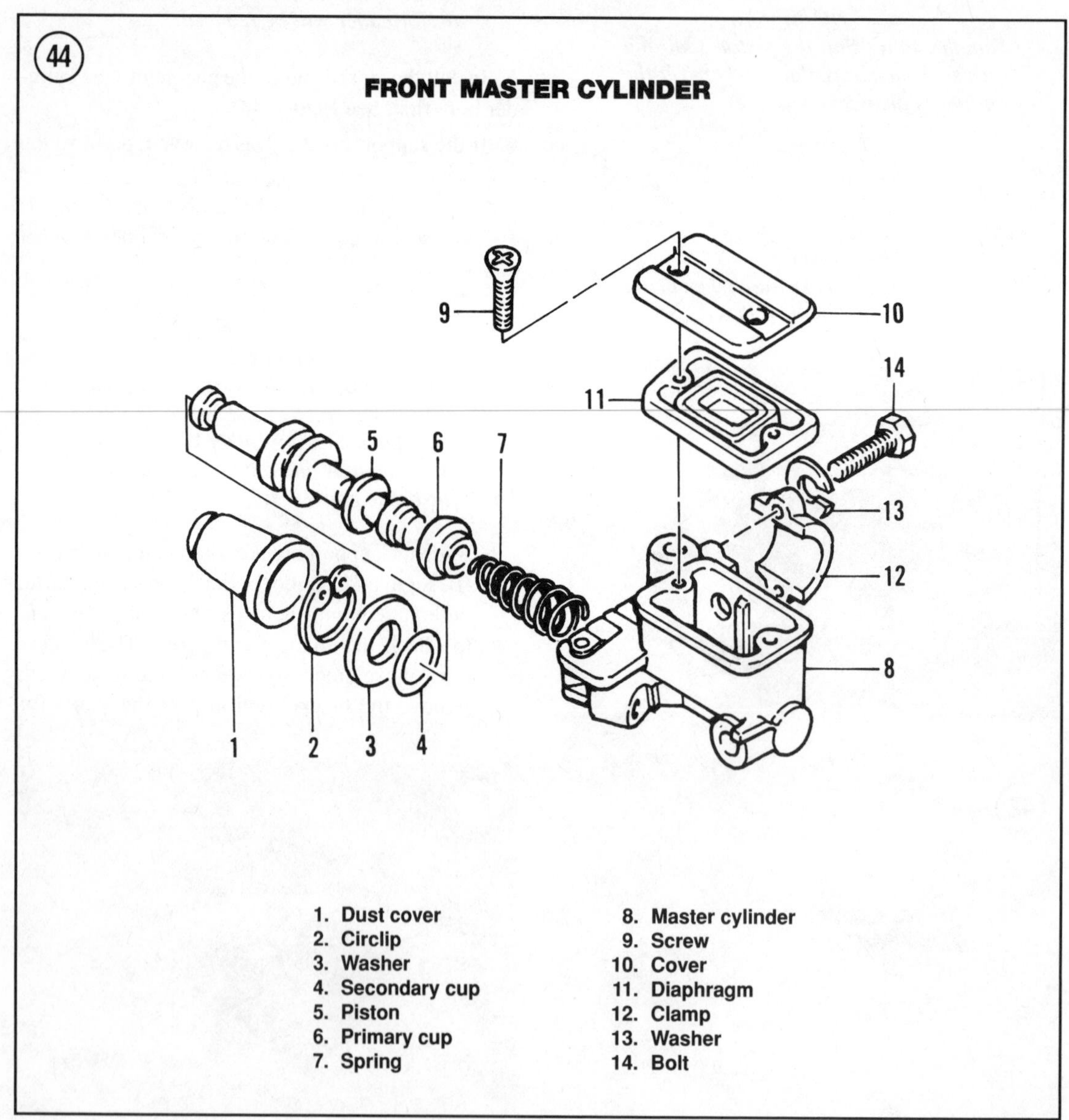

2. Cover the area under the master cylinder to prevent brake fluid from damaging any component that it might contact.

CAUTION

If brake fluid should contact any surface, wash the area immediately with soapy water and rinse completely. Brake fluid will damage plastic, painted and plated surfaces.

3. To remove brake fluid from the reservoir:
   a. Remove the master cylinder cover and diaphragm.
   b. Use a clean syringe and remove the brake fluid from the reservoir. Discard the brake fluid.
4. Pull the rubber cover away from the brake hose at the master cylinder.
5. Remove the banjo bolt (**Figure 45**) and the washers securing the brake hose to the master cylinder. Seal the brake hose to prevent brake fluid from dripping out.
6. Remove the 2 bolts and the clamp (**Figure 46**) holding the master cylinder to the handlebar and remove the master cylinder.

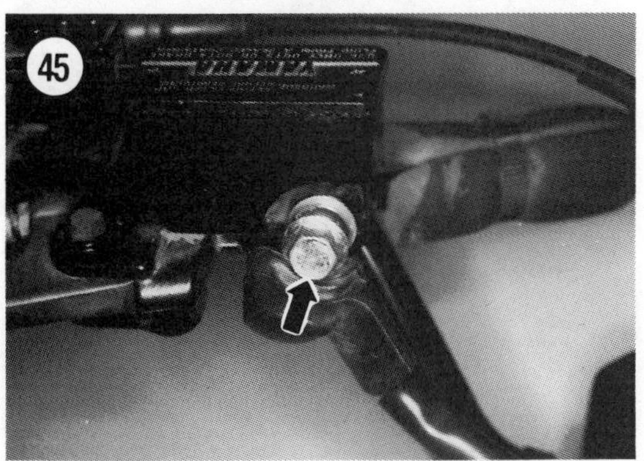

45

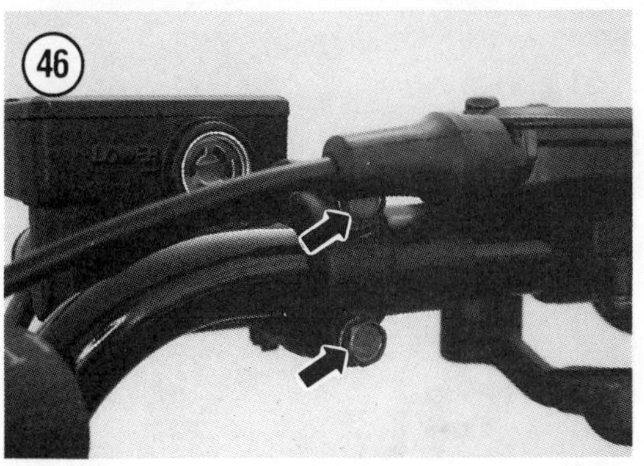

46

7. If necessary, service the master cylinder as described in this chapter.
8. Clean the handlebar, master cylinder and clamp mating surfaces.
9. Position the master cylinder onto the handlebar. Then install its clamp (arrow mark facing up) and install the 2 mounting bolts (**Figure 46**). Then position the spacer so that the notch in the spacer fits into the alignment tab on the throttle housing as shown in **Figure 47**. Slide the master cylinder over so that it contacts the spacer. Position the master cylinder brake lever to best suit your riding position and tighten the master cylinder mounting bolts securely.
10. Install the brake hose onto the master cylinder, using the banjo bolt (**Figure 45**) and the 2 washers; a washer should be installed on each side of the hose. Tighten the banjo bolt to the torque specification listed in **Table 3**.
11. Refill the master cylinder with DOT 4 brake fluid and bleed the front brakes as described in this chapter.

WARNING

Do not ride the vehicle until the front brakes are working properly. Make sure the that the brake lever travel is not excessive and that the lever does not feel spongy—both indicate that the bleeding operation needs to be repeated.

Disassembly

1. Remove the master cylinder as described in this chapter.
2. Remove the brake lever pivot bolt and nut from the master cylinder.

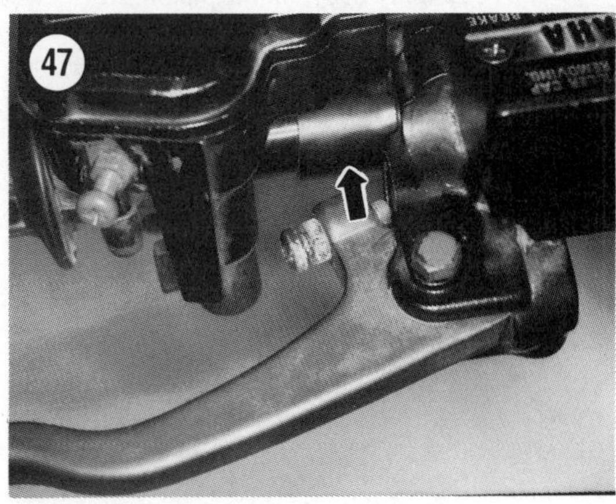

47

3. Remove the brake lever and spring (**Figure 48**) from the master cylinder.
4. Remove the master cylinder cover screws and remove the cover and diaphragm from the caliper.
5. Carefully remove the dust cover (**Figure 49**) from the groove in the end of the piston. See **Figure 50**.

NOTE
If there is brake fluid leaking at the front of the piston bore, the piston cups are worn or damaged. Replace the piston assembly during reassembly.

6. Compress the piston and remove the circlip (**Figure 51**) from the groove in the master cylinder.
7. Remove the circlip, washer and piston assembly (**Figure 52**) from the inside of the cylinder.

Inspection

Worn or damaged master cylinder components (**Figure 53**) will prevent proper brake fluid pressure from building in the brake line. Reduced pressure will cause the brake to feel weak and it will not hold properly.

1. Wash the piston and cylinder with clean DOT 4 brake fluid.
2. The piston assembly is identified in **Figure 54**:
   a. Spring.
   b. Primary cup.
   c. Secondary cup.
   d. Piston.

CAUTION
*Do not attempt to remove the secondary cup (C, **Figure 54**) from the piston. Removal will damage the cup, requiring replacement of the piston assembly.*

3. Check the piston assembly (**Figure 54**) for the following defects:
   a. Broken, distorted or collapsed piston return spring (A, **Figure 54**).
   b. Worn, cracked, damaged or swollen primary (B, **Figure 54**) and secondary cups (C, **Figure 54**).
   c. Scratched, scored or damaged piston (D, **Figure 54**).
   d. Corroded, weak or damaged circlip (E, **Figure 54**).
   e. Worn or damaged dust cover (F, **Figure 54**).

If any of these parts are worn or damaged, replace the piston assembly.

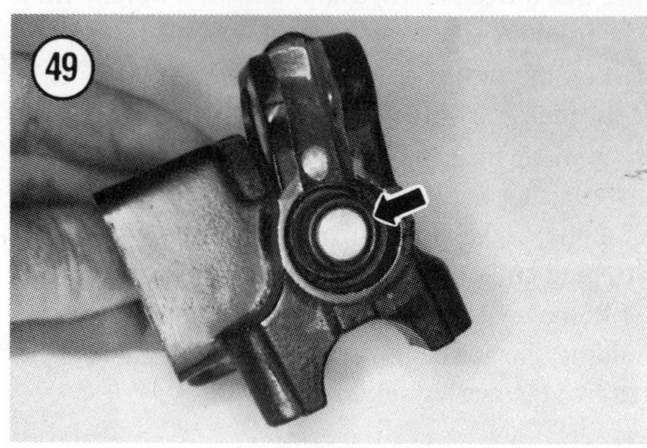

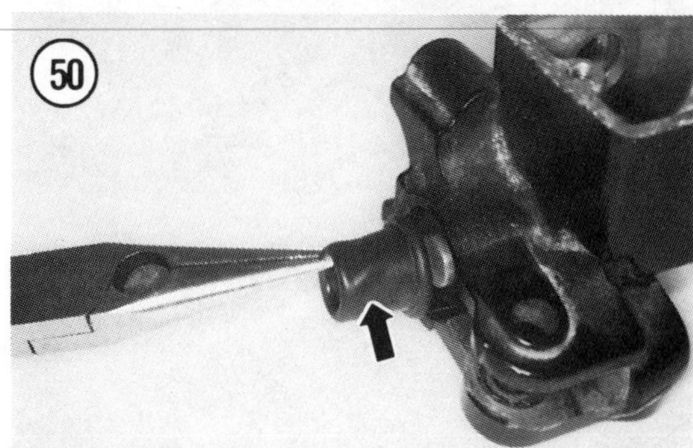

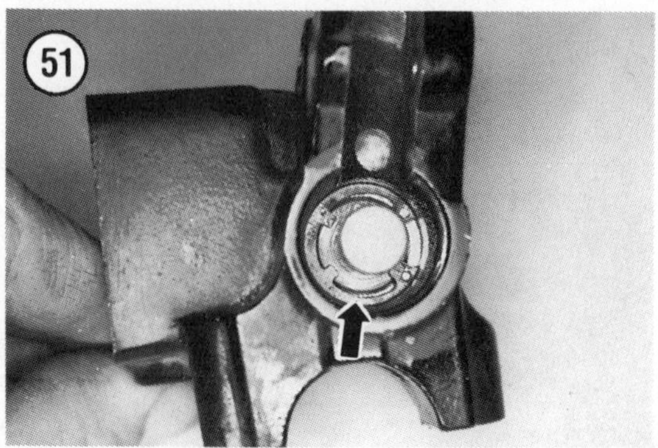

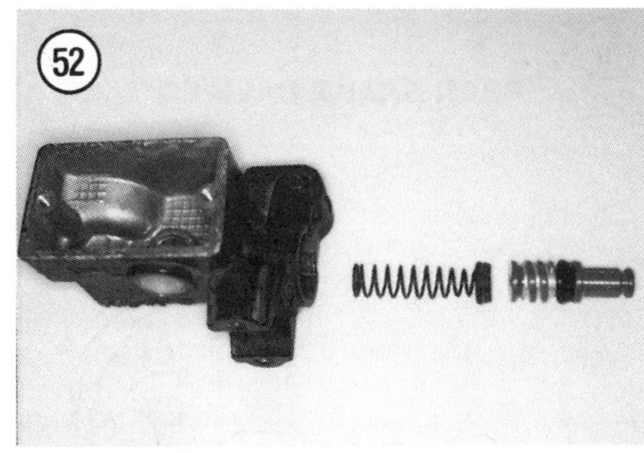

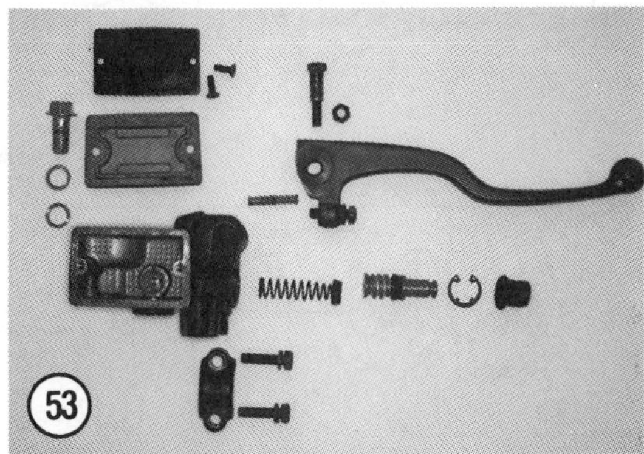

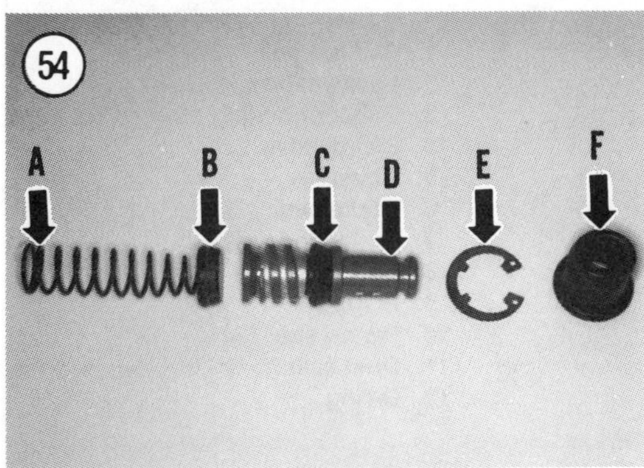

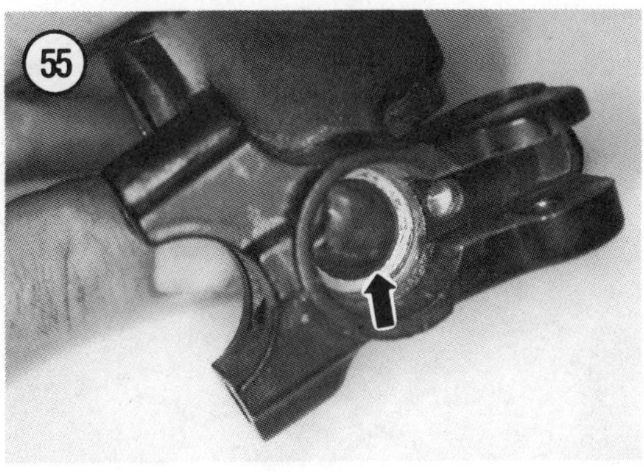

4. Inspect the master cylinder bore (**Figure 55**). If the bore is corroded, scored or damaged in any way, replace the master cylinder assembly. Do not hone the master cylinder bore to remove scratches or other damage.
5. Check for plugged supply and relief ports in the master cylinder. Clean with compressed air.

NOTE
A plugged relief port will cause the pads to drag on the disc.

6. Check the brake lever, pivot bolt and spring (**Figure 56**) for severely worn or damaged parts.
7. Check the reservoir cap and diaphragm for damage. Check the diaphragm for cracks or deterioration. Replace damaged parts as required.
8. Check all of the threaded holes in the master cylinder. Clean with compressed air. The small Phillips screws used to secure the reservoir cover can strip easily; check the screw heads and threads for damage and replace or repair if necessary.

Assembly

Use new, DOT 4 brake fluid when brake fluid is called for in the following steps.
1. If you are installing a piston repair kit, note the following:
   a. Check the repair kit to make sure that it contains all of the necessary new parts.
   b. Wash the new parts in new brake fluid.
2. Lightly coat the piston assembly and cylinder bore with brake fluid.
3. Assemble the piston assembly as shown in **Figure 54**. The primary cup fits onto the return spring.

CAUTION
When installing the piston assembly in Step 4, make sure the primary and sec-

13

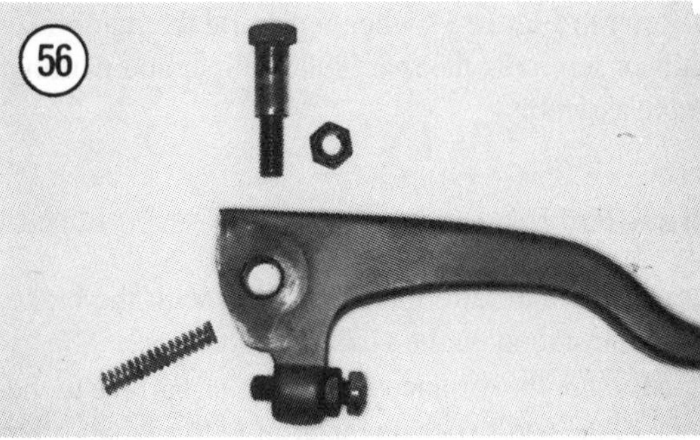

ondary cups do not tear or turn inside out—both cups are slightly larger than the bore.

4. Insert the piston assembly into the master cylinder bore in the direction shown in **Figure 52**.
5. Compress the piston assembly and install the washer (if used) and circlip. Make sure the circlip seats in the master cylinder groove completely (**Figure 51**). Push and release the piston a few times to make sure it moves smoothly in the cylinder bore.
6. Slide the dust cover (**Figure 50**) over the piston. Seat the cover in the cylinder bore and in the piston groove.
7. Insert the spring (**Figure 48**) into the brake lever and install the brake lever onto the master cylinder. Lightly grease the pivot bolt shoulder and install the bolt through the master cylinder and brake lever. Install the nut and tighten securely. Then, operate the hand lever, making sure the lever moves freely with no sign of binding and that the adjust screw on the lever contacts the piston correctly.
8. Install the master cylinder as described in this chapter.

REAR CALIPER

The rear brake caliper is mounted onto the rear axle housing. The parking brake assembly is mounted onto the rear brake caliper.

The only factory replacement components available for the rear brake caliper are those parts shown in **Figure 57**. The rear parking brake assembly (**Figure 58**) and the brake caliper dust boot and friction boot assemblies are not available separately. If these items are damaged, the entire rear brake caliper assembly will have to be replaced. When servicing the rear caliper in the following sections, handle these items carefully so that you do not damage them.

Refer to **Figure 57** when replacing the rear brake pads or servicing the rear brake caliper and parking brake assembly.

Brake Pad Inspection

You can measure brake pad wear with the brake caliper installed on the vehicle as follows.

1. Measure the distance from the disc surface to the back of the pad's friction material with a small ruler

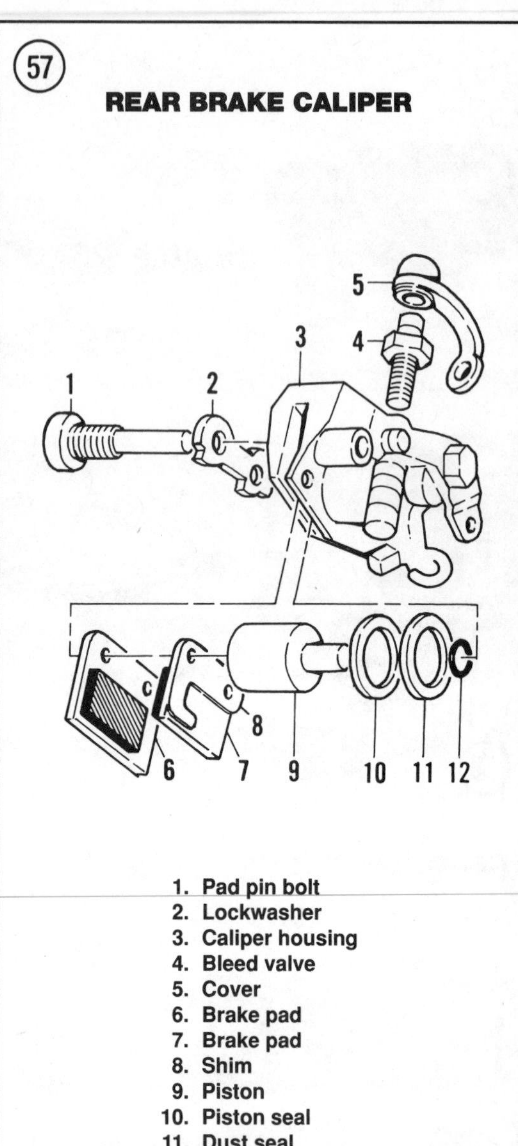

1. Pad pin bolt
2. Lockwasher
3. Caliper housing
4. Bleed valve
5. Cover
6. Brake pad
7. Brake pad
8. Shim
9. Piston
10. Piston seal
11. Dust seal
12. O-ring

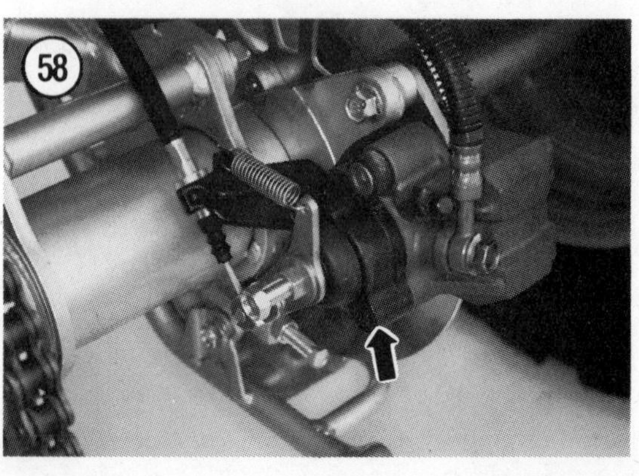

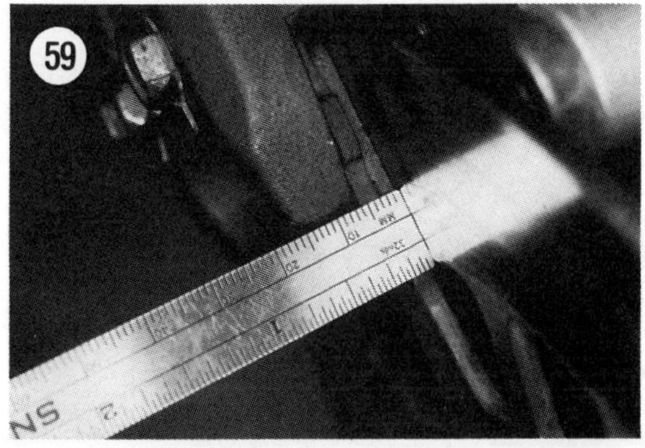
59

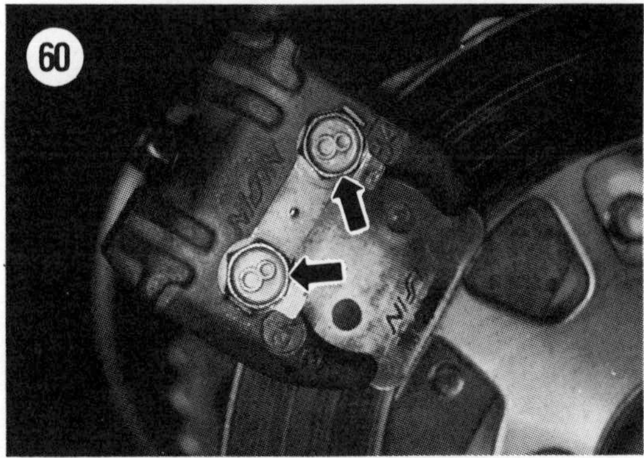
60

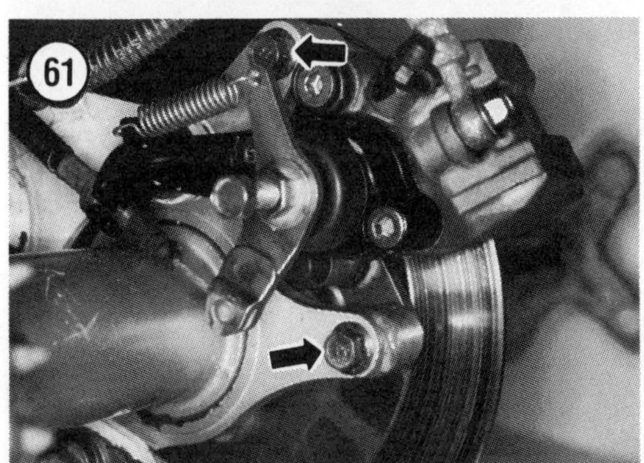
61

62

as shown in **Figure 59**. The brake pads should be replaced when the friction material thickness is equal to or less than the service limit specification in **Table 2**.

2. If necessary, replace the brake pads as described in the following section.

Rear Brake Pad Replacement

There is no recommended time interval for changing the friction pads in the front brakes. Pad wear depends greatly on riding habits and conditions.

To maintain an even brake pressure on the disc always replace both pads in the caliper at the same time.

1. Read the information listed under *Disc Brake* in this chapter.
2. Support the vehicle with all 4 wheels on the ground. Block the front wheels to prevent the vehicle from rolling forwards or backwards.
3. Release the parking brake.
4. Pry back the lockwasher tabs from the 2 brake pad mounting bolts (**Figure 60**). Then loosen, but do not remove, the 2 brake pad mounting bolts.
5. Remove the 2 bolts (**Figure 61**) that hold the brake caliper to the axle housing. Then slide the brake caliper off of the brake disc.
6. Remove the 2 brake pad mounting bolts (**Figure 62**) and lockwasher.
7. Remove the brake pads from the caliper as shown in **Figure 63**.
8. Support the brake caliper with a Bunjee cord or heavy wire hook.

NOTE

If the pads are to be reused, mark each pad so that they can be reinstalled in their original mounting positions. Note

63

*that an L-shaped shim is installed on the inside brake pad (**Figure 64**).*

9. Check the pad spring (**Figure 65**) in the caliper.

NOTE
*Currently, Yamaha does not sell the pad spring (**Figure 65**) as a replacement item. Handle the pad spring carefully so that you do not damage it.*

10. Measure the thickness of each brake pad (**Figure 66**). Replace the brake pads if the thickness of any one pad is equal to or is less than the service limit in **Table 2**. Replace both brake pads as a set.
11. Inspect the brake pads (**Figure 67**) for uneven wear, damage or grease contamination. Replace the pads as a set.
12. Check the end of the piston (**Figure 68**) for fluid leakage. If the dust seal is damaged and/or if there is fluid leaking from the caliper, overhaul the brake caliper as described in this chapter.
13. Check the pad pin bolts (**Figure 67**) for corrosion, bending or other damage.
14. Replace the lockwasher (**Figure 67**) if damaged.
15. Check the brake disc for wear as described in this chapter.
16. To make room for the new pads, the piston (**Figure 68**) must be pushed back into the caliper. This will force brake fluid to backup through the hose and fill the master cylinder reservoir. To prevent the reservoir from overflowing, remove some of the brake fluid as follows:
    a. Clean the top of the master cylinder of all dirt.
    b. Remove the cover and diaphragm from the master cylinder.
    c. Temporarily install the inside brake pad into the caliper and slowly push the piston back into the caliper.
    d. Constantly check the reservoir to make sure brake fluid does not overflow. Siphon fluid, if necessary, before it overflows.

WARNING
Brake fluid is poisonous. Do not siphon with your mouth.

    e. The caliper piston should move freely. If not, the caliper should be removed and overhauled as described in this chapter.
    f. Push the caliper piston in all the way to allow room for the new pads.

64

65

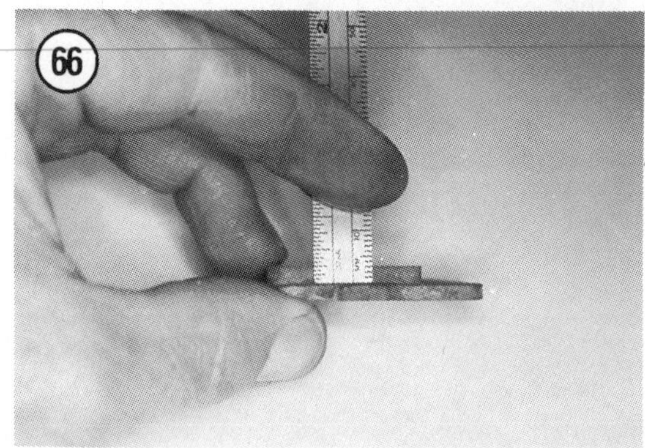
66

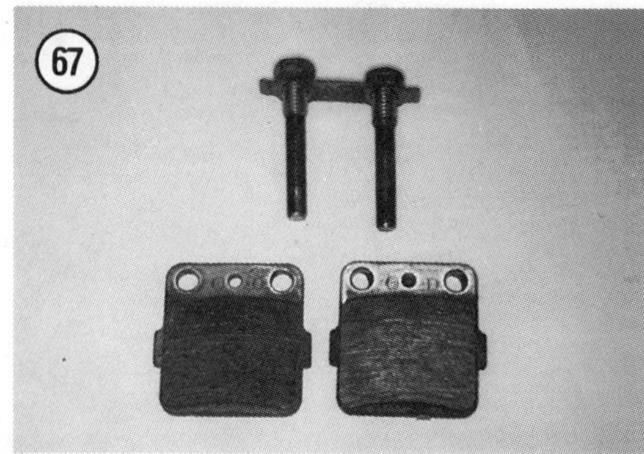
67

g. Remove the inside pad.

17. Install the brake pads as follows:

a. If you are installing new brake pads, hook the pad shim onto one of the brake pads as shown in **Figure 69**. This is now the inside brake pad.

WARNING
Do not use grease on the pad shim to hold it in place. Heat produced during braking will melt the grease and cause it to run onto the brake pads and contaminate them and the brake disc.

b. Install the inside brake pad (with pad shim) into the caliper so that the pad shim faces toward the caliper piston; see **Figure 69** and **Figure 70**.

c. Install the outside brake pad into the caliper. The friction material on both brake pads must face toward each other.

18. Compress both brake pads and install the lockwasher and the 2 pad pin bolts (**Figure 62**) through the brake pads. Tighten the bolts finger-tight at this time.

19. Slide the brake caliper over the brake disc. Then install the bolts that hold the brake caliper to the axle housing (**Figure 61**) and torque to the specification in **Table 3**.

20. Torque the brake pad pin bolts (**Figure 60**) to the specification in **Table 3**.

WARNING
Use new brake fluid clearly marked DOT 4 from a sealed container.

21. Install the master cylinder reservoir diaphragm and top cover. Tighten the cover screws securely.

22. Press and release the rear brake lever a few times to seat the pads against the disc, then recheck the brake fluid level in the reservoir. If necessary, add fresh DOT 4 brake fluid.

WARNING
Do not ride the vehicle until you are sure that the rear brake is operating correctly with full hydraulic advantage. If necessary, bleed the rear brake as described in this chapter.

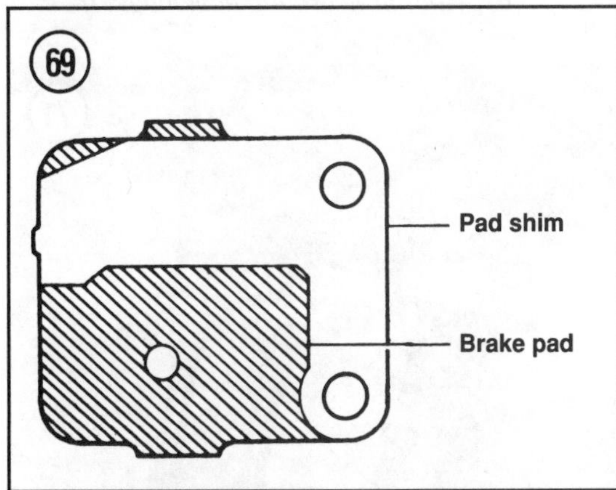

Brake Caliper Removal/Installation (Caliper Will Not Be Disassembled)

If the brake caliper is to be removed without disassembling it, perform this procedure. If the caliper is to be disassembled, refer to *Caliper Removal/Piston Removal* in this chapter.

1. Support the vehicle with all 4 wheels on the ground. Block the front wheels to prevent the vehicle from rolling forwards or backwards.

2. Release the parking brake. Then pull back the rubber cover and loosen the parking brake cable

(**Figure 71**) at the handlebar cable adjuster. Disconnect the parking brake cable at the rear brake caliper.

3A. If the caliper is to be completely removed from the vehicle, perform the following:

a. Loosen the brake hose banjo bolt (A, **Figure 72**) at the caliper.
b. Remove the bolts (B, **Figure 72**) that hold the brake caliper to the axle housing. Then lift the caliper off the brake disc.
c. Remove the banjo bolt and the 2 washers and remove the brake caliper. Seal the hose so that brake fluid does not drip out.

3B. If the caliper is only being partially removed and it is not necessary to disconnect the brake line at the caliper, perform the following:

a. Remove the bolts (B, **Figure 72**) that hold the brake caliper to the axle housing. Then lift the caliper off the brake disc.
b. Insert a wooden or plastic spacer block in the caliper between the brake pads.

NOTE

The spacer block prevents the piston from being forced out of the caliper if the brake lever is pressed while the caliper is removed from the brake disc. If the brake lever is pressed, the piston will be forced out. If this happens, the caliper will have to be disassembled and then reassembled to properly reseat the piston. Bleeding the system will also be required.

c. Support the caliper with a Bunjee cord or a wire hook. Do not allow the caliper to hang by its hose.

4. Install the caliper by reversing these steps, while noting the following.

5A. If the caliper was completely removed from the vehicle:

a. Check that the brake pads are not contaminated with brake fluid. Wipe the caliper housing off with a clean rag.
b. Route the brake hose across the top of the caliper as shown in **Figure 72**.
c. Place a washer on each side of the brake hose. Then install the bolt into the caliper (A, **Figure 72**). Tighten the banjo bolt finger-tight at this time.
d. Carefully install the caliper assembly over the brake disc. Be careful not to damage the leading edge of the pads during installation.
e. Install the 2 bolts that hold the brake caliper to the axle housing. Then torque the bolts to the specification in **Table 3**.
f. Torque the brake hose banjo bolt to the specification in **Table 3**.
g. Refill the master cylinder and bleed the rear brake as described in this chapter.

5B. If the caliper was only partially removed from the vehicle:

a. Remove the spacer block from between the brake pads.
b. Disconnect the caliper from its hanger and carefully install the caliper over the brake disc. Be careful not to damage the leading edge of the pads during installation.
c. Install the 2 bolts that hold the brake caliper to the axle housing. Then torque the bolts to the specification in **Table 3**.
d. Press the brake lever a few times to seat the pads against the brake disc.

WARNING

Do not ride the vehicle until you are sure that the rear brake is operating correctly with full hydraulic advantage. If

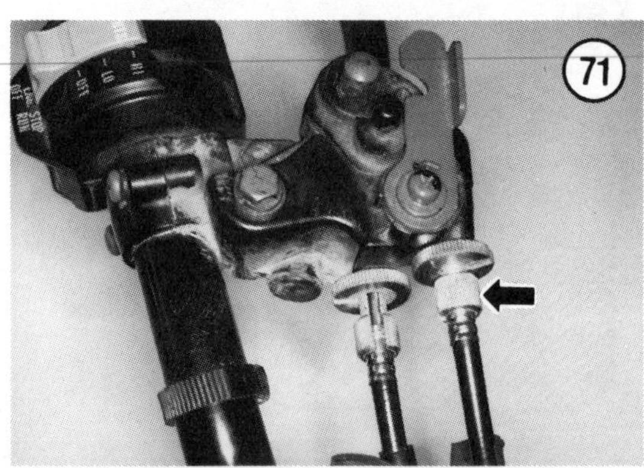

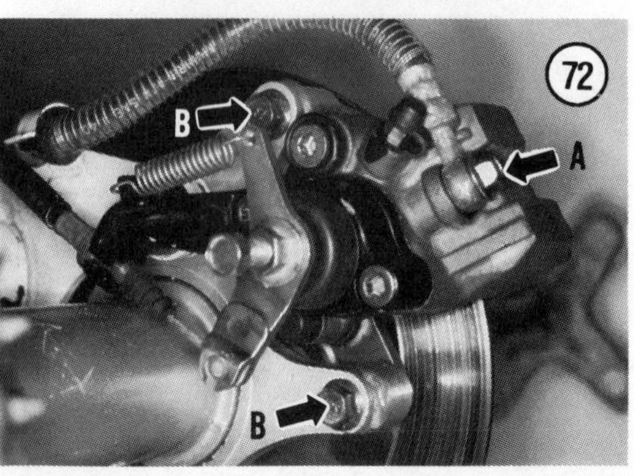

necessary, bleed the rear brake as described in this chapter.

6. Reconnect the parking brake cable. Then adjust the parking brake as described in Chapter Three.

Caliper Removal/Piston Removal (Caliper Will Be Disassembled)

If the caliper is to be completely disassembled, force will be required to remove the piston from the caliper. Force can be supplied by hydraulic pressure in the brake system itself, or compressed air. If you are going to use hydraulic pressure, you must do so before the brake hose is disconnected from the caliper. This procedure describes how to remove the piston while the caliper is still mounted on the vehicle.

1. Release the parking brake. Then pull back the rubber cover and loosen the parking brake cable (**Figure 71**) at the handlebar cable adjuster.

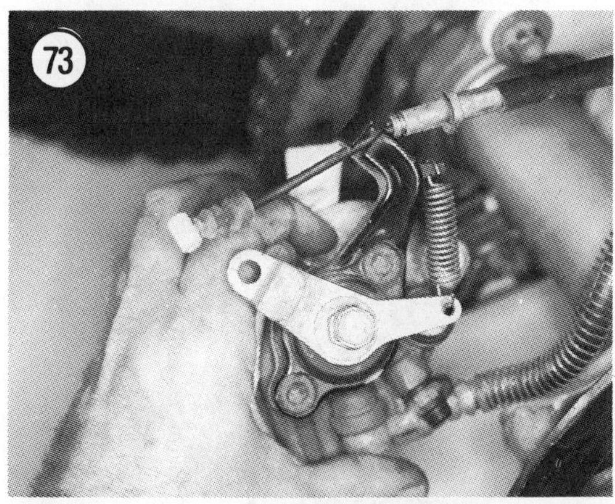

73

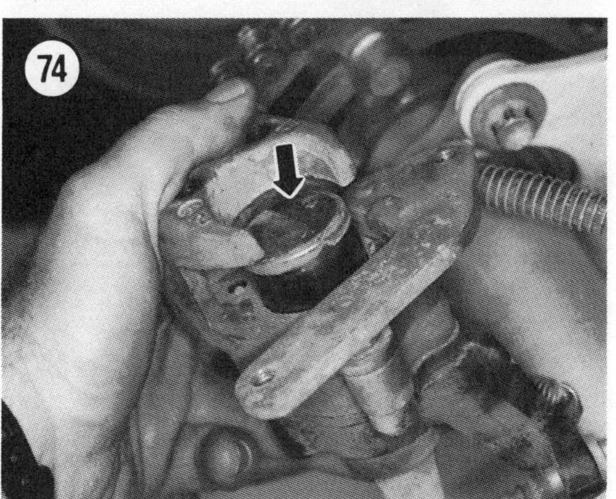

74

2. Remove the brake pads as described in this chapter.
3. Disconnect the parking brake cable at the lever mounted on the rear brake caliper (**Figure 73**).
4. Hold the caliper so that your hand and fingers are placed away from the piston.
5. Operate the rear brake lever to force the piston (**Figure 74**) out of the caliper cylinder. Remove the piston.

NOTE

If the piston will not come out, you will have to use compressed air to remove it. Refer to ***Disassembly*** *in this chapter.*

6. Support the caliper. Then loosen the caliper banjo bolt (**Figure 75**) and remove the bolt and its 2 washers from the caliper. Seal the brake hose to prevent brake fluid from dripping out.
7. Take the caliper to a workbench for further disassembly.

Disassembly

1. Remove the caliper as described in this chapter.

WARNING

The piston will be forced out of the caliper with considerable force. Do not try to cushion the piston with your fingers, as injury could result.

2. Cushion the caliper piston with a shop rag, making sure to keep your fingers and hand away from the piston area. Then apply compressed air through

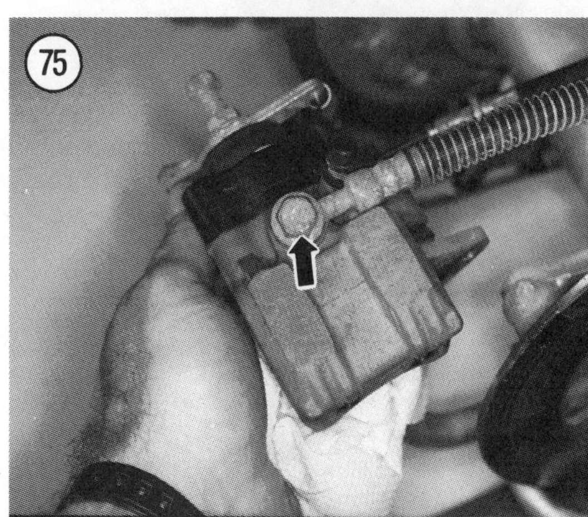

75

the brake line port (**Figure 76**) to remove the piston. See **Figure 77**.

3. Using a wooden or plastic rod with a flat, narrow tip, remove the dust seal (A, **Figure 78**) and piston seal (B, **Figure 78**) from the inside of the cylinder.
4. Remove the small O-ring (C, **Figure 78**) from the inside of the parking brake housing.
5. To remove the rear parking brake assembly, perform the following:
   a. Measure the length of the exposed threads on the parking brake adjust bolt as shown in **Figure 79**. Record the measurement for reassembly.
   b. Remove the return spring (A, **Figure 80**).
   c. Loosen the locknut (B, **Figure 80**) and remove the adjust bolt (C, **Figure 80**).
   d. Remove the parking brake lever (**Figure 81**).

NOTE
Remove the parking brake housing carefully in the following step to avoid damaging the gasket installed between the housing and brake caliper. Factory replacement gaskets are not available. If the gasket is damaged, you will have to make a new one.

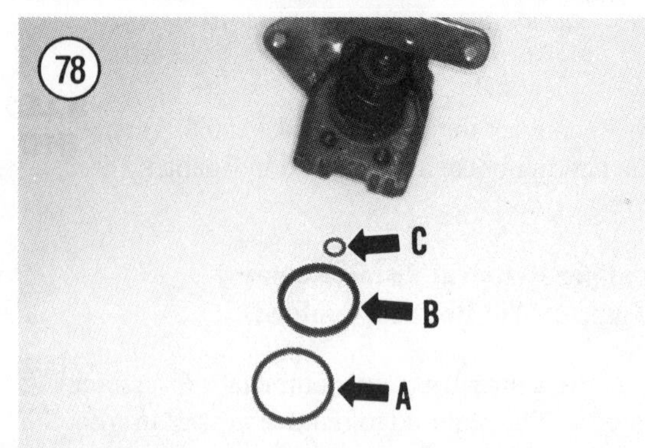

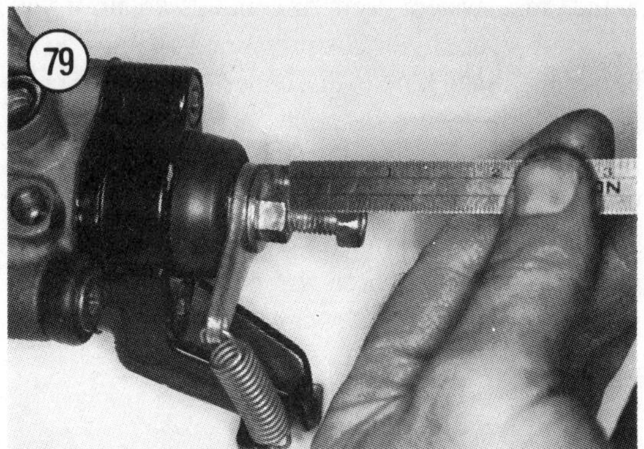

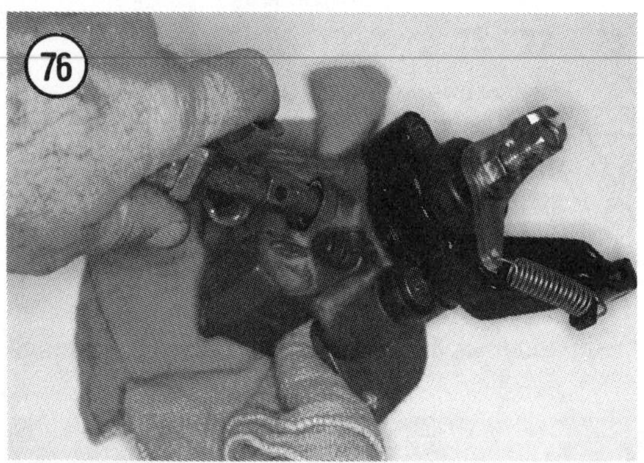

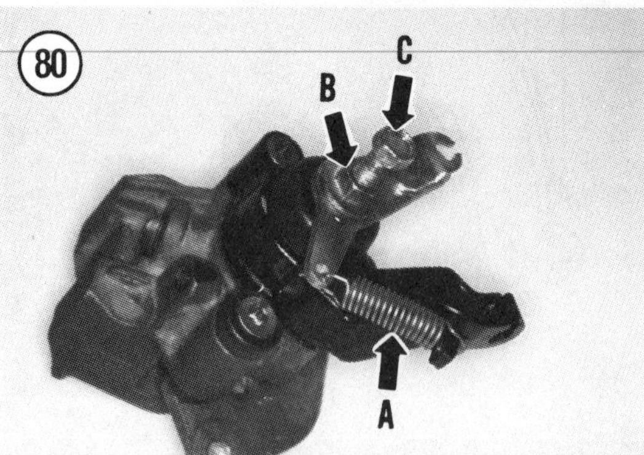

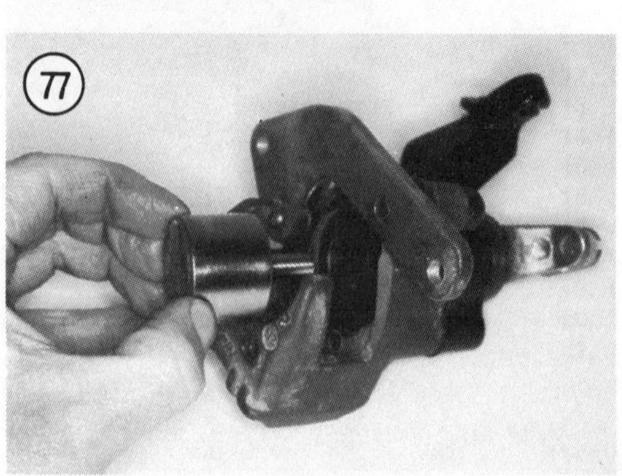

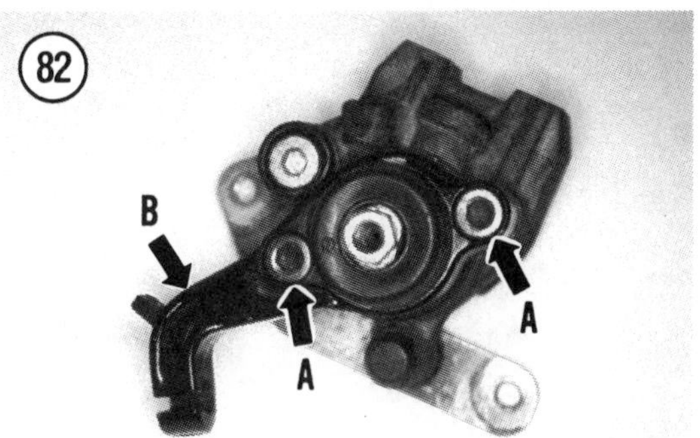

82

83

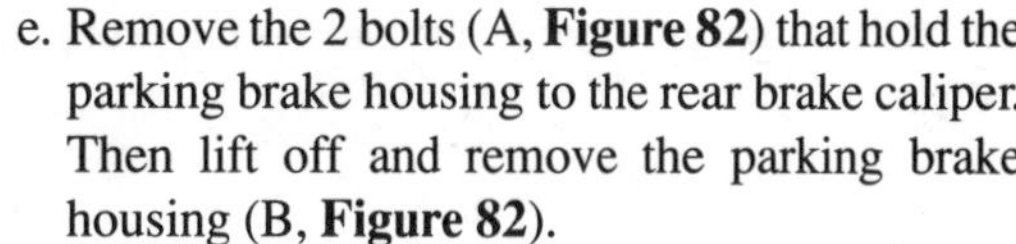

e. Remove the 2 bolts (A, **Figure 82**) that hold the parking brake housing to the rear brake caliper. Then lift off and remove the parking brake housing (B, **Figure 82**).

f. Remove the gasket (**Figure 83**).

6. Loosen the bolt (A, **Figure 84**) that holds the support bracket to the rear brake caliper. Then pull the support bracket (B, **Figure 84**) out of the brake caliper. Remove the washer (**Figure 85**) from the bolt threads.

NOTE

Factory replacement friction boots and dust covers are not available from Yamaha. Handle the caliper carefully so that you do not damage them in the following steps.

7. If necessary, remove the friction boot (**Figure 86**) from the brake caliper.

8. If necessary, remove the caliper bracket bolt (A, **Figure 87**) and both dust covers (B, **Figure 87**) from the brake caliper.

9. Remove the bleed valve and its cover from the caliper.

84

86

85

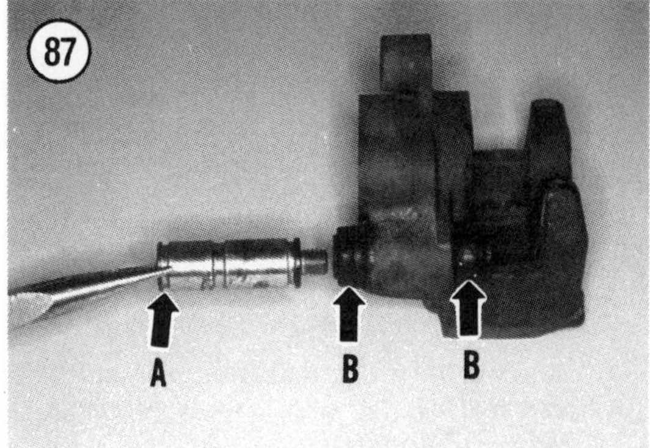

87

10. If necessary, remove the pad spring from the caliper.

Brake Caliper Inspection

1. Clean the outside of the caliper housing in alcohol-based solvent. Remove stubborn dirt with a soft brush, but do not brush the cylinder bores as this may damage them. Clean the dust and piston seal grooves with a plastic-tipped tool so that you do not damage them or the cylinder bore. Then clean the caliper in hot soapy water and rinse in clear, cold water. Dry with compressed air.
2. Clean the piston in clean DOT 4 brake fluid.
3. Check the piston and cylinder bore (**Figure 88**) for deep scratches or other obvious wear marks. Do not hone the cylinder. If the piston or cylinder is damaged, replace the caliper assembly.
4. Clean the bleed valve with compressed air. Check the valve threads for damage. Replace the dust cap if missing or damaged.
5. Clean the banjo bolt (**Figure 89**) with compressed air. Check the threads for damage. Replace worn or damaged washers.
6. Check the caliper friction boot and dust covers (**Figure 90**). If swollen, cracked or severely worn, the entire brake caliper will have to be replaced.
7. Check the support bracket shafts and bolt (**Figure 90**) for severe wear, damage or uneven wear (steps). The shafts must be in good condition for the caliper to slide back and forth. Remove all grease residue from the bracket. If the support bracket is damaged, the entire brake caliper will have to be replaced.
8. Measure the thickness of each brake pad (**Figure 66**) with a vernier caliper or ruler and compare to the specification in **Table 2**. If the pad thickness is equal to or less than the wear limit, replace the pads as a set.
9. Inspect the brake pads for uneven wear, damage or grease contamination. Replace the pads as a set, if necessary.
10. Replace the piston seal, dust seal and parking brake O-ring as a set.

NOTE

Yamaha states that the piston seal and dust seal must be replaced whenever the caliper is disassembled.

Parking Brake Housing Inspection

The rear parking brake assembly components (**Figure 91**) are not available separately. If these items are damaged, the entire rear brake caliper assembly will have to be replaced. When servicing the rear caliper in the following sections, handle these items carefully so that you do not damage them.

Refer to **Figure 91** when servicing the parking brake assembly.

NOTE
*Do not wash the parking brake housing (**Figure 92**) in solvent as this will wash the grease out of the housing.*

1. Inspect the spring in the parking brake housing. If the spring is damaged, replace the entire brake caliper assembly.
2. If the parking brake housing gasket (**Figure 91**) is damaged, cut out a new gasket, using gasket material.
3. Clean the parking brake lever, adjust bolt and nut, small return spring and the 2 Allen bolts in solvent. Dry with compressed air.

92

93

Assembly

NOTE
Use new, DOT 4 brake fluid when brake fluid is called for in the following steps.

1. If removed, install the 2 dust covers and caliper bracket bolt as shown in **Figure 87**.
2. If removed, install the friction boot through the caliper as shown in **Figure 86**.
3. Install the washer onto the caliper bracket bolt installed in Step 1. See **Figure 85**. Lubricate the support bracket shafts with a thin coat of PBC (Poly Butyl Cuprysil) grease (or equivalent). Then slide the support bracket into the brake caliper as shown in **Figure 93**. Torque the caliper bracket bolt (A, **Figure 84**) to the specification in **Table 3**.

CAUTION
PBC grease (or equivalent) is a special high temperature, water-resistant grease that can be used in braking systems. Do not use any other kind of lubricant as it may thin out and contaminate the brake pads.

4. If removed, install the parking brake housing assembly as follows:
   a. Install the gasket (**Figure 83**) onto the brake caliper.
   b. Place the parking brake housing (B, **Figure 82**) onto the brake caliper, aligning the mounting holes and gasket.
   c. Apply Loctite 242 (blue) onto the parking brake housing mounting bolts prior to installation. Then install the bolts (A, **Figure 82**) and torque to the specification in **Table 3**.
   d. Align the 2 dot marks (**Figure 94**) and install the parking brake lever onto the parking brake shaft.

94

e. Install the adjust bolt (C, **Figure 80**). Then set the bolt so that the original length of the threads, as recorded during disassembly (**Figure 79**), are exposed. Tighten the locknut (B, **Figure 80**).

f. Hook the spring between the parking brake lever and parking brake housing as shown in A, **Figure 80**.

5. Soak the dust seal, piston seal and parking brake housing O-ring (**Figure 78**) in brake fluid for approximately 5 minutes.

6. Install the new parking brake O-ring (A, **Figure 95**) into the groove in the back of the parking brake housing. See **Figure 96**.

7. Lightly coat the piston and cylinder bore with brake fluid.

8. Install a new piston seal (B, **Figure 95**) into the second groove in the cylinder bore.

9. Install a new dust seal (C, **Figure 95**) into the front groove in the cylinder bore.

NOTE

Check that both seals fit squarely into their respective cylinder bore grooves. If a seal is not installed properly, the caliper assembly will leak and braking performance will be reduced.

10. Install the piston (shoulder end first) into the cylinder bore. See **Figure 97**.

11. If necessary, install the bleed screw and its dust cover. Tighten securely.

12. If removed, install the pad spring into the brake caliper.

13. Install the brake caliper assembly and brake pads as described in this chapter.

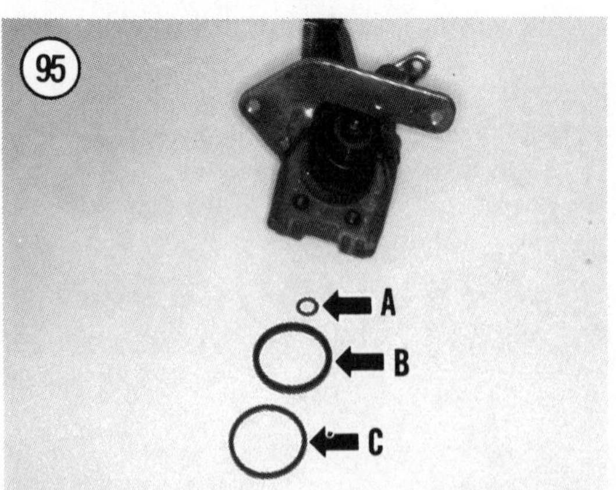

REAR MASTER CYLINDER

Refer to **Figure 98** when servicing the rear master cylinder in this section.

Read the information listed under *Disc Brake* in this chapter before servicing the master cylinder.

Removal/Installation

1. Park the vehicle on level ground. Block the front wheels so that the vehicle cannot roll in either direction.

2A. To remove brake fluid from the reservoir:

a. Remove the master cylinder cap and diaphragm. See A, **Figure 99**.

b. Use a clean syringe and remove the brake fluid from the reservoir. Discard the brake fluid.

2B. To drain the reservoir and brake hose:

a. Insert a tube onto the rear brake caliper bleed valve (**Figure 100**). Insert the other end of the tube into a clean container.

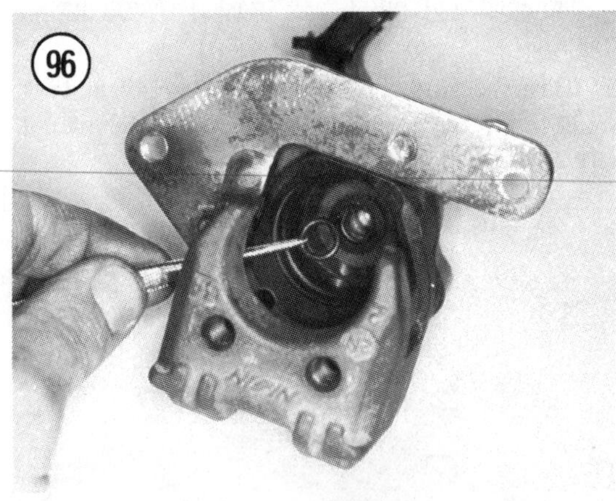

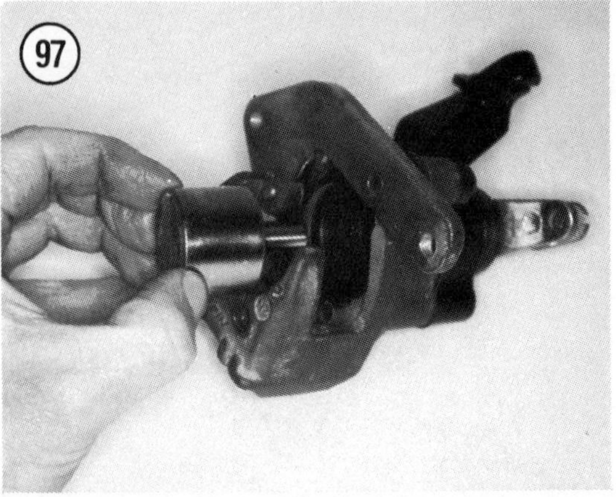

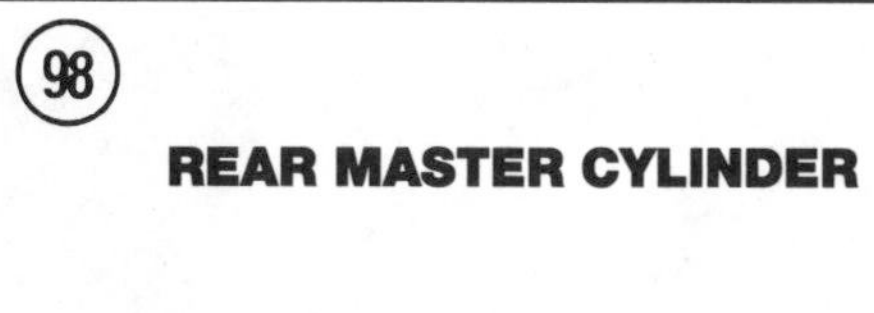

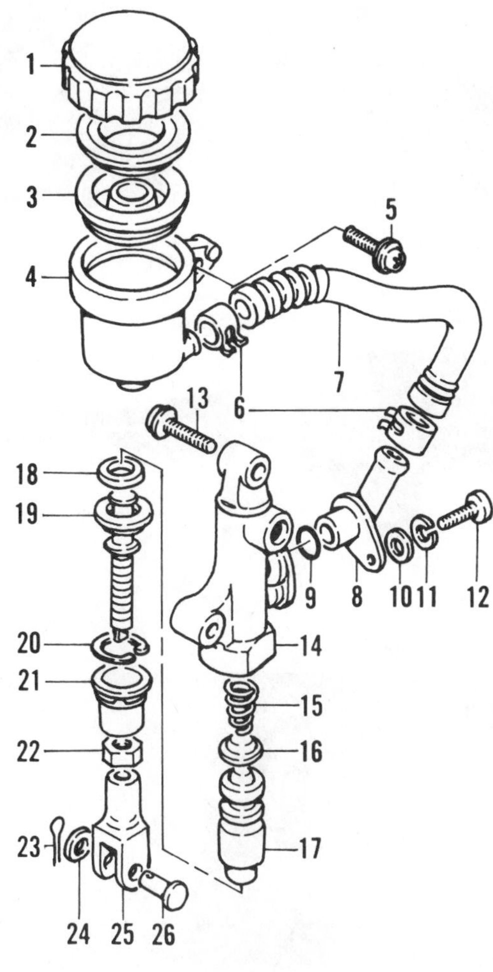

1. Cap
2. Diaphragm bushing
3. Diaphragm
4. Reservoir
5. Screw
6. Hose clamp
7. Hose
8. Hose joint
9. O-ring
10. Washer
11. Lockwasher
12. Screw
13. Screw
14. Master cylinder
15. Spring
16. Primary cup
17. Piston
18. Secondary cup
19. Pushrod/washer assembly
20. Circlip
21. Boot
22. Nut
23. Cotter pin
24. Washer
25. Connector
26. Clevis pin

b. Open the bleed valve and operate the rear brake lever to drain the master cylinder and brake hose of all brake fluid.

c. Close the bleed valve and remove the tube.

d. Discard the brake fluid.

3. Disconnect the brake pedal at the master cylinder pushrod. Remove the cotter pin (A, **Figure 101**) that locks the clevis pin between the pushrod and brake

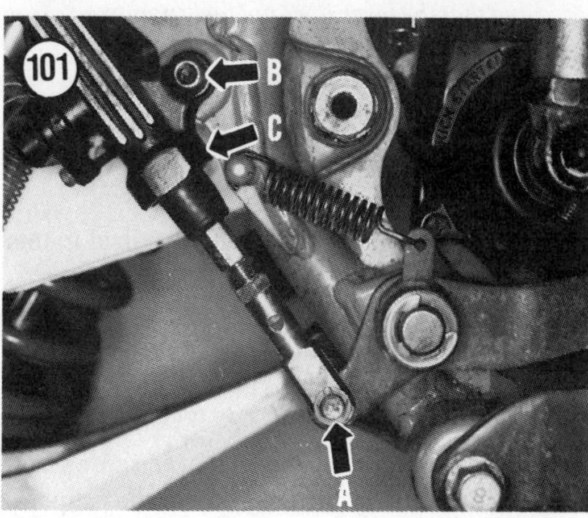

lever. Then remove the washer and pull out the clevis pin. Discard the cotter pin.

4. Loosen the master cylinder banjo bolt (**Figure 102**) and remove the bolt and its washers. Seal the brake hose to prevent brake fluid from dripping out.

5. Remove the brake fluid reservoir mounting screw (B, **Figure 99**).

6. Remove the master cylinder mounting screws (B, **Figure 101**), then remove the master cylinder and reservoir (C, **Figure 101**) from the frame.

7. If necessary, service the master cylinder as described in this chapter.

8. Mount the master cylinder housing onto the frame. Install and torque the screws (C, **Figure 101**) to the specification in **Table 3**.

9. Mount the brake fluid reservoir hose onto the frame and secure with its mounting screw. See B, **Figure 99**, typical.

10. Install the brake hose onto the master cylinder (**Figure 102**), using the banjo bolt and the 2 washers; a washer should be installed on each side of the hose. Tighten the banjo bolt to the torque specification in **Table 3**.

11. Connect the brake lever to the master cylinder pushrod with the clevis pin, washer and a new cotter pin (A, **Figure 101**). Bend the cotter pin arms over to lock it.

12. Refill the master cylinder with DOT 4 brake fluid and bleed the brake as described in this chapter.

13. Adjust the brake pedal height as described in Chapter Three.

WARNING

Do not ride the vehicle until the rear brake is working properly. Make sure the that the lever travel is not excessive and that the lever does not feel spongy—both indicate that the bleeding operation needs to be repeated.

Disassembly

1. Remove the master cylinder as described in this chapter.

2. Remove the screw and washers that secure the reservoir hose joint to the master cylinder; see 12, **Figure 98**. Then remove the hose joint (8, **Figure 98**) and the O-ring (9, **Figure 98**).

3. Remove the master cylinder cover screws and remove the cover and diaphragm from the caliper.

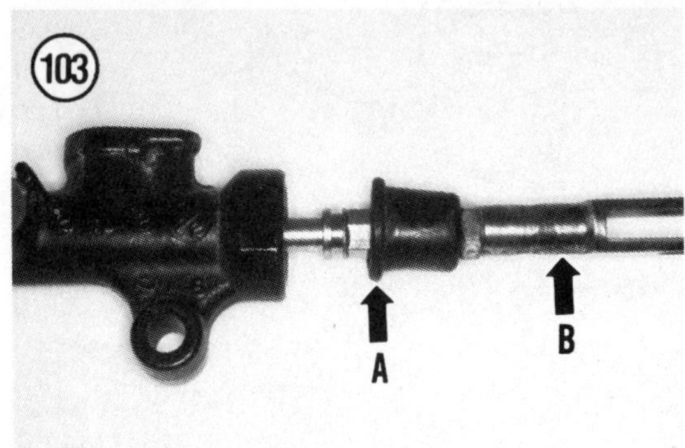

4. Carefully pull the dust cover (A, **Figure 103**) out of the piston bore.

NOTE
If there is brake fluid leaking at the front of the piston bore, the piston cups are worn or damaged. Replace the piston assembly during reassembly.

5. Compress the piston and remove the circlip (**Figure 104**) from the groove in the master cylinder.

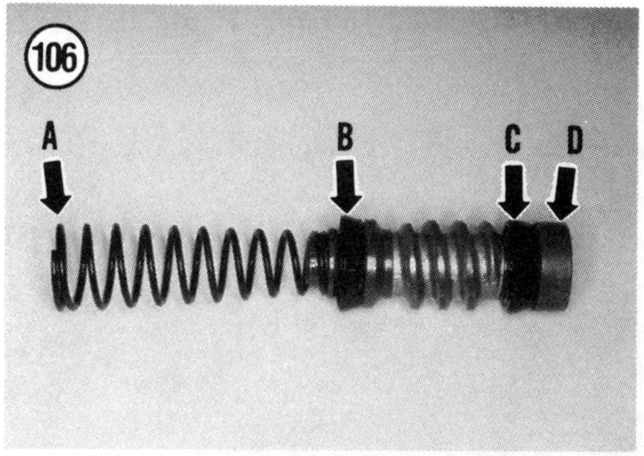

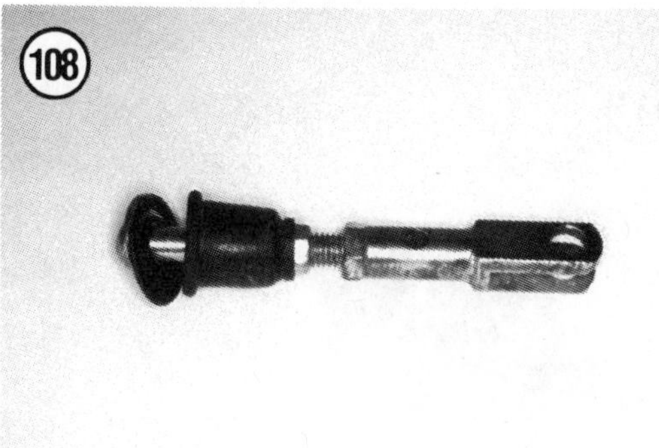

6. Remove the pushrod assembly along with the washer and circlip (B, **Figure 103**) from the cylinder.
7. Remove the piston assembly (**Figure 105**) from the cylinder.

Inspection

Worn or damaged master cylinder components will prevent proper brake fluid pressure from building in the brake line. Reduced pressure will cause the brake to feel weak and it will not hold properly.

1. Wash the piston and cylinder with clean DOT 4 brake fluid.
2. The piston assembly is identified in **Figure 106**:
   a. Spring.
   b. Primary cup.
   c. Secondary cup.
   d. Piston.

CAUTION
*Do not attempt to remove the secondary and primary cups (**Figure 106**) from the piston. Removal will damage the cups, requiring replacement of the piston assembly.*

3. Check the piston assembly (**Figure 106**) for the following defects:
   a. Broken, distorted or collapsed piston return spring (A, **Figure 106**).
   b. Worn, cracked, damaged or swollen primary (B, **Figure 106**) and secondary cups (C, **Figure 106**).
   c. Scratched, scored or damaged piston (D, **Figure 106**).

   If any of these parts are worn or damaged, replace the piston assembly.
4. Check the master cylinder bore (**Figure 107**) for severe wear, scratches or other damage.
5. Check the pushrod assembly (**Figure 108**) for the following defects:
   a. Cracked or damaged bracket. Stripped or damaged bracket nut.
   b. Severely worn or damaged pushrod.
   c. Worn, cracked or swollen dust boot.
   d. Bent or damaged circlip.
   e. Bent or damaged washer.

   If any of these parts are worn or damaged, replace the pushrod assembly. The circlip can be purchased separately.

13

6. Check for plugged supply and relief ports in the master cylinder (**Figure 109**). Clean with compressed air.

NOTE
A plugged relief port will cause the pads to drag on the disc.

7. Check the reservoir cap and diaphragm for damage. Check the diaphragm for cracks or deterioration. Replace damaged parts as required.
8. Check all of the threaded holes in the master cylinder. Clean with compressed air.
9. Clean and blow dry the reservoir and hose assembly. Replace the O-ring if worn, cracked or damaged.

Assembly

Use new, unused DOT 4 brake fluid when brake fluid is called for in the following steps.

1. If you are installing a piston repair kit, note the following:
   a. Check the repair kit to make sure that it contains all of the necessary new parts. Compare to the exploded view in **Figure 98**.
   b. Wash the new parts in new brake fluid.
2. Lightly coat the piston assembly and cylinder bore with brake fluid.
3. Assemble the piston assembly as shown in **Figure 106**. The return spring is tapered; fit the smaller end onto the piston as shown in **Figure 106**.

CAUTION
When installing the piston assembly in Step 4, make sure the primary and secondary cups do not tear or turn inside out—both cups are slightly larger than the bore.

4. Insert the piston assembly into the master cylinder bore, spring end first, as shown in **Figure 105**.
5. Install the pushrod ball into the end of the piston (**Figure 110**) and compress the piston slightly. Slide the washer down the pushrod so that it rests below the circlip groove in the cylinder. Install the circlip (**Figure 104**), making sure it seats in the cylinder groove completely. Push and release the piston a few times to make sure it moves smoothly in the cylinder bore.
6. Pull the dust cover down the pushrod and fit it into the cylinder bore as shown in **Figure 111**.
7. Install the brake hose O-ring (9, **Figure 98**) into the master cylinder.
8. Insert the hose joint (8, **Figure 98**) into the master cylinder and secure it with the screw, lockwasher and flat washer.
9. Install the master cylinder as described in this chapter.

BRAKE HOSE REPLACEMENT

The brake hoses should be replaced when they show signs of wear or damage. The front brake hoses and their fittings are shown in **Figure 112** (1987-1989) or **Figure 113** (1990-on).

109

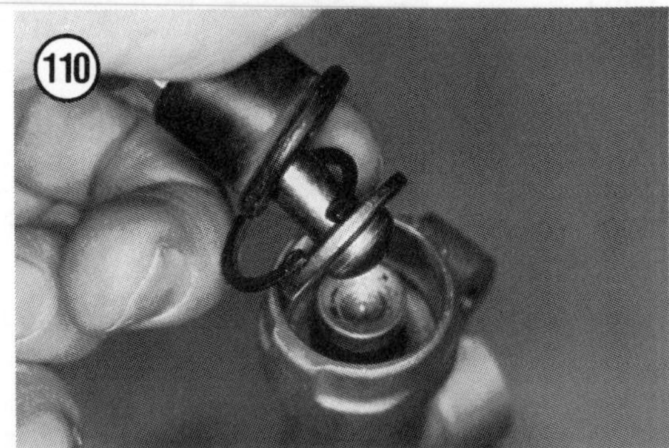
110

111

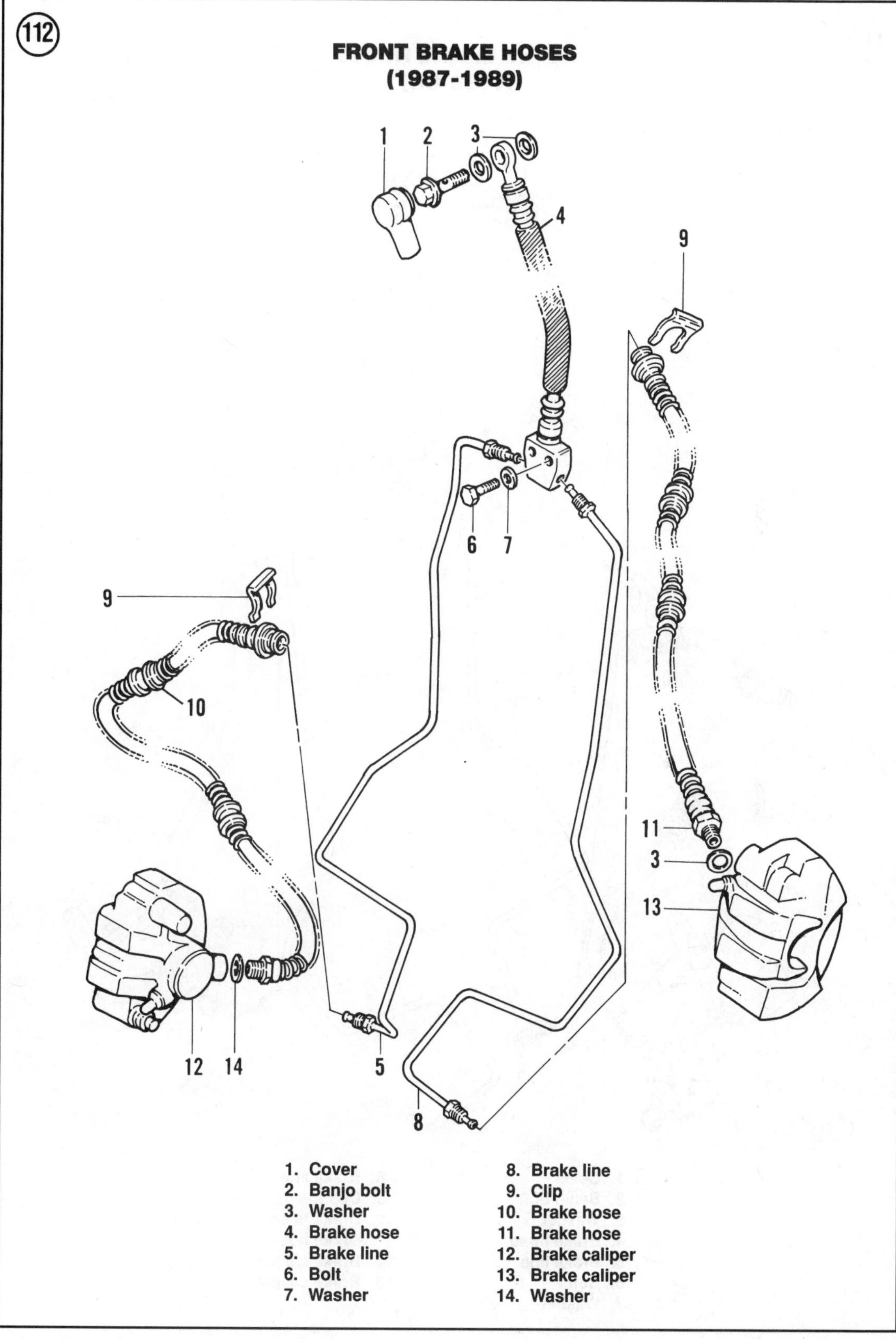
112
FRONT BRAKE HOSES
(1987-1989)
1
2
3
4
9
6
7
9
10
11
3
13
12
14
5
8
1. Cover
2. Banjo bolt
3. Washer
4. Brake hose
5. Brake line
6. Bolt
7. Washer
8. Brake line
9. Clip
10. Brake hose
11. Brake hose
12. Brake caliper
13. Brake caliper
14. Washer

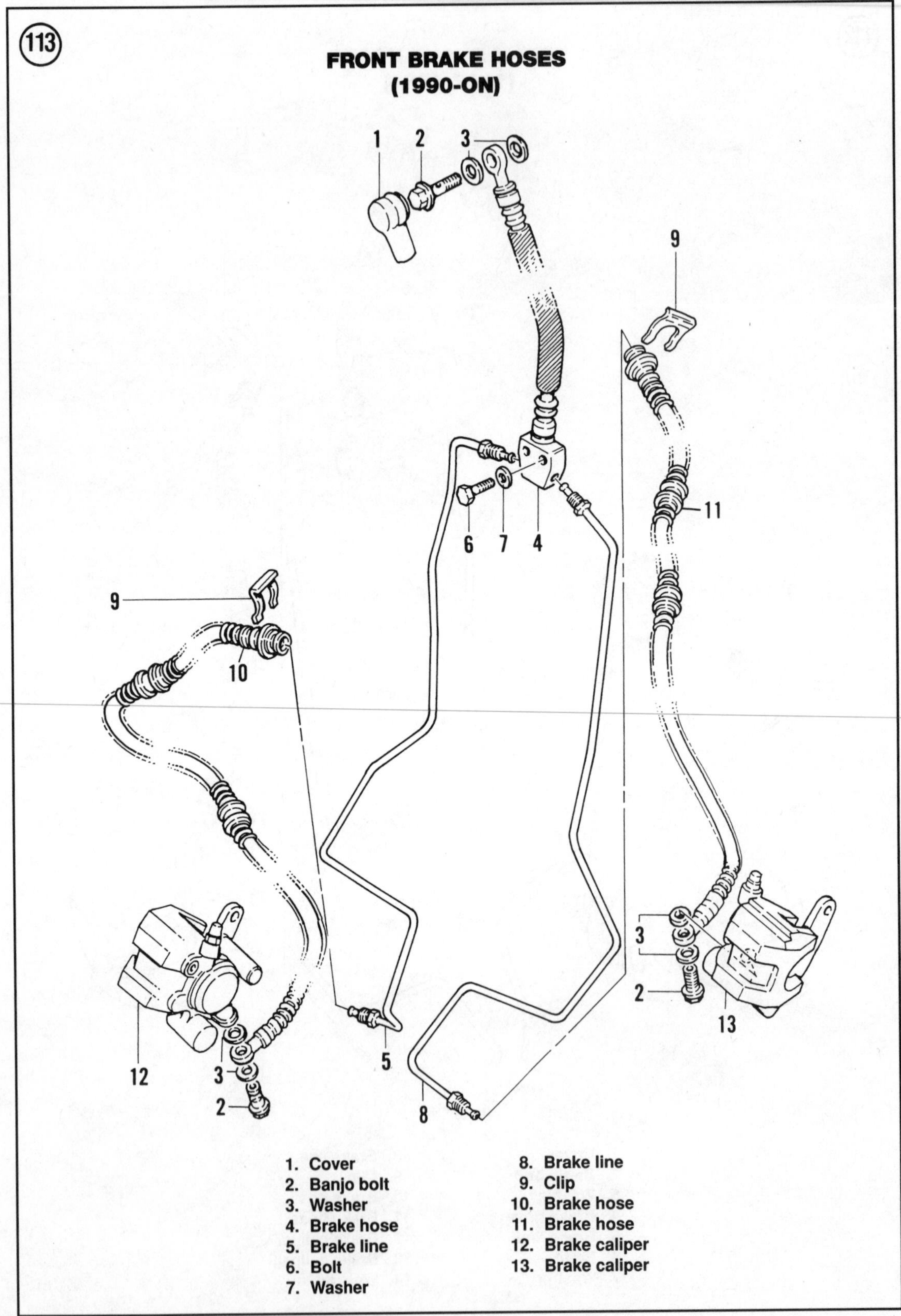
113
FRONT BRAKE HOSES
(1990-ON)
1
2
3
9
11
6
7
4
9
10
3
2
13
12
3
2
5
8
1. Cover
2. Banjo bolt
3. Washer
4. Brake hose
5. Brake line
6. Bolt
7. Washer
8. Brake line
9. Clip
10. Brake hose
11. Brake hose
12. Brake caliper
13. Brake caliper

114

115

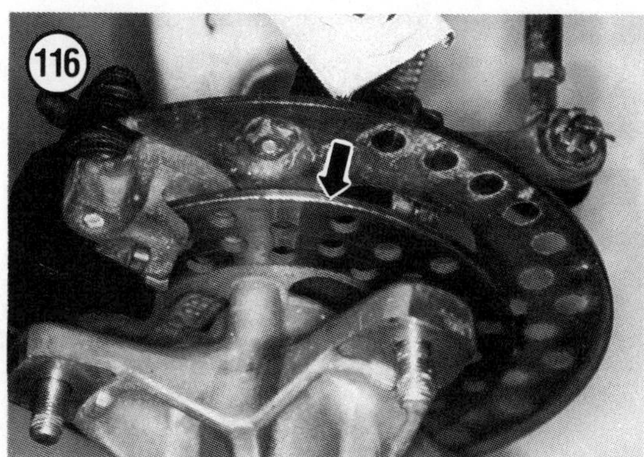
116

117

1. Place a container under the brake line at the caliper. Remove the banjo bolt and sealing washers at the caliper or master cylinder. See **Figure 114**, typical.
2. On compression fittings, hold the brake hose with a wrench and loosen the bolt. Separate the hose from the bolt.
3. Place the end of the brake hose in a clean container. Operate the brake lever to drain the master cylinder and brake hose of all brake fluid. Dispose of this brake fluid—never reuse brake fluid.
4. Install a new brake hose in the reverse order of removal. Install new sealing washers and banjo bolts (**Figure 115**) if necessary.
5. Tighten the banjo bolts to the torque specification in **Table 3**.
6. On compression fittings, thread the bolt onto the brake hose. Tighten the compression nut securely.
7. Refill the master cylinder with fresh brake fluid clearly marked DOT 4. Bleed the brake as described in this chapter.

WARNING
Do not ride the vehicle until you are sure that the brakes are operating properly.

BRAKE DISC

The front brake discs (**Figure 116**) are mounted onto the front hubs. The rear brake disc (**Figure 117**) is mounted onto a splined hub that is installed onto the rear axle.

Inspection

It is not necessary to remove the disc to inspect it. Small marks on the disc are not important, but radial scratches deep enough to snag a fingernail reduce braking effectiveness and increase brake pad wear. If these grooves are evident, and the brake pads are wearing rapidly, the disc should be replaced.

Yamaha lists standard and wear limit specifications for the brake discs; see **Table 1** and **Table 2**. When servicing the brake discs, do not have the discs reconditioned (ground) to compensate for warpage. The discs are thin and grinding will only reduce their thickness, causing them to warp quite rapidly. If a disc is warped, the brake pads may be dragging on the disc, causing the disc to overheat. Overheating can be caused when there is unequal brake pad pressure on both sides of the disc. Four main causes of unequal pad pressure are: the floating caliper is binding on the caliper bracket shafts, thus preventing the caliper from floating (side-to-side) on the disc; the brake caliper piston seal is worn or damaged; the small master cylinder relief port is plugged; and the primary cup on the master cylinder piston is worn or damaged.

1. Support the vehicle with all 4 wheels off the ground.
2. Remove the front wheels as described in Chapter Eleven.
3. Measure the thickness around the disc at several locations with a micrometer (**Figure 118**). The disc must be replaced if the thicknesses at any point is less than the thickness specified in **Table 1** or **Table 2**.
4. Make sure the disc bolts are tight prior to performing this check. Using a magnetic stand, install the dial indicator and position its stem against the brake disc as shown in **Figure 119**. Then zero the dial gauge. Slowly turn the axle or hub to measure runout. If the runout exceeds 0.15 mm (0.006 in.), the disc must be replaced.
5. Clean the disc of any rust or corrosion and wipe clean with lacquer thinner. Never use an oil-based solvent that may leave an oil residue on the disc.

Removal/Installation

1A. To remove the front brake disc:
   a. Remove the front hub(s) as described in Chapter Eleven.
   b. Remove the screws securing the disc to the wheel and remove the disc (**Figure 120**).

1B. To remove the rear brake disc:
   a. Set the parking brake to lock the rear axle.
   b. Loosen, but do not remove, the bolts securing the rear brake disc to the axle hub.
   c. Block the front wheels. Then support the vehicle with both rear wheels off the ground.
   d. Remove the right-hand rear wheel as described in Chapter Twelve.
   e. Remove the brake caliper as described in this chapter.
   f. Remove the brake disc screws and remove the brake disc.

2. Install by reversing these removal steps. Torque the disc brake screws to the specification in **Table 3**.

CAUTION

The disc brake screws are made out of a harder material than similar screws that are not used in the braking system. When replacing these screws, make sure to purchase the correct type.

BRAKE BLEEDING

This procedure is necessary only when the brakes feel spongy, there is a leak in the hydraulic system,

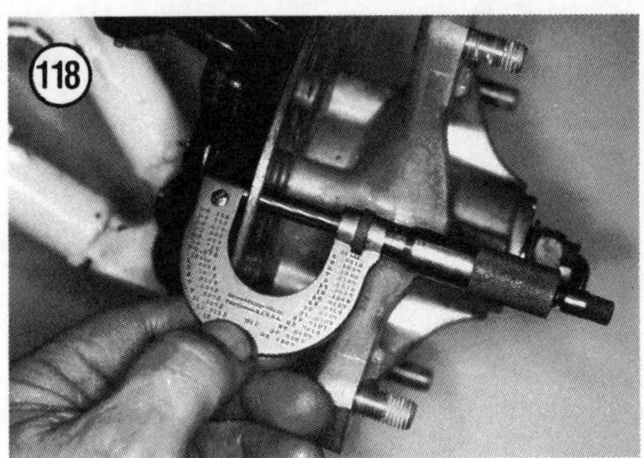

118

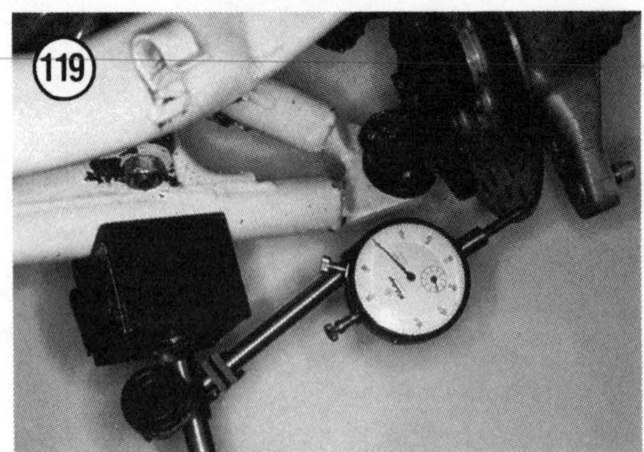

119

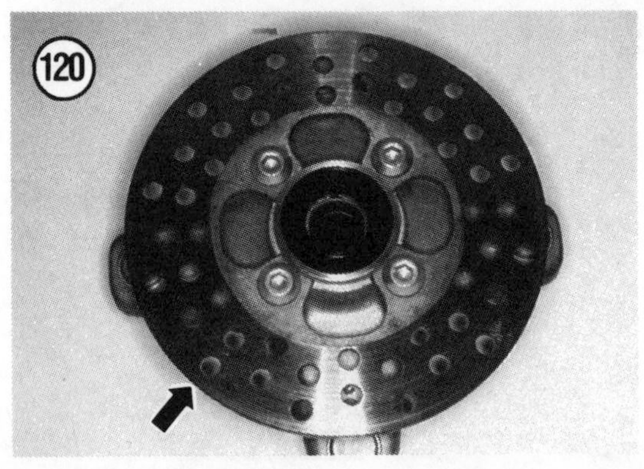

120

a component has been replaced or the brake fluid has been replaced.

NOTE
During this procedure, all the hose junctions in the brake system will be bled of air. It is important to check the fluid level in the master cylinder frequently. If the reservoir runs dry, air will enter the system which will require starting over.

1. Flip off the dust cap from the brake bleeder valve.
2. Connect a length of clear tubing to the bleeder valve on the caliper (**Figure 121**). Place the other end of the tube into a clean container. Fill the container with enough fresh brake fluid to keep the end submerged. The tube should be long enough so that a loop can be made higher than the bleeder valve to prevent air from being drawn into the caliper during bleeding.

CAUTION
Cover all parts which could become contaminated by the accidental spilling of brake fluid. Wash any spilled brake fluid from any surface immediately, as it will destroy the finish. Use soapy water and rinse completely.

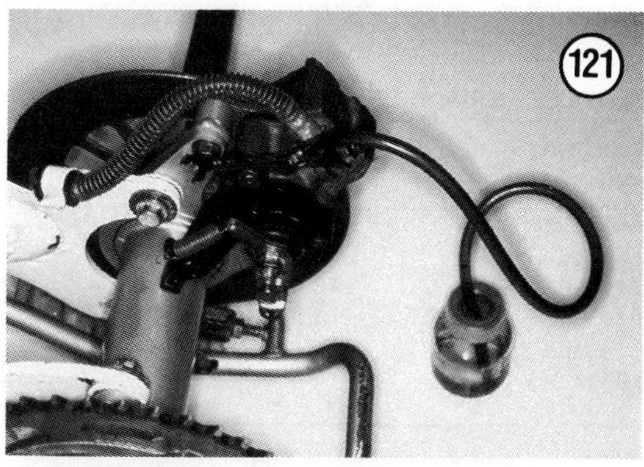

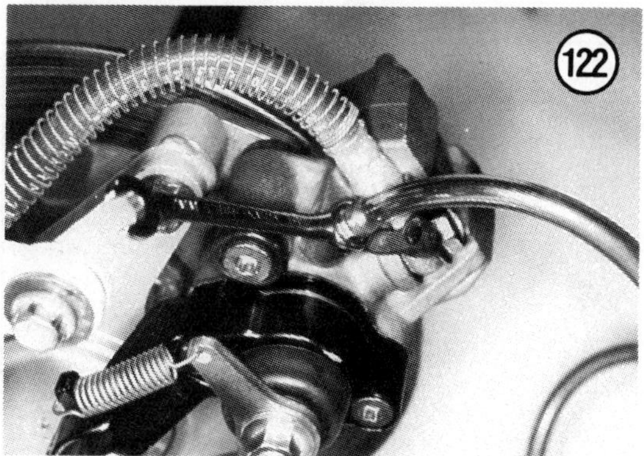

3. Clean the top of the front master cylinder or the rear reservoir cap of all dirt and foreign matter. Remove the cap and diaphragm. Fill the reservoir to about 10 mm (3/8 in.) from the top. Insert the diaphragm to prevent the entry of dirt and moisture.

WARNING
Use brake fluid clearly marked DOT 4 only. Others may vaporize and cause brake failure. Always use the same brand name; do not intermix the brake fluids, as many brands are not compatible.

NOTE
During this procedure, it is important to check the reservoir fluid level periodically to make sure it does not run dry. If the reservoir should run dry, air will enter the system and you'll have to start over.

4. Hold the brake lever in the applied position and open the bleeder valve (**Figure 122**) about 1/2 turn—do not release the brake lever while the bleeder valve is open. When you open the bleeder valve, you will feel the lever loosen a bit as it moves to the limit of its travel. At this point, tighten the bleeder screw, then release the brake lever.

NOTE
As the brake fluid enters the system, the level will drop in the master cylinder reservoir. Maintain the level at about 10 mm (3/8 in.) from the top of the reservoir to prevent air from being drawn into the system.

5. Repeat Step 4 until the system is bled. If you are replacing the fluid, continue until the fluid emerging from the hose is clean.

NOTE
If bleeding is difficult, it may be necessary to allow the fluid to stabilize for a few hours. Repeat the bleeding procedure when the tiny bubbles in the system settle out.

6. Hold the lever in the applied position and tighten the bleeder valve. Remove the bleeder tube and install the bleeder valve dust cap.

7. If necessary, add fluid to correct the level in the master cylinder reservoir. It must be above the level line.

8. Install the cap and tighten the screws (front master cylinder).

9. Test the feel of the brake lever. It should feel firm and should offer the same resistance each time it's operated. If it feels spongy, it is likely that air is still in the system and it must be bled again. When all air has been bled from the system and the brake fluid level is correct in the reservoir, double-check for leaks and tighten all fittings and connections.

WARNING

Before riding the vehicle, make certain that the brake is working correctly by operating the lever or pedal several times. Then make the test ride a slow one at first to make sure the brake is working correctly.

Table 1 FRONT DISC BRAKE SERVICE SPECIFICATIONS

	Standard mm (in.)	Service limit mm (in.)
Disc		
Outer diameter	161 (6.34)	–
Thickness	3.5 (0.138)	–
Brake pad thickness		
1987-1989	6.0 (0.236)	0.8 (0.031)
1990-on	4.5 (0.18)	1.0 (0.04)
Master cylinder inside diameter	14 (0.55)	–
Brake caliper inside diameter	31.75 (1.25)	–

Table 2 REAR DISC BRAKE SERVICE SPECIFICATIONS

	Standard mm (in.)	Service limit mm (in.)
Disc		
Outer diameter	220 (8.66)	–
Thickness	3.5 (0.14)	3.0 (0.12)
Brake pad thickness	4.5 (0.177)	1.0 (0.040)
Master cylinder inside diameter	12.7 (0.50)	–
Brake caliper inside diameter	33.96 (1.34)	–

Table 3 BRAKE TIGHTENING TORQUES

	N•m	ft.-lb.
Front brake caliper mounting bolts	28	20
Rear brake caliper		
Mounting bolts	23	17
Bracket bolt	23	17
Brake pad pin bolts	18	13
Brake disc (front and rear)	28	20
Brake hose banjo bolts	25	18
Brake hose at brake caliper	25	18
Brake hose joint at brake line	18	13
Rear master cylinder	20	14
Parking brake housing mounting bolts	28	20

CHAPTER FOURTEEN

BODY

This chapter contains removal and installation procedures for body panels and seat.

It is suggested that as soon as the part is removed from the vehicle, all mounting hardware (i.e. small brackets, bolts, nuts, washers, etc.) be reinstalled onto the removed part.

SEAT

Removal/Installation

1. Lift the seat latch (**Figure 1**) and remove the seat.
2. To install the seat, insert the front seat lobe underneath the frame bracket, then push the rear of the seat down to lock it in place.

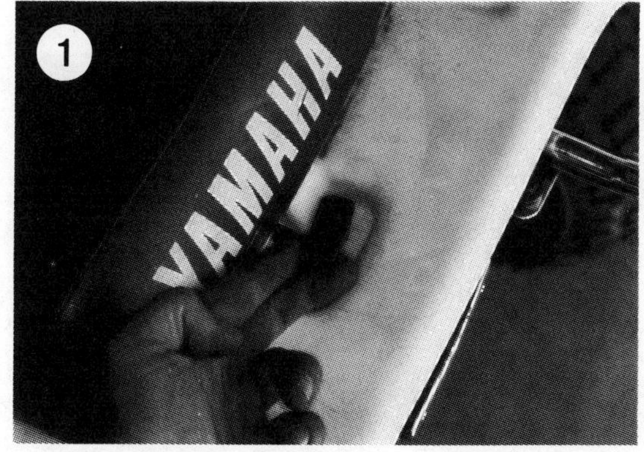

3. Lift up on the seat and make sure it is properly secured at both ends.

FRONT PANEL AND SIDE COVERS

Refer to **Figure 2**.

Removal/Installation

1. Remove the seat as described in this chapter.
2. Remove the front panel mounting screws and remove the front panel (A, **Figure 3**).
3. Remove the side cover mounting screws. Then slide the side cover toward the rear of the vehicle to disconnect its mounting tabs (**Figure 4**) and remove the side cover (B, **Figure 3**).
4. Install by reversing these steps.

FRONT FENDER

Refer to **Figure 5**.

Removal/Installation

1. Remove the seat, front panel and side covers as described in this chapter.
2. Remove the bolts and washers securing the front fender to the frame. See **Figure 6** and **Figure 7**.

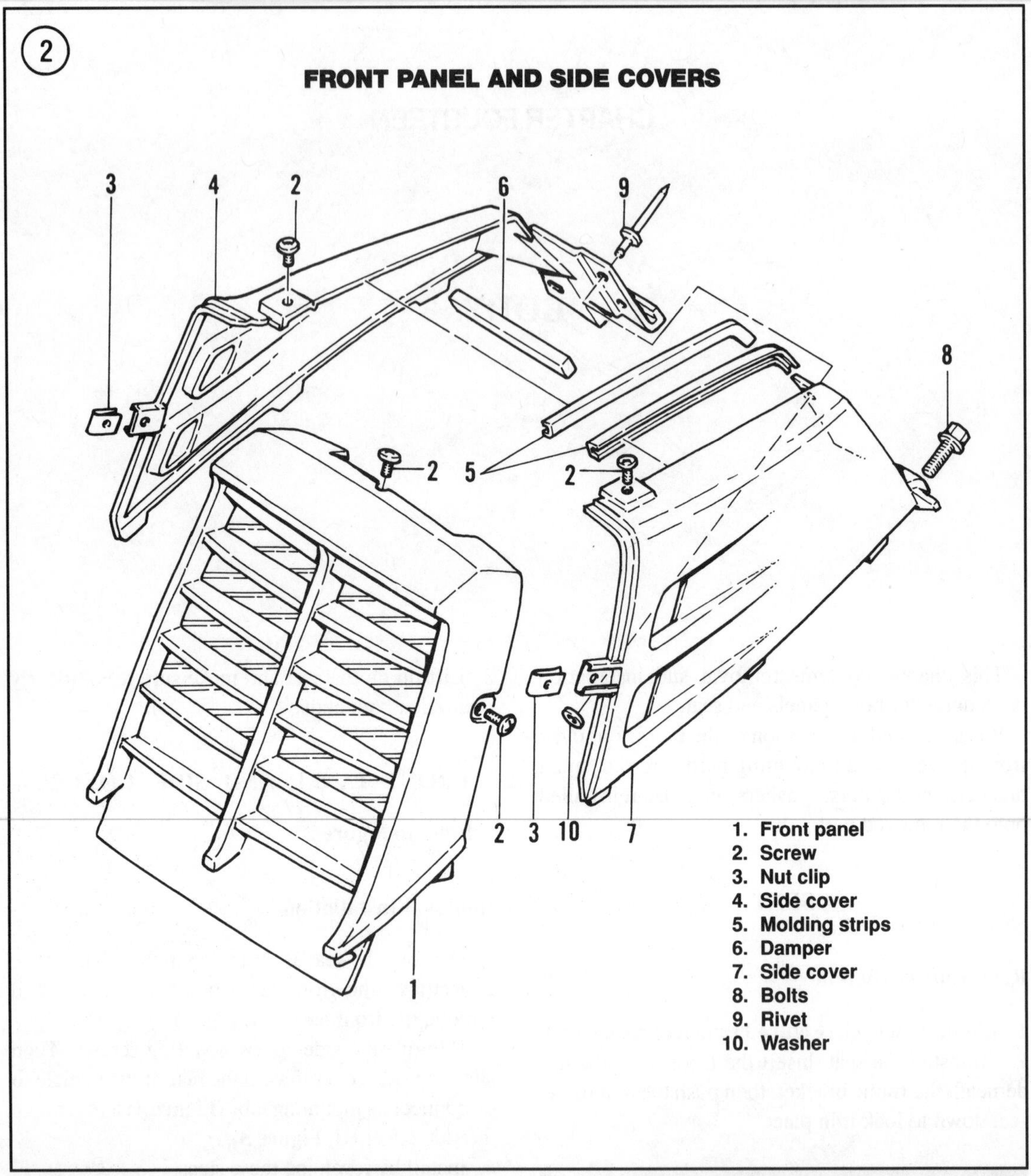

2
FRONT PANEL AND SIDE COVERS
3
4
2
6
9
8
2
5
2
2
3
10
7
1
1. Front panel
2. Screw
3. Nut clip
4. Side cover
5. Molding strips
6. Damper
7. Side cover
8. Bolts
9. Rivet
10. Washer

3
B
A

4

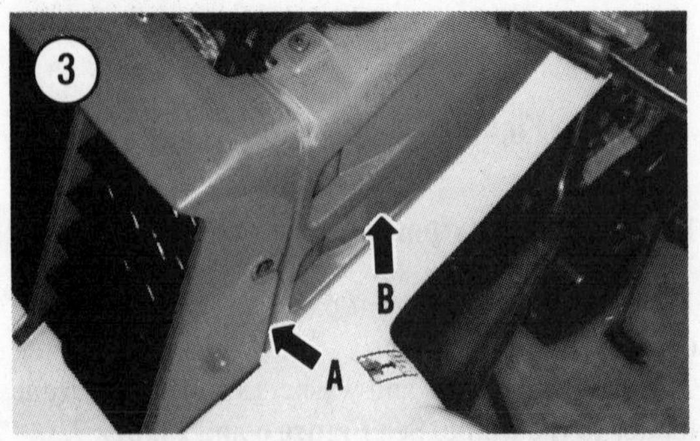

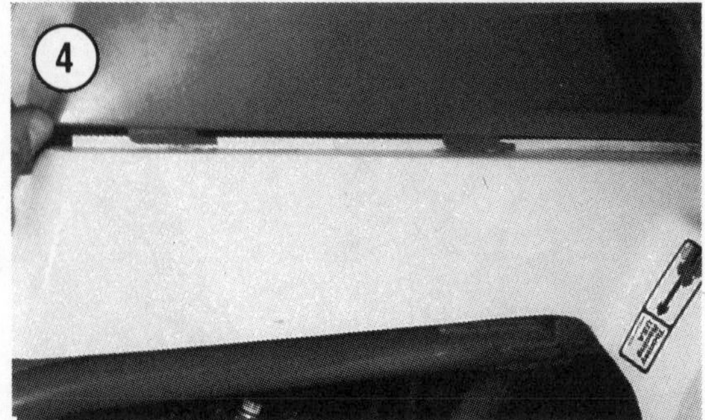

(5)

FRONT FENDER

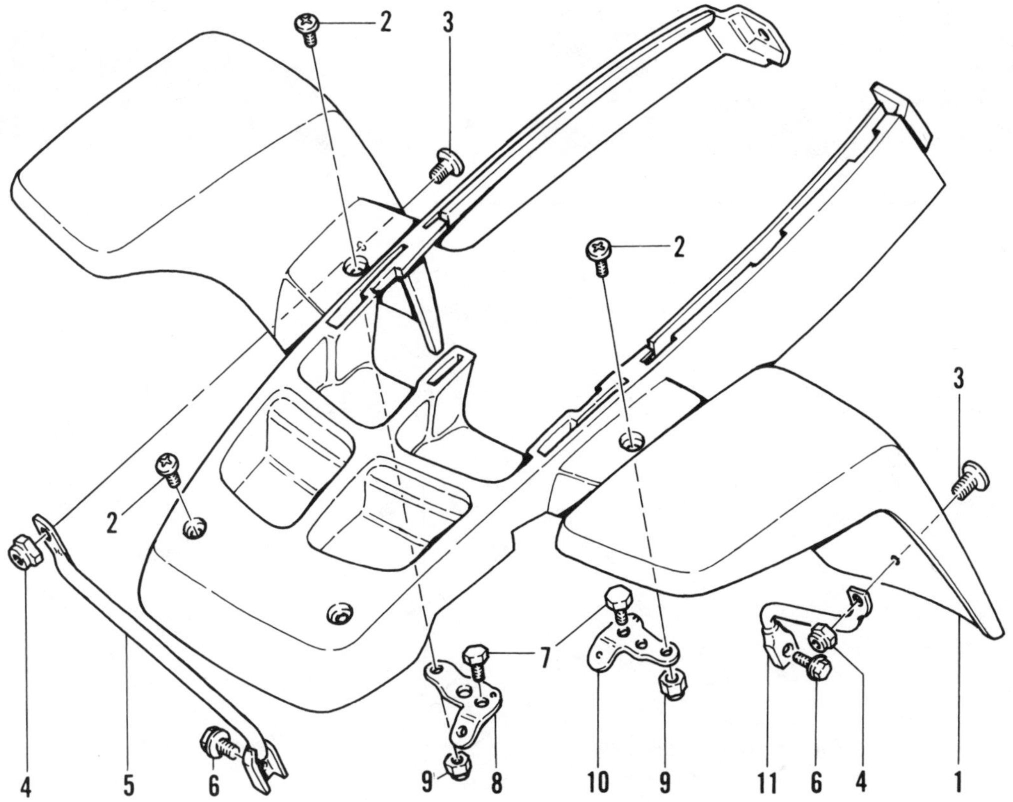

1. Front fender
2. Screw
3. Screw
4. Nut
5. Bracket
6. Bolt
7. Bolt
8. Bracket (right-hand)
9. Nut
10. Bracket (left-hand)
11. Bracket

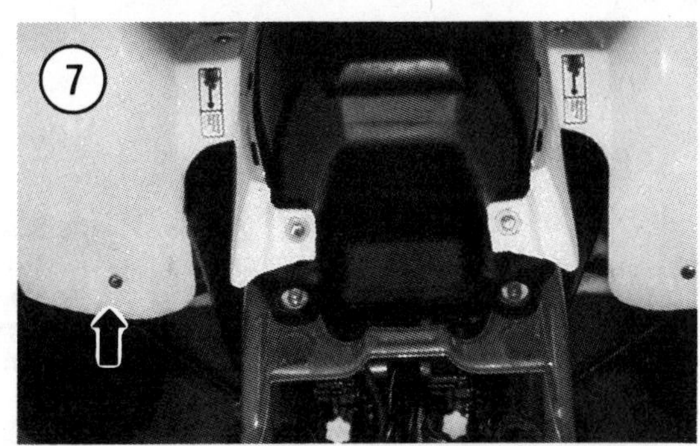

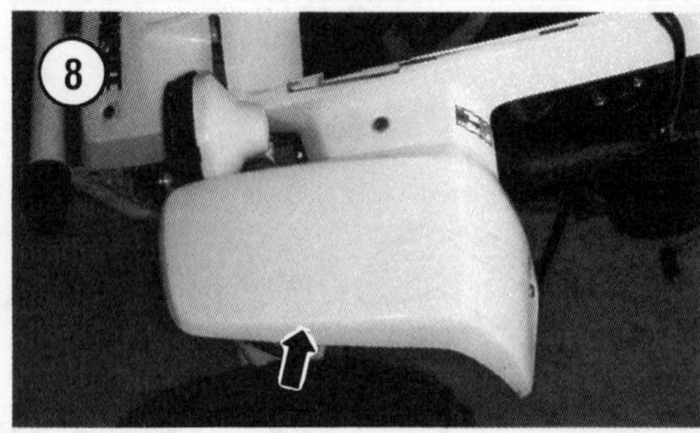
8

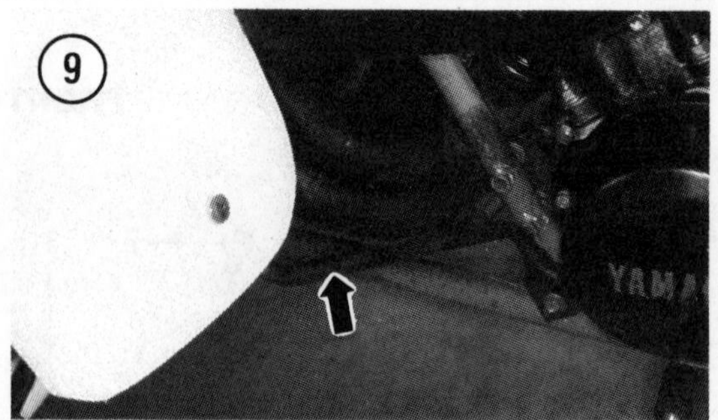
9

10

REAR FENDER
(1987-1989)

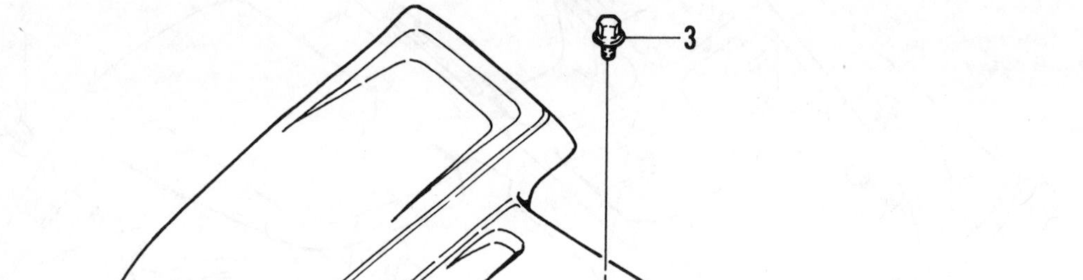

1. Rear fender
2. Screw
3. Bolt
4. Washer
5. Nut

3. Carefully pull the front fender (**Figure 8**) away from the frame. Then move the front fender up and toward the front. Spread the rear portion of the front fender out and pull it from the frame.
4. If necessary, remove the front fender mounting brackets (**Figure 9**).
5. Install by reversing these removal steps, noting the following.
6. Do not overtighten the bolts as the plastic fender may fracture.

REAR FENDER

Refer to **Figure 10** (1987-1989) or **Figure 11** (1990-on).

Removal/Installation

1. Remove the seat as described in this chapter.
2. Remove the rear fender mounting bolts. See **Figure 12**, typical.

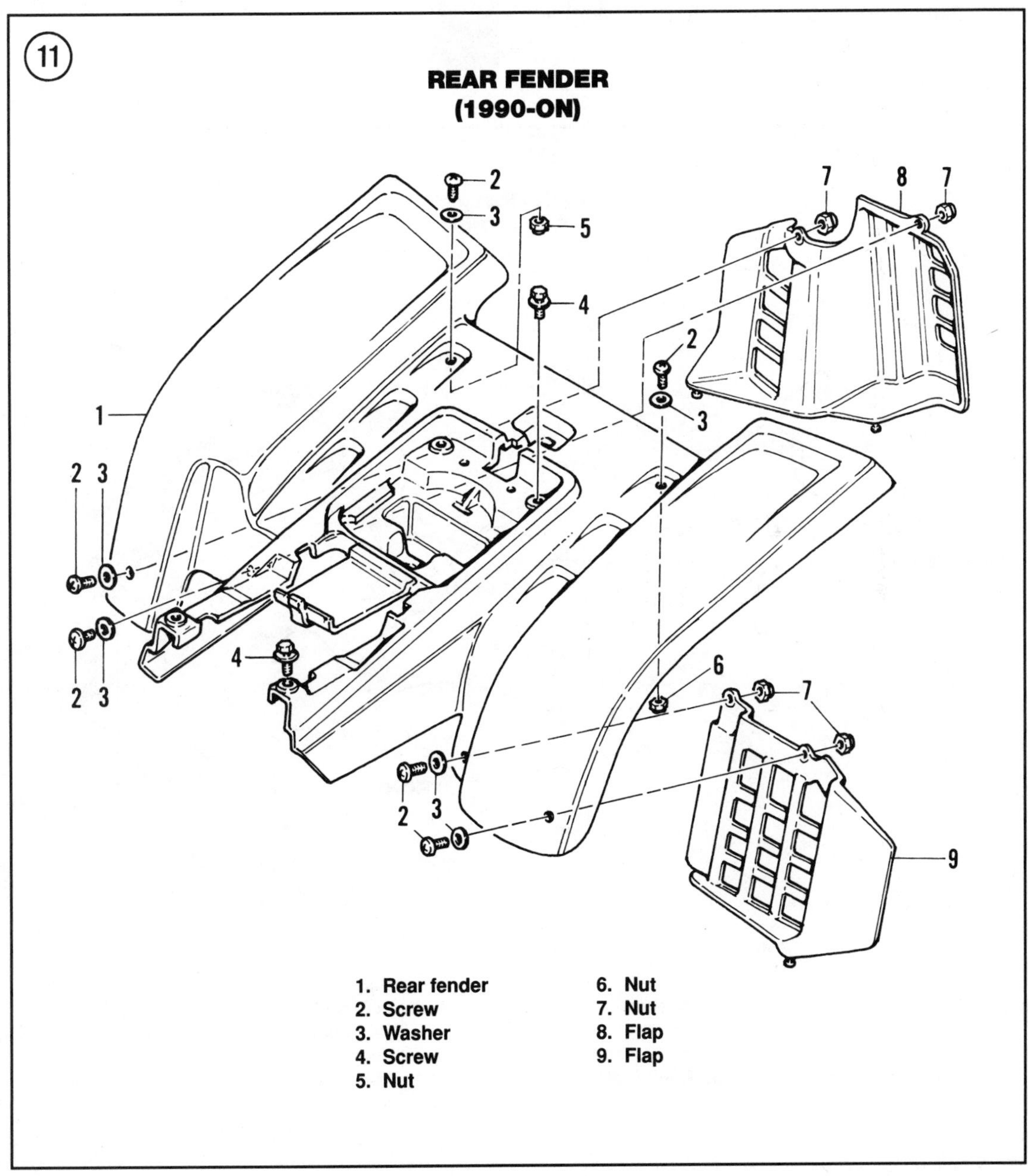

3. On 1990-on models, remove the bolts securing the rear fender to the footpeg assemblies.
4. Remove the rear fender.
5. Install by reversing these steps.

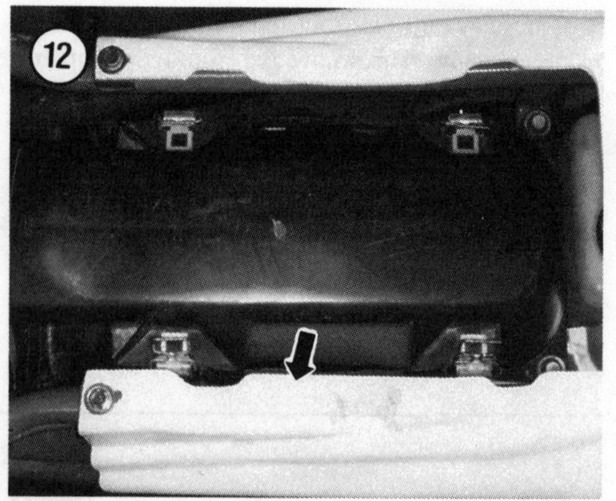

FOOTPEGS

Removal/Installation

Refer to **Figure 13** or **Figure 14** when removing and installing the footpeg assemblies. Tighten the footpeg-to-frame mounting bolts to 55 N•m (40 ft.-lb.).

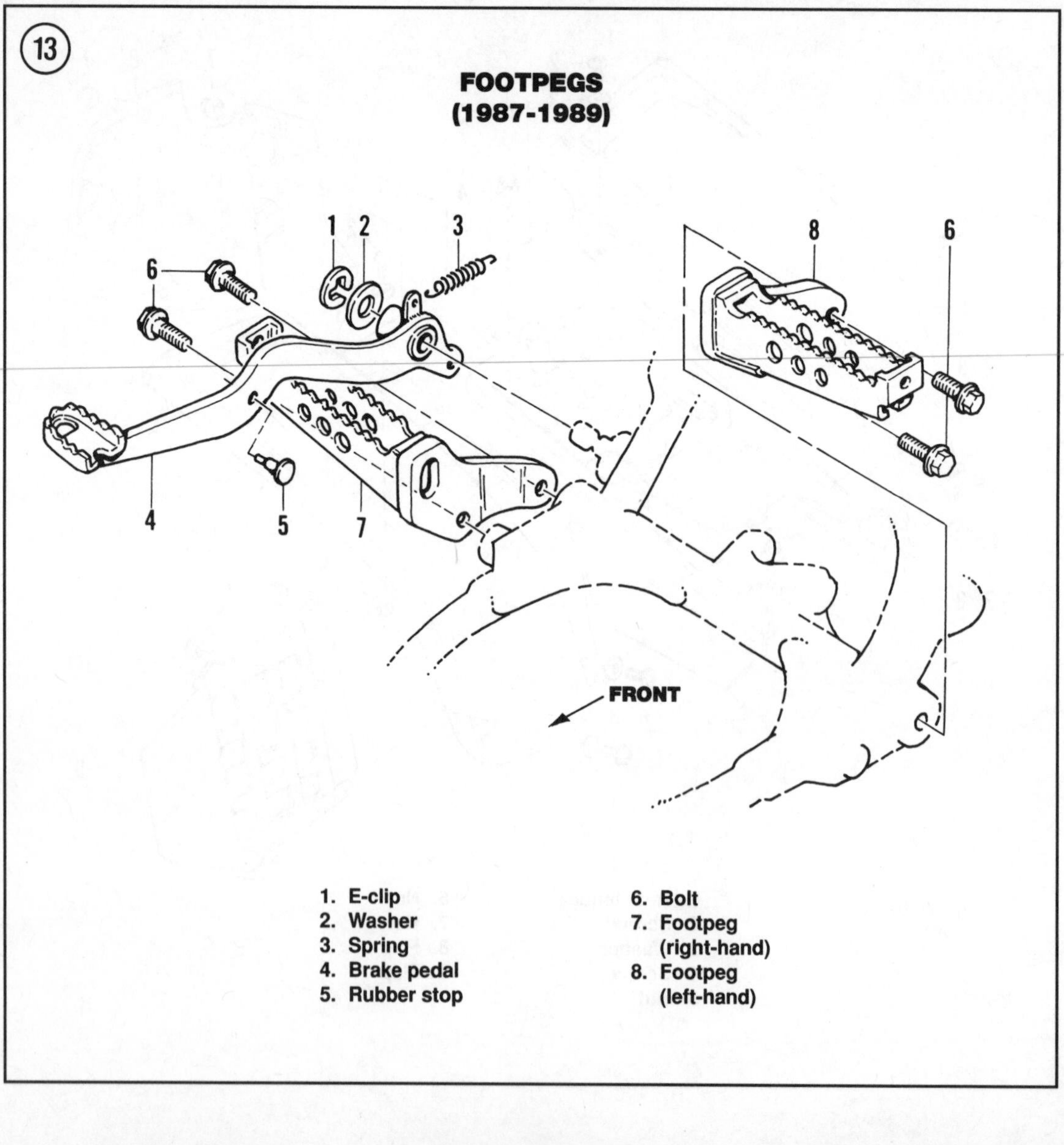

13

FOOTPEGS (1987-1989)

1 2 3 6 8 6 4 5 7 FRONT

1. E-clip
2. Washer
3. Spring
4. Brake pedal
5. Rubber stop
6. Bolt
7. Footpeg (right-hand)
8. Footpeg (left-hand)

(14)

FOOTPEG ASSEMBLY
(1990-ON)

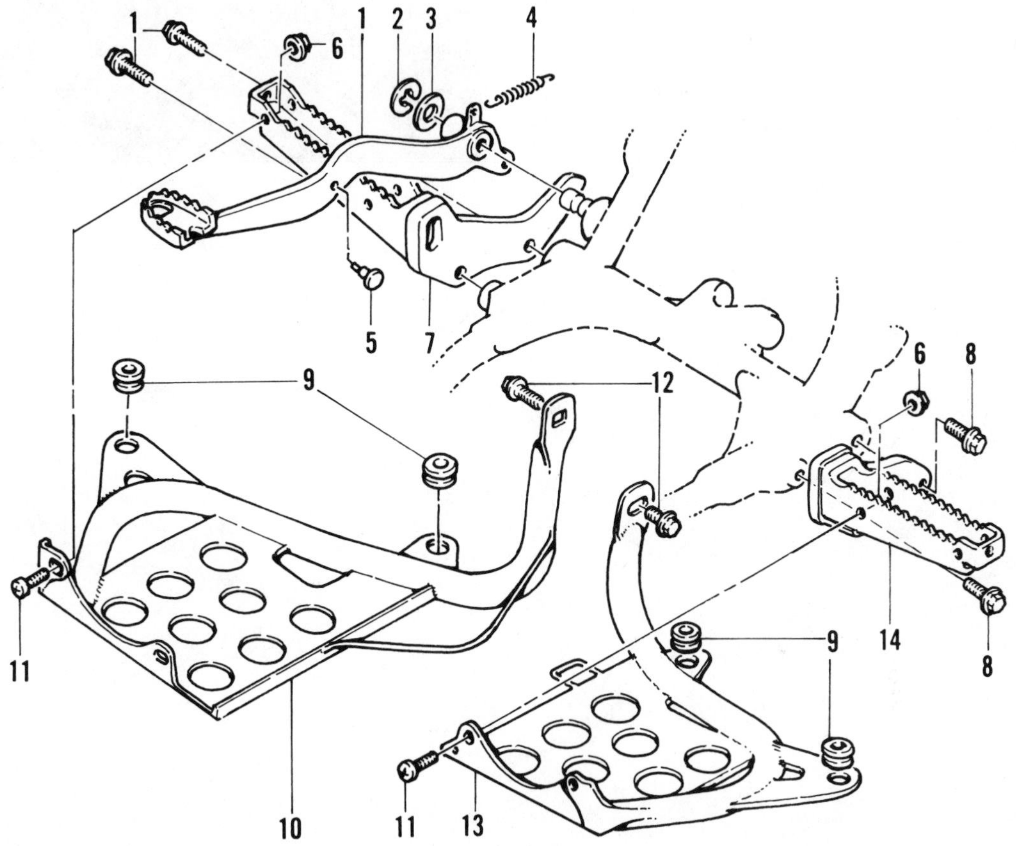

1. Brake pedal
2. E-clip
3. Washer
4. Spring
5. Rubber stop
6. Nut
7. Footpeg (right-hand)
8. Bolt
9. Grommet
10. Guard plate (right-hand)
11. Screw
12. Bolt
13. Guard plate (left-hand)
14. Footpeg (left-hand)

FRONT BUMPER

Removal/Installation

The front bumper (**Figure 15**) is secured to the frame with 4 mounting bolts. Tighten the bolts to 23 N•m (17 ft.-lb.).

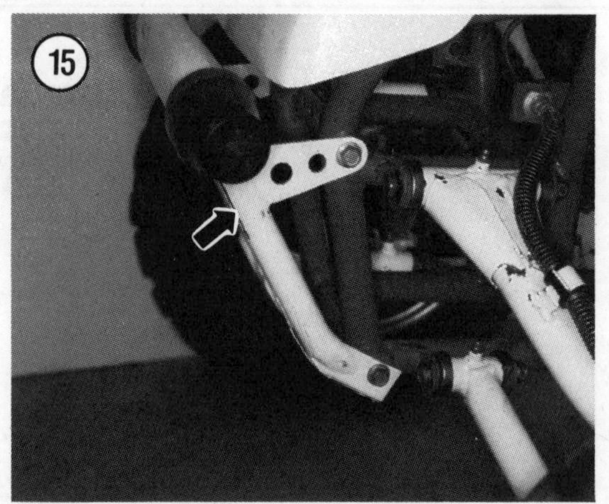

REAR BUMPER

Removal/Installation

The rear bumper is secured to the frame with 4 mounting bolts. Tighten the bolts to 23 N•m (17 ft.-lb.).

INDEX

A

B

C

D

E

F

G

H

I

K

L

M

N

O

P

R

S

T

V

W

YFZ350 (1987-2001)

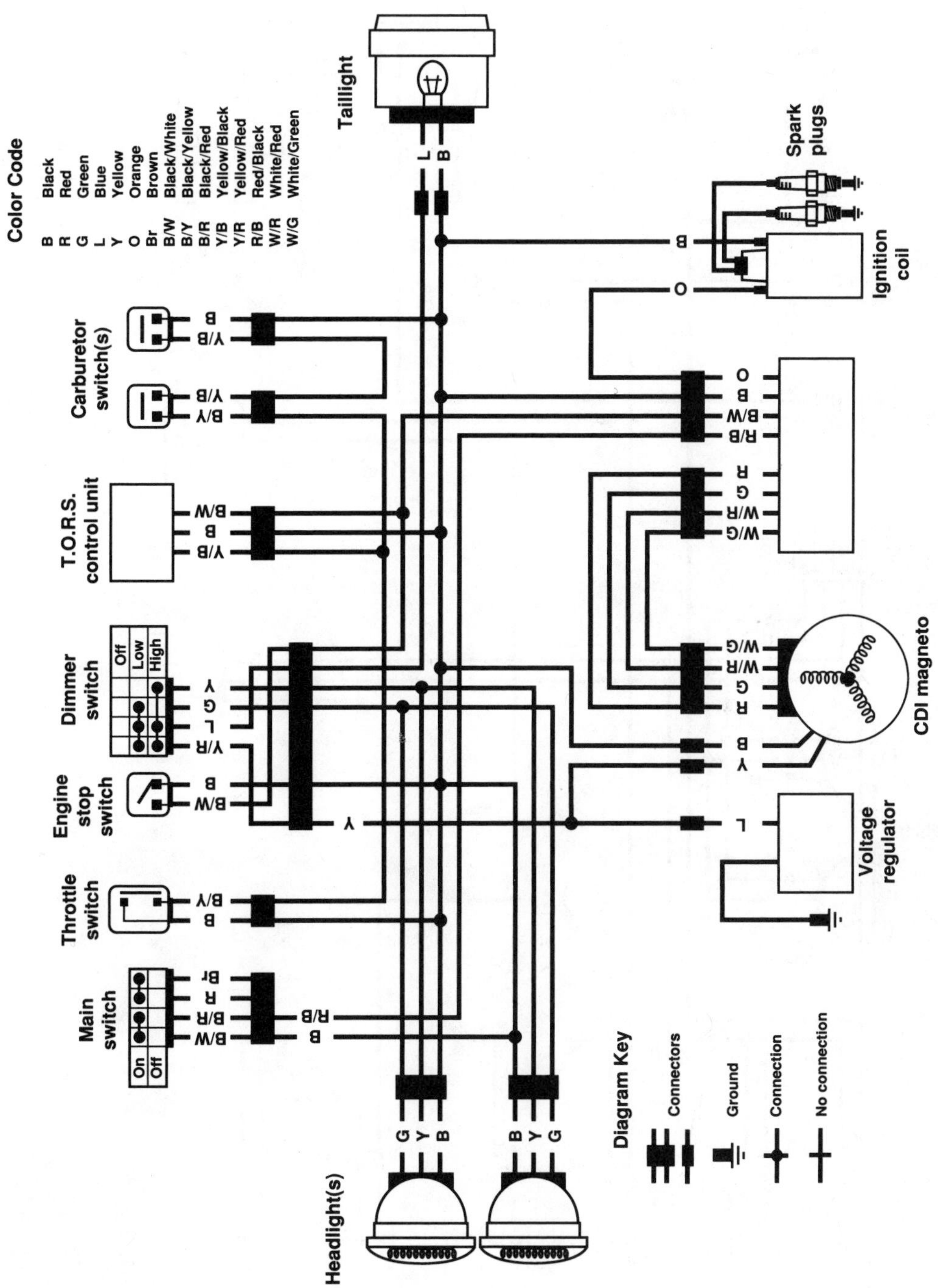

YFZ350 (2002-2004)

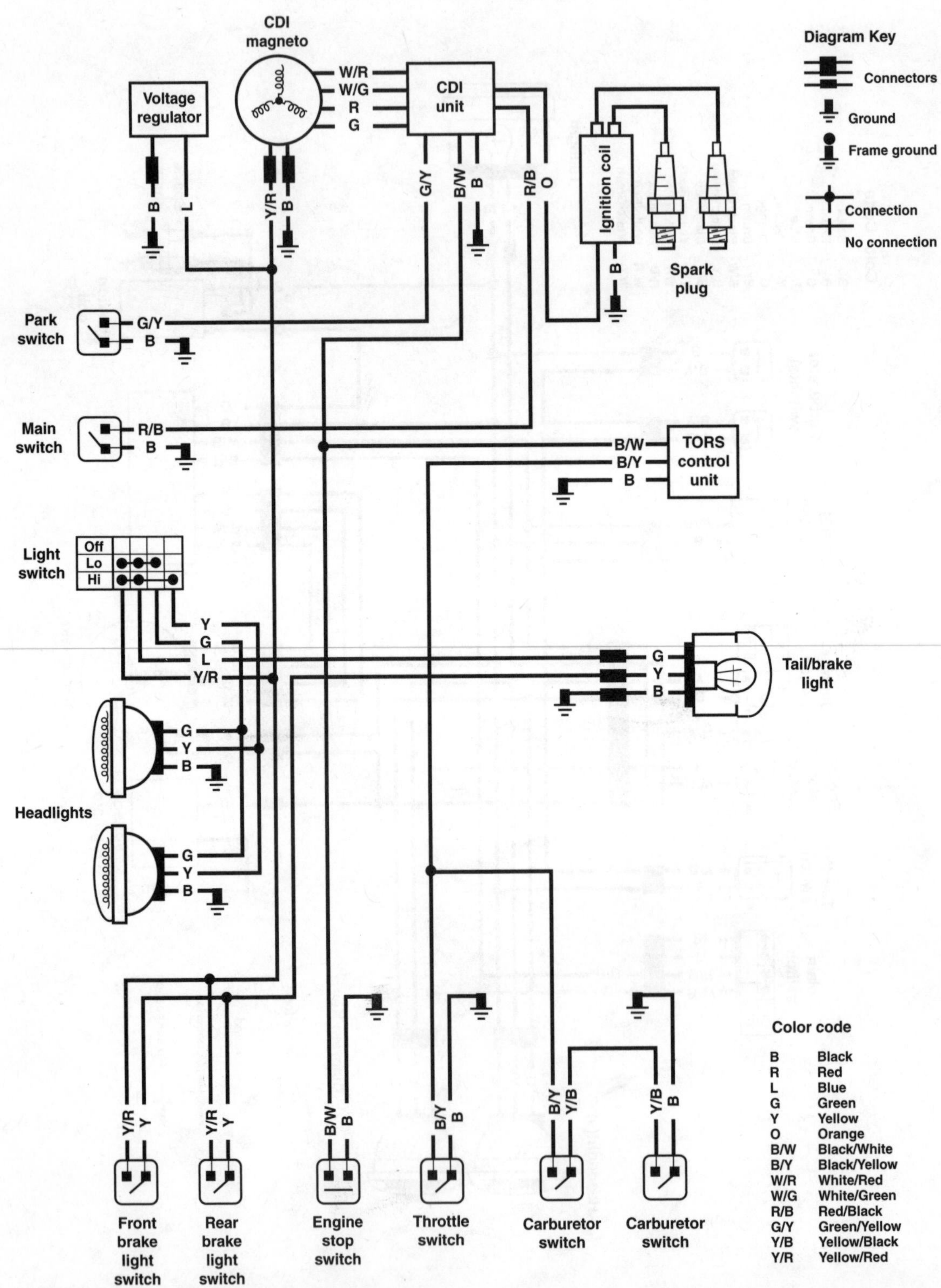

NOTES

NOTES

NOTES

NOTES

MAINTENANCE LOG

Date	Miles	Type of Service

CLYMER®

Check out *clymer.com* for our full line of powersport repair manuals.

BMW

M308 500 & 600 CC Twins, 55-69
M309 F650, 1994-2000
M500-3 BMW K-Series, 85-97
M502-3 BMW R50/5-R100 GSPD, 70-96
M503-2 R850, R1100, R1150 and R1200C, 93-04

HARLEY-DAVIDSON

M419 Sportsters, 59-85
M428 Sportster Evolution, 86-90
M429-4 Sportster Evolution, 91-03
M418 Panheads, 48-65
M420 Shovelheads,66-84
M421-3 FLS/FXS Evolution,84-99
M423 FLS/FXS Twin Cam 88B, 2000-2003
M422 FLH/FLT/FXR Evolution, 84-94
M430-2 FLH/FLT Twin Cam 88, 1999-2003
M424-2 FXD Evolution, 91-98
M425-2 FXD Twin Cam, 99-03

HONDA

ATVs

M316 Odyssey FL250, 77-84
M311 ATC, TRX & Fourtrax 70-125, 70-87
M433 Fourtrax 90 ATV, 93-00
M326 ATC185 & 200, 80-86
M347 ATC200X & Fourtrax 200SX, 86-88
M455 ATC250 & Fourtrax 200/ 250, 84-87
M342 ATC250R, 81-84
M348 TRX250R/Fourtrax 250R & ATC250R, 85-89
M456-3 TRX250X 87-92; TRX300EX 93-04
M446 TRX250 Recon 97-02
M346-3 TRX300/Fourtrax 300 & TRX300FW/Fourtrax 4x4, 88-00
M200 TRX350 Rancher, 00-03
M459-3 TRX400 Foreman 95-03
M454-2 TRX400EX 99-03
M205 TRX450 Foreman, 98-04

Singles

M310-13 50-110cc OHC Singles, 65-99
M319 XR50R-XR70R, 97-03
M315 100-350cc OHC, 69-82
M317 Elsinore, 125-250cc, 73-80
M442 CR60-125R Pro-Link, 81-88
M431-2 CR80R, 89-95, CR125R, 89-91
M435 CR80, 96-02
M457-2 CR125R & CR250R, 92-97
M464 CR125R, 1998-2002
M443 CR250R-500R Pro-Link, 81-87
M432-3 CR250R, 88-91 & CR500R, 88-01
M437 CR250R, 97-01
M312-13 XL/XR75-100, 75-03
M318-4 XL/XR/TLR 125-200, 79-03
M328-4 XL/XR250, 78-00; XL/XR350R 83-85; XR200R, 84-85; XR250L, 91-96
M320-2 XR400R, 96-04
M339-7 XL/XR 500-650, 79-03

Twins

M321 125-200cc, 65-78
M322 250-350cc, 64-74
M323 250-360cc Twins, 74-77
M324-5 Twinstar, Rebel 250 & Nighthawk 250, 78-03
M334 400-450cc, 78-87
M333 450 & 500cc, 65-76
M335 CX & GL500/650 Twins, 78-83
M344 VT500, 83-88
M313 VT700 & 750, 83-87
M314 VT750 Shadow, 98-03
M440 VT1100C Shadow , 85-96
M460-3 VT1100C Series, 95-04

Fours

M332 CB350-550cc, SOHC, 71-78
M345 CB550 & 650, 83-85
M336 CB650,79-82
M341 CB750 SOHC, 69-78
M337 CB750 DOHC, 79-82
M436 CB750 Nighthawk, 91-93 & 95-99
M325 CB900, 1000 & 1100, 80-83
M439 Hurricane 600, 87-90
M441-2 CBR600, 91-98
M445 CBR600F4, 99-03
M434 CBR900RR Fireblade, 93-98
M329 500cc V-Fours, 84-86
M438 Honda VFR800, 98-00
M349 700-1000 Interceptor, 83-85
M458-2 VFR700F-750F, 86-97
M327 700-1100cc V-Fours, 82-88
M340 GL1000 & 1100, 75-83
M504 GL1200, 84-87
M508 ST1100/PAN European, 90-02

Sixes

M505 GL1500 Gold Wing, 88-92
M506-2 GL1500 Gold Wing, 93-00
M507 GL1800 Gold Wing, 01-04
M462-2 GL1500C Valkyrie, 97-03

KAWASAKI

ATVs

M465-2 KLF220 & KLF250 Bayou, 88-03
M466-3 KLF300 Bayou, 86-04
M467 KLF400 Bayou, 93-99
M470 KEF300 Lakota, 95-99
M385 KSF250 Mojave, 87-00

Singles

M350-9 Rotary Valve 80-350cc, 66-01
M444-2 KX60, 83-02; KX80 83-90
M448 KX80/85/100, 89-03
M351 KDX200, 83-88
M447-2 KX125 & KX250, 82-91 KX500, 83-02
M472-2 KX125, 92-00
M473-2 KX250, 92-00
M474 KLR650, 87-03

Twins

M355 KZ400, KZ/Z440, EN450 & EN500, 74-95
M360-3 EX500, GPZ500S, Ninja R, 87-02
M356-3 Vulcan 700 & 750, 85-04
M354-2 Vulcan 800 & Vulcan 800 Classic, 95-04
M357-2 Vulcan 1500, 87-99
M471-2 Vulcan Classic 1500, 96-04

Fours

M449 KZ500/550 & ZX550, 79-85
M450 KZ, Z & ZX750, 80-85
M358 KZ650, 77-83
M359-3 900-1000cc Fours, 73-81
M451-3 1000 &1100cc Fours, 81-02
M452-3 ZX500 & 600 Ninja, 85-97
M453-3 Ninja ZX900-1100 84-01
M468 ZX6 Ninja, 90-97
M469 ZX7 Ninja, 91-98
M453-3 900-1100 Ninja, 84-01
M409 Concours, 86-04

POLARIS

ATVs

M496 Polaris ATV, 85-95
M362 Polaris Magnum ATV, 96-98
M363 Scrambler 500, 4X4 97-00
M365-2 Sportsman/Xplorer, 96-03

SUZUKI

ATVs

M381 ALT/LT 125 & 185, 83-87
M475 LT230 & LT250, 85-90
M380-2 LT250R Quad Racer, 85-92
M343 LTF500F Quadrunner, 98-00
M483-2 Suzuki King Quad/ Quad Runner 250, 87-98

Singles

M371 RM50-400 Twin Shock, 75-81
M369 125-400cc 64-81
M379 RM125-500 Single Shock, 81-88
M476 DR250-350, 90-94
M384-2 LS650 Savage, 86-03
M386 RM80-250, 89-95
M400 RM125, 96-00
M401 RM250, 96-02

Twins

M372 GS400-450 Twins, 77-87
M481-4 VS700-800 Intruder, 85-04
M482-2 VS1400 Intruder, 87-01
M484-3 GS500E Twins, 89-02
M361 SV650, 1999-2002

Triple

M368 380-750cc, 72-77

Fours

M373 GS550, 77-86
M364 GS650, 81-83
M370 GS750 Fours, 77-82
M376 GS850-1100 Shaft Drive, 79-84
M378 GS1100 Chain Drive, 80-81
M383-3 Katana 600, 88-96 GSX-R750-1100, 86-87
M331 GSX-R600, 97-00
M478-2 GSX-R750, 88-92 GSX750F Katana, 89-96
M485 GSX-R750, 96-99
M338 GSF600 Bandit, 95-00
M353 GSF1200 Bandit, 96-03

YAMAHA

ATVs

M499 YFM80 Badger, 85-01
M394 YTM/YFM200 & 225, 83-86
M488-4 Blaster, 88-02
M489-2 Timberwolf, 89-00
M487-5 Warrior, 87-04
M486-5 Banshee, 87-04
M490-2 YFM350 Moto-4 & Big Bear, 87-98
M493 YFM400FW Kodiak, 93-98
M280 Raptor 660R, 01-03

Singles

M492-2 PW50 & PW80, BW80 Big Wheel 80, 81-02
M410 80-175 Piston Port, 68-76
M415 250-400cc Piston Port, 68-76
M412 DT & MX 100-400, 77-83
M414 IT125-490, 76-86
M393 YZ50-80 Monoshock, 78-90
M413 YZ100-490 Monoshock, 76-84
M390 YZ125-250, 85-87 YZ490, 85-90
M391 YZ125-250, 88-93 WR250Z, 91-93
M497-2 YZ125, 94-01
M498 YZ250, 94-98 and WR250Z, 94-97
M406 YZ250F & WR250F, 01-03
M491-2 YZ400F, YZ426F, WR400F WR426F, 98-02
M417 XT125-250, 80-84
M480-3 XT/TT 350, 85-00
M405 XT500 & TT500, 76-81
M416 XT/TT 600, 83-89

Twins

M403 650cc, 70-82
M395-10 XV535-1100 Virago, 81-03
M495-3 V-Star 650, 98-04
M281 V-Star 1100, 99-04

Triple

M404 XS750 & 850, 77-81

Fours

M387 XJ550, XJ600 & FJ600, 81-92
M494 XJ600 Seca II, 92-98
M388 YX600 Radian & FZ600, 86-90
M396 FZR600, 89-93
M392 FZ700-750 & Fazer, 85-87
M411 XS1100 Fours, 78-81
M397 FJ1100 & 1200, 84-93
M375 V-Max, 85-03
M374 Royal Star, 96-03
M461 YZF-R6, 99-04
M398 YZF-R1, 98-03

VINTAGE MOTORCYCLES

Clymer® Collection Series

M330 Vintage British Street Bikes, BSA, 500–650cc Unit Twins; Norton, 750 & 850cc Commandos; Triumph, 500-750cc Twins
M300 Vintage Dirt Bikes, V. 1 Bultaco, 125-370cc Singles; Montesa, 123-360cc Singles; Ossa, 125-250cc Singles
M301 Vintage Dirt Bikes, V. 2 CZ, 125-400cc Singles; Husqvarna, 125-450cc Singles; Maico, 250-501cc Singles; Hodaka, 90-125cc Singles
M305 Vintage Japanese Street Bikes Honda, 250 & 305cc Twins; Kawasaki, 250-750cc Triples; Kawasaki, 900 & 1000cc Fours